Praise for *The Uses and Misuses of Politics*

"An insightful examination of the mastermind behind George W. Bush's presidency. William G. Mayer's grasp of Karl Rove's strategic vision, however flawed, is second to none. Mayer's interpretation is likely to remain the authoritative account of the architect of a 'durable' Republican realignment that vanished before George W. Bush even left the White House."
—**Stephen F. Knott**, author of *The Lost Soul of the American Presidency: The Decline into Demagoguery and the Prospects for Renewal*

"A carefully researched and lucid analysis of politics and policy-making in the George W. Bush administration, this book is highly instructive for presidency studies and American politics. It demonstrates the critical importance of executive leadership in White House decision-making to ensure clearly defined responsibilities for political strategists and policymakers."
—**Meena Bose**, Peter S. Kalikow Chair in Presidential Studies and professor of political science, Hofstra University

"This excellent book provides a thorough and thoughtful analysis of the George W. Bush presidency. It looks beyond personalities to dig deep into political history and public policy. For readers across the political spectrum it offers bracing lessons about the limitations facing presidents and their staffs."
—**John J. Pitney Jr.**, author of *After Reagan: Bush, Dukakis, and the 1988 Election*

"In this deep dive into the travails of the George W. Bush administration, scholar William G. Mayer methodically shows that it isn't always true that 'good politics is good policy.' Sometimes, 'good politics' isn't even good politics. There are important lessons here for future occupants of the White House and the people around them."
—**Andrew E. Busch**, author of *Reagan's Victory: The Presidential Election of 1980 and the Rise of the Right*

"In the long history of American politics, the number of successful campaign managers is small. They live in the shadows, mostly uncredited and unknown. But there are three who are known and well-credited because they are also the only campaign managers to win two successive elections for their candidates: Mark Hanna for William McKinley in 1896 and 1900, Jim Carville for Bill Clinton in 1992 and 1996, and Karl Rove for George W. Bush in 2000 and 2004. Thanks to Bill Mayer's fascinating and insightful exploration of Karl Rove's career, we are now able to learn how 'George Bush's brain' shaped the early decades of twenty-first-century American politics."
—**Garrison Nelson**, Elliott A. Brown Green and Gold Professor of Law, Politics, and Political Behavior, Emeritus, University of Vermont

"In this comprehensive study of 'the architect' of George W. Bush's ascent to the White House and the strategy that shaped his two terms in office, William Mayer reveals how Karl Rove's unprecedented joining of politics and public policy ravaged his ambition to forge a new Republican majority. Hoping their partnership would birth a historic political realignment, Bush and Rove instead presided over the collapse of the Republican establishment—leaving in their wake a party ripe for a hostile takeover by a clever demagogue. Anyone tempted to romanticize the George W. Bush years amid the disruption of Donald Trump's presidency will be disabused by this clear-eyed account of a presidency destroyed by a multitude of unforced errors."
—**Sidney M. Milkis**, White Burkett Miller Professor in the Department of Politics, University of Virginia

The Uses and Misuses of Politics

The Uses and Misuses of Politics

Karl Rove and the Bush Presidency

William G. Mayer

 University Press of Kansas

Published by the University Press of Kansas
(Lawrence, Kansas 66045), which was organized
by the Kansas Board of Regents and is operated and
funded by Emporia State University, Fort Hays State
University, Kansas State University, Pittsburg State
University, the University of Kansas, and Wichita
State University.

Library of Congress Cataloging-in-Publication Data

Names: Mayer, William G., author.
Title: The uses and misuses of politics : Karl Rove and
    the Bush presidency / William G. Mayer.
Description: Lawrence : University Press of Kansas, 2021. |
    Includes bibliographical references and index.
Identifiers: LCCN 2020026474
    ISBN 9780700630530 (cloth)
    ISBN 9780700630547 (epub)
Subjects: LCSH: United States—Politics and government—
    2001–2009. | Rove, Karl. | Rove, Karl—Influence. | Bush,
    George W. (George Walker), 1946– | Republican Party
    (U.S. : 1854–)—History—21st century. | Political
    consultants—United States.
Classification: LCC E902 .M384 2021 | DDC 973.931092—dc23
LC record available at https://lccn.loc.gov/2020026474.

British Library Cataloguing-in-Publication Data
is available.

Printed in the United States of America

10 9 8 7 6 5 4 3 2 1

The paper used in this publication is recycled and
contains 30 percent postconsumer waste. It is acid
free and meets the minimum requirements of the
American National Standard for Permanence of
Paper for Printed Library Materials Z39.48–1992.

To my mother, Mary Rose Mayer,
and to the memory of my father,
Joseph C. Mayer (1918–2006)

And still the wonder deepens

Contents

Acknowledgments

When this book was still at an early stage, I was fortunate to have Gerald Pomper and Marc Landy participate in a seminar at Northeastern University, organized at the instigation of Mitchell Orenstein, at which both gave the then-partially completed manuscript a thorough reading and critique. I also benefited enormously from the comments of Kathryn Dunn Tenpas and Andrew Busch, who reviewed the full manuscript for the University Press of Kansas. Deserving of special praise is Woody Kay, friend and polymath, who read and commented on the entire book for no reason except that he is a good guy and a great friend. John Portz, Chris Bosso, Bob Gilbert, Costas Panagopoulos, Jim Campbell, Joseph Cooper, Ralph Whitehead, Mark Jamrozik, Garrison Nelson, and Matt Dickinson also provided important help with parts of the analysis.

As readers will discover, this book contains a lot of survey data (see especially chapters 2, 6, and 8). Like virtually everything else I have published, my ability to access these data owes a great deal to the Roper Center for Public Opinion Research and the two people most responsible for establishing and maintaining its wonderful iPOLL database, Lois Timms-Ferrara and Marc Maynard. My thanks also to Karlyn Bowman of the American Enterprise Institute for sharing her remarkable collection of survey materials on public opinion toward the war in Iraq.

For making the publication process as smooth and painless as possible, I would also like to express my gratitude to the many good people at the University Press of Kansas—David Congdon, Colin Tripp, Mike Kehoe, Derek Helms, Karl Janssen, and especially Irina du Quenoy, who has restored my faith in copyeditors.

When my first book was published almost thirty years ago, I called it a triumph of family. My family has grown much larger since then, and, sadly, lost a few much-loved members as well, but I am still amazed and grateful for all the love and support they give me without stint. In that spirit I offer my inadequate thanks to: Joseph and Rita Farrell Mayer and their children, Lauren and Mike; Mary Beth and the late Joe King and their children, Allie and Kate; Jack and the late Mary Weiler Mayer; Tom and Christine Lobo Mayer and their son, Joseph; and Rosemary and Scott "the Iron Man" Kryk and their children, Andy, Steve, Dana, and Renee.

I would also like to thank Loretto Carr and the late Jack Carr for their support and assistance throughout my undergraduate and graduate school years.

In the final stages of my first book, a woman I had just started dating helped with the proofreading, alerting me, among other things, to the fact that the word "accomodate" actually has two m's. Two years later, we were married (her proofreading skills were among the least of her many virtues). Amy and our two children, Natalie and Thomas, have given me what have been, incontestably, the best twenty-six years of my life. They have also managed to put up with my quirks and work habits with a remarkable mixture of love, tolerance, and good humor.

Among Amy's many great contributions to my life is making me a member of her family. For their warm welcome and continuing affection and encouragement, I am grateful to the late Natalie and Maury Logan; Brian and Coralee Hirsch Logan; Erin Hirsch; Lori Hirsch and her daughter, River; Bill and Maureen Logan Ferrari and their children, Andrew and Christina; Nancy Logan; and Adam and Katie Logan and their children, Audrey, Sarah, and Grant.

Like my first book, this is dedicated to my parents, Mary Rose Mayer and the late Joseph Mayer. Having been a parent myself, my admiration, love, and respect for them has only grown greater over the years. Age deepens the wonder.

1

Introduction: Karl Rove and
the President Makers

This is a story of politics done wrong.

When George W. Bush moved to Washington in January 2001 to become the nation's forty-third president, he, like every other modern president, brought with him a small army of aides, advisors, friends, and associates to help carry out the manifold responsibilities of his new job. Among the best-known and most controversial new occupants of the "presidential branch" was a fifty-year-old political consultant named Karl Rove.

We live in an age of cheap superlatives. Short-lived fads, minor celebrities, and events of small consequence are routinely called "the biggest," "the best," "the worst," "the most amazing." Usually, such descriptions testify only to the limited historical knowledge of so many of our journalists and commentators. And yet, there really is something rare and remarkable about the career of Karl Rove.

A rough measure of Rove's prominence and reputation may be glimpsed by comparing the number of books written about him with the number written about other modern presidential campaign managers and strategists. As of early 2020, when this book was being finished, no one had yet written a book about Hamilton Jordan, Jimmy Carter's top political advisor and manager. (This count does not include three autobiographical books by Jordan himself.) There is one book on Lee Atwater, often seen as the paradigm of a certain type of contemporary political consultant. James Baker, perhaps the most successful political manager of modern times, has zero books written about him. (Like Jordan, Baker has written two books about his own career; his wife has also written an autobiography.) Michael Deaver, Ronald Reagan's chief image minder, and David Axelrod, Barack Obama's principal political strategist, are both bookless, again excepting their own works. James Carville has written at least ten books on politics and political strategy, but no one else has thought Carville sufficiently interesting to write a book about him. By contrast, there are already seven books about Karl Rove, not counting his autobiography, his book on the 1896 election, or the present volume.

There is, of course, nothing new about the basic role that Rove filled. Political consultants have been a ubiquitous feature of presidential campaigns since at least the 1960s; well before that, political managers of various types performed many of the same tasks that are now entrusted to consultants. And many of these consultants, if they worked for the winning candidate, continued to provide the new president with advice and assistance after he was sworn into office. Many were also given formal positions on the White House staff or in other parts of the executive branch. All such surface similarities conceded, Rove nevertheless stands out from his look-alikes in at least three major ways.

Strategist in Chief

The first measure of Rove's distinctiveness is the totality of his direction over Bush's political career. Simply put, George W. Bush never won an election, of any kind, in which Rove was not the dominant, even sole campaign strategist. Before putting Rove in charge of his political destiny, Bush had run for public office just once—for US representative from the Nineteenth District in Texas—and lost. An indifferent student, a failure in almost all his business enterprises, Bush had impressed almost no one as a suitable occupant of the governor's office, much less the presidency, until he became Karl Rove's principal client. And then, with Rove in the driver's seat, Bush's political career suddenly took off. In 1994, he won an upset victory over a popular Democratic governor. In 1998, he was overwhelmingly re-elected, establishing several records in the process.[1] By early 2001, he was president.

Rove's role in nurturing George Bush's political career has often been compared to that played by Marcus Alonzo Hanna in the career of William McKinley in the closing years of the nineteenth century. But this comparison, though frequently made, is fundamentally mistaken.[2] By the standards of the late 1800s, McKinley was a model presidential candidate: a Civil War hero, utterly devoted to his invalid wife, a person of great reserve and dignity, with no significant scandals attached to his name. Hence, Democratic newspapers of the time decided that the best way to attack McKinley was to portray him as the puppet and plaything of Mark Hanna, the wealthy Cleveland businessman who managed McKinley's 1896 and 1900 presidential campaigns and had also helped him get elected governor of Ohio in 1891 and 1893.[3] This image of Hanna as the real power behind the McKinley facade still lingers in the popular and journalistic imagination—but I am not aware of any serious modern historian of Gilded Age politics who accepts it as accurate.[4]

To be sure, Hanna was, by all evidence, a highly skilled manager, organizer, and fundraiser. But McKinley was also a person of considerable ability and substance. Though Hanna and McKinley first met in the 1870s, it was not until 1889 that Hanna made any significant effort to promote McKinley's political career. (Hanna spent most of the 1880s trying, without success, to advance the presidential fortunes of a different Ohio Republican: US senator John Sherman.) By that time, McKinley had already been elected to Congress six times and had established himself as one of the most prominent and highly regarded Republicans in the House of Representatives.

Even in 1896, the election that made Hanna's reputation as a "president maker," McKinley played a much more active, hands-on role in directing the campaign than is often recognized. To take the most noteworthy example, it was McKinley rather than Hanna who decided to conduct the now-famous "front-porch campaign," in which McKinley never left his hometown of Canton, Ohio, and large numbers of voters were brought there to see him.[5] Stanley Jones, in a comprehensive history of the 1896 election, has provided the following description of how the McKinley campaign made decisions with respect to the 1896 Republican convention:

> Though McKinley remained in Canton, the overall strategy and the decisions on all important matters were in his hands to the very last. Hanna and the other members of the McKinley team were entrusted with the work of guiding the McKinley forces in the convention, as they had been entrusted with the work of the pre-convention canvass, only after receiving careful, detailed instructions from McKinley. Thus, each of the McKinley workers at St. Louis went to Canton to talk with McKinley before he went to the convention.[6]

More generally, Jones concluded,

> The popularly accepted picture of Hanna's domination [over McKinley] was not true. Though McKinley did leave to Hanna the immensely complicated and exceedingly arduous task of organizing the campaign and though he usually deferred to Hanna's judgment in this area, he himself retained control of the general structure and program. Nothing was done without his approval. Hanna raised money, hired men, set up headquarters offices, bought literature, with the same drive and skill

that he managed his business. He was confident of his mastery of that kind of operation, but he never ceased to defer to McKinley's mastery of the grand strategy of politics.[7]

For those seeking a historical precedent for the relationship between Bush and Rove, a better fit, at first glance, might be the partnership between Franklin Delano Roosevelt and Louis McHenry Howe.[8] Howe met Roosevelt in 1911, shortly after FDR had first been elected to the New York state senate, started working for him in 1912, and was the campaign manager and principal strategist for every campaign Roosevelt ran for the next twenty years, including his successful quest for the presidency in 1932. Howe also served as Roosevelt's principal deputy during the latter's eight-year stint as assistant secretary of the navy under Woodrow Wilson.

There is no doubt that Howe was a talented political operative and fiercely dedicated to Roosevelt, even living with the Roosevelt family during the bleakest period of FDR's struggles with polio. Yet it is difficult to argue that Howe "made Roosevelt presidential" in the same way that Rove transformed the political career of George W. Bush. Before meeting Howe, Roosevelt had already been elected to the state senate and emerged as a leader of the anti-Tammany forces within the state Democratic Party. More importantly, Howe died in April 1936 (and had been hospitalized for a considerable period before that), yet Roosevelt went on to win three more presidential elections, all by substantial margins.

With the possible exception of George Washington, no one has ever been elected president without a lot of help. Indeed, one mark of a good president is precisely the ability to attract, select, and retain talented subordinates. When reading biographies of McKinley and Roosevelt, however, one always gets the sense that they were firmly in charge of their own careers—that as one historian has written of McKinley, "Hanna was a complement to his skill, not a substitute for it."[9] When examining the relationship between Karl Rove and George W. Bush, one is much less certain that this was the case.

Of all the campaign managers and strategists in American history, the only one I know of whose lifework parallels that of Karl Rove—who established a close, early relationship with an aspiring politician and then devised the strategies that brought him to the White House—is Hamilton Jordan, who directed all of Jimmy Carter's major campaigns.[10] Jordan first met Carter in the summer of 1966, when Carter was running for governor of Georgia (he had already served two terms in the state senate). Jordan served as youth coordinator in that campaign, which Carter lost. When Carter ran for governor again in 1970, Jordan was his campaign manager—

and this time Carter won. Jordan then became the new governor's executive secretary. In 1972, Jordan wrote a famous memo to Carter that outlined, in remarkable and prescient detail, the strategy that Carter would use to propel himself from the governor's office to the White House.[11] Jordan then managed Carter's 1976 presidential campaign, as well as his unsuccessful 1980 reelection effort.

Of all the campaigns Jordan managed, it is Carter's drive for the 1976 Democratic presidential nomination that is surely the most noteworthy. When the former Georgia governor announced his candidacy in December 1974, he was an almost hopeless long shot: unknown outside his own state, relatively inexperienced, from a region of the country that had rarely produced serious presidential contenders, with almost no support from other party leaders. Carter won because his campaign substantially outperformed all the others.

The 1976 nominating contests took place at a moment of great strategic uncertainty: the rules governing the presidential nomination process had just been thoroughly recast, in two major ways.[12] First, the McGovern-Fraser Commission (1969–1970) had systematically rewritten the Democratic Party's delegate selection rules. Then Congress (in 1974) completely refashioned the laws that regulated fundraising and spending in presidential campaigns. Yet, without precedents or guidelines, the Carter campaign devised and implemented a strategy, the basic principles of which quickly became the standard way of running for president in the contemporary era. Announce early. Campaign everywhere. Target Iowa and New Hampshire. In particular, have the candidate spend lots of time in both states meeting voters in small groups and town meetings. Don't worry about national media attention as long as the campaign is doing well with local media. Count on momentum to propel the campaign through the rest of a crowded primary and caucus schedule.

Jordan was not the sole author of this strategy. Gerald Rafshoon, Carter's long-time media advisor, developed a plan for "establishing [Carter's] national image." Tim Kraft was primarily responsible for getting the campaign to focus on Iowa. (Jordan's original memo had only targeted New Hampshire and Florida.) The decision to run everywhere is usually attributed to Carter himself.[13] Still, it was Jordan who fit all the pieces together and then presided over the apparatus that put the plan into practice. Without his leadership, it is most unlikely that Carter would have come anywhere near a first-ballot convention victory.

Politics and Policy

A second important difference between Karl Rove and other major presidential campaign strategists was the role that Rove played in helping formulate policy after Bush became president. As I will document in more detail in chapter 4, Rove was one of Bush's principal domestic policy advisors. Informed observers called him "the only power center on the domestic side of the Bush administration" and the first presidential aide "to tackle two big jobs—dispensing political advice to his boss and controlling the policy levers inside the White House."[14]

Rove's influence on Bush administration policy separates him even more sharply from Hanna and Howe. Neither McKinley nor Roosevelt can be accused of trying to govern "above politics," yet both also recognized that there was a difference between campaigning and governing. Whatever Hanna's skills as a campaign manager, there is no evidence that he ever served as a significant policy advisor to President McKinley. Even during the 1896 campaign, Stanley Jones has noted, Hanna "left in the hands of McKinley and his political entourage the decisions regarding the ideas [i.e., the policy positions] of the campaign."[15] After McKinley won that election, he offered to make Hanna postmaster general—a cabinet post that was a major source of patronage but *not* one that would have allowed Hanna to make important policy decisions. Hanna decided instead that he wanted to become a United States senator—an ambition that McKinley made possible by appointing one of Ohio's existing senators to his cabinet and then pressuring the Ohio governor to appoint Hanna to the vacancy. Even in the Senate, however, Hanna was not among the leaders of his party, nor did he play a role as semiofficial spokesman for the White House. Of all the major policy controversies of the McKinley presidency— the currency question, the Spanish–American war, the postwar occupation of the Philippines, the growing public concern over trusts—Hanna appears to have had a significant impact on none of them.[16] Though Hanna did visit McKinley at the White House on occasion, these meetings were apparently about patronage rather than policy.

Louis Howe's influence on Roosevelt administration policy was only marginally more substantial. After FDR's triumph in 1932, Howe was named secretary to the president and actually moved into the White House with the Roosevelts, living in the Lincoln bedroom. But only a small number of New Deal initiatives bear Howe's imprint—in particular, the Civilian Conservation Corps and the Subsistence Home Experiment. During the 1932 campaign, Howe's efforts were confined to matters of strategy, organization, and publicity. Roosevelt's policy positions were developed by a "brain trust" headed by Columbia University professor Raymond Moley.

At first glance, Hamilton Jordan might once again appear to provide a closer match to the policy role filled by Karl Rove. After Carter won the 1976 election, Jordan quickly established himself as the most powerful of Carter's many aides and advisors. Over time, his responsibilities—especially with regard to policy—steadily increased, until finally, in July 1979, Carter formally named Jordan his White House chief of staff.[17]

Yet Jordan, unlike Rove, never seems to have used his growing powers as an opportunity to push *his own* policy views. Instead, he saw his role in considerably more restricted terms as that of trying to assess the political feasibility of *Carter*'s preferred policies and then coordinating the administration's efforts to achieve those policies. As Nicholas Lemann argued in an insightful profile of Jordan published in 1978:

> Jordan is still very much a non-expert, a man of instinct and common sense, someone who helps the Carter administration meet its goals rather than helping to formulate those goals. The latter role he hasn't taken on because everyone—including Jordan himself—seems convinced that it's not his kind of thing. People bring matters to Jordan after they're finished, and he looks at them and decides whether or not they'll work politically. Or Jordan holds meetings, where he listens quietly and attentively to everyone's point of view and decides which way will work best. Or he plans campaigns like the one for the [Panama Canal] treaties, with much detailed manipulating of the press, politicians, and celebrities. . . . The matter of whether the course is a wise one, Jordan leaves to others. He is reputed to be genuinely idealistic, to care about the people of America and about humanity generally, but the specifics of his ideology all come from Carter.[18]

Later histories of the Carter presidency also support this conclusion. Jordan is often mentioned for commenting on the political effects of various policy proposals, rarely for pronouncing on their policy soundness.[19]

In Search of the Next Realignment

Karl Rove is noteworthy, finally, for the scope of his ambitions. While most "president makers" were concerned merely with getting their favorite candidate elected to the highest office in the land, Rove set his sights even higher. He hoped to create a durable Republican majority that would dominate American politics for the next several decades.

To fully appreciate the nature of Rove's ambition, one must first understand the concept of a *partisan realignment*. The story begins in the mid-1950s, when an eminent political scientist named V. O. Key Jr. wrote an article called "A Theory of Critical Elections." "Even the most fleeting inspection of American elections," Key argued,

> suggests the existence of a category of elections in which voters are . . . unusually deeply concerned, in which the extent of electoral involvement is relatively quite high, and in which the decisive results of the voting reveal a sharp alteration of the pre-existing cleavage within the electorate. Moreover, and perhaps this is the truly differentiating characteristic of this sort of election, the realignment made manifest in the voting seems to persist for several succeeding elections.[20]

From this small seed, a much larger literature soon began to grow, as numerous other scholars developed more systematic methods for identifying such elections or tried to apply the theory's insights to other states and historical periods than the ones Key had analyzed. Though there were always dissenting voices and qualifications, the basic argument gradually came to assume the following form:[21] American electoral and political history has consisted of a number of distinct periods of relative stability, often called *party systems*, in which the identities of the two major parties, the relative electoral success of these parties, and the composition of the party coalitions don't change very much. One party may do unexpectedly well in an election or two, but soon the forces of continuity and stability reassert themselves and the normal pattern of electoral politics returns. And then, quite suddenly, the existing party system breaks down and a new one emerges to take its place. Over a period of just one or two elections, the balance of strength between the parties changes and the composition of each party's regular, core supporters is substantially recast. Once established, this new regime—the new party system—lasts for about twenty-eight to thirty-six years, until it too is overturned by the next realignment. These realignments, it was further argued, tend to be characterized by a high level of voter interest and participation, an unusually intense concern with policy issues, a shift in the major line of cleavage between the parties, and important subsequent changes in public policy. The elections that were usually singled out as critical or realigning elections were those of 1800, 1828, 1860, 1896, 1932, and (maybe) 1968.

For present purposes, the most significant of these earlier realignments was the one that took place in the mid-1890s. The years between 1876 and 1892 were a time of remarkably even competition between Republicans and Democrats.[22] Republicans won three of the five presidential elections held during this period, but all five contests were very close, at least in the popular vote.[23] At the other end of Pennsylvania Avenue, congressional elections generally produced a divided outcome. Democrats won a majority of House seats in seven of nine elections, but Republicans won a majority in the Senate on seven of nine occasions. And then, in 1893, the United States fell into a deep and prolonged economic depression. In 1894, the Republicans seized control of both houses of Congress, gaining an additional 125 seats in the House of Representatives, the largest midterm seat swing in American history. In 1896, the GOP also won back the presidency, as William McKinley scored a decisive victory over William Jennings Bryan. This shift in party fortunes, moreover, was not just a temporary phenomenon. In retrospect, the 1894–1896 results were the beginning of a prolonged period of Republican dominance that lasted, with one interruption, until 1930. Between 1894 and 1928, the Republicans won seven of nine presidential elections and a majority of seats in both houses of Congress fourteen of eighteen times.

In the beginning, most discussions of the realignment phenomenon were confined to the sorts of books and journals that only academics read. In 1969, however, the subject suddenly became of much more practical concern. Kevin Phillips, a young lawyer who had been a special assistant to the national campaign manager in Richard Nixon's just-concluded presidential campaign, published a book called *The Emerging Republican Majority*. As its title indicates, Phillips's thesis was that the next realignment had already begun: 1968 marked the end of the New Deal party system and the start of a new political era that would be dominated by the Republicans.[24] To say the least, this claim was not universally accepted. Over the next half-decade, there was an outpouring of good books on the upheavals of the American political system and which party (if either) was most likely to benefit from the changes.[25]

For now, the most important consequence of that debate was that the realignment concept came out of the ivory tower and became part of mainstream American political discourse. Ever since then, realignment has been a standard part of the conceptual apparatus that journalists, politicians, and political consultants use for interpreting elections. Virtually every decisive presidential election (and some that were not so decisive) has prompted a wave of speculation about whether a realignment was now beginning or continuing.

One person who was clearly steeped in this literature was Karl Rove.

Though Rove never graduated from college, he is, as even his critics concede, extraordinarily well-read, especially on matters of politics and history. This reading gave a particular shape to Rove's ambitions. Simply put, Rove wanted to engineer the next realignment: to have future historians see the Bush presidency as the beginning of a long period of Republican electoral successes.

As many readers of this book will know, in 2002 the theory of party realignments suffered a major body blow. David Mayhew, a Yale political scientist whose work is universally respected within the profession, published a book arguing that the whole realignment concept was fatally flawed. Thinking about American political history as a sequence of realignments and party systems often distorted the facts of history and added "little or no illumination" while blinding us to many other productive ways of understanding and interpreting the past. All of which supplied "a good argument for abandoning the [realignment] terminology entirely."[26] I am not convinced by Mayhew's critique, though any attempt to explain why would require a lengthy analysis of both conceptual issues and electoral data that would take us far beyond the subject matter of this book.[27] For present purposes, it is enough to say that, Mayhew notwithstanding, Karl Rove *did* believe in the theory of party realignments and that this belief is key to understanding the way he approached his job.

It is Rove's interest in party realignments that explains, for example, his special fascination with the presidency of William McKinley. Most historians have rated McKinley as, at best, a slightly above average president. Even Lewis Gould, who has called McKinley "the first modern president" (and whom Rove studied under at the University of Texas), concludes his highly regarded history of the McKinley presidency with the judgment that "greatness is appropriately reserved for only a few presidents, a group in which McKinley does not belong."[28] But all that paled beside one overriding fact: McKinley had been president during the last clear pro-Republican realignment.[29] Thus, when Rove gave a speech in 2002 titled "What Makes a Great President," most of the presidents he mentioned as examples were the usual suspects: Lincoln, Washington, and Franklin and Theodore Roosevelt. But Rove ended his speech with a tribute to McKinley, whom he depicted as the best answer to the question, "Who are the great presidents we don't know are great?"[30] Since leaving the White House, Rove has written two books: one a memoir of his career in politics, the other about McKinley's victory and "why the election of 1896 still matters." (A review of Rove's book on McKinley, which examines the parallels between Rove's interpretation of the 1896 campaign and what he himself tried to do for Bush, can be found in the appendix to this book.)

Not only did Rove admire McKinley, he also saw important similarities between the situation that McKinley encountered in 1896 and the situation facing George W. Bush in 2000. As Nicholas Lemann noted in a profile of Bush published in early 2000:

> Karl Rove has a riff, which he gives to anybody who will listen, entitled "It's 1896." Every national political reporter has heard it, to the extent that it induces affectionate eye-rolling when it comes up. . . . Here's the theory, delivered at Rove's mile-a-minute clip: "Everything you know about William McKinley and Mark Hanna . . . is wrong. The country was in a period of change. McKinley's the guy who figured it out. Politics were changing. The economy was changing. We're at the same point now: weak allegiances to parties, a rising new economy."[31]

Another reporter, writing an article about Rove in 2007, quoted these lines and then added:

> Rove was suggesting that the electorate in 2000, as in 1896, was ripe for realignment, and implying, somewhat immodestly, that he was the guy who had figured it out. . . . Earlier political realignments resulted from historical accidents or anomalies, conditions that were recognized and exploited after the fact by talented politicians. Nobody ever planned one. Rove didn't wait for history to happen to him—he tried to create it on his own. "It's hard to think of any analogue in American history," says David Mayhew, a Yale political scientist who has written a book on electoral realignments, "to what Karl Rove was trying to do."[32]

What Lies Ahead

At one level, this book is an analysis of Karl Rove's performance as a presidential advisor: the roles he played, the kinds of advice he gave to President George W. Bush, and how the Republican Party fared when Rove was its principal strategist. For all the books that have been written about Rove, this aspect of his career has been strangely ignored. Virtually all previous work has focused either on the various dirty tricks he allegedly committed or about how, long after the end of the Bush presidency, Rove is still purportedly hatching plans to take over the country.

But I am also interested in exploring a second and larger set of questions: What is the proper role of politics in the contemporary presidency? When does politics enhance a nation's long-term welfare and when does it detract from it? And what positive contributions can political advisors make to a modern-day president?

Among the more persistent elements in American political culture is a tradition of regarding politics as something dirty and sordid, which should therefore be kept as far as possible from governing in general and from the Oval Office in particular. As historian Richard Current observed: "Among Americans the words *politics* and *politician* long have been terms of reproach. Politics generally means 'dirty' politics, whether the adjective is used or not. Politicians, then, are dirty politicians unless they happen to be statesmen, and in that case they are not politicians at all."[33] Even Abraham Lincoln, by all odds the best politician America ever produced, once defined politicians as "a set of men who have interests aside from the interests of the people, and who . . . are, taken as a mass, at least one long step removed from honest men."[34]

One consequence of this tradition was that for the first hundred years or so after the adoption of the Constitution, aspirants for the presidency were rarely allowed to acknowledge their ambitions in public. Convinced that the lust for power was one of the strongest and least easily restrained of human passions, most Americans seem to have believed that it was simply inappropriate for any person to campaign actively for the presidency. The office was supposed to seek the person, not the reverse. Of course, with the notable exception of George Washington, there is little evidence that this norm actually resulted in a line of pure, selfless presidents devoid of personal ambition. Though major party nominations were occasionally conferred on men who had not actively sought to be a presidential candidate, most presidential elections between 1796 and the end of the nineteenth century were contested by a group of candidates who were probably about as ambitious as present-day aspirants. The only difference was that, quite deceptively, they were unwilling or unable to acknowledge this fact.

Today, of course, we have long since passed the time when presidential aspirants decline to acknowledge their ambitions. For the last fifty years, no one has been elected president without devoting almost two full years to a very public campaign, shaking every hand in sight and pleading for every vote and financial contribution. But if this sort of behavior is now regarded as (mostly) legitimate, much of our civic discourse seems to be based on the premise that politics should end on election night. Once the voters have rendered their decision, politics should be replaced by a pure concern for the public good and (at least in some versions) the disinterested rule of experts. This is the major appeal of the frequently proposed constitutional amendment that would limit presidents to a single, six-year term. After their election, it would—allegedly—prevent presidents from worrying about politics.[35]

The 1976 presidential campaign provided a nice demonstration of how potent the antipolitics element in our national culture continues to be. That year, Democratic presidential candidate Birch Bayh ran television commercials that featured the tagline "It takes a good politician to make a good president." However much one might admire Bayh's honesty, this was plainly not a message that most voters wanted to hear. As Bayh's pollster told me later, most voters he surveyed disagreed with the campaign's slogan. (You know your campaign is in trouble when most voters don't even like your slogan.) Instead, the Democrats nominated Jimmy Carter, a man who regularly insisted that he was not a politician, even though he had spent the previous fourteen years either holding public office or seeking his next one.

Is politics really such a rank undertaking? The answer depends to a great extent on what one means by that elusive word *politics*. A standard dictionary definition holds that politics is "the art or science of government," which sounds harmless enough.[36] For those seeking a more attractive, more ennobling definition, there is the one proposed by Robert Maynard Hutchins: politics "is the science of the common good. . . . The task of politics is to define the common good and to organize the community to achieve it."[37] Neither of these definitions, however, helps us to understand the image that politics holds in our culture—why Carter denied that he was a politician and why Bayh's open embrace of that term was almost certainly a tactical mistake. For the purposes of this book, I therefore adopt a less exalted but, I believe, more realistic definition: *politics is the art of acquiring and keeping power*.

Some readers might object that this definition is notably amoral: that it says nothing about the ends for which politics is used. But this, in my judgment, merely reflects the way politics works and, thus, the way the word is used. There are many people who are described as brilliant politicians who used their power for entirely reprehensible purposes. Joseph Stalin, to take just one example, was undoubtedly one of the most brutal tyrants of the twentieth century, but he was also clearly a very skilled politician. Anyone who fails to acknowledge this would be hard put to explain how he managed to outmaneuver several rivals to become Lenin's successor and how he was then able to wage a campaign of terror against the Russian population at large and many of his top associates, without ever losing his grip on power.

Besides its descriptive accuracy, one of the principal merits of this definition is that it helps explain the dilemma that confronts anyone who hopes to be successful in politics. As Americans have long recognized—a recognition central to the ideology that lay behind the American Revolution—political power is dangerous but necessary.[38] On the one hand, as I have just noted, power can be used in all sorts of oppressive, unfair, and corrupt ways. As the Founders also recognized, there is something about power that is almost addictive. Of all the passions that are supposed to motivate human behavior, the lust for power, they believed, was among the least easily controlled. One of the most popular books of the revolutionary era put it this way: "Almost all men desire power, and few lose any opportunity to get it. . . . We know, by infinite examples and experience, that men possessed of power, rather than part with it, will do anything, even the worst and the blackest to keep it."[39]

But power can also be used—indeed, has to be used—to protect the country from external enemies, preserve law and order, help make the nation more prosperous, assist the disadvantaged and vulnerable, protect the environment, and more. Someone who does not know how to get and use power may make a tolerably good prophet, but not a successful politician.

What I hope to do in this book, then, is to explore and defend a middle ground: to argue that there are both appropriate and inappropriate uses for politics and that one task of a good president—and a good presidential advisor—is to appreciate the difference. The old aphorism, which Rove himself sometimes quoted, that "good government is good politics, and vice versa," is true in some circumstances, but there are also many ways in which good politics and good policy are in conflict. Chapters 3 through 10 are thus each designed to convey one major lesson that I have derived from a close study of the Bush presidency. As these chapters will indicate, I have faulted Rove (and Bush) for errors of both kinds: for being too concerned with immediate electoral needs in some cases and for ignoring the importance of political considerations in others.

In the interests of full disclosure, I should finally say something about my own, very limited involvement in the events examined in this book. Shortly after the 2000 election was resolved, I wrote a letter to Karl Rove in which I said that I knew a number of Republican and Republican-leaning political scientists who specialized in the study of voting and elections and offered to organize a group of such people who would meet periodically with Rove and other major Republican Party strategists and provide them with any advice or assistance that might be gleaned from our research. This group, later called the Academic Advisory Committee, was duly put together and met with various White House and Republican National Committee staffers, including Rove, on four or five occasions between 2001 and 2005.[40]

(For those who think that money is the root of all evil, it should be noted that we were never paid for our work.) Several members of the group (I was not among them) contributed to the development of the Republican Party's extensive 2004 voter mobilization program. That aside, I am not aware that the committee had any significant impact on the administration's political strategy or behavior.

I do not believe that this "brush with history" has influenced or contaminated the analysis presented here, but those who think otherwise cannot complain that they have not been forewarned.

2

The Rove Record

We should begin by assessing Rove's performance on his preferred terrain, his home turf. Whatever else he may have morphed into, Rove's roots—his entrée into presidential politics and then the White House—have always been firmly planted in the world of political consulting. And political consulting, unlike many areas of public policy, has a single, clear goal. Whatever else political consultants may say in defense of their profession, its overriding purpose—the *sole* reason candidates hire consultants—is to win elections. And as profiles of the Bush political brain trust invariably noted, few consultants subscribed to this "just win" philosophy as completely as Karl Rove.

Hence the unavoidable question: How often did Karl Rove win? How well did the Republican Party fare while Rove was the principal person plotting its strategies and directing its fortunes and was also one of the president's top domestic policy advisors? The purpose of this chapter is to take a closer look at the elections of 2000 through 2008 and at how public perceptions of the Bush presidency have continued to affect American politics after he left the White House.

The 2000 Nomination Campaign

For analytical purposes, it is useful to divide the 2000 nomination campaign into two phases: the invisible primary, the extended period of campaigning that preceded the Iowa caucuses; and the primary and caucus season, when the national convention delegates were actually selected.

Of Rove's performance during the 2000 invisible primary, it is hard not to speak in superlatives. Simply put, it was perhaps the most brilliantly executed campaign of its type in recent history. By the time it was over, Bush had the largest lead over his competitors of any nonincumbent presidential candidate since the nomination rules were rewritten in the early 1970s.[1]

The 2000 Bush campaign really began in 1998, when Rove correctly anticipated that he could significantly enhance Bush's presidential prospects by not just getting the Texas governor reelected but by running up a huge margin of victory. (The Democrats nicely cooperated by nominating a weak candidate to run against Bush.) When the dust settled, Bush had received 68 percent of the total vote, including, according to the network exit polls, 49 percent of the Hispanic vote, 27 percent of the black vote, and 31 percent of the votes cast by Democrats and liberals. In a year when Republicans in general fell short of their preelection expectations, Bush's victory sent a potent message to victory-hungry Republicans. Here, it said, was one candidate who wasn't tarred by the excesses of the Republican Congress, who could appeal to groups outside of the usual Republican coalition.

Through the first five months of 1999, as the other Republican candidates engaged in a typical, all-out scramble for money and support, Rove found a more dignified and attractive way to showcase his candidate. Taking advantage of Bush's large early lead in name recognition and media attention, Rove ran what was variously called a "front-porch" or "Yellow Rose Garden" campaign. Reputedly modeled on the general election campaign that William McKinley ran in 1896, Rove kept Bush in Austin, Texas, as long as the Texas state legislature was in session and brought the campaign to him. A steady procession of Republican Party leaders, fundraisers, allied interest group leaders, and policy intellectuals made the pilgrimage to Austin, where they met with Bush in small groups and then (usually) expressed their support for his still-not-formally-declared presidential candidacy or at least said flattering things about him.

Meanwhile, Rove was using Bush's family connections and his own base in Texas politics to assemble what can only be described as the most potent campaign fundraising machine in contemporary American history. I will review the achievements of that operation in a moment. For now, it is worth emphasizing how Bush's fundraising success enhanced the other aspects of his campaign, heightening the sense that he was the strongest and most attractive candidate in the Republican field and thereby convincing other party leaders and activists to jump on the bandwagon. So complete was Bush's domination of Republican fundraising that many of his early rivals found it difficult or impossible to get the money they needed to run even a minimally competitive campaign. As one political scientist noted at the time, "This is the political equivalent of bombing the supply lines. There's only so much political money out there, and every dollar that goes to [Bush] is a dollar that doesn't go anywhere else."[2] Between July and October 1999, six GOP presidential candidates were compelled to withdraw from the race before a single vote was cast, including Dan Quayle, Elizabeth Dole, Lamar Alexander, and John Kasich.

In work that a number of other scholars and I have published over the last two decades, two major indicators have generally been used to assess the rival candidates' progress during the invisible primary period.[3] The first is the candidates' relative standing in surveys of the national party electorate. Almost from the moment that one presidential election concludes, pollsters ask national samples of Democrats and Republicans whom they would like to see nominated as their party's next presidential candidate. The last such poll taken before the Iowa caucuses, the traditional start of the delegate selection process, has been shown to be a good predictor of who will eventually win the nomination (though its predictions were wrong in 2004 and 2008). Whatever their forecasting value, these polls provide a useful picture of how well the candidates are managing to get their name and message out to potential primary voters.

As shown in table 2.1, Bush was always a major contender for his party's 2000 nomination. By September 1997, he already had a small lead over the rest of the Republican field. The more impressive pattern in table 2.1, however, is how Bush's support among the nation's Republicans grew over time—from 21 percent in September 1997 to 39 percent in October 1998, to 52 percent in March 1999, to 61 percent in August 1999. To provide some perspective on these figures, the top half of table 2.2 compares Bush's standing in the final pre-Iowa poll with that of the pre-Iowa front-runners in every other contested presidential nomination race held between 1980 and 2016. As these figures demonstrate, not only was Bush well ahead of his rivals for the 2000 nomination, he had a more dominating position than any other nomination front-runner of the modern era. Bush in early 2000 was considerably more popular among his party's adherents than was Ronald Reagan in 1980, Walter Mondale in 1984, George H. W. Bush in 1988, or Hillary Clinton in 2016.

The second indicator of the candidates' standing during the invisible primary is their ability to raise campaign money, as revealed by the reports they file every quarter with the Federal Election Commission (FEC). Though multivariate models typically show that money has little or no independent effect on nomination outcomes once poll standings are accounted for, a substantial campaign war chest is nonetheless an important prerequisite for a successful nomination campaign. More to the immediate point, the so-called money primary is widely regarded by candidates, journalists, and consultants as an important indicator of how a nomination race is progressing. Howard Dean, for example, first drew the attention of the national press corps because of his fundraising success during the second quarter of 2003.

In 1999 the Bush campaign raised $67,631,000, approximately double

Table 2.1. Presidential Nomination Preferences of National Republican Identifiers during the 2000 Invisible Primary

"Next, I'm going to read a list of people who may be running in the Republican primary for president in the year 2000. After I read all the names, please tell me which of those candidates you would be most likely to support for the Republican nomination for president." Question was asked of Republicans and Republican-leaning independents.

Survey date	Bush (%)	McCain (%)	Forbes (%)	Dole (%)	Quayle (%)	Buchanan (%)	Hatch (%)
All Republicans							
Sept. 6–7, 1997	21	—	9	—	10	4	—
May 8–10, 1998	30	4	7	14	9	3	—
Oct. 23–25	39	—	6	18	12	—	—
Jan. 8–10, 1999	42	8	5	22	6	—	—
March 12–14	52	3	1	20	9	4	—
April 13–14	53	5	6	16	7	4	—
April 30–May 2	42	4	6	24	6	5	—
May 23–24	46	6	5	18	7	6	—
June 4–5	46	5	5	14	9	6	—
June 25–27	59	5	6	8	6	3	2
Aug. 16–18	61	5	4	13	6	3	1
Sept. 10–14	62	5	5	10	5	3	2
Oct. 8–10	60	8	4	11	—	3	2
Oct. 21–24	68	11	8	—	—	—	3
Nov. 4–7	68	12	6	—	—	—	2
Nov. 18–21	63	16	6	—	—	—	4
Registered voters only							
Nov. 18–21	63	16	6	—	—	—	4
Dec. 9–12	64	18	7	—	—	—	2
Dec. 20–21	60	17	9	—	—	—	1
Jan. 7–10, 2000	63	18	5	—	—	—	2
Jan. 13–16	61	22	5	—	—	—	1
Jan. 17–19	63	19	6	—	—	—	1

Source: Gallup Poll.
Note: An em dash indicates that a candidate's name was not listed in the survey question, either because they were not thought to be running for president or had already withdrawn from the race.

what multimillionaire Steve Forbes had contributed to his campaign and more than four times the amount of money that John McCain was able to raise. Again, a historical comparison can help give perspective to the Bush campaign's achievement. The bottom half of table 2.2 shows the total amount of money raised in the year before the election by the most successful fundraiser in each contested nomination race between 1980 and 2000, adjusted for inflation.[4] The Bush total dwarfs that of Al Gore, then the incumbent vice president, and of every campaign that preceded it.

The 2000 invisible primary, in short, was a remarkable triumph for Karl

Table 2.2. Historical Comparison of George W. Bush with Other Early Front-Runners in Contested Presidential Nomination Races

A. National Poll Standings

Year and party	Top candidate in last national poll before Iowa	Percentage	Margin over his/her nearest competitor (%)
1980 Republican	Ronald Reagan	41	27
1980 Democratic	Jimmy Carter	51	14
1984 Democratic	Walter Mondale	49	36
1988 Republican	George H. W. Bush	45	15
1988 Democratic	Gary Hart	23	7
1992 Democratic	Bill Clinton	42	26
1996 Republican	Robert Dole	47	31
2000 Republican	George W. Bush	63	44
2000 Democratic	Al Gore	60	33
2004 Democratic	Howard Dean	25	6
2008 Republican	Rudy Giuliani	27	11
2008 Democratic	Hillary Clinton	45	18
2012 Republican	Mitt Romney	24	1
2016 Republican	Donald Trump	37	16
2016 Democratic	Hillary Clinton	55	19

B. Fundraising

Year and party	Top fundraiser in the year before the election	Total net receipts	Inflation-adjusted receipts*
1980 Republican	John Connally	$9,160,000	$21,020,000
1980 Democratic	Jimmy Carter	5,752,000	13,199,000
1984 Democratic	Walter Mondale	11,448,000	19,148,000
1988 Republican	George H. W. Bush	19,058,000	27,949,000
1988 Democratic	Michael Dukakis	10,371,000	15,210,000
1992 Democratic	Bill Clinton	3,304,000	4,041,000
1996 Republican	Robert Dole	24,612,000	26,905,000
2000 Republican	George W. Bush	67,631,000	67,631,000
2000 Democratic	Al Gore	27,829,000	27,829,000

Source: All poll results are taken from the Gallup Poll except 2016, which are taken from ABC News/*Washington Post*. Fundraising data are taken from the Federal Election Commission reports submitted by the candidates, available at fec.gov.
*In 1999 dollars.

Rove (and, of course, for George W. Bush). By the time it was over, half of the original Republican candidates had already withdrawn and Bush had a commanding, apparently prohibitive lead over all his remaining rivals.

Unfortunately for Rove and Bush, the Republicans decided to hold their 2000 primaries and caucuses anyway, and here Rove's performance was much less impressive. In particular, Rove seems to have completely misread the nature of the campaign in the critical early states of Iowa and New Hampshire. Both states have long prided themselves on being the last vestiges of retail politics in the presidential nomination process: two places where the voters insist on meeting the candidates up close and in person and having a serious discussion of the issues. Yet, Rove inexplicably chose to run a glitzy, vacuous, mass media-focused campaign in both states.

Rove got away with it in Iowa, largely because Bush's only real opponent in that state was Steve Forbes. Even then, Bush's margin of victory was unexpectedly small. New Hampshire, where Bush squared off against John McCain for the first time, was a different story.

The contrast between the Bush and McCain campaigns in New Hampshire is nicely captured in two events that I witnessed on the Saturday before the primary. McCain was in Windham, New Hampshire, that evening, holding one in a series of more than one hundred town meetings across the state. After a few introductory remarks, McCain spent the next ninety minutes fielding questions on any and all topics from the audience of ordinary voters. And while many of his listeners might have disagreed with the positions he took, his answers were invariably clear, straightforward, and nonevasive. (Also unscripted.) If McCain often received positive press coverage from such events, one can only say he deserved it.

Earlier that day, by contrast, the Bush campaign had held its major event for the day in the massive indoor tennis court space at a country club in Milford. The location is itself significant: most New Hampshire campaign events are held in town halls or school gymnasiums. But such pedestrian surroundings apparently struck the Bush high command as insufficiently regal; hence, they chose the considerably more expensive option of renting out a private country club. The event began with Texas-style line dancing, led by two people from a commercial DJ service. Next, there was a short country-western concert by the Bellamy Brothers. After an interlude of cheerleading directed by a short, fat kid with a loud voice, Bush himself took the stage. He spoke for perhaps five minutes, thanking some prominent local supporters and saying how much he liked the enthusiasm of his New Hampshire campaign. Then he introduced his parents. Barbara Bush spoke for about forty-five seconds, the former president for a minute and a half, both saying how proud they were of their son.

And that was it. During the entire exercise, there was not a single mention of *any* substantive issue. Any undecided voters attracted by curiosity, civic duty, or the music were never given a single reason why they might actually want to support George Bush. As I noted in an op-ed published several days later, it was "the most vacuous, content-free political rally" I had seen in twenty-five years of observing and participating in campaigns.[5]

For a campaign that was already facing questions about whether its candidate had enough intelligence and experience to handle the presidency, holding such an event was a shockingly bad strategic decision. Nor was this particular event unrepresentative of what the Bush campaign had been doing for the previous six months. As Dan Balz wrote in the *Washington Post* two days after the primary, both Republicans and Democrats had characterized the Bush New Hampshire campaign as "long on photo ops and endorsements and short on substance and energy."[6] In the week before the primary, most polls had shown Bush and McCain running about even in New Hampshire. In the actual primary, McCain trounced Bush, 48 percent to 30 percent.

Suddenly—but quite predictably—Rove's carefully laid plans for an easy, consensual Bush coronation had come undone, and the Republican nomination contest turned into a dogfight. In South Carolina, site of the next major Republican primary, Bush had once led McCain by 62 percent to 15 percent. Three days after New Hampshire, the polls read McCain 44 percent, Bush 40 percent.[7]

The 2000 South Carolina primary had a simple narrative arc. Stunned by the magnitude of its loss in New Hampshire, the Bush campaign abandoned its previous resolution to run a "positive campaign" and attacked McCain; McCain responded in kind. Soon the charges and accusations and mud were flying fast and furious. Press reports on the campaign featured headlines like "Accusations Fly of False Advertising"; "Bush and McCain Exchange Sharp Words over Fund-Raising"; "GOP Rivals Escalate Fight"; "Spotlight Turns on Ugly Side of Politicking"; and "Harsh, Incessant Wave Crosses South Carolina."[8] As the chairman of the South Carolina Democratic Party happily observed, "It's an electronic charnel house. Bush and McCain have not only taken the gloves off, they've put the brass knuckles on."[9]

And then McCain blinked. On February 11, eight days before the primary, McCain was sufficiently disturbed by the tone of the campaign that he announced he was pulling all his negative television ads and would run only positive commercials for the rest of the South Carolina campaign. The Bush campaign had no such scruples. As the *New York Times* reported on the day before the primary, "'Winning ugly' may be taking on new meaning in the closing days of the South Carolina primary campaign, as the airwaves fill with a new round of acrimonious commercials, virtually all directed toward Senator John McCain of Arizona. . . . Since Mr. McCain's renunciation of his own attack ads last week, and especially in recent days, Mr. Bush's advertisements have become almost unrelentingly aggressive. If anything, they are tougher now than before Mr. McCain pulled back."[10]

The Bush campaign even attacked McCain for engaging in negative campaigning.

The McCain campaign apparently pinned its hopes on the prospect that voters would be turned off by the negative tone of the Bush campaign and reward the Arizona senator for his more positive approach. To no avail: On February 19, Bush beat McCain rather handily in the South Carolina primary, 53 percent to 42 percent. And with that loss, the McCain insurgency effectively fizzled out. Though McCain won a number of other primaries (mostly in New England), he never again seriously threatened to derail the Bush juggernaut. The overwhelming assets that Bush had amassed during the invisible primary period were simply too much to overcome.

The 2000 General Election

On the surface, 2000 did not look like a particularly good year to be the Republican presidential nominee. The country was at peace; the US economy was dazzlingly prosperous; and though President Clinton had been tarnished by personal scandal, his job approval ratings, the conventional way of measuring the president's standing with the public, were quite high. Under such circumstances, the incumbent party generally wins reelection.

Perhaps the most vivid testimonial to how much circumstances seemed to favor Al Gore in 2000 was provided by a subfield in political science known as election forecasting. In the mid-1980s, American political scientists began to develop statistical models that claimed to be able to predict the results of a presidential election months before the actual voting took place. Using such variables as the approval rating of the incumbent president and the state of the economy, these models generate a numerical forecast, usually of the two-party division of the popular vote.

The Super Bowl of presidential election forecasting occurs every four years at the American Political Science Association's national convention, held over the Labor Day weekend, when every political scientist with a presidential forecasting model is given five minutes to explain how it works and then reveal his prediction for the upcoming election. In 2000, there were seven modelers, who made the following forecasts as to the percentage of the two-party popular vote that Al Gore would receive:

Holbrook	60.3
Lockerbie	60.3
Lewis-Beck and Tien	55.4
Wlezien and Erikson	55.2

Norpoth	55.0
Abramowitz	53.2
Campbell	52.8
Actual Result	50.3

The forecasters, that is to say, uniformly predicted that Gore would fare *a lot* better than he actually did. Had Gore matched even the lowest of these predictions, he would have spent the next four years in the White House, regardless of whatever did or did not take place in Florida.

The 2000 presidential forecasting debacle received a great deal of after-the-fact scrutiny from political scientists.[11] A long list of possible culprits was identified. I list them here in order of increasing general acceptance—that is, the explanations that were most widely credited by academic analysts are listed last:

- the third-party candidacy of Ralph Nader, who drew more votes from Gore than Pat Buchanan drew from Bush;
- a noticeable decline in economic conditions during the third quarter of 2000 (for reasons of timing, forecasting models can only include economic data up through the *second* quarter of the election year);
- the impact of Clinton's personal scandals, which do not seem to have affected his approval rating, a variable frequently used in forecasting models, but did cause a large decline in the number of Americans who viewed him favorably as a person;
- the likelihood that Gore received only partial credit for the Clinton-era economic prosperity, since Gore was, after all, only the vice president;
- the fact that the Gore campaign made almost no attempt to emphasize or claim credit for the health of the economy, choosing instead to run on a theme of economic populism that probably struck many voters as too liberal in tone.

The last of these explanations deserves particular attention. Since election forecasts are made before most of the general election campaign takes place, forecasters are compelled to argue that campaigns have minimal and generally predictable effects: that both major party campaigns make their share of good and bad decisions and that the net effects of the campaign are therefore pretty much a wash.[12] In *most* years. But perhaps 2000 was different—maybe in this case, the campaigns were mismatched. Maybe one campaign (i.e., Bush's) was substantially better run than the other (Gore's), with the result that in 2000, the campaigns mattered a lot more than they usually do. Among the people apparently inclined to this view was Karl Rove himself, who often called attention to the forecasters' failure as proof of his own managerial prowess.[13]

Unfortunately for Rove's place in history, the argument that was usually made in postelection commentary concerned how *poorly* the *Gore* campaign had been managed. No academic analyst I know of gave Bush or Rove credit for having run an exceptionally brilliant campaign. To the contrary, Rove, too, came in for his share of criticism. Questions were raised especially about the Bush campaign's decision to expend so much time and money in California during the closing weeks of the campaign—a state that Bush had no realistic chance of winning. During the final eight days of the general election campaign, Bush devoted a significant part of two days' personal campaigning to California; and, according to one report, spent more money on television advertising in California than in any of the major battleground states.[14] Yet, in the end, Bush lost California by 11 percentage points and 1.2 million votes. The Bush campaign has also been faulted for not acting earlier to disclose Bush's 1976 arrest for drunk driving—which instead was made public just five days before Election Day and thus, according to some reports, helped dampen turnout among social conservatives and evangelical voters.

Still, if the 2000 Bush general election campaign was not entirely mistake-free, it was, in general, very well run. Many important strengths of the Bush campaign, moreover, involved advance planning rather than spur-of-the-moment decisions made in the heat of the fall campaign—and were, therefore, easy for analysts to overlook. Bush would never have achieved his narrow victory in the electoral college, for example, had Rove not had the foresight to target a number of states that a less prescient strategist might have written off, such as the hitherto-Democratic bastion of West Virginia[15] or Tennessee, Gore's home state. As I will argue in a subsequent chapter, Rove also understood the need to soften some of the rough edges associated with traditional conservatism.

The bottom line is that Rove won an election against enormous odds and deserves great credit for doing so. If the 2012 Romney campaign had been as well managed, Barack Obama would have been a one-term president.[16]

The 2002 Midterm Election

Through most of American history, one of the most reliable, time-tested patterns in politics has been that the party of the president loses seats in

Congress at midterm elections. Between 1880 and 1996, the only exception to this regularity had occurred in 1934, in the middle of what was later recognized as the New Deal realignment. Against that background, the results of the 2002 midterm elections, in which the Republicans actually *gained* eight seats in the House and two in the Senate, would have been regarded as an historic achievement—except that Bill Clinton and the Democrats had done pretty much the same thing four years earlier, picking up five seats in the House and breaking even in the Senate. As they say in comedy, timing is everything.

Record-breaking or not, however, there is good reason to think that the 2002 Republican midterm campaign was very skillfully managed, and that Karl Rove, who directed the campaign at a remarkable level of detail, deserves much of the credit. Rove's efforts probably helped his party in at least three major ways. First, in a number of states, including Minnesota and Georgia, Rove personally selected the Republican candidate for Senate—and successfully discouraged other Republican aspirants from entering the race.

Second, and easy to overlook, Rove and the president's other political advisors deserve considerable credit for the fact that Bush was as popular as he was. In early September 2001, Bush had an approval rating in the low to mid-50 percent range, about average for recent presidents at a similar point in their first terms. And then, on September 11, terrorists attacked the World Trade Center and the Pentagon, killing thousands of Americans in the process. Within days, Bush's approval rating shot up to 86 percent, and then to 90 percent.[17]

Neither Bush nor Rove can claim credit for this increase, nor have they. What is often called the "rally-round-the-flag" effect is a well-known and frequently recurring phenomenon in American politics—and as Nelson Polsby once noted, seems to occur "regardless of the wisdom of the policies [the president] pursues."[18] More noteworthy for present purposes is how long this increase lasted. According to political scientists Marc Hetherington and Michael Nelson, the post-9/11 rally "lasted longer than any in the history of polling."[19] Not until November 2003, more than two years later, did Bush's approval rating return to something like its pre-9/11 level. By way of comparison, George H. W. Bush, the president's father, had enjoyed an 89 percent approval rating in early March 1991, in the immediate aftermath of the Gulf War. Yet just ten months later, the elder Bush had lost all of his postwar "bounce" and more. By mid-December 1991, Bush's approval rating was down to 50 percent; by February 1992, it had declined to 39 percent.

George W. Bush has been criticized—with considerable justification—

for many of the decisions he made in conducting the war on terror. (For my own criticisms, see chapters 7, 8, and 9.) So it is only fair to note the many steps he took immediately after the 9/11 attacks that helped preserve and enhance national unity—and also had the effect of bolstering his own popularity. First, Bush declined to blame the attacks on his predecessor or on any other members of the Democratic Party. Second, Bush refused to criticize or stigmatize Muslims as a group, instead insisting that Islam's teachings were "good and peaceful"[20] and forbidding anything that might have been construed as racial or ethnic profiling. Third, he resisted considerable public pressure for an immediate response to the attacks, waiting until there was clear, strong evidence showing who was really at fault. Fourth, the military campaign against the Taliban in Afghanistan was conducted with a remarkably low level of US troop involvement and, thus, a very low number of American casualties.[21] The upshot was that during the fall 2002 campaign, Bush's approval rating hovered between 62 and 70 percent.

Finally, Rove tried to take maximum advantage of the president's popularity by convincing Bush to assume an unusually active and visible role in the 2002 fall campaign. As political commentator Larry Sabato noted:

> Most presidents have learned to be extremely cautious, and not to take unnecessary risks. Thus, the usual behavior of a president in midterm elections is to raise money for party candidates early in the year, then make occasional appearances in September and October for favored nominees, avoiding too close identification with candidates who may lose. George Bush decided to set a new precedent, however. He campaigned extensively for party candidates from Labor Day onwards, braving criticism that he was "spending too much time on politics." He criss-crossed the country over and over, appearing a half-dozen times or more in the states with key races. He barnstormed for House candidates, not just Senate and gubernatorial contenders. In the last ten days he never left the trail, spending long days and nights jetting to contests that the latest tracking polls showed he could influence.[22]

Terry McAuliffe, then-chairman of the Democratic National Committee, offered a more laconic explanation for his party's losses: "We faced a very popular president who campaigned more than any other president."[23] Several good studies have since confirmed what most observers suspected at the time: that Bush's campaigning provided a significant boost to his party's House and Senate candidates.[24]

Table 2.3 shows one measure of how well Rove's tactics worked. In eight

Table 2.3. Expressed Support and Opposition to the President in Midterm Exit Polls

Vote for Congress was meant to . . .

Year	Express support for the president	Express opposition to the president	President not a factor	Net effect (% support – % opposed)
1982	35	40	25	−5
1990	20	16	64	+4
1994	17	27	55	−10
1998	18	20	62	−2
2002	37	18	45	+19
2006	22	37	39	−15
2010	20	34	47	−14
2014	19	33	45	−14

Source: All data are taken from midterm exit polls conducted by CBS/*New York Times* (1982); Voter Research and Surveys (1990); Voter News Service (1994, 1998, 2002); and Edison Media Research/Mitofsky International (2006, 2010, 2014).
Note: From 1990 to 2014, the question was worded as follows: "Was one reason for your vote for Congress today: to express support for [name of current president]; to express opposition to [current president]; [current president] was not a factor." In 1982, question read: "Do you think of your vote for U.S. House today a vote for or against Ronald Reagan? for Reagan; against Reagan; Reagan not a factor." Question was not asked in 1986.

of the last nine midterm elections, a major media exit poll has included a question of the form: "Was one reason for your vote for Congress today: to express support for [the president]; to express opposition to [the president]; [the president] was not a factor." Of all the elections shown in this table, Bush in 2002 had the largest margin of support over opposition.

The 2004 Election

In the immediate aftermath of the 2004 elections, both Rove and Bush were clearly anxious to portray the result as not just a win for Bush—which it indisputably was—but as a significant and decisive triumph. Bush called it "an historic victory" and later told a press conference, "I earned capital in the campaign, political capital, and now I intend to spend it."[25] Several days after that, Rove spoke at a reporters' lunch where, one participant later recounted, "before taking questions, [Rove] removed a folded piece of paper from his pocket and rattled off a series of numbers that made clear how he wanted the election to be seen: not as a squeaker but a rout."

This was an extraordinary election. [Bush won] 59.7 million votes, and we still have about 250,000 ballots to count. [Bush's final total was actually 62.0 million.] Think about that—*nearly 60 million votes!* The previous largest number was Ronald Reagan in 1984, sweeping the country with 49 states. We won 81 percent of all the counties in America. We gained a percentage of the vote in 87 percent of the counties in America. In Florida, we received nearly a million votes more in this election than in the last one.[26]

A more disinterested look at the 2004 results, however, makes such a verdict impossible to sustain. Running against a Democratic opponent whom Republicans had repeatedly ridiculed for being stiff, aloof, inconsistent, ineffectual, and ultraliberal, the president actually came rather close to losing. The precariousness of Bush's victory becomes particularly clear when one compares his showing in 2004 with the results of the fourteen other presidential elections held between 1948 and 2004.[27]

Table 2.4 provides three possible ways of looking at the numbers. Measured by the percentage of the *two-party popular vote*, Bush's showing—51.2 percent—is clearly well below average. Using the percentage of the *total popular vote* (i.e., taking third-party votes into account), as shown in the next section of table 2.4, makes Bush look a little better, but not dramatically so. He still ranks below the median. Measured finally in terms of the percentage of the *electoral vote*, Bush's showing was the second weakest in the previous half century, exceeding only his even narrower victory in 2000. Put most bluntly, a candidate who beats his opponent by less than 2.5 percent of the total vote cannot claim to have won an "historic victory." Nor, as Bush would learn in the succeeding months, will he earn any significant amount of "political capital."

As for the various numbers that Rove "rattled off" to reporters in an attempt to demonstrate the decisiveness of the 2004 vote, all of them dissolve on closer inspection. The fact that Bush won "nearly 60 million votes," at the time the largest number ever received by a presidential candidate, shows only that the US population is growing and, thus, so is the size of the electorate. John Kerry, as it turned out, also won more votes than Ronald Reagan had in 1984, but that hardly proves that Kerry was more popular or a better vote-getter than Reagan. Bush won "81 percent of all the counties in America" because Republican candidates tend to do well in small, rural counties that are more numerous—but have fewer votes—than the large, urban counties that provide the core support for Democratic candidates. In Illinois, for example, Bush won a plurality of the vote in 87 of the state's 102 counties. But the fact that Bush carried Brown County (which recorded 2,614 votes), Clay County (6,770 votes), and Jasper County (5,395 votes) does not offset Kerry's decisive margin in Cook County (2,088,727 ballots

Table 2.4. How Bush's Vote in the 2004 Presidential Election Compares to That of Other Postwar Presidents

A. Ranked by Percentage of the Two-Party Popular Vote

Richard Nixon 1972	61.8
Lyndon Johnson 1964	61.3
Ronald Reagan 1984	59.2
Dwight Eisenhower 1956	57.8
Dwight Eisenhower 1952	55.4
Ronald Reagan 1980	55.3
Bill Clinton 1996	54.7
George H.W. Bush 1988	53.9
Bill Clinton 1992	53.5
Harry Truman 1948	52.4
George W. Bush 2004	**51.2**
Jimmy Carter 1976	51.1
Richard Nixon 1968	50.4
John Kennedy 1960	50.1
George W. Bush 2000	49.7

B. Ranked by Percentage of the Total Popular Vote

Lyndon Johnson 1964	61.1
Richard Nixon 1972	60.7
Ronald Reagan 1984	58.8
Dwight Eisenhower 1956	57.4
Dwight Eisenhower 1952	55.1
George H.W. Bush 1988	53.4
Jimmy Carter 1976	50.1
Ronald Reagan 1980	50.75
George W. Bush 2004	**50.73**
John Kennedy 1960	49.7
Harry Truman 1948	49.6
Bill Clinton 1996	49.2
George W. Bush 2000	47.9
Richard Nixon 1968	43.4
Bill Clinton 1992	43.0

C. Ranked by Percentage of the Electoral College Vote

Ronald Reagan 1984	97.6
Richard Nixon 1972	96.7
Ronald Reagan 1980	90.9
Lyndon Johnson 1964	90.3
Dwight Eisenhower 1956	86.1
Dwight Eisenhower 1952	83.2
George H.W. Bush 1988	79.2
Bill Clinton 1996	70.4
Bill Clinton 1992	68.8
Harry Truman 1948	57.1
John Kennedy 1960	56.4
Richard Nixon 1968	55.9
Jimmy Carter 1976	55.2

| George W. Bush 2004 | 53.2 |
| George W. Bush 2000 | 50.4 |

Source: All figures are taken from *America Votes* (Washington, DC: Elections Research Center, Congressional Quarterly), various issues.

cast, resulting in a Kerry plurality of 842,319 votes). Thus, even though Kerry lost 85 percent of Illinois counties, he still carried the state quite comfortably, 55 percent to 44 percent.[28] In sum, data on the number of counties won by the respective candidates is a pretty meaningless statistic.

Finally, Bush "gained a percentage of the vote in 87 percent of the counties in America" due to the confluence of two factors. First, Bush had run relatively poorly in the 2000 election, when, it will be recalled, he won the electoral college even though he lost the popular vote. Second, as Louis Bean first pointed out in the 1940s, when a party or candidate gains votes, its percentage of the vote tends to increase across the board, rather than going up in some places and down in others.[29]

The 2004 elections, in short, had given George Bush the right to occupy the White House for four more years. The Republicans also posted small gains in Congress, winning three more seats in the House, four in the Senate. All of this gave the GOP ample cause for celebration. But for someone like Rove, who hoped to launch the next Republican realignment, the story of the vote should have been less reassuring. Especially if one compared the 2004 Bush vote to the Roosevelt vote in 1936 or the Reagan vote in 1984, it was hard to sustain the fiction that a new Republican majority was starting to coalesce. By 2004, Bush was not a particularly popular president. Far from sending a message of "Full speed ahead," the 2004 results should have alerted the administration to the need for substantial course corrections. Unfortunately for the Republican Party, there is no evidence that they did.

There is one final point worth noting about the 2004 presidential election. In 2000, as we have seen, Rove proudly called attention to the fact that the Bush campaign had substantially outperformed the predictions of the academic election forecasters. In 2004, those same forecasters tried to predict the outcome of the Bush–Kerry contest. Their forecasts for the Bush popular vote were as follows:

Lockerbie	57.6
Norpoth	54.7
Holbrook	54.5
Campbell	53.8
Abramowitz	53.7

Wlezien and Erikson	51.7
Lewis-Beck and Tien	49.9
Actual Result	51.2

This time, in other words, the Bush campaign fared *worse* than six out of seven forecasters had predicted.

The 2006 Midterm Election

Had Karl Rove been concerned solely with his own historical reputation, he should have retired immediately after the 2004 elections. By that time, some commentators were convinced that the long-awaited, much-promised Republican realignment had effectively been accomplished. Perhaps the most outspoken proponent of this view was Fred Barnes, then the executive editor of the *Weekly Standard*. As early as October 2003, Barnes had proclaimed that "realignment is already here, and well advanced."[30] Several weeks after the 2004 election, Barnes was even more emphatic:

> Karl Rove said last year that the question of realignment—whether Republicans have at last become the majority party—would be decided by the election of 2004. And it has. Even by the cautious reckoning of Rove . . . Republicans now have both an operational majority in Washington (control of the White House, Senate, and the House of Representatives) and an ideological majority in the country (51 percent popular vote for a center-right president). They also control a majority of governorships, a plurality of state legislatures, and are at rough parity with Democrats in the number of state legislators. . . . So Republican hegemony in America is now expected to last years, maybe decades.[31]

In doing the research for his article, Barnes had interviewed Walter Dean Burnham, one of the most prominent academic proponents of realignment theory. Burnham, if we may assume that Barnes quoted him accurately, was equally convinced that a pro-Republican realignment was pretty much a fait accompli:

> The 2004 election, [Burnham] says, "consolidates it all"—that is, it solidifies the trend that has favored Republicans over the past decade. To Burnham, it means there's "a stable pattern" of Republican rule. "If Republicans keep playing the religious card along with the terrorism card, this could last a long time," he says. . . . Burnham says the 2004 election

"may be the most important of my lifetime." (He's 75.) The reelection of Bush plus pickups in the Senate and House was "a very, very impressive showing, given the past." Democrats will have enormous difficulties overcoming "the huge weight of Republican strength," he says.[32]

Rove himself was a bit more restrained—but only a bit. As Dan Balz and Mike Allen of the *Washington Post* reported on the weekend after the 2004 election,

> Rove's assessment is that the 2004 election pushed the country away from deadlock, where it had come to rest after the disputed election four years ago. "We now clearly are not the country that was 49–49," he said. "We're now at 51–48 and may be trending to 51–47. It is incremental but small, persistent change. We saw it in 2002, and we saw it again this year. . . . It tells me we may be seeing part of a rolling realignment."[33]

Against that background, Rove might have been well-advised to follow the recommendation that Senator George Aiken once offered with respect to the Vietnam War: "Declare victory and go home." Basking in the afterglow of all his successes, Rove could have settled into the far easier role of a media pundit: approving or disapproving the decisions his successors made only after it was already clear whether or not they worked; making bold predictions that no one would remember if they turned out wrong.

To Rove's credit, however, he stuck it out—and things went to hell in a handbasket. It is difficult to think of anything that went right for the Bush administration in 2005 and 2006. American casualties in Iraq continued to mount, with no end in sight; the federal government's response to Hurricane Katrina was widely regarded as a disaster; the president's plan to partially privatize Social Security, the top item on his legislative agenda, went nowhere, nor did he succeed in reforming the tax code, reauthorizing his signature education legislation, or enacting comprehensive immigration reform; the federal budget was way out of balance; and vice presidential aide Lewis Libby was indicted for perjury and obstruction of justice by a special counsel who had been appointed to investigate how the identity of a CIA operative had been leaked to a reporter. As one reflection of all these setbacks and missteps, the president's approval rating fell from 51 percent in mid-January 2005 to 38 percent in early November 2006. And to top it all off, there were the 2006 elections. Republicans suffered significant losses in the House and the Senate—thirty seats in the lower house, six seats in the upper house—in both cases turning a Republican majority into a Democratic one. Republicans also lost six governorships and more than three hundred state legislative seats.

In his memoirs, published in 2010, Rove tried his best to argue that the 2006 election results had not been a decisive repudiation of the Bush presidency. On the one hand, he contended that the Republican losses in 2006 were not particularly large; actually, they were "about average for second-term midterms."[34] Rove reached this conclusion by comparing 2006 with all second-term midterm elections in the twentieth century, including those held in 1906, 1918, and 1938. But as numerous analysts have shown, the magnitude of seat losses in congressional elections has declined dramatically since the early 1900s. Beginning in the mid-1960s, the advantages of incumbency increased, congressional elections became steadily less competitive, and, as a result, the number of seats that the major parties typically gained or lost every two years also fell sharply.[35] According to data computed by James Campbell, the median seat swing in US House elections between 1900 and 1924 was thirty-two seats. That is to say, in a typical congressional election held during the first quarter of the twentieth century, one party or the other lost thirty-two seats. But the median seat swing then dropped to thirty-one seats in 1926–1950, to twenty seats in 1952–1974, and then to just eight seats in 1976–2000.[36] In light of this finding, a better vantage point for evaluating the 2006 results is to compare them to the seventeen congressional elections held between 1984 and 2016, as shown in table 2.5. The norm in recent years, it will be noted, is very small seat swings. In thirteen of seventeen cases, the victorious party gained fewer than fifteen seats. By that standard, a loss of thirty seats[37] looms quite large—the worst Republican congressional showing since the post-Watergate debacle of 1974. The 2006 outcome, in short, was not just business as usual.

Rove also argued that "underneath the surface," the 2006 election "was a lot closer than [the number of seats lost in the House and Senate] portrayed. Control of the Senate came down to 2,847 votes [actually, 3,562] out of 61.2 million cast in Senate races—that was Democrat Jon Tester's margin over Montana senator Conrad Burns. . . . The fourteen closest races that settled control of the House of Representatives were decided by a margin of 27,022 votes out of 81 million cast in all House races."[38]

At one level, Rove's assertion is correct: change a few thousand votes in Montana and the Republicans would have held on to a narrow majority in the Senate, which in turn might have affected the fate of some of Bush's judicial nominations. Yet even if Burns had won and the GOP had lost "just" five seats in the Senate and thirty in the House, the result would still have been seen as a significant rejection of the Bush presidency. To

Table 2.5. Seat Swings in Congressional Elections, 1984–2016

Year	Net change in House seats	Net change in Senate seats
1984	14R	2D
1986	5D	8D
1988	2D	0
1990	9D	1D
1992	10R	0
1994	52R	8R
1996	3D	2R
1998	4D	0
2000	1D	5D
2002	8R	1R
2004	3R	4R
2006	31D	6D
2008	21D	8D
2010	64R	6R
2012	8D	2D
2014	13R	9R
2016	6D	2D
Median absolute seat swing	8	2

Source: "Vital Statistics on Congress," https://brookings.edu/multi-chapter-report/vital-statistics-on-congress (accessed August 24, 2020).
Note: "14R" means the Republican Party gained fourteen seats; "2D" means the Democratic Party gained two seats.

have altered *that* verdict would have required changing a lot more than a few thousand votes. Moreover, the kind of argument Rove made can cut both ways. Add or subtract a few votes here and there and the Republicans could have fared even worse. In particular, there were fifteen House races in 2006 where the winner's margin of victory over his or her closest opponent was 2 percent or less of the total vote. Republicans won ten of these fifteen contests. In short, the Republicans might easily have lost thirty-six or forty-one House seats.[39]

Finally, Rove argued that such losses as the Republicans did suffer in 2006 were due to the misbehaviors of congressional Republicans, not the performance of the Bush administration. The evidence supports the first half of this assertion, but not the second. Many GOP congressmen were tainted by scandals of various sorts, which certainly contributed to the party's electoral difficulties. But to suggest that Bush's mistakes weren't also a major factor in 2006 is to ignore a great deal of evidence to the contrary.

In the best study of the scandal issue in the 2006 midterm elections, Hendry, Jackson, and Mondak identified twenty-six House Republicans who were tainted in one way or another by scandal. Ten of the twenty-six lost their bids for reelection; three others were so badly tarnished that they resigned from the House and Democrats were then elected to fill their now-open seats. In all thirteen cases, Hendry, Jackson, and Mondak concluded, "scandal may have been decisive."[40] This is clearly a significant number of seats—though if this had been the limit of Republican losses in 2006, the GOP would still have retained a narrow majority in the House. Scandal played a lesser role on the Senate side. All six Senate seats that the Republicans lost in 2006 were due to the defeat of incumbent senators, only one of whom, Conrad Burns in Montana, had been implicated in any kind of congressional scandal. Since Burns lost so narrowly—by less than 1 percent of the vote—it is surely reasonable to conclude that scandal was decisive there as well. Moreover, as the authors of this study note, these estimates represent only the *direct* effects of the scandals. They do not include all the votes the Republicans may have lost because of the general perception that their congressional party had allowed a "culture of corruption" to develop.

So congressional scandals were undoubtedly *part* of the explanation for Republican losses in 2006. Yet even in the fourteen cases just mentioned, where the influence of scandal would appear to be especially strong and obvious, it was not just scandals that were hurting Republican candidates. Being implicated in a scandal is never good news for an incumbent member of Congress, but neither should it be regarded as a certain political death sentence. In a particularly good study published in 1997, Welch and Hibbing identified eighty-eight incumbent House members from both parties who had been charged with "corruption" of various kinds between 1982 and 1990. Of that number, 10 percent resigned or chose not to run for reelection. Another 25 percent were defeated in either the primary or the general election. In other words, *fully 65 percent of incumbents charged with corruption were nonetheless reelected.*[41]

Scandal, then, is just one of many factors voters take into account when deciding how to cast their ballots. It *does* matter, but its effects can be offset or increased by a myriad of other considerations: partisanship, ideology, service to the district, the quality of the challenger, and so forth. In 2006, one of those "other considerations" was a strong national tide that affected all Republican candidates, whether or not they were personally touched by scandal. In the 409 congressional districts where the Republican candidate had not been tarnished by scandal, the Republican Party won 50.5 percent of the two-party vote in 2004, but only 45.4 percent in 2006.[42] What was responsible for this anti-Republican tide? The evidence overwhelmingly indicates that much of it was a reaction to the perceived mistakes and failures of the president.

To start with the most basic point: by 2006, George W. Bush, whose approval rating had once hit 90 percent, was no longer a popular president.

Table 2.6. Presidential Approval Ratings (Percentage) Just before the Midterm Elections, 1950–2010

Year	Incumbent president	First poll after Labor Day	Last poll before Election Day
1950	Truman	35	39
1954	Eisenhower	66	62
1958	Eisenhower	56	57
1962	Kennedy	63	62
1966	Johnson	46	44
1970	Nixon	57	58
1974	Ford	66	53
1978	Carter	42	49
1982	Reagan	42	42
1986	Reagan	63	62
1990	Bush	76	59
1994	Clinton	39	46
1998	Clinton	63	66
2002	Bush	66	63
2006	Bush	39	38
2010	Obama	46	45

Source: All data are from the Gallup Poll.

Table 2.6 shows the approval rating of the incumbent president in every midterm election since 1950, as measured at two points in time: the first poll after Labor Day and the last poll before Election Day. Depending on which poll one finds more meaningful, Bush in 2006 was either the most or second most unpopular president to face a midterm electorate in the last 65 years.

Did voters draw a link between their feelings about Bush and the candidates they supported in the 2006 elections? Again, there is a great deal of evidence to indicate that they did. One piece of data bearing out this conclusion can be found back in table 2.3, which shows whether exit poll respondents in eight of the last nine midterm elections viewed their congressional vote as an expression of support for or opposition to the president. In 2002, it will be recalled, survey respondents gave Bush the most positive balance of support over opposition of any election in which this question was asked. In 2006, by contrast, Bush had the most *negative* balance: 37 percent said they had used their vote to express opposition to Bush; just 22 percent said they were expressing support for the president. In a similar vein, Gary Jacobson has shown that the correlation between presidential approval and congressional vote was stronger in 2006 than in any midterm election for which comparable data exist. Even more than in past elections, people who approved of the president's performance voted for House candidates of his party; people who disapproved—who in 2006 were far more numerous—voted for candidates from the other party.[43]

As one final test of this point, I have conducted a more systematic examination of the influences on the 2006 vote, using data from the National Election Pool exit poll. The full analysis is presented in an appendix to this chapter, but the results can be summarized in two propositions. First, much as Rove argued, there is evidence that congressional scandals and corruption hurt Republican congressional candidates generally, not just those who were specifically tainted by scandal, though the effect is significantly weaker in Senate elections. Second, every analysis I have made shows that attitudes about Bush and his performance in office imposed a major cost on Republican candidates, in both House and Senate elections. Rove's protestations notwithstanding, the evidence indicates that the record of the Bush administration was the most important factor weighing down Republican House and Senate candidates in 2006.[44]

Yet so confident was Rove in his diagnosis that several days after the election he told the *Washington Post*, "The Republican philosophy is alive and well and likely to reemerge in the majority in 2008."[45]

The 2008 Election

Rove was wrong, of course. From the Republican Party's perspective, things only got worse in 2008. The Republicans lost twenty-one more seats in the House and eight more seats in the Senate. And they lost the White House. Barack Obama's victory was not a landslide, at least by historical standards, but it was far more decisive than either of George W. Bush's presidential wins. The largest number of electoral votes Bush ever received was 286; Obama won 365. And if winning 51.2 percent of the two-party popular vote, as Bush did in 2004, was an "historic" and "extraordinary" victory, what adjectives should be applied to a candidate who received 53.8 percent of the vote?

Since Rove left the Bush administration on August 31, 2007, he can be held only partly responsible for the 2008 debacle. The recession technically began in December 2007, but it reflected policies and decisions that had taken place (or had not been changed) during the time that Rove was still a member of the Bush high command. The wholesale financial collapse that occurred in the fall of 2008 was something that virtually no one had anticipated. Certainly the 2008 results cannot be blamed on the misbehaviors of congressional Republicans. Might the 2008 campaign have turned out better for Republicans if Rove had been directing party strategy? In light of the 2006 results, which undeniably did take place on

Rove's watch, it is hard to argue that Rove's presence would have made a material difference in 2008.

It is a telling measure of how far Republican fortunes had declined in the four last years of the Bush presidency that in the final months of 2008 there was talk once again of realignment—only this time it was a *pro-Democratic* realignment that was said to be in the offing. For example:

Harold Meyerson: Even though Obama's victory was nowhere near as numerically lopsided as Franklin Roosevelt's in 1932, his margins among decisive and growing constituencies make clear that this was a genuinely realigning election. . . . Republicans stumble from Tuesday's contest, then, in worse shape than they've been in decades.

John Judis: [Obama's] election is the culmination of a Democratic realignment that began in the 1990s, was delayed by September 11, and resumed with the 2006 election. This realignment is predicated on a change in political demography and geography. Groups that had been disproportionately Republican have become disproportionately Democratic, and red states like Virginia have turned blue. Underlying these changes has been a shift in the nation's "fundamentals"—in the structure of society and industry, and in the way Americans think of their families, jobs, and government. The country is no longer "America the conservative."

Hendrik Hertzberg: This election was so extraordinary in so many ways that its meaning will take many years to play out and many more to be understood. But there is already the feel of the beginning of a new era. As in 1932 and 1980, a crisis in the economy opened the way for the rejection of a reigning approach to government and the forging of a new one. Emphatically, comprehensively, the public has turned against conservatism at home and neoconservatism abroad. The faith that unfettered markets and minimal taxes on the rich will solve every domestic problem, and that unilateral arrogance and American arms will solve every foreign one, is dead for a generation or more. And the electoral strategy of "cultural" resentment and fake populism has been dealt a grievous blow.[46]

Over the next eight years, the 2010, 2014, and 2016 election results would make predictions of a Democratic realignment seem just as fanciful as the predictions of a Republican realignment that had been pronounced in 2004. Yet, in the immediate aftermath of the 2008 election, one can hardly say that expectations of a durable Democratic majority were unreasonable. In 2004, when Republican fortunes in the Bush-Rove era were at their zenith and the Rove realignment project was allegedly succeeding, the GOP held 232 seats in the House of Representatives and 55 seats in the Senate. In 2008, the comparable Democratic numbers were 257 seats in the House and 59 in the Senate. To borrow Rove's formulation, we were, by all appearances, no longer a 49–49 nation.

Presidential Approval Ratings

As one way of summarizing the political record of the forty-third president—and of his chief political advisor—figure 2.1 shows Bush's presidential approval ratings for the eight years he was in office. One noteworthy feature of these data, which I have already mentioned in connection with the 2002 elections, is how long the post-9/11 bounce lasted. Not until the final months of 2003 did Bush's ratings return to their pre-9/11 level. The most conspicuous pattern in figure 2.1, however, is the large, almost uninterrupted decline in Bush's job approval that began shortly after 9/11 and continued all the way to the end of his presidency. There are two brief "hiccups" in the time series associated with the beginning of the Iraq war in March 2003 and the capture of Saddam Hussein in December 2003. Other than that, the line marking Bush's job approval runs straight downhill.

There is, it is important to point out, nothing inevitable or irreversible

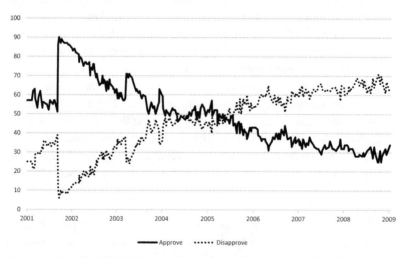

Figure 2.1. Bush Presidential Approval Ratings, 2001–2009. Question wording was: "Do you approve or disapprove of the way George W. Bush is handling his job as president?" *Source*: Gallup Poll.

Table 2.7. Three Examples of Presidents Recovering from a Decline in Approval Ratings

President	Decline	Recovery
EISENHOWER		
Change in approval ratings	78% to 48%	48% to 67%
Dates	Dec. 1956–April 1958	April 1958–Aug. 1959
NIXON		
Change in approval ratings	64% to 49%	50% to 62%
Dates	Feb. 1970–April 1971	Jan. 1972–May 1972
REAGAN		
Change in approval ratings	68% to 35%	35% to 61%
Dates	May 1981–Jan. 1983	Jan. 1983–Dec. 1984

Source: All data are from the Gallup Poll.

about a decline in presidential approval ratings. Lots of presidents have suffered a significant decline in popularity that they were able to halt and then turn around—all without the aid of a major international crisis. Table 2.7 gives several examples. Much like his father, however, George W. Bush was quite good at basking in widespread popular applause but had no idea what to do when the public started turning against him. Nor, it appears, did Karl Rove know what to do in this type of situation.

Everything taken into account, Bush was the most unpopular president in the history of polling.[47] In October 2008, 71 percent of Americans disapproved of Bush's performance as president, the highest disapproval number in the history of the Gallup Poll.[48] But what really stands out in the Bush record is the long, uninterrupted period in which Americans overwhelmingly repudiated his presidency. The last time his approval numbers exceeded his disapproval numbers was in late July of 2005. Not once during his final year in office did even 35 percent of Americans rate his performance positively, while 60 percent or more routinely said they disapproved. Richard Nixon also suffered very low approval ratings beginning in July 1973, a predicament that was ended, however, by his resignation in August 1974. Harry Truman's longest period of sustained disapproval lasted for about fourteen months. In the contemporary era of polarized parties, presidents like Obama and Trump have often registered approval ratings in the single digits among members of the opposite party, but they have made up for this by gaining the approval of 80–90 percent of their own party members. By the end of Bush's presidency, by contrast, even a substantial proportion of his fellow partisans disapproved of how he was handling his job. In two polls conducted in October 2008, just 55 and 57 percent of Republicans approved of Bush's performance.

The Post-Presidential Image of George W. Bush

In February 2010, a billboard was put up in Wyoming, Minnesota, that showed a smiling picture of George W. Bush along with the words "Miss Me Yet?" This sign summarizes one view of the Bush presidency that was entertained by many Republicans. Yes, they conceded, Bush was unpopular when he left office (approval ratings consistently below 35 percent make this hard to deny). But after watching the Obama-led Democrats in action, it was alleged, Americans came to have a new appreciation for the virtues and strengths of the forty-third president. The available polling data, however, provide little support for this view. The American people *have* revised their opinion of Barack Obama's abilities significantly downward, but this has not caused them to fundamentally alter their assessment of George W. Bush.

The best measure of how the public views Bush *as a president* is provided by a set of Gallup Poll questions that asked respondents how "each of the following [eight] presidents will go down in history—as an outstanding president, above average, average, below average, or poor?"[49] As shown in table 2.8, in early January 2009, just before Bush left office, he was clearly seen as the worst occupant of the Oval Office in the last forty years. Even Jimmy Carter and Richard Nixon were rated higher than Bush.

How did things look when Gallup posed the same battery of questions to a national sample in February 2012? As indicated earlier, the biggest change concerned views of Barack Obama. In 2009, before he actually took office, 62 percent of Americans thought Obama would be an outstanding or above average president, making him the second most highly rated of the presidents Gallup asked about, just a notch below Ronald Reagan. By late 2013, by contrast, only 28 percent thought history would view Obama as an outstanding or above average president, dropping him to sixth place. That change notwithstanding, assessments of George W. Bush's presidency had barely budged. He had moved ahead of Richard Nixon but was still rated lower than Jimmy Carter—and Barack Obama. In 2017, when this question sequence was asked yet again, Bush's ratings had inched up slightly, but he was still seen as the second worst president of the last half century. Only Nixon was rated lower.

Did the American people miss George W. Bush? No, actually, they didn't.

The Gift That Keeps On Giving: The Bush Legacy in 2012

Unlike the public's views of Richard Nixon and Jimmy Carter, opinions about George W. Bush were of more than historical interest. Indeed, the

Table 2.8. Public Assessments of How Recent Presidents Will Go Down in History

	Outstanding (%)	Above average (%)	Average (%)	Below average (%)	Poor (%)	Don't know (%)	Overall assessment
Jan. 9–11, 2009							
Ronald Reagan	25	39	26	4	5	2	3.76
Barack Obama	24	38	25	5	6	3	3.70
Bill Clinton	13	37	29	10	10	*	3.33
Gerald Ford	4	19	58	7	4	8	3.13
George H.W. Bush	5	23	49	10	11	2	3.01
Jimmy Carter	6	20	39	15	14	5	2.88
Richard Nixon	2	13	32	23	25	4	2.41
George W. Bush	4	13	23	23	36	*	2.25
Feb. 2–5, 2012							
Ronald Reagan	27	42	20	6	4	1	3.83
Bill Clinton	18	42	28	7	5	*	3.61
George H. W. Bush	6	29	44	11	9	1	3.12
Gerald Ford	5	16	54	15	4	6	3.03
Barack Obama	10	28	26	17	18	1	2.95
Jimmy Carter	5	20	34	22	16	3	2.75
George W. Bush	7	18	28	22	25	*	2.60
Richard Nixon	3	11	28	32	23	3	2.37

(continued on the next page)

Table 2.8. *Continued*

	Outstanding (%)	Above average (%)	Average (%)	Below average (%)	Poor (%)	Don't know (%)	Overall assessment
Jan. 4–8, 2017							
Ronald Reagan	20	43	21	11	3	1	3.67
Bill Clinton	10	33	33	17	6	1	3.24
Barack Obama	18	29	18	17	18	1	3.12
George H.W. Bush	6	21	51	12	8	1	3.05
Gerald Ford	5	14	54	15	3	9	3.03
Jimmy Carter	7	21	36	18	12	5	2.93
George W. Bush	6	16	36	26	15	*	2.72
Richard Nixon	4	9	27	34	22	4	2.36

Source: Gallup Poll.

Note: Question wording was, "How do you think each of the following presidents will go down in history—as an outstanding president, above average, average, below average, or poor?" "Overall assessment" figures were computed by assigning a value of 5 for "outstanding" responses, 4 for "above average," 3 for "average," 2 for "below average," and 1 for "poor," and then calculating a mean value for each president. "Don't know" responses were not included in the calculations. An asterisk indicates that that response was given by less than 0.5 percent of respondents.

Bush image probably played an essential role in the reelection of Barack Obama in 2012. Faced that year with an economy that wasn't performing very well, Barack Obama turned back to the strategy that had worked so well for him in 2008: he ran against George Bush. From the Democrats' perspective, the Bush presidency was the gift that kept on giving.[50]

In recent decades, political scientists and economists have devoted considerable energy to devising numerical measures of how well the nation's economy has fared during a president's term, so as to be able to estimate its impact on election results. The unemployment and inflation rates and real change in gross domestic product and per capita disposable income have all been used; such indicators can also be measured over varying periods of time. But all the measures forecasters have used agree on one conclusion: that the economy had performed very poorly during Obama's first term—well below the level that presidents must normally achieve in order to get reelected.

Political economist Douglas Hibbs, for example, has long argued that the growth of real per capita disposable income is the best single measure of the electorate's economic well-being, and that its effect on the vote is best captured by a weighted average of the quarterly results throughout a president's term. Hibbs's income index grew, on average, by 1.8 percent during all presidential terms since 1949. At least through the second quarter of 2012, Obama's weighted-average growth rate was 0.1 percent, the second worst of the sixteen terms Hibbs examined. James Campbell, by contrast, used real growth in gross domestic product as his economic measure and calculated average growth rates for every president since 1952 who was running for reelection. He also excluded results from the first year in a president's term, on the quite reasonable grounds that first-year economic results are primarily due to the conditions that a president inherits from his predecessor. By this measure, Obama was the eighth worst of the ten presidents Campbell studied. The two presidents who did worse—George H. W. Bush from 1990 to 1992 and Gerald Ford from 1974 to 1976—both lost.[51]

Fortunately for Obama's reelection prospects, he had a ready excuse for the economy's weak performance: It was Bush's fault. More specifically, Obama said that he had inherited an unprecedented economic catastrophe from his predecessor and that his policies had, in fact, done a creditable job under the circumstances. In purely economic terms, there are lots of reasons to be skeptical about this argument. While Obama undoubtedly did inherit an economic mess from Bush, it is by no means obvious that it was worse than, for example, the economy that Jimmy Carter bequeathed to Ronald Reagan in 1981. As for the post-2009 economic recovery, not only has it been extraordinarily weak by historical standards, it also falls far below the forecasts the Obama administration itself made when arguing in favor of the 2009 stimulus bill.

The more important point for the moment, however, is that the American public largely accepted Obama's assertion. The 2012 National Election Pool exit poll included a question asking voters who was "more to blame for current economic problems," Obama or Bush. Just 38 percent of 2012 voters blamed the incumbent president; 53 percent felt Bush was more at fault. Numerous other polls that asked about this issue yielded similar results.[52] Nor was this the only Obama-era problem for which the public largely blamed Bush. In January 2012, a CBS News/*New York Times* survey asked respondents who was "mostly to blame for most of the current federal budget deficit." Three years after Bush left office, 43 percent of the American public still felt that his administration was mostly to blame for the deficit; just 14 percent blamed the Obama administration. (Nineteen percent blamed Congress.) Even on issues where conservatives were particularly apt to find fault with Obama, the public rated Bush as no better or even worse than his successor. In October 2014, the public was evenly split when asked how "President Obama's handling of foreign policy" compared to George W. Bush's: 35 percent said Obama was better, 33 percent said Bush was better, 28 percent thought they were "about the same." Asked in June 2014 who was more to blame "for the situation in Iraq," 51 percent put the onus on Bush, versus 27 percent who held Obama responsible.

The Bush Legacy in 2016

One final casualty of the Bush presidency deserves mention: the 2016 presidential candidacy of his brother Jeb.[53] Though John Ellis Bush did not formally announce his candidacy until June 15, 2015, it had been clear since at least the previous December that he was interested in pursuing the presidency—sufficiently so that his name was regularly included in polls on the Republican nomination race. Indeed, for the first six months of 2015, Jeb may reasonably have been described as the front-runner for his party's 2016 nomination—but he was a distinctly weak front-runner. According to the Roper Center's iPOLL database, there were twenty-one national polls conducted from January through June 2015 in which Republican respondents were asked which candidate they favored in the 2016 nomination contest. Bush was in first place or tied for first in fourteen of these polls. On average, however, he was supported by just 15 percent of his party's rank-and-file members. In no poll conducted during this period did even a quarter of Republicans say that they wanted Jeb to be the party's next presidential standard-bearer. By contrast, as we saw in table 2.1, during the first six months of 1999, George W. Bush had been routinely supported by between 40 and 60 percent of Republican identifiers.

As it so happened, Donald Trump announced his presidential candidacy one day after Jeb threw his hat in the ring, and Jeb soon lost his never-terribly-impressive front-runner status. By late July, Trump had a clear lead in every national poll of Republican identifiers. By January 2016, on the eve of the primary and caucus season, Jeb was supported by just 5 percent of the potential Republican electorate, putting him in fifth place behind Trump, Cruz, Rubio, and Carson.

Bush fared no better in the delegate selection season. In the Iowa caucuses, after spending $14 million on television ads, Jeb came in sixth, supported by just 2.8 percent of the caucus attendees. Eight days later, he finished fourth in the New Hampshire primary, with 11 percent of the vote—not exactly an electrifying performance, but good enough (at least in his eyes) to keep him in the race for one more contest. But his showing in the South Carolina primary was almost exactly the same as in New Hampshire—fourth place and 11 percent. He withdrew from the race that night.

Why did the second son of the forty-first president fare so poorly in 2016? While the race was still in progress, many commentators opined that Jeb wasn't as dynamic or charismatic a campaigner as his older brother had been when he sought the nomination. Having seen both Bushes on the stump, I think this is nonsense. Jeb was far better than his brother in town hall meetings and in the televised debates. The big difference between his candidacy and George W.'s was that in 1999 and 2000, the Bush name was still an honored one in American politics. By 2015, the last thing most Americans wanted was another President Bush. The only way Jeb might have been a competitive candidate in 2016 was if he had opened his campaign with a speech in which he detailed a half dozen or so major mistakes his brother had made and explained how he would have done things differently. That he was unwilling to make such a speech made him a good brother but a poor presidential candidate.

The most shocking aspect of the 2016 Republican nomination race, of course, was not the collapse of Jeb Bush's campaign but the triumph of Donald Trump's. And here, too, George W. Bush's presidency left its mark. Lest my point be misunderstood, I am not arguing that Bush was primarily responsible for Trump's startling success. Were one to make a list of the major reasons Trump won, most items on the list would have nothing to do with the Bush presidency: the Republican Party's long-standing antigovernment ideology, which tends to denigrate the value of previous governmental experience and to exalt the work of the private sector; Trump's own remarkable capacity for self-promotion; the media's decision to give Trump an extraordinary amount of coverage, utterly disproportionate to his standing in the polls or the quality of what he had to say; the huge number of Republican presidential candidates who entered the 2016 race, which made it more difficult for any one contender to acquire the resources or publicity necessary to emerge as a serious rival to Trump; and the weaknesses of the other candidates and their campaigns, which made numerous mistakes—in particular, their collective failure to take Trump's candidacy seriously until it was too late.[54]

But George W.'s eight years in the White House helped add one final item to the list: the substantial delegitimization of the Republican establishment, which allowed Trump to win the nomination even though he was supported by virtually no major Republican Party leaders or elected officials.[55] In the battle for the 2000 Republican nomination, Bush had been the clear favorite of the party leadership. Before a single primary or caucus had taken place, Bush had been endorsed by all thirty Republican governors and thirty-six of the fifty-five GOP senators; his chief competitor, John McCain, had the support of just four of his fellow senators. The Republican governors, in particular, had rallied behind Bush out of frustration with the recent performance of congressional Republicans. Governors, they were convinced, were better problem solvers and therefore had a more inclusive appeal than the crowd in Washington.[56] When Bush turned out to be neither popular nor a great problem solver, the value of elite endorsements almost certainly took a significant hit.

As I will show in more detail in chapter 10, the emergence of the Tea Party in 2009 and 2010 was a reaction to the policies of Barack Obama, but also to the record of George W. Bush. Bush had run for the presidency as a conservative—a compassionate one, to be sure, but a conservative nonetheless. He had fought off the challenge of John McCain largely by portraying himself as more consistently conservative and more within the party mainstream. Yet once in office, he had dramatically expanded the federal role in education, added a major new entitlement to Medicare, and turned a hefty budget surplus into an even larger deficit. Perhaps nothing infuriated the Republican base more than Bush's position on immigration, which showed no appreciation for the large number of rank-and-file Republicans who were genuinely concerned about the problem of illegal immigration. Instead, Bush proposed to create a big new guest worker program and grant amnesty to those who were already here illegally—and offered nothing in return except some vague promises of stepped-up enforcement. Add in all the other failures of the Bush presidency, and the party was ripe for a "populist"-style rebellion. To his credit, Trump understood this mood better than any of his major competitors.

Conclusion

The presidency of George W. Bush was a disaster for the Republican Party. There is no other way to put it. Whatever modest gains the party made between 2001 and 2004—and emphasis should be placed on the word *modest*—were entirely erased by the 2006 and 2008 elections. More than that, the 2006 and 2008 results appeared to wipe out most of the Republican advances that had been so painstakingly achieved in the 1980s and 1990s. By the time Barack Obama was sworn in as president:

- Republican strength in the House of Representatives had been reduced to its lowest level since 1993;
- Republican strength in the Senate had been reduced to its lowest level since 1979; and
- Obama had received the highest percentage of the total popular vote of any Democratic candidate since 1964.

In the words of political scientist John Kenneth White, "It took thirty years to build the Reagan coalition. It has taken George W. Bush just two years to destroy it."[57]

But the Reagan coalition proved to be more resilient than White and many others anticipated. In the 2010 elections, the Republicans gained back all of the ground they had lost in the House; in 2014, they reclaimed their majority in the Senate; and in 2016 they won the presidency. Yet there was nothing inevitable about these outcomes, still less should they be taken as vindication of Bush and Rove's stewardship of the party. As it so happened, the 2008 Democratic presidential nominee turned out to be a weak officeholder and a poor party leader.[58] Had they chosen someone with more experience and ability, the Democrats might still hold sizable majorities in both houses of Congress. And if the Obama health care law (technically, the Patient Protection and Affordable Care Act) proves difficult or impossible to repeal, as seems to be the case, Republicans should remember that this bill would almost certainly never have passed without the huge Democratic Senate majority established largely in reaction to the failures of the Bush presidency.

Appendix

The 2006 National Election Pool exit poll employed two different question-naires, and many of the questions relevant to this analysis were included in one questionnaire but not the other. I am also interested in trying to under-stand the variation in two different dependent variables: a respondent's vote in the election for the House of Representatives and his or her vote in the election for the US Senate (in states where one was held). Table 2.9 ac-cordingly shows the results of four separate logistic regression equations, one for each vote-questionnaire combination.

The independent variables are of three types: attitudes toward President Bush and his policies; attitudes toward Congress and its behavior and leadership; and party identification and ideology, which are included as controls. The exact wordings for each question are shown below. As noted in the table, all independent variables are coded so that higher values indicate pro-Republican attitudes: for example, approving the president's performance; believing the condition of the economy was excellent or good; or being enthusiastic or satisfied with the Republican leaders in Congress. A positive coefficient thus means that a variable had an effect in the expected direction.

To summarize the results of these four equations: the variables mea-suring attitudes toward the president were *always* both substantively and statistically significant, in every equation. Republican House and Senate candidates were less likely to be supported by those who: disapproved of President Bush's performance; thought the condition of the economy was not so good or poor; disapproved of the war in Iraq; and felt dissatisfied or angry about the Bush administration. (In every one of these questions, those who were critical of the president and his policies significantly out-numbered those who were supportive.) Attitudes about Congress had an uneven and generally weaker effect on the vote. Those who disapproved of how Congress was doing its job were no more likely to vote Democratic than those who approved. Believing that corruption and the scandals in government were important had no effect on Senate elections and a small effect on House elections that just barely crossed the threshold of statisti-cal significance. On the other hand, being dissatisfied or angry about the Republican leaders in Congress and disapproving of how Republican lead-ers dealt with Mark Foley and the congressional page scandal did affect voting in both types of elections, though the effects were much stronger in the House equation.

Table 2.9. How Attitudes about Bush and the Republican Congress Affected Voting in the 2006 Midterm Elections

Variable	House elections		Senate elections	
	Coefficient	Stnd. error	Coefficient	Stnd. error
Questionnaire version 1				
Approve of Bush	0.861	0.070***	0.602	0.075***
Condition of national economy	0.275	0.071***	0.312	0.076***
Approve of war in Iraq	0.232	0.064***	0.366	0.067***
Importance of scandals and corruption	0.088	0.053*	0.015	0.056
Approve of Congress	0.072	0.066	0.081	0.069
District with scandal-tainted incumbent	−0.221	0.176		
Party identification	1.737	0.065***	1.263	0.069***
Ideology	0.492	0.079***	0.760	0.084***
Constant	−7.957	0.305***	−7.770	0.281***
Percent correctly predicted				
Null	54		57	
Model	90		88	
Pseudo R²	.76		.70	
(N)	(5,417)		(3,973)	
Questionnaire version 2				
Enthusiastic or angry about Bush	0.644	0.094***	0.698	0.101***
Approve of war in Iraq	0.220	0.065***	0.442	0.068***
Enthusiastic or angry about Republican congressional leaders	0.794	0.093***	0.354	0.099***
Approve handling of Foley page scandal	0.252	0.061***	0.140	0.065**
District with scandal-tainted incumbent	−0.237	0.189		
Party identification	1.735	0.071***	1.221	0.073***
Ideology	0.636	0.087***	0.874	0.093***
Constant	−9.226	0.318***	−8.292	0.277***
Percent correctly predicted				
Null	55		57	
Model	90		88	
Pseudo R²	.78		.72	
(N)	(5,079)		(3,650)	

Source: 2006 National Election Pool exit poll
Note: All independent variables are coded so that higher values indicate pro-Republican attitudes, i.e., all regression coefficients are hypothesized to be positive.
* $p < .05$
** $p < .01$
*** $p < .001$

House and Senate votes: 1 indicates a vote for a Republican candidate, 0 a vote for a Democrat. Votes for other parties (of which there were very few) were excluded, as were votes in uncontested House races.

"Do you approve or disapprove of the way George W. Bush is handling his job as president? Strongly approve; somewhat approve; somewhat disapprove; strongly disapprove."

"Do you think the condition of the nation's economy is: Excellent; good; not so good; poor."

"How do you feel about the US war in Iraq? Strongly approve; somewhat approve; somewhat disapprove; strongly disapprove."

"In your vote for US House, how important were corruption and scandals in government: Extremely important; very important; somewhat important; not at all important."

"Do you approve or disapprove of the way Congress is handling its job? Strongly approve; somewhat approve; somewhat disapprove; strongly disapprove."

"No matter how you voted today, do you usually think of yourself as a: Democrat; Republican; independent; something else." (Those answering "something else" were excluded from the analysis.)

"On most political matters, do you consider yourself: Liberal; moderate; conservative."

"Which comes closest to your feelings about the Bush administration: Enthusiastic; satisfied, but not enthusiastic; dissatisfied, but not angry; angry."

"Which comes closest to your feelings about the Republican leaders in Congress: Enthusiastic; satisfied, but not enthusiastic; dissatisfied, but not angry; angry."

"How do you feel about the way Republican leaders in Congress handled Mark Foley and the congressional page scandal? Strongly approve; somewhat approve; somewhat disapprove; strongly disapprove."

3

Presidents Need Political Help

In his acceptance speech at the 2000 Republican National Convention, George W. Bush declared, "I believe great decisions are made with care, made with conviction, not made with polls. I do not need to take your pulse before I know my own mind."[1] Though the wording varied a bit from speech to speech, this avowal was a frequent theme in Bush's campaign against Al Gore. Seeking to draw a contrast with the Clinton administration, whose policy agenda was reputedly heavily poll-driven (at one point, Clinton strategist Dick Morris had even conducted a poll to determine where the president should go on vacation),[2] Bush repeatedly pledged that polls would not play such a role in his presidency. "I really don't care what polls and focus groups say," he insisted at another point. "What I care about is doing what I think is right."[3]

At first glance, this might seem to be one campaign promise that the second president Bush kept. Neither of Bush's pollsters from the 2000 campaign—Jan van Lohuizen and Fred Steeper—was a prominent figure in George W. Bush's White House. None of the inside accounts of the Bush presidency published to date speaks of him eagerly poring over the latest polling results. Just below the surface, however, there are indications that the Bush administration, like all its immediate predecessors, paid considerable attention to the polls. Based on public records available from the Federal Election Commission, political scientist Kathryn Dunn Tenpas has shown that the Republican National Committee (RNC) paid Lohuizen and Steeper $1.7 million for presidential polling in 2001 and 2002. This is less money than the national party committees had paid to Ronald Reagan's and Bill Clinton's pollsters during their first two years in office—but more than the RNC had paid to Robert Teeter, who did polling for the first president Bush. George W. Bush himself may not have actually seen any of the results from these polls, but Karl Rove surely did. So did Matthew Dowd, who helped coordinate polling during the 2000 campaign and then became a "senior adviser" at the Republican National Committee. It is difficult to believe that the RNC spent $1.7 million on polls that had no consequences at all for presidential or White House behavior. More likely, as I will try to show in subsequent chapters, the polls had a strong if generally indirect effect on Bush, shaping the ideas of people like Rove, which were then incorporated into the advice they gave the president. As Tenpas concludes, what seems most distinctive about the Bush presidency is not its actual use of polling, but its level of "secrecy and denial."[4]

The moral of this story, some observers might argue, is that George Bush should have tried even harder to live up to the standard he had set forth during the 2000 campaign and thus prevented his presidency from being contaminated by even the slightest hint of polling data. I would suggest a different lesson: that the standard never should have been enunciated in the first place. Presidents need high-quality political information and advice; and while polling is not the only form such information can take, public opinion surveys can tell a president much that is valuable for him to know. Instead of trying to deny himself access to all such data, a far better approach would have been for the president to recognize that there are proper and improper ways of using polls and then discipline himself to use them in appropriate ways.

The point I have just made with respect to polls applies to politics more broadly. A great deal of harm has been done to American government by the widespread acceptance of the ridiculous notion that presidents and other elected officials should somehow seek to govern above or without politics. In fact, the greatest American presidents have always been highly skilled, often brilliant politicians.[5] This is certainly true, for example, of Abraham Lincoln, generally ranked today as the single greatest American president. To study Lincoln's presidency closely is to observe a man who was always keenly aware of the political constraints he faced and was accordingly anxious to use every political resource at his disposal. A President Lincoln without the real Lincoln's political skill would today be regarded as, at best, a second-rate occupant of the White House: someone who correctly tried to limit the expansion of slavery but was, regrettably, unable to prosecute the war to a successful conclusion and thus ensured the establishment of a new Confederate nation dedicated to the subjugation of blacks.

To argue that presidents should be skillful politicians is not, of course, to fly off to the opposite extreme and urge the election of demagogues, pure political animals whose only goal is to maintain themselves in power. A moral politician—the phrase is not a contradiction in terms—is someone who always keeps one eye on the long-term policy goals he hopes to achieve and one eye on the political situation he faces, and recognizes that it is only through politics, through the acquisition and use of power, that he is likely to accomplish those goals.

And to return to the central lesson of this chapter, if presidents are to be effective politicians, they need political help. They need people to give them political information and advice and to help them carry out the more purely political aspects of their work. This information and assistance can—and does—take a number of forms and come from a variety of sources. Many top political operatives and advisors from a successful presidential campaign are brought directly onto the White House staff. Others continue to advise the president from outside the government. The national party committees are another traditional source of political expertise and assistance, and another place to stash once and future campaign staffers. After the first two years of a president's first term, many of these people will be put on the payroll of the president's reelection campaign. Whatever the mechanism, *all* modern presidents have made sure that they continued to receive political help after the formal campaign was over.[6] In the rest of this chapter, I discuss some of the major purposes for which a president needs political help—and therefore needs people like Karl Rove.

Defining the Boundaries of the Possible

Politics, according to a frequently quoted adage, is the art of the possible. Like many adages, it is basically good advice. But acting on that advice immediately runs into one major roadblock: it is often far from clear just what is and is not possible. Many bills that informed observers believed would sail through Congress have fallen short of passage. Others that were thought to have no chance of enactment unexpectedly caught fire. Yet, if politics is never fully predictable and the precise limits of the possible are always uncertain, those advisors who can help the president reduce this uncertainty—who can tell him which battles are potentially winnable and which are not—are clearly providing the president with a very valuable service.

Time is among the most limited and unforgiving of presidential resources. Theoretically, a newly elected president who takes office with a long list of things he wants to accomplish has at least four years, more likely eight, in which to fulfill his goals. In fact, to judge from the experiences of the last five presidents, the period in which a president stands a good chance of enacting significant and controversial legislation is remarkably short: the first year or so after his first inauguration and (sometimes) the first couple months of his second term. Reagan's tax and budget cuts, Clinton's effort to cut the deficit, George W. Bush's tax cuts, the Patriot Act, and No Child Left Behind, and Obama's stimulus bill and the Affordable Care Act were all passed during this quite narrow window. After that, these presidents were successful in getting major legislation through Congress only in the increasingly rare case where a bill enjoyed bipartisan support.

This might not be such a limiting problem for presidents if they could send a long list of bills up to Congress at the same time. Actually, as numerous students of contemporary American politics have noted, the American political system is apparently incapable of dealing with more than a very small number of issues simultaneously.[7] Thus, when a president makes a major push for one piece of legislation, the time, energy, and agenda space devoted to that issue are taken away from other, competing priorities. Against that background, presidents would obviously prefer not to waste their time working for a bill that has no realistic chance of passing.

To amplify the points just made, and to demonstrate what happens when a president fails to receive or act on good political advice, consider an extended example from George W. Bush's second term in office. In mid-February 2006, Dubai Ports World, a port management company controlled by the emirate of Dubai, bought a British shipping company called Peninsular and Oriental Steam Navigation (P&O). P&O was, at that point, playing a substantial role in the management of six major American ports, including the ports of New York City, Philadelphia, New Orleans, and Miami. Thus, less than five years after the events of 9/11, at a time when US ports in general were seen as a key area of vulnerability against future terrorist attacks, operations at six major American ports were to be managed by an Arab state-run company.

Before this transaction, the United Arab Emirates (UAE), of which Dubai is a part, had what may fairly be called a mixed record in fighting terrorism. Officially, the UAE was an American ally, with a US airbase just outside its capital, and had taken a number of significant steps to cooperate with the US-led war on terror. But the 9/11 Commission, which conducted the official, congressionally sanctioned investigation of the attacks on the Pentagon and the World Trade Center, had sharply criticized the UAE, noting that "the vast majority of the money funding the Sept. 11 attacks flowed through the UAE."[8] As one homeland security expert further noted, the UAE "was one of only three countries in the world that recognized the Taliban regime [in Afghanistan]. And Dubai was an important transshipment point for the smuggling network of Abdul Qadeer Khan, the Pakistani scientist who supplied Libya, Iran, and North Korea with equipment for making nuclear weapons."[9]

Since 1975, any foreign investment that might affect American national security has to be reviewed by the Committee on Foreign Investment in the United States (CFIUS), an interagency committee that includes representatives from twelve different departments and agencies, including

Treasury, Defense, State, the National Security Council, and, since 2002, Homeland Security. When the company making the investment is controlled by a foreign government, there is supposed to be a special, forty-five-day investigation, with the final decision then made by the president. In September 2005, the Government Accountability Office, an investigative arm of Congress, had criticized the CFIUS for using "an overly narrow definition of national security threats." True to form, the committee approved the pending DP World deal in mid-January, without asking for further investigation and with little apparent understanding of the powder keg it was about to ignite.[10]

Congress was notably less acquiescent. Within a very few days after the deal was made public, a small army of senators and representatives were denouncing it, expressing sentiments that ranged from strong reservations to complete opposition. Particularly noteworthy was the resistance from congressional Republicans, who had previously supported almost anything the Bush administration proposed to do or at least confined their objections to private meetings. This time, however, both House Speaker Dennis Hastert and Senate Majority Leader Bill Frist publicly criticized the deal and suggested that it should at least be "put on hold . . . until this decision [i.e., the one by CFIUS] gets a more thorough review."[11]

Yet the Bush administration showed little apparent recognition of how deeply the Committee on Foreign Investment's decision had touched on American sensitivities and security concerns, treating the opposition instead as a small kerfuffle that would disappear in a day or two after the media got bored and cooler heads prevailed. Though Bush himself had reportedly not known about the deal or the CFIUS decision until the weekend after the controversy began, he immediately voiced his support for the DP World takeover. Even more striking, he threatened to veto any congressional legislation that sought to block the deal—a significant gesture given that Bush had, to that point, not vetoed a single bill during more than five years in office. Nor did the administration make any effort to accommodate congressional concerns, instead falling back on the legalistic excuse that the committee's decision was final and there was no way to reopen the case.[12] To make matters worse, the CFIUS's deliberations were conducted in secret, yet the administration made no attempt to disclose what had or had not been discussed, offering instead the bluff assurance that, as President Bush put it, "If there was any chance that this transaction would jeopardize the security of the United States, it would not go forward."[13] Coming from a man who had also assured the country that Iraq had weapons of mass destruction, it is unlikely that many found the president's statement convincing.

Whether having an Arab state-run company involved in running American ports really posed a substantial threat to US national security might have made an interesting topic of discussion for an academic debating society. Informed authorities with no obvious ax to grind could be found on both sides of the question.[14] Some argued that many US ports were already under foreign management (though not by Arab companies), that virtually all of the people working at these ports would continue to be American citizens, and that actual port security would be handled not by the company but by US Customs and the Coast Guard. Others insisted that the risks of foreign infiltration were too great and that the new DP World position might give potential terrorists much greater knowledge of American security arrangements.

But this was not an academic exercise. The position the administration had to defend was exactly the kind of intricate, nuanced argument that is difficult or impossible to get across in the contemporary mass media; the opponents' argument was much simpler, easily expressed in a ten-second sound bite. And the Democrats had no incentive to make things easier. Having spent much of the previous four years suffering from the imputation that they were insufficiently concerned about defending American national security, they delightedly seized on an issue that allowed them to reverse the accusation.

As the controversy proceeded, a significant number of survey organizations conducted polls about the issue. A sampling of their results is shown in table 3.1. Quite consistently, regardless of the organization or question wording, about 70 percent of the public opposed allowing the deal to go through. But this was a case where the polling data were almost superfluous. As anyone with the least bit of political sensitivity should have realized, less than five years after the events of September 11, it was impossible to convince the American public that an Arab company should play a role in any matter even remotely connected to US national security.

Yet for almost three weeks, the Bush administration continued to trumpet its support for the deal and repeat its veto threat. Belatedly, DP World, perhaps under prodding from the administration, began to offer some concessions to its critics. The company first promised that it would not "exercise control" over its American operations until Congress was satisfied, then said it would "voluntarily" ask the administration to conduct the lengthier, forty-five-day review that many members of Congress insisted had been legally required all along. But by then it was too late. The final straw came on March 8, when the House Appropriations Committee, by a slap-in-the-face vote of sixty-two to two, added an amendment to an emergency spending bill blocking the transaction entirely. One day later, DP

Table 3.1. Public Opinion on the Dubai Ports World Transaction

1. CBS NEWS, Feb. 22–26, 2006: "As you may know, the Bush Administration has agreed to let a company from the United Arab Emirates run six shipping ports in the U.S., including ports in New York and New Orleans, that are now being run by a British company. Critics of the plan say that allowing a company from an Arab country to operate U.S. shipping ports is dangerous to national security. The Bush Administration says security will be protected by the U.S. Do you think the U.S. should or should not let a United Arab Emirates company operate U.S. shipping ports?"

Should	21%
Should not	70%
Don't know	9%

2. FOX NEWS/OPINION DYNAMICS, Feb. 28–March 1, 2006: "As you may know, there has been some public debate about a United Arab Emirates–owned company called Dubai Ports World taking over commercial management of some U.S. ports. From what you've heard and read, do you support or oppose allowing a United Arab Emirates company to manage operations at some U.S. ports?"

Support	17%
Oppose	69%
Don't know/depends	13%

3. ABC NEWS/*WASHINGTON POST*, March 2–5, 2006: "As you may know, a company owned by the government of a nation called the United Arab Emirates is in a merger deal that will give it management of six U.S. ports. Do you think this company should or should not be allowed to manage these ports?"

Should	23%
Should not	70%
No opinion	7%

4. PEW RESEARCH CENTER, March 8–12, 2006: "As you may know, recently a company from the United Arab Emirates made a deal to run six shipping ports in the United States. Would you approve or disapprove of the government allowing this company to operate U.S. ports?"

Approve	14%
Disapprove	73%
Don't know	13%

World announced that it would sell its American operations to an American entity.[15]

Clearly, the Bush administration committed a number of significant mistakes in its handling of the Dubai Ports World episode. As one business communications consultant observed, "They couldn't have botched this any worse if they had tried."[16] For the moment, however, I wish to concentrate on those mistakes that were due to a lack of awareness of the political constraints surrounding the DP World transaction. Ideally, the controversial nature of the pending deal would have been recognized by someone on the Committee on Foreign Investment well before it was finalized. A number of early steps might then have been taken to ease public and congressional anxieties and limit the political and diplomatic consequences of rejection. Dubai could have been warned that the deal might not go through; Congress could have been briefed in advance (even the White House conceded that this should have been done);[17] a more thorough and public investigation of the issues could have been undertaken. Yet, in this highly political administration, no one on CFIUS seems to have thought about the matter from this perspective.

There is an interesting sidelight to the CFIUS decision that was, so far as I can tell, never mentioned in the mainstream media and that underlines the importance of political sensitivity. The head of the Committee on Foreign Investment was Deputy Treasury Secretary Robert Kimmitt. Kimmitt was also the person chosen by George H. W. Bush in 1988 to supervise the "vetting process" when the elder Bush was looking for a vice-presidential running mate. Here, too, Kimmitt seems to have done a perfectly good job of reviewing Dan Quayle's legal and financial records, but apparently never recognized—and never warned Bush and his campaign advisors about—the potentially explosive nature of Quayle's service in the Indiana National Guard.[18] Whatever his legal skills, it is hard not to conclude that Kimmitt's political antennae are simply dreadful.

Since no one in the Bush political apparatus served on CFIUS, they cannot be blamed for this initial mistake. But one can legitimately wonder whether and when Rove et al. made any attempt to alert Bush as to the potential political consequences of this developing debacle.[19] Within days after the controversy broke, someone should have taken Bush aside and told him, as bluntly as possible, "Look: This is an issue we can't win. There's no way Congress and the American public will agree to let an Arab government run our ports. Less than a year after Hurricane Katrina and the Harriet Miers Supreme Court nomination, you cannot afford another major incident that raises serious questions about your judgment. *Don't* draw lines in the sand; *don't* threaten a veto; *start* looking for a way to get out of this mess."[20]

This case is also instructive in another regard. As the quotations at the beginning of this chapter indicate, Bush prided himself on doing what he thought was right, regardless of the political consequences. (The reality, as we will see in later chapters, is quite different.) But in this case (and many others), disregarding the politics of the issue led to consequences that were, from the Bush administration's perspective, almost wholly negative, in both political *and* policy terms. The deal did not go through; relations with an important Middle Eastern ally were needlessly agitated; and Bush's own approval ratings, according to a CBS News poll, fell by 8 percentage points.[21]

Assessing Support and Opposition

Defining the boundaries of the possible can be thought of as a special case of a more general function for which presidents need political help: assessing the level and sources of support and opposition the president is likely to encounter before he makes a decision or announces a policy. A few things a president wants to do will be almost universally popular, such as Bush's original decision to depose the Taliban government in Afghanistan or Obama's decision to authorize the Navy Seals to kill Osama Bin Laden. In the far more typical case, however, presidential decisions will meet with some degree of opposition—frequently from the other party, but sometimes from the president's own party or from interest groups usually allied with the president. A president's political advisors should help him anticipate and understand the lay of the political landscape before he decides what course to pursue, instead of leaving him to learn about such matters only after he has already taken a public position.

How should the president deal with this sort of information? This is a remarkably difficult subject about which to generalize. It is certainly not the case, for example, that a president should forego a particular action just because it arouses strong opposition. Whether an unpopular policy or a potentially controversial decision should be abandoned depends on a host of other factors, such as how important the issue is to the president, whether he needs congressional approval to authorize or implement the policy, whether he believes that opponents can be persuaded to change their minds or conciliated in other ways, and whether there are other, "second best" alternatives available that might arouse less opposition. But a president cannot begin to weigh and assess these factors unless he has such information *before* he makes his decision.

The importance of this function is perhaps easiest to appreciate when it is performed poorly. In October 2005, George Bush nominated White House Counsel Harriet Miers to become an associate justice of the United States Supreme Court. Judged solely on the merits, there were many strong reasons to question this decision. As Robert Bork, the intellectual godfather of the conservative judicial movement, summed up the case against her, "This is a woman who's undoubtedly as wonderful a person as they say she is, but so far as anyone can tell she has no experience with constitutional law whatever."[22] For now, the more important point is that Bush genuinely seems to have believed that the Miers nomination would be widely popular. On the one hand, a number of Democratic senators had commended Miers's work in John Roberts's nomination to the Court, which Bush interpreted—quite wrongly—as a commitment that they would vote for her own confirmation. Bush also believed—even more fatuously—that conservatives and Republicans would endorse her nomination because he himself knew and trusted her. Relying on personal assurances was precisely the mistake conservatives had made with respect to David Souter's nomination. Yet, as Bush would later note in his presidential memoirs, several of his top aides "told me bluntly that she [Miers] was not the right choice. None told me to expect the firestorm of criticism we received from our supporters."[23] In fact, once Miers's nomination was announced, it quickly became clear that she had virtually no support on either side of the aisle. The result was that, less than four weeks later, her nomination had to be withdrawn.

Would Bush have made this nomination if he had any idea how little support it would generate, especially from conservatives? Probably not— though Bush, like a number of other recent presidents, had a well-known stubborn streak such that he might have persuaded himself that once senators got to know her as well as he did, they would become her enthusiastic supporters. But by all accounts, Bush completely misjudged the reception Miers's nomination would receive. And while much of the blame for this certainly lies with Bush himself, Rove too bears some of the responsibility, as he admits in his memoirs: "But what made sense to us [Bush and his top advisors] didn't to our usual allies. In that respect, I didn't serve the president well. My job, after all, included outreach to the groups interested in the Court. . . . My antennae should have been sharper. We expected to be hit by adversaries, but it was our friends who carried the fight against Harriet."[24]

Selling the President's Program—And the President

I am not aware of any American politician who has ever admitted to taking a poll in order to determine where he or she stands on a policy question (though there is considerable anecdotal evidence to suggest otherwise).[25] Even Dick Morris, often depicted as the evil genius who wrote Bill Clinton's policy agenda in 1995–1996, has denied doing this.[26] Where pollsters and other political advisors come in—or so they say—is *after* an elected official has already determined which policy is best. Only then do the political advisors help the official figure out the most effective way to persuade other officials and political actors to support the decided-upon policy. There was a time when selling the president's program chiefly required an intimate knowledge of Congress and consisted primarily of behind-the-scenes bargaining with a relatively small number of congressional leaders. Increasingly, however, the sales job is a very public enterprise, both in its target and in its methods—and one that requires precisely the sorts of skills and expertise possessed by political consultants.

The most influential single analysis of modern-day presidential salesmanship is *Going Public*, by University of California, San Diego, political scientist Samuel Kernell. Traditional bargaining between the president and Congress, Kernell argued, had become increasingly difficult and unproductive. Congress was too fractionalized; the contemporary presidential selection process produced "outsider" candidates unfamiliar with Washington and thus ill-equipped to participate in such bargaining. So to build support for their programs, contemporary presidents used a bank shot: appealing for support directly to the American public, who in turn would apply the pressure to Congress, holding over congressional heads the one incentive that all members took seriously: the threat of defeat at the next election.[27]

Subsequent scholarship has raised serious questions about just how well "going public" works for the president. George Edwards has argued that the power of the "bully pulpit" is greatly overrated, that presidents really don't have much capacity to lead or shape public opinion.[28] Marc Bodnick showed that the passage of Ronald Reagan's budget and tax program in 1981, often cited as the archetypal example of a president successfully going public, actually owed more to traditional bargaining than to the Great Communicator's ability to persuade and mobilize public opinion.[29] On the other hand, Page and Shapiro have produced evidence showing that persuasive efforts by *popular* presidents do have a measurable impact on public attitudes. Unpopular presidents, however, "have no effect at all or maybe even a negative impact."[30]

However successful going public really is at passing the president's program, it is remarkably accurate as a description of presidential behavior. Every recent president has devoted considerable time and energy to sustained direct appeals for public support.[31] The administration of George W. Bush, in particular, treated going public almost like a religion. As one account of the Bush presidency noted:

Soon after taking office, he [Bush] launched a massive public relations campaign on behalf of his priority initiatives. At the core of this effort was the most extensive domestic travel schedule of any new president in American history. Bush spoke in 29 states by the end of May [2001], often more than once. The president also used his Saturday radio addresses to exhort the public to communicate their support for his tax cut and education plans to Congress. . . . The Bush administration has never looked back—and never slowed down—in its efforts to win public support for its policies.[32]

During his second term, when Bush sought to add a private account option to Social Security, the administration began the effort with another huge public relations campaign, tellingly dubbed "60 Stops in 60 Days."

Political consultants can and do assist such efforts in a variety of ways. Some of their work involves supervising phone calls, direct mail, and email solicitations, similar to what goes on in field organizations and phone banks during an election campaign. At the level of a Karl Rove or a Dick Morris, however, most of the work concerns the content of the president's message. Of the many possible arguments that might be made in support of a president's policies, which would be most likely to persuade or mobilize the average American? Before any major presidential public appeal is launched today, every major element in it has almost certainly been pretested in polls and focus groups.

One of the better-documented examples of consultants' labors concerns the specific words that are used to describe a particular problem or policy. In 2007, when President Bush decided to increase the number of American troops fighting in Iraq, he was remarkably successful at getting the media and even his partisan opponents to call the new policy a "surge," which almost certainly sounded more appealing to many Americans than an "increase" or "escalation" of the US military effort (which is what it was). In the battle to restructure Social Security, the Bush administration tried— less successfully—to describe its plan as the creation of "personal" rather than "private" accounts, since the former word reportedly drew a more positive response from focus groups and survey respondents. Congressional Democrats, meanwhile, with assistance from their political consultants, claimed that the problems facing Social Security were not a "crisis," as Bush often said, but a "challenge," a word that made the whole issue seem less pressing and accorded better with the Democrats' reluctance to offer a reform plan of their own.[33]

Political consultants and advisors not only help sell the president's program, they also help sell the president. The two enterprises are, of course, closely related. By and large, a president's personal popularity rises and falls with the success or failure of his policies, especially on issues of peace and prosperity. The notion that a warm smile and a good television presence can somehow delude the public into overlooking the ravages of recession or war is a myth. That said, the statistical models that try to explain the ups and downs of presidential popularity leave a great deal of variation unaccounted for. The way a president is presented to the public, the way he is portrayed in the mass media, the kind of image he projects, may matter at the margins—and in some cases, those margins may be relatively large or may spell the difference between victory and defeat in the next election. (This is one lesson of the Trump presidency. Based on past experience, a president who presided over the lowest unemployment rate in fifty years and who had not waged a war with substantial American casualties should have had a lot more public support than Trump had before the COVID-19 lockdown took effect.) Not surprisingly, every recent president has employed a large number of people whose principal occupation is to fret about the president's public image.

Whether selling the president or his policies, a great deal of the political help presidents need concerns communication. And since much of what presidential campaigns do also involves communication—about the candidate, his policies, his personal attributes, and his opponent(s)—it should come as no surprise that the White House communications apparatus is staffed largely by former campaign personnel and public relations consultants. Presidential press secretaries, in particular, have often served a previous stint as a presidential *campaign* press secretary. Among those who have taken this path to the White House podium are Jody Powell, Dee Dee Myers, Mike McCurry, Joe Lockhart, Ari Fleischer, Scott McClellan, and Robert Gibbs.

Monitoring the Nation's Political Pulse

This fourth function of political advisors overlaps a bit with the preceding one, but for a number of reasons deserves separate mention and examination. Like anyone else engaged in a complex, ongoing enterprise, a president needs feedback: regular information that tells him how well he is doing, what is working, and what is not. Much of that feedback is concerned strictly with policy matters. The US economy, in particular, generates a remarkable profusion of statistics that measure various aspects of recent economic performance: quarterly estimates of economic growth; monthly readings of inflation, unemployment, consumer confidence, factory inventories, and new housing starts; and weekly data on first-time claims for unemployment insurance. The same principle applies to foreign policy. Every president during wartime should do what, by all accounts, George W. Bush did not do: monitor the progress of the war through a variety of sources, both official and unofficial. (This is one of many reasons a president ought to read a daily newspaper.)

But the president also needs political feedback: information about how he and his policies are faring with the president's numerous significant constituencies, especially the mass public, but also interest groups, members of Congress, and the activists within his own party. Simple as this point may sound, doing it successfully can be a complicated undertaking. For a variety of reasons, the members of a president's inner circle are often reluctant to confront the president with the truth about his mistakes and shortcomings. The "bubble" that was said to surround President Bush and isolate him from the perceptions and concerns of the average citizen probably operates to a greater or lesser extent for all presidents. Special efforts are sometimes needed, in short, to ensure that a president hears his critics as well as his admirers.

This is another justification for having presidential pollsters—and for making sure that the president himself is made aware of what the polls say. As any novice politico knows, polls have a long list of shortcomings and pitfalls: things they measure poorly, ways they can be misinterpreted, problems in drawing a representative sample.[34] Yet after saying everything bad that can be said about polls, the simple truth is that polls provide presidents (and everybody else) with far more accurate information about the state of public opinion than any other alternative. The mail that presidents and other elected officials receive, for example, has frequently been shown to come from a small and unrepresentative segment of the public—primarily people who like and support that particular official.[35] Nor does one get a reliable portrait of public opinion by observing the size and enthusiasm of the crowds that show up at presidential speeches and motorcades, as George W. Bush seems to have believed. (This was particularly true in his case. Throughout the Bush presidency, there were recurrent reports that the crowds the president encountered on his trips outside Washington had been carefully screened and selected by his advance and security teams so as to be friendly to Bush, while critics and those carrying hostile signs were kept as far away from the president—and the media—as possible.)[36]

Together, the concern with the president's image and the need to monitor the fluctuations in public opinion have produced one of the more remarkable phenomena in modern American politics—what has sometimes been described as a "perpetual election" or a "continuous referendum on the president." The catalyst for this development was a survey question that the Gallup Poll began asking on a regular basis in 1945. Called the presidential approval question, it reads, "Do you approve or disapprove of the way _____ is handling his job as president?" where the blank is filled with the name of the current president. When Harry Truman was president, this question was asked about nine times a year.[37] But as other public and media polling firms were created, most of them borrowed the question to include in their surveys, and Gallup began to ask it more often; soon it had become the most frequently reported survey question in all of American politics. During George W. Bush's first year in office, it was asked in 127 different polls spaced rather evenly throughout the year. In other words, about once every three days, a new poll was released showing George Bush's latest approval rating. By 2006, there were 194 distinct surveys measuring presidential approval, about one every two days.[38] And for those who did not have the time, energy, or expertise to pull together the results from all these separate surveys and survey organizations, there were three websites that performed this service for them, producing, in effect, a continuous daily index of presidential approval.[39] At the start of the Obama presidency, both the Gallup and Rasmussen polls carried this mania one step further by conducting a "presidential approval tracking poll," where the question was asked on a daily basis and every day thus brought a new estimate of presidential job approval.

Is presidential approval really worth all the fuss? All presidents, of course, would prefer to be popular—but is there any tangible political pay-off to these numbers? The evidence on this question is decidedly mixed.

One point that is quite well established is that presidential approval ratings taken *in June of a presidential election year* are a very good predictor of who will win the upcoming presidential election.[40] Since 1956, every incumbent president with an early summer approval rating of 46 percent or higher has gone on to win reelection; every incumbent with an approval rating of 45 percent or lower has been defeated. The question's track record is not quite so good when the incumbent president is not himself a candidate for reelection. As Richard Nixon in 1960 and Al Gore in 2000 both learned, a president's personal popularity does not necessarily transfer to his vice president. But the failures and disappointments of an *unpopular* president, it appears, do affect whatever candidate his party nominates to succeed him. This, more than anything else, explains the losses of Adlai Stevenson in 1952, Hubert Humphrey in 1968, and John McCain in 2008.

But the key to understanding this particular use of presidential approval ratings is the italicized phrase: "in June of a presidential election year." Presidential approval ratings taken during the first two and a half years of a presidential term are *not* a very good predictor of the next election. As shown in table 3.2, not until December of the third year does a

Table 3.2. Correlation between Presidential Approval Ratings and the Vote in the Next Presidential Election at Fourteen Points during a Presidential Term, 1952–2016

March of the first year	.29
June of the first year	.28
September of the first year	.33
December of the first year	.31
March of the second year	.37
June of the second year	.39
September of the second year	.22
December of the second year	.40
March of the third year	.23
June of the third year	.36
September of the third year	.38
December of the third year	.56*
March of the fourth year	.71***
June of the fourth year	.82***
(N)	(17)

Source: All approval ratings are taken from the Gallup Poll.
Note: Figures are the correlation between the president's approval rating at the time indicated and the percentage of the two-party popular vote received by the candidate of the incumbent president's party in the next presidential election. Where more than one poll was conducted in a given month, I have averaged the results.
* sign. at .05 level
** sign. at .01 level
*** sign. at .001 level

president's approval rating become significantly correlated with the outcome of the next presidential election. For the first eleven quarters of the typical presidential term, approval ratings explain, on average, a scant 10 percent of the variance in election results.

What about midterm elections? Here, too, the picture is mixed. On the one hand, there is evidence showing that midterm elections serve, *in part*, as a referendum on the performance of the president and that a president's approval rating in the summer before the election bears some relationship to the number of seats his party will lose in the House and the Senate.[41] But the strength of this relationship is a good deal weaker than the relationship between approval ratings and presidential elections. Presidential popularity helps establish the general environment in which the midterm takes place—but the qualities of the individual congressional candidates, the particular issues being debated, and the dynamics of the campaign all matter as well. To take a prominent recent example, in 2010 the Democrats lost sixty-three seats in the House of Representatives, the largest midterm seat loss in postwar American history. Yet Barack Obama's approval ratings were not particularly low that year. His approval rating in June 2010 was 48 percent, about average for postwar presidents at that point in the election cycle. In June 1978, Jimmy Carter's approval rating was 43 percent—but that year the Democrats lost just fifteen House seats. In statistical terms, presidential approval ratings explain 71 percent of the variance in presidential election results, but just 45 percent of the variance in House elections and 12 percent of the variance in Senate elections.[42]

A final assertion about the importance of presidential approval ratings is that as a president's ratings go up, so does his success in dealing with Congress. As one long-time Senate staffer observed, "It's an absolute rule up here: popular Presidents get what they want; unpopular ones don't." Lyndon Johnson, who knew a thing or two about Congress, subscribed to the same belief: "Presidential popularity is a major source of strength in gaining cooperation from Congress."[43] Political scientists have subjected this proposition to considerable testing—with remarkably little consensus. Edwards, Rivers and Rose, Ostrom and Simon, Brace and Hinckley, and Canes-Wrone and Marchi all claim to find evidence showing that highly-rated presidents do indeed fare better with Congress.[44] But Bond and Fleisher, Peterson, Mouw and MacKuen, and Collier and Sullivan all reached the opposite conclusion.[45] As Bond and Fleisher put it, "The President does not win more votes nor does he receive higher levels of support when he is popular than when he is unpopular."[46] At best, the relationship appears to be a relatively modest one. Edwards, for example, estimates that a 10 percent increase in public approval increases a president's success rate in congressional roll call votes by about 2 percentage points.[47] In concrete terms, this means that the Watergate scandal, which reduced Richard Nixon's approval ratings by about 30 percentage points, thereby diminished his success rate in Congress by just 6 percent.

When all the evidence has been assessed and weighed, I am not convinced that there is adequate reason for a polling firm to conduct a daily presidential approval tracking poll. Except in exceptional circumstances, once every week or two is enough. But the evidence clearly *is* sufficient to explain why the president and his advisors ought to monitor this indicator and various other measures of popular support on some kind of regular basis. Of course, the surveys must be interpreted with care. No administration should panic, for example, if the president's approval rating falls early in his first term; this happens to almost all presidents. In terms of the long-run prospects of the administration, early approval ratings, high or low, are a reliable harbinger of nothing.

To say that presidents should monitor the state of public opinion, moreover, is not to imply that there are simple and easy ways to respond to what they learn. As shown in the previous chapter, many presidents have reversed a slide in popular approval—but many others just kept doing the same things that got them in trouble in the first place. When Jimmy Carter's approval ratings fell precipitously after his first two-and-a-half years in office, he and his top political aides reportedly concluded that Carter needed to spend more time traveling outside Washington and return to the themes and appeals that had worked so well for him during the 1976 campaign. But as Nelson Polsby has persuasively argued, Carter probably would have had more success doing just the opposite: staying in Washington and learning how to work more effectively with a heavily Democratic Congress.[48]

But no president can make these sorts of choices if he is unaware of the problem. Presidents need to have some mechanism for staying in touch with public opinion, and for that to be done well, they need exactly the sort of help provided by many of the same people they used for that purpose during the campaign.

Outreach to Interest Groups

Contemporary presidents have exhibited a strikingly ambivalent attitude toward interest groups. While they often complain about the powerful "special interests" who oppose their policies, they eagerly seek out and accept the assistance of those groups that support the administration and its programs. Here, for example, is one political scientist's description of the relationship between the Bush administration and a variety of business and conservative groups in the fight to restructure Social Security:

> In addition to their own efforts, the White House and the Republican National Committee worked closely with the same outside groups that helped Bush win reelection in 2004. . . . As President Bush began his second term, the alliance had become an institutional fixture, providing both money and manpower to further the Bush agenda and strengthen the Republican party apparatus. Thus, corporations, the financial services industry, conservative think tanks, much of the Washington trade association community, and GOP lobbyists and consultants prepared to spend $200 million or more on lobbying, television advertising, grassroots campaigning, letter-writing, and phone calls to help the president obtain passage of his priority domestic policy proposals, the most important of which was personal accounts under Social Security.[49]

Presidents seek out interest group support for a variety of purposes: to help pressure Congress; to support their reelection; to bolster their public image. Whatever the precise mixture of purposes, presidents have gradually come to conclude that they cannot sit back and hope that these groups will get involved on their own volition and then work together efficiently and effectively. Instead, presidents must actively reach out and cultivate group support and then help coordinate their efforts.[50]

By 1974, interest group liaison work had become a sufficiently important and regular part of presidential politicking that Gerald Ford established a distinct unit within the White House to direct such efforts: the Office of Public Liaison (OPL). (In 2009, Barack Obama renamed it the Office of Public Engagement.) The function of the OPL/OPE, as John Hart nicely phrased it, is to "lobby the lobbies. It reaches out to important non-government constituencies such as business, labor, ethnic, religious, and women's groups to sell the president's policies and build coalitions in support of them."[51] The OPL is not the only entity in the White House that has conducted such outreach, and its influence has varied over time. In some instances, such as the Carter presidency, it played the lead role in such efforts. In other cases, such as during the Reagan administration, it was much less significant.

Whether performed in the OPL or elsewhere, interest group liaison work need not be performed exclusively by political consultants and former campaign personnel in the same way that polling is performed exclusively by pollsters. But working with groups to advance the president's program is recognizably similar to the work that goes on in many campaigns: seeking group endorsements; using group-based membership lists and communication networks to solicit votes, money, and volunteers; and using group endorsements to show that a candidate's policies are beneficial to group members. It should come as no surprise, then, that the OPL has often been headed by people with extensive experience in campaigning. Prominent examples include Midge Costanza, Anne Wexler, David Demarest, and Minyon Moore. In the Bush White House, the Office of Public Liaison was one of several units specifically under the direction of Karl Rove.

Planning for the Next Election

When viewed in comparative perspective, one of the more distinctive features of American politics is the frequency with which we hold elections.[52] Where a British prime minister must face the voters about once every four or five years, in the United States another election is always looming just over the horizon. As the head of his party, the president cannot simply stand by and enjoy the spectacle. In a variety of ways, he and his advisors are inevitably pulled into every election that happens on his watch: recruiting candidates, raising money, devising the party message, campaigning in person, and, after it is all over, trying to shape the way the election results are interpreted. For a president, life in the White House really is a "permanent campaign."

From this perspective, a summary view of a president's first term looks like this:

Year One: Even as the president is settling into his new job and trying to reach the flat part of a very steep learning curve, gubernatorial and state legislative elections are being held in New Jersey and Virginia. And even though there is scant evidence that these contests really do serve as a referendum on the president's own performance, that is, as the president's strategists know, one of the ways they are often interpreted.

Year Two: At stake in the midterm elections are 435 representatives, 33 senators (at least), 36 or so governors, and thousands of state legislative seats and lower-level offices. The results will have a major impact on the president's success rate in Congress over the next two years.

Year Three: There will be gubernatorial elections in Louisiana, Mississippi, and Kentucky, but that is the least of the president's concerns. Of far greater moment is the next *presidential* election. Though all of the formal steps in that election occur in Year Four, it is universally recognized that much of the activity takes place in the third year of a president's term.[53] It is then that even a relatively popular president and his top political advisors must devise an overall strategy (knowing, however, that much of it may need to be updated and revised), begin putting together a national organization, raise a great deal of money, and make sure that the president is formally entered into the next year's presidential primaries and that suitable delegate slates are put together.[54] If the president faces the possibility of a serious challenge for his own party's nomination, these tasks become even more urgent. At one time, much of this work could be safely delegated to the national party committees and their state and local affiliates. But the wholesale changes in the delegate selection rules and campaign finance laws that took place in the early 1970s now require these tasks to be carried out by the president's personal campaign organization.[55]

Year Four: However much presidential campaigning occurs in Year Three, it pales beside the frenetic pace of activity in the president's fourth year in office, when, as one presidential press secretary observed, "the campaign overwhelms the White House."[56] In particular, data drawn from the public papers of the president show that Year Four brings a huge increase in the number of presidential public appearances, with consequently greater demands upon the president's schedulers, speechwriters, and advance people.[57]

Like outreach to interest groups, planning for the next election was institutionalized in the form of a separate unit within the White House: the Office of Political Affairs (OPA), established in 1981.[58] The OPA has had a more controversial existence than the Office of Public Liaison, however, since its workload is more actively and explicitly political and thus, many have argued, inappropriate for persons on a governmental payroll. After the 2006 midterm elections, the Bush OPA became a particular target of investigation by the House Committee on Oversight and Government Reform. An Office of Special Counsel report would later accuse OPA employees of having "violated the Hatch Act through a number of practices that were prevalent during the months leading up to the 2006 elections" and with transforming the OPA "from an advisory office to the President into a campaign organization."[59] In 2008, Republican presidential nominee John McCain promised to abolish the office entirely and transfer its functions to the Republican National Committee.[60] Barack Obama made no such commitment, however, and the OPA continued in existence through the first two years of the new administration—doing, by some reports, many of the same things for which the Democrats had criticized the Bush administration just a few years earlier. In January 2011, Obama announced that he was closing the Office of Political Affairs, just a few months ahead of the time when most OPA employees would have left the public payroll anyway and joined Obama's reelection campaign.[61] In January 2014, the Obama White House announced the creation of a new Office of Political Strategy and Outreach that seemed to be, in most respects, just the same old OPA with a different name on the letterhead. And, quite predictably, within months after the new office commenced operations, it was accused of conducting illegal campaign activity.[62]

As a general proposition, McCain's promise from the 2008 campaign strikes me as a good idea: Given their partisan and electoral character, the kinds of activities and persons that were once housed in the OPA should probably be transferred to the national committees. But whatever specific form future presidents employ, there is little doubt that they will create some institutional capacity to do the things done by the OPA. Those features of the American political system known as the permanent campaign have affected the presidency every bit as much as they have impacted Congress, interest groups, and the press.

4

Good Politics Doesn't Always Mean Good Government, or Never Make a Political Consultant One of Your Top Policy Advisors

To summarize the point of the last chapter: No president who hopes to be successful can afford to operate as if politics isn't important to his job. And presidents therefore need the help of political advisors and political consultants to help them navigate the minefields—to provide them with the kind of information that will allow them to make better decisions and sustain their political support. But there's an important caveat to all this: political advisors need to be kept in their proper place. Concern with elections and political standing can easily become not just one of many elements that a president considers but the *dominant* or even the *only* thing that matters. For all elected officials, there appears to be a political equivalent of Gresham's Law, which holds that "Absent special effort to the contrary, political motives of the crassest kind will tend to drive out any concern with sound public policy." Or in simpler terms, "Political considerations drive out policy ones."

Almost every recent president has been criticized at one time or another for being "overly political," but George W. Bush, I will argue, had a particular problem in this regard, at least with respect to domestic policy. For unlike other contemporary presidents, Bush not only invited many of his former campaign consultants and political advisors into the White House, he actually put one of them in charge of the policy-making machinery. In a way that has no real precedent that I am aware of, Karl Rove served as a top *policy* advisor to President Bush.

"Good government is good politics, and good politics is good government." Growing up in Chicago, I remember hearing this aphorism a lot; it was a favorite saying of the legendary Mayor Richard J. Daley. In this chapter, I take a close look at the second half of this adage: Does good politics really result in good government? Undoubtedly, there are lots of cases where it does. Reducing the unemployment rate is both popular with the voters and, except in highly unusual circumstances, good public policy.[1] Depending on how they are achieved, the same can usually be said about lower crime rates, peace, and price stability.

There are lots of instances, however, where the kinds of strategies and tactics that are likely to be pushed by political consultants make for bad public policy. In this and the following chapter, I will delineate four important differences between the incentives and practices of campaign consultants and the requisites of good government.

1. Campaign consultants tend to deal with issues only in the broadest and most general terms, but in policy-making, details matter and usually spell the difference between effective and ineffective policy.
2. Campaign consultants often make use of issues that have great symbolic or emotional content, but relatively little policy impact.
3. Campaign consultants frequently employ strategies that are targeted at small, discrete subgroups of the electorate by promising them special benefits of one kind or another, such as subsidies, tax exemptions, or protection from economic competition. Such policies are, however, very difficult to justify on their substantive merits.
4. Campaign consultants are focused on winning the next election. They are therefore likely to look unfavorably on any policy that might impose significant short-term costs even if it provides substantial long-term benefits.

Of course, consultants are not the only people in politics who engage in symbolic appeals and short-term thinking or who are overly submissive to special interest groups. Elected officials are quite capable of doing these things on their own initiative. But political consultants are, in general, more likely to advocate these sorts of actions than people whose expertise and background is in policy-making. And a White House dominated by consultants and a consultant mentality will therefore resort to such expedients more frequently than one in which the voices of consultants are less prominent. Such, in a nutshell, was one major shortcoming of the Bush presidency.

The Rove Portfolio

In the pages that follow, I will examine Rove's role in a number of specific policy controversies. For now, I wish to take notice of the general point: that virtually every serious examination of the inner workings of the Bush White House found Karl Rove to be a major, central, even dominant player in the formulation and making of domestic policy decisions. (For a variety of reasons, Rove had a much more limited role in foreign policy, especially after the terrorist attacks of September 2001.) He was called "the busiest man in the White House"; "one of the most powerful and controversial advisors in this or any White House"; the first presidential aide "to tackle two big jobs—dispensing political advice to his boss and controlling the policy levers inside the White House"; "the only power center on the domestic side of the Bush administration"; a man who "plays a much heavier role in domestic policy than any previous occupant of his position"; "arguably the most powerful political consultant in American history."[2] Is there any other presidential political advisor—any other presidential aide of any kind—who has been described in terms like the following?

No one, with the possible exception of the President, will be more responsible for the success or failure of Bush's presidency.

White House tours don't pass through Karl Rove's office, but most everything else around the president does. Rove determines which lobbyists and supporters get access to the White House, and he weighs in with Bush on every major domestic-policy decision, from stem cells to farm subsidies.

Forget the title: he's the White House C.O.O. [chief operating officer]—the inside operator; everything reports up to him.

Little happens on any issue without Karl's okay, and often he supplies such policy substance as the administration puts out.

There are few decisions, from tax cuts to judicial nominations to human cloning, in which Rove is not directly involved. 'It's not a real meeting if Karl isn't there,' says a senior member of the domestic-policy staff.

Everybody knows that in terms of putting it all together, in terms of the politics, in terms of strategy positions and also policy, that Karl is the hub, the central node of activity that surrounds the presidency.

No other [presidential] aide since the 1940s had been given such a vast White House portfolio. No one made any decision on anything without at least considering what Karl would think about it. Andy Card was the technical White House chief of staff but Karl was the chief of all White House staff.

Rove likes to have his hands in just about everything, relishing policy shaping as much as political strategizing. He views governing and politics as completely interconnected, and he occupied a key seat at the center of both in Bush's White House.[3]

And lest one dismiss these comments as coming only from journalists and others who were not actually present when important decisions were being made, it should be pointed out that two of the above quotations come from former White House staffers, while a third was made by the then-majority leader of the US Senate.

Rove's influence on Bush administration policy is partly, though imperfectly, reflected in his job titles. In previous administrations, as we saw in the last chapter, political consultants were generally consigned to the Office of Political Affairs or the party's national committee or advised the president from the outside. Rove, by contrast, was named senior advisor to the president and put in charge of several major subunits within the White House, including both the Office of Political Affairs and the Office of Public Liaison. More significantly, an entirely new unit was created to help support and coordinate Rove's work: the Office of Strategic Initiatives (OSI). OSI, as one early report noted, was "an effort to solve the problem that consistently dogs White House staffs: the pressure to respond to unexpected events and to react to daily news cycles, which causes presidential advisors to lose sight of the big picture."[4] Plainly, that "big picture" involved both politics and policy. Rove himself characterized OSI as "an operation that sets the agenda, prepares the notebooks and materials, and does the research." Andrew Card, Bush's first chief of staff, called it a "think tank."[5] Its practical effect was bluntly summed up by Ed Gillespie, a Republican strategist who had worked with Rove on the 2000 campaign: "Basically, Karl Rove has carte blanche to stick his nose into anything he deems appropriate or necessary."[6]

If there were any lingering doubts about the broad boundaries of Rove's empire, they were resolved shortly after Bush's narrow reelection victory in 2004, when Rove was named deputy chief of staff *for policy* (emphasis added). The new title, the next day's *New York Times* noted, was "a move that formally gives him [Rove] what he has had in practice all along, a substantial voice in nearly every issue before the administration."[7] As presidential press secretary Scott McClellan explained, Rove would keep his previous title (senior advisor to the president) and all of its responsibilities but would also now "coordinate the work of the National Economic Council, the Domestic Policy Council, the National Security Council, and the Homeland Security Council."[8] (In April 2006, new White House chief of staff Josh Bolten forced Rove to give up his day-to-day control of the policy development process in order to concentrate his attention on the upcoming midterm election, though he seems to have retained a substantial measure of input on domestic policy issues until he left the administration in August 2007.)[9]

A System That Magnified His Powers

The power that Rove exercised through the first six-and-a-half years of the Bush presidency was partly a function of his own interests, abilities, and personality—but it was also a reflection of the administration in which he worked, especially the characteristics and operating style of the president. Over the last half century, one of the major themes in research and writing about the presidency, to which both scholars and practitioners have contributed, concerns the signal importance of *information* to the successful performance of that office. "The first essential need" of a president, declared Richard Neustadt, probably the most influential and respected student of the modern presidency, "is information."

> To help himself [the president] must reach out as widely as he can for every scrap of fact, opinion, gossip, bearing on his interests and relationships as President. He must become his own director of his own central intelligence. For that directorship two rules of conduct can be drawn from the case studies in this book. On the one hand, he never can assume that anyone or any system will supply the bits and pieces he needs most; on the other hand, he must assume that much of what he needs will not be volunteered by his official advisers.[10]

Subsequent scholarship has devoted considerable energy to examining the ways that different presidents have actually interacted with their staff, department heads, and other sources of advice and information, and how these different systems have affected presidential decision-making.[11] Unfortunately for the country, the Republican Party, and his own historical reputation, George W. Bush organized his presidency as if this entire large body of knowledge was either wrong, irrelevant, or nonexistent.

When Bush took the presidential oath of office in January 2001, he had, as even many of his supporters conceded, little previous acquaintance with many of the issues he would now be required to contend with. Though he had spent a good deal of time in and around *campaigns*, he had a grand total of just six years' experience in *government*, the last two of which had been devoted largely to his presidential campaign. The state of Texas, moreover, is generally characterized as having a relatively weak gubernatorial office, in which "broad powers over the legal system, state budget and finances, education, transportation, agriculture, public utilities, and land development" are entrusted not to the governor but to a number of other, independently elected executive officials.[12] And like all governors, Bush had never been required to make decisions or grapple seriously with issues of foreign policy. Bush might have remedied these deficiencies by having an omnivorous thirst for knowledge—but few except the most ardent loyalists would describe George W. Bush in these terms. To the contrary, profiles of the forty-third president frequently characterized him as "incurious" and "intellectually lazy."[13]

The one notable exception to this pattern was that Bush does seem to have been an avid book reader, even at one point holding a contest with Karl Rove to see who could read the most books. It is unclear, however, how much that reading helped fill the significant gaps in his knowledge of contemporary government and public policy. Much of this reading seems to have been confined to history books. By one report, Bush read fourteen separate biographies of Abraham Lincoln during his time in the White House.[14] Though Lincoln is generally regarded as our greatest president and much can be learned from studying his presidency, one wonders how much additional insight Bush gained after the first four or five biographies. Bush may have read all these books less for what they taught him about statesmanship and more for the psychological comfort they provided. Like Bush, Lincoln had waged a long and costly war in spite of substantial domestic opposition and criticism but had refused to yield, won the war in the end, and was ultimately vindicated by history. As Bush himself observed, "Abraham Lincoln motivated me a lot. He was a great president. Abraham Lincoln understood the president's need to stand on principle no matter how tough the politics might be."[15] (For a quite different reading of Lincoln's presidency, see chapter 8.)

One wishes Bush had read more books like Thomas Ricks's *Fiasco* or Larry Diamond's *Squandered Victory*. Bush apparently did read Eliot Cohen's *Supreme Command*, about how chief executives should relate to their nation's military in a time of war, but doesn't seem to have acted on its central recommendation until late 2006.[16] Frank Bruni, who covered Bush during the 2000 campaign and in the White House, credits Bush with being "a pretty steady consumer of books." "And yet," he concluded, "despite these indications of a moderately active mind, Bush betrayed gaping holes in his knowledge during his conversations with us [reporters]. . . . We constantly made references to recently reported facts or details that he had somehow missed."[17]

Starting from an initial information deficit, Bush needed, even more than his immediate predecessors, to establish a set of procedures and work routines that were specifically designed to keep him informed and expose him to a wide range of viewpoints. Instead, Bush's general operating style only made the problem worse. Space does not permit an extended discussion of the internal operations of the Bush White House and the routines and procedures the president used to keep himself informed. Suffice it for here to say that virtually every major channel of information that other presidents have traditionally relied upon was in some significant way closed off or distorted. Bush seems to have been an irregular newspaper reader (how irregular is a matter of some disagreement) and rarely watched television news; he had a short attention span and didn't like lengthy memos or long briefings. According to Condoleezza Rice, his first national security advisor and later secretary of state, the thing Bush least liked to hear her say was, "This is complex."[18] Though his administration created the usual assortment of cabinet councils, decision memoranda, and clearance procedures, he frequently bypassed or undermined these devices when making important decisions; he used his cabinet not to help him make policy decisions but to support and implement the policies he had already decided upon; and he rarely consulted with outside advisors.[19] It is, in short, difficult to gainsay the conclusion reached by Evan Thomas and Richard Wolffe in 2005: "Bush may be the most isolated president in modern history."[20]

All of which has one very important implication for the present analysis: the few people who *did* advise Bush on a regular basis—the small circle of close advisors whom he did consult—could have enormous influence on his decisions. Rove was, of course, not the only member of this circle, but unlike most of the other members, he wasn't shy about pushing his own views on policy. As one top White House staffer observed:

There were other influential power centers [in the Bush White House], but none had as much impact on White House governing, policy, and operations [as Rove did]. Unlike Karen Hughes, whose goal was to help the president shape his message in ways that would appeal to ordinary Americans . . . and unlike Andy Card, the chief of staff who served as an honest broker among various political points of view, Rove was a central player who was anything but neutral in his political and ideological views.[21]

Bush proudly called himself the "decider," and in a purely formal sense, this was no doubt true. What Bush never seems to have recognized was that his capacity to truly decide an issue, in any kind of independent and meaningful sense, was heavily dependent on the quantity and quality of information he received. Consider an analogy: Two men—call them Smith and Jones—want to have dinner together. They will talk that night about which restaurant they will eat at but agree that Smith will make the final choice. So is Smith the "decider" on this matter? Maybe—but now suppose that Smith knows very little about the restaurants in the area, whereas Jones knows a great deal about them. Assume further that Jones knows a lot about Smith's tastes—knows, for example, that he dislikes spicy foods but likes restaurants with extensive wine lists. If Smith is unable or unwilling to learn more about his potential choices, Jones can, if he wants, pretty much dictate which restaurant they go to just by manipulating the information he provides to Smith.

Lest the preceding scenario be dismissed as entirely fanciful, consider now an important, real-world example. On November 13, 2001, George W. Bush signed a military order stating that al-Qaeda members who were accused of committing or abetting acts of terrorism would be tried by "military commissions," under rules of procedure set by the secretary of defense, with no possibility of appeal to any other US or foreign court.[22] This order had been secretly prepared by David Addington, legal counsel to Vice President Dick Cheney, who had consulted only with a small number of like-minded government attorneys. Among those who were never informed about the order—and probably would have opposed it in whole or in part—was an impressive list of top Bush administration officials, including the secretary of state, the national security advisor, the attorney general, the director of the CIA, and the legal advisor to the National Security Council. George W. Bush also apparently knew nothing about the draft order until Cheney told him about it during one of their weekly lunches but quickly decided to approve it without ever listening to any counterarguments or considering its full implications. The text of the order was then sent to the deputy White House staff secretary so that it could be prepared for immediate signature, "with emphatic instructions to bypass staff review." The staff secretary, after first insisting that "he had handled thousands of presidential documents without ever bypassing strict procedures of coordination and review," finally relented, and less than an hour later Bush officially signed the soon-to-be controversial document. Colin Powell and Condoleezza Rice first learned about the order's existence when they heard about it in on the news later that evening.[23]

Much the same thing had happened eight months earlier, when Bush signed and made public a letter drafted by Cheney renouncing the Kyoto climate change treaty and opposing a cap on carbon dioxide emissions, the latter position being contrary to a promise he had made during the 2000 campaign. Here, too, Bush acted without an effort to consult anyone else in his administration, including Powell, Rice, and Christine Todd Whitman, head of the Environmental Protection Agency.[24]

It is hard to examine episodes such as these and not conclude that Bush was, in many cases, the "decider" only in the most perfunctory sense. The person who really formulated the administration's position with respect to trying terrorists was Dick Cheney; Bush merely signed on at the end. Or as former assistant secretary of defense Richard Perle summarized the situation, "The machinery of government that he [Bush] nominally ran was actually running him."[25] After observing Bush's performance as governor, University of Texas political scientist Bruce Buchanan noted the same problem: "Bush's biggest weakness is that he might not be in a position to discern the credibility of the options his advisors lay out for him."[26]

The principal blame for establishing such an obviously dysfunctional advising system clearly rests with Bush himself. Yet there is little evidence that Karl Rove made any significant effort to alter Bush's work routines or strengthen the policy-deliberating capacity in the White House. As Bush's friend and close advisor, Rove might have urged him to consult with a wider range of sources, especially those who had a stronger background in analyzing and implementing policy, or at least read a daily newspaper. As director of the Office of Strategic Initiatives, Rove might have tried to make it into a real "think tank," staffed by a large complement of genuine policy experts. As deputy chief of staff for policy, he might have devised a way to seek out information and advice from a variety of sources and then condense them into a form that Bush might have found congenial.

So far as one can tell from existing accounts (including his own), Rove did none of these things. To the contrary, Rove actually seems to have been quite pleased with a system that, while it may have weakened the administration as a whole, almost certainly enhanced his own power. And this, too, is characteristically Rovian. "If there is one aspect of Rove's personality that his friends and enemies agree on," a Texas political reporter found, "it is his aggressive territoriality." Put simply, Rove didn't like rivals and competitors. "Karl is extremely turf-sensitive," said a "close friend and associate." "He often feels threatened when there is no threat. He has an inexplicable insecure streak."[27]

In campaigns, Rove had the reputation of being, as several people told me, a "control freak"—someone who wanted not only to be the principal strategist but to control every aspect of the campaigns he worked on. Melinda Henneberger of the *New York Times* reached a strikingly similar conclusion: "When I asked people who have worked with Rove in Texas what makes a classic 'Karl campaign,' they all used the same word: control."[28]

When Karen Hughes left the White House in 2002 and thus lost most of her capacity to offset Rove's influence, Rove was described as "giddy" about the opportunity he now had to expand his power.[29] There are also reports that other staff recognized Rove's power and sensitivities and were, as a result, reluctant to disagree with him: "Some staff members, senior and junior, are awed and cowed by Karl's real or perceived powers. They self-censor lots for fear of upsetting him, and, in turn, few of the president's top people routinely tell the president what they really think if they think that Karl will be brought up short in the bargain."[30]

The result was a domestic policy development process dominated to a remarkable degree by Rove and his acolytes—dominated, that is to say, by people whose background and training was largely in political consulting.

A Brief Word about Dick Cheney

The argument I have just made—that Karl Rove exercised enormous influence over the policy decisions that were formally made by George W. Bush—is one that has also been made about Bush's vice president, Dick Cheney. It is, of course, no accident that the administration that produced "the most powerful political consultant in American history" also begot the person often described as the most powerful vice president in our nation's history.[31] Both descriptions are eloquent testimony to the president's own substantial weaknesses: his lack of information about many topics and issues, his unwillingness to seek out additional information or encourage vigorous debate among his top advisors, his proclivity for bypassing formal decision-making procedures. What one observer said about Rove could also be said of Cheney: "Rove wouldn't be Rove . . . were Bush not Bush."[32]

Did these two very powerful subordinates check and balance one another and thus increase the range of advice and information given to the president? (Franklin Roosevelt was notorious for giving the same assignment to several different subordinates, in order to retain the power of final decision in his own hands.) The answer, unfortunately, is no. According to Peter Baker, Rove and Cheney had a "tacit arrangement" to avoid "issues where the other specialized."[33] Cheney did make one major foray into domestic policy: in the early months of the administration, he led a task force charged with developing a national energy plan. The politics of this effort were handled very clumsily, however, and the plan produced went nowhere, at least during Bush's first term. After that, and especially after the terrorist attacks in September 2001, Cheney seems to have confined his influence efforts largely to foreign and defense policy.[34] Rove, on the other hand, concentrated his labors on domestic policy, perhaps because that was where his interests and expertise lay, perhaps because realignments have historically turned on domestic issues. In Shirley Warshaw's study of what she calls the "co-presidency of Bush and Cheney," she argues that Cheney's experience as Gerald Ford's chief of staff led him to recognize the powers and prerogatives of the White House staff and therefore to be especially careful not to "threaten [its] role in making policy."[35] Whatever the explanation, accounts of the Bush presidency rarely if ever mention clashes between Rove and Cheney.

Political Consultants versus Policy Analysts: The Difference It Makes

What is wrong with turning political consultants into policy advisors? After all, it might be argued, political consultants are in the business of trying to please the voters—which, to a fair extent, is also what elected officials aim to accomplish. So why not make consultants central players in the policy development process?

The answer is that, whatever the surface similarities, the jobs of a policy analyst and a political consultant are fundamentally quite different. While both deal in a broad sense with the needs and concerns of the voters and potential voters, they approach such matters in very different ways, asking different questions and evaluating policy by different standards. In saying this, I do not mean to argue that there is a hard, rigid line separating the two professions, such that persons from one camp are entirely incapable of doing or appreciating the work of the other. But there is, as I will attempt to show in the following pages, a sharp difference in basic perspective.

In his book *Bureaucracy*, James Q. Wilson has shown that the work performed by a governmental agency is strongly affected by the types of people hired to work in it—in particular, by their "prior experiences" and "professional norms."[36] The basic nature of the Central Intelligence Agency (CIA), to take one of Wilson's examples, owes a great deal to the fact that many of its first employees were drawn from a World War II spy agency called the Office of Strategic Services (OSS). Though the authorizing legislation suggested that the CIA was intended primarily to synthesize and coordinate the intelligence gathered by other agencies, the OSS veterans had little experience in that sort of endeavor. What the OSS men did know how to do, "because they had done it for many years," was how to "manage spies and conduct covert operations behind enemy lines."[37] As a result, the CIA soon began doing the same kind of work performed earlier by the OSS.

As one history of the agency summarized its early development, "Although the Agency was established primarily for the purpose of providing intelligence analysis to senior policymakers, within three years clandestine operations became and continued to be the Agency's preeminent activity."[38]

In a similar way, the organizational mission of the National Highway Traffic Safety Administration (NHTSA) has been influenced to a significant degree by the professional composition of its work force. Charged in the most general terms with reducing deaths and injuries on the nation's highways, the NHTSA might have carried out that directive in a variety of ways: by improving driver education, for example, or by reducing drunk driving or increasing the quality and availability of safety resources for motorists, such as emergency medical treatment for accident victims.[39] "But to a remarkable degree," Wilson reports, the agency "has favored changing the automobile rather than the driver" or the highway environment.[40] In the beginning, this focus may have made sense—but the agency continued to operate this way, even as evidence accumulated that the later changes in auto safety it promulgated were having no measurable effect on highway fatalities and that other approaches might have been more productive.

Why did the NHTSA behave this way? According to a study by Charles Pruitt, the answer had much to do with the fact that the NHTSA was staffed largely by engineers. Engineers are good at designing autos and other complex machinery; they have no special skill or training in teaching people how to drive or deploying emergency medical resources. Hence, most of the agency's resources—including, for example, the disbursement of research money—were narrowly focused on finding ways to make cars safer, while generally ignoring the myriad other ways of meeting the agency's goals.[41]

In an analogous way, I will argue in this and the next chapter, a presidential administration dominated by political consultants and a consultant mentality will do its work differently than an administration where the task of policy formulation is entrusted primarily to policy specialists. Four such differences are particularly worth noting.

A Difference of Detail

To start with the most basic point, political consultants are experts in politics, not policy. They are, of course, required to know some general propositions about the major issues facing the country and what the voters think about them. But given the relatively low level of public knowledge about governmental affairs and the news media's equally limited interest in such matters, election campaigns are rarely required to deal with policy issues at any great level of detail. On an issue such as health care, a candidate for Congress or the presidency who says that he supports a government-run health insurance program that covers every American has probably gotten as specific and concrete as he needs to get for purposes of the campaign. Perhaps he may be forced to provide more detailed answers to a few specific questions: Does he favor a mandate? Will his plan require a tax increase? Yet even here, he will probably be able to get away with blithe assurances ("No, there won't be a mandate") or standard clichés ("We'll pay for it by taxing the rich and cutting out waste and fraud") that virtually every serious student of the issue recognizes are highly problematic. What the candidate will almost certainly *not* be required to do is provide a draft bill of sufficient specificity that it could plausibly be enacted into law.[42]

Policy analysis plainly marches to a different drummer. A great deal of policy analysis is precisely about details: about how to design and implement a national health insurance program; about how to simplify the tax code; about how the federal government can get state and local school systems to perform more effectively; about how (and how not) to negotiate arms control treaties or provide foreign aid or bring peace to the Middle East.

This difference between political consultants and policy analysts is strikingly illustrated by an incident that occurred during John DiIulio's brief tenure as the first head of the White House Office of Faith-Based and Community Initiatives. DiIulio, a Princeton University professor and, by universal recognition, a serious student of public policy, was at one point told by a "senior staff member": "John, get a faith bill [i.e., a bill that would have allowed faith-based groups to participate more actively in delivering certain kinds of social welfare services], any faith bill."[43] This is, to say the least, a remarkable request. It is difficult to imagine any serious authority on tax policy telling a subordinate, "Get a tax bill, any tax bill." Or an arms control expert saying, "Get a treaty, any treaty." The senior staff member's comments suggest that either (a) he had no concept of the complexities and nuances of the issue, or (b) he did not care since the purpose of the legislation was purely symbolic anyway and was not intended to have a serious policy impact. Either alternative speaks volumes about the staff member's interest in, and understanding of, public policy.

Unfortunately, this was not an isolated incident. A remarkable number of people who worked in the upper reaches of the Bush presidency came away complaining about the poor quality of policy thinking inside the White House. The kind of criticism I am referring to here, it is important to emphasize, was *not* that the Bush White House was too conservative or too liberal (though it was frequently criticized on these grounds as well). The criticism was that nobody thought much about policy, period, except in terms of its immediate electoral impact.

One of the first and most publicized criticisms came from DiIulio:

There is no precedent in any modern White House for what is going on in this one: a complete lack of a policy apparatus. What you've got is everything—and I mean everything being run by the political arm. . . . I heard many, many staff discussions but not three meaningful, substantive policy discussions. There were no actual policy white papers on domestic issues. There were, truth be told, only a couple of people in the White House who worried at all about policy substance and analysis, and they were even more overworked than the stereotypical nonstop, twenty-hour-a-day White House staff. Every modern presidency moves on the fly, but on social policy and related issues, the lack of even basic policy knowledge, and the only casual interest in knowing more, was somewhat breathtaking.[44]

Presidential speechwriter David Frum, in an otherwise admiring book about Bush, made much the same point:

If you looked more narrowly at the White House staff, there was again a dearth of really high-powered brains. One seldom heard an unexpected thought in the Bush White House or met someone who possessed unusual knowledge. Aside from the witty and ingenious Mitch Daniels at the Office of Management and Budget and of course Karl Rove, who played the unusual dual role of political guru and leading intellectual, conspicuous intelligence seemed actively unwelcome in the Bush White House.[45]

When Treasury Secretary Paul O'Neill left the administration in December 2002, he too scored the White House for its woefully deficient policy analytic capabilities. As he told reporter Ron Suskind, the policy formulation process in the Bush administration "was a broken process . . . or rather no process at all; there seemed to be no apparatus to assess policy and deliberate effectively, to create coherent governance."[46]

Though it is often difficult to draw a precise link between the policy procedures of the Bush presidency and any particular policy outcome, it is hard not to notice the general pattern: that the administration was repeatedly criticized—including, in the end, by many Republicans—for the ineptness with which it pursued many of its objectives. The most glaring example of this shortcoming occurred in foreign policy. As I will argue in a later chapter, even if one supports the decision to invade Iraq—indeed, *especially* if one supports the decision to invade Iraq[47]—it is hard not to conclude that the postwar occupation was appallingly mishandled, in a variety of distinct ways.

Karl Rove was not, in general, a major player in formulating or implementing Bush's foreign policy and thus cannot be blamed for the occupation debacle (though, as I will suggest later, he might have done more to warn Bush about the consequences of the developing quagmire). But the same sorts of missteps also occurred regularly in domestic policy—even in education, one of the few policy areas that Bush reputedly did know and care about.

In late 2001, the final version of the No Child Left Behind (NCLB) bill sailed through both houses of Congress with large, bipartisan majorities. Yet, just a few years later, this act had become one of the most uniformly unpopular laws on the federal statute books, with the brickbats coming from both sides of the partisan divide and every point on the ideological spectrum. Representative George Miller (D-CA), who played a major role in writing the legislation, said in 2007 that NCLB "may be the most tainted brand in America."[48]

To be fair to Bush and his advisors, the bipartisan criticism of NCLB was, in part, a backhanded tribute to how difficult it was to pass the law in the first place.[49] The Bush high command skillfully took advantage of a singularly favorable constellation of circumstances. Republicans, who had spent most of the past decade arguing for a smaller federal role in education, swallowed their ideological reservations in order to give an important victory to the new president; Democrats were at least willing to give Bush's pleas for bipartisanship a cautious trial. Both sides were also anxious to demonstrate a spirit of unity in the immediate aftermath of the 9/11 attacks. As the normal rhythms of Washington politics resumed, however, and as Bush's once-stratospheric approval ratings fell back to earth, both sides came to have second thoughts. The Democratic recantation was particularly rapid. By March 2002, just two months after the bill was signed into law, Senator Edward Kennedy was already complaining that the Bush administration was significantly underfunding the law. In January 2003, on the law's one-year anniversary, forty-two Democratic senators who had voted for the bill sent a letter to the president in which they predicted that the law would fail "without a substantial increase in resources."[50] Most Republicans took a little longer to sour on NCLB, but by 2007, sizable numbers were indicating agreement with the comments of then-House minority whip Roy Blount (R-MO): "I always had misgivings. But I did vote for it on the basis that maybe he [Bush] was right and this was his big domestic initiative and let's give him a chance. But all my concerns . . . have proven to be justified."[51]

Early in his second term, in a remarkable (but not atypical) misreading of the political tea leaves, President Bush actually urged Congress to extend NCLB's basic framework to high school. Whereas the original law had only required students to be tested once in high school, Bush now wanted to have students take evaluation tests in the ninth, tenth, and eleventh grades. He also proposed creating a new federal program to increase high school graduation rates among at-risk students.[52] Congress, however, was unwilling even to reauthorize the original legislation. In March 2007, a group of fifty-seven Republican senators and representatives introduced legislation that would have allowed states to opt out of the NCLB testing and accountability mandates, in effect gutting the whole law.[53] Nor were Democrats receptive to working out another compromise with a president now widely viewed as untrustworthy. When told that Bush would increase education spending if the Democrats agreed to reauthorize the law, George Miller replied, "I bought a horse from that man once. I'm not going to buy another horse from him."[54] The Bush presidency came to an end with its most publicized domestic achievement still not reauthorized. (In 2015, large, bipartisan majorities in both houses of Congress passed the Every Student Succeeds Act, which retained NCLB's testing requirements but turned most of the accountability questions over to the states.)

However much one wishes to concede to the vagaries of American politics, much of the controversy surrounding No Child Left Behind is attributable to a far more basic problem: the law just wasn't very well designed. As Frederick Hess of the American Enterprise Institute has observed, "NCLB leavened 1990s-style accountability with Great Society-style ambition and race-conscious rhetoric, while lacking attention to the program design that characterized Clinton-era efforts to reform welfare and 'reinvent government.' The resulting law relied more on moral exhortation than on calculated goals, metrics, or incentives."[55]

In virtually every major review of NCLB's performance, two features have been singled out for special criticism. First, the basic architecture of NCLB centered around an effort to set standards and then hold states and local schools accountable for meeting them. Unlike past federal educational programs, there would be real consequences for failure. But while the law established federal accountability, *it actually allowed the states to set the standards*. Each state was allowed to define for itself what students should know in reading and math at each relevant grade level, what tests would be used to assess student achievement, and, perhaps most importantly, what level of achievement on the test would constitute "proficiency." The obvious problem with this arrangement was that it gave states a clear incentive to lower their sights: to achieve 100 percent proficiency and thus avoid federal penalties not by doing a better job of educating students, but by setting a less demanding standard of proficiency.[56]

The upshot was vividly revealed in a 2006 study by the Education Trust, a nonprofit think tank, which compared the percentage of students rated as proficient in state exams and in the National Assessment of Educational Progress (NAEP), a highly regarded and carefully constructed national test that played, however, no role in the NCLB accountability system. In Colorado, 89 percent of fourth graders were rated proficient in math on the state test—but only 39 percent achieved proficiency on the national test. In West Virginia, the state exam showed 71 percent of eighth-graders proficient in math—but only 18 percent were rated proficient on the NAEP.[57] In a similar study published in 2008, Peterson and Hess found that only three states (Massachusetts, South Carolina, and Missouri) had established "world-class standards" that were reasonably comparable to those demanded by the NAEP and by most other countries. The other forty-seven states had a lower standard of proficiency—in many cases, dramatically lower.[58]

As states became more familiar with the law, moreover, state standards were lowered even further. According to one study, among states that significantly changed their proficiency "cut scores" after 2002, more than 70 percent made their tests even easier.[59] (A cut score is the minimum test score that a student must achieve in order to be judged proficient in a subject.) William Bennett and Rod Paige, both of whom served as secretary of education under a Republican president, cite the example of Oklahoma. "In one year the number of schools on [the state's] 'needs improvement' list dropped by 85 percent—not because they improved or their students learned more but because a bureaucrat in the state education department changed the way Oklahoma calculates 'adequate yearly progress' under the federal law."[60]

The second widely noted design flaw in NCLB was the inflexibility of its accountability procedures.[61] In the early months of his presidency, Bush repeatedly insisted that he wanted "local control of schools," that "real reform . . . does not try to run the schools from a central office in Washington."[62] At times, he even insisted that his plan would "pass power out of Washington," that there would be "*more* flexibility . . . at the local level."[63] It is difficult to believe that any fair-minded observer would say that the final bill came close to meeting this objective. Not only were all schools and school districts required to undertake a heavy new regimen of annual testing, those schools that did not make "adequate yearly progress" toward the goal of 100 percent proficiency in 2014 were also subject to a series of specific and increasingly significant penalties. A school that did not make adequate yearly progress two years in a row had to offer all students the option of transferring to another public school in the same district that was not deficient. After three years of inadequate progress, a school was required to offer "supplemental educational services" (e.g., after-school or weekend tutoring). After four years, the schools had to take various kinds of "corrective action." After six years, they had to implement a "restructuring plan." In both of the last two situations, schools did have some options as to what kind of "corrective action" to take or how to "restructure" themselves, but the options were limited and some kind of major response was mandated.[64] Most of the "increased flexibility" provisions, by contrast, were scrapped at some point during the congressional deliberations. To say, against that background, that No Child Left Behind did not represent a huge increase in federal control over the nation's elementary and secondary schools seems a blatant denial of reality. A more accurate assessment was provided by Harvard education professor Richard Elmore, who called NCLB "the single largest—and the single most damaging—expansion of federal power over the nation's education system in history."[65] Andy Rotherham, a Clinton education advisor, reached a similar conclusion: NCLB "represents the high water mark of federal intrusion in education."[66]

The NCLB penalties, it should be added, applied not only to schools that failed to make adequate yearly progress for students as a whole. The penalties also kicked in if there was insufficient progress in *any* of the tested grades (third through eighth) or for *any* of a myriad of specific subgroups (for example, blacks, Hispanics, the disabled, English-language learners, or the economically disadvantaged). As Finn and Hess have noted, "Larger or more diverse schools are at greater risk simply because they have more such subgroups whose scores will fluctuate. Some schools can have 40 or more subgroups, yet there is no distinction between a school that failed to make AYP in 35 and another that fell short in just one."[67] Many of the "remedies," moreover, were difficult to apply in certain kinds of local circumstances. The option of transferring to another *public* school, in particular, was of little or no help to students in rural areas, where there might not be another such school a convenient distance away, or in many urban areas, where a large number of schools were failing to make adequate yearly progress and those that did meet this benchmark were unwilling to accept substantial numbers of transfer students.

While trying to drum up support for his education reform plan during the first half of 2001, Bush had repeatedly insisted that "one size does not fit all when it comes to educating children."[68] Turns out he was right.

The result was a law that in significant respects proved to be exactly the opposite of what Bush had promised. While he had promoted his program as offering "high standards" and "local control," NCLB as it was actually passed and implemented provided low standards and a dramatic increase in federal control. In Bush's defense, it should be acknowledged that some of these problems were the inevitable byproduct of a legislative process that required the president to secure a majority vote in a closely divided House of Representatives and sixty votes in a majority Democratic Senate. Yet as numerous commentators have noted, Bush and his advisors were so fixated on getting a "bipartisan" bill that they agreed to numerous provisions and compromises that almost certainly weakened the final product. And just as John DiIulio had found, the administration seemed so concerned about getting "a bill, any bill" that most details were considered unimportant. Andrew Rudalevige noted in his history of the bill's formulation and passage:

> The president's core accountability priority was annual testing. What was in the tests, and how they were used, was less critical. Vouchers were less critical still. . . . The administration had thus set itself up to claim credit at the end of the process while Congress squabbled over the specifics. As one Democratic staffer put it, "The White House had orders: don't get bogged down in details."[69]

After the bill was passed, moreover, the administration "stoutly defended NCLB as enacted, refusing to acknowledge that it needed revising and resisting sensible regulatory modifications until backed into a corner."[70] In 2006, the Secretary of Education told reporters, "I like to talk about No Child Left Behind as Ivory soap. It's 99.9 percent pure. There's not much needed in the way of changes."[71]

A Difference in Measurement Standards

Another important difference between political consultants and policy analysts is the yardsticks they use to measure the value of a policy. Policy analysis, whatever its specific form, is centrally concerned with estimating the impact of a given policy or procedure on the outputs of government. Policies thus become valuable or attractive according to the effect they have on reducing some problem or promoting some set of desired goods. Political consultants, by contrast, are focused on winning elections—and therefore tend to evaluate policies according to their electoral impact: how many votes will be won or lost by adopting one policy rather than another.

In general, these two criteria are probably correlated. A policy that significantly reduces a major problem is likely to move more votes than a policy that produces a smaller effect or deals with a less important problem. An economist who finds a way to substantially reduce unemployment will be heartily welcomed by both policy analysts and political consultants. But there are also lots of exceptions: issues or policies that have a high emotional or symbolic content and thus the capacity to influence many voters, even though their policy significance is quite limited. In such cases, political consultants are likely to advocate policy positions or issue emphases that are difficult to defend strictly on policy grounds.

Consider an example from Bush's successor. On June 29, 2011, Barack Obama held a press conference in which he used his opening statement to argue that tax increases needed to be part of any serious effort to reduce the federal deficit. As he stated his position:

> There's been a lot of discussion about revenues and raising taxes in recent weeks, so I want to be clear about what we're proposing here. I spent the last two years cutting taxes for ordinary Americans, and I want to extend those middle-class tax cuts. The tax cuts I'm proposing we get rid of are tax breaks for millionaires and billionaires, tax breaks for oil companies and hedge fund managers and corporate jet owners.[72]

And then, just in case reporters did not get the point, Obama mentioned his desire to eliminate tax breaks for "corporate jet owners" five more times over the next several minutes. (Obama's specific proposal, which was not described in detail during the press conference, was to change the depreciation period for corporate-owned jets from five to seven years.)

From the moment I first heard about this press conference, I was virtually certain about one thing: the people who pushed Obama to adopt and then publicize this proposal were his political advisors, not his economic or tax experts. (This supposition was later confirmed in several news reports and in a conversation I had with a major Washington political reporter.)[73] This is not to say that Obama's proposal was without merit: plausible arguments can certainly be made in favor of it. But the most conspicuous characteristic of this proposal was the gross disproportion between its potential political appeal and its likely policy impact. In subsequent discussion of the issue, it was widely agreed that the president's proposal would have produced about $3 billion in additional revenue over ten years, or about $300 million per year.[74] While this is more than some political scientists earn, measured against the size of the federal deficit—$1.3 trillion in fiscal year 2010—lengthening the depreciation period for corporate aircraft would have had only the most trivial impact on the problem Obama was supposedly addressing. As one political columnist pointed out, "If you collect that tax for the next 5,000 years . . . it would equal the new debt Obama racked up last year alone."[75] Had Obama charged his economic advisors with finding ways to reduce the deficit, anyone who came back boasting about a proposal that cut the deficit by 0.02 percent would not have kept his job very long. What was attractive about the proposal, in short, was its symbolic appeal, which allowed Obama to say, in effect, "The Republicans are so rigid on this issue and so subservient to the very rich that they're even fighting to preserve tax breaks for corporate jet owners."

The same sort of divergence between political and policy values was clearly visible at a number of points during the Bush presidency. The preceding section of this chapter has provided one example. In formulating the No Child Left Behind law, the White House was so fixated on having a bill that could be advertised as "bipartisan" that it agreed to a series of major compromises with congressional Democrats—compromises that significantly undercut the purposes that the law was supposed to serve.

Another instance where political symbolism trumped policy substance occurred in late 2003 and early 2004, when the Bush high command was beginning to gear up for the president's reelection campaign. To his credit, Rove has always prided himself on running issue-oriented campaigns.[76] In this instance, Rove felt that the president could not just run on his past record as, for example, Ronald Reagan had in 1984. Bush needed to lay out an agenda of things he hoped to accomplish in a second term. Needless to say, Rove was the person put in charge of developing this agenda.[77]

And what kind of programs and policies was Rove seeking? In a word, Rove was looking for *big* initiatives. As a senior administration official explained to the *Washington Post*, "Bush's closest aides are promoting big initiatives on the theory that they contribute to Bush's image as a decisive leader even if people disagree with some of the specifics. 'Iraq was big. AIDS [i.e., Bush's program to combat AIDS in Africa] is big,' the official said. 'Big works. Big grabs attention.'"[78]

No doubt big ideas do often have electoral appeal. But as the Iraq war example illustrates (did the senior administration official really not see the irony in his comments?), from a policy perspective big initiatives often lead to big problems:

- Big initiatives tend to cost more than small initiatives, a not insignificant consideration when the federal government was running a $400 billion deficit.

- Big initiatives tend to involve more issues, affect more interests, and entail a greater departure from the status quo—and are thus more difficult to get approved by Congress.
- Big initiatives also tend, for many of the same reasons, to be more difficult to implement and administer.
- Big initiatives tend to be more complicated and thus more likely to produce unanticipated consequences.[79]

To be fair, some of the big initiatives Bush promoted over the next few months were policies he had already endorsed in his 2000 campaign, such as the partial privatization of Social Security, which he presumably favored for other reasons. But one such initiative had little precedent in anything Bush had said earlier in his presidency or during the 2000 campaign: in January 2004, Bush announced an ambitious proposal to reinvigorate the American space program. Specifically, Bush promised to: "develop and test a new spacecraft" by 2008; "complete the International Space Station by 2010"; and "return to the moon by 2020 . . . with the goal of living and working there for increasingly extended periods of time." Finally, using the moon as a base, the United States would undertake "human missions to Mars and to worlds beyond."[80]

Besides the fact that it was big and might provide Bush with what his aides called a "Kennedy moment,"[81] the benefits of an expanded space program were far from obvious. Certainly there was nothing pressing about the matter, such that it had to be dealt with immediately as opposed to, say, five or ten or twenty years in the future. Moreover, even many who supported the general goals Bush had outlined—exploring space and extending the human presence in the solar system—wondered if his plan was the best way to proceed. Two issues were particularly controversial. First, should the United States send *humans* to Mars? Though manned spaceflight is more glamorous and emotionally stirring, critics have long argued that unmanned, robotic probes are just as scientifically productive, at a fraction of the cost.[82] Second, what was the proper mix of governmental and private sector actors in carrying out the missions? Once the Cold War was over and the United States was no longer involved in a head-to-head competition with the Soviet Union, many conservatives began to complain that the traditional, NASA-led space program was exactly the sort of "big government" initiative that they criticized in most other nondefense-related policy areas. As Rand Simberg has argued: "In order to defeat a state-socialist enterprise, we ourselves set up something resembling one: a hugely funded government space agency. Although we wanted to disprove the Kremlin's continuous bluster about the inherent superiority of social-ism, the great irony of space history is that we created a massive, central-ized, command-and-control agency to get the job done."[83]

Ronald Reagan, in particular, *had* noticed the inconsistency and had worked hard to shift major parts of the American space program to the private sector, thereby "fundamentally reshap[ing] the nature of the U.S. space program."[84] From this perspective, Bush's proposal seemed like a de-cided step backward: an attempt to put government back at the center of space exploration. Yet, however difficult these issues might be for space policy experts, from the perspective of the 2004 Bush campaign they were easy to resolve: unmanned, private ventures in space just aren't as big and dramatic as a national, governmentally run effort to land a man on Mars. Q.E.D.

Looming over the whole enterprise was the huge, inescapable question of costs. Though Bush himself never mentioned it, his proposal was strik-ingly similar to one his father had made in July 1989. Like his son, Bush the elder had promised to complete a space station, return to the moon, and then undertake "a manned mission to Mars."[85] The Bush I proposal went nowhere, largely because of concerns about its cost, which then-budget director Richard Darman had estimated to be about $400 billion.[86] As one writer summarized the proposal's reception, "No funding was allocated to the initiative [by Congress] in fiscal years 1991, 1992 or 1993. By fiscal year 1994, with a new president, Bill Clinton, in the White House, the Space Exploration Initiative [the official name of the Bush proposal] had disap-peared altogether."[87]

If the George W. Bush administration learned anything from this earlier episode, the lessons seem to have been almost entirely about packaging. Unlike his father, Bush II refused to give a total price tag for his project. Instead, Bush dealt with the cost issue in the same way that, as we will see in the next chapter, he handled the costs of his prescription drug bill: by fobbing off the difficult choices onto future presidents. Bush did urge Congress to increase NASA's budget by "roughly a billion dollars, spread out over the next five years." He also called on the agency to "reallocate" $11 billion from its existing budget. (At least some of the money would be freed up by another proposal Bush made in this speech: to retire the space shuttle from service in 2010.) But these two steps hardly solved the cost problem. Bush himself noted, "This increase, along with refocusing of our space agency, is a solid beginning to meet the challenges and the goals that we set today. It's only a beginning. Future funding decisions will be guided by the progress we make in achieving these goals."[88] An editorial in the next day's *New York Times* was more blunt: "What Mr. Bush has really done is promise the moon (literally) while leaving future presidents and Congresses to figure out how to pay the potentially large future bills."[89]

In the end, the Bush II space initiative fizzled in a quite predictable manner. As long as Bush himself was in office, NASA worked on what was now called the Constellation program, including the development of two new launch vehicles, a new crew capsule, and a lunar lander. Once Barack Obama took office, however, the yawning gap between the space program's goals and its resources could no longer be ignored. In May 2009, the new president appointed a Review of US Human Spaceflight Plans Committee, headed by Norman Augustine, a former aerospace executive who had chaired a similar committee for the first president Bush. The Committee's central conclusions were clearly stated in the first paragraph of its report, released in October 2009:

> The U.S. human spaceflight program appears to be on an unsustainable trajectory. It is perpetuating the perilous practice of pursuing goals that do not match allocated resources. Space operations are among the most complex and unforgiving pursuits ever undertaken by humans. It really *is* rocket science. Space operations become all the more difficult when means do not match aspirations. Such is the case today.[90]

The upshot was that when Obama released his 2011 budget in early 2010, he tried to kill Constellation entirely. As the *Washington Post* described Obama's proposal, "NASA's grand plan to return to the moon, built on President George W. Bush's vision of an ambitious new chapter in space exploration, is about to vanish without a whimper."[91] But Constellation, like many another government program, proved difficult to kill—not because Congress was dazzled by the force of Bush's vision but because representatives from states like Florida and Texas, where much of the space program was located, sought to keep the federal gravy flowing to their districts. Finally, in October 2010, a compromise was reached that canceled most of the Constellation program, including the planned visits to the moon and Mars, but continued work on the crew capsule and a single heavy-lift rocket. By that time, NASA had already spent an estimated $10 billion on Bush's proposal.[92]

5

Good Politics Doesn't Always Mean Good Government, Part II

Two other important conflicts between good political strategy and good public policy remain to be explored.

A Different Perspective on Group Interests

American campaign managers have long been fascinated by group-based political strategies. Perhaps it is the country's size and demographic diversity—the sheer number of religions, industries, occupations, and ethnic groups[1]—that has so often led strategists to think about the electorate in segmented terms. Whatever the cause, no one who studies the reality of American election campaigns can fail to notice the imprint this has left on our politics.

In recent years, a number of political scientists and economists have developed formal theories and abstract models that try to explain how and why group appeals work.[2] But the basic idea has been apparent to political strategists since the beginning of the republic. Rather than looking for a few big ideas or policies that a majority of the voters will support, group-based strategies search for issues and appeals that are more narrowly targeted at a series of discrete subgroups. From a political strategist's perspective, the ideal group-based appeal involves a policy or issue position with two characteristics. First, the issue is of overwhelming, dominant concern to the members of one particular group, who largely agree on how to handle it (i.e., what policy to adopt or at least the general direction that policy should take). Second, the rest of the voting population *doesn't* care about the issue—or at least, doesn't care enough to take it into account when deciding how to cast their ballots.

Suppose, for example, that when farmers participate in politics, the one issue that matters most to them, the one consideration that dominates everything else in determining their votes, is farm policy. Given a choice between a candidate who supports generous farm subsidies and one who doesn't, farmers will almost always vote for the candidate who advocates aid to farmers, even if they disagree with his or her position on just about everything else. Assume further that the rest of the electorate doesn't care much about farm policies, doesn't know how they work or how much they cost, perhaps even has a vaguely positive attitude toward them based on the (mis)perception that most of the money goes to small, family-owned farms.

Under these conditions, a political strategist might reasonably conclude that, whatever other policies his or her candidate supports, generous farm subsidies must be part of the package. Even if the group in question is quite small—by the early twenty-first century, only about 2 percent of American adults worked on farms—support for farm subsidies is, from a purely electoral perspective, a no-lose proposition. And if the rest of the electorate is evenly divided between the two major parties, that 2 percent of the vote may spell the difference between victory and defeat. Or it can be combined with similar sorts of appeals to a variety of other groups—affirmative action for blacks, increased educational spending and opposition to vouchers for teachers, protectionism and closed-shop laws for union members, support for Israel to attract Jewish voters, easier access to abortion for feminists—thereby cobbling together a majority coalition whose members may have little in common besides voting for the same candidate. Small wonder, then, that group appeals have long been a ubiquitous feature of American election campaigns.

If political strategists in general are attracted to policies that appeal to narrow group interests, Karl Rove seems to have had a particular obsession with them. As numerous books and articles about him have noted, Rove regularly and instinctively viewed the electorate in group terms. David Frum, who worked as a presidential speechwriter during the first year of the Bush presidency, saw this proclivity as the principal difference between Rove and Karen Hughes, "the two dominant personalities in the pre-9/11 White House." Hughes "perceived the American electorate as something like the television audience in the days before cable, an undifferentiated mass of people whose attention could all be held by a simple story with big themes." By contrast,

> When Rove thought of the American electorate, he saw an enormous bag of toy magnets. Some of the magnets were white, and some were black or brown; some were rural, some were urban; some married, others single. No politician could ever hope to scoop up all the magnets in his hands. There were too many: If he tried to grab them all, he would

end up with none. . . . The job of a political strategist was to gather together the maximum feasible number of magnets.[3]

Many other portraits of Rove have noted the same tendency:

> Most of the reliable indicia of what [Rove is] up to involve his cultivating close political relations with specific groups, in particular locales, that know exactly what they want from government. If you have an idea involving a hitherto undiscovered but distinct group of voters that the Republican Party might be able to attract, chances are that you have heard from Rove.

> The instinct for categorization—for finding, probing, classifying, and ultimately harvesting voters according to minute gradations of preference—has made Karl Rove the power in politics that he is today. . . . For Rove, all politics is partitive, and there is almost nothing he can't explain by slicing up the electorate and slotting it into place.

> Rove never pushed for a policy unless he saw a group of big funders or a significant electoral constituency which it might bring to the Republican Party. Social Security privatization was supposed to attract middle-class people whose pensions had been invested in the stock market; immigration reform to attract Latinos and small-business owners; the No Child Left Behind law public-school parents; and so on. Conversely, Rove was always looking for neglected constituencies . . . and trying to figure out what mix of government goodies and organizing techniques would bring them into the Republican fold.[4]

An interesting example of Rove's tendency to view the electorate in group terms is his analysis of William McKinley. As we have seen in chapter 1, Rove had a particular fascination with McKinley, who not only won the presidential elections of 1896 and 1900 but also presided over a major realignment of the American party system that ushered in a three-decade-long era of Republican dominance. What is especially worth noting here, however, is Rove's analysis as to *why* McKinley was so successful. According to Rove, McKinley's triumph was largely a result of his group-based appeals to previously Democratic constituencies. As Rove argued in a speech he gave at the University of Utah in 2002, "He [McKinley] attempted deliberately to break with Gilded Age politics. He was inclusive and he was the first Republican candidate for president to be endorsed by a leader in the Catholic hierarchy. The Protestant Anglo-Saxon Republicans were scandalized by his 1896 campaign, in which he paraded Portuguese fishermen and Slovak coal miners and Serbian iron workers to Canton, Ohio, to meet him. He just absolutely scandalized the country."[5]

This is, to say the least, an idiosyncratic reading of the mid-1890s realignment. According to most historians and election scholars, McKinley and the Republicans triumphed not because of their skill and boldness in making group-based appeals but because the big national issues worked strongly in their favor. Grover Cleveland, McKinley's Democratic predecessor, had presided over what was probably the second worst depression in American history, which began in 1893 and could easily therefore be blamed on the Democrats. And in mid-1897, shortly after McKinley took office, the American economy began to recover and then grew steadily for the next ten years. (For further details on the state of the economy in the 1890s and its role in the 1896 presidential election, see the review of Rove's book *The Triumph of William McKinley* in the appendix to this volume.) The fact that McKinley hobnobbed with Portuguese fishermen and met with the Catholic archbishop of Minnesota and published election materials in Croatian and Yiddish[6] may have added a few votes around the edges, but it is difficult to credit the argument that group-based appeals were a major explanation for the Republican realignment. Another piece of evidence bearing out the same conclusion is the fact that the shift to the GOP actually began in the congressional elections of 1894, a year and a half before the Republicans chose McKinley as their standard bearer, when the party gained the astounding total of 120 seats in the House of Representatives, the largest midterm seat swing in American history.

In the next chapter, I will raise some questions about how successful Rove's group-based appeals actually were in purely electoral terms. At the moment, however, I wish to make a different point: Even if group appeals do work in the *electoral* arena, they are not a good guide for making *policy* decisions. There may be some cases in which a policy that particularly concerns the members of a well-defined group is also in accord with the public interest as a whole. During the 1960s, for example, the top item of concern to most black voters and political organizations was the passage of strong civil rights legislation that would ban racial discrimination in employment, public accommodations, and voting. Most Americans today would say that in addition to helping blacks, such laws were also in the broader public interest, in that they promoted basic justice and pushed the country to live up to its founding principles. Outlawing racial discrimination truly benefited all of us.

In general, however, there is no guarantee that policies that provide special benefits to one group will also help the rest of the population or at least leave them no worse off. In most cases, indeed, we would expect the opposite. Most of the policy interventions that groups conventionally demand—subsidies, tariffs, restrictions on competition—are widely regarded as economically inefficient, in that they stimulate production beyond the level that the public would otherwise demand or raise prices higher than they would be otherwise. More generally, few interest groups take account of the interests of nonmembers or of the nation as a whole when formulating their demands. Their general mindset is to get as much as they can for their own members. If that imposes costs on everybody else—well, that's their problem. All interest groups *claim*, of course, that they are only seeking what is "fair" and "just," and that their particular industry, occupation, or interest is so important to the nation as to necessitate special treatment. But few such arguments stand up to close scrutiny.

The problems associated with such policies, it should be added, are not just that some groups are advantaged and others are not. Thus, expanding the list of favored groups will not alleviate the difficulties. If a tariff for one product or industry is bad, extending such protection to lots of other products does not make the system work better; it merely multiplies the inefficiencies.

Policy analysts have not been entirely immune from the attractions of special-interest policies (especially if their research is funded by an interest group). In general, however, most forms of policy analysis (equilibrium analysis in economics is perhaps the best example) force the analyst to view such policies from a more general perspective and thus to recognize that a system that provides special benefits to one group must impose the costs of these benefits on the rest of the population, in the form of higher taxes, higher prices, reduced employment, and so forth. (This is the insight behind the aphorism that there's no such thing as a free lunch.)

Unfortunately, there is abundant evidence that Rove applied his group-based political vision to policy as well as to election campaigns. In numerous instances, he successfully pushed the administration to support policies that may have had a short-term political payoff but were difficult or impossible to defend in policy terms. Consider three examples:

STEEL TARIFFS

One of the clearest examples of the triumph of group politics over sound public policy was Bush's 2002 decision to impose tariffs on imported steel. It is not accurate to say that all economists support free trade. It is fair, however, to say that the vast majority of economists believe that trade benefits all nations that take part in it and that almost all of the dissenters come from the left side of the political spectrum. There may have been a time in the nineteenth century when many Republicans sincerely (though wrongly) believed that the key to national prosperity was to erect high tariff walls against virtually every type of foreign goods. Today, however, the appeal of protectionism is almost entirely political, in the pejorative sense of the word.

Such, at any rate, was what happened in early 2002, when the president had to consider a demand by the steel industry and organized labor that he impose substantial tariffs on imported steel. Though the various accounts of the Bush administration's internal deliberations differ a bit on the details, all agree that the issue basically pitted Bush's policy advisors against his political advisors.[7] In opposition to the tariff was virtually every one of Bush's major economic policy advisors, including Glenn Hubbard, chairman of the Council of Economic Advisors; Larry Lindsey, director of the National Economic Council; Treasury Secretary Paul O'Neill; Mitch Daniels, the director of the Office of Management and Budget; and Federal Reserve Chairman Alan Greenspan. Secretary of State Colin Powell also weighed in against the tariff, apparently out of concern that it would complicate efforts to build a broad international coalition against terrorism.[8]

On the other side were Karl Rove and his political acolytes. Rove's motives were, by all accounts, narrowly electoral. By 2002, steel producers only employed about 160,000 people—as compared with about 8 million workers in the steel-using sector.[9] Fortunately for its political clout, however, the steel industry was located primarily in swing states such as West Virginia, Pennsylvania, and Ohio, whose votes were thought to be critical to both the 2002 midterms and Bush's own reelection plans. There were also three hundred thousand retired steelworkers in Florida, who depended upon the industry for their pensions and health care benefits. As political scientist Douglas Brattebo has observed, "It is hard to imagine that legislators and presidents would be so responsive to this constituency if its members lived in states that consistently tipped to one party or the other in presidential elections."[10]

His protestations about always doing the right thing regardless of politics notwithstanding, Bush sided with Rove and the political arm of his administration, imposing tariffs of between 8 and 30 percent for three years on most types of imported steel. In a press conference, Bush described his decision as providing "temporary relief so that the industry could restructure itself."[11] But as numerous commentators noted at the time, the steel industry had been complaining about foreign competition since at least the 1960s, and though many presidents had already granted them protection of one form or another on the premise that they would use the "temporary safeguards" as an opportunity to adjust and adapt to foreign imports, the industry never seemed to do the requisite adjusting. No sooner had one set of trade restrictions ended than the steel industry would demand another round.[12] It is perhaps worth recording that when faced with similar pressures from the steel industry in the late 1990s, the oh-so-unprincipled Bill Clinton, whom the Bush people loved to mock for "governing by poll," refused to abandon his free-trade convictions and accommodate the industry's demands.

The policy fallout from Bush's decision was almost entirely negative. Though the administration apparently hoped to be able to help the steel industry without hurting American steel users, this proved impossible. News reports were soon filled with stories about auto parts manufacturers and other domestic industries, mostly small businesses, that were shutting down or unable to expand because of sharply increased steel prices.[13] Quite predictably, most economists argued that the tariffs cost far more jobs than they saved—jobs that a nation still struggling to emerge from a recession could ill afford to sacrifice. Another wholly predictable consequence of the tariffs was that once Bush had shown a willingness to abandon free-trade principles when importuned by one well-connected group, many other industries also demanded protection, including textiles and agriculture. More surprising, by all accounts, was the level of anger expressed by other countries, including some of the United States' strongest allies in Europe and Asia. From the day the tariffs were first imposed, steel producers from around the world were vowing to fight the plan through the World Trade Organization (WTO).[14] Some countries went further. The Russian foreign ministry reportedly warned the US ambassador in Moscow that the steel tariffs could have a "serious impact on Russian-American relations."[15]

The beginning of the end for the steel tariffs came on November 10, 2003, when the WTO ruled that the US action was illegal, thereby allowing the European Union (EU) to impose $2.3 billion in tariffs on American exports to Europe. In a telling signal that the EU understood the political roots of Bush's decision, the retaliatory tariffs were aimed at goods that were also produced in states thought to be vital to Bush's reelection plans, such as southern textiles and Florida citrus. With many other countries warning of an impending trade war, on December 4 Bush backed down and announced that he was lifting the tariffs on imported steel.[16]

FARM SUBSIDIES

Depending on which economist you talk to, there may once have been a solid justification for federal programs that provided significant aid to

America's farmers. When 25 percent of Americans lived on farms, when the typical farm was small and farm poverty was widespread, when most economists believed that certain characteristics of the agricultural sector tended to result in chronically low and unstable farm incomes,[17] a plausible case could perhaps have been made for something like the McNary-Haugen bill in the 1920s or the Agricultural Adjustment Act of 1933. By the beginning of George W. Bush's presidency, however, there was, if anything, even wider agreement that the circumstances and conditions that had once justified special government support for farmers no longer applied. American farming had been thoroughly transformed by a series of major technological, economic, and social changes,[18] and careful studies had shown that many of the claims traditionally made on behalf of agricultural subsidy programs were wrong or misleading. Though there was still a case to be made for federal spending on agricultural research and environmental conservation programs, the most prominent and expensive farm aid programs seemed to be just one more example—and a particularly glaring one—of special interest politics run riot.

To cite just a few of the pertinent facts: While the average income of American farmers had once lagged well behind that of nonfarm households, by the 1990s "farm households attained . . . income levels equal to or exceeding those of the nonfarm population."[19] Statistics also show that farmers today are substantially wealthier than their nonfarm counterparts. As of 2007, "the median net worth of a farm household [was] $460,000. That is nearly five times the $92,000 median net worth for all U.S. households."[20] There is, to be sure, still a significant amount of *rural* poverty, but rural is no longer synonymous with *agricultural*. By 1990, farm families accounted for just 7 percent of the rural population.[21] In 1989, according to US Department of Commerce data, 11.1 percent of farm households were poor, compared to 12.9 percent for nonfarm households and 18.1 percent in central cities.[22]

Though farm subsidies are often justified as helping save small family farms, the structure of the programs essentially guarantees that they cannot perform this function. Since farm commodity payments are "roughly proportional to production of program crops," such payments flow largely to big farms and, thus, to "individuals who are relatively wealthy compared to most Americans."[23] Farm subsidies, in short, are Robin Hood in reverse: they take money from working-class and middle-class taxpayers and largely transfer it to "a small group of fairly well-off farm businesses and landowners."[24] In this way, farm subsidy programs have actually *reduced* the number of family farms, by providing larger farms and farm businesses with the incentive and resources to buy up their smaller, less-subsidized neighbors.

The extent to which farm commodity programs produced this perverse result became clearer starting in 2001, when the Environmental Working Group (EWG), using US Department of Agriculture data, began releasing reports on the concentration and major recipients of commodity subsidies. "In 1995," the EWG noted, "the top 10 percent of American farmers received 55 percent of government subsidies; in 2001 their share rose to 67 percent."[25] By 2012, after the two Bush-era farm bills had done their work, the top 10 percent were receiving 75 percent of all commodity payments.[26] A 2002 investigation by the *Los Angeles Times* similarly found that:

> Here in the heart of California's farm belt, the list [of commodity payment recipients] includes wealthy doctors, lawyers, home builders and a man named Ed Donaghy, who built his fortune as a major distributor of Budweiser beer. . . . It includes beef baron John Harris and members of the wine-making Gallo family—power brokers who donate large sums of money to state and national politicians. . . . The Woolf family, which farms about 15,000 acres in Fresno County and owns three vacation homes overlooking the Pacific in Santa Cruz, has received nearly $1 million in subsidies since 1996.[27]

Any argument that ending subsidy programs would deliver a life-threatening blow to American agriculture is further belied by another relevant fact: many important farm sectors have rarely or never received direct subsidies, yet seem to be doing quite well without them. For reasons that made sense back in the 1930s, the vast majority of federal farm aid has always been directed at a narrow set of crops, including wheat, rice, corn, cotton, peanuts, and soybeans. Most fruits and vegetables have never been on the target list; indeed, according to EWG data, 62 percent of American farmers received no federal commodity payments between 1995 and 2012. Yet Americans are nevertheless able to buy US-grown apples, lettuce, carrots, potatoes, tomatoes, and onions, all at generally reasonable prices.

The result, as the eminent agricultural economist Bruce Gardner noted in 1996, has been "a significant change in the thrust of commodity policy recommendations" made by agricultural economists. "Until about 1950 the most carefully considered recommendations focused on judicious intervention by government to improve the functioning of markets. By 1990 recommendations for such intervention had virtually ceased."[28]

Consider, for example, the judgment rendered by economist Daniel Sumner, director of the University of California Agricultural Issues Center:

For generations no one has been able to maintain any plausible reason to support [farm] prices, subsidize business insurance, or distribute government payments, mainly to farmers of grains, oilseeds and cotton, while perpetuating convoluted regulations for milk marketing and trade barriers to subsidize sugar producers. Rationales that might have sounded credible in 1950—e.g., farmers tend to be poor; the free market just doesn't work—were shown over the decades to be weak rationalizations for transfers to the wealthy. Other stories, such as that farm subsidies aid rural economies, are similarly at odds with basic facts. Farms account for a tiny share of rural employment, and subsidies do not go to poor regions.[29]

David Orden, Robert Paarlberg, and Terry Roe, two economists and a political scientist, reached a similar conclusion in 1999:

As the technological and economic transformation of agriculture progressed, the "temporary" farm policies improvised in the 1930s thus became unsuited for the farm sector that emerged. Supply-control and price- and income-support programs did not have much long-term effect on the earnings of farm labor, or on the rate of return to farm capital, but continuation of these programs was costly to taxpayers and consumers, and the benefits of the policies were concentrated in the asset values of a decreasing number of increasingly wealthy farm owners.[30]

Hovering in the background as Congress and the president formulated the 2002 farm bill was the last major farm bill, the "Freedom to Farm" Act of 1996.[31] Regarded by many observers as one of the few real accomplishments of the so-called Republican Revolution of the mid-1990s, the Freedom to Farm law was widely portrayed as having tried to "wean" the nation's farmers off federal subsidies.[32] At the heart of the 1996 law was a kind of bargain: farmers would receive a set of fixed "contract payments" that were expected to be less on average than what they would have received under existing law, in return for which they would be largely freed from government restrictions on their planting and acreage decisions. In fact, the Freedom to Farm Act never lived up to its promise. Farmers accepted the fixed payments as long as crop prices were high and the payments were thus a kind of unearned windfall. When commodity prices declined in 1998, 1999, and 2000, however, farmers and their lobbyists sought—and received—billions of dollars in "supplemental" appropriations. Still, by most reckonings, the 1996 law had been a step in the right direction; and based on his rhetoric during the 2000 campaign, when he said that "the best way to ensure a strong, growing, and vibrant agricultural sector is through a more market-driven approach,"[33] one might have expected George W. Bush to see the law's expiration as an opportunity to further diminish the government's role in agriculture. As late as November 2001, Agriculture Secretary Ann Veneman criticized a bill then being developed in the Senate on the grounds that it would create "pressure for more government payments, thereby creating a self-defeating and ultimately unsustainable cycle."[34]

The actual writing of the Farm Security and Rural Investment Act of 2002 can be briefly summarized.[35] Starting in mid-2001, the House Agriculture Committee, packed with members whose constituents had benefited from past subsidy programs, wrote a bill that significantly expanded subsidy spending and restored many of the more objectionable subsidy programs that had been eliminated during the Clinton administration. The Senate Committee on Agriculture, Nutrition, and Forestry, similarly constituted, did pretty much the same thing. Then a House-Senate conference committee put together a compromise bill that seemed to combine the worst features of both bills. A *Washington Post* editorial provided several sad examples:

> Both House and Senate had voted to cap payments to individual farmers—the Senate legislation set a limit of $275,000, the House had passed a nonbinding resolution supporting the idea of caps. But the bill that emerged from conference had no effective cap, so a handful of vast agro-industrial operations will continue to pocket millions of dollars, perhaps using them to buy out the small family farmers whose traditional livelihood the bill's backers claim to preserve. Similarly, the original Senate bill had promised high subsidies but then blunted the damage by saying that farmers could not expand production onto unspoiled grasslands. The conferees kept the high payment levels but scrapped that safeguard.[36]

The Bush administration made a few attempts to push the bill-writers in a less free-spending, more free-market direction, then gradually changed its tune to lukewarm and then enthusiastic support. By May 2002, one farm lobbyist said that "you will have to be a 9-foot greyhound" to catch up with Bush and Sen. Tom Harkin (D-IA) in their race to "tak[e] credit for this bill."[37] Behind Bush's change of heart, contemporary observers of all stripes agreed, was politics in its crassest form. As Mike Allen of the *Washington Post* reported, "A senior Republican official said Bush, after opposing the bill's costliest provisions last fall, capitulated because the most fertile ground for gaining the one Senate seat needed for a Republican takeover lies in the farm states of South Dakota, Montana, Minnesota, Missouri, Iowa and Georgia."[38] Sen. Richard Lugar (R-IN), himself a farmer, similarly attributed the bill to "a concern among lawmakers of both parties that power in Congress could hinge on a few races in heavily subsidized agricultural regions."[39] John McCain had a pithier explanation: "This is all about votes."[40]

Bush deserves particular reproach for his conduct during the conference committee negotiations. Had he spoken up against the kind of bill that was plainly emerging—in particular, had he threatened to veto it—he might still have had a significant impact on the bill's final form. Press coverage at the time indicates that there was a considerable amount of Republican opposition to the bill, almost certainly enough to sustain a veto in one house or the other. A majority of Senate Republicans voted against the bill; "key House Republican leaders" were also said to be opposed to it.[41] In fact, according to numerous accounts, while the bill was in conference the Bush administration was "silent" about all of the bill's most egregious features. The president pushed for just two small changes, one of which was to make the bill even more expensive, by repealing a provision of the 1996 welfare reform law that had barred legal immigrants from receiving food stamps.[42]

At a time when the American political media are at least as polarized as the members of Congress, the 2002 farm bill achieved the rare feat of uniting critics from across the political spectrum. The bill was denounced by editorials in the *New York Times*, the *Washington Post*, and the *New Republic*, and by columnists in the *Weekly Standard*, *Newsweek*, *U.S. News*, and *Business Week*.

A war is on and there's again a huge deficit, yet Washington is back to its old ways, gorging on spending. The era in which big government was over is over.

Never has so much money been showered on so few with so little consideration.

Congress . . . has passed, and President Bush has signed, one of the worst pieces of legislation of the past decade. . . . Its collateral damage on the nation's foreign policy and budgetary priorities will be substantial.

You would think that if there was one clear benefit to having an economic conservative in the White House, it would be the opportunity to dismantle government programs that are both wasteful and unnecessary. In the case of George W. Bush, you'd be wrong.

Mr. Bush did not create the awful farm bill. But he failed to contain Congress's runaway extravagance, and in signing it he put the votes of farm states that could tip the balance in the midterm elections ahead of policy or principle.[43]

The final bill, which was signed into law on May 13, 2002, was estimated to increase farm spending by 80 percent, or $45.1 billion over the six-year life of the law.[44] Among its distinctive features was to reestablish three subsidy programs that everyone except the subsidy recipients agreed were particularly worthless: those for wool, mohair, and honey. At the signing ceremony, Bush conceded, "It's not a perfect bill." But the only specific criticism he offered was that it did *not* include farm savings accounts—which, their name notwithstanding, were actually another form of government subsidy.[45] Bush also lauded the bill for providing a "safety net" for farmers "without encouraging overproduction and depressing prices. It will allow farmers and ranchers to plan and operate based on market realities, not Government dictates." In fact, as virtually everyone who wasn't on the White House payroll recognized, the bill did precisely the opposite.[46]

Besides busting the budget and sending a clear signal that well-organized special interests would get a sympathetic hearing at the White House, the 2002 farm bill also had an adverse impact on US trade policy. In November 2001, the United States and 150 other members of the World Trade Organization had started a new series of trade talks, usually referred to as the Doha round, which were supposed to focus on expanding trade between developed and developing nations. In addition to the costs they impose on taxpayers and consumers, the kinds of agricultural subsidies maintained by the United States and most European countries generally lead these countries to "dump" their surplus crops on the international market. And precisely because they are subsidized, the crops grown in wealthier nations are often able to undersell those grown in poorer countries. In response, developing countries have often erected strict trade barriers that keep out the manufactured goods produced by developed economies.

Against this background, the basic shape of a mutually beneficial trade deal clearly emerged: developed countries like the United States would cut or eliminate their agricultural subsidies, in return for which they would gain greater access to Third World markets. In fact, as Laura D'Andrea Tyson, one of President Clinton's top economic advisors, noted in June 2002, "For years, the U.S. government has lectured the rest of the world, especially Europe, to slash agricultural subsidies. . . . Now the US is doing the opposite of what it has been preaching. This about-face has dealt a severe blow to American credibility [on trade issues] around the world. . . . The new farm bill threatens to kill the negotiations before they have even begun."[47]

Economics writer and Reagan policy advisor Bruce Bartlett, writing in 2006, reached a similar conclusion: "Once Bush signed a massive increase in U.S. [farm] subsidies right at the start of the trade talks, he lost all credibility on the issue and it became a foregone conclusion that no agreement would be reached on the central topic of the [Doha] negotiations."[48]

George W. Bush has received considerable praise—deserved, in my opinion—for his decision to dramatically increase US spending to combat AIDS in Africa.[49] But an even more effective way to assist the worst-off Africans would have been to reduce American agricultural subsidies. In July 2003, the presidents of Mali and Burkina Faso wrote an op-ed in the *New York Times* calling attention to the fact that US cotton subsidies were making it substantially more difficult for poor African nations to sell their cotton on world markets. "Thus, the payments to about 2,500 relatively well-off [American] farmers has the unintended but nevertheless real effect of impoverishing some 10 million rural poor people in West and Central Africa."[50] Laura Tyson was even more emphatic: "Cutting agricultural subsidies, which depress global agricultural prices and reduce farm incomes in the developing world, would be the single most effective way for the U.S. and the other developed countries to help the world's poorest citizens."[51]

IMMIGRATION

The third example of how group-based electoral appeals translated into special interest policies under the Bush administration is perhaps less clear-cut than the preceding two. Unlike steel tariffs and farm subsidies, there are solid, intellectually respectable arguments that can be made in defense of the kind of "comprehensive immigration reform" that the Bush administration repeatedly tried to enact between 2004 and 2007. Yet Bush himself rarely made such arguments—and most of those who did were thorough-going liberals or hard-core libertarians who started from premises that the president would not have accepted.

The arguments the administration *did* make were generally dubious or misleading.[52] A particularly good example was Bush's repeated assertion that, if large numbers of additional immigrants were admitted to the United States through a guest worker program, they would only "fill jobs that Americans will not do."[53] This argument is problematic on at least two counts. First, if Bush and Rove had half the respect for and understanding of free markets that they claimed to have in other circumstances, they would have recognized that there are few if any jobs that Americans won't do; there are only jobs that Americans won't do *at the wages US employers are now paying*. Most Americans admittedly do not covet work picking fruits and vegetables. But if employers facing a labor shortage were compelled to pay higher wages and offer reasonable benefits and working conditions, many Americans would be quite willing to fill such jobs.[54] Indeed, one of the arguments often made against current levels of immigration is that they reduce the wages of the least well-paid and most economically vulnerable native-born workers, while the benefits of such policies (e.g., the lowered costs of housekeeping and landscaping services) accrue largely to the wealthiest Americans. Harvard economist George Borjas has estimated that current levels of immigration are responsible for a 7 percent drop in earnings among native-born high school dropouts.[55]

Second, even if there were jobs Americans were unwilling to do at any foreseeable wage, there is no way that one can introduce a large number of economically and socially vulnerable workers into a nation's economy and then guarantee that these workers will take *only* those jobs. Some immigrants might pick fruits and vegetables—but others would underbid native-born workers and thus take jobs that American workers would be delighted to hold. In fact, as the Center for Immigration Studies showed in an analysis of 2005–2007 Census data, immigrants are *not* concentrated in a small number of occupations made up entirely or largely of immigrant workers. There were four occupations in which the work force was majority immigrant—but these four occupations together accounted for less than 1 percent of employed immigrants. The other 99 percent were employed in occupations in which the majority of workers were native-born. Native-born Americans held a majority of the jobs even in many occupations often thought to be dominated by immigrants, such as maids and housekeepers, taxi drivers and chauffeurs, construction workers, and janitors.[56]

It is hard to avoid the conclusion, then, that the Bush administration's immigration policies were driven more by electoral considerations than by a concern with good public policy. To bring his new Republican majority into being, Rove—and many other commentators—saw Hispanics as a particularly significant voting bloc.[57] As an unnamed "senior Republican" recounted, "Karl mentioned the first day or the first few days of the Bush presidency that, to get reelected, Bush would have to get a significantly higher percentage of Hispanic voters, just looking at demographic trends."[58] According to the national media exit polls, the Hispanic share of the presidential electorate had grown from 1 percent in 1980 to 3 percent in 1988, to 6 percent in 2000, and then to 8 percent in 2004.[59] There was, Rove and others concluded, no way the Republicans could dominate presidential and congressional elections if the Democrats consistently won the overwhelming share of the Hispanic vote. And, Rove apparently also concluded, the key to courting Hispanics was to adopt a permissive posture with regard to immigration issues. Most businesses, a key component of the Rove fundraising machine, were also part of the expanded-immigration lobby. The US Chamber of Commerce, the National Restaurant Association, agribusiness, and Silicon Valley all saw immigrants as a source of cheap labor that were less likely to join unions or push for better working conditions.

The Bush immigration policy had three central components. The first was a "temporary-worker program" that would allow "foreign workers to enter our country . . . for a limited period of time."[60] (The precise period of time varied a bit from bill to bill, but a typical congressional proposal, which Bush seems to have found acceptable, would have allowed temporary workers to get a three-year visa with a single three-year renewal.[61]) I have already noted the problematic nature of Bush's assertion that these guest workers would only "fill jobs that Americans will not do." An equally grave shortcoming involved Bush's assurance that these workers would "return to their home country at the conclusion of their stay." Though the most publicized face of illegal immigration is those who enter the country illegally, an estimated 40 percent of illegal aliens actually enter the United States legally—as tourists or students, for example—and then stay on illegally after the expiration of their visas.[62] Allowing in a huge number of additional "temporary" workers would, of course, only make this problem a great deal worse. That had been the experience in a number of small-scale guest worker programs that were already in operation. In 2004, for example, a North Carolina company found that more than 10 percent of their temporary workers "took off to live in the U.S. without returning home to Mexico." For many illegals, said a company official, a guest-worker program was simply "a foot in the door."[63]

Bush claimed that the temporary worker program would be strictly enforced by, among other things, issuing a new "tamper-proof" identification card to every legal foreign worker. But tamper-proof IDs (even if we assume they were truly tamper-proof) would have only restrained those immigrants who actually used them. They might prevent an illegal immigrant from falsely claiming to be a temporary worker. But they would not block someone from entering the country legally as a temporary worker and then staying on after his or her guest-worker visa expired by claiming to be a citizen—and then producing forged documents of the sort that, as

Bush admitted, were already in widespread use by illegal aliens.[64] If a job applicant claimed to be a citizen, in other words, he or she would also be claiming not to have or need one of the new ID cards. This problem could perhaps have been remedied by requiring *all* job applicants to produce proof of citizenship via a tamper-proof ID—but Bush never made any such proposal. And if, as Rove argued, the country was unwilling to bear the financial and moral costs of deporting large numbers of illegal immigrants, why would it be willing to insist that guest workers be required to leave, most of whom would have spent six years in the United States?[65]

Second, Bush sought a way to, as he put it, "resolve the status of illegal immigrants who are already here." Illegal immigrants "who have been here for years" and "have roots in our country," the president argued, should be allowed to stay and eventually become citizens if they fulfilled a number of conditions, such as paying a fine, paying their taxes, learning to speak English, and proving that they had held a job "for a number of years."[66]

Much of the controversy surrounding this provision concerned how to label it. Bush always insisted that he was not advocating amnesty, because his proposal did not give illegals "an automatic path to citizenship." Literally every speech Bush gave on immigration thus included a sentence in which he declared, in unqualified terms, "I oppose amnesty."[67] But even if longtime illegal immigrants did not automatically become citizens, neither would they be deported. As one opponent of the Bush plan correctly noted, "Any legislation that does not require those who break the law to abide by it, but instead suspends the normal penalty and in some way changes the law to accommodate the violator is an amnesty."[68] However one chooses to resolve the semantic issue, the essential point was that Bush was proposing to legalize a whole lot of people—seven to ten million, by most estimates— who were in the country illegally.

Moreover, though Bush always insisted that one of his goals was to stem the tide of illegal immigration, any program that offered legal status to those who had come to or stayed in the country illegally would almost certainly have made the problem worse. To those who might be thinking about violating US immigration laws, Bush was offering an additional incentive. Americans, his proposal effectively said, have no great commitment to enforcing their immigration laws, especially if it involves deportation. Once in the United States, most illegal immigrants will eventually be legalized.

In sum: the first two components of the Bush immigration plan allowed more immigrants to enter the country and gave legal status to those who were here illegally. Both of these components were thus plainly designed to please proimmigration groups. What did it offer to the substantial number of Americans, especially within Bush's own party, who thought that current levels of immigration were already too high and that illegal immigration was hurting the country in a variety of significant ways? The short answer is: not much. Bush did promise that he would "secure the borders," but for a variety of solid reasons, such promises were widely seen as noncredible.

For all its rhetoric to the contrary, the record shows that the Bush administration made little effort to enforce existing immigration laws. Consider, for example, the data in table 5.1, which shows the total number of illegal aliens apprehended in every year between 1993 and 2008. During the last five years of Bill Clinton's presidency, the Border Patrol and the Immigration and Naturalization Service caught, on average, 1.68 million illegal immigrants every year. During the first five years of the Bush administration, by contrast, these agencies apprehended just 1.21 million illegals per year, a drop of 28 percent. In the final two years of the Bush presidency, the number of aliens apprehended fell even further, to just 876,000 per year. Throughout the spring of 2006, in another example of the fundamentally misleading way that Bush conducted the debate on immigration, the president repeatedly told audiences that in the five years since 2001, the Border Patrol had "caught and sent home about 6 million illegal immigrants."[69] Somehow, he always forgot to mention that during the last five years of the Clinton administration, federal authorities had apprehended 8.4 million illegal immigrants. Though Bill Clinton was never known as an anti-immigration zealot, he plainly enforced the law a lot more vigorously than George W. Bush ever did.

In defense of the administration's record on immigration enforcement, both Bush and Rove often pointed out that they had "doubled the size of the Border Patrol and tripled its budget."[70] But the significance of this claim is substantially undercut by one pertinent fact: In the wake of 9/11, the mission of the Border Patrol had been expanded to include antiterrorism responsibilities. As the Border Patrol's own website announced, "The priority mission of the Border Patrol is preventing terrorists and terrorists' weapons, including weapons of mass destruction, from entering the United States."[71] In short, even if there were more Border Patrol agents, a lot less of their time and energy was devoted to immigration enforcement.

Another telling indication of the Bush administration's lack of commitment to reducing the flow of illegal immigrants was the people the president appointed to lead the principal immigration enforcement agency. Bush's first nominee to head what was then called the Immigration and Naturalization Service (INS) was James Ziglar.[72] Ziglar was a person of some substance and accomplishment, but as the *New York Times* reported on the day before his confirmation hearings, he "readily admits he knows next to nothing about immigration."[73] More impressive to the Bush people, apparently, was the fact that Ziglar was a boyhood friend of Senate Minority Leader Trent Lott (R-MS) and had previously served as the Senate's sergeant-at-arms.

But Ziglar does seem to have understood that the Bush high command did not want him to enforce the immigration laws too strictly. In the wake of the September 11 terrorist attacks, for example, Ziglar encouraged illegal immigrants to seek disaster relief from the state and federal governments without fear of retribution.[74] His most embarrassing moment came in mid-March 2002, when it was revealed that the INS had sent out notices to a Florida flight school saying that the agency had approved student visas for Mohamed Atta and Marwan al-Shehhi—this in spite of the fact that both men were by then (a) well-known terrorists who had participated in the 9/11 hijackings and (b) dead.[75] Five months later, Ziglar resigned.

A prime lesson of Ziglar's tenure, one might have thought, concerned the necessity of staffing immigration agencies with people who had a substantial measure of knowledge about and experience with immigration issues. In June 2005, however, Bush made a remarkably similar appointment when he nominated thirty-six-year-old Julie Myers to head the agency now known as Immigration and Customs Enforcement (ICE).[76] Though Myers had held a variety of government jobs, she, too, had no experience in immigration-related issues. As the president of a union representing 7,800 ICE agents told the *Washington Post*, "It appears she's got a tremendous amount of experience in money laundering, in banking and the financial areas. My question is: Who the hell is going to enforce the immigration laws?"[77] Unlike most appointive positions in the federal government, the head of ICE was statutorily required to have at least five years' experience in both management and law enforcement. Myers met the former requirement only by counting her time in the White House Personnel Office, where she had managed, by her own account, "up to three deputies as well as support staff and interns."[78]

Like Ziglar, however, Myers had sterling political connections. She was a special assistant to the president at the time of her appointment; her uncle was General Richard Myers, then-chairman of the Joint Chiefs of Staff; her fiancé was chief of staff to the secretary of homeland security. As *National Review* commented in an editorial opposing her appointment, "Naming her at this stage in her career, especially given her connections, smacks of cronyism. Her nomination highlights the administration's desire to keep immigration enforcement on a short leash, lest some rogue official embarrass the White House by actually enforcing the immigration law."[79]

Hovering in the background as these issues were being debated was

Table 5.1. Two Measures of Immigration Enforcement, 1993–2008

Year	Deportable aliens apprehended	Aliens removed or returned
1993	1,327,261	1,285,952
1994	1,094,719	1,074,781
1995	1,394,554	1,364,688
1996	1,649,986	1,643,108
1997	1,536,520	1,555,116
1998	1,679,439	1,744,940
1999	1,714,035	1,757,977
2000	1,814,729	1,864,343
2001	1,387,486	1,538,397
2002	1,062,270	1,177,284
2003	1,046,422	1,156,392
2004	1,264,232	1,407,241
2005	1,291,142	1,343,351
2006	1,206,457	1,324,355
2007	960,756	1,210,772
2008	791,568	1,171,058
Administration averages:		
Clinton: 1993–2000	1,526,405	1,536,363
Bush: 2001–2008	1,126,292	1,291,106
Clinton to Bush change (percent)	−26	−16

Source: Office of Immigration Statistics, US Department of Homeland Security, *2010 Yearbook of Immigration Statistics* (Washington, DC: US Government Printing Office, 2011), table 33, p. 91 and table 36, p. 94.

the country's experience with the Immigration Reform and Control Act (IRCA) of 1986. Though Bush never acknowledged it, the deal he was proposing in 2005–2006 was strikingly similar to one that had been struck twenty years earlier. On the one hand, the IRCA had created two different amnesty programs (and had actually called them *amnesty* programs). One aimed at legalizing any illegal immigrants who had lived in the country continually for the last five years; the other granted legal status to any alien who had done at least sixty days of seasonal agricultural work during the previous year. In return, those who thought that amnesty simply rewarded lawbreakers were promised that the federal government would "secure the border once and for all."[80] More resources would be devoted to the Border Patrol, and for the first time, sanctions would be imposed on employers who hired illegal aliens.

In practice, however, the "deal" turned out to be very one-sided. The amnesty half of the bargain was duly carried out. Some 2.7 million immigrants were legalized, substantially more than had originally been anticipated, largely because of widespread fraud in the agricultural workers program. But the employer sanctions turned out to be weak and easily evaded, and more resources didn't begin to flow to the Border Patrol until the mid-1990s.[81] The failure of the 1986 act is most emphatically demonstrated by the size of the illegal alien population. In 1986, there were an estimated five million illegal immigrants in the United States. By 2006, twenty years after the border was supposed to be secured "once and for all," the illegal population had more than doubled, to an estimated eleven million.[82]

If Bush declined to take note of this experience, it was a major concern to those who were actually committed to reducing the flood of illegal immigrants. As one former INS official summed up the lesson: "It has been said many times, but bears repeating: Don't accept so-called trade-offs that consist of amnesty immediately, with empty promises of fences, technology, enhanced border security, and interior enforcement to follow once amnesty is complete. That was one of the false premises of IRCA, and everyone fell for it."[83] Many congressmen drew the same conclusion. The *New York Times* reported in May 2006, "The 1986 amnesty has cast a long shadow over the [2006 amnesty] legislation. It is the invisible enemy lurking in nearly every Congressional debate, challenging and dogging even the most eloquent champions of immigrants. These days, skeptical senators pepper their speeches with repeated references to its failures."[84]

In the end, Bush and Rove were never able to convince the opponents of illegal immigration that they took their concerns seriously. Though most antiamnesty groups were staffed by conservatives and Republicans, I am not aware of anyone from that side of the argument who thought that Bush could be trusted to follow through on his promises of stepped-up enforcement. As Mark Krikorian of the Center for Immigration Studies commented, "For his entire administration, George W. Bush has presided over what can only be described as a Silent Amnesty, refusing to enforce the law as it's written today, and even taking steps to help illegal aliens embed themselves in American society."[85] James Edwards of the Hudson Institute said much the same thing: "The enforcement part of [Bush's] message lacks credibility because this administration has failed. They have to really show they will enforce laws on the books before anyone takes them seriously."[86] Had Bush and Rove truly wanted to reach a compromise solution to the immigration crisis that was acceptable to most Americans, they should have secured the border first; then the country probably would have been willing to enact some kind of amnesty for those illegals who remained in the country. But that sort of approach was less likely to bring increased support from Hispanic voters.

While the Senate passed a bill in 2006 that closely followed Bush's specifications, the House passed a far more conservative bill that concentrated on improved border security and tougher workplace enforcement. No compromise between the two approaches was possible. The newly Democratic Senate tried again in 2007 but couldn't find enough votes to invoke cloture.

A Difference in Time Horizon

Candidates hire political consultants to help them win elections. Obviously, this tends to make consultants a great deal less concerned with anything that happens after election day. Even if the consultant hopes to have a continuing relationship with the candidate, the likelihood of doing so depends largely on winning the next election. Has any political consultant ever told one of his or her clients, "The voters won't be pleased if you take such-and-such a position—but don't worry, long after you've been voted out of office, historians will recognize that you were right"?

The result is to give political consultants a very distinctive conception of political time. Simply put, any action or policy position that looks good on election day is likely to be viewed very favorably, even if it creates a lot of significant problems in the months and years after the election. And any policy that imposes immediate pain will be strongly disfavored, no matter what kinds of long-term benefits it provides. Without meaning to ignore the numerous shortcomings of many policy analysts, they at least tend to assume a more long-range perspective when thinking about policy than political consultants do. Though policy advisors sometimes advocate short-sighted policies—conservative policy mandarins often level this charge against their liberal counterparts—and are sometimes pushed by their political superiors to devise quick fixes and short-run gimmicks, nothing in the basic craft of policy analysis encourages them to adopt the kind of restricted time horizon that is an inescapable feature of election consulting.

Few issues show the dangers of a foreshortened time perspective quite so vividly as the handling of the federal deficit. In saying this, I do not mean to argue that consultants are uniquely or even primarily responsible for the federal deficits of the last fifty years. Elected officials are quite capable of creating deficits on their own. At those moments when presidents have tried to grapple seriously with the deficit, however, they have generally found their political advisors arguing against it.

Consultants are unlikely to urge their clients to undertake a serious deficit reduction effort for the simple reason that it generally does not have much immediate political payoff. In most years, the deficit—as distinct from other economic issues—just doesn't rank very high on the public's list of major national problems. Table 5.2 shows the percentage of Americans who told the Gallup Poll that the federal deficit was the country's "most important problem" in the months immediately preceding each of the last fourteen national elections (presidential and midterm). Not once has even 15 percent of the adult population claimed that the deficit was the nation's leading problem. From 2002 through 2008, when the Bush administration regularly racked up deficits of $150 billion or more, only about 2 percent of the public put the issue at the top of their list of concerns.

Even when the deficit does assume a somewhat greater salience, voters are unlikely to embrace any of the major realistic solutions for it, such as serious cuts in spending or significant, broad-based tax increases, instead contenting themselves with the comforting thought that deficits can be eliminated just by cutting out "waste, fraud, and abuse" or by "taxing the rich." By contrast, the benefits of deficit reduction are generally long-term, indirect (e.g., lower deficits *may* lead to lower interest rates which *may* generate a higher rate of economic growth), and intangible (such as leaving a lesser burden on the backs of future generations). The only presidential candidate of the last thirty years to propose a serious deficit reduction plan *during the campaign* was Walter Mondale in 1984—and by all indications, he paid dearly for it.[87] It should come as no surprise, then, that during the presidencies of George H. W. Bush and Bill Clinton, discussions of the federal deficit tended to pit policy advisors against political consultants.

George Bush Sr.'s battle with the federal deficit really began in the summer of 1988, when he and some of his top advisors were writing his acceptance speech for the Republican National Convention.[88] A controversy soon developed over the stance Bush should take toward taxes and the deficit. At the urging of Jack Kemp, Bush speechwriter Peggy Noonan had inserted a line in an early draft that committed Bush not to increase taxes under any circumstances. As eventually delivered at the Republican convention, the line read: "My opponent won't rule out raising taxes. But I will. And the Congress will push me to raise taxes, and I'll say no, and they'll push, and I'll say no, and they'll push again. And I'll say to them: Read my lips. No new taxes."[89] Who urged Bush to make such an iron-clad commitment against tax increases? Besides Noonan, a speechwriter who had worked in government but never in a policy-making capacity, its principal proponents were political consultants: media strategist Roger Ailes and pollster Robert Teeter. And who opposed it? Richard Darman, former deputy secretary of the treasury and the odds-on favorite to become Bush's director of the Office of Management and Budget; and Craig Fuller, Bush's

Table 5.2. The Salience of the Federal Deficit as an Election Issue, 1984–2012

Month(s) and year	Percentage mentioning the federal deficit as the country's most important problem	Number of surveys including most important problem question
Sept.–Oct. 1984	8	2
July and Sept. 1986	13	2
Sept. 1988	12	1
Oct.–Nov. 1990	14	2
Aug.–Sept. 1992	9	1
July–Aug. 1994	3	2
July 1996	8	1
Sept. 1998	2	1
Oct. 2000	*	1
July–Sept. 2002	1	4
July–Nov. 2004	3	5
July–Oct. 2006	2	4
July–Oct. 2008	2	4
July–Nov. 2010	7	5
July–Oct. 2012	9	4

Source: All data are from the Gallup Poll and are based on all surveys conducted between July 1 and November 7 that included the "most important problem" question and specifically distinguished responses concerning the "federal budget deficit" from other economy-related issues. When more than one survey was conducted during this time period, the number shown is an average of the surveys.
Note: The question was "What do you think is the most important problem facing this country today?" An asterisk indicates that the federal deficit was mentioned by less than 0.5 percent of all respondents.

vice presidential chief of staff. Noonan, Ailes, and Teeter liked the line because it made a good sound bite and would give the Bush campaign a nice issue with which to flog his Democratic opponent. Darman and Fuller, by contrast, read the speech with at least one eye on its governing implications and immediately decided that it was, as Darman put it, "stupid and irresponsible." As the two men correctly sensed, given the heavily Democratic Congress and Bush's own reluctance to propose deep cuts in *any* major category of spending, "read my lips" effectively meant "I promise to do nothing about the deficit." In this initial skirmish between the consultants and the policy people, the consultants prevailed. Running significantly behind his Democratic opponent in every major poll, Bush stifled his own reservations about the line and approved its inclusion in his acceptance speech.

Two years later, of course, Bush repudiated this commitment and agreed to a sizable tax increase. In the deliberations and negotiations that preceded this decision, the principal advocates of a tax increase were once again people who actually had some responsibility for making and implementing policy: in particular, OMB director Darman and Treasury Secretary Nicholas Brady. This time, however, the voice of the consultants was largely stilled. Both Noonan and Ailes no longer worked for Bush. Teeter still did polling for the president but was not a major presence in the administration. The one political consultant whose opinion might have mattered to Bush was his former campaign manager, Lee Atwater, who had become chairman of the Republican National Committee. But Atwater had been diagnosed with brain cancer in March 1990, and from then until his death in March 1991 ceased to be an important factor in the Bush White House. And according to some observers, Atwater's absence may have played a key role in Bush's decision:

> It was at this juncture [i.e., when Atwater's health started to deteriorate], according to [Paul] Weyrich, [an influential figure on the Republican right,] that Bush began to get into trouble with conservatives. Whenever issues had come up touching on their sensitivities including talk of a possible tax increase, Weyrich said later, Atwater was there to say to Bush: "Okay, you're the president. But do you really want to do this? Because if you do, you're gonna have problems with your base." With Atwater gone, Weyrich said, "I think that lack of that, arguing in political terms, really was the beginning of the problem. There was nobody over there who understood politics."[90]

A similar line of division emerged during the early budgetary deliberations of the Clinton presidency. The principal advocates of a major deficit reduction initiative were the members of the Clinton economic policy team, especially Treasury Secretary Lloyd Bentsen, OMB director Leon Panetta, and Alice Rivlin, OMB's deputy director. Its principal opponents were the political consultants who had worked for Clinton in the 1992 campaign, particularly Paul Begala, Stan Greenberg, and Mandy Grunwald.[91]

There is no evidence that Karl Rove was a major architect of the Bush administration fiscal policy. On the other hand, neither is there any indication that he was an aggressive internal critic of the exploding federal deficits. Actually, in another compelling demonstration of the weakness of the Bush policy development process—and of the triumph of politics over policy—there is remarkably little indication that there was ever a sustained debate at the top ranks of the administration about the size and consequences of the deficit. Presidents Ford, Carter, Reagan, and George H. W. Bush all ran up sizable budget deficits. But in each of these administrations, there was a vigorous debate about whether these deficits were acceptable and how to bring them down, resulting in several major deficit-reduction efforts. By contrast, of the numerous accounts of the Bush presidency that have been published to date, not one records a major Oval Office show-down between "deficit hawks" and their opponents or any other serious effort to challenge or rethink the policies that put the federal budget so deep in the red. Paul O'Neill's quasi-memoir about his time as secretary of the treasury mentions one meeting in which he tried to convince Bush to scale back the size of his first tax cut. Bush listened with a "flat, inexpressive stare," then finally said, "I won't negotiate with myself. . . . It's a closed issue."[92] O'Neill also opposed a second tax cut that Bush eventually pushed through Congress in 2003.[93] If there were any other significant attempts to persuade the president to adopt a more responsible fiscal policy, no one has seen fit to record them.

In recent years, defenders of the Bush presidency and supporters of Barack Obama have engaged in a spirited game of finger-pointing, with each accusing the other of running up the federal deficit. It is time to acknowledge that both sides' accusations have merit. On issues of budget-balancing and fiscal responsibility, the Bush administration had a terrible record. Against all odds, Obama managed to do even worse.

A thorough analysis of the Obama budgets is beyond the concerns of this book. As for George W. Bush, the hard, inescapable deficit numbers are shown in table 5.3. It cannot be mentioned too often that, unlike his six immediate predecessors, George Bush inherited a government that actually had a huge budget *surplus.* In Bill Clinton's last full fiscal year (2000), the federal government took in $236 billion more than it spent. After less than one year in office, Bush had cut the surplus in half. By 2002, the federal budget was already $157 billion in debt; by 2003, the deficit had ballooned to the then-record total of $377 billion. Nor was this a temporary condition: the closest the Bush administration came to achieving a balanced budget was in fiscal year 2007, when the federal accounts were still $160 billion in the red.

How did the Bush administration manage to create such a massive fiscal mess in such a short period of time? The simple but sufficient answer is that they saw little political payoff in fiscal responsibility, particularly when compared to all the other things they wanted to do that (they believed) *were* likely to yield additional votes. Four major policies were consequently adopted:

1. They enacted two major tax cuts.
2. They substantially increased defense spending and, after 9/11, spending for homeland security.

3. They pursued and won sizable increases in numerous categories of nondefense discretionary spending, including education, food stamps, agricultural subsidies, and a program to combat AIDS in Africa.
4. They created the first major expansion of entitlement spending since the 1960s, by adding prescription drug coverage to Medicare.

Except for some of the items in number three, any one of these policies was defensible by itself. What was indefensible was to have pursued *all* of them at the same time, with little apparent concern for their cumulative fiscal implications. In particular, if the Bush team truly believed it was necessary to increase spending on defense and homeland security and so many other things, at least they should have had the courage and integrity to take Paul O'Neill's advice and scale back the size of the tax cuts.

Bush's unwillingness to consider a smaller tax cut, much less a tax increase, owes much to the experience of his father. Within the Bush family, it is widely believed that George H. W. Bush's failure to win reelection in 1992 could be blamed largely on the president's decision to break his famous "no new taxes" promise from the 1988 campaign. (Most disinterested analysts, it might be noted, think that the elder Bush could readily have survived this episode if he had only reacted earlier and more decisively to the economic downturn that began in July 1990.)[94] Whatever the truth of the matter, George W. operated as if the following maxim had been emblazoned on the Oval Office wall in large letters: "UNDER NO CIRCUMSTANCES SHALT THOU INCREASE TAXES." Though an argument might have been made that there was a significant difference between increasing taxes and reducing the size of a tax cut, Bush showed no interest in exploring such territory.

In terms of sheer budgetary recklessness, it is hard to top the Medicare prescription drug plan that Bush and the Republican Congress enacted in 2003, an initiative often attributed to Karl Rove.[95] For some time, experts at all points along the political spectrum had recognized that Medicare was financially out of balance, with unfunded liabilities estimated at $45 trillion. Yet Bush now added onto that a huge new set of expenses—*all without the slightest attempt to figure out a way to pay for it.* If Bush is looking for a policy achievement to bolster his historical reputation, the prescription drug bill is an unlikely candidate. Robert Samuelson, a widely respected economics columnist, has concluded, "Far from a triumph, the Medicare drug benefit is one of the worst pieces of social legislation in decades."[96] Former US comptroller general David Walker was similarly harsh: "The prescription drug bill was probably the most fiscally irresponsible piece of legislation since the 1960s."[97]

Table 5.3. Size of the Federal Surplus or Deficit, 1996–2009

President	Fiscal year	Surplus or deficit (in billions of dollars)
Bill Clinton	1996	−107.4
	1997	−21.9
	1998	69.3
	1999	125.6
	2000	236.2
Transition year	2001	128.2
George W. Bush	2002	−157.8
	2003	−377.6
	2004	−412.7
	2005	−318.3
	2006	−248.2
	2007	−160.7
	2008	−458.6
Transition year	2009	−1,412.7

Source: Office of Management and Budget, Historical Tables, table 1.1, at whitehouse.gov/omb/historical-tables (accessed August 12, 2020).

In his memoir, Rove defends the drug bill by noting, "The Medicare prescription drug benefit is the only major government health initiative that has cost less than was originally estimated."[98] When the full consequences of the bill are taken into account, however, this defense loses most of its power. To begin with, the extent of the "savings" depends very much on the standard of comparison one uses. At the time the bill was being debated and voted on in Congress, the official Congressional Budget Office estimate said that the prescription drug program would cost just under $400 billion during its first ten years of operation (2004–2013).[99] But a month and a half after Bush signed the bill, administration officials revealed that the estimated costs would be far greater: about $530 billion for the first ten years.[100] In the end, a report by the Medicare trustees put the 2004–2013 costs at $367.8 billion—31 percent lower than the revised estimate but not dramatically different from the figure Congress relied on when it passed the program.[101]

No matter which comparison one uses, however, Medicare Part D, as the prescription drug program is officially known, cost the federal government about $40 billion a year when it first went into effect and is now costing about $70 billion per annum—all money that neither the Medicare trust fund nor the federal general treasury can readily afford to pay. In that sense, Rove's boast that the program came in under budget basically amounts to saying, "Well, it could've been even worse." Or as conservative commentator Mark Levin put it, "All that proves is that an already unsustainable program will become unsustainable a little later, yet still sooner than otherwise would have occurred but for the Bush prescription drug program."[102]

Another item that vividly symbolizes the spendthrift spirit of the Bush years is the fabled "Bridge to Nowhere." As many readers will recall, the Bridge to Nowhere was a project authorized by an earmark in a 2005 transportation bill, which would have built a $223 million bridge between Ketchikan, Alaska, population 7,900, and Gravina Island, population 50. Eventually the project became so widely publicized and so controversial that in November 2005, Congress de-earmarked it. This last act was largely symbolic, however. As the *Washington Post* noted at the time, "Alaska will get to keep the $454 million that Congress set aside for [the Bridge to Nowhere and another equally dubious bridge], and technically the state can use the transportation funds for any project it chooses—including the bridges."[103]

In his book, Rove blames this episode on congressional Republicans, concluding that "Even though Congress repealed the 'Bridge to Nowhere' after public outcry, the reputation of congressional Republicans had been badly damaged—and by extension, ours [i.e., that of the Bush administration]."[104] But Rove's summary leaves out an important fact: While the Bridge to Nowhere earmark was indeed the work of congressional Republicans, *so was the opposition to it*. So far as I can determine, no one in the Bush administration, including Bush himself, ever criticized the bridge or any of the other six thousand or so earmarks in the transportation bill, much less threatened to veto it.[105] The remarks Bush made on signing the bill contain not a single caveat or complaint. To the contrary, he actually praised the bill for accomplishing its goals "in a fiscally responsible way."[106] That the bridge was later defunded (sort of) was due entirely to the efforts of such congressional critics as Senators John McCain (R-AZ) and Tom Coburn (R-OK).

In this respect, the Bridge to Nowhere is symptomatic of another telling indicator of the Bush administration's fundamental lack of commitment to a balanced budget. In the aftermath of the 2006 and 2008 elections, many observers blasted the Republican members of Congress for the way they had conducted themselves, with special attention to their record of fiscal profligacy. No doubt congressional Republicans deserved the brickbats. But as any serious student of American politics should have known, congressional behavior of this sort is the normal, expected pattern, no matter which party is in the majority. Congress has always had what might be called a "part-whole" problem: individual members pursue policies that are good for their districts and thus their reelection prospects, but the total result is often bad for the country as a whole.[107]

To avoid this trap, the American system has depended primarily on *executive* leadership, since the president is the only official elected by the country as a whole and is thus held responsible for national policies and outcomes. But George W. Bush entirely failed to exercise such leadership. In particular, as congressional Republicans loaded up the bills they passed with a record number of earmarks, he *never* vetoed any of these bills— the first president since the nineteenth century who failed to cast a single veto during his first five years in office.[108] Bush's behavior in this respect contrasts sharply with that of Ronald Reagan, the president he most often cited as his role model. In 1987, Reagan vetoed a highway and mass transit bill because it included 152 earmarks. In 2005, the congressional transportation bill contained 6,371 earmarks—yet Bush signed it.[109]

Inevitably, Bush's forbearance sent a clear signal to Congress that its misbehavior would be tolerated. As one commentator noted, "His [Bush's] rhetoric against runaway spending may be tough, but in his actions, he's been an enabler. To get his priorities approved on Capitol Hill, the president has shown he's willing to buy votes with an unprecedented level of pork-barreling."[110]

Conclusion

To put the various issues and incidents examined in this and the previous chapter in their proper perspective, one additional set of questions needs to be asked: What were the *political* consequences of the choices Bush made? Did Bush or his party gain any political advantage from passing No Child Left Behind or imposing steel tariffs or failing to take significant action against illegal immigration? These questions are the subject of the next chapter.

For the moment, however, several conclusions are worth underlining. First, good politics—more specifically, good electoral strategy—does not always yield good policy. In too many ways, the incentives and criteria of good electoral strategy diverge from those of good public policy.

Second, for all his self-righteous posturing about "doing the right thing, for the right reason" and "put[ting] the interests of the American people ahead of politics," policy-making in the Bush administration frequently put political considerations and partisan interests ahead of policy and principle. In policy terms, it is remarkably difficult to justify the president's decisions on steel tariffs, farm subsidies, space exploration, the federal budget, and many other issues. All are quite easy to explain, however, in terms of the president's short-term electoral objectives. Of course, Bush is far from being the only president who can be criticized on this count. Every president sometimes agrees to make this sort of tradeoff. But the presidency of George W. Bush had, I believe, a special problem in this regard, not because Bush himself was more nakedly political than his predecessors, but because the normal policy development and advising apparatus was so stunted.

Finally, there is one conclusion that should *not* be drawn from the analysis in this chapter. I am *not* arguing that political advisors and consultants should be kept as far from the policy development process as possible. As I have tried to show in chapter 3, political advisors definitely deserve a place at the table when important policy decisions are made.

In particular, there are two major contributions that political advisors can make to policy discussions. First, they can provide important information about the likely political reception a policy will meet. Even the best-designed policy is of little use to a president if it requires congressional approval and cannot receive it, or if it requires cooperation from other countries or other levels of government that will not be forthcoming. And presidents do need to keep one eye on their short-term electoral concerns. If vetoing a farm bill will complicate his party's efforts to retake the Senate, if passing a particular program will help him get reelected even though it deepens the federal deficit, the president really does need to know about such things.

In addition, political advisors, precisely because they are not steeped in the minutiae of policy analysis, can sometimes bring an important element of common sense and hard-eyed realism to the policy development process. The purpose of this chapter has been to examine the shortcomings of political advisors as policy analysts. But policy analysts have their own set of problems and limitations. They are often too attached to theoretical models that have an uncertain application to the real world. Because their egos and reputations are closely wrapped up in their writings and recommendations, they are generally reluctant to admit they are wrong or to acknowledge their level of uncertainty. Being experts on some topics, they sometimes claim authority on issues that lie beyond the purview of their research.[111]

The result is that many of the worst policy mistakes in recent American history were based on the best current scholarly thinking, provided by experts with sterling credentials. The Community Action Program in the war on poverty drew upon the latest social science research about the causes of and cures for poverty. The war in Vietnam may not literally have been launched by "the best and the brightest," but its major architects did include a "whiz kid" who had previously served as president of the Ford

Motor Company, the former dean of the Harvard faculty, and a secretary of state who had considerable previous experience in East Asian affairs.

Whatever else may be said of the war in Iraq, its primary advocates were, as such things are conventionally measured, an impressive and highly credentialed group. Donald Rumsfeld's resume was at least as distinguished as that of Hillary Clinton, who was sometimes touted as the most qualified person ever to run for president. Before becoming secretary of defense under George W. Bush, Rumsfeld had served in Congress, been ambassador to NATO, was presidential chief of staff, and served an earlier stint as secretary of defense; he also had substantial private sector experience, having served as a top executive for three different corporations. Paul Wolfowitz had a PhD in political science from the University of Chicago, along with previous service in the defense department. Douglas Feith was a magna cum laude graduate of both Harvard College and Georgetown Law School. Bush's decision to select Dick Cheney as his running mate was widely heralded at the time for the "gravitas" that Cheney brought to the Republican ticket. Prior to the 2000 campaign, Cheney had been White House chief of staff; served five terms in the House of Representatives, including a stint as chair of the House Republican Conference; was secretary of defense during the first Gulf War; was director of the Council on Foreign Relations; and served as the chief executive officer of a multibillion dollar corporation. (He is also the coauthor of an article published in the *American Political Science Review*.) As these and other top policy makers explained all the ready benefits of deposing Saddam Hussein, it would have been nice if at least one person had asked some tough, basic questions about what would happen if all Iraqis didn't greet the American army as liberators or whether the transition to a stable democracy would really be so easy.

Unfortunately, as we will see in chapter 7, no one did.

6

You Can't Nickel and Dime Your Way to

a Realignment

In an often-quoted passage in *Federalist,* no. 68, Alexander Hamilton declared that the constitutional provisions regarding presidential selection "afforded a moral certainty" that the presidency "will seldom fall to the lot of any man who is not in an eminent degree endowed with the requisite qualifications":

> Talents for low intrigue, and the little arts of popularity, may alone suffice to elevate a man to the first honors in a single State; but it will require other talents, and a different kind of merit, to establish him in the esteem and confidence of the whole Union, or of so considerable a portion of it as would be necessary to make him a successful candidate for the distinguished office of President of the United States.[1]

Hamilton never defined precisely what he meant by the "little arts of popularity," but I think we may safely conclude that most of the Bush administration policies examined in the two previous chapters would fit comfortably under this rubric. Proposing a dramatically expanded space program on the grounds that it would look big and bold and then refusing to provide adequate funding; adopting policies that contradicted the president's own, often-expressed principles in order to cultivate the support of steel workers and farmers; pursuing an unsustainable fiscal policy because any problems it created could be fobbed off on future presidents and Congresses—it is difficult to imagine Hamilton maintaining that these were model examples of presidential decision-making. Hamilton would have looked more favorably upon an ambitious attempt to reform the American system of public education, but he would also have insisted that the details mattered and that a poorly designed program in pursuit of a worthy goal was nothing to brag about.

In chapters 4 and 5, I argued that a policy-making process driven by immediate, short-term electoral calculations is likely to produce bad policies.

In this chapter, I wish to pose the question begged by the Hamilton quotation: Do such policies work *politically*? Did the space initiative and the steel tariffs and the push for so-called comprehensive immigration reform enhance the president's image or produce extra votes from steel-making states and districts or Hispanic voters? A close look at each of the major policy episodes examined in the two previous chapters yields surprisingly little evidence of political payoff.

Education

In *Courage and Consequence,* his autobiography and memoir of his service in the Bush administration, Karl Rove cites education as a premier example of how Bush's domestic policies paid off politically: "The law [No Child Left Behind] has also brought political benefits to the GOP. In 1996, only 16 percent of voters for whom education was the top issue voted for Bob Dole over Bill Clinton. After Bush talked about education endlessly during his 2000 presidential campaign, he received 44 percent of the vote from those for whom education was their top issue."[2]

So far as it goes, Rove's analysis is accurate. Table 6.1 shows the complete data upon which Rove based his argument. In 1996, 2000, and 2004, the national media exit polls presented voters with a list of issues and asked them, "Which one issue mattered most in deciding how you voted for President?"[3] And just as Rove said, 44 percent of 2000 voters who said that education was the issue that mattered most to them voted for George W. Bush, whereas Bob Dole had won just 16 percent of education-minded voters in 1996.

What Rove neglected to mention was that Bush's electoral gains with respect to education proved to be extremely short-lived. In the 2004 Bush-Kerry contest, fully 73 percent of those who said education was their most important issue voted for John Kerry, even though the Massachusetts senator had no real record of leadership on education issues. Bush won just 26 percent of education voters when he ran for reelection.

Why did the No Child Left Behind law have such an evanescent effect on public support for Bush? The history of the act's passage and implementation suggests several possible explanations. After being approved by large, bipartisan congressional majorities, NCLB soon came under heavy criticism—from both sides of the political and ideological spectrums as well as from many of the education "experts" who appear on talk shows and get quoted in news stories and whose views thus sometimes filter into popular discourse. In addition, those who had children in elementary and secondary school had a certain amount of direct experience with the law as they saw it implemented in their local schools. For one or both reasons, perhaps the American public also turned against the law—or may never have supported it in the first place. Alternatively, the American public may have accepted the somewhat less thoroughgoing criticism leveled by many Democrats: that the NCLB law was basically sound but had been significantly underfunded. Since Kerry made precisely this argument and also promised to create a "trust fund" that would provide NCLB with full, guaranteed funding, a voter who held this view would (all other things equal) probably have voted for Kerry.

As to the first of these explanations, polling data indicate that public opinion did turn sharply against No Child Left Behind, but most of the change took place after the 2004 election. The best single set of questions on this issue comes (as it usually does) from the Gallup Poll. As shown in table 6.2, on seven occasions between 2003 and 2009 Gallup asked national samples of American adults if they had a favorable or unfavorable opinion of the act, or if they didn't "know enough about it to say." In 2003, more than a year after the act was passed, fully 69 percent of the Gallup respondents said they didn't know enough about the law to offer an assessment; but among those who did have an opinion, favorable responses outnumbered unfavorable ones by about a three to two margin, or 18 percent to 13 percent. By 2009, however, the balance of popular sentiment had shifted strongly against the law, with 48 percent expressing an unfavorable opinion versus just 28 percent favorable (and 24 percent still saying they didn't know enough to say). As of 2004, however, public opinion on the law still seems to have been slightly favorable.

It is more difficult to say how many Americans accepted the Democratic argument that No Child Left Behind was badly underfunded. To start with the most basic point, the American public has long expressed the conviction that not enough money is being spent on education. In eleven separate polls conducted between 1990 and 2008, the National Opinion Research Center at the University of Chicago asked its survey respondents if we were spending "too much," "too little," or "about the right amount" on "improving the nation's education system." On average, 70 percent of Americans thought we were spending too little on education, as against 23 percent who felt spending was about right and just 5 percent who said we were spending too much. There is no evidence, however, that NCLB had any effect on this opinion. Neither the Republican claim that Bush had increased federal education spending far more than any of his recent predecessors nor the Democratic argument that NCLB appropriations did not match authorized spending levels had any perceptible impact on attitudes about future levels of spending.

Given the large number of Americans who said they didn't know enough about the No Child Left Behind law to express even the most basic sort of evaluation, it was almost certainly unrealistic to ask the public to sort through the complexities of how much federal education spending had been or should have been increased. And as often happens when pollsters ask about issues on which the level of public knowledge is quite low, questions about funding for No Child Left Behind have produced widely varying results, depending on how the question is phrased. Asked in January 2003 whether "schools will need more money, less money, or about the same money to meet the requirements of No Child Left Behind?" 75 percent said more money was needed. But in May 2004, only 40 percent of respondents said that the public schools in their district did "not have enough resources to meet the standards set by the No Child Left Behind Act," while 39 percent said their local schools did have the resources. And in July 2003, when asked to choose between two statements about NCLB, 50 percent said that the No Child Left Behind Act "gives more federal funding to schools than ever before," while just 37 percent endorsed the position that "states are facing massive budget problems that make it impossible to fulfill those [NCLB] obligations without federal help. This is just an unfunded mandate."[4]

The data and analysis just presented carry, I believe, two important lessons. First, in developing legislation, the details do matter. No Child Left Behind was a poorly designed law, and both public opinion and a substantial part of elite opinion eventually woke up to that fact. As the final two items in table 6.2 indicate, the trend of declining public support for NCLB continued up through at least 2012, by which time less than 20 percent of Americans thought that No Child Left Behind was making the public schools better.

Second, it is difficult to reshape a long-established party image. For many years, most Americans have believed that Democrats have a better record than Republicans in dealing with education issues. One can readily think (as I do) that this perception is largely mistaken; but no one should base a campaign strategy on the premise that such a belief can be easily changed. By talking about education "endlessly" during the 2000 campaign, Bush apparently did convince many voters (though not a majority) that the issue was very important to him and that he was, in that respect, "a different kind of Republican." Bush continued to talk about education and NCLB in 2004, but whatever he said about the issue was overshadowed (especially in press coverage) by the debates about Iraq, the war on terror, and the state of the economy. And without the constant reminder, many Americans apparently fell back upon their traditional party images, even

Table 6.1. Presidential Vote by Issue Concerns, 1996–2004

	Percentage voting for			Percentage saying that
Year and issue	Dole	Clinton	Perot	issue mattered most
1996				
Taxes	73	19	7	14
Medicare/Social Security	26	67	6	18
Foreign policy	56	35	8	5
Federal budget deficit	52	27	19	15
Economy/jobs	27	61	10	26
Education	16	78	4	14
Crime/drugs	50	40	8	8

	Bush	Gore		
2000				
World affairs	54	40		14
Medicare/prescription drugs	39	60		8
Health care	33	64		9
Economy/jobs	37	60		21
Taxes	80	17		16
Education	44	52		17
Social Security	40	58		16

	Bush	Kerry		
2004				
Taxes	56	43		6
Education	26	73		5
Iraq	26	73		16
Terrorism	86	14		20
Economy/jobs	18	80		21
Moral values	80	18		24
Health care	23	77		9

Source: Voter News Service National Exit Polls, 1996 and 2000; National Election Pool Exit Poll, 2004.
Note: Question was: "Which one issue mattered most in deciding how you voted for president?" Question was also asked in 2008 and 2012 exit polls, but "education" was not included on the list of issues. Percentages may not sum to 100 percent because of votes cast for independent and third-party candidates.

though, as already noted, Kerry himself had never taken a leading role in educational policy-making.

Space Exploration

If the plan to reinvigorate the American space program that Bush announced in January 2004 played any role in securing his reelection ten months later, it is news to both political reporters and election scholars. So far as I can determine, there is not a single book on the 2004 election whose author(s) thought the Bush space proposal worth mentioning, much less accorded it a major role in explaining the election's outcome.[5] It would also, I suspect, come as news to the Bush campaign, which rarely mentioned the issue again during the remainder of 2004 and certainly made no effort to highlight it in Bush's campaign commercials or in his debates with John Kerry.[6] One of the space proposal's chief critics within the Bush high command was Karen Hughes; at her urging, all references to the plan were dropped from the 2004 State of the Union speech. As one presidential advisor explained her reasoning, "The policy gesture didn't pass the communications straight-face test."[7] Even in his nationally televised acceptance speech at the Republican convention, when Bush talked about his positions, promises, and achievements on a long list of issues, there was nary a word about the space program.[8]

Did Bush at least get a temporary "bounce" in the polls from his "big" space plans, even if the bounce didn't last very long? Here, too, there is no evidence that he did. Throughout Bush's eight years in office, the Real-ClearPolitics website pulled together presidential approval question results from every major public pollster and computed a daily average approval rating. According to this index, Bush's average approval rating in the four days immediately preceding the January 14, 2004, announcement of his space initiative was 56.4 percent. In the four days following his speech, his average approval rating was 55.4 percent.[9] Bush's approval rating had been trending downward for a considerable period of time prior to this speech, so I do not think these data show that the space exploration plan *caused* a decline in his popularity. But neither did the plan halt that decline, much less reverse it, even temporarily.

Actually, the space program was always a strange issue to use for boosting the Bush reelection campaign. For all the program's superficial aura of glamour and boldness, spending on space exploration has never been very popular with the general public. A few months after Bush announced his space exploration proposal, the General Social Survey, a highly regarded academic opinion poll, asked a national sample of American adults whether we were spending "too much," "too little," or "about the right amount" on seventeen different issues and problem areas. As shown in table 6.3, the "space exploration program" ranked *next to last* in public support. Only 14 percent of Americans thought we were spending too little on space exploration, while 37 percent said we were already spending too much. The only type of spending that was less popular was "foreign aid"; even "welfare" did better. Nor were the 2004 results atypical. In twenty-three other General Social Surveys conducted between 1973 and 2002, the *largest* proportion of the American public that favored increased spending on the space program was 18 percent (in 1980 and 1988). Another vivid demonstration of the limited public support for the space program comes from a Harris Poll conducted immediately after Bush announced his space initiative, in which respondents were asked how to spend the "hundreds of billions of dollars" that the space program was estimated to cost: should it be spent on "improving education, balancing the budget, cleaning up the environment, space exploration, [or] enlarging the military?" Only 9 percent opted for space exploration.[10]

Aside from its "bigness," then, it is difficult to come up with a plausible explanation as to how or why a plan to reinvigorate the space program would help the president's reelection prospects. In fact, by all indications, it didn't.

Steel Tariffs

So many things went wrong with Bush's decision to impose tariffs on imported steel that it is difficult to know where to begin. As recounted in chapter 4, the president imposed the tariffs in March 2002 but was forced to rescind them in December 2003, in response to an unfavorable ruling by the World Trade Organization. In an ideal world—ideal, that is, from Bush's perspective—the president would have received credit from the steel industry for his original decision to provide protection, and then credit from steel users and consumers for his decision to dismantle the trade barriers. In actuality, there is no evidence that either decision worked much to Bush's benefit.

Though many Republicans from steel-producing states applauded Bush's decision to institute the tariffs, most Democrats attacked the president for not erecting an even higher tariff barrier. Representative Richard Gephardt (D-MO), the House minority leader, released a statement saying that he was "disappointed" that the tariffs averaged less than 30 percent: "Last week the steel companies and the steel worker unions agreed that 40 percent was the minimum average tariff needed to stabilize the industry."[11] On the same day, the *New York Times* quoted Ed O'Brien, a steel union official who was the Democratic candidate in a steel-producing congressional district, as saying that the president's plan "sends a signal to the rest of the world that the U.S. is really afraid to stand up and defend its industries, and that we can be bullied."[12]

If Rove expected some measure of payback from the steelworkers' union, this, too, failed to materialize. On August 5, 2003, well before the

Table 6.2. Public Attitudes toward the No Child Left Behind Act (in Percentages)

1. GALLUP: "From what you know or have heard or read about the No Child Left Behind Act, do you have a very favorable, somewhat favorable, somewhat unfavorable, or very unfavorable opinion of the act—or don't you know enough about it to say?"

Sampling dates	Very or somewhat favorable	Very or somewhat unfavorable	Don't know enough to say	(N)
May–June 2003	18	13	69	(1,011)
May–June 2004	24	20	56	(1,003)
June 2005	28	27	45	(1,000)
June–July 2006	32	31	37	(1,007)
June 2007	31	40	29	(1,005)
June–July 2008	32	33	35	(1,002)
June 2009	28	48	24	(1,003)

2. GALLUP: "Just your impression, how would you rate the overall impact of the No Child Left Behind program on the public schools in your community? Would you say it is helping, hurting, or making no difference in the performance of the local public schools?"

Sampling dates	Helping	Hurting	No difference	Don't know
June–July 2006	26	21	37	16
June 2007	26	27	41	6
June–July 2008	25	22	34	19
June 2009	24	29	43	4
June 2010	22	28	45	5

3. GALLUP: "How familiar are you with the No Child Left Behind Act, the federal education law passed in 2002—very familiar, somewhat familiar, not too familiar, or not familiar at all?" [IF RESPONDENT WAS VERY, SOMEWHAT, OR NOT TOO FAMILIAR WITH THE ACT] "From what you have heard or read, do you think the No Child Left Behind Act has generally made the education received by public school students in the United States better, has it not made much difference, or has it made it worse?"

Sampling dates	Better	Not much difference	Worse	Don't know/ not familiar
Aug. 2009	18	38	25	19
Aug. 2012	16	38	28	18

tariffs were rescinded, the United Steelworkers of America (USW) endorsed Congressman Gephardt for president. Sticking the knife in just a bit deeper, USW president Leo Gerard called the 2004 Democratic presidential field "an embarrassment of riches, any of whom we can support over the reactionary policies of the current administration."[13]

Table 6.3. Public Attitudes about Government Spending on Seventeen Issue Areas in 2004 (in Percentages)

	Too little	About right	Too much	Average rating
Improving and protecting the nation's health	78	17	4	2.74
Improving the nation's education system	73	21	5	2.69
Social Security	64	28	5	2.61
Improving and protecting the environment	63	29	6	2.58
Halting the rising crime rate	56	36	5	2.52
Assistance for childcare	54	33	6	2.51
Dealing with drug addiction	53	34	9	2.46
Solving the problems of the big cities	39	38	13	2.29
Supporting scientific research	38	45	12	2.28
Mass transportation	34	50	10	2.26
Parks and recreation	31	60	7	2.25
Improving the conditions of Blacks	32	46	14	2.20
Highways and bridges	29	55	13	2.17
The military, armaments, and defense	34	38	25	2.09
Welfare	23	34	40	1.82
Space exploration program	14	43	37	1.76
Foreign aid	10	25	61	1.47

Source: National Opinion Research Center, 2004 General Social Survey.
Note: Question wording was: "We are faced with many problems in this country, none of which can be solved easily or inexpensively. I'm going to name some of these problems, and for each one I'd like you to tell me whether you think we're spending too much money on it, too little money, or about the right amount." "Average rating" was computed by assigning respondents who said "too little" a value of 3, those who said "about right" a value of 2, and those who said "too much" a value of 1, and then computing an average value for each issue area. "Don't know" responses are not shown in this table or included in the average rating calculations.

When deciding to impose the steel tariffs, Bush and his political advisors apparently expected the issue to play out politically as most special interest policies generally do. Bush, that is to say, would get credit from the groups that received visible, concentrated benefits (i.e., the steel industry and steelworkers), while the costs to other Americans would be sufficiently small and dispersed so as not to attract much attention or opposition.[14] In fact, lots of steel *users* found that the tariffs had a noticeable effect on their costs and competitive position—and proved quite good at publicizing their grievances. As the *Wall Street Journal* noted in September 2002, "Steel consumers used to be a disparate group with little might in Washington. But in the past six months, they've hired public-relations firms, staged protests and offered Mr. Bush tales of financial hardship."[15] According to another *Journal* article, "Anger is spreading across the industrial belt as manufacturers complain that the president's bid to help one industry is hurting hundreds of companies that employ far more workers."[16] The *Washington Post* commented, "The tariffs alienated thousands of small businessmen who run steel-consuming companies," then quoted the chief executive of a small manufacturing company as saying, "He [Bush] didn't win the steelworkers over, and he sure as hell didn't win the users over, and there are a hell of lot more of us."[17] Contemporary news reports were filled with estimates that for every job saved in the steel industry, the Bush tariffs had cost the country seven or eight or fourteen times as many jobs elsewhere in the economy.[18] By September 2003, according to the *Post*, "key administration officials have concluded that Bush's order has turned into a debacle."[19]

By ruling against the American steel tariffs, in short, the World Trade Organization probably did Bush a considerable favor, allowing him to rescind the tariffs without having to admit what every unbiased observer already recognized: that his decision had been a mistake from the very beginning.

Farm Subsidies

Few policy decisions during the Bush presidency had such a clear, direct electoral tie-in as the 2002 farm bill. Not only was it universally agreed that Bush had backed down from his early opposition to increased subsidies in order to win a larger share of the farm vote—most contemporary press coverage localized whatever effect the bill would have to seven key farm-state Senate races that were to be held later in 2002: those in Montana, South Dakota, Minnesota, Iowa, Missouri, Arkansas, and Georgia.[20] An embattled Republican incumbent was struggling to hold on to a seat in Arkansas; in the other six states, the Republicans were trying to dislodge a Democratic incumbent. In the end, Republicans did pick up two Senate seats in the 2002 midterm elections and thus reclaimed their Senate majority. But it is far from obvious that Bush's support for the farm bill had anything to do with bringing about this result.

The six races with Democratic incumbents played out as follows:

Montana: Democratic incumbent Max Baucus was easily reelected, with 63 percent of the total vote.

South Dakota: Democratic incumbent Tim Johnson was narrowly re-elected, beating challenger John Thune 49.6 percent to 49.5 percent.

Iowa: Democratic incumbent Tom Harkin was handily reelected, with 54 percent of the vote.

Minnesota: Republican Norm Coleman won this seat, but only after Democratic incumbent Paul Wellstone was killed in a late October plane crash. Former vice president Walter Mondale was then chosen to run in Wellstone's place. Coleman beat Mondale, 49 percent to 47 percent, partly in response to the perception that the Democrats turned Wellstone's funeral into a political pep rally. Prior to Wellstone's death, he was leading in most polls.

Missouri: Democratic incumbent Jean Carnahan, who had been appointed to fill the seat when her husband died just prior to the 2000 election, was defeated by Republican Jim Talent, 50 percent to 49 percent.

Georgia: Democratic incumbent Max Cleland was defeated by his Republican challenger, 53 percent to 46 percent.

Meanwhile:

Arkansas: Republican incumbent Tim Hutchinson was defeated by Democratic challenger Mark Pryor, 54 percent to 46 percent.

In short, three of the six Democratic incumbents won anyway, and a fourth probably would have if he had not been killed. And the farm bill didn't save the Republican incumbent in Arkansas, who had been tarnished by a personal scandal (in 1999–2000, he divorced his wife of three decades in order to marry one of his aides).

How would these races have played out if the 2002 farm bill hadn't passed or had been significantly scaled back? I know of no plausible way to answer this question in any kind of scientific or rigorous manner. The farm bill does not seem to have been a major point of contention in any of these races, but, one could argue, that was exactly what the Bush political team wanted: to prevent the Democrats from painting Republicans as "anti-farm" and thus allow the election to be fought on other grounds, such as the war on terror. But two facts may help put the 2002 results in perspective.

First, while the Republicans did gain two Senate seats in 2002, they also gained a net of two Senate seats in 1996, right after passing a farm bill that was widely portrayed as an attempt to "undo New Deal-era farm programs and move agriculture partially to a free market."[21] Among the Republican pickups in 1996—states where Republicans won seats previously held by Democrats—were three states where agriculture was a major industry: Alabama, Arkansas, and Nebraska.

Second, the Republicans were not the only ones desperate to pass the 2002 farm bill. Democrats made it clear that they, too, regarded it as a top priority. In early December 2001, Senate Majority Leader Tom Daschle (D-SD) called the bill "must do" legislation, which the Congress needed to enact before the end of the year.[22] He then took the unusual step of appointing himself to the conference committee. Much like Bush, Daschle's handling of the issue reeked strongly of election-year politics. As Richard Cohen and Corine Hegland noted in an article on the farm bill's "winners and losers":

> It wasn't just the farmers who got what they wanted. In the Senate, Daschle made sure to accommodate the political imperatives of several of his members in farm-sensitive states who face difficult re-election challenges in November. Sen. Max Cleland, D-Ga., won a new peanut subsidy. Sen. Timothy P. Johnson, D-S.D., got an expansion of country-of-origin labeling. [Sen. Tom] Harkin [D-Ia.] created the new, conservation-based entitlement and added several energy-related measures.[23]

It is hard to imagine the Democrats so anxious to pass a bill that clearly benefited Republicans. In fact, the bill was designed so that embattled Democrats like Cleland, Johnson, and Harkin could go back to their states and claim that they were "bringing home the bacon" and looking out for the needs of a major constituency.

Immigration

One of the prouder boasts of the Bush political team concerned their success at attracting the votes of Hispanic Americans. Table 6.4 shows some basic numbers on the Hispanic vote in recent presidential elections, as derived from the national media exit polls, which have become in recent years the quasi-official source for measuring such matters. In 1992 and 1996, the Republican presidential candidates had won just 25 and 21 percent of the Hispanic vote. But George W. Bush won 35 percent of that vote in 2000, and then 44 percent in 2004. To put the latter figure in perspective, prior to 2004 the best showing among Hispanic voters by a Republican presidential candidate had come in 1984, when Ronald Reagan won 37 percent. But that came in a landslide election, in which Reagan won 59 percent of the national popular vote and carried 49 of 50 states. Bush's 44 percent, by contrast, came in an election in which he won just 51 percent of the popular vote.

For many Republican leaders, these numbers contained an important strategic lesson. If Republicans were to be a viable national party in the future, these leaders concluded, they had to win a reasonable share of the Hispanic vote—certainly a good deal larger than the 27 percent share received by Mitt Romney in 2012. And that, in turn, will require Republicans to adopt something like the Bush/Rove position on immigration. In March 2013, for example, the Republican National Committee released a special report on the state of the party in the aftermath of the 2012 elections. While noting that the party was doing quite well at the gubernatorial level, the report warned that the Republicans' "federal wing is increasingly marginalizing itself, and unless changes are made, it will be increasingly difficult for Republicans to win another presidential election in the near future." Several pages later, the report declared: "We are not a policy committee, but among the steps Republicans take in the Hispanic community and beyond, we must embrace and champion comprehensive immigration reform. If we do not, our Party's appeal will continue to shrink to its core constituencies only."[24] All of which raises two important questions:

1. Did Bush really win 44 percent of the Hispanic vote in 2004?
2. Did Bush's position on immigration have anything to do with his showing?

The estimate that Bush won 44 percent of the Hispanic vote came from the National Election Pool (NEP) exit poll, and it quickly became a subject of considerable contention. On the one hand, questions were raised about the NEP sample, which allegedly overestimated the size of the Bush Hispanic vote in Texas and/or included too many south Florida precincts and, thus, a disproportionate number of Republican-leaning Cuban Americans.[25] Meanwhile, the William C. Velasquez Institute, an organization that does research on Latino economic and political participation, had conducted its own exit poll, exclusively of Hispanic voters, the results of which were significantly different. According to the Velasquez Institute poll, Bush received just 33 percent of the Hispanic vote in 2004, which was actually *less* than he had received in 2000.[26]

Though some recent commentators have asserted that the NEP results have been "discredited,"[27] I have a different reading of the controversy. To begin with, the National Election Pool was not the only source that had Bush winning a record-breaking share of the Hispanic vote. The *Los Angeles Times* also conducted a national exit poll in 2004, which put the Bush

Table 6.4. Hispanic Presidential Vote as Recorded in the National Media Exit Polls, 1980–2012

Year	Percentage Hispanic in the entire electorate	Percentage voting Republican	Percentage voting Democratic	Percentage voting Other	(N)
1980	1	33	59	8	(252)
1984	2	37	62	1	(227)
1988	3	30	69	1	(442)
1992	2	25	61	14	(432)
1996	5	21	72	7	(715)
2000	6	35	62	3	(868)
2004	8	44	53	3	(1,037)
2008	8	31	67	2	(1,542)
2012	10	27	71	2	(2,572)

Sources: All results are taken from national exit polls, as conducted by CBS News/*New York Times* (1980, 1984, 1988); Voter Research and Surveys (1992); Voter News Service (1996, 2000); and National Election Pool (2004, 2008, 2012).

Hispanic vote at 45 percent. In addition to its national sample, the National Election Pool in 2004 had also conducted separate polls in all fifty states and the District of Columbia. The Pew Hispanic Center combined these fifty-one state polls, weighted by state turnout, to produce an estimate that Bush won 40 percent of the Hispanic vote.[28] Political analysts Ruy Teixeira and Steve Sailer, after a close look at both exit polls and the actual vote in a number of heavily Hispanic areas, both estimated that Bush received about 39 percent of the Hispanic vote.[29]

There are also good reasons to question the accuracy of the Velasquez Institute poll.[30] Unlike the National Election Pool, the Velasquez Institute did not construct—did not attempt to construct—a national sample of voters. Since it was only interested in studying Hispanic voters, the Velasquez Institute poll was limited to heavily Latino precincts in heavily Latino states. It thus excluded the considerable number of Hispanics who lived in predominantly Anglo areas. From the institute's perspective, this allowed them to interview a large number of Hispanic voters for a relatively modest expenditure of research money—but it also meant that their sample was probably unrepresentative of the full Hispanic electorate. When there are specific attitudes and behaviors associated with group membership, those norms are more likely to be communicated to and accepted by people who are closely tied in with the group than by those who are not. For example, one would almost certainly overestimate the Democratic percentage of the union vote if one only interviewed people who regularly attended union meetings. In general, Hispanics who live in heavily Hispanic areas will be more likely to read Hispanic newspapers, belong to Hispanic organizations, and meet Hispanic political leaders. Hence, if the norm among Hispanics is to vote Democratic, those who live in heavily Hispanic areas will be more likely to adhere to this norm.[31]

Everything considered, then, Bush probably won around 40 percent of the Hispanic vote, and possibly even a bit more. This was undoubtedly a significant achievement for a Republican presidential candidate—but did Bush's stance on immigration have anything to do with it? There is little evidence that it did.

All three of the 2004 exit polls mentioned earlier included a question in which respondents were given a list of major issues in the campaign and then asked to "check" the one or two issues that were "most important to you in deciding how you would vote for president." Unfortunately for my purposes, neither the NEP nor the *Los Angeles Times* poll included immigration as one of the issues on their list. But the Velasquez Institute did include "immigration policy" as one of its thirteen issues. The results the institute obtained are shown in table 6.5. With all due allowance for whatever sampling problems the Velasquez Institute poll may have encountered, the results clearly demonstrate that immigration was *not* a major voting issue for Hispanics in 2004.[32] Like other racial and ethnic groups, Hispanics were principally concerned about the economy, the war in Iraq, and the war on terrorism; more than most other groups, Hispanics also took the abortion issue into account. Just 3 percent, however, checked the box next to "immigration policy," making it the eighth most important of the thirteen issues.

Much the same result was registered by the 2004 American National Election Study (ANES), which asked respondents if there was "anything in particular about George W. Bush that might make you want to vote for him?" Though the ANES sample included only eighty-seven Hispanic respondents, its findings parallel those of the Velasquez Institute survey. While 51 percent of Hispanics had at least one positive thing to say about Bush (a good showing for a Republican), only two respondents (3 percent of the weighted Hispanic sample) specifically mentioned the immigration issue.[33] Most gave answers that could have been given—in many cases were given—just as readily by non-Hispanic white respondents. They approved of Bush's handling of the war on terrorism; they admired him for his sincerity, his religiosity, and his idealism.[34] Another set of questions in the 2004 ANES showed, not unexpectedly, that Hispanics liked the Democratic Party better than the Republican Party. But when asked what they liked about the Democrats, only 2 percent of Hispanic respondents cited the immigration issue. Most mentioned the kinds of issues that, as we will see in chapter 10, have long been the strength of the Democratic Party with voters of all races:

that Democrats are more concerned with the interests of working people and the poor and that they do a better job of handling economic issues.

The argument that Bush fared well among Hispanics because he supported immigration "reform," and that Romney fared poorly because he opposed it, also fails to explain why John McCain won only 31 percent of the Hispanic vote in 2008. When Bush pushed Congress to rewrite the immigration laws in 2006 and 2007, McCain had been among the most prominent supporters of the Bush policy. Yet, when compared to Bush's showing in 2004, McCain's losses among Hispanic voters (13 percentage points) were more than double the rate of his losses in the rest of the electorate (5 percentage points). In a similar way, George Hawley's analysis of voting in the 2006 House elections found that Republican representatives who voted for expanded immigration levels (i.e., those who said they supported the Bush proposal) did not win a larger share of the Latino vote than Republicans who had voted for restrictionist immigration policies.[35]

Finally, even if Bush's position on immigration did help increase his share of the vote among Hispanics, those gains would need to be balanced against the gains he might have registered among non-Hispanic white voters by taking a tougher stance on illegal immigration. As becomes clear every time Congress takes up the immigration issue, and as Donald Trump would show even more vividly in 2016, there is a large and vocal segment of the electorate that believes that the lax enforcement of current immigration laws imposes substantial costs upon the country, such as increased crime rates, greater expenditures on welfare and other social services, lower wage rates and increased unemployment among low-skilled Americans, and greater vulnerability to foreign terrorism. Many of these voters are conservatives and Republicans who probably would have voted for Bush anyway, but many are independents or weak Democrats who might have voted Republican if Bush had shown a greater willingness to take their concerns seriously. In an analysis of voting in the 2016 presidential election, James Gimpel concluded that "tapping into widespread discontent with the trajectory of U.S. immigration policy was a winning strategy" for Trump. While he may have lost votes among proponents of expansive immigration policies, he gained even more votes among women, the well-educated, and weak Democrats who advocated a tougher line on illegal immigration. Moreover, "contrary to the post-election conclusions of Romney's advisers, Romney would likely have done better, not worse, by campaigning more vigorously for immigration control."[36]

In comparing the votes to be won and lost from taking various positions on the immigration issue, it is important to recognize that relatively small increases in the non-Hispanic white vote can have a greater total impact

Table 6.5. Issues That Mattered Most to Hispanic Voters in the 2004 Presidential Election

Issue	Percentage mentioning that issue
Economy/jobs	20
Iraq war	20
War on terrorism	9
Abortion	9
Health care	8
Bilingual education	4
Public education	3
Immigration policy	3
Crime/drugs	2
Same-sex marriage	2
Taxes	2
Gun control	1
Environment	1

Source: William C. Velasquez Institute Exit Poll, 2004.
Note: Question wording was: "Which one issue mattered most in deciding how you voted for president?" N = 850.

than much larger increases in the Hispanic vote. According to the 2004 exit poll, whites accounted for 77 percent of the electorate while just 8 percent were Hispanic. Whites outnumbered Hispanics, in other words, by more than nine to one. So a 2 percentage-point increase in the white vote would have provided Bush with more total votes than an 18 percentage-point increase in the Hispanic vote.

The Federal Deficit

Of all the issues examined in the last two chapters, it is probably most difficult to assess the long-term political effects of Bush's budget policies. On the one hand, there are ample indications that the American public noticed and disliked the speed and recklessness with which Bush converted the Clinton-era surpluses into large and persistent deficits. Consider, in particular, the data in table 6.6. By the second half of 2003, when Bush's overall approval ratings were still quite good, a clear majority of Americans said that they disapproved of the way Bush was handling the federal budget; only a third approved his performance in that area. Over the next five years, as table 6.6 also shows, the public's judgment on Bush's budgetary policies grew even more negative. One consequence of these assessments was that when Bush ran for reelection in 2004, polls during the fall campaign consistently showed that the public thought John Kerry would do a better job than Bush of dealing with the federal deficit, even though Kerry had proposed several hundred billion dollars in additional spending, with no way to pay for it except taxes on the rich. In a mid-October 2004 Gallup poll, for example, 53 percent of the respondents said that Kerry "would better handle . . . the federal budget deficit," while just 42 percent preferred Bush for that task.[37]

Not surprisingly, Bush's spendthrift ways, in conjunction with the equally unrestrained spending habits of many congressional Republicans, soon cast a shadow over the entire party. As shown in table 6.7, in 2002 Republicans and Democrats were seen as equally good—or equally bad—at dealing with the federal deficit. By the end of Bush's second term, however, the American public had decided that the Democrats offered a substantially better prospect of reducing the deficit. This perception carried over to the 2008 presidential campaign. Though John McCain had an admirable record of opposing earmarks and special-interest giveaways, it was Barack Obama whom the public saw as better able to cope with the deficit—and by a substantial margin. A Pew Research Center poll conducted just a few weeks before the election, for example, found that 50 percent of likely voters thought that Obama "would do the best job of reducing the budget deficit," versus 30 percent who favored McCain.[38]

There is no doubt, then, that the Bush-led Republican Party developed a highly negative image on issues of budgeting, deficits, and fiscal responsibility. What is less clear is how much, if any, political price they paid for this image. Fortunately for Bush and the Republicans, there is little evidence to show that the deficit was an important voting issue in 2004—or in 2002, 2006, or 2008. With so much else dominating the headlines—the war on terror, the war in Iraq, the ups and downs of the economy, the aftermath of Hurricane Katrina—the federal deficit never made it to the front burner of public concerns. In four Gallup polls conducted between August and early November 2004, the largest number of respondents who said that the federal deficit was the country's "most important problem" was 4 percent, ranking it well behind the war in Iraq, the war on terrorism, the economy, unemployment, health care, education, and moral decline. In the 2004 American National Election Study, 62 percent of respondents were able to name at least one thing they disliked about George W. Bush. But only 3 percent made any reference to deficits or wasteful spending. The major sources of public irritation with Bush were, not surprisingly, the war in Iraq, the state of the economy, doubts about his honesty and intelligence, and the perception that he was too sympathetic to the concerns of big business. In chapter 5, I argued that political consultants—and most politicians—are reluctant to recommend a concerted attack on the federal

Table 6.6. Public Opinion about How George W. Bush Was Handling the Federal Budget Deficit (Yearly Averages)

Year	Approve	Disapprove	Don't know	(Number of surveys)
2001	50	42	7	(3)
2002	52	37	11	(5)
Jan.–June 2003	44	46	10	(7)
July–Dec. 2003	34	55	10	(10)
2004	34	58	8	(5)
2005	33	58	10	(6)
2006	26	66	9	(5)
2007	26	63	11	(3)

Sources: Based on surveys conducted by Gallup, ABC News/*Washington Post*, *Los Angeles Times*, Princeton Survey Research Associates, CBS News/*New York Times*, and Greenberg Quinlan Rosner.
Note: From 2001 through February 2003, the survey question was: "Do you approve or disapprove of the way George W. Bush is handling the federal budget?" From March 2003 through 2007, the question was usually: "Do you approve or disapprove of the way George W. Bush is handling the federal budget deficit?" No question of this type was asked in 2008.

deficit because there is so little short-term benefit from a serious deficit reduction program, and relatively little short-term cost for avoiding action. At least while Bush was in the White House, this disheartening diagnosis almost certainly held true. In that minimal sense, Bush "got away with" his budget policies.

The Republican Party may not have been so fortunate. One consequence of the Bush fiscal legacy was to make it considerably more difficult for Republicans to oppose the Obama deficits. By the end of Obama's first term, the federal deficit had started to creep up on the list of public priorities. In four separate Gallup polls conducted between August and November 2012, 10 percent of Americans now cited the deficit as the country's most important problem, generally putting the issue in third place behind unemployment and the economy. Yet, even as Obama racked up three consecutive trillion-dollar deficits, Americans consistently told pollsters that they blamed Bush more than Obama for the "current federal budget deficit." In January 2012, three years after Bush had moved out of the White House, a CBS News/*New York Times* poll asked a national sample of American adults this question: "Who do you think is mostly to blame for most of the current federal budget deficit—the Bush administration, the Obama administration, Congress, or someone else?" The results were: Bush administration, 43 percent; Obama administration, 14 percent; Congress, 19 percent; someone else, 9 percent.[39] Not until March 2012 is there finally

Table 6.7. Public Opinion about Which Party Is Better at Handling the Federal Deficit

Survey date	Republicans	Democrats	(N)
Aug. 2002	37	43	(1,372)
Dec. 2002	39	38	(1,305)
Feb. 2006	28	48	(900)
Sept. 2007	29	52	(557)
Jan. 2008	31	52	(624)

Sources: Surveys were conducted by the *Los Angeles Times*, Opinion Dynamics, and ABC News/*Washington Post*.
Note: Question wording varied slightly across surveys, but in most cases was: "Which party, the Democrats or the Republicans, do you think can do a better job handling the budget deficit?"

a poll in which, by a 26 percent to 25 percent margin, more people held Obama rather than Bush responsible for the federal deficit.[40]

Conclusion

The first conclusion to be drawn from the analysis in this chapter is that most of the policies discussed in chapters 4 and 5—which were pretty clearly adopted for reasons of politics rather than principle—probably didn't pay off politically. Any advantage Bush gained by promising a huge expansion of the federal role in elementary and secondary education had evaporated by 2004; the benefits of his big and bold plan for space exploration were either microscopically small or nonexistent; "key officials" from his own administration concluded that the steel tariffs were a "debacle"; and the 2002 farm subsidy bill probably helped Democrats as much as Republicans (if it helped anybody). Bush did run very well in both 2000 and 2004 among Hispanic voters, but it is unclear if this was because of his permissive stand on illegal immigration or if he might have won even more votes by enforcing the immigration laws more vigorously.

To be fair to Rove, not only are there important differences between political consultants and policy analysts, there are also major differences between political practitioners and political scientists. In particular, the penalties for being wrong are radically different for these two groups. Take the case of the 2002 farm bill. I cannot find any evidence to show that Republican Senate candidates benefited from the bill's passage, but neither can I conclusively disprove the claim that by supporting the bill, Bush made sure that Democrats could not exploit the farm issue in 2002 and thus made possible the victories of Jim Talent in Missouri and Saxby

Chambliss in Georgia. If I am wrong, however, and the farm bill really did matter, the worst that is likely to happen to me is that some eager graduate student will publish an article in some little-read academic journal challenging my methods or my data. (Since many academics measure a book's "impact" by the number of times it is cited, regardless of whether it is cited positively or negatively, having such an article published might actually be a small plus for my career.) If, by contrast, the farm bill mattered and Rove made the wrong decision, the Bush administration would have had to deal with a Democratic-majority Senate in 2003–2004, almost certainly making it a lot more difficult to pass important legislation or confirm conservative judicial nominees. Maybe if I had been in Rove's position, I would have played it safe and made the same decision he did.

Maybe. But a second point should also be made here: that a great deal of what passes for "wisdom" among political consultants is more folklore than science.[41] Though many consultants are reluctant to acknowledge it, political consulting in the early twenty-first century is in approximately the same position that medicine was in the seventeenth. At that time, medical "knowledge" consisted not of a scientifically demonstrated body of conclusions but of a series of propositions accepted because they had been recommended by various "authorities" of uncertain reliability or because somebody thought they had worked in the past. And one became a medical practitioner not by undergoing a thorough, well-grounded course of study in a certified medical school but by apprenticing with an existing practitioner or just by hanging out a shingle and hoping to attract clients. Against that background, it is not amiss for somebody to point out that many tried-and-true electoral strategies may not work as well as advertised.

And if the art of political management has its limitations, these limitations are particularly severe at the level of the presidency. Put another way, I believe that the passage from Alexander Hamilton quoted at the beginning of this chapter is fundamentally correct. One can build a perfectly good career in Congress through the "little arts of popularity": taking care of constituency services, posing as a champion of whatever special interests are most important to the state or district, criticizing the policies of the executive branch without putting forward a specific or realistic alternative, being especially good at getting one's face on television. But the presidency, at least in the modern era, is about getting the big issues right: peace, prosperity, security, the *general* welfare. To be sure, one can get elected president the first time by campaigning against the failures of one's predecessor. If those failures are substantial enough, one may even use them as an excuse to get reelected, as Barack Obama successfully proved in 2012. But eventually, the presidency has a way of calling a politician's bluffs, of revealing the essential emptiness of many a nice-sounding speech.

This is an important perspective for every presidential advisor to keep in mind, but one might have thought it especially useful for an advisor who hoped to bring about a full-scale party realignment. Even more than ordinary presidential elections, realignments hinge on finding solutions to an era's most pressing policy problems. You can't nickel and dime your way to a realignment. If Bush and Rove believed their own rhetoric, it is hard not to think that they would have been better off in the long run by trying to show that free trade really did work to a country's advantage, by making a good-faith effort to enforce border security, by trying to govern agriculture according to free-market principles, by sincerely attempting to be fiscally responsible. The little arts of popularity might have saved them a congressional seat here or there (maybe), but they were plainly insufficient to bring about a sustained era of Republican dominance.

7

When an Administration Is in Crisis and the President Refuses to Acknowledge It, a Political Advisor May Be the Best Person to Warn the President

Politics, as I have suggested in chapter 1, has both its proper and improper uses. A president who allows his policy development process to be run by a political consultant is asking for trouble—but so is a president who tries to pretend that politics is irrelevant to his job. This chapter deals with one kind of situation where a president's political advisors do have an important role to play—a role that Rove and his cohorts failed to perform.

Crisis and Denial

The kind of situation I have in mind is when an administration faces a genuine crisis—and the president refuses to recognize or respond to it. The word I want to emphasize here is *crisis*. Every administration encounters minor setbacks, makes small miscalculations, suffers brief bouts of unfavorable publicity. For all the breathless prose that is sometimes expended on such episodes, most will be quickly forgotten and be of so little long-term consequence as never to be mentioned in the standard presidential histories. But some issues and incidents are of far greater significance. They are crises in the full, dictionary sense of that term: "an unstable or crucial time or state of affairs in which a decisive change is impending, especially one with the distinct possibility of a highly undesirable outcome."[1] Or to provide a somewhat more operational definition, a crisis is the kind of situation that, if not properly dealt with, threatens to cripple the administration's future effectiveness and impose significant costs on the president and his party.

When an administration faces a genuine crisis, one might think that the president would be the first person to see the impending danger and seek some kind of corrective action. The history of the presidency, however, shows that this is often not the case. Whether out of stubbornness or "groupthink"[2] or confirmation bias[3] or an inadequate knowledge of the facts, presidents sometimes cling to the notion that things are working just fine, no matter what their growing army of critics say. Indeed, the very fact that a problem has escalated to the crisis stage may itself be an indication that the president and many of his top advisors have failed to recognize the seriousness of the situation.

The history books are, in any event, replete with examples of this kind of presidential myopia. Lyndon Johnson pursued the same basic policy in Vietnam for three years before he was finally willing to admit that it wasn't working. Nixon and his closest aides seem to have believed for a long time that they could successfully cover up their involvement in the Watergate affair. George H. W. Bush ignored the country's economic problems until they had pretty much doomed any chance he had of getting reelected and even then failed to make more than cosmetic changes. Bill Clinton seems never to have appreciated the severe risk he took by allowing his administration's health care plan to be devised by a task force headed by his wife.[4]

When a president refuses to recognize that his administration faces a crisis, a political advisor is not the only person who can or should try to shake him out of his stupor. Cabinet members and other top policy advisors sometimes undertake the same task. Yet for a variety of reasons, a political advisor is often the best person to shoulder this responsibility.

To begin with, the political consequences of presidential missteps are often more visible—and more difficult to deny—than their policy effects. The "bubble" that was frequently said to isolate George W. Bush from critical news reports and unpleasant realities is probably true, to a greater or lesser extent, for all presidents. All are surrounded by aides and advisors who tend to have a highly favorable view of the president, whose egos and reputations are heavily invested in past decisions, and whose access and influence depend on maintaining good relations with the president. All White Houses tend to develop an us-versus-them mentality; none like receiving or passing on bad news. Given the complexities of most policy problems, it is therefore all too easy to ignore the evidence of policy failure and instead to find some measure(s) that shows the policy is actually succeeding, to insist that the policy will work if only it is given more time, or to believe that all other policy choices will only make things worse.

By contrast, the signs of political failure—in particular, declining poll ratings and substantial election losses—become at some point more difficult to brush aside. While many commentators argued that Bill Clinton was governing well to the left of his 1992 campaign platform and had grossly mishandled the health-care issue, he himself declined to recognize his mistakes until his party lost control of both houses of Congress in the 1994 midterms. George H. W. Bush did not acknowledge the problem of economic stagnation and drift until his approval rating had fallen by almost 40 percentage points. And it is no accident that Lyndon Johnson announced a change in his Vietnam policy just a few weeks after Eugene McCarthy almost defeated him in the New Hampshire presidential primary.[5] The Bush presidency, as we will see later in this chapter, added another example to this list. After years of insisting that the United States was making progress in Iraq, that no major changes in policy were necessary, and that Donald Rumsfeld was doing a splendid job as secretary of defense, Bush reversed course and publicly acknowledged the need for change only after his party suffered major losses in the 2006 elections.

Presidents respond to evidence of political failure for a simple reason: however much they may sometimes posture to the contrary, presidents are fundamentally politicians. Dwight Eisenhower and Donald Trump excepted, no one has been elected president in the twentieth or twenty-first centuries without spending most of his adult life in and around politics. Even Eisenhower was a substantially more "political" person than is sometimes recognized. As a general during World War II, Eisenhower was noted less as a strategist or battlefield commander than for his ability to secure some measure of cooperation from a group of remarkably headstrong military and governmental leaders.[6]

To argue that a political advisor should intervene in the policy process when an administration faces an unacknowledged crisis is not to suggest that he or she needs to present the president with a fully developed, ten-point plan for restarting a stagnant economy, remodeling the American health care system, or negotiating an end to the Vietnam war. As I have argued in chapter 4, political advisors rarely have anything like the knowledge and skills requisite to such an undertaking. Instead, an advisor should aspire to be (in what I concede is an overused phrase) a catalyst for change. His or her goal should be to make the president aware that an important initiative or policy isn't working, that continuation of the present course is starting to impose significant costs on the president and his party, and that something different needs to be done. If the advisor also has some useful insights as to the specific sorts of changes the president should make—well, that's pure gravy.

In the sense defined above, the presidency of George W. Bush faced, I believe, two authentic crises: one involving the war in Iraq, the other concerning Hurricane Katrina. Though a lot of people can reasonably be blamed for the disaster that followed in the wake of Katrina—at every level of government—I would not put Rove's name on the blacklist. Had Rove been omniscient, he might have raised some warnings about the way that Bush had turned the Federal Emergency Management Agency (FEMA) into a dumping ground for political hacks or about the dangers of transferring FEMA to the new Department of Homeland Security, but to make this argument is to hold Rove to an impossibly high standard. Bush's own response to the events in New Orleans was slow and often maladroit, but this was largely because FEMA had virtually no one actually stationed in the city and consequently believed that the levees had held and that little flooding had occurred. By the time Bush's political advisors and image managers realized how bad conditions were in New Orleans and how inept FEMA's performance had been, the damage had already been done. The only mistake that can be charged directly to Rove was the decision to have Bush's plane fly over the flooded city rather than actually visiting the affected area and then allow Bush to be photographed looking out the plane window.[7] The resulting pictures reinforced the image of Bush as distant and out-of-touch, but that image would have taken hold even if such pictures had never been taken. Had FEMA done its job properly, one photo-op gone bad wouldn't have mattered.

But there was ample time for Rove to alert Bush to the disaster that was developing in Iraq and the need to make some kind of significant change in US policy. Yet on this key issue, the generally hyperactive Rove was strangely passive.

The War in Iraq

Fifty or a hundred years from now, how will historians view the war in Iraq that George W. Bush launched in March 2003? The answer to this question depends in part, of course, on the future character of the history profession. Unless there is a sharp change in the nature of American intellectual life, it seems likely that many future historians (especially academic historians) will pronounce a negative judgment on any exercise of American military power, no matter what the circumstances, especially if it was undertaken by a Republican president.[8] But among those historians capable of taking a more dispassionate view of events, I suspect they will draw a distinction between the initial decision to invade Iraq and the way that decision was carried out, especially the occupation and reconstruction period that followed the end of major combat operations.

About the original decision to invade Iraq, the best historians will probably express mixed judgments. Knowing that Saddam Hussein didn't have an active nuclear, biological, or chemical weapons program in 2003, taking account of all the problems that followed in the wake of the invasion, many will no doubt conclude that Bush's decision to go to war was a serious and tragic mistake. But other historians, I believe, will conclude that there were defensible reasons to remove Saddam from power.[9] Saddam Hussein was not just a dictator but a very brutal and cruel one, who killed hundreds of thousands of his subjects and single-handedly crippled what had once been, by Third World standards, a fairly prosperous economy. Unlike other Middle Eastern despots, moreover, Saddam had regularly shown that he was not content to sit back within his own borders, oppress his people, and otherwise leave the world alone. To the contrary, he had started, without obvious provocation, two major wars against his neighbors, invading Iran in 1980 and Kuwait in 1990. (He may also have come close to invading Kuwait again in 1994.)[10] Both attacks were motivated in part by his desire to gain control of a commanding share of the world's oil reserves. As for weapons of mass destruction, once the mention of George Bush's name no longer causes a sizable number of academics to foam at the mouth, historians will be compelled to admit that Bush was not the only person who claimed that Saddam possessed such weapons: that Bill Clinton and the intelligence services of virtually every other Western democracy also subscribed to this belief. Those who make a serious attempt to understand the information that was and was not available to Bush at the time he decided to invade Iraq will also appreciate the difficulties of learning anything very definite about the internal workings of a closed and highly secretive regime, and that when US intelligence had made errors in the past, they had almost always underestimated the progress other countries were making toward developing nuclear weapons. (I will expand on all of these points in a later chapter.)

And if Saddam was a serious threat, the other policy options (besides a full-scale military invasion of Iraq) were all highly problematic. The sanctions regime that had been established in the wake of the first Gulf War was clearly breaking down and would have been difficult to resuscitate. Conventional deterrence strategies, of the kind that restrained the Soviet Union during the Cold War, would not obviously work with Saddam, particularly if he acquired nuclear weapons. Covert action or support for internal opposition groups was unlikely to be successful. While there is ample reason to believe that the Bush administration substantially underestimated the risks and difficulties of a military invasion, all of the other strategies that might have been employed against Saddam also had their flaws and dangers.

Whatever verdict future historians render about the decision to invade

Iraq, however, I predict that virtually no one, regardless of ideology or partisanship, will try to defend the conduct of the postwar occupation. Without any exception I am aware of, accounts of US policy in Iraq between May 2003 and late 2006 reveal an operation characterized by an appalling level of recklessness and incompetence.[11]

Though present purposes do not require a detailed reexamination of how the Bush administration bungled the postwar occupation, a brief recounting may help provide some context for the analysis that follows.

1. Convinced that American forces would be greeted as "liberators" and that the occupation and reconstruction period would not be difficult, the administration gave shockingly little attention to planning what would or should happen after Saddam was deposed. As a Rand Corporation study noted in 2005, "Post-conflict stabilization and reconstruction were addressed only very generally, largely because of the prevailing view that that task would not be difficult." A lieutenant general who worked for the Joint Chiefs of Staff similarly observed, "I was there for all the planning, all the execution. I saw it all. . . . There was no real plan. The thought was, you didn't need it. The assumption was that everything would be fine after the war, that they [the Iraqis] would be happy they got rid of Saddam."[12]

2. Planning for the occupation was further undermined by Bush's decision to put the Defense Department in charge of postwar Iraq, rather than the State Department, which had handled such responsibilities in every other "postconflict situation" since World War II.[13] As numerous analyses would later conclude, the Defense Department lacked the experience and expertise to handle such matters effectively.[14]

3. Even worse, the Defense Department was the redoubt of Defense Secretary Donald Rumsfeld, whose record for arrogance, personal pettiness, and bureaucratic in-fighting was unmatched in the Bush presidency. Though his own department put little effort into postwar planning, he nevertheless did his best to make sure that other departments and agencies didn't usurp this prerogative and that any offers of advice or assistance were spurned. In one celebrated instance, Jay Garner, who led the principal occupation planning agency in the Pentagon, wanted to add Tom Warrick to his staff, for the quite good reason that Warrick had headed up an early postwar planning effort in the State Department and seemed to have more detailed knowledge about such issues than anyone else. But when Rumsfeld heard that Warrick was from the State Department, he ordered Garner to "take [him] off the team."[15]

4. Warrick's removal was part of a larger pattern: in selecting personnel for the occupation effort, ideological commitment was too often preferred over competence and experience. For example:

A twenty-four-year-old who worked at a real estate firm and had never been to the Middle East was assigned to rebuild the [Iraqi] stock exchange. An army officer busied himself rewriting Iraq's traffic laws by cutting and pasting from Maryland's code. A twenty-one-year-old who had yet to finish college and whose most significant job until then had been ice-cream truck driver was among those charged with purging the Interior Ministry of militia members.[16]

5. Acting against the advice of numerous top generals and military leaders, Rumsfeld drastically reduced the size of the force that ultimately invaded Iraq. The result, just as these experts had warned, was that there were enough troops available to depose Saddam but not enough to accomplish the numerous other tasks that would have laid the foundation for a smooth transition: preventing disorder and looting; safeguarding important public ministries and the electrical grid; securing the large number of caches of conventional weapons that Saddam had stockpiled all over the country; and sealing off the borders to Iran and Syria.

6. One month after the fall of Baghdad, the Bush administration further nullified the value of such planning as had taken place by appointing L. Paul Bremer as head of the Coalition Provisional Authority (CPA), the new civilian governing authority in Iraq. Bremer was, as one of his staff would later describe him, "brilliant and yet had only a limited understanding of Iraq."[17] Though an experienced diplomat, Bremer had no combat experience, didn't speak Arabic, and had never before been to Iraq. He also had not participated in any of the prewar planning and ignored most of its major recommendations.

7. Almost immediately after getting to Iraq, Bremer issued two orders that have been almost universally criticized in subsequent analyses. The first removed all "full members" of the Baath Party from their current posts and banned them from holding positions in any future Iraqi government. The second disbanded the Iraqi army. Together, these decisions ensured a large supply of ready recruits for any insurgency: that is to say, they created a large body of men who were unemployed, resentful, armed, and convinced that they would fare worse under the new regime than they had under Saddam. One US official would later say of these decisions, "That was the week we made 450,000 enemies on the ground in Iraq."[18]

De-Baathification had the additional effect of removing from government service a large proportion of its most competent and knowledgeable employees—what one US official called "the brains of the government."[19] While some were Saddam loyalists, many had been compelled to join the Baath Party as a condition of employment. In either case, Bremer's order dramatically reduced the effectiveness of the government ministries that dealt with such basic services as electricity, water and sewage treatment, and education. In both cases, moreover, Bremer's orders contradicted the policies that Bush and his top advisors back in Washington had decided upon earlier—yet the president made no attempt to countermand his appointee.

8. Bremer also decided to substantially delay the creation of an interim Iraqi government and canceled a number of previously scheduled local elections.[20] In a way that Bremer and most other top officials in the Bush administration never fully appreciated, the United States faced a delicate situation in postwar Iraq.[21] Though Saddam Hussein was widely hated, history had also left the Iraqis with a deep suspicion of the United States and the West in general. As time went on, one historian has observed, many Iraqis "began to wonder if the U.S. and U.K. were trying to establish a colony and if Bremer was the new proconsul."[22]

The result was vividly shown in two surveys of the Iraqi public. The first, taken shortly after the war ended, found that 46 percent of Iraqis already viewed Coalition forces as "occupying powers," versus 43 percent who saw them as liberators. As Bremer continued to put off the transfer of sovereignty, and after the United Nations Security Council formally declared Great Britain and the United States to be "occupying powers,"[23] things only got worse. By October 2003, two-thirds of Iraqis saw the Coalition as an occupying power, while just 15 percent still viewed them as liberators.[24]

9. Partly because of the lack of American troops and partly because the Iraqi army had been disbanded, it soon became clear that postwar Iraq was characterized by an extraordinary level of violence, disorder, and lawlessness. And that, in turn, made it immensely more difficult to carry out all the other economic, social, and governmental functions of the reconstruction. As early as May 2003, Iraqi leaders had warned the White House that "it would be foolish to start experimenting with democracy without making people feel secure enough to go back to work or school, and without giving them back at least the basic services they received during Saddam Hussein's brutal rule."[25] Larry Diamond, a political scientist who worked for the CPA, made the same point in more philosophical terms: "We cannot get to Jefferson and Madison without going through Thomas Hobbes. You can't build a democratic state unless you first have a state, and the essential condition for a state is that it must have an effective monopoly over the means of violence."[26]

10. In yet one more example of the triumph of wishful thinking over realistic planning, the Bush administration seems to have believed that once major combat operations were concluded and Saddam had been deposed,

lots of other countries would be willing to supply sizable quantities of troops and money and thus assume much of the burden of occupation and reconstruction.[27] Given the general unpopularity of the war and the widespread sense that the United States had shown contempt for world opinion in its prewar planning, this belief was never a realistic one. But the postwar violence and disorder made other countries and nongovernmental organizations even less likely to become or stay involved in Iraq. A particularly severe setback occurred on August 19, 2003, when a truck bomb destroyed a substantial part of the United Nations headquarters building in Iraq, killing twenty-two people, including the chief of the UN mission, and injuring seventy others. The attack, said one Marine colonel, "convinced the organization that continuing to operate in Iraq would be too costly." The upshot was that the UN almost completely withdrew from Iraq, reducing its staff from eight hundred to fifteen. In the following weeks, other international organizations, such as the World Bank, the International Monetary Fund, and Oxfam, also began to pull out.[28]

Table 7.1 shows the number of monthly fatalities suffered by American forces in Iraq between 2003 and 2010. As has often been noted, the initial invasion of Iraq was completed with relatively little loss of American lives: in March and April 2003, 139 Americans were killed. The problem was that after the end of what Bush called "major combat operations," large numbers of US soldiers continued to die. In the months immediately after April 2003, a policy maker might reasonably have assumed that this level of violence was temporary, a dying gasp from a small number of Saddam loyalists and other "dead-enders" that would soon wither away. One might also be forgiven for thinking/hoping that American casualties would decline after Saddam Hussein was finally captured in December 2003, or after sovereignty was handed over to the Iraqis in late June 2004. But by early 2005 at the very latest, it should have been clear to any fair-minded observer that there was something seriously wrong with US policy in Iraq, and that merely giving existing policy more time was unlikely to solve the problem.

And yet, all through this period, George W. Bush remained in what Bob Woodward has accurately called a "state of denial": a strange and remarkable unwillingness to recognize the inadequacy of American policy in Iraq. Even relatively minor modifications were resisted. At one point during the spring of 2004, Paul Bremer sent a special message to Rumsfeld asking that two more divisions, or thirty to forty thousand additional soldiers, be sent to Iraq. Yet Bush and Rumsfeld never seriously considered the request, much less agreed to it, because it had not been sent through the proper chain of command.[29] Declining to make any substantive changes,

Bush instead delivered a series of speeches throughout the summer of 2006 in which he merely urged the country to "stay the course."[30]

Bush's refusal to face reality was probably attributable to three major factors. First, Bush, like a number of other recent presidents, was always reluctant to admit that he had made a mistake. Second, as noted in chapter 4, Bush had, deliberately or otherwise, shut himself off from most of the sources of information that might have told him what was really going on in Iraq. Without much attention to or trust in the American news media, declining to consult with outside advisors, he seems, instead, to have received most of his military news from official sources, particularly Donald Rumsfeld and one or two top generals, all of whom tended to present an overly optimistic picture of the occupation.

In an interview with Brit Hume conducted in September 2003, Bush declared:

> I have great respect for the media. I mean, our society is a good, solid democracy because of a good, solid media. But I also understand that a lot of times there's opinions mixed in with news. . . . I appreciate people's opinions, but I'm more interested in news. And the best way to get the news is from objective sources. *And the most objective sources I have are people on my staff who tell me what's happening in the world.*[31]

Not to mince words, this is an appallingly ill-informed thing for a president to say. As anyone familiar with bureaucracies—or human nature—ought to know, when a policy isn't working, the people responsible for devising and implementing that policy are *least* likely to provide the president with objective reports about their own failings. This is one reason that Richard Neustadt and numerous other presidential scholars have all but unanimously advised presidents to seek information from a wide variety of sources. Though Bush seems to have followed this advice during the period immediately after the 9/11 attacks and when he was looking for an alternative Iraq policy after the 2006 elections, he was, by all accounts, substantially more isolated during the time when the Iraq intervention was moving from victory to disaster. Joseph Nye, a Harvard political scientist who served in Jimmy Carter's state department and Bill Clinton's defense department, commented:

> [Ronald] Reagan in his first term was very successful. Reagan in his first half of his second term was a disaster. But Reagan had the sense to recover in his last two years. He did that because he listened to people who were telling him what was wrong. Nobody's done for Bush what

Table 7.1. Monthly Fatalities of American Forces in Iraq, 2003–2010

	2003	2004	2005	2006	2007	2008	2009	2010
January	—	47	107	62	83	40	16	6
February	—	20	58	55	81	29	17	6
March	65	52	35	31	81	39	9	7
April	74	135	52	76	104	52	19	8
May	37	80	80	69	126	19	25	6
June	30	42	78	61	101	29	15	8
July	48	54	54	43	80	13	8	4
August	35	66	85	65	84	23	7	3
September	31	80	49	72	66	25	10	7
October	44	64	96	107	38	14	9	2
November	82	137	84	70	37	17	11	2
December	40	72	68	112	23	14	3	1
TOTAL	486	849	846	823	904	314	149	60

Source: Iraq Coalition Casualty Count, http://icasualties.org/Iraq/ByMonth.aspx (accessed October 19, 2012).

Howard Baker, David Abshire, and Ken Duberstein did for Reagan.[32]

Finally, Bush seems to have believed that any effort on his part to re-think American policy in Iraq would only signal weakness and indecision and thus encourage the insurgents and terrorists. As Bush told one reporter:

> A president has got to be the calcium in the backbone. If I weaken, the whole team weakens. If I'm doubtful, I can assure you there will be a lot of doubt. If my confidence level in our ability declines, it will send ripples throughout the whole organization. I mean, it's essential that we be confident and determined and united. I don't need people around me who are not steady. . . . And if there's kind of a hand-wringing attitude going on when times are tough, I don't like it.[33]

Bush also seems to have viewed "staying the course" as a test of his personal strength and leadership ability. As he told one White House visitor, "The American people are watching—do I have the will to do what I'm doing or will I lose my nerve. I will not lose my nerve."[34] The president, a "senior administration official" told a reporter, thinks that "change shows weakness. Doing what everyone knows has to be done shows weakness."[35]

This, too, is a highly dysfunctional thing for a president to believe. A president's refusal to second-guess any of his previous decisions makes sense only if he thinks that there is little or no chance that his original decisions were wrong—in other words, that he is for all practical purposes infallible. Otherwise, it effectively says that maintaining confidence and steadiness are more important than getting the decision right. Even if Bush had decided, for what he believed were good reasons, that it was crucial to see the mission in Iraq through to completion, the posture he took toward criticism and dissent assumed that there were only two options available: continuing the present policy and complete withdrawal. In fact, of course, there were—there almost always are—other alternatives. In particular, it was possible to pursue the same long-term goals via a different set of strategies and tactics. The new Iraq policy Bush finally announced in January 2007 is a good example. Far from evincing weakness and irresolution, the new policy, which required an increase in US force levels, probably communicated a sense of *greater* American resolve and determination. Unfortunately, there is no indication that Bush ever seriously considered this option until after the 2006 elections, though many critics had been recommending it since mid-2003.

Where Was Rove?

Karl Rove was *not*, I should make clear, responsible for the mistakes and tragedies just recounted. The principal culprits in this story were Donald Rumsfeld, Paul Bremer, and, of course, George W. Bush, the man who hired Rumsfeld and Bremer and then failed to hold them accountable. Rumsfeld, in particular, is almost certainly the worst secretary of defense in American history. Rove's work and influence, as I have stressed in previous chapters, were generally limited to domestic policy.

By early 2005, however, the more appropriate question was: Why *wasn't* Rove involved? To repeat a point made earlier, I am not suggesting that Rove should have tried to become the de facto secretary of defense and devise a detailed new military/governing strategy for Iraq. But given Bush's isolation from news reports and general unwillingness to acknowledge mistakes, Rove *should* have been pushing Bush to recognize the crisis that was undermining his presidency. Formulating a solution for that crisis was not Rove's job, but shaking the president out of his isolation and complacency clearly should have been.

A good description of the role Rove should have played can be found, ironically, in Rove's own memoirs. In discussing the development of the new Iraq policy in the final months of 2006, Rove comments, "I didn't pretend to be Carl von Clausewitz or Henry Kissinger, but I knew the Iraq War wasn't going well, that the Bush presidency was in peril, and that unless we made changes, public support would crater. If that happened, we would lose not only Iraq but our ability to prevail against terrorism. I expressed these views to the president."[36]

Rove also used his reading of public opinion to urge Bush to widen his search for alternative policies:

[The Iraq strategy review conducted by National Security Advisor Stephen Hadley] was way out of my lane, but Bush and I did talk often about how to sustain political support for the war. I told him that as long as Americans were convinced the administration was committed to victory and our soldiers were not set up as targets on street corners for creative bomb makers, we would soon find enough support to sustain the effort. But we had to show progress. What was often lost in the analysis of public opinion and the war is that many of those who disapproved of Bush's handling of the war were not antiwar. Rather, many wanted to win and didn't think we were serious about it.[37]

All of this is entirely correct and appropriate—but why did Rove wait until late 2006 to tell Bush that his "presidency was in peril"? Had Rove pushed Bush to reevaluate his Iraq policy a year or two earlier, Bush's second term would have had a very different trajectory. In particular, Republican losses in the 2006 midterm elections would almost certainly have been a good deal smaller.

Had Rove really been looking out for his client's best interests, he might have gone even further and warned Bush in advance—*before going to war*—about the precautions he needed to take if he wanted to maintain popular support for both the war and his own presidency. As of 2002, when the Bush administration was gearing up for the war in Iraq, there were several major schools of thought about the types of factors that affected public support for an American military mission. The earliest important study of this issue—and still probably the most frequently cited—was an examination of public attitudes toward the wars in Korea and Vietnam published by political scientist John Mueller in the early 1970s. Analyzing a set of Gallup questions that had been asked repeatedly throughout both conflicts, Mueller showed that public support for both wars fell in direct proportion to the cumulative number of American casualties. As the total number of US soldiers who were killed or wounded went up, support for the wars went down.[38] Indeed, so strong was this relationship that Mueller's work was sometimes interpreted to mean that there was little presidents could do to maintain support for foreign military engagements except to limit the number of casualties.

In the 1990s, however, a number of international relations scholars began to take another look at this issue. After examining a considerably larger number of incidents than were available to Mueller,[39] many scholars concluded that the picture was a lot more complicated than he had acknowledged, that public opinion about American military interventions was influenced by more than just the number of US casualties. Among the factors singled out by this second wave of scholarship were the following:

- whether or not American vital interests were at stake;
- whether the intervention showed some reasonable prospect of success;
- the principal policy objective that the United States was seeking to accomplish—in particular, whether the American military was being used to restrain an aggressive foreign power or for humanitarian purposes, as opposed to effecting internal change in another country's government;
- whether American political and intellectual elites were united or divided in supporting the intervention; and
- whether the United States was acting alone in its use of military force or whether it had significant multilateral support, especially from the United Nations.[40]

In short, there are a number of things Rove might have pushed Bush to do in order to maintain public support for the Iraq war, such as making sure the United States had a better-planned exit strategy, being a little less high-handed in his treatment of world opinion, and avoiding any appearance of a protracted military stalemate. In fact, by early 2005 it was clear that Bush had stumbled into precisely the kind of conflict that *every one* of the viewpoints just listed would have urged him to avoid: a long war with steadily accumulating casualties, uncertain multilateral support, an increasingly sharp division between the major parties, and few obvious signs of progress.

There is no evidence I am aware of, however, to indicate that Rove warned Bush about the dangers of a poorly planned occupation or that he was an early internal critic of the administration's Iraq policy. In the many good books that have been written about the war in Iraq, Rove is a distinctly minor character (as, in general, he should have been).[41] He did play some role in the more explicitly political aspects of the war: deciding how to "market" the war to the public and convincing members of Congress to support it.[42] But he is only recorded as having made three interventions in the policy process—and in all three cases, he was on what may reasonably be described as the wrong side. In the lead-up to the war, Rove wrote a memo in which he predicted that the war would be a boon to the president's reelection campaign. (By early February 2004, he was already having second thoughts.)[43] And in both early 2005 and April 2006, Rove helped persuade Bush to retain Donald Rumsfeld as secretary of defense— a decision that effectively guaranteed that existing policies in Iraq would continue unchanged.[44]

Not until the second half of 2006 did George Bush seriously begin to entertain the idea that some kind of significant change in American policy toward Iraq might be necessary. Even then, it is difficult to say how far this reexamination would have proceeded had the 2006 elections not intervened. By the fall of that year, committees and study groups had been organized within the National Security Council (NSC), the State Department, and the Pentagon, all with the goal of conducting an "Iraq strategy review."[45] Bush himself, however, was notably uninvolved in these efforts, allowing them to go forward (when he even knew about them) but not actually participating in their deliberations or communicating any great sense of urgency. ("Did you give them [the Iraq strategy review team in the NSC] a deadline at this point?" Bob Woodward asked the president in a later interview. "I don't think I did," the president replied. "This is nothing that you hurry.")[46] The existence of these reviews, moreover, was a closely guarded secret—meaning, among other things, that no public expectations were raised and that it would therefore have been easier to end the process by concluding that no change in policy was needed. Finally, no major change was likely to take place as long as Donald Rumsfeld was secretary of defense—and just six days before election day, Bush told a group of reporters that he intended to keep Rumsfeld at the Pentagon until he left office in 2009.[47]

Visible indications of change, accompanied by a proper sense of urgency, came only after American voters had delivered what Bush himself called a "thumping" to the Republican Party, electing Democratic majorities to both the House and the Senate.[48] Just one day after the 2006 elections, Bush announced Rumsfeld's resignation. Of equal importance, Bush himself now took a considerably more active role in the Iraq strategy review and did begin to set some deadlines. And once involved, Bush performed quite creditably. He consulted widely with experts from both inside and outside the administration. He also showed considerably better judgment than those who advocated an immediate withdrawal of American forces or who thought that major progress could be achieved by negotiating with Iran and Syria.

Enter the Surge

The new Iraq strategy, formally known as the "New Way Forward" but more often called the "surge," was announced in a nationally televised address on January 10, 2007.[49] It had three major, interrelated components. First, Bush finally acknowledged (if only implicitly) that the United States had not sent enough troops for the original mission. Now, he pledged to send twenty thousand additional American troops to Iraq. Second, almost all of the top personnel responsible for devising and implementing US policy in Iraq were replaced. The most important changes were the sacking of Donald Rumsfeld (he was succeeded by Robert Gates) and the appointment of Lieutenant General David Petraeus, who had just rewritten the Army's manual on counterinsurgency, to become the commander of US forces in Iraq. Finally, there was a significant change in the strategy employed by the military, focused on an effort to provide greater security and improved services to the Iraqi population and thereby win greater support and cooperation from them.[50]

To say that the new strategy was successful is, in my opinion, a significant understatement. The surge, as we have seen, was announced in January 2007, but General Petraeus did not get to Iraq until February and the full complement of additional troops did not arrive until June. Yet as the data in table 7.1 indicate, a noticeable decline in American fatalities was already visible by the end of the year: October, November, and December 2007 saw the lowest number of fatalities of any three-month period since the war began. And the improvements continued through 2008, 2009, and 2010.

Table 7.2 shows one way of summarizing the new strategy's effect on three major indicators of the level of violence in Iraq: the number of American military fatalities, the number of Iraqi civilian fatalities, and the number of Iraqi police and military who were killed. As a measure of pre-surge violence, I have calculated the average number of fatalities that occurred per year from 2004 through 2006. To measure the level of post-surge violence, I have computed the average yearly number of fatalities for 2009 through 2011. As table 7.2 indicates, the "New Way Forward" brought about

- a 90 percent reduction in the number of American military fatalities
- a 76 percent reduction in the number of Iraqi civilian fatalities
- and a 76 percent reduction in the number of Iraqi police and military fatalities.

In many years of studying American politics, I know of few other cases in which a change in policy had such a clear, positive effect on the problem it was supposed to address.

Progress on the political and governmental front was, not unexpectedly, slower and more fitful. Yet progress did occur. A law passed by Congress in May 2007 established eighteen "benchmarks" to measure governmental success in Iraq. In September 2007, a study by the Government Accountability Office concluded that the Iraqi government had fully met three of the eighteen, partially met four, and not met eleven.[51] This record was widely criticized at the time,[52] but given the short time the new strategy had then been in effect, it might easily have been interpreted as a sign of progress. There was, in any event, evidence of continued improvement after that. In July 2008, two scholars at the Brookings Institution, using a different set of eleven benchmarks and a somewhat different scoring system, found substantial progress on three benchmarks and partial progress on five, yielding a score of 5.5 on an 11-point scale. By December 2008, in its last report issued during the Bush presidency, Brookings gave the Iraqi government a score of 7 (substantial progress in five areas, partial progress in four).[53]

So the surge, as even most Democrats came to recognize (though they rarely acknowledged it publicly), was a major success. Yet its very success only raises further questions about George W. Bush's leadership. Why didn't he send more troops in the first place? Why didn't he replace Rumsfeld sooner? And why didn't one of Bush's top advisors—Karl Rove, Andy Card, Condoleezza Rice—push him to reexamine his Iraq policy earlier, in 2004, say, rather than late 2006?

Conclusion

In chapters 4 and 5, I have criticized Karl Rove for some of the ways he did intervene in the policy process. Now I am criticizing him for not intervening soon enough. So is he damned if he does and damned if he doesn't? Am I holding him to an impossible standard?

One answer to these questions is that this is the nature of politics, which is preeminently a matter of balance and proportion. Operating without regard to politics is just as problematic as being overly political.

The war in Iraq, moreover, was not just one more in a long list of issues, events, and challenges that George W. Bush faced during his eight years in office. It was, in a real sense, the defining issue of the Bush presidency. Bush made many mistakes while in office, but if one is looking for the *one* issue that torpedoed Rove's hopes for a lasting era of Republican electoral dominance, it was the Iraq war and its aftermath. And if the person who was Bush's top political advisor did not warn him about the political conse-

Table 7.2. The Effect of the "New Way Forward" on Three Measures of Violence in Iraq

	2004–2006 yearly average	2009–2011 yearly average	Percentage increase or reduction
Number of US military fatalities	839	88	−90
Number of Iraqi civilian fatalities	19,282	4,570	−76
Number of Iraqi police and military fatalities	2,318*	562	−76

Sources: Calculated by the author from data drawn from the following sources: US military fatalities: Iraq Coalition Casualty Count, http://icasualties.org/Iraq/ByMonth.aspx (accessed October 19, 2012). Iraqi civilian fatalities: Iraq Body Count, https://www.iraqbodycount.org/database (accessed March 10, 2010). Iraqi police and military fatalities: Michael E. O'Hanlon and Ian Livingston, "Iraq Index: Tracking Variables of Reconstruction & Security in Iraq," July 2012, p. 4, http://www.brookings.edu/iraqindex.
*Figure for Iraqi police and military fatalities covers 2005 and 2006 only.

quences of the policy he was pursuing there, that it was putting his whole presidency "in peril," what point is there in having a political consultant as senior advisor to the president and (from 2004 to 2006) deputy chief of staff for policy?

George W. Bush being the sort of person he was, perhaps he would have ignored any advisor who tried to tell him before late 2006 that his policy in Iraq was seriously flawed, dismissing it as just the kind of "hand-wringing attitude" he said he didn't like. But in all the accounts of the war that I have examined, there is no indication that Rove even tried.

8

Never Forget That War Is a Political Endeavor

At some point shortly after 9/11, George Bush seems to have decided that, no matter how central a role politics played in the formulation of his domestic policies, it had no place in the war on terror. "Politics has no role" in the war against terrorism, he reportedly told his aides in early 2002. "Don't talk to me about politics for a while."[1] Bush seems to have reached this conclusion partly because of the seriousness of the issues involved, partly because he and many of his top advisors entertained a quite grandiose view of their place in history, a sense of Destiny that made them unwilling to be diverted from their course by public opinion or the objections of lesser mortals. Bush reached this decision on his own. So far as I can determine, Karl Rove made no attempt to challenge this perspective—Rove, after all, had his own lofty ambition to be the Architect of the Next Great Realignment. But even if Rove had tried to change Bush's mind, he might not have succeeded.

However the decision was made, I will argue in this chapter, it was a major mistake.

War as a Political Enterprise

As the previous chapter has shown, history will almost certainly regard George W. Bush as an exceedingly poor war president. The initial decision to go to war in Iraq may have been defensible, given the information then available to the president; the surge was clearly a very good decision. It is hard to say a positive word about almost everything else. In recent years, a number of good books have been written that have tried to identify the many specific duties and responsibilities that an effective war president needs to perform.[2] As one such work has concluded, "Bush mishandled nearly all of the tasks a wartime president faces."[3]

In this chapter, I wish to examine one particular war-related failing of the Bush presidency, which I single out because it is explicitly and unavoidably political in nature. In a democracy, a war president must be concerned about *sustaining political support for the war effort*.[4] Most wars do not end with the total destruction of one side's army and fighting capacity. More often, wars end because one of the combatants (or both) decides that the end no longer justifies the sacrifices in lives and money, or because one side concludes that it has no reasonable chance of winning. A president who hopes to bring a war to a successful conclusion must therefore make sure that there is enough support for the war—at both the elite and mass levels—to sustain the military effort. In the contemporary United States, presidents have assumed broad powers to declare and fight wars on their own initiative, and sometimes act as if they alone have the power to determine the country's military and defense policies, no matter what anyone else thinks. Yet even the most stubborn president eventually learns that an unpopular war can impose significant costs on his party's congressional candidates—and on its next presidential ticket. (Of the three recent presidents who are most associated with fighting an unpopular war—Harry Truman, Lyndon Johnson, and George W. Bush—all were succeeded by a president from the other party.) Lack of popular support can also retard US military efforts in a variety of other ways: by depriving the military of volunteers and raising the costs of conscription, for example, or by undermining military morale.

The fragile and uncertain nature of political support has been especially characteristic of the wars and battles the United States has fought since the end of World War II, only one of which—the war in Afghanistan that began in late 2001—came in response to a direct attack on American soil. In every other case, there was a less explicit, more tenuous connection between our military effort and our national security—and thus ample room to challenge its wisdom. Whether we were willing to continue fighting a war like the one that took place in Korea in the early 1950s depended on the answers to questions like: Were American national interests really threatened if North Korea took over South Korea? No doubt we would have preferred a noncommunist South Korea—but was it worth the cost of thirty-six thousand American lives? And how far should the war have been pursued? Was it enough to repel the North Korean invasion and restore South Korea to its prewar situation—or should we have tried to effect "regime change" in North Korea and thereby ensure that South Korean security would not be similarly threatened in the future? The president is, of course, not the only person charged with answering these sorts of questions. But given his role as our country's commander in chief and chief diplomat, and given the disproportionate media coverage the president invariably receives, his is surely the most important voice.

Carl von Clausewitz's *On War*, widely regarded as the best book ever written on the nature and conduct of war, is well known for the assertion that "war is not a mere act of policy but a true political instrument, a continuation of political activity by other means."[5] Most often, this statement has been interpreted to mean that a nation's political leadership must make sure that its military strategy is properly aligned with its foreign policy and diplomatic objectives (another thing Bush notably failed to do).[6] But it also means that political leaders must recognize the political roots of the war effort and ensure that the country is willing to continue supplying the resources needed to fight the war. Since Clausewitz has a notably obscure prose style, it is worth quoting a more straightforward statement of the same point, this from an early biography of Abraham Lincoln written by his two principal secretaries:

> Military writers love to fight over the campaigns of history exclusively by the rules of the professional chess-board, always subordinating, often totally ignoring, the element of politics. This is a radical error. Every war is begun, dominated, and ended by political considerations; without a nation, without a Government, without money or credit, without popular enthusiasm which furnishes volunteers, or public support which endures conscription, there could be no army and no war— neither beginning nor end of methodical hostilities. War and politics, campaign and statecraft, are Siamese twins, inseparable and interdependent; and to talk of military operations without the direction and interference of an administration is as absurd as to plan a campaign without recruits, pay, or rations.[7]

If the "war" in question involves only a brief military engagement, sustaining political support may not require a great deal of presidential attention and effort. When the United States sent troops into Grenada in 1983 and Panama in 1989, the fighting was pretty much over by the time the public and most members of Congress found out about it. The active combat phase of the 1991 war to liberate Kuwait lasted less than a month and a half. The Bush administration war planners initially assumed that the war in Iraq would be similarly short. By early 2004, however, it had become clear that there would be nothing quick and easy about the war in Iraq. Even if the fighting in Iraq had gone more smoothly, moreover, the Iraq war had always been presented as just one piece of a larger war on terrorism. As Bush himself said in a nationally televised speech delivered nine days after the attacks on the Pentagon and the World Trade Center:

Our war on terror begins with Al Qaida, but it does not end there. It will not end until every terrorist group of global reach has been found, stopped, and defeated. . . . This war will not be like the war against Iraq a decade ago, with a decisive liberation of territory and a swift conclusion. . . . *Americans should not expect one battle but a lengthy campaign, unlike any other we have ever seen.*[8]

Had Bush heeded his own warning, he would thus have fought the Iraq war with one eye on the future: After this war was concluded, would the country be willing to undertake the *next* major battle in the war on terrorism?

It seems to be a prominent characteristic of wars, moreover, that they never go exactly as planned, that they often develop in unexpected ways. This means that many of the policies and objectives that a president and other political leaders believe they have explained and justified will later need to be redefined or reargued. To take a quite famous example (which will be examined more fully in the next section), when the Civil War began, Abraham Lincoln always insisted that it was a war to preserve the Union, *not* a war to end slavery. Indeed, he said, he had neither the desire nor the legal power to end slavery in those states where it already existed. But once Lincoln decided to issue the Emancipation Proclamation— purportedly as an act of military necessity—emancipation and the Union war effort were inseparably tied together. Now, as Lincoln acknowledged in the Gettysburg Address, the war was somehow about the proposition that "all men were created equal," which it manifestly had not been when the war started.

The Lessons of History

To get a more tangible sense of how presidents can build and sustain support for a war, we should examine how this task was performed by our two greatest war presidents, Abraham Lincoln and Franklin Roosevelt.

ABRAHAM LINCOLN AND THE CIVIL WAR

Historians have long disagreed about how good Lincoln was as a military strategist.[9] What virtually no one contests, however, is his political genius. Given the North's advantages in population, resources, and industry, there was never any great chance that the South could prevail in an all-out war of attrition. The real question was whether the North would be willing to continue fighting until the South gave in or its armies were destroyed. That the North did persevere, in spite of enormous casualties, numerous early defeats, and protracted periods of stalemate, was largely due to Lincoln— and to accomplish that feat, he used every political resource and trick at his disposal.

When the Civil War began and the North started mobilizing its military resources, Lincoln insistently characterized his actions as an effort to *preserve the Union*. There is no mention in any of his early presidential speeches and letters of a need or desire to eliminate slavery. To the contrary, his inaugural address, delivered at a time when seven states had already seceded, included an explicit assurance that "I have no purpose, directly or indirectly, to interfere with the institution of slavery in the States where it exists. I believe I have no lawful right to do so, and I have no inclination to do so."[10] Why did Lincoln frame the issue this way? Probably he believed what he said, though as I have argued elsewhere, the arguments he made against secession and in defense of preserving the Union hold up rather poorly to close scrutiny.[11] The more telling point is that this was the only argument that showed promise of bringing the North into the war on a relatively united basis. As the eminent Civil War historian James McPherson has written, "The goal of preserving the Union united the Northern people, including border-state Unionists. The issue of slavery and emancipation divided them. To maintain maximum support for the war, Lincoln initially insisted that it was a war solely for preservation of the Union and not a war against slavery."[12]

Lincoln took several other early steps to build support for the Northern war effort. First, he contrived to have the war begin by having the South fire the first shot. He did this by deciding to send provisions, but not additional men or ammunition, to the embattled federal garrison at Fort Sumter, one of the few southern forts then still in the control of the national government. (He also sent a letter to the governor of South Carolina explicitly informing him of his intentions.) This allowed Lincoln—and the Northern press—to portray the South as the aggressor, trying to obstruct a mission that was clearly nonaggressive in nature. To quote McPherson again, "The attack on Fort Sumter united a previously divided Northern people more than they would ever be united again. War fever swept the free states."[13]

Lincoln also appointed a substantial number of what have often been called "political generals": generals who were given their commands not because of long prior service in the military but because they represented important political or ethnic groups. While some of these generals proved to be deficient as battlefield commanders, their appointment, especially in the early stages of the war, helped bring additional support to the Northern war effort. As Eliot Cohen has observed, "Politician-generals occasionally received patronage from Lincoln, but rarely without a reason. In many ways the Union resembled a coalition more than an integral state, and often in order to sustain support for the war the president had to turn to political representatives of important constituencies."[14] Lincoln made a special effort to appoint Democrats to important military positions and thus ensure that the Civil War could not be dismissed as a "Republican war." Lincoln also made ample use of patronage in nonmilitary federal departments, as a way of cementing support in Congress and from Republican governors, who were responsible for recruiting most of the Union troops. The adroit use of patronage also helped ensure Lincoln's own renomination in 1864.[15]

Lincoln's efforts notwithstanding, it soon became clear that the slavery issue was too important to be ignored or swept aside. On the one hand, the South derived an enormous advantage from having slaves do their farming and make their munitions, thus freeing large numbers of white men for military service. Lincoln also began to receive pressure from the Radicals within his own party to take a firmer stand against slavery and make at least some move toward ending it.

There was also an international dimension to consider. Throughout the early years of the war, one of Lincoln's recurrent worries concerned the possibility that the Confederacy would win recognition and assistance from one or more European governments, just as the new United States had received aid from France during the American Revolution. Great Britain seemed an especially good prospect for such help, since British textile mills relied heavily on Southern cotton and many British leaders looked with disfavor on the American experiment in republican government. Such a turn of events would have had an enormous impact on the war's probable outcome. "If the South has now secured the alliance of England," historian and diplomat John Lothrop Motley informed one correspondent in late 1861, "a restoration of the Union becomes hopeless."[16] Many Northerners and Union sympathizers, however, believed that emancipation would make European governments less likely to intervene on behalf of the South, by adding an important moral dimension to what otherwise could be portrayed as a simple exercise in power politics. As a delegation of Chicago ministers told Lincoln in September 1862, "To proclaim emancipation would secure the sympathy of Europe and the whole civilized world, which now saw no other reason for the strife [i.e., the Civil War] than national pride and ambition, an unwillingness to abridge our domain and power. No other step would be so potent to prevent foreign intervention."[17]

The Emancipation Proclamation that Lincoln finally issued on the first day of 1863 was a masterpiece of political legerdemain. Knowing that many in the North were not yet prepared to embrace the antislavery cause, Lincoln famously couched the proclamation as an act of "military necessity." Nowhere in the text does he suggest that slavery was evil and inhumane. Indeed, as has often been noted, the proclamation was written in a deliberately dry, matter-of-fact style, with none of the soaring rhetoric one finds in all of Lincoln's other great state papers. In order to retain the support of three major slave states that had *not* seceded (Missouri, Maryland, and Kentucky), the proclamation applied only to those states that were "in rebellion against the United States."[18] Finally, Lincoln heeded the advice of Secretary of State William Seward and delayed issuing the proclamation until it could be "supported by military success." Otherwise, it would be perceived as "the last measure of an exhausted government, a cry for help."[19]

Like most of Lincoln's political gambits, emancipation worked—brilliantly. On the one hand, there is plentiful evidence that the proclamation really did aid the Northern war effort, just as Lincoln had promised it would. After the war was over and Secretary of War Edwin Stanton was trying to explain the causes of the Union victory, the first item on his list was:

> The steadfast adherence of the President to the measures of emancipating the slaves in the rebel States. . . . The hopes of freedom, kindled by the Emancipation Proclamation, paralyzed the industrial power of the rebellion. Slaves seized their chances to escape, discontent and distrust were engendered, the hopes of the slave and the fears of the master . . . shook each day more and more the fabric built on human slavery.[20]

At the same time, Radicals and abolitionists understood that whatever rhetorical genuflections Lincoln was making to the preserve-the-Union crowd, they were getting most of the substance they wanted. The proclamation effectively signaled the end of slavery in America. Many Northern whites opposed the measure, just as Lincoln had been warned, but not enough to cause dissension in the military or to precipitate any new state secessions. Finally, though the preliminary proclamation that Lincoln released in September 1862 sparked some unfavorable comment from British leaders, the actual proclamation "gradually became the [British] government's principal rationale for *not* intervening."[21] Henry Adams, writing from London in late January 1863, summed up the British reaction:

The Emancipation Proclamation has done more for us here than all our former victories and all our diplomacy. It is creating an almost convulsive reaction in our favor [i.e., the Union's favor] all over this country. . . . [P]ublic opinion is very deeply stirred here and finds expression in meetings, addresses to President Lincoln, deputations to us, standing committees to agitate the subject and to affect opinion, and all the other symptoms of a great popular movement.[22]

Throughout the Civil War, Lincoln took seriously the need to educate, persuade, and mobilize public opinion. Though he gave very few formal speeches during his time in the White House—not until the early twentieth century did presidential speech-making become a common way of selling the president's program—Lincoln communicated his ideas in numerous other ways. One of Lincoln's favorite vehicles was the so-called public letter: an ostensibly private communication, usually sent to a public official or newspaper editor, that, Lincoln knew, would be widely published in contemporary newspapers. In the eight months after issuing the Emancipation Proclamation, for example, Lincoln wrote four public letters in which he attempted to explain and justify his decision.[23] A significant number of newspapers could also be counted upon to reprint in their entirety Lincoln's major proclamations and messages to Congress, which would presumably then be read by a sizable proportion of the literate and politically active citizenry.

But as Lincoln scholars have recently started to appreciate, his formal statements and letters are only the tip of the iceberg.[24] From quite early in his political career, Lincoln had always made a great effort to cultivate the notice and favor of the press: meeting with editors and reporters when he visited the many cities and small towns in Illinois and surrounding states, and going to news offices to make sure his speeches had been accurately transcribed and typeset. In 1859, he actually became the principal owner of a German-language newspaper in Illinois, a paper that, needless to say, devoted much of its column space to promoting both the Republican Party and Lincoln's own career.[25] As president, Lincoln held no formal press conferences, an innovation that would not develop until the early twentieth century, but he did meet with reporters and editors individually on a regular basis. He also attempted to influence the tenor of his press coverage in ways that, if practiced today, would widely be regarded as improper or even scandalous. John Hay, one of Lincoln's private secretaries, wrote anonymous articles for various Northern newspapers. In 1864, in an effort to win the support of the *New York Herald*, one of the most widely read and influential papers in the country, Lincoln offered what was essentially a bribe: he promised to make its owner-editor the next US minister to France.

It would be easy to criticize many of the actions, statements, and positions just recounted as being "wrong on the merits" or as "temporizing with evil." But it was precisely these sorts of decisions that allowed Lincoln to hold together an uncertain, unwieldy coalition long enough both to win the war *and* to end slavery. A lesser politician might have kept his conscience clean, won the whole-hearted approval of Radical Republicans (and most twenty-first century historians)—and lost the war in the process.

FRANKLIN D. ROOSEVELT AND WORLD WAR II

Compared to Lincoln, Franklin Roosevelt had a far easier time maintaining support for World War II. The Japanese attack on Pearl Harbor saw to that. Roosevelt's political skills were put to their greatest test in the twenty-six months before the United States declared war on Japan, Germany, and Italy. From September 1939 to December 1941,[26] Roosevelt faced a very difficult political quandary: how to provide desperately needed aid to Great Britain (and before May 1940, France) at a time when a large part of the American population was still strongly isolationist and determined not to get involved in another European war. FDR met this challenge through a series of actions, many of which required congressional approval, that were carefully calibrated to provide as much assistance as the current state of congressional and public opinion would allow, without having the United States become an active participant in the fighting. Major steps along this path included:[27]

- The Neutrality Act of (November) 1939, which repealed the embargo on selling arms to belligerent nations and thus permitted the United States to supply Britain and France with arms and munitions.
- FDR's creative redefinition of the "Western Hemisphere," which established an American defensive zone up to three hundred miles from the eastern coast of the United States and authorized US "patrols" (though not convoys) throughout this area. In April 1941, the US defensive perimeter was pushed out to twenty-five degrees west longitude, about halfway in between the eastern border of Greenland and the western coast of Africa.
- The September 1940 decision to transfer fifty destroyers to Britain in return for the right to establish US military bases on various British possessions in the Western Hemisphere.

- The Lend-Lease Act of March 1941, which allowed the United States to lend or lease military equipment to "any country whose defense the President deems vital to the defense of the United States," without requiring immediate cash payment.
- The extension of US military assistance to the Soviet Union after that country was invaded by Nazi Germany in June 1941.
- The renewal of the Selective Service Act in August 1941, which passed by just a single vote in the House of Representatives. The new law extended the term of service for previous draftees by eighteen months.
- FDR's announcement in a September 1941 fireside chat that the United States would "protect all merchant ships—not only American ships but ships of any flag—engaged in commerce in our defensive waters"—that is, anywhere in the Atlantic Ocean west of twenty-five degrees west longitude. In the same speech, Roosevelt established what has often been described as a "shoot on sight" policy (though FDR never actually used those words) toward any "German or Italian vessels of war" found in American defensive waters.[28]
- A final set of revisions to the neutrality acts, passed in November 1941, that permitted the arming of US merchant vessels and repealed virtually all of the remaining restrictions on American commerce with belligerent nations.

To accomplish all this required political dexterity of a high order: a fine feel for what Congress would and would not approve and a willingness to settle for less when he had to; an ability to lead and shape public opinion without getting too far out in front of it; and the creativity that allowed him to find innovative ways to assist the British. And while all this was taking place, FDR also managed to get himself elected to an unprecedented third term as president. While no one can say for certain what would have transpired in Europe if a less politically skillful person had been in the White House during this period, Britain would certainly have had a far more difficult time surviving the Nazi onslaught.

Though FDR was widely denounced by the isolationists of his own time, present-day historians are more likely to criticize him from the opposite perspective: for not moving fast enough to assist Britain and restrict trade with Japan, for not getting into the war sooner. Roosevelt, these critics claim, significantly overestimated the extent of American isolationism, which by the early 1940s was a minority viewpoint, and was thus reluctant to challenge it more aggressively. At least some members of Roosevelt's administration shared this view:

[Secretary of War Henry] Stimson, [Secretary of the Navy Frank] Knox, and a great many others were very sure that Roosevelt . . . overestimated greatly the strength of isolationist sentiment in general. Most of such strength as isolationism had was due to Roosevelt's obviously fearful respect for it, they said. He conceded far more than was necessary in his public speech, blurring issues that should be sharply defined . . . and through the cloud of doubt and confusion thus raised in the public mind, isolationism loomed a far larger phenomenon than it actually was. The illusion would be instantly dissipated, reality would be revealed in the clear light of frank and honest discourse, if ever the President again performed his sacred duty *to lead*.[29]

I disagree. While contemporary poll results can be cited showing substantial anxiety about events in Europe and some willingness to aid Britain and France, these surveys also show that there were distinct limits on what Americans were willing to do in support of their concerns. It should also be noted that Roosevelt, as compared to more recent presidents in both parties, took a much more restrictive view of presidential war powers, that is, of the kinds of actions a president could undertake on his own initiative. Much of what he wanted to do, he and virtually everyone else at that time believed, required the consent of Congress, and there is ample evidence that Roosevelt did *not* overestimate the level of congressional isolationism.

A good example of the constraints Roosevelt faced as he maneuvered to support France, Great Britain, and later the Soviet Union came in mid-1941, when his administration sought to make two amendments to the Selective Service Act that Congress had passed one year earlier. The first amendment would have removed a provision in the original legislation which said that draftees could not serve outside the Western Hemisphere. The second amendment would have extended the term of service for draftees. Under the original law, draftees were only required to serve one year— which meant that all those who entered the army in 1940, having received a full year of training, would soon be discharged and replaced by a new cohort of raw recruits. Such a development, Army Chief of Staff George Marshall told Congress, would have a "disastrous effect" on the American military.[30]

During the summer of 1941, the Gallup Poll asked specific, well-worded questions about both of these amendments; and just five months before Pearl Harbor, with the Nazis controlling most of Western Europe and apparently on the verge of adding the Soviet Union to their list of conquests, the polls showed nothing like overwhelming support for either proposal. Asked whether Congress should "change the law which says drafted men cannot be sent to fight outside of North or South America," the results were 40 percent "yes," 52 percent "no." Should "drafted men . . . be released at the end of one year, or should they be kept in active service for longer than one year?" A bare 51 percent favored longer terms; 45 percent wanted draft service to last just one year.[31]

And at least in this instance, Congress seems to have reflected public opinion quite faithfully. Meeting with Democratic congressional leaders in July, FDR was flatly informed that Congress would never approve an amendment that permitted draftees to be stationed outside the Western Hemisphere. So that proposal was dropped. As for the amendment that lengthened the draftees' term of service, after a good deal of debate it passed the Senate rather comfortably (the vote was 45–30), but just barely squeaked through the House of Representatives, 203–202.

As a result of the attack on Pearl Harbor, the United States entered World War II with a level of national unity and support for the war that has probably never been equaled. The vote to declare war on Japan was 82–0 in the Senate, 388–1 in the House. On the other hand, Roosevelt faced a number of political challenges that Lincoln never had to contend with: coordinating strategy with foreign allies; providing aid to a country, the Soviet Union, that most Americans viewed as evil and untrustworthy; treating Germany as the most serious threat to American security (both Roosevelt and Churchill felt this way) even though the United States had been attacked by Japan.

In any event, Roosevelt never took popular support for granted, instead taking numerous steps to make sure that it continued. Well before Pearl Harbor, he had tried to encourage bipartisan support for a military build-up and a more internationalist foreign policy by bringing two prominent Republicans into his cabinet: Henry Stimson as secretary of war and Frank Knox as secretary of the navy. (Stimson had been Hoover's secretary of state; Knox was the Republican vice-presidential candidate in 1936.) Knowing that it would take a long time for the United States to mobilize its full resources, Roosevelt pushed his top military advisors to make some early attempts to engage in offensive warfare against Japan and Germany, so that Americans would not grow dissatisfied with the apparent lack of progress. It was primarily for this reason that FDR supported both the bombing raid on Tokyo led by Jimmy Doolittle in April 1942 and the American invasion of North Africa in November 1942. Though neither action was militarily significant, both probably helped to maintain the American public's interest in and commitment to the war effort. In Joseph Persico's words, Roosevelt "could now exclaim, 'We're striking back.'"[32] FDR also made a commendable effort to assure the nation that the burdens of the war effort were being equitably distributed—and that those doing the fighting would be appropriately taken care of when they returned. His signature achievement in this area was, of course, the passage of the GI Bill of Rights, one of the most effective and widely applauded pieces of social legislation in American history.

Like Lincoln, Roosevelt also devoted a good deal of time and effort to educating and persuading public opinion. Taking advantage of the still relatively new medium of radio, FDR delivered five nationally broadcast "fireside chats" on the growing crisis in Europe between September 1939 and September 1941, gave another one two days after Pearl Harbor, and then delivered twelve more fireside chats between February 1942 and January 1945, all devoted to the progress of the war effort, conditions and developments on the home front, and what ordinary Americans could do to support the military.[33] Roosevelt also held 208 press conferences between America's entry into the war and his death in April 1945—more than one every six days.

How well did Roosevelt succeed in maintaining popular support for World War II? Unlike Lincoln and the Civil War, in Roosevelt's case we have data from public opinion polls to help answer this question. These data are far from ideal, survey research then being in its infancy, but they are sufficient to show both the overwhelming support for the US war effort and, more importantly, that this support showed no signs of flagging as the war continued.

The first item in table 8.1, taken from the Gallup Poll, is one of the few questions that was asked repeatedly—that is, with the same wording— over a substantial part of the early war period. The question asked respondents how they would react to a hypothetical peace proposal from Adolf Hitler that would have "offered peace to all countries on the basis of not going farther, but of leaving matters as they are now." In other words, this question marked out those who were so opposed to the war that they were willing to accept "peace at any price." When this question was first asked, in late December 1941, the American public decisively rejected any suggestion of a peace that left Germany in possession of its previous conquests: just 10 percent favored peace under such conditions, 87 percent opposed it. More noteworthy is the finding that public opinion on this issue didn't change over the next year and a half. In August 1943, after seventy thousand Americans had been killed or wounded, 8 percent favored a peace that left "matters as they are now," 89 percent were opposed.

On five occasions between January 1944 and March 1945, the Office of Public Opinion Research asked a question about a peace proposal that was less obviously favorable to Germany: "If Hitler offered to discuss peace now, should the Allies accept this offer and discuss peace terms with Hitler?" (table 8.1, item 2). Though this question didn't commit the Allies to anything except *discussing* peace terms with Hitler, it surely implied, at the very least, a willingness to end the war at some point short of the "unconditional surrender" goal to which Roosevelt and Churchill had committed their countries in January 1943. Only about 15 percent of the American public favored peace under such circumstances, a number that may have increased very slightly in the months before the Normandy invasion but was otherwise unaffected by contemporaneous military developments. The final item in table 8.1 asked specifically about unconditional surrender, and found that in both February 1944 and February 1945, about 80 percent of Americans wanted to continue fighting until that objective was achieved.

In sum, American support not only started out at a high level, it stayed that way to the end of the war.

Maintaining Support for the War in Iraq

How well did George W. Bush fulfill his responsibility to sustain political support for the war in Iraq? By most measures, he got off to a reasonably good start. In surveys by five different polling organizations conducted in the two weeks immediately before the war began on March 19, 2003, about two-thirds of the American public supported US military action (see table 8.2). The Gallup Poll, for example, found that 64 percent of its respondents favored "invading Iraq with U.S. ground troops in an attempt to remove Saddam Hussein." In a PSRA poll for *Newsweek*, 70 percent supported "using military force against Saddam Hussein and his military in Iraq." The public also expressed general approval of the process by which the Bush administration had brought the country to war. Two days before the onset of hostilities, 68 percent of the public told Gallup interviewers that "the United States [had] done all it [could] to solve the crisis with Iraq diplomatically." On the same day, 72 percent of an ABC News/*Washington Post* sample said that "the Bush administration [had] done enough to try to win support from other countries." In a PSRA survey conducted on March 27–28, 63 percent said that "the United States should have begun military action against Iraq when it did," versus 32 percent who said it "should have waited longer to try to achieve its goals in Iraq diplomatically." In a CBS News poll on March 17, just 32 percent thought "Bush should have waited for specific United Nations approval of military action."

Perhaps because they had read the polling data, both houses of Con-

Table 8.1. Public Support for Continued Fighting in World War II

1. GALLUP: "If Hitler offered peace now to all countries on the basis of not going farther, but of leaving matters as they are now, would you favor or oppose such a peace?"

Survey date	Favor	Oppose	No opinion	(N)
Dec. 20–25, 1941	10	87	4	(1,500)
Feb. 5–11, 1942	8	88	4	(1,500)
May 23–28, 1942	6	91	2	(1,500)
Jan. 29–Feb. 3, 1943	4	92	4	(1,500)
Aug. 19–24, 1943	8	89	3	(1,500)

Note: Sample sizes are approximate.

2. OPOR: "If Hitler offered to discuss peace now, should the Allies accept this offer and discuss peace terms with Hitler?"

Survey date	Yes	No	No opinion	(N)
January 1944	16	78	6	(1,269)
March 1944	22	73	4	(1,264)
April 1944	19	77	5	(1,289)
June 1944	16	80	4	(552)
August 1944	15	82	3	(1,258)
March 1945	15	80	5	(1,263)

Note: Specific sampling dates for these polls have not been reported.

3. NORC/OPOR: "Do you think we should demand an unconditional surrender from Germany before we stop fighting, or not?

Survey date	Yes	No	No opinion	(N)
NORC: Feb. 1944	81	10	9	(2,532)
OPOR: Feb. 1945	83	13	4	(802)

gress also voted solidly in favor of the resolution authorizing the war. In the House, the vote was 297–133; in the Senate, 77–23. At a time when American politics is invariably described as highly polarized, what is particularly striking is the level of Democratic support for the war: 39 percent of House Democrats and 58 percent of Democratic senators voted for war. And it wasn't just southern Democrats or those facing a tough reelection contest who voted for regime change in Iraq. Particularly in the Senate, the prowar contingent was pretty much a Who's Who of current and future Democratic party leaders, including Hillary Clinton, John Kerry, Tom Daschle, Joe Biden, Harry Reid, and Chuck Schumer.

To track the state of public opinion after the war began, figures 8.1 to 8.4 show the trend in four survey questions that were asked repeatedly between mid-March 2003 and the end of the Bush presidency in January

2009. The questions employed a variety of wordings: one asked if the war was a "mistake"; another asked if the war was "worth it"; a third simply asked respondents if they favored or opposed the war. All can be regarded as fair and reasonable measures of how the American public evaluated the US military action in Iraq.

All four questions show that the war began with strong public support. In every case, about 70 percent of the public chose the prowar answer. That level of support held up, moreover, throughout the period of "major combat operations" that ended with the fall of Baghdad on April 10. Unfortunately, as we have seen in the previous chapter, the end of major combat operations did not bring an end to the fighting—or to American casualties. To the contrary, 347 more Americans died between May 1 and December 31, 2003, followed by 849 US military fatalities in 2004, 846 in 2005, and 823 in 2006. To make matters worse—a lot worse—the principal justification for the war had collapsed. The claim that Saddam Hussein's Iraq possessed an ample store of weapons of mass destruction that it might use against the United States or pass on to terrorists was not the only argument the Bush administration had made during the lead-up to the war—but by any reasonable measure it was the most salient and important argument. By January 2004, the team charged with the search for these weapons had concluded that there were none to be found.

The result, as figures 8.1 to 8.4 demonstrate, was that support for the war began a long, slow, but ultimately quite large decline. To take just one example: the number of Americans who told the Gallup Poll that they "favor[ed] the U.S. war in Iraq" fell from about 70 percent when the war began, to 54 percent in late 2003, to 40 percent in early 2006, to about 30 percent in the summer of 2008. Where supporters of the war had once outnumbered opponents by about three to one, for the last two years of the Bush presidency opponents outnumbered supporters by two to one.

That the war in Iraq became progressively more unpopular will come as no surprise to anyone who lived through the Bush presidency. What received less attention at the time was the effect of the "New Way Forward"—the surge—on American public opinion. As I have shown in chapter 7, the surge had a transformative effect on the level of violence and casualties in Iraq. But the surge came too late to have much impact on public attitudes. After three thousand US military fatalities, most of the public had already concluded that the Iraq war was a bad mistake. According to all four of the questions in figures 8.1 to 8.4 (and many other questions whose results I have not reported), the surge largely halted the increase in opposition to the war, but *did not reverse it*. Table 8.3 makes this point more clearly by showing, for all four questions, the average result for the three final polls

Table 8.2. Public Support for Military Action in Iraq Just before the Beginning of the War

	Pro-war response	Anti-war response
ABC News, March 5–9, 2003: "Would you favor or oppose having U.S. forces take military action against Iraq to force Saddam Hussein from power?"	65	30
GALLUP: March 14–15, 2003: "Would you favor or oppose invading Iraq with U.S. ground troops in an attempt to remove Saddam Hussein from power?"	64	33
CBS News, March 15–16, 2003: "Do you approve or disapprove of the United States taking military action against Iraq to try and remove Saddam Hussein from power?"	67	29
Fox News/Opinion Dynamics, March 11–12, 2003: "Do you support or oppose U.S. military action to disarm Iraq and remove Iraqi President Saddam Hussein?"	71	20
PSRA/*Newsweek*: March 13–14, 2003: "In the fight against terrorism, the Bush administration has talked about using military force against Saddam Hussein and his military in Iraq. Would you support using military force against Iraq, or not?"	70	24

Note: The war in Iraq began on March 19, 2003.

conducted in 2006, just before the surge was announced, and the three final polls in 2008, after the surge had brought about a significant decline in both American and Iraqi casualties. One of the Gallup questions shows no change between 2006 and 2008; the other three show a continued, albeit small, drop in public support—about 3 to 5 percentage points.

What might the Bush administration have done to maintain support for the war in Iraq? The first imperative was to recognize the difficult position they were in by early 2004. As we have seen in the previous chapter, Americans are generally quite willing to support a war when they see a definite link between the fighting and our own national security. Once it was clear that Iraq did not have an active WMD program, however, that link became a great deal more tenuous. Other justifications for the war could be given, but none was likely to have the strong, visceral appeal provided by the threat of chemical, biological, or nuclear weapons. In particular, there was little reason to think that Americans would be willing to endure significant US casualties in order to pursue an exercise in nation building—which, whether Bush was willing to admit it or not, was exactly what the United States was by then pursuing in Iraq.

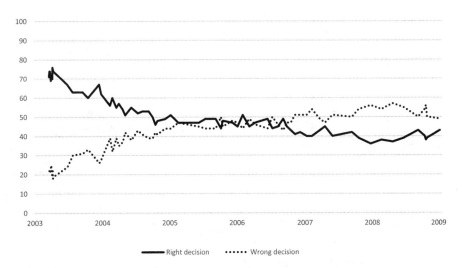

Right decision ••••••Wrong decision

Figure 8.1. Right or Wong Decision to Go to War in Iraq? Question wording was: "Do you think the U.S. made the right decision or the wrong decision in using military force against Iraq?" *Source*: Princeton Survey Research Associates.

All of which should have sent a clear signal that the American public's patience with the war was likely to be quite limited. Urging Americans to "stay the course" and tolerate three successive years in which more than eight hundred Americans were killed was not a winning strategy. Like Abraham Lincoln in the first years of the Civil War, George W. Bush needed to be more impatient, to goad Rumsfeld and his top advisors to make a quicker and more vigorous effort to reduce the level of violence in Iraq. And if Rumsfeld failed to deliver—as he plainly did—Bush should have fired him, just as Lincoln did with his first six commanders of the Army of the Potomac.

Second, Bush needed to do a better job communicating with the American public. Bush took the communication function seriously during the lead-up to the war, giving a series of major speeches on the threat posed by Iraq and getting many top members of his administration to do likewise. As I will show in the next chapter, however, Bush and his advisors apparently saw little reason to keep explaining and justifying the war after the end of so-called major combat operations. They were particularly poor at responding to the charge that Bush had deliberately exaggerated the state of Iraq's weapons of mass destruction program and thereby "lied the nation into war."

As I will also emphasize in the next chapter, however, the Bush high command needed to be realistic about what a good public education campaign could accomplish. From mid-2003 to late 2006, the administration regularly issued statements claiming that "progress" was being made in

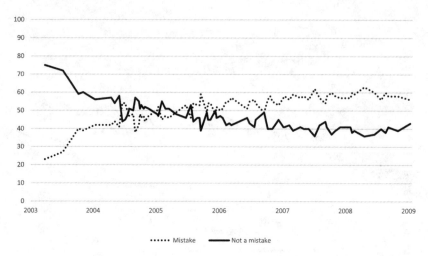

Figure 8.2. Was It a Mistake to Send Troops to Iraq? Question wording was: "In view of developments since we first sent our troops to Iraq, do you think the United States made a mistake in sending troops to Iraq, or not?" *Source*: Gallup Poll.

Iraq.[34] But this message, no matter how often and effectively it was trumpeted, would be of little value if US casualty figures continued their long, steady increase. An effective communications campaign must have some substantial basis in reality. One reason the Tet Offensive had such a pronounced effect on American public opinion about the war in Vietnam is that it had been preceded by a major public relations campaign, dubbed

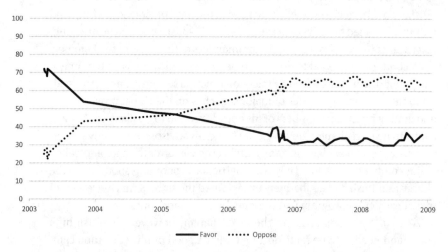

Figure 8.3. Favor or Oppose War in Iraq? Question wording was: "Do you favor or oppose the U.S. war in Iraq?" *Source*: Gallup Poll/ORC.

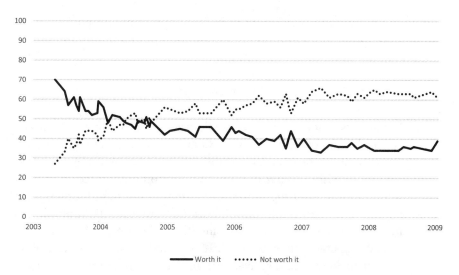

Figure 8.4. Was the War in Iraq Worth Fighting? Question wording was: "All in all, considering the costs to the United States versus the benefits to the United States, do you think the war with Iraq was worth fighting, or not?" *Source*: ABC/*Washington Post*.

Table 8.3. Effect of the Surge on Support for the War in Iraq

	PRE-SURGE Last three polls of 2006	POST-SURGE Last three polls of 2008
1. PSRA: Did the U.S. make the right or wrong decision in using military force against Iraq?		
Right decision	42	39
Wrong decision	50	53
2. GALLUP: Did the U.S. make a mistake in sending troops to Iraq?		
Yes, mistake	55	59
No, not a mistake	42	39
3. CNN/ORC: Favor or oppose the war in Iraq?		
Favor	32	34
Oppose	64	64
4. ABC/*Washington Post*: Considering the costs and benefits to the United States, was the war in Iraq worth fighting?		
Yes, worth fighting	40	35
No, not worth fighting	57	63

the "Success Offensive," that was designed to convince the public that the United States was finally on the verge of winning that war.[35]

Seeking Congressional Involvement

Finally, Bush should have borrowed a page from Lincoln and Roosevelt and made a greater effort to involve Congress, especially the Democrats in Congress, in the planning and execution of the war. In fact, Bush did exactly the opposite. Even in cases where he almost certainly could have received congressional approval, Bush was determined to go it alone. Three important hallmarks of the war against terrorism were initially established by presidential fiat: the military commissions that were to be used to try enemy combatants; the surveillance of communications between people in the United States and suspected foreign terrorists without a court order; and the rules governing the interrogation of suspected terrorists and other people in US custody.[36]

By all accounts, the principal mover behind this approach was Vice President Cheney, though Bush was apparently quite sympathetic to the idea. Having served as chief of staff for President Gerald Ford at the height of the congressional reaction against Vietnam and Watergate, Cheney came away convinced that the presidency had been seriously weakened and that there was a desperate need to restore the power and authority of the executive branch.[37] I think Cheney was wrong on the merits. The so-called congressional resurgence of the 1970s went much less far than its proponents had hoped, and the presidents after Ford gradually reclaimed whatever ground had been lost.[38] Cheney's views on presidential power are also difficult to square with the kind of originalist interpretation of the Constitution that Cheney and Bush claimed to support in other areas of government policy and procedure.

In keeping with the overall theme of this book, however, what I wish to emphasize for the moment are the *political* problems connected with Bush's unilateralist approach. It is unclear if the best way to restore presidential powers is to have a president simply assert them without obvious congressional authorization or judicial sanction. What seems more certain is that a president who devises and implements a policy entirely on his own initiative leaves himself in a very exposed political position. If the public reacts unfavorably to the commissions or the surveillance, if "enhanced interrogation" leads to brutal treatment of prisoners, the president has no one to share the blame with. There was also the danger that if the war on terrorism did not end with the Bush presidency—and Bush himself had told Americans to expect a "lengthy campaign"—the next president might reverse or decline to follow through on many of Bush's policies, especially if that next president came from the other party.

There may be instances where a president believes that an issue is sufficiently important and the legal and constitutional warrant sufficiently strong to allow him to act on his own initiative, in the absence of congressional sanction or even in opposition to Congress's expressed preferences. But this should be the method of last resort—not the preferred alternative, as it so often was during the Bush presidency. What Justice Jackson said with reference to the president's legal authority is also, in general, true with respect to his political power: it is at its maximum when he "acts pursuant to an express or implied authorization of Congress."[39]

The exception that proves the rule—the most conspicuous case where Bush *did* seek explicit congressional approval—was the initial decision to commence war against Saddam Hussein. Like all other recent presidents, Bush claimed to have the authority to use military force without congressional permission. And at least some administration officials were concerned that asking for a congressional vote of support would appear to undermine this claim. As one official told the *Washington Post*, "We don't want to be in the legal position of asking Congress to authorize the use of force when the president already has that full authority. We don't want, in getting a resolution, to have conceded that one was constitutionally necessary." But others argued that "while there is not a legal necessity to seek [a vote from Congress], as a matter of statesmanship and politics and practicality, it's necessary—or at a minimum, strongly advisable—to do it."[40]

The latter view eventually prevailed. In early September 2002, Bush announced that his administration would "fully participate in any hearings that the Congress wishes to have on this subject [the threat posed by Saddam Hussein]" and that he would "go to Congress to seek approval" for whatever was "necessary to deal with the threat." (At the same time, he refused to say that he was granting Congress a "veto" over his Iraq policy.)[41] About five weeks later, Congress dutifully fell in line, as both the House and the Senate voted, by wide margins, to give Bush a free hand to use the armed forces in any way he deemed "necessary and appropriate" to "defend the national security of the United States against the continuing threat posed by Iraq."

The decision to seek congressional approval, even in such qualified form, paid major political dividends for the Bush administration. In the short term, it helped assuage the concerns of those who worried that the country was rushing into war, or who felt that the president alone should not be making such a fateful decision. As one survey analyst has noted,

"Strong majorities of Americans wanted Congress involved in the decision to go to war [in Iraq]. The polls were unanimous on this point."[42]

The congressional vote also assisted Bush during the 2004 presidential campaign. By the fall of that year, the war in Iraq had become the strongest counterargument to Bush's claim that he was the candidate best qualified to fight an effective war against terrorism. In two Gallup polls conducted in September and October 2004, the American public strongly endorsed the way Bush was "handling terrorism," with 60 percent on average approving and 38 percent disapproving. Asked about his handling of the "situation in Iraq," however, the public gave the president a negative grade: 47 percent approved, 50 percent disapproved.[43] Against that background, Democratic presidential nominee John Kerry would no doubt have preferred to run the kind of campaign that Barack Obama would wage in 2008: criticizing the war in Iraq as a catastrophic decision while complaining that Bush was neglecting the more important fight in Afghanistan. There was, however, one huge problem with this strategy: Kerry had voted *for* the resolution authorizing the Iraq war. The result was that he spent most of the general election campaign flailing about for a defensible position, sometimes claiming that the war was a great mistake, while at other times insisting that Saddam Hussein had been a serious threat and that his vote to authorize the war had been the correct one. In three National Annenberg Election Surveys conducted in the fall of 2004, most Americans doubted that George W. Bush had a "clear plan for bringing the situation in Iraq to a successful conclusion": 38 percent said he did, 55 percent said he didn't. But the public was even more skeptical that Kerry had a sure sense of direction: just 29 percent were convinced that he had a clear plan for Iraq, 58 percent thought he lacked one.[44]

If Bush had tried to seek congressional authorization for various aspects of the war on terror, would he have received it? Was this, in other words, a case where good politics conflicted with good public policy? Actually, as subsequent events would prove, Congress, including sizable numbers of congressional Democrats, would probably have granted the president virtually everything he tried to do without their authorization.

A good example of this type of outcome involved the procedures used to try enemy combatants who had been captured by the American military. The story begins on November 13, 2001, barely two months after the attacks on the Pentagon and World Trade Center, when President Bush issued a military order on the "Detention, Treatment, and Trial of Certain Non-Citizens in the War against Terrorism." In it, Bush declared that any non-citizen whom he determined was a member of al-Qaeda or had engaged in or abetted an act of terrorism would be tried by a military commission to be established by the secretary of defense, and that such trials could not be appealed to any US court.[45] In a subsequent order issued in March 2002, Secretary Rumsfeld laid out detailed ground rules for the structure and operation of these commissions. Among the most controversial items in this order was a provision that allowed the presiding judge to exclude the accused and his civilian counsel from hearing or even learning about evidence if the judge believed that giving them access to that evidence would compromise classified information, intelligence sources and methods, or other national security interests. In other words, the accused might never have the chance to become aware of, much less refute, some of the witnesses or other types of evidence that could be used to convict him. The commissions were also allowed to admit any evidence that "would have probative value to a reasonable person," including evidence obtained through so-called enhanced interrogation techniques.[46]

In June 2006, however, in a case called *Hamdan v. Rumsfeld*, the Supreme Court ruled that Bush lacked the legal authority to establish such commissions on his own initiative. The court also held that military commissions were bound by the requirements of the Geneva Conventions—in particular, by a provision that any adjudicatory system must provide defendants with "all the judicial guarantees [i.e., procedural rights] which are recognized as indispensable by civilized peoples."[47] All of which compelled the Bush administration to seek congressional authorization for its military commissions. At a time when Congress is often accused of gridlock and stalemate—and when most Americans had lost confidence in Bush's capacity as a wartime president—Congress responded with impressive speed. Bush asked Congress to send him the requisite legislation in a speech on September 6, 2006, and the bill had cleared both houses by September 29.

The Military Commissions Act of 2006 granted Bush virtually everything he wanted. The president was now authorized to establish military commissions to try "alien unlawful enemy combatants engaged in hostilities against the United States." Evidence obtained via "torture" was not admissible, but statements obtained through "coercion" could be used if the presiding judge decided that they were reliable and of probative value and that "the methods used to obtain the statements [did] not amount to cruel, inhuman, or degrading treatment." In an attempt to ward off future *Hamdan*-like decisions, the law also prevented US courts from considering habeas corpus petitions from any detainee and declared that the Geneva Conventions could not be used as a "source of rights" in any US court.[48] As the *New York Times* summarized the substance of the new law:

Rather than reining in the formidable presidential powers Mr. Bush and Vice President Dick Cheney have asserted since Sept. 11, 2001, the law gives some of those powers a solid statutory foundation. In effect it allows the president to identify enemies, imprison them indefinitely and interrogate them—albeit with a ban on the harshest treatment— beyond the reach of the full court reviews traditionally afforded criminal defendants and ordinary prisoners.

Taken as a whole, the law will give the president more power over terrorism suspects than he had before the Supreme Court decision this summer. . . . The bill . . . does not just allow the president to determine the meaning and application of the Geneva Conventions; it also strips the courts of jurisdiction to hear challenges to his interpretation.[49]

Not surprisingly, most of the votes needed to pass this legislation came from Republicans, but twelve Democratic senators and thirty-two Democratic representatives also voted in favor of it.[50] Of course, Democratic support would almost certainly have been much greater had Bush asked for such legislation in 2001 or 2002.

Lest one dismiss Congress's handling of the military commissions issue as a fluke, almost the same thing happened when Bush needed legislation to continue his administration's electronic surveillance program. In the 1970s, in the aftermath of the Watergate scandal, congressional investigators discovered that every president since Franklin Roosevelt had used the various entities concerned with foreign intelligence gathering— the National Security Agency, the Central Intelligence Agency, the FBI— to spy on their domestic political opponents. In an effort to prevent this sort of activity, Congress passed and President Carter signed the Foreign Intelligence Surveillance Act of 1978 (FISA). There had never been any controversy about the American government's authority to monitor communications that passed exclusively among foreign governments, groups, or individuals; the protections of the Fourth Amendment did not apply to them. But what if such communications went to or from a person in the United States? Though FISA did allow this sort of surveillance without judicial sanction in certain limited circumstances (e.g., in the fifteen days after the beginning of a war), in general it required the federal government to get a warrant any time it wanted to monitor communications between a foreign source and an American citizen or resident alien. To make sure that warrant requests were kept secret and dealt with expeditiously, the act also created a special Foreign Intelligence Surveillance Court to handle warrant applications.[51] By all accounts, that court was highly sympathetic to government claims about national security interests. From 1978 to 2005, the court rejected just 5 of the 18,748 government requests for wiretaps or search warrants.[52]

This legal framework notwithstanding, shortly after the terrorist attacks of September 11, 2001, President Bush secretly ordered the National Security Agency (NSA) to undertake an extensive new program of electronic surveillance of American citizens who were in various ways linked to suspected foreign terrorists—without seeking warrants from the FISA court. Though a few congressional leaders were informed about this initiative, Americans generally, including most members of Congress, did not find out about it until December 2005, when its existence was revealed in a front-page story in the *New York Times*.[53]

The administration's initial reaction to the *Times* story was to insist that Bush had the authority to institute the warrantless surveillance program without the permission of the legislative or judicial branches, either as a consequence of his powers as commander in chief or because Congress had already granted him that power when it passed the Authorization to Use Military Force in September 2001.[54] But many in Congress didn't buy it, and as the extent of the congressional opposition became apparent, the White House changed its strategy. In February 2006, in an effort to avoid a public airing of the program's nature and methods, the administration indicated its willingness to seek retroactive congressional authorization for the NSA program.[55] In August, a federal district court judge in Detroit gave the administration another incentive for seeking legislative approval when she declared the program unconstitutional.[56] Any lingering hopes that the issue would somehow lose salience or could be papered over with a few cosmetic changes were dealt a death blow by the 2006 midterm elections, which gave the Democrats majority control in both houses of Congress.

Before the new Democratic Congress could seize the initiative, the Bush administration took preemptive action. On January 17, 2007, Attorney General Alberto Gonzales sent a letter to the leaders of the congressional intelligence and judiciary committees in which he said that the Justice Department had worked out a new arrangement with the FISA court and that, as a result, "any electronic surveillance that was occurring as part of the Terrorist Surveillance program will now be conducted subject to the approval of the Foreign Intelligence Surveillance Court."[57] Then, in mid-April, the administration sent a bill to Congress that significantly relaxed some of the restrictions on electronic surveillance within the United States.[58] The need to pass some kind of new legislation acquired additional urgency in July, when the FISA court apparently ruled—the actual text of the decision was kept secret—that any communications between two foreign sources required a warrant if it was routed through the United States.[59]

Though initial reports suggested that the administration bill would encounter stiff opposition in the Democratic Congress, many Democrats were apparently reluctant to deny the president a power he claimed was necessary for protecting American national security. After some contentious debate and a few failed attempts to write an alternative bill, in early August both houses passed a bill very similar to the one the White House had drafted. As the *New York Times* summarized this legislation the day after Bush signed it:

> [Those familiar with the law] said that [it] for the first time provided a legal framework for much of the surveillance without warrants that was being conducted in secret by the National Security Agency and outside the Foreign Intelligence Surveillance Act. . . . "This more or less legalizes the N.S.A. program," said Kate Martin, director of the Center for National Security Studies in Washington, who has studied the new legislation.[60]

Presidential scholar James Pfiffner reached a similar conclusion: "The new law essentially made legal the surveillance that the administration had been carrying out since 2001."[61]

From the administration's perspective, the 2007 law had one major shortcoming: its provisions expired in six months. This convinced many observers that the new law was only a "stopgap" measure passed just before a congressional recess and that the Democrats would eventually pass a bill that contained much tougher restrictions on domestic surveillance. As *Congressional Quarterly* observed, "Despite the win President Bush scored on legislation expanding the administration's eavesdropping authority, Democrats appear determined to make it a temporary victory."[62] Once again, however, the expected congressional opposition failed to materialize. By July 2008, Congress had passed legislation that granted the Bush administration the two things it reportedly wanted most: "enhanced executive branch spying powers" and "retroactive legal protection" for telephone companies that had cooperated with the NSA's previous surveillance efforts. To quote *Congressional Quarterly* again: "Democratic efforts to confront President Bush over electronic surveillance laws ended abruptly in July, with the White House the clear winner and Democrats dropping the fight for the duration of the Bush presidency."[63] The support for this bill, moreover, can reasonably be described as bipartisan: 105 House Democrats voted for the legislation, along with 21 Democratic senators.[64]

Would Congress have been similarly willing to authorize the "enhanced interrogation techniques" that were used against some suspected terrorists? Certainly not in Bush's second term. In 2005, the House and Senate both passed, by large, veto-proof majorities, an amendment to the Defense Department authorization bill that banned torture and all other forms of "cruel, inhuman, and degrading treatment."[65] Had the Bush administration broached the same topic in late 2001 or early 2002, however, they might have encountered a very different reception. In 2002, a number of members of Congress, including then-House Minority Whip Nancy Pelosi, were briefed about the interrogation techniques the CIA was using against suspected terrorists in American custody, including waterboarding, and none raised any objection. As one official present during the briefings described the congressional reaction, "There was no objecting, no hand-wringing. The attitude was, 'We don't care what you do to those guys as long as you get the information you need to protect the American people.'"[66]

In short, in two of the three most celebrated cases where the Bush administration tried to assert unilateral presidential powers, Congress ended up giving them these powers via legislation; and had they sought authorization for "enhanced interrogation techniques" in a timely fashion, that might have been granted as well. Had Bush truly been interested in leading a united nation in a war against terrorism, he should have avoided all the contention and charges of secrecy and presidential aggrandizement and sought congressional approval from the very beginning. Quite belatedly, Bush himself reached the same conclusion. As he stated in his presidential memoirs, "In retrospect, I probably could have avoided some of the controversy and legal setbacks by seeking legislation on military tribunals, the TSP [Terrorist Surveillance Program], and the CIA enhanced interrogation program as soon as they were created."[67]

The Vietnam Syndrome Revisited

One final political consequence of the Bush Iraq policy deserves a close examination. The prolonged violence and disorder and the steady accumulation of American casualties not only hurt the Republican Party and made the last five years of Bush's own presidency more difficult, it will almost certainly continue to haunt future presidents as they try to wage war on terrorism. By greatly mishandling the initial invasion of Iraq and, even more, the postwar occupation, Bush gave new life to the Vietnam syndrome.

The Vietnam syndrome has been defined as "a fundamental reluctance to commit American military power anywhere in the world, unless it is absolutely necessary to protect the national interests of the country." And:

"the belief that foreign military intervention is unwinnable and therefore a 'quagmire' to be avoided; the inability to make and follow through with overseas commitments."[68] Especially in the years immediately after the end of the Vietnam War, American public opinion was highly ambivalent about using the military even to repel a direct attack on some of our closest and most important allies. In a 1974 Gallup poll, only 48 percent of a national sample wanted to help defend our "major European allies" if they were attacked by the Soviet Union. Just 37 percent supported defending Japan if that country were attacked by either "Soviet Russia" or "Communist China."[69]

Throughout the 1980s, any suggestion that the United States should provide assistance to the anticommunist forces in Central America was met with the rejoinder that such aid would only lead to "another Vietnam." As one legislator noted in 1983, whenever Congress considered Central American-policy issues, Vietnam was a "ghostly presence; it's there in every committee room, at every meeting."[70] Memories of Vietnam also exerted a powerful influence on public opinion. In a series of Gallup surveys conducted in 1983, 70 percent of those who had heard or read about the situation in El Salvador said that it was either "very likely" or "fairly likely" that "U.S. involvement in El Salvador could turn into a situation like Vietnam." Only about 25 percent thought that such an outcome was "not very" or "not at all" likely. In two Harris polls from the same year, 70 percent agreed that "U.S. involvement in El Salvador looks too much as though it could turn out to be another Vietnam." When ABC News offered respondents two ways to describe "the war in El Salvador," 54 percent said that it "is much like the war in Vietnam"; only 31 percent thought that "it is not at all like the war in Vietnam."[71]

Against this background, one of George H. W. Bush's genuine achievements in the 1991 Gulf War was to show that all American wars did not degenerate into Vietnam-like quagmires, that it was possible for the United States to wage war successfully, for a limited purpose, with a limited number of casualties. On the day that the US ground offensive ended, the first president Bush delightedly told a group of state legislators, "It's a proud day for America. And, by God, we've kicked the Vietnam syndrome once and for all." Later the same day, in a radio address to the armed forces stationed in the Persian Gulf region, Bush declared, "The specter of Vietnam has been buried forever in the desert sands of the Arabian Peninsula."[72]

As it turned out, Bush's eulogy for the Vietnam syndrome was premature. Indeed, his own administration's most controversial Iraq-related decision—the decision to halt the ground offensive without deposing Saddam Hussein and then not to support the Shiite and Kurdish revolts in Iraq—seems to have been dictated largely by the desire to avoid a Vietnam-like entanglement. As then CIA-director Robert Gates would later comment about any attempt to depose Saddam, "Therein lay Vietnam, as far as we were concerned."[73] Bill Clinton's presidency was haunted by the same specter, especially after the October 1993 firefight in Somalia in which eighteen American soldiers were killed, an event interpreted partly through the lens of Vietnam. Though Vietnam and Somalia were actually very different kinds of events, both suggested that even limited military missions could gradually, almost imperceptibly become larger and more dangerous, creating a mindset that one US diplomat would call the "Vietmalia syndrome."[74] The result was that "the [Vietnam] syndrome was on full display during the 1990s, when pundits and politicos rushed to compare American interventions in Haiti, Bosnia, and Kosovo, which resulted in no American casualties, to the worst military defeat in our history."[75] On the other hand, the available survey data, while not fully comparable with polls taken during the Reagan presidency, suggest that public concerns about "another Vietnam" had diminished somewhat; Bush's celebratory conclusion was not entirely fanciful. In an April 1999 Fox News/Opinion Dynamics poll, for example, 49 percent of the respondents said that it was "very" or "somewhat" likely that "Kosovo will turn into another Vietnam," a number significantly smaller than the number who were concerned about the Reagan policy toward El Salvador.[76]

If the first Gulf War did not vanquish the Vietnam syndrome, it seemed, at first glance, that the September 11 terrorist attacks might finally do the trick. As the respected Vietnam historian George Herring would later write:

> For the first time since 1814, the continental United States had come under attack, and much of the intellectual and emotional baggage from Vietnam seemed swept aside in a surge of grief, anger, and fear. Patriotism was fashionable again. . . . Just as Pearl Harbor had wiped away the bitter memories of World War I that had been the basis for isolationism in the 1930s, so also the terrorist attacks on September 11 appeared to sweep aside memories of America's failure in Vietnam and inhibitions against the use of military force.[77]

The most dramatic sign of the new mood was the two resolutions passed by Congress to authorize the wars in Afghanistan and Iraq. With a level of unity that hadn't been seen on military issues since the Tonkin Gulf resolution in 1964, the vote to authorize "all necessary and appropriate force" against those who had "planned, authorized, committed, or aided the terrorist attacks" was 420–1 in the House, 98–0 in the Senate. Such overwhelming support was perhaps to be expected, given that the vote took place just three days after the attacks. But the same cannot be said about the vote, thirteen months later, that authorized the war in Iraq. Though there was a vocal opposition to the war, the resolution was approved by a two to one margin in the House and by three to one in the Senate, with strong Democratic support in both chambers. As a further indication of just how completely the Vietnam syndrome seemed to be a thing of the past, only one public pollster saw fit to ask a question about the Vietnam analogy in any national poll conducted between September 11, 2001, and the start of the Iraq war on March 19, 2003. (The question is reported in table 8.4 and will be discussed below.)

By early 2004, however, Vietnam seemed like an increasingly apt analogy with what was taking place in Iraq: a steady accumulation of American casualties; repeated claims by the incumbent administration that we were making "progress" but few tangible signs of this on the battle front; and no easy or obvious way to extricate ourselves from the conflict. The best indicator of the resurgence of the Vietnam syndrome within American public opinion is provided by a set of survey questions posed by ABC News (sometimes in conjunction with the *Washington Post*). In five different foreign policy controversies that took place between 1982 and 2009—El Salvador, Nicaragua, Bosnia, Afghanistan, and Iraq—ABC asked an identically worded question about whether the United States was "heading for the same kind of involvement" in that country "as it had in the Vietnam War." The full results are shown in table 8.4. Forty-six percent of the public thought that El Salvador was likely to become another Vietnam. Only 30 percent expressed similar misgivings about Nicaragua and Bosnia, and in March 2002, just 18 percent thought that the war in Afghanistan bore a close resemblance to Vietnam. By June 2005, however, 45 percent of Americans said that our involvement in Iraq was heading toward a Vietnam-like quagmire (or had already reached that point). There was also a significant increase in the number who worried that our war in Afghanistan would succumb to the Vietnam syndrome. By the end of the Bush presidency, in short, the Vietnam syndrome was alive and well and once again haunting American foreign policy.

As many readers will already have concluded, the Vietnam syndrome has both its positive and negative aspects. If it encourages policy makers not to undertake military interventions too lightly, if it reminds them of the limitations of military power and the difficulties in devising an easy exit from a mission once it has been started, the Vietnam syndrome is all to the good. (On the basis of the analysis presented in the previous chapter, I think it is clear that Bush, Rumsfeld, and many other top US policy makers did not heed these lessons when launching the war in Iraq.) But as all but complete pacifists recognize, American military power also has its constructive uses, and the Vietnam syndrome may work to discourage even the most prudent, limited, and well-justified military missions.

The experience of the Clinton administration is instructive in this regard. Clinton and almost all of his top foreign policy advisors had opposed the war in Vietnam and were presumably pleased when its "ghostly presence" helped restrain the Reagan administration from intervening more actively in Central America. Once in office, however, the Clintonites quickly came to realize that many of the principal challenges they faced also required some role for the American military—and that the Vietnam syndrome they had previously invoked against Reagan and Bush Sr. was now being used against them.

A particularly poignant example of this predicament involved the American response to the Rwandan genocide of 1994.[78] In a little less than one hundred days, Hutu soldiers, militia, and ordinary citizens slaughtered an estimated eight hundred thousand Tutsi and moderate Hutu in an effort to eliminate the Tutsi from the Rwandan population. Though some form of American intervention might have saved hundreds of thousands of lives, one critic has noted, "Clinton had shown virtually no interest in stopping the genocide, and his Administration had stood by as the death toll rose into the hundreds of thousands."[79] Believing that there was little public support for any kind of US intervention, anxious not to give congressional Republicans another opportunity to criticize Clinton's foreign policy, the administration not only opposed sending reinforcements for the existing United Nations peacekeeping mission; it actually lobbied for a significant *decrease* in UN forces. It even turned down a proposal that the US military jam a Rwandan radio station that was broadcasting hate-filled propaganda and urging the Hutu to murder their Tutsi neighbors, on the grounds that such action was too expensive and might be a violation of international law. The administration also refused to call the Rwandan tragedy a "genocide" for more than two months after the killing began. In his memoirs, Clinton would call "the failure to try to stop Rwanda's tragedies . . . one of the greatest regrets of my presidency."[80]

And just as Clinton battled a "Vietmalia" syndrome through most of his presidency, there is good reason to think that a "Viet-Iraq" syndrome had a noticeable effect on the foreign policy of Barack Obama. As a matter of ideology, the Obama administration had always envisioned a less vigorous use of the American military than the administrations that preceded it. Yet there clearly were times when Obama was inclined to approve some kind of US military intervention but stopped short or scaled back his plans be-

Table 8.4. The Rise, Fall, and Resurgence of the Vietnam Syndrome

"Do you think the United States is heading for the same kind of involvement in
_____ as it had in the Vietnam War, or do you think the United States will
avoid that kind of involvement this time?"

	Same as Vietnam	Not the same	Don't know	(N)
"El Salvador"				
March 18–21, 1982	46	49	5	(1,218)
"Nicaragua"				
March 6, 1986	30	61	9	(543)
"Bosnia"				
Nov. 29, 1986	33	61	6	(523)
"Afghanistan"				
March 7–10, 2002	18	77	5	(1,008)
Oct. 15–18, 2009	35	58	7	(1,004)
"Iraq"				
June 2–5, 2005	45	52	3	(1,002)
Oct. 19–22, 2006	45	50	5	(1,200)
Jan. 10, 2007	43	50	6	(502)

Source: All surveys were conducted by either ABC News or ABC News and the Washington Post.

cause of what he perceived as a lack of political support for such policies. In October 2015, one White House correspondent offered this analysis of Obama's policy toward Syria:

> The U.S. military footprint in the [Mideast] region is growing. But each step is on a small scale, so as to reassure Americans that Obama isn't plunging their country into another large, open-ended conflict. While the strategy may help ease them back into the realities of war, experts and some of Obama's political allies say his slow ramp-up may not be enough to defeat the fast-moving militants. . . . Obama repeatedly has used the costly and unpopular Iraq War as an example of what he's tried to avoid.[81]

9

Communication Is Important, but Don't

Expect Miracles

In the early twenty-first century, poor communications has become the excuse of choice for elected officials with low approval ratings or unpopular policies. Rather than admit that their policies are flawed or that they themselves have made poor decisions, embattled politicians claim that the public just doesn't understand what they're doing and how much they've really accomplished. And that lack of public understanding can, in turn, be blamed on the fact that (choose one or more): the media are biased against them; their opponents have presented a false picture of what they're doing; they themselves are too busy thinking about the big issues to waste their time making speeches; the people are just not very smart.

Donald Trump has been an especially ardent practitioner of this subterfuge, but, lest we forget, the stratagem was also much in vogue during the presidency of Barack Obama.[1] In July 2011, when only about 45 percent of Americans approved of his job performance, Obama offered this explanation of his predicament: "Over the first two years, I was so focused on policy and, you know, getting the policy right, that sometimes I forgot part of my job is explaining to the American people why we're doing this policy and where we're going."[2] Asked in July 2012 about his biggest mistake as president, he said much the same thing: "The mistake of my first term . . . was thinking that this job was just about getting the policy right. And that's important. But the nature of this office is also to tell a story to the American people that gives them a sense of unity and purpose and optimism, especially during tough times."[3]

Pressed in November 2013 about why the new health-care law was forcing so many Americans to lose their doctor or their health care plan, contrary to his repeated promises that this would not happen, the most Obama would concede was that he hadn't explained the law very well: "I regret very much that what we intended to do—which is to make sure that everybody is moving into better plans because they want them, as opposed to because they're forced into it—that, you know, we weren't as clear as we needed to be in terms of the changes that were taking place."[4]

Why did the Democrats suffer such significant losses in the 2014 midterm elections, according to Obama?

> When you start governing, there is a tendency sometimes for me to start thinking, "As long as I get the policy right then that's what should matter." I think that one thing I do need to constantly remind myself and my team is, it's not enough just to build the better mousetrap. . . . We've got to sell it, we've got to reach out to the other side and where possible persuade. And I think there are times, there's no doubt about it, where, you know, I think we have not been successful in going out there and letting people know what it is that we are trying to do and why this is the right direction.[5]

And when the president was criticized in late 2015 for an insufficiently aggressive response to terrorism, he said—you guessed it—that his policy was just fine, the problem was poor communication. As the *Washington Post* reported:

> As President Obama flew home from Asia aboard Air Force One in late November [2015], he scolded his aides about how poorly the administration was communicating the U.S.-led strategy against the Islamic State.
>
> Throughout the nine-day trip, . . . they had all heard critics at home and abroad charge that he had no coherent game plan, Obama said.
>
> But while many outside the administration found the strategy itself lacking, Obama felt what they really needed was to do a better job of explaining it. He ordered what [a senior administration official] called an "uptick in our communications tempo."[6]

Contra Obama, I do not intend to argue in this chapter that the principal problem of George W. Bush's presidency was poor communications and that he would have been wildly popular if only he had "told the story" properly. Reality has a nasty way of undermining even the best-told stories about bungled military missions, poorly designed education laws, or insufficient immigration enforcement. Yet neither will I claim that presidential communications fall entirely "on deaf ears," to quote the title of one recent book on the subject. A good communications strategy cannot turn failure into success; but it may have some effect on how the public interprets a particular outcome or whether the public understands the reasoning behind a given policy. For those who wish to examine the impact of presidential communications, moreover, George W. Bush's presidency provides an especially interesting case study. As I will demonstrate in this chapter, on many important issues and controversies, the Bush administration didn't just respond weakly to its critics—it didn't respond at all.

The Bush Communications Operation: An Overview

As a political consultant, Karl Rove was known for developing very detailed campaign plans before a race actually got underway—and then trying to stick to those plans no matter what else was taking place. Having decided, after a great deal of research, what issues he wanted to talk about and which groups and geographical areas he needed to target, Rove was determined not to be sidetracked by what the other campaign was saying or the preoccupations of the media. In the White House, Bush and his top advisors tried to create a communications operation organized along similar principles. They would make news based on what *they* wanted to say, what messages *they* wanted to get out, and not worry about the topics the media were asking them to address.

As Martha Joynt Kumar has noted in her award-winning study of White House media operations, this approach had both its pluses and minuses. On the one hand:

The Bush [communications] operation did a good job planning ahead on policy and establishing a disciplined White House staff that held presidential information very closely. Bush's staff thought through how to develop publicity for the issues he wanted to discuss and focus on what they thought was important. The communications staff emphasized the issues they thought crucial and avoided discussing what was on the minds of others. Considerable effort went into prioritizing issues, creating events to emphasize a limited number of priorities, and rounding up people to talk about them.[7]

During the transition period, for example, Rove developed a 180-day plan for implementing the goals and policies Bush had discussed during the campaign. "As soon as he was inaugurated, Bush began to introduce this governing agenda by devoting a week" to each of his major goals.[8] Bush's effort in the fall of 2002 to convince the Congress and the country to go to war against Iraq has also been given high marks for effectiveness by most observers. (Its truthfulness will be examined later in this chapter.)

But this single-minded devotion to pursuing their own agenda also had a significant downside:

> Where the Bush team proved less responsive was in listening to others, including members of Congress, and developing a communications operation that could adjust to changing circumstances. . . . The Bush operation did not prove adept at taking advantage of unanticipated opportunities and dealing with unexpected problems. When information crises arose, it often took weeks for the White House staff to get the matter off the front pages of the newspapers and off the evening news programs.[9]

Not until the start of Bush's second term did the White House create a specific "rapid response" unit.[10]

At the beginning of the Bush presidency, the person most responsible for developing and implementing the administration's communications strategy was Karen Hughes, a former television reporter who had worked closely with Bush since his first gubernatorial campaign in 1994. In the White House organizational chart, she oversaw all the various units with communications responsibilities: the press office, speechwriting, media affairs. Reports on the early Bush White House often noted that Bush had a level of personal comfort with and trust in Hughes that he accorded to no other of his top advisors. As one Bush advisor commented, "There are a hundred decisions he [Bush] has to make every day, big decisions, with a lot riding on each one. So he'll give twenty of them to Karen to make. He trusts her completely. He trusts her like he trusts no one." A "longtime observer of the Bush operation" put it this way: "Bush reveres Karl; he depends on Karen."[11]

But Rove also played an important role in presidential communications. One could hardly be the president's chief political strategist and not have some concern with how the administration was communicating its plans and accomplishments, both to the public and to other elites. Rove, said a top member of the Bush communications team, "liked to have his hands involved in, if not controlling, anything and everything that could affect Bush's approval ratings."[12] In particular, it was Rove who chaired the so-called Strategery Group, which met every week to develop a unified vision as to how policy, politics, and communication fit together.

The result for the first eighteen months of Bush's first term was said to be a rough balance between the influence exerted by Hughes and Rove over White House communications issues.[13] In June 2002, however, Hughes left Washington and went back to Texas in order to accommodate her husband and fifteen-year-old son, both of whom were said to be "homesick." Hughes's West Wing office and one of her titles (director of communications) were given to Dan Bartlett, yet another Texan who had worked for Bush since his initial run for governor.[14] But Bartlett never developed anything like Hughes's relationship with the president or, therefore, with other top administration figures. In the case studies that follow, Bartlett often plays a bit part but rarely seems to have been a major strategist or decision maker.

Press reports at the time of Hughes's departure claimed that she would still be an important advisor to the president, who would speak with her regularly by telephone.[15] In fact, Hughes's removal to Texas confirmed what presidential scholars have long believed: that simple physical proximity to the president is an important source of power and influence. Hughes continued to play an important role in writing Bush's major speeches—something she could do from afar—but she was not there to affect the myriad other decisions that inevitably confront a modern president, often with little advance warning.

An interesting test of Hughes's postdeparture influence was her role in the so-called sixteen words controversy, which first became a major news story in July 2003 and was thus one of the first great communications crises in the Bush presidency. A full discussion of that episode will be provided later in this chapter. For now, it is enough to note that in writing that section, I consulted eight major accounts of the controversy, written by both major participants and some of the journalists who covered it—and *not one* mentions Karen Hughes, even in passing.[16] The president himself was accused of taking the country to war under deliberately false pretenses and Hughes seems to have played no role in determining how the administration responded to the charges.

If Hughes's influence on White House communications was diminished by her departure—well, you don't need a PhD in political science to deduce the likely outcome. As Scott McClellan, who served as Bush's press secretary from 2003 to 2006, would confirm in his memoirs, "Rove's controlling personality and substantial influence over policy, strategy, political communications, and message expanded unchecked, *particularly after the departure of Karen Hughes*."[17] This is not to say, however, that Rove was solely in charge of administration communications policy after July 2002 and that all of the problems and mistakes detailed in the rest of this chapter can be laid directly at his doorstep. In some of the cases that follow, a more apt characterization is that *no one* was in charge: no individual seems to have had the power to decide upon a single communications strategy and then get the rest of the administration to fall in line behind it.

The vice president's office, in particular, was often a loose cannon, which dealt with communications issues based on Dick Cheney's opinions and priorities, even if these conflicted with what others believed was in the president's best interests. In August 2002, for example, Cheney gave a highly publicized speech about the developing situation in Iraq in which he assumed a substantially more bellicose posture than the president had yet taken and made assertions that went well beyond the available intelligence. "There is no doubt that Saddam Hussein now has weapons of mass destruction," he said. And: "Many of us are convinced that Saddam will acquire nuclear weapons fairly soon." At a time when Bush was thinking about taking the issue to the United Nations, Cheney clearly suggested that such an approach was futile, that getting inspectors back into Iraq "would provide no assurance whatsoever of his [Saddam's] compliance with U.N. resolutions. On the contrary, there is a great danger that it would provide false comfort that Saddam was somehow back in his box." Remarkably, Cheney's speech had not been cleared in advance by the State Department, the CIA, or anybody in the White House. On another occasion, Cheney signed an amicus curiae brief on a gun control case that directly contradicted the position taken by the Justice Department.[18] Unfortunately for the administration, neither Bush nor Cheney nor anyone else in the White House political or communications shops seems to have appreciated the problems such a situation posed for the Bush presidency.

However one chooses to apportion the responsibility, there is little doubt that communication—selling the president and his program—is a quintessentially political function.

The Response to Corporate Scandal

Besides being a careful planner, Rove's reputation as a political consultant was that of a man with a fierce determination to win—and who wasn't shy about pushing the ethical envelope in order to do so. Most books about Rove are filled with stories about dirty tricks he allegedly played on political opponents and bad things that happened to opposition candidates and their supporters.[19]

That history and reputation notwithstanding, there is no recent president who has been as kind and gentle to his opposite-party predecessor as George W. Bush was to Bill Clinton. In making this statement, I am not referring to the gracious speech that Bush delivered in June 2004 when Clinton returned to the White House for the unveiling of his presidential portrait, nor to the fact that Bush appointed Clinton and his own father, ex-president George H. W. Bush, to head the fundraising efforts for the victims of the South Asian tsunami in 2004 and Hurricane Katrina in 2005. What I have in mind, instead, is the remarkable unwillingness of the Bush administration to point out how often the policy problems they encountered were actually due to the mistakes and failures of the Clinton presidency. For reasons that are difficult to fathom, Bush and his advisors acted as if blaming a problem on their predecessors was a sign of weakness on their own part.

An archetypal example of this strange proclivity was the administration's response to the string of corporate scandals that became a major news story and, thus, an important political issue in late 2001 and early 2002. The most celebrated of these scandals concerned the Enron Corporation, a once highly regarded Houston energy company that filed for bankruptcy in December 2001 and quickly became the subject of numerous congressional and criminal investigations. As the extent of Enron's fraud and misbehavior became apparent, media attention—with a healthy assist from congressional Democrats—soon came to focus on the purported connections between the corporation and several top officials in the Bush administration, including the president.

During his career in politics, it was widely reported, Bush had received more money from Enron and its employees than from any other company (though the reports were unable to agree on just how much they had given him).[20] Ken Lay, chairman of the Enron board of directors and its former chief executive officer, had personally contributed $10,000 to the Florida recount effort and another $100,000 to the Bush-Cheney inaugural. While Bush was governor of Texas, Lay had been the head of the Governor's Business Council. Bush knew Lay well enough to have given him the nickname "Kenny Boy." When Cheney was putting together the administration's national energy policy, he himself had met with Lay. His aides had met with Enron officials on four other occasions. At least thirty senior administration officials had at one point owned substantial amounts of Enron stock.[21]

The Bush administration finally answered most of these accusations, though it took them a while to get their act together. Though Enron filed for bankruptcy on December 2, 2001, not until January 10, 2002, did the White House disclose that, just before filing, Lay had spoken by telephone with two different Bush cabinet secretaries. Not until January 22 did Bush tell the press that he himself was "outraged" by Enron's conduct.[22] Eventually, however, the administration got its talking points in order. Yes, Enron had given a lot of campaign money to Bush, but it had also given a substantial amount to Democrats, including many of the president's sharpest critics. And while Lay had spoken to two cabinet officers, the essential point was that they had refused to do any special favors for him. At the same time, administration assertions of transparency and full disclosure were being undermined by Cheney's unwillingness to release the full list of energy industry executives who had met with his task force.[23]

As a result of this damage-control effort, polls suggest that Enron inflicted no more than a light bruise on Bush's public image. There was considerable suspicion about the administration's honesty. In a February 2002 Gallup Poll, 47 percent of the sample said that the Bush administration was "cooperating as much as possible in letting the public know about its contacts with Enron," while 43 percent thought the administration was "trying to cover up its contacts with Enron." At almost the same time, CBS News offered its respondents three options, and found that 13 percent felt that "members of the Bush administration" were "telling the entire truth," 55 percent said they were "mostly telling the truth but hiding something," and 20 percent said they were "mostly lying." On the whole, however, the public was reluctant to blame the corporate scandals on the Republicans alone. According to a *Washington Post* survey, just 12 percent of the public thought Republicans bore "more responsibility for the Enron situation," while 32 percent thought "both parties" were at fault, 44 percent said "neither party" and 3 percent put the onus on the Democrats alone. All told, a Princeton Survey Research poll in September 2002 showed that 51 percent approved of the way Bush was handling "corporate scandals like Enron, WorldCom, and Tyco," versus 34 percent who disapproved, though this came as a time when Bush's overall approval rating was about 65 percent.[24]

So much for playing defense. What the administration really needed, however, was an offensive game plan. Once the general outlines of the Enron scandal became clear, the Bush communications shop should have been pushing the argument that any "connections" between Bush and Enron were a red herring that obscured the real issue: who was in charge of the regulatory and prosecutorial machinery of government when the corporate malfeasance actually occurred? The answer, in every case, was that while the scandalous behavior came to light during the Bush presidency, it took place while Bill Clinton was in the White House. Far from being a defensive effort to make the best of a potentially embarrassing situation, Bush should have been able to sell the whole episode as a substantial achievement, in which, by exposing and prosecuting the guilty and then passing the Sarbanes-Oxley Act, he had cleaned up a mess left by his predecessor.[25]

Consider, in this light, the three most infamous corporate scandals from this period: Enron, Tyco, and WorldCom.

While many issues connected with Enron's collapse are still a matter of dispute, virtually everyone who has written about the episode has pointed to two major sets of problems that pushed a once thriving company into bankruptcy and dissolution.[26]

First, though its name is now synonymous with the worst sorts of corporate misbehavior, Enron was originally a legitimate success story. Created in 1985 by the merger of two gas pipeline companies, the new entity found an innovative way of bringing order and flexibility to the newly deregulated natural gas market. Rather than undertaking new gas explorations or building additional gas-fired power plants, Enron adopted an "asset-lite" strategy, in which they served an intermediary role between producers and consumers.

After this initial success, however, Enron executives quickly developed an extraordinary level of overconfidence—it is almost impossible not to use the word hubris—that convinced them they could apply the same business model to just about any commodity or situation that seemed superficially similar. The result was a series of ill-considered, money-losing ventures. In 1993, Enron signed a contract to build the Dabhol power plant in India, with little apparent recognition of the important political and cultural differences between India and the United States. In 1996, it purchased Portland General Electric for $2.1 billion, which quickly turned into another white elephant. In 1998, Enron executives somehow convinced themselves that they could make a fortune in the water business, as they spent $2.4 billion to acquire a small water company in England. In 1999, the company launched an expensive foray into the broadband market. These four ventures alone—all of which, be it noted, were undertaken during the Clinton presidency—resulted in estimated total losses of $5.8 billion.[27]

Second, lots of companies have made foolish business decisions. What set Enron apart from its confreres was its wholesale attempt to hide its mistakes and losses from its shareholders, outside analysts, and even many of its own employees. For this purpose, Enron made extensive use of so-called special purpose entities (SPEs). Like many of the controversial practices in which Enron engaged, SPEs are a legitimate business vehicle in some circumstances. But Enron created a string of special purpose entities in which they claimed—falsely—that part of the funds were provided by outside investors and then used these SPEs to pump up their earnings and keep losses and underperforming assets off the company's balance sheets. The result was to disguise how limited Enron's earnings were and how large was its indebtedness.

In what is probably the most thorough analysis of the Enron mess published to date, former Harvard Business School professor Malcolm Salter has identified 1997 as the "tipping point" in the Enron story—the time when Enron "crossed the line between limits testing and out-and-out deception."[28] The same year was singled out by the corporation's bankruptcy examiner as "the beginning of Enron's major GAAP [generally accepted accounting principles] violations."[29] Such a precise year was, of course, not selected at random. In 1997, Enron created Chewco, the first of its deceptive SPEs. This was quickly followed by a succession of similarly fraudulent entities: LJM1 and LJM2 in 1999, the Raptors in 2000. I need hardly add that all this activity took place during Bill Clinton's second term.

In short, by the time George W. Bush was sworn into office in January 2001, Enron was a house of cards just waiting to collapse. That collapse occurred during the Bush presidency, but all the major mistakes and misrepresentations took place while Clinton was in the White House.

TYCO

Tyco International was a small, New Hampshire–based conglomerate until 1992, when L. Dennis Kozlowski became its chief executive officer.[30] It then embarked on a very ambitious acquisitions program that over the next ten years led the company to spend some $65 billion in "at least 120 large transactions" and numerous smaller ones. The early results seemed strikingly positive. The price of Tyco stock rose 30 percent each year between 1993 and 1996, then jumped an additional 50 percent in 1997. By the end of the 1990s, "Kozlowski was becoming a corporate legend for his ability to cut costs and increase earnings, while successfully digesting the company's many acquisitions."[31] In early 2001, *BusinessWeek* named Tyco the top performing company of 2000; a year later, it named Kozlowski as one of the "Top 25 Managers of the Year."[32]

Not all of Tyco's press was positive, however. In 1999, an influential investment analyst accused the company of using accounting gimmicks to hide its real financial picture.[33] These allegations, in combination with the recession that began in March 2001, caused Tyco's share price to fall by more than 75 percent during 2001 and the first half of 2002, raising fears that Tyco would be the "next Enron." Such concerns proved to be exaggerated, however. An outside investigation of the company would later conclude that "Tyco's accounting, though aggressive, generally conformed to accepted accounting principles and required only a modest restatement of earnings."[34] Or as one legal commentator observed in 2005, "Tyco is not

Enron. Tyco is a real company with a real business plan that still employs thousands of people. . . . There are no retirees eating cat food because of Dennis Kozlowksi."[35] Of all the major corporate scandals of the early 2000s, Tyco's was the only one that did not result in a declaration of bankruptcy.

The Tyco affair seemed, instead, to be a story of how Kozlowski and a few other top company officials had used corporate assets for their own personal benefit. (It should be noted, however, that the only book written to date about the Tyco scandal concludes that Kozlowski was innocent of the charges for which he was eventually sent to prison.)[36] Initial reports focused on two episodes that clearly did occur during the Bush presidency. From August to December 2001, Kozlowski bought a number of expensive paintings for display in a Fifth Avenue New York apartment but (allegedly) claimed that they were purchased for Tyco headquarters in New Hampshire and even had empty boxes shipped there, thereby evading more than $1 million in state and local sales taxes. This led to his indictment in June 2002 and his resignation as Tyco CEO.

The second episode was a week-long birthday party that Kozlowski threw for his second wife in June 2001. Held at a resort on Sardinia, the affair is inadequately described by words like opulent and garish. One of the most conspicuous details, mentioned in virtually all subsequent press accounts, was a full-size ice sculpture based on Michelangelo's David, with expensive vodka flowing from David's penis. All told, the party cost more than $2 million; since a number of top Tyco executives attended the party, and since Kozlowski claimed to have conducted some business meetings during the week, Tyco paid for about half of the total bill.[37]

As the scandal progressed, however, it soon became clear that Kozlowski's excesses, real or alleged, began well before George W. Bush was elected president. This point is made most emphatically by a second indictment, this one targeting both Kozlowski and Tyco chief financial officer Mark Swartz, that a Manhattan grand jury handed down in September 2002. The essence of this second indictment was that Kozlowski and Swartz had operated a "criminal enterprise" that systematically looted Tyco without the knowledge or approval of the board of directors. This enterprise, as the second sentence of the indictment makes clear, ran "from on or about January 1, 1995, through on or about September 9, 2002."[38] The alleged misbehavior, in other words, began halfway through Bill Clinton's *first* term.

As the rest of the indictment shows, these dates were not adopted merely to be as inclusive as possible. One of the "pattern acts" detailed in the indictment, for example, was Kozlowski's inappropriate use of two no-interest loan programs the company had established to help cover executives' moving expenses and the income taxes they owed after the vesting of their stock options. The indictment then went on to list 68 "overt acts" of this type, only ten of which (15 percent) took place while Bush was president. One occurred in 1995, thirty-one between 1997 and 1999, and another twenty-six in 2000.[39]

In the two trials that followed—the first one ended in a mistrial—a great deal of attention was focused on $121.5 million in bonuses that Kozlowski and Swartz had received after the conclusion of four major transactions—without the Tyco board's knowledge, said the prosecution; with its approval, according to the two executives. Kozlowski and Swartz each received one such bonus in 1999, two in 2000—and only one (the smallest of the four) in 2001.[40]

WORLDCOM

When Enron sought chapter 11 protection in December 2001, it was, as measured by the company's total assets, the largest bankruptcy filing in US history. Enron didn't keep that title for long, however. In July 2002, WorldCom, a Mississippi-based telecommunications company with assets almost double those of Enron, also filed for bankruptcy.[41] By that time, most of the accoutrements of scandal were already visible: the resignations of the company's chief executive officer, its chief financial officer, and other top executives; a precipitous drop in share prices; and, most relevant to this discussion, allegations of shoddy and misleading accounting practices.

Much like Tyco, first reports of the WorldCom scandal seemed to indicate that the wrongdoing had taken place entirely during the Bush presidency. In late June 2002, WorldCom announced that it had overstated its cash flow during 2001 and the first quarter of 2002 by more than $3.8 billion. (Specifically: it had treated operating costs as capital investments, thus allowing the company to substantially reduce its reported expenses and inflate its profits.) Instead of a profit of more than $1.5 billion during those five quarters, WorldCom had actually lost money. Just as with Tyco, however, it soon became clear that WorldCom's problems did not suddenly commence when George W. Bush entered the White House. In early August 2002, the corporation announced an additional $3.3 billion in improperly accounted expenses, this time beginning in 1999. In November, the Securities and Exchange Commission filed additional fraud charges against WorldCom, alleging $2 billion more in accounting manipulations, again beginning in 1999. In sum, WorldCom started cooking its books when there were still two years left in Clinton's second term.[42]

Far from being an example of how corporations run wild whenever a

Republican is in the White House, then, the corporate scandals of the early 2000s were really a symptom of the "irrational exuberance" that took hold of the American economy during Bill Clinton's second term. Enron, Tyco, and WorldCom were all very successful companies at one point in their histories, which led their executives to believe that almost anything they touched would turn to gold. It also tempted them to cross a lot of ethical and legal boundaries they might have respected earlier in their careers.

None of this means that Bill Clinton is the real villain in all these scandals—though if one is determined to find some top government official to cast in that role, Clinton is a far more plausible candidate than George W. Bush. Corporate scandals were simply the downside of what otherwise was a time of remarkable economic prosperity. On the other hand, in studying the messes that developed at Enron, Tyco, and WorldCom, one never gets the sense that top executives were restrained by the fear of hypervigilant federal regulators and prosecutors. Had a profusion of corporate scandals taken place in 1993, at the beginning of the Clinton presidency, the major news media would almost certainly have interpreted them as just one more example of the "excesses" of the Reagan era. The notion that a Republican president might have to clean up after the corporate scandals of a Democratic administration, however, didn't fit the prevailing media narrative. If the White House wanted to make this argument a prominent part of the national discussion, they would need to push it themselves.

And for whatever reason, they almost entirely failed to do so. Though Enron's travails had been a major news story since November 2001, and though Bush had been forced to address the issue on a number of occasions,[43] not until a July 8, 2002, press conference did the president offer even the most subtle suggestion that the most serious instances of corporate wrongdoing had occurred before he entered the White House. His words were: "There had been a period of time when everything seemed easy. Markets were roaring; capital was everywhere; and people forgot their responsibilities." A few minutes later, when a reporter's follow-up question gave Bush a golden opportunity to sharpen his criticism and make explicit its partisan implications, he refused to take the bait:

Q: Sir, you said, in your speech tomorrow you're going to talk about some of the excesses of the 1990s, when a lot of money was flying around, people were playing a lot of games with money.
The President: That's right.
Q: You weren't President then: Bill Clinton was President. Do you think in some way he contributed to that, set a moral tone in any way?
The President: No.[44]

In a much-ballyhooed speech on corporate responsibility that Bush delivered one day later, his only reference to the timing of corporate misbehavior was these two sentences: "The lure of heady profits in the late 1990s spawned abuses and excesses. . . . Nearly every week [now] brings better economic news and a discovery of fraud and scandal, problems long in the making but now coming to light."[45] As White House communications advisors should have anticipated, these statements, buried in a twenty-minute speech, received very little attention in subsequent news reports.

Whether any of Bush's aides tried to push the theme that the corporate scandals were really a product of the Clinton years is more difficult to determine, since much of this sort of activity occurs in one-on-one, off-the-record conversations. But after examining a small mountain of contemporary press coverage about the scandals, I have found exactly one sentence that refers to this theme. In late January 2002, the *New York Times* reported that "White House officials are questioning why regulators in the Clinton administration did not pick up on the transgressions at Enron."[46] Apparently, these officials did not ask such questions very often or very prominently.

More of the Same: Assigning Blame for 9/11

The Bush administration's messaging strategy with regard to corporate scandals is, as I have suggested earlier, part of a larger pattern. Another example of their strange unwillingness to criticize the Clinton administration was their response to the 9/11 terrorist attacks. In the immediate aftermath of those attacks, the administration wisely chose not to point fingers or raise questions about how al-Qaeda had grown so powerful. At that juncture, the country sought unity, not division. But by the spring of 2004, it should have been clear that the gloves were off and the brief period of nonpartisanship was over. Its passage was most clearly marked by former White House counterterrorism coordinator Richard Clarke's testimony before the 9/11 investigating commission on March 24, 2004, in which he claimed that while "fighting terrorism, in general, and fighting al-Qaeda, in particular, were an extraordinarily high priority in the Clinton administration—certainly no higher priority," the Bush administration, in its first eight months in office, "considered terrorism an important issue, but not an urgent issue."[47] He followed this with a description of a series of incidents and anecdotes designed to show the Bush high command asleep at the wheel until the attacks on the Pentagon and World Trade Center jolted them awake.

In response, the White House and other Republicans mounted a major effort to undermine Clarke's credibility and challenge his characterization of their pre-9/11 antiterrorism efforts. But they never made any attempt to dispute the first part of Clarke's argument, that the Clinton administration had a very good record in dealing with terrorism. The only major Bush official who took exception to this assertion was Attorney General John Ashcroft, who told the 9/11 commission that "the single greatest structural cause for the Sept. 11 problem was the wall that segregated or separated criminal investigators and intelligence agents"—a wall that had been erected by the Clinton Justice Department in 1995.[48] More specifically, Deputy Attorney General Jamie Gorelick (who was also a member of the 9/11 investigating commission) had promulgated a set of guidelines and procedures that made it virtually impossible for the FBI and CIA to share information about potential terrorists.

Yet when Ashcroft's Justice Department posted the relevant documents on its website, presidential press secretary Scott McClellan told reporters that "the president is disappointed in this." "The president does not believe we ought to be pointing fingers in this time period. We ought to be working together to help the commission complete its work."[49] In the wake of Clarke's testimony—and the willingness of Democratic commission members to defend and exploit it—calls for "working together" seem incredibly naive.

Had the Bush administration chosen to press the issue, there was a lot of additional evidence they could have pointed to, showing that terrorism had not, in fact, been a particularly high priority of the Clinton presidency and that the Clintonites had in numerous ways helped prepare the path for al-Qaeda's attacks:

- With the Cold War at an end, Clinton shortsightedly decided to make significant reductions in the CIA's budget, as if major, external threats were at an end. As CIA director George Tenet told a congressional committee in 2002, "During the 1990s our intelligence community funding declined in real terms—reducing our buying power by tens of billions of dollars over the decade. We lost nearly one in four of our positions."[50]
- To make matters worse, the CIA also adopted a new set of rules that made an important aspect of intelligence gathering significantly more difficult. In 1995, in reaction to reports that a paid CIA informant had been involved in the murder of two Americans, then-CIA director John Deutch, a Clinton appointee, instituted new guidelines for field agents who were attempting to recruit human intelligence sources who had committed serious criminal or human rights

violations. While the so-called Deutch Rules did not entirely prohibit the recruiting of such sources, they did establish a cumbersome bureaucratic procedure, under which CIA case officers were required to send a substantial amount of information to headquarters, which would then decide if "the value of the intelligence that might be obtained from a particular asset outweighed the risk to the United States that resulted from dealing with the asset."[51]

Though this policy may sound reasonable in the abstract, in practice there is good reason to think that it greatly hindered the work of CIA field operatives. The problem, simply put, is that the sorts of people who are most likely to be able to provide useful information about terrorists and their activities are other terrorists—who are, of course, not likely to have unblemished personal histories. As James Woolsey, Deutch's predecessor as CIA director, observed, "To deter CIA officers who are trying to penetrate terrorist groups from recruiting people with violence in their past is like telling FBI agents that they should penetrate the mafia, but try not to put any actual crooks on the payroll as informants. There's nobody in the mafia but crooks and there's nobody in terrorist organizations but terrorists."[52]

In June 2000, the National Commission on Terrorism recommended that the Deutch guidelines "no longer apply to recruiting terrorist informants."

The guidelines set up complex procedures for seeking approval to recruit informants who may have been involved in human rights violations. In practice, these procedures have deterred and delayed vigorous efforts to recruit potentially useful informants. The CIA has created a climate that is overly risk averse. This has inhibited the recruitment of essential, if sometimes unsavory, terrorist informants and forced the United States to rely too heavily on foreign intelligence services. The adoption of the guidelines contributed to a marked decline in Agency morale unparalleled since the 1970s, and a significant number of case officers retired early or resigned.[53]

But the Clinton administration declined to implement this or any other of the commission's recommendations.

- When a terrorist truck bomb decimated the Khobar Towers in Saudi Arabia in June 1996, killing nineteen American servicemen and injuring hundreds of others, President Clinton vowed to "make sure those responsible are brought to justice," with the FBI assuming principal responsibility for that task. But as the hunt for the terrorists proceeded, FBI director Louis Freeh became increasingly convinced that the Clinton administration "wasn't fully committed to investigating the attack," since doing so would have interfered with other goals, such as developing better relations with Iran and Clinton's futile quest for an Israeli-Palestinian peace treaty.[54] As one FBI official would later comment, "Director Freeh was the only one in Washington pushing for direct access to suspects, pushing for records, pushing for identities of the people, wanting this investigation to succeed. We got a lot of lip service from people who said that they were behind us, but we knew for a fact that when certain Saudi officials came into town and it was the right time to push them for things the Bureau wanted, we know from other people that the issue wasn't even raised. It was crystal clear to some of us that they were hoping that this whole thing would just go away."[55]

- Shortly after taking office, the Clinton administration dramatically mishandled the situation in Somalia, first allowing what had originally been a humanitarian intervention to turn into an exercise in nation building, and then, after eighteen American soldiers were killed in a firefight with the followers of a local warlord, withdrawing from the country entirely. Osama bin Laden would later tell an ABC News reporter that Clinton's actions convinced Muslim fighters that "the American soldier was a paper tiger and after a few blows ran in defeat."[56]

- Those like Al Gore who are convinced that a competent president (read: Clinton or Gore) would have heeded the available but ambiguous warning signs and prevented the attacks of September 11[57] should consider the Clinton administration's record with regard to the August 1998 bombing of the US embassy in Nairobi, Kenya. As Miller, Stone, and Mitchell conclude, "Though . . . intercepting 100 percent of all terror attempts is an impossibility, no one can seriously argue that the horrors of August 7, 1998, couldn't have been prevented." American intelligence agencies were well aware of the al-Qaeda cell in Kenya, had even raided the home of one of its leaders and seized his papers and computer, yet "failed to penetrate the rest of the cell, or arrest or detain any of its remaining members." The US embassy in Nairobi was known to be in a highly exposed position and the ambassador there had applied to the State Department for money to improve security—but her request was turned down. In May 1998, Osama bin Laden had even told an interviewer that the next attack on a US target would take place "within the next several weeks." But the bombing occurred nonetheless, killing 213 people and injuring thousands of others.[58]

In a controversial speech delivered before the Republican National Committee in January 2002, Rove had been quite open about the political advantages Republicans could derive from the terrorism issue. In his words: "Americans trust the Republicans to do a better job of keeping our communities and our families safe. We can also go to the country on this issue because they trust the Republican Party to do a better job of protecting and strengthening America's military might and thereby protecting America."[59] One might have thought that the effectiveness of this argument would have been significantly enhanced if, in addition to playing up Bush's record on national security issues, the White House had also called attention to the Democrats' shortcomings. But the Bush high command decided otherwise.

The Sixteen Words Controversy

The Bush presidency had the reputation of having a very disciplined communications operation, which decided just what it wanted to say and how and when it wanted to say it and then made sure that all the departments and agencies in the executive branch stayed on message and spoke with one voice. As I have suggested earlier in this chapter, this characterization has considerable validity when applied to issues that were drawn from the administration's own, carefully planned agenda. When dealing with issues and controversies that had not been anticipated, however, a very different picture emerges: one of an administration that might fumble and stumble for weeks before finally coming up with a minimally effective response.

A good venue for observing this pathology was the uproar that developed over sixteen words that had appeared in Bush's 2003 State of the Union address, delivered to a joint session of Congress on January 28, 2003. A substantial part of that speech was, not surprisingly, devoted to an attempt to justify the war against Saddam Hussein's Iraq, which loomed on the horizon. (The war actually began less than two months later, on March 20.) Amid many other arguments and assertions was this sentence: "The British Government has learned that Saddam Hussein recently sought significant quantities of uranium from Africa."[60]

This statement initially attracted little attention. In the days immediately following Bush's speech, it received one brief mention in the *New York Times* and two in the *Washington Post*. What pushed this claim into the center of the national discourse was an op-ed published in the *New York Times* on July 6, 2003. Written by former ambassador and career foreign service officer Joseph C. Wilson, it revealed that Wilson had been asked by the CIA to go to Niger to investigate a report that Iraq had negotiated a "memorandum of agreement" to purchase yellowcake uranium. (Yellowcake is a type of partially processed uranium ore that is, for that reason, easier to enrich into a form that can be used in nuclear weapons.) In February and March 2002, Wilson had talked with a number of current and former government officials and other people associated with Niger's uranium business and concluded that "it was highly doubtful that any such transaction had ever taken place." Moreover, Wilson asserted, he had "every confidence that the answer I provided was circulated to the appropriate officials within our government." In particular, since his mission had been undertaken at the request of Vice President Cheney, there would have been "a specific answer from the agency to the office of the vice president."

Viewing Bush's State of the Union address against that background, Wilson concluded that "some of the intelligence related to Iraq's nuclear weapons program was twisted to exaggerate the Iraqi threat" and that "a legitimate argument" could be made "that we went to war under false pretenses."[61] In an interview with the *Washington Post* that was published on the same day, Wilson adopted an even harsher tone: "It really comes down to the administration misrepresenting the facts on an issue that was a fundamental justification for going to war. It begs the question, what else are they lying about?"[62]

Before proceeding further, it is worth taking a closer look at the famous sentence that generated all the controversy. The first point worth noting is that Bush only claimed that Saddam Hussein had "sought" to buy uranium, not that he had actually acquired any or even finalized a deal. This is a distinction that Joseph Wilson never seems to have appreciated. His op-ed and a book he published in 2004 both contain numerous references to the "alleged sale" of uranium, the "uranium deal," and the "secret transaction," as well as a detailed discussion of all the safeguards that would have prevented an off-the-books transaction.[63] But no "sale" or "deal" was ever alleged. Of course, a finding that Iraq had successfully purchased uranium would have been more disturbing than the claim that that country had only tried to acquire it. But even an unsuccessful effort—assuming it took place—would have shown that the Iraqi government was still actively trying to develop a nuclear weapon, which was the point Bush sought to make.

Second, Bush specifically attributed this claim to the "British Government." That attribution would not permit the president to pass on a claim that he knew to be false. But it does suggest that the administration should have been held to a somewhat lower standard of proof. Implicitly, I would argue, Bush's phrasing says, "The British Government has made this claim and we think they are a credible source. We can't verify the claim on our own, but neither do we have the evidence to disprove it."

There were two plausible ways that the Bush White House might have responded to Wilson's accusations that were broadly consistent with the facts. One was to concede that the sentence at issue was inaccurate, but that none of the relevant agencies had objected to it at the time the State of the Union speech was being prepared and that Bush had therefore believed it to be true when the speech was delivered. A second option was to claim that the sentence was in fact correct: that the British government *did* say that Saddam Hussein had sought significant quantities of uranium from Niger. The CIA had at one point tried to persuade the British that this claim was false and should be dropped from its official intelligence reports— but the British had rejected the US recommendation, saying that they had "separate intelligence" to confirm the allegation, intelligence that was not available to the Americans and, for various reasons, could not be shared.[64]

Whatever strategy the administration chose, certain imperatives were clear. Given the "feeding frenzy" that had immediately erupted over Wilson's column and his appearance the same day on *Meet the Press*, the administration needed to get its version of the story out as quickly as possible. On the other hand, they also needed to make sure that this version was relatively complete and that they were not forced to modify or retract it as new information became available. It was also important that the administration's response be unified and coordinated: that all the various entities involved in drafting and reviewing the speech—the White House, the CIA, the National Security Council—agree on what had happened and why.

Yet it was precisely this lack of central planning and direction that is perhaps the most conspicuous feature of the administration's response to the sixteen words controversy. Commentary on administration communications efforts during this period often uses words like "clumsy," "disjointed," and "disarray."[65] Indeed, there is no agreement among the major players as to whether a meeting was ever held to agree on a unified strategy. Condoleezza Rice claims in her memoir that she, the president, the vice president, and CIA director George Tenet met on the day Wilson's column was published and decided to "take the issue off the table and say that the claim should not have been included in the President's speech." But Tenet, in his memoir, said that "I know of no meeting that was convened to come to this decision." Dick Cheney, in his autobiography, says that there was "at least one discussion in the Oval Office, about whether we should apologize" for the sixteen words (he does not say who participated in the meeting) but adds that he "was under the impression that the president had decided against a public apology."[66]

To be fair to the Bush White House, the Niger uranium controversy caught them at a moment of particular vulnerability. Wilson's column, as noted above, was published on July 6. On July 7, Bush took off for a long-planned trip to Africa, taking Condoleezza Rice, presidential press secretary Ari Fleischer, and White House communications director Dan Bartlett along with him. A day or two later, Tenet flew to Sun Valley, Idaho, to deliver a speech and take a short vacation. On July 11, Karl Rove also left town, driving to Mississippi "through places with spotty cell coverage."[67] Obviously, agreeing on a unified strategy would be much more difficult with so many of the principals scattered around the globe. But that only accentuates the fact that no one person or entity seems to have had the authority to whip all the participants into line.

Whether agreed upon in advance or not, most of the major players in the Bush administration opted for the first strategy. In a press briefing held on the morning of July 7, Fleischer initially tried to downplay the whole issue but stumbled over the question of whether the administration was now conceding that Bush's original claim was wrong. That issue was apparently resolved later that evening, when a "senior Bush administration official" released a statement to the Washington Post that said: "Knowing all that we know now, the reference to Iraq's attempt to acquire uranium from Africa should not have been included in the State of the Union speech." The article that resulted carried an unambiguous headline: "White House Backs Off Claim on Iraqi Buy."[68]

But if some Bush advisors thought that this admission would "take the issue off the table"—Condoleezza Rice was a particular proponent of this view—they were very wrong. (Rice acknowledges this in her memoir.)[69] Instead, it merely prompted a flood of new questions—questions that the White House was, at this time, unprepared to answer. How did the offending sentence get included in the State of the Union speech, a major speech that was supposed to be carefully reviewed and "cleared" by all of the agencies whose policies and programs were mentioned? Was it in fact the case, as Joseph Wilson had asserted, that the White House knew the claim was wrong and used it anyway, thus deliberately exaggerating the Iraqi threat?

After several days of relentless questioning from the sizable press contingent that had accompanied the president to Africa, on July 11 Rice, who was not an expert in media relations and should never have been making communications decisions on her own initiative, made another attempt to calm the waters. Speaking to reporters on Air Force One while flying to Uganda,

Rice declared, "If the CIA, the director of central intelligence, had said, 'take this out of the speech,' it would have been gone, without question." Though the CIA had requested a number of minor changes, "the agency cleared [the final text] and cleared it in its entirety."[70] Later the same day, in answer to a reporter's question, Bush himself said that "I gave a speech to the Nation that was cleared by the intelligence services."[71] Together, these statements were obviously designed to deflect blame from the president. But they also had the (apparently unintended) consequence of seeming to place full responsibility for the erroneous sixteen words on the CIA, an attribution that was not well-received by agency officials. As would eventually become clear, the White House was not entirely without fault in the affair.

To further complicate matters, not everyone in the Bush administration conceded that the sixteen words were mistaken. The vice president's office, in particular, continued to argue that there was solid evidence that Iraq had indeed tried to purchase uranium from Niger. One of their key talking points was the claim that a National Intelligence Estimate (NIE) prepared in October 2002 indicated "no doubts about Iraq's efforts to buy uranium." (In fact, the NIE had mentioned reports of the purported Iraq-Niger transaction but was equivocal about whether any such attempt had actually occurred.)[72]

Meanwhile, back in Idaho, CIA Director Tenet was trying to draft a statement that, he assumed, would be one part of an acknowledgment of "shared responsibility": the CIA had made some mistakes, but so had some members of the White House.[73] After going through seventeen drafts, the final statement was released late on Friday July 11. It began with a clear acknowledgment that the CIA had, in fact, approved the State of the Union speech before it was delivered and that "the President had every reason to believe that the text presented to him was sound."[74] It then contained one block of material that should have pleased the White House and one section that the White House disliked.[75]

On the positive side, Tenet's statement included a brief but thorough rebuttal to Joseph Wilson's op-ed piece. Specifically, the CIA director provided at least four solid bases for challenging Wilson's criticisms:

1. Wilson's mission had not been undertaken at the vice president's request. He had been sent to Niger by the "CIA's counterproliferation experts, on their own initiative."
2. This was significant because it meant that the CIA made no special effort to inform the vice president about Wilson's findings, as they almost certainly would have if Cheney had been the instigator. Indeed, Wilson's "every confidence" notwithstanding, the results of his

mission were never communicated to "the President, Vice-President, or other senior Administration officials."

3. Wilson's column was not entirely forthcoming about what he had learned in Africa. In June 1999, a former Nigerien official told Wilson, a businessman had "insisted" that the official meet "with an Iraqi delegation to discuss 'expanding commercial relations' between Iraq and Niger." Though the meeting never occurred, the former official had interpreted the overture as an attempt to purchase uranium. Given the nature and priorities of the Iraqi government and the short list of Nigerien exports, there were few other plausible commodities that Iraq might have been interested in obtaining. As a result, the CIA actually concluded that Wilson's report "did not resolve whether Iraq was or was not seeking uranium from abroad." Yet Wilson said not one word about this encounter in his article or subsequent interviews.

4. Contrary to Wilson's interview with the *Washington Post*, the claim that Iraq had tried to buy uranium from Niger was not a "fundamental justification for going to war." In the October 2002 National Intelligence Estimate, the CIA had actually cited *six* reasons for believing that "Iraq was reconstituting its nuclear weapons program" and the alleged Niger-uranium connection hadn't been one of them.[76]

Unfortunately for the White House, virtually none of these points came through in subsequent press coverage. Part of the problem was that Tenet had released his statement on a Friday evening, traditionally regarded by most politicians and press-watchers as the ideal time to make something public if one's goal was to ensure as *little* coverage as possible. To make matters worse, the opening paragraph of Tenet's statement, along with Rice's and Bush's comments from earlier in the day, meant that the dominant theme in news stories was the apparent effort to blame the whole mess on the CIA. The *New York Times* story, for example, was headlined "C.I.A. Chief Takes Blame in Assertion on Iraqi Uranium." The *Washington Post*'s story was titled "Bush, Rice Blame CIA for Iraq Error." Neither story included any mention of the many ways in which Tenet had contradicted Wilson.[77]

As for the part the White House didn't like: Tenet's statement also attempted to provide some "perspective" and "history" on the Niger-uranium question. The gist of this material was that there had long been questions about the reliability of the claim that Iraq had sought uranium from Africa and that, for that reason, "the subject was not included in many public speeches, Congressional testimony and the Secretary of State's United Nations presentation in early 2003."[78] In other words: only the White House somehow never got the message.

Though many in the White House were apparently disappointed by Tenet's statement, it did everything they might reasonably have expected. Besides acknowledging his agency's error in unmistakable terms, the CIA director had provided a solid basis for a counterattack against Wilson—though to do so would have required a concerted effort by the Bush communications team to highlight some of the nonheadline portions of the statement. Whether the White House made such an effort is unclear. If they did, it had no visible impact on the substance of contemporary press coverage. What the White House *did* turn into a major talking point was a claim that Tenet had not made: that Joseph Wilson had been recruited for the Niger mission by his wife, Valerie Plame Wilson, who worked for the CIA.

In retrospect, one of the more puzzling aspects of the whole sixteen words controversy is why anyone thought that attributing Wilson's mission to his wife was an especially powerful or persuasive argument. There *was* a valid reason for pointing out that the mission hadn't been undertaken at the behest of Vice President Cheney, because this helped explain why Wilson's findings were never reported to the top officials in the White House, as Wilson had claimed. But whether Wilson's name was suggested by his wife or someone else was of questionable relevance.[79] Whoever first proposed him for the mission to Niger, he was clearly qualified for the job. Though he had no background in nuclear proliferation issues, he had spent twenty-three years in various foreign service jobs, including extended stints in both Iraq and Niger. In the period immediately prior to the 1991 Gulf War, Wilson was the top American diplomat remaining in Iraq, in which capacity he had managed to ensure that several hundred Americans were able to leave that country safely before the war started. Nor could he or his wife be accused of organizing a "junket" and thus using their relationship for personal benefit: he had performed the Niger mission without being paid for it.

In going after Wilson's wife, moreover, the White House was playing with fire—and possibly engaging in criminal activity. The Intelligence Identities Protection Act of 1982 had made it a crime to intentionally disclose the identity of a "covert agent."[80] To be fair to the persons who first called attention to Valerie Wilson's role in the affair, it is not clear that they were fully aware of her status. Though she was undeniably a "covert agent" as defined in the law, her position at the CIA was probably better described as that of an "analyst" rather than a "spy."[81] Still, as this White House should have known, any disclosures connected to the CIA involved significant potential dangers. Whatever the reasoning, shortly after Wilson's op-ed piece was published, a number of high-level White House figures told reporters that Wilson had been sent to Niger by his wife who worked for the CIA, obviously hoping that this information would be printed or broadcast. Exactly how far this effort extended—how many Bush administration personnel were involved and how many reporters were contacted—has, so far as I can determine, never been conclusively settled. But a general description has been provided by Special Counsel Patrick Fitzgerald in April 2006: "[Fitzgerald] reported . . . that 'multiple officials in the White House' . . . discussed Plame's CIA employment with reporters before and after publication of her name on July 14, 2003 . . . Fitzgerald said the grand jury has collected so much testimony and so many documents that 'it is hard to conceive of what evidence there could be that would disprove the existence of White House efforts to 'punish Wilson.'"[82]

One White House informant was Press Secretary Ari Fleischer, who had been told of Valerie Wilson's position by both I. Lewis "Scooter" Libby, Vice President Cheney's chief of staff, and communications director Bartlett. While still in Africa with the president, Fleischer relayed this information to reporters from NBC News and *Time* magazine. (Neither thought the revelation significant enough to report it.)[83] Bartlett himself also encouraged at least one reporter to investigate who had sent Wilson on his mission.[84]

By all accounts, however, it was Vice President Cheney who, without any apparent attempt to coordinate his efforts with the rest of the White House communications shop, was at the center of the campaign to "discredit, punish, or seek revenge against" Joseph Wilson.[85] Though Wilson's op-ed had been, in the most direct sense, a broadside against George W. Bush, Cheney seems to have interpreted the piece as an attack on his own honor and credibility. Scooter Libby was particularly active in carrying out Cheney's directions, telling at least three reporters that it was Wilson's wife who had sent him on his errand.

How active Rove was in the campaign against Wilson's wife is a matter of some dispute. Valerie Wilson's work for the CIA and her purported role in sending her husband to Niger were first made public in a syndicated column by Robert Novak that was published on July 14. The key sentences in this column read: "[Joseph] Wilson never worked for the CIA, but his wife, Valerie Plame, is an agency operative on weapons of mass destruction. Two senior administration officials told me that Wilson's wife suggested sending him to Niger."[86] The original source for this revelation, Novak would later disclose, was Deputy Secretary of State Richard Armitage. Armitage was not a White House intimate nor, by all accounts, was he seeking revenge against Wilson and his wife. (He was actually an early opponent of the Iraq war.) He was simply a guy who liked to gossip. The other "senior administration official" was Rove—but Rove's role was, according to both Rove and Novak, a quite passive one. It was Novak who first mentioned Wilson's wife and said that he had heard she worked for the CIA. Rove merely responded "Oh, you know about that, too" (Novak's version) or "I've heard that, too" (Rove's version). Novak interpreted Rove's response as an "affirmation" of what he had learned earlier from Armitage, though Rove has denied that that was his intention.[87] Rove also mentioned Valerie Wilson's place of employment in a telephone conversation with a *Time* reporter.[88] Finally, Rove had a disputed conversation with MSNBC host Chris Matthews. According to Matthews, Rove said that the Wilsons "were trying to screw the White House so the White House was going to screw them back." "Wilson's wife," Rove added, "is fair game." (This last phrase would eventually become the title of Valerie Wilson's autobiography.) According to Rove, it was Matthews who asked if Wilson's wife was "fair game"; Rove only said that it was fair "to assess Wilson's claim that he was sent to Africa at the request of Vice President Cheney's office."[89]

In July 2003, the role of Valerie Wilson in her husband's Niger mission was a minor sideshow to the larger controversy about whether the sixteen words should have been included in the State of the Union speech and, if not, who was to blame. The latter story continued to be a front-page issue until July 22, when deputy national security adviser Stephen Hadley told a press conference that the CIA had sent him two memoranda in October 2002 "warning him that evidence about Iraqi efforts to obtain uranium in Africa was weak." Hadley said that he had not remembered receiving these memos and that they had only been discovered "in the last 72 hours." "I should have asked that the 16 words be taken out," Hadley acknowledged. "I failed in that responsibility."[90] With the White House finally shouldering its share of the blame, the story finally petered out several days later.

But not for long. Though Novak's column had generated only a small amount of response when it first appeared, it was catapulted onto the front page in late September 2003 by reports that George Tenet had asked the Justice Department to look into the allegation that "administration officials [had] leaked the name of an undercover CIA officer to a journalist."[91] The charge that the Bush White House had leaked the name of a covert agent and perhaps "put [her] life in danger"[92] quickly became a scandal in its own right—one that would plague the Bush administration for the next several years. It led to the appointment of a special counsel, the near indictment of Karl Rove, and the indictment and conviction of Scooter Libby.

The uproar over the attacks on Wilson and his wife also had the effect of prolonging what might otherwise have been a relatively brief front burner story. As shown in table 9.1, Wilson's original op-ed and its associated revelations generated a flurry of coverage over the subsequent three weeks: twenty-four stories in the *New York Times*, forty in the *Washington Post*. And then the media seem to have lost interest in the issue. Over the next two months, there were just two stories about the Niger-Iraq uranium connection in the *Times*, six in the *Post*—and only one of these was on the front page. It wasn't until Tenet requested a Justice Department investigation of the White House leaks that media interest in the topic picked up again.

One final episode in this tangled saga deserves mention. Having suffered a great deal of negative press for those infamous sixteen words in Bush's 2003 State of the Union speech, in July 2004, almost exactly one year after the publication of Wilson's op-ed, the administration actually received two pieces of good news. The first came on July 9, with the publication of a report on prewar intelligence by the Senate Select Committee on Intelligence. The main thrust of that report, not surprisingly, was that the US intelligence community had been almost entirely wrong in its estimates of the state of Iraq's nuclear, chemical, and biological weapons programs. In particular, most of the "key judgments" in the 2002 National Intelligence Estimate were "either overstated, or were not supported by, the underlying intelligence reporting."[93]

But the report also contained a number of findings that significantly undercut the claims of Joseph Wilson. Contrary to Wilson's assertion that he had definitively "debunked" the claim that Iraq was seeking uranium from Niger, most American intelligence analysts believed that his trip "did not provide substantial new information." If anything, however, Wilson's finding that an Iraqi delegation had traveled to Niger in 1999 seemed to provide "some confirmation" for the allegations that the United States had picked up from foreign intelligence services. And contrary to Wilson's repeated denials, "the plan to send the former ambassador to Niger was suggested by the former ambassador's wife." Finally, Wilson admitted to committee staff that he had made statements on matters about which "he had no direct knowledge" and about which he was, instead, "drawing on . . . unrelated past experiences or [had] no information at all. For example, when asked how he 'knew' that the Intelligence Community had rejected the possibility of a Niger-Iraq uranium deal, as he wrote in his book, he told Committee staff that his assertion may have involved 'a little literary flair.'"[94]

The other bit of good news appeared on July 14, when a British committee headed by Lord Butler released its "Review of Intelligence on Weapons of Mass Destruction." Like its American counterpart, the British committee documented serious and extensive failures in prewar intelligence. But not

Table 9.1. Articles on the Niger-Uranium Story in the New York Times and Washington Post, July 6–October 15, 2003

	New York Times	Washington Post
July 6–27, 2003	24	40
July 28–Sept. 27	2	6
Sept. 28–Oct. 15	15	23

Source: Based on a count of all stories including the words *Niger* and *uranium* in the Nexis Uni database during the specified time periods (accessed August 11, 2020).

all of that intelligence was deemed to be in error. The British government's "statements on Iraqi attempts to buy uranium from Africa" and thus, by extension, "the statement in President Bush's State of the Union Address" were declared to be "well-founded."[95]

Conservative commentators and media outlets were delighted by these revelations.[96] Their joy would turn to anger and frustration, however, when they saw that the attacks on Wilson were receiving little attention from the mainstream media—certainly nothing like the saturation coverage that had been given to Wilson's attacks on Bush. According to *Washington Post* media reporter Howard Kurtz, NBC television aired forty stories about Wilson's original allegations—but just one story about the Senate committee's criticisms of him. ABC did eighteen stories on the Wilson op-ed and the fallout from it, as against one story on the committee report. CBS had the worst record: thirty stories on Wilson's allegations, including fifteen in which Wilson was allowed to speak on camera—and not a single story on the Senate committee's findings.[97]

This striking imbalance admits of a number of explanations. Media critics and scholars have frequently complained that an attack, no matter how dubious, often gets more coverage than the rebuttal to it. (This is one explanation for the rise of Joe McCarthy.) And, yes, it would be surprising if media bias didn't have something to do with it. But another reason why these two stories were so significantly underreported was that the Bush administration made no discernible effort to publicize them. All presidential press secretary Scott McClellan would say was, "I think those reports speak for themselves on that issue." According to the *New York Times*, one reason that administration officials "were not crowing about the reports" was that "both reports were highly critical of most of the prewar intelligence . . . and to embrace one aspect of the reports would make it more difficult to dispute other findings."[98] But it was by then universally accepted that the prewar intelligence was in error. At this point in Bush's presidency, the key question was not whether many of the administration's assertions about weapons of mass destruction were wrong—they clearly were—but whether those errors were deliberate. The two reports that came out in July 2004 might have helped Bush repair at least some of the damage that his personal reputation had suffered. But as Martha Kumar has noted, not only was the Bush White House maladroit in coping with unanticipated bad news, they were also often inept in responding to unexpected good news.[99]

The Case of the Missing WMDs

There are a number of critical milestones in the downward slide of the Bush presidency. One, of course, was the decision to invade Iraq with a poorly conceived battle plan and no real idea what to do during the post-war occupation. Another was the inept response to Hurricane Katrina. A less obvious turning point occurred in late January 2004, when David Kay, who led the Iraq Survey Group, the entity that directed the search for weapons of mass destruction in Iraq, publicly reported his conclusion that the prewar intelligence had been "almost all wrong." Large stockpiles of biological and chemical weapons didn't exist: "I don't think there was a large-scale [WMD] production program [in Iraq] in the '90s."[100] Unlike Joseph Wilson's op-ed, Kay's conclusion should not have come as a total surprise to the White House. For months, administration critics had been raising questions about the failure to find ready evidence of such weapons. Yet, especially when compared to some of his earlier reports, which had struck a somewhat more optimistic tone, the interviews and congressional testimony Kay gave in late January seemed to put a final, official seal on the issue.

Kay's announcement posed a substantial threat to the future of the Bush presidency on at least two major levels. Most conspicuously, it took away what had been the principal public justification for the war in Iraq. The threat that Saddam Hussein would use weapons of mass destruction against the United States and its allies or would give them to terrorists was not the only reason Bush had given for effecting regime change in Iraq, but it was clearly the most prominent and politically potent reason.[101] With US casualties in Iraq slowly but steadily mounting, Bush now needed to rejustify the war.

The failure to find weapons of mass destruction in Iraq also threatened to undermine what many voters had long seen as one of George W. Bush's most attractive personal traits: his honesty and integrity. This image was partly an inheritance from his father. Especially when compared to his predecessor and his successor, George H. W. Bush's time in the White House had been remarkably scandal-free. When running for president in 2000,

George W. had played on this perception by repeatedly promising that "when I put my hand on the Bible, I will swear to not only uphold the laws of our land, I will swear to uphold the honor and dignity of the office to which I have been elected, so help me God."[102] Well after Bush entered the White House, at least in the opinion of his political handlers, a reputation for personal integrity continued to be one of Bush's greatest assets. When Scott McClellan became the president's press secretary in July 2003, Karen Hughes told him, "Your most important job, in my view, will be to make sure the president maintains his credibility with the American people. It's one of his greatest strengths. People trust him. His 'honest and trustworthy' numbers in polls have always been very high."[103] In May 2003, for example, a Pew Research Center survey had asked respondents to provide the one or two words that best described George W. Bush. The most popular answer, given by 29 percent, was "honest."[104]

David Kay's findings thus created a predicament that cried out for a major, prime-time television address to the nation. That address should have started by conceding that Kay's conclusion was accurate: that no large stockpiles of biological or chemical weapons were to be found in Iraq and that its efforts to develop a nuclear weapon had made far less progress than previous intelligence had indicated. If a large cache of WMDs were later discovered, the White House would have no trouble calling attention to that finding and acknowledging that Bush's concession had been premature. But insisting that the weapons might still be found, after nine months of unsuccessful searching, only helped Bush acquire a well-deserved reputation as someone who hated to admit his mistakes.

That matter settled, Bush could then have correctly pointed out that, once one got past the headlines and ten-second sound bites, much of what Kay said actually supported the claim that Saddam Hussein posed a real danger to other Middle Eastern countries and to the world. Certainly, there could be no doubt about Saddam's intentions—or his compliance with UN mandates. In Kay's words: "We have discovered hundreds of cases, based on both documents, physical evidence, and the testimony of Iraqis, of activities that were prohibited under the initial U.N. Resolution 687 and that should have been reported under [Resolution] 1441, with Iraqi testimony that not only did they not tell the U.N. about this, they were instructed not to do it and they hid material."[105]

And even if there was little evidence that Saddam's regime had cooperated with al-Qaeda or other terrorist groups, there was still a real danger that Iraqi material and know-how could have been put in the hands of terrorists. As Kay explained: "We know that terrorists were passing through Iraq. And now we know that there was little control over Iraq's weapons capabilities. I think it shows that Iraq was a very dangerous place. The country had the technology, the ability to produce, and there were terrorist groups passing through the country—and no central control."[106]

Next, Bush should have confronted head-on the assertion, immediately popular among Democrats, that his administration had "cooked the books" and "lied us into war": that it had deliberately falsified and distorted the "evidence" purporting to show that Iraq had weapons of mass destruction. The great problem with this argument was that the Bush administration was far from the only entity that had made this claim. Lots of foreign governments, who had their own intelligence services, also believed that Saddam had such weapons. Even countries such as France and Germany, who declined to support the American-led war effort, never disputed the existence of an active Iraqi WMD program.

In his memoir, Karl Rove tried to refute the "Bush Lied, Thousands Died" charge by pointing out that a large number of major Democrats, including Al Gore, Jay Rockefeller, and Bob Graham, had made statements in 2002 and 2003 indicating that they, too, believed that Saddam possessed such weapons.[107] But this line of argument permitted an easy response: that when they made these statements, Democrats were relying on intelligence produced by various agencies within the executive branch, which were therefore susceptible to influence and pressure from the president, the vice president, and other Bush appointees. A far more effective tactic would have been to emphasize that Bill Clinton, whose power over these same agencies had been at least as comprehensive as Bush's, had also been convinced that Iraq had an active WMD program.

Had Bush actually given a prime-time speech on the subject, he could have—and should have—quoted extensively from Clinton's public speeches and messages. Here, for example, is an excerpt from a Clinton speech at the Pentagon in February 1998:

> In 1995, Hussein Kamel, Saddam's son-in-law and the chief organizer of Iraq's weapons of mass destruction program, defected to Jordan. He revealed that Iraq was continuing to conceal weapons and missiles and the capacity to build many more. Then and only then did Iraq admit to developing numbers of weapons in significant quantities and weapons stocks. . . .
>
> What did it admit? It admitted, among other things, an offensive biological warfare capability, notably 5,000 gallons of botulinum, which causes botulism; 2,000 gallons of anthrax; 25 biological-filled Scud warheads; and 157 aerial bombs. And I might say, [United Nations] inspectors believe that Iraq has actually greatly understated its production.[108]

In a nationally televised speech in December 1998, Clinton made clear both the threat this posed and the inability of the United Nations inspectors to keep Saddam in check:

> In short, the inspectors are saying that, even if they could stay in Iraq [they had just been kicked out], their work would be a sham. Saddam's deception has defeated their effectiveness. Instead of the inspectors disarming Saddam, Saddam has disarmed the inspectors. . . .
>
> Without a strong inspections system, Iraq would be free to retain and begin to rebuild its chemical, biological, and nuclear weapons programs in months, not years. . . . [Saddam] will surmise that he has free rein to rebuild his arsenal of destruction. And some day, make no mistake, he will use it again, as he has in the past.[109]

And later in the same speech, Clinton claimed, "The hard fact is that so long as Saddam remains in power, he threatens the well-being of his people, the peace of his region, the security of the world. The best way to end that threat once and for all is with a new Iraqi Government, a Government ready to live in peace with its neighbors, a Government that respects the rights of its people."[110]

Lest one think that Clinton changed his mind during his final year in office as new intelligence became available, his last communication to Congress on the issue, dated July 28, 2000, said in no uncertain terms, "The Government of Iraq continues to engage in activities inimical to stability in the Middle East and hostile to United States interests in the region. Such Iraqi actions pose *a continuing unusual and extraordinary threat to the national security and foreign policy of the United States.*"[111]

For those who are inclined to dismiss all this as mere rhetoric, designed only to insulate Clinton from charges that he was "weak on defense," the most telling demonstration of Clinton's beliefs about weapons of mass destruction in Iraq is the fact that his wife, then-senator Hillary Clinton, voted in favor of the resolution authorizing President Bush to use American armed forces in Iraq in any way he deemed "necessary and appropriate." Surely, if Clinton had any doubts about the WMD issue, he would have warned her not to vote in support of the war. As it was, a strong case can be made that that one vote, as much as anything else, cost her the 2008 Democratic presidential nomination and with it the White House.

Finally, Bush should have tried to put the Iraqi war intelligence failure in historical context, for this was certainly not the first time that US intelligence agencies had badly missed the mark. As Professor Peter Feaver of

Duke University noted in a remarkable op-ed piece that could easily have served as the first draft of a Bush speech:

> The [US] intelligence community has a sorry record of assessing just how advanced an incipient WMD program really is. In fact, there is a striking pattern. In each of [the following] cases, new evidence turned out to rebut the established consensus of the intelligence community: the Soviet Union in 1949, China in 1964, India in 1974, Iraq in 1991, North Korea in 1994, Iraq in 1995, India in 1998, Pakistan in 1998, North Korea in 2002, Iran in 2003 and Libya in 2003. In each of these cases, the WMD program turned out to be *more advanced* than the intelligence community thought.[112]

The pattern Feaver describes was set early in the atomic era, when US intelligence significantly underestimated the progress of the Soviet Union in developing an atomic bomb. As President Truman has recorded in his memoirs, the American "monopoly [on atomic weaponry] came to an end sooner than the experts had predicted. An atomic explosion took place in Russia in August 1949. The intelligence experts had different opinions about it, but in general none of them had looked for the Russians to detonate any atomic device before 1952."[113]

The most significant of Feaver's examples, however, was Iraq in 1991. When the first president Bush and his top advisors were planning the first Gulf War, they knew that Saddam Hussein had chemical and biological weapons: he had used them against the Iranians and the Kurds. It was also known that Saddam *wanted* to acquire a nuclear weapon, but virtually no one in the US government or among its allies thought he was pursuing that quest very actively or was close to achieving his goal.

Fortunately for the United States, Israel, and the rest of the Middle East, after the fighting ended, the United Nations Security Council passed a resolution requiring Iraq to rid itself of all chemical and biological weapons and agree not to acquire or develop nuclear weapons. More importantly, the UN established a Special Commission, named UNSCOM, to make sure that Iraq lived up to these stipulations. After an exchange of letters with the Iraqi foreign minister, UNSCOM was given broad powers to go anywhere it wanted in Iraq and examine and analyze anything it deemed relevant.[114]

The UNSCOM inspectors soon discovered that the Iraqi nuclear program was far larger and more advanced than previous intelligence had believed. As the *Washington Post* summarized the situation in October 1991:

Until recently, Iraq was able to conceal from the outside world the origins, dimensions and operation of the [atomic] bomb program, its extensive connections to foreign suppliers and even the identity of . . . its native mastermind. . . . Despite repeated warnings and Saddam's own public statements, Western experts consistently underestimated Iraq's scientific and technical capabilities. Inspection officials now believe Iraq was only 12 to 18 months from producing its first bomb, not five to ten years as previously thought.[115]

A front-page article in the *New York Times* trumpeted the same conclusion: "Overall, the Iraqi bomb program was more ambitious, advanced and deadly than had previously been suspected, analysts said. A top former intelligence official said its enterprising nature and vast scale showed that the West's intelligence failure had been extensive. . . . From the evidence gathered by United Nations inspectors, it is now believed that Iraq could have been making atomic bombs in as little as a year."[116]

As the *Times* notes, this was not a small mistake. At the start of the Gulf War, the Iraqi nuclear program was a large operation, employing by some estimates as many as twenty thousand people and consuming several billion dollars in Iraqi government funds.[117] Yet US intelligence had only the sketchiest idea of what was going on. When the allied bombing campaign began, according to Michael Gordon and Bernard Trainor, the United States knew of just two nuclear facilities or test sites that were designated as bombing targets. Eventually, thirty-nine such facilities were discovered at nineteen separate locations.[118] These sorts of misjudgments continued throughout the war. One week into the air war, President Bush had declared, "Our pinpoint attacks have put Saddam out of the nuclear bomb-building business for a long time." General Norman Schwarzkopf also claimed that the air attacks had "destroyed all their nuclear-reactor facilities." In fact, postwar inspections found that the allies had "underestimated the size of Iraq's nuclear program and overestimated the damage they had inflicted on it." At the complex that constituted the "nerve center" of Saddam's nuclear program, for example, only about 15 percent of the buildings had been hit.[119] All told, said one Israeli military analyst, "This was a colossal international intelligence failure."[120]

The Gulf War intelligence failure deserved an extended discussion for at least two reasons. First, it helps explain why people like Vice President Dick Cheney and Deputy Secretary of Defense Paul Wolfowitz were inclined to downplay or ignore those intelligence analysts who disagreed with the consensus position and believed that Iraq did not have an active WMD program in the early 2000s. Both Cheney and Wolfowitz had held senior positions in the administration of George H. W. Bush, Cheney as secretary of defense, Wolfowitz as undersecretary of defense for policy. Both no doubt had vivid memories of just how bad the intelligence had been in the first US war against Saddam. Against that background, both men might reasonably have suspected that some of the intelligence might be equally wrong this time around (which it was, though in a different direction) and that especially in the wake of 9/11, the safest course was to assume that Saddam's WMD program was *at least* as dangerous as the bulk of current intelligence indicated. Analysts at the CIA viewed Iraqi intelligence from much the same perspective. As CIA Director George Tenet would later observe, "Inevitably, the judgments [the CIA made about the state of Iraq's WMDs in 2001 and 2002] were influenced by our underestimation of Iraq's progress on nuclear weapons in the late 1980s and early 1990s—a mistake no one wanted to repeat."[121]

Second, drawing attention to the intelligence failure in the first Gulf War would have served an important educational function. Simply put, assessing the state of a clandestine weapons program in a closed, highly secretive society is always going to be a difficult, mistake-prone task. Reforming the intelligence system (assuming it was done correctly) might help at the margins, but even then, every estimate of a WMD-development program in a totalitarian country needs to come with a large "error margin" attached to it. As Condoleezza Rice once suggested, the only "certain intelligence" about a country's nuclear capability comes when it actually explodes an atomic bomb.

Such a predicament obviously does not mean that the United States should declare war on every unfriendly nation it suspects may be developing a nuclear weapon. But when dealing with a country like Iraq, which was known to have possessed and used chemical weapons in the past, which had started two previous wars with little provocation or advance warning, Bush's general approach was clearly a defensible one: putting the burden of proof on Saddam, demanding that *he* show that he neither possessed nor was actively developing weapons of mass destruction. Had such a policy been properly executed, it would have sent a strong signal to other, similarly situated countries: that the United States meant what it said, that its threats and demands were to be taken seriously, that a dictator who hoped to stay in power would be more likely to do so by abandoning plans to develop chemical, biological, or nuclear weapons. Unfortunately, the aftermath of the Iraq war was sufficiently disastrous that countries such as Iran knew quite well that the United States was unlikely to pursue WMD disarmament in any other setting. Yet even with all the missteps described in chapter 7, the US invasion of Iraq was sufficient to persuade Libyan dictator Moammar Qadhafi to announce in December 2003 that he was end-ing his country's WMD program.

The outlines of a speech Bush might have given should now be clear. He could have admitted his mistake; insisted that it really was a mistake and not a deliberate attempt to mislead the public; pointed out that in most past situations US intelligence had erred on the opposite side, underestimating the state of a country's nuclear capability; and explained the stark choices that this posed for American foreign policy. Unfortunately, no such speech was ever given. In fact, the Bush administration made surprisingly little attempt in 2004 to defend its handling of the pre–Iraq war intelligence.

For an administration that always aspired to be "on message" and to speak with one voice, its response to the Kay report was notably confused and uncoordinated. In October 2003, David Kay had told Congress that "we have not yet found stores of weapons [of mass destruction]," though he added that "we are not yet at the point where we can say definitively . . . that such weapons stocks do not exist."[122] Yet no one in the White House political shop or in Rove's vaunted Office of Strategic Initiatives seems to have asked the obvious question: What do we do if the Iraq Survey Group never does find any weapons of mass destruction?

Since Kay had acknowledged that as of January 2004 the postwar search for weapons of mass destruction was still only 85 percent complete, many administration officials insisted that the weapons would be found in that last 15 percent or, at least, that it was too early to draw any firm conclusions. Presidential press secretary Scott McClellan, for example, re-sponded to initial press reports by saying, "Yes, we believe he [Saddam Hussein] had them [weapons of mass destruction], and yes we believe they will be found. We believe the truth will come out."[123] Noting that it had taken American forces ten months to find Saddam Hussein, Donald Rumsfeld told a congressional hearing that, "It's too early to come to final conclusions, given the work still to be done."[124]

Given the significance of the issues involved, George W. Bush himself clearly needed to play a major role in articulating the administration's response. Yet Bush was noticeably reluctant to say much of anything on the subject. The first news reports of Kay's findings were aired on the network evening newscasts on January 23; similar stories were on the front page of both the *New York Times* and the *Washington Post* on January 24. But the next few days had been designated as a time when the president would talk about health care, and no matter what was going on in Iraq or on the network evening news programs, administration planners were determined to stick to the script. So Bush gave a radio address on health care on January 24, held a town meeting in Arkansas on health care on

January 26, then delivered a lengthy speech in Washington on the same subject on January 28.[125] The only time during this period when Bush mentioned the WMD issue was on January 27—and then only because the subject was raised by reporters during a press availability that took place when Bush met with the president of Poland. In the brief interchange that followed, Bush had two major talking points, both of which he repeated several times. First, Saddam Hussein was a "gathering threat" to America and the world. Second, it was "very important . . . to let the Iraq Survey Group do its work so we can find out the facts," a statement that seemed to echo McClellan's conviction that the weapons would eventually be found.[126]

And so it continued for the next week. Though the failure to find weapons of mass destruction was one of the dominant issues in the mainstream media—between January 24 and February 5, it was the subject of nine front-page articles in the *New York Times*—George Bush did his level best to ignore the whole subject. He talked about it only when the press brought it up.[127] Even when circumstances effectively compelled him to say *something* about the war in Iraq, he managed to discuss that conflict without any reference to the Iraq Survey Group and its findings. At a "Bush-Cheney Reception" in Connecticut on January 29, for example, the president offered a wide-ranging defense of his record in office, including his handling of the economy, education, faith-based programs, and, unavoidably, the war on terrorism. In a speech that, in its printed form, ran forty paragraphs, Bush accordingly devoted three paragraphs to the war in Iraq. He said, quite correctly, that Iraqis would "never again have to fear the brutality of Saddam Hussein." He held out the prospect of a "free and democratic and peaceful Iraq," while acknowledging that achieving this goal would not be an easy task. But as to his highly publicized, frequently repeated claim that Iraq had an active program for the production of chemical, biological, and nuclear weapons, Bush said nary a word.[128]

Meanwhile, the candidates for the 2004 Democratic presidential nomination were delightedly attacking the president for what they alleged was a deliberate effort to hoodwink the country into war. Since most of the Democratic contenders had voted *for* the war, which was now highly unpopular with the Democratic base, the charge that Bush had purposely distorted the prewar intelligence was a godsend—a way the candidates could explain their change in position while making themselves appear blameless. As eventual nominee John Kerry said in a televised debate on January 29, "I could run a long list of clear misleading, clear exaggeration. They [the Bush administration] are really misleading all of America . . . in a profound way."[129]

Not until February 5, almost two weeks after Kay first announced his conclusions, did Bush finally offer a partial response to his critics. In a speech delivered in Charleston, South Carolina, the president quoted the chief weapons inspector as saying, "We have not *yet* found the stockpiles that we thought were there" (emphasis added). Or as the next day's *Washington Post* reported, "President Bush edged closer . . . to admitting that some of his prewar allegations about Saddam Hussein may have been mistaken," but stopped short of embracing that conclusion.[130]

Bush then offered a brief summary of some of Kay's other findings:

> Yet, the [Iraq] Survey Group has uncovered some of what the dictator was up to. We know Saddam Hussein had the capability to produce weapons of mass destruction. He had the scientists and technology in place to make those weapons. We know he had the necessary infrastructure to produce weapons of mass destruction because we found the labs and dual use facilities. . . . We know he was developing the delivery systems, ballistic missiles that the United Nations had prohibited. We know Saddam Hussein had the intent to arm his regime with weapons of mass destruction, because he hid all those activities from the world until the last day of his regime.

After noting that Saddam Hussein had a "record of using weapons of mass destruction" against both his enemies and his own people, Bush concluded:

> Knowing what I knew then and knowing what I know today, America did the right thing in Iraq. We had a choice: Either take the word of a madman, or take action to defend the American people. Faced with that choice, I will defend America every time.[131]

As a defense of Bush's handling of the prewar intelligence, the South Carolina speech was okay, though certainly not great. He did call attention to the many ways in which the Iraq Survey Group had shown Saddam to be a continuing danger, although quoting Kay directly rather than paraphrasing him might have been more effective. And he did point out the difficult choices Saddam posed for American policy in a post-9/11 world. But Bush made no attempt to rebut the charge that his administration had deliberately overstated the threat that Iraq posed; nor did he put the Iraq issue in historical context by pointing out that in most previous cases American intelligence had erred in the opposite direction. And the administration continued to deliver a mixed message. Even as Bush himself came close to admitting that Kay might have been right, Defense Secretary Rumsfeld and CIA Director George Tenet were giving speeches in which they insisted that there was still lots of work to be done and that those elusive weapons might yet be found.[132]

Apparently recognizing that they hadn't dealt with the WMD controversy very effectively, the Bush high command made one final attempt to respond to its growing army of critics. On February 7, the president sat for an extended, one-on-one interview with NBC's Tim Russert, which was aired the next day on "Meet the Press." As the Bush people almost certainly expected, more than half of the interview dealt with the war in Iraq and, in particular, the failure to find weapons of mass destruction.

As a vehicle for influencing public opinion and the larger public debate about the war in Iraq, an interview of this sort had its advantages and disadvantages. On the plus side, it suggested that the president had nothing to hide. A president who could demonstrate a solid command of the facts and respond effectively to unexpected questions could also reassure the public that their chief executive was intelligent, capable, and well-informed—but these were, in general, not Bush's strong points. When asked, for example, why the United States was now engaged in "nation-building" even though Bush had repeatedly condemned such activity during the 2000 campaign, Bush replied that in the case of Iraq, we were "fighting a war so that they [the Iraqis] can build a nation," an answer that few of his listeners probably understood, much less found persuasive.

On a more substantive level, Bush repeated the argument he had made two days earlier about how America could not "stand by and hope for the best from a madman." But he made only a few brief references to the fact that his "predecessor" and the "international community" also believed that Saddam had weapons of mass destruction, and said nothing about the nature of previous intelligence failures. On whether the weapons would eventually be found, Bush offered another mixed message. When Russert said that Saddam apparently did not possess and conceal WMDs, Bush replied, "Correct." But a minute later, he suggested that the weapons "could be hidden" or might have been "transported to another country."[133]

In a speech at Fort Polk, Louisiana, on February 17, Bush finally made a somewhat more concerted attempt to remind the nation that he was not alone in believing that Iraq had an active WMD program: "My administration looked at the intelligence information, and we saw a danger. Members of Congress looked at the same intelligence, and it saw a danger. The United Nations Security Council looked at the intelligence, and it saw a danger. We reached a reasonable conclusion that Saddam Hussein was a danger."[134]

This passage or some close variant of it would later become part of Bush's stock campaign speech over the next few weeks.[135] But without any details, without mention of how the Clinton administration had reached the same conclusion or the findings of the many foreign intelligence services, and with the debatable assertion that Congress had looked at the same intelligence, it was unlikely that many Americans were persuaded. Moreover, since this passage was usually stuck in the middle of a boilerplate list of the administration's major policy achievements, it was unlikely that most Americans were even aware of Bush's new argument.

And then the administration moved on to other topics. Particularly when compared to the long and systematic campaigns that were made to sell the president's tax cut and Social Security reform plans, it is remarkable how little effort was made to refute the charge that the president had deliberately led the nation into war under false pretenses.

I am not the only one to criticize the Bush administration's response to this issue. Karl Rove himself belatedly reached the same conclusion. As he says in his memoirs, published two years after Bush left office:

> Our weak response in defense of the president [on the WMD issue] and in setting the record straight, is, I believe, *one of the biggest mistakes of the Bush years*. When the pattern of the Democratic attacks became apparent in July 2003, we should have countered in a forceful and overwhelming way. This assault was worthy of significant attention by the entire White House, including a rebuttal delivered in a presidential address. We should have seen this for what it was: a poison-tipped dagger aimed at the heart of the Bush presidency (emphasis added).

One paragraph later, Rove made another significant admission: "So who was responsible for the failure to respond? I was. I should have stepped forward, rung the warning bell, and pressed for full-scale response. I didn't. Preoccupied with the coming campaign and the daily schedule in the West Wing, I did not see how damaging the assault was. There were others who could have sounded the alarm, but regardless, I should have."[136]

I think this second passage is correct on all counts. Rove made a serious mistake—and, at least in my opinion, a rather obvious one. But so did Karen Hughes and Dan Bartlett and Scott McClellan and, for that matter, George W. Bush himself. Somebody should have recognized the danger of letting such a major charge go unanswered.

The Effect on Public Opinion

Given the communications missteps examined in the last two sections of this chapter, it should come as no surprise that public assessments of

Bush's honesty and integrity, which the president's political advisors had once viewed as one of his greatest assets, took a dramatic nosedive during his last five-and-a-half years in office. Table 9.2 shows two measures of public opinion on this issue, both posed initially by the Gallup Poll. The first question asks specifically about Bush's honesty with respect to the war in Iraq. When this question was first posed to a national sample in early June 2003, 31 percent of the respondents said that the Bush administration had "deliberately misled the American public" about Iraqi WMDs, but 67 percent rejected that charge. By February 2008, a small majority of Americans—53 percent—thought that Bush had deliberately distorted the prewar intelligence while just 42 percent denied the accusation.

The second item in table 8.2 asks in more general terms whether one would describe George W. Bush as "honest and trustworthy." Just as Karen Hughes had told Scott McClellan, honesty had once been one of Bush's strengths. In three different surveys conducted between February and July 2001, before the 9/11 terrorist attacks sent the president's ratings soaring on virtually every dimension, two-thirds of the public consistently said that Bush was honest and trustworthy. (His overall approval rating at this time generally hovered between 55 and 60 percent.) Starting in late 2003, however, Americans became progressively more skeptical that Bush's word could be trusted. One month before Bush left office, only 37 percent believed he was honest and trustworthy.

What would these numbers have looked like if the Bush communications operation had done its job more effectively? This question is difficult to answer in a rigorous way. Of course, no communications campaign, no matter how well designed and executed, would have been 100 percent effective. In a nation where many people believed that Bush knew in advance about the terrorist attacks on the World Trade Center, many Americans would have doubted Bush's honesty regardless of what the White House said in his defense. But there are also strong reasons to think that many of those who came to doubt Bush's honesty might have been persuaded to render a different judgment.

Table 9.3 breaks down the responses to these two questions by party identification and ideology. Not surprisingly, given what we have learned about the dynamics of public opinion,[137] Democrats and liberals were most responsive to the charges against Bush: that is, they exhibited the biggest change. Republicans and conservatives were substantially more resistant, though even these two groups became significantly less trusting. But moderates and independents changed almost as much as Democrats and liberals. In the battle for "swing voters"—for those who were not strongly predisposed for or against Bush—the administration was a decisive loser.

As noted in chapter 3, many scholars have argued that presidential attempts to sell their policies—the practice of "going public"—have less effect on public opinion than one might infer from all the time and energy that are devoted to them. In many cases, polls conducted before and after a major presidential media campaign show little or no movement—or movement in the wrong direction.[138] Public opinion about policy issues, the leading study on this topic has concluded, usually moves very slowly— if it moves at all.[139] But a principal reason for such stasis is that in most controversies, the flow of messages reaching most Americans is two-sided. When an abortion-related controversy develops, most news reports will quote one pro-choice spokesperson and one pro-life person. The messages largely neutralize each other, with the result that American attitudes about abortion have stayed essentially constant for the last forty-five years. But when communication is largely one-sided—as it often is, for example, in certain kinds of foreign policy crises—a different dynamic is at work, and presidents can sometimes receive a significant boost in their approval ratings.[140] A good communications operation can't work miracles, but an administration that fails to answer its critics or answers them inadequately is asking for trouble.

Conclusion

Space has permitted me to analyze just four instances of the Bush communications operation in action. But they are four significant cases, and many more could be added to the list: the unwillingness to meet with Cindy Sheehan a second time, thereby creating a media sensation and antiwar hero; the administration's inability to mount an effective response to the claim that Bush had "banned" embryonic stem cell research; and the failure when announcing the Troubled Asset Relief Program to mention that he had tried on numerous occasions to impose stricter regulations on Fannie Mae and Freddie Mac and thereby undercut the claim that his administration was uniquely responsible for the economic mess.

Why did the Bush messaging shop mishandle so many of the issues it confronted? One explanation, developed earlier in this chapter, concerned the way the Bush high command had conceptualized its task. Karl Rove, Karen Hughes, et al. entered the White House determined to communicate on their own terms rather than having their agenda dictated by the media or their political opponents. They would plan much of their messaging activity in advance and then try to stick to those plans no matter what else intervened. The downside of this strategy, of course, was that they were

Table 9.2. Changing Public Attitudes about George W. Bush's Honesty

1. GALLUP: "Do you think the Bush administration deliberately misled the American public about whether Iraq has weapons of mass destruction, or not?"

Sampling dates	Yes, misled	No, did not mislead	Don't know
May 30–June 1, 2003	31	67	2
June 9–10, 2003	31	64	5
June 27–29, 2003	37	61	2
July 18–20, 2003	39	58	3
Jan. 29–Feb. 1, 2004	43	54	3
July 19–21, 2004	45	52	3
Oct. 9–10, 2004	47	51	2
April 1–2, 2005	50	48	2
July 22–24, 2005	51	47	2
Oct. 28–30, 2005	53	45	2
Jan. 20–22, 2006	53	46	1
March 10–12, 2006	51	46	3
Feb. 21–24, 2008	53	42	5

2. GALLUP/ORC: "Thinking about the following characteristics and qualities, please say whether you think it applies or doesn't apply to George W. Bush. How about . . . is honest and trustworthy?"

Sampling dates	Applies	Does not apply	Don't know
GALLUP			
Feb. 9–11, 2001	64	29	7
April 20–22, 2001	67	29	4
July 10–11, 2001	66	31	3
April 29–May 1, 2002	77	20	3
July 26–28, 2002	69	26	5
Jan. 10–12, 2003	70	27	3
April 5–6, 2003	73	25	2
June 27–29, 2003	65	33	2
Nov. 14–16, 2003	59	40	1
Feb. 16–17, 2004	55	42	3
Jan. 14–16, 2005	56	41	3
April 1–2, 2005	56	42	2
July 22–24, 2005	54	44	2
Aug. 28–30, 2005	51	47	2
Sept. 16–18, 2005	47	50	3
Oct. 28–30, 2005	49	48	3
Nov. 11–13, 2005	46	52	2
Jan. 20–22, 2006	49	49	2
Feb. 28–March 1, 2006	47	52	1
April 28–30, 2006	41	56	3
ORC			
April 21–23, 2006	40	55	5
Aug. 18–20, 2006	44	54	2
Dec. 15–17, 2006	45	53	2
March 9–11, 2007	43	52	5
Dec. 19–21, 2008	37	62	1

Table 9.3. Changes in Public Opinion about George W. Bush's Honesty, by Party Identification and Ideology

Percentage Who Think Bush Deliberately Misled the Public

	May–June 2003	February 2008	Change
Republicans	9	15	+6
Independents	31	57	+26
Democrats	51	80	+29
Conservatives	14	29	+15
Moderates	33	58	+25
Liberals	56	84	+28

Percentage Who Say That Bush Is Not Honest and Trustworthy

	February 2001	Feb.–March 2006	Change
Republicans	6	14	+8
Independents	31	58	+27
Democrats	49	80	+31
Conservatives	18	33	+15
Moderates	33	58	+25
Liberals	41	77	+36

Source: All data are from the Gallup Poll.

much less adept at dealing with unplanned issues and events, such as the matters examined in this chapter.

The communications problems of the Bush White House may also reflect an inability to appreciate the differences between campaigning and governing. Devising a plan that indicates precisely which issues will be talked about when may be a reasonable way of conducting an election campaign. It is much less useful as an approach to governing, especially at the presidential level, where so much of a president's agenda is unplanned or dictated by outside events. The White House may not have wanted to talk about the missing weapons of mass destruction in late January 2004, but that, and not health care, was the topic that needed to be addressed— especially since the president's message on health care said little that had not been said many times before and was of uncertain relevance to the fall campaign.

Finally, many of the mistakes discussed in this chapter may simply represent a failure of imagination and ability. In selecting people for his White House staff—and for many other executive departments and agencies—Bush too often acted as if personal loyalty was more important than competence. (This also explains why he appointed Michael Brown to be the head of the Federal Emergency Management Agency and nominated Harriet Miers to the Supreme Court.) Other than Rove, presidential speechwriter David Frum was struck by the "dearth of really high-powered brains" on the White House staff.[141] Though Bush had some first-rate speechwriters, there was no one responsible for presidential image-making who compared with David Gergen and Michael Deaver, the men primarily responsible for handling such tasks during Ronald Reagan's first term.

10

It's Hard to Have Ideological Heirs When You Don't Have Much of an Ideology

Two days after the 2008 elections, while flipping through the buttons on my car radio, I came across a talk show whose host, apparently a conservative, posed this question to his listeners: "What, if anything, is worth saving from compassionate conservatism?" A far better question, I remember thinking at the time, was whether there was anything there in the first place.

The Need for Presidential Ideology

Though it rarely ranks very high on the standard lists of presidential do's and don'ts, a strong case can be made that any president who hopes to be successful in his job needs some kind of reasonably clear, overarching philosophy of government. Every president, of course, is required to take positions on a myriad of specific issues, both as a candidate and when in office. But a good president must also be able to fit all these individual policies into some kind of larger, more comprehensible whole. Call it vision, call it ideology, call it a sense of the big picture—a president who lacks it is unlikely to accomplish very much or leave a lasting imprint.

Certainly this is one lesson that emerges from a careful study of those presidents generally regarded as great. Presidents such as Washington, Jefferson, Lincoln, and Franklin Roosevelt left their legacies not only in the policies they adopted and the institutions they created but also in the ideas and principles they made a part of the American political tradition. As Marc Landy and Sidney Milkis have shown in their book *Presidential Greatness*, each of the great presidents was also a great teacher, "taking the people to school" and explaining, by both word and deed, the nature of democracy, the meaning of the Constitution, and the roles and responsibilities of presidents and ordinary citizens.[1] Winning the Civil War was a substantial achievement, but that alone is not enough to explain why

Abraham Lincoln is so widely revered today. What gives Lincoln plausible title to being the greatest American president was his ability to give larger meaning to the North's victory: to insist that it was not just a fight to preserve the Union (as he himself had once claimed) but a war to establish the proposition that all men are created equal.

Some readers might wish to argue that Franklin Roosevelt is an exception to the claims just made. In a speech delivered in May 1932, Roosevelt declared that the country demanded "bold, persistent experimentation,"[2] and according to some observers, he fulfilled this promise all too well. So anxious was he to do *something* about the Great Depression, these critics contend, that all the policies he adopted and the agencies he created ultimately lacked any kind of overall coherence. But this reading of the Roosevelt record has always struck me as greatly overstated. While there was much about the New Deal that was new and experimental, what strikes one in retrospect is how much in common all the "experiments" shared: almost all involved significant expansions in federal spending on and/or regulation of matters previously left to the decision of private businesses and individuals or to state and local governments. And if many important acts of the First Hundred Days defy easy ideological classification, the same cannot be said for the major products of the Second New Deal, such as Social Security and the National Labor Relations Act. Like Lincoln, Roosevelt's most enduring legacy was not the policies he enacted (many prominent New Deal programs, including the National Recovery Administration, the Works Progress Administration, and the Civilian Conservation Corps, were terminated in the late 1930s or early 1940s) but the principles that lay behind them. Since 1936, no major-party presidential nominee save perhaps Barry Goldwater has seriously challenged the proposition that the federal government has extensive, direct responsibilities for the economic and social welfare of the nation's citizens.

But even presidents with less exalted ambitions (or a lesser probability of achieving them) need a guiding philosophy for governing. Any president who hopes to be an effective communicator—a task that virtually everyone agrees is an essential feature of the contemporary presidency—must do more than announce and explain his preference for individual policies. He must also be able to set these policies into some larger context, drawing connections across apparently disparate issues and explaining why a particular problem is more deserving than its competitors of space on the national agenda. A sense of vision can also give direction to the president's own administration. Without this sort of guidance, a president is apt to stumble from one crisis to another, allowing external events and other political leaders to set the agenda, thereby sacrificing the ability to frame issues in a more advantageous way and to consider a broader array of alternative policies. A clear ideology can also help unify the executive branch, reducing (though never entirely eliminating) the likelihood that presidential appointees will pursue policies at variance with the president's own.[3]

The consequences of failing to possess a clear guiding philosophy are best illustrated by the presidency of George H. W. Bush. Throughout the 1988 presidential campaign, Bush was repeatedly criticized for lacking what he himself sometimes disparaged as "the vision thing." The following comment, drawn from a profile of Bush written in early 1987, is typical:

> Ideas and ideologies do not move Bush. People and their problems do. Domestic issues, in particular, stir him little. . . . Colleagues say that while Bush understands thoroughly the complexities of issues, he does not easily fit them into larger themes.
>
> This has led to the charge that he lacks vision. It rankles him. Recently he asked a friend to help him identify some cutting issues for next year's campaign. Instead, the friend suggested that Bush go alone to Camp David for a few days to figure out where he wanted to take the country. "Oh," said Bush in clear exasperation, "the vision thing."[4]

It turned out, however, that the critics were right. Particularly in domestic affairs, Bush showed little interest in doing much of anything. This is a major theme in virtually everything that has been written about the elder Bush's presidency.[5] One of the few significant domestic initiatives he pursued involved a complete repudiation of his most conspicuous 1988 campaign promise. An especially telling indicator of the Bush "agenda" occurred in November 1990. Where every other recent president has complained about the slow pace with which Congress acted on his legislative recommendations, just two years into his presidency Bush's chief of staff declared, "There's not another single piece of legislation that needs to be passed in the next two years for this president. In fact, if Congress wants to come together, adjourn, and leave, it's all right with us."[6] Even in foreign policy, where Bush generally received high marks from the public, he seemed content to grapple with individual crises and challenges as they presented themselves, with no obvious larger goal than short-term stability.

In the end, it was this lack of vision, more than anything else, that explains why the first George Bush was one of only three elected postwar presidents who failed to win a second term. In retrospect, the recession of 1990–1991 was not particularly severe or long-lasting; academic writings on the 1992 election have often argued that, by historical standards, the economy was doing well enough to have given Bush a reasonable probability of being reelected.[7] Indeed, election forecasting models that relied heavily on economic indicators generally predicted that Bush would *win* the 1992 contest.[8] The more serious impediment, from a political perspective, was Bush's complete inability to convince the American public that he recognized the problems they were facing or had any clear idea what to do about them. With little or no positive message coming from the White House, it is small wonder that the public had such a pessimistic view of the economy in 1992.

Compassionate Conservatism: The Strategic Imperative

As the presidential campaign of George W. Bush began to take shape in early 1999, then, one question that inevitably hovered over the water-testing concerned the Texas governor's general approach to questions of government and public policy. Did the son possess the sense of vision that his father so conspicuously lacked? More generally, just what, if any, political ideas and principles was he truly committed to?

This question assumed even greater prominence because Bush, as a governor, began his presidential odyssey with a substantially greater measure of ideological "flexibility" than is generally granted to US senators and representatives. However much senators and representatives might wish to claim that their approach to governing is new and unconventional, that the existing ideological labels simply don't apply to them, their record in national politics usually foils their efforts. Just by holding the offices they do, they will have been required to cast votes on a host of difficult and controversial issues, even if they themselves would have preferred to pose a different set of choices or frame the issues in a different way. Governors must also make difficult choices, of course, but in many cases, the precise meaning and significance of those choices may not be fully apparent to voters, reporters, and interest group leaders from outside the state. At the national level, by contrast, every major vote is invariably scrutinized and evaluated by a host of interest groups. Like it or not, senators and representatives acquire ratings from groups like Americans for Democratic Action (ADA) and the American Conservative Union (ACU) that allow them to be placed, with a fair measure of confidence, along the conventional liberal-conservative spectrum.

From the very beginning, the Bush campaign had a two-word answer to the ideology and vision question: George W. Bush was a "compassionate conservative." This was more than an isolated phrase that a few reporters plucked out of context from one of Bush's speeches. Bush's formal declaration that he intended to run for president, delivered in Iowa on June 12, 1999, was plainly designed to showcase this slogan:

> I'm running because our country must be prosperous. But prosperity must have a purpose. The purpose of prosperity is to make sure the American dream touches every willing heart. The purpose of prosperity is to leave no one out . . . to leave no one behind. I'm running because my party must match a conservative mind with a compassionate heart . . .
>
> I know this approach [compassionate conservatism] has been criticized. But why? Is compassion beneath us? Is mercy below us? Should our party be led by someone who boasts of a hard heart? . . . I am proud to be a compassionate conservative. I welcome the label. And on this ground I'll take my stand.[9]

But what exactly was compassionate conservatism? And why did Rove, who carefully stage-managed every major aspect of the Bush campaign, choose to present the Texas governor to the national electorate in this way?

The latter question is more easily answered. Whatever else one may say about compassionate conservatism, it was undoubtedly a clever political gambit. In fact, compassionate conservatism served at least two strategic needs for the Bush campaign. On an immediate level, it helped to separate Bush from the increasingly unpopular Republican Congress, then reeling from the fallout of both the 1995–1996 budget battle and the impeachment of President Clinton. In various polls conducted during the first two months of 1999, only 35 percent of Americans gave the "Republicans in Congress" an excellent or good rating, versus 60 percent who rated their performance as fair or poor. By a 51 percent to 27 percent margin, the public said that President Clinton had "better ideas for how to solve [the country's] problems" than the Republican Congress. In an ABC News poll, only 35 percent believed that congressional Republicans "understand the problems of people like you."[10] Plainly, any Republican presidential candidate who was linked too closely to his copartisans in Congress would have difficulty winning a general election.

But Rove had larger ambitions for compassionate conservatism. Though Bush's opponents for the 2000 Republican nomination dismissed the slogan as "silly and insulting,"[11] Rove had, at least, a more acute reading of the American electorate. In fact, ever since the New Deal, the Republican Party has suffered from a problem that, while somewhat broader than a perceived lack of compassion, plainly has some connection to that image. Consider two pieces of survey evidence:

Perhaps the best single indicator of this problem is provided by data taken from the American National Election Studies (ANES), a series of academic election surveys conducted almost every two years since 1952 by the University of Michigan. Near the beginning of their presidential election-year surveys, the ANES have always included a set of four open-ended questions that ask respondents, in simple, nondirective terms, if there is "anything in particular" that they like and dislike about the Democratic and Republican Parties.

Table 10.1 shows the top five answers that were given to these questions in the surveys taken in 1960 and 2000. Though these surveys were conducted forty years apart, they tell a remarkably consistent and politically significant story about the public images of the two major American parties. Notice first that in both years—and in all the years in between—the Democrats were viewed more favorably than the Republicans. In 2000, for example, American adults found more to like than dislike about the Democrats, 56 percent to 43 percent. For the Republicans, by contrast, negatives slightly outnumbered positives, 51 percent to 45 percent.

And despite all the momentous changes that had taken place in America and the world between 1960 and 2000, the source of the Democratic advantage was essentially the same in both years. The principal issue working in the Democrats' favor is what might best be described as *economic fairness*. The Democrats are seen as being more responsive to the interests of the "common people," the "little people," the needy, the working class. Republicans, by contrast, are criticized for being overly solicitous of "big business," the upper classes, the corporate rich, Wall Street. Moreover, as Mark Brewer has shown, this perception of the parties' relative concern for different social classes held true in *every* ANES presidential-year survey conducted between 1952 and 2004.[12]

A second manifestation of this Republican problem appears in public assessments of the personal qualities of recent presidential candidates—in particular, the extent to which they demonstrate a quality usually referred to as *empathy*. Empathy may be defined as the capacity of a presidential candidate or other political figure to understand, sympathize with, and then work in behalf of the problems and concerns of their constituents. According to several recent studies, it is one of the most important personal characteristics that American voters look for in a potential president.[13] Since 1984, this attribute has been measured in the American National Election Studies by a set of questions that ask survey respondents whether each of the major party presidential candidates "really cares about people like you."[14] The results are shown in table 10.2. In every instance, the Democratic candidate was rated more favorably than the Republican.

I have thought these results worth emphasizing because many conservative and Republican commentators apparently believe that it is the Republicans who generally score better on this dimension. Democrats, it is claimed, have often nominated candidates perceived by the voters as stiff and aloof, whereas Republican nominees seem more plain-spoken and "down-to-earth." In 2004, for example, many Republicans were delighted by the results of an Opinion Dynamics poll which had asked its respondents, "If you were at a picnic this Memorial Day, which of the presidential candidates would you rather sit down and have a beer or soda with—Bush or Kerry?" By a 42 percent to 36 percent margin, the public preferred Bush over Kerry.[15] Unfortunately for Republicans, there is no evidence that this sort of superficial, nonpolitical appeal has any measurable effect on voting decisions. Ronald Reagan may have been viewed as genial and avuncular, but as shown in table 10.2, it was Walter Mondale who was seen as more in touch with the concerns of the average voter. Michael Dukakis may not have provided a particularly compelling answer to a hypothetical question about his wife's rape and murder, but he was still seen as significantly more caring than George H. W. Bush. To judge from the stability of responses across elections, Americans form an opinion about a presidential candidate's empathy not on the basis of how he talks or behaves in staged media events, but on the basis of his *policies*, which are in turn inferred largely from the candidate's *party identification*.[16] In every election for which we have survey data, this has worked to the Republicans' disadvantage.

The data in tables 10.1 and 10.2 obviously do *not* mean that Republicans cannot win elections. In spite of this disadvantage in public perceptions, Republicans managed to win five of the six presidential elections held between 1968 and 1988; in 1994, they also, at long last, won a majority of seats in both houses of Congress. But for someone like Rove, who hoped to usher in a new era of Republican dominance like the one that began in 1896, tables such as these surely identified one of the major obstacles standing in his way. And though Rove may never have examined data from the American National Election Studies, he clearly appears to have reached the same conclusion: that to set a realignment in motion, and to increase his chances of winning the 2000 election, he had to convince the electorate that George Bush was, as Rove himself put it, "a different kind of Republican."[17] Hence, compassionate conservatism.

But what exactly did this tantalizing phrase mean? In what specific ways did Bush aspire to be different than the various incarnations of conservatism that had gone before him? Most importantly, is compassionate

Table 10.1. Public Images of the Democratic and Republican Parties: What Americans Liked and Disliked about the Parties in 1960 and 2000

A. 1960

	Percentage mentioning
Like about the Democratic Party	
1. Democrats good for the common people, poor people, the working class	22
2. Traditional vote (I've always been a Democrat)	10
3. Party of prosperity, times are better under Democrats	7
4. Democrats bring higher wages, more jobs	6
5. I just like them; it's a good party	5
Total mentioning at least one thing they like about the Democratic Party	**57**
Dislike about the Democratic Party	
1. Too much government spending, deficit spending	8
2. Democrats are the war party, always a war when Democrats are in office	5
3. Too radical, creeping socialism, welfare state	3
4. Can't trust Democrats; don't keep their promises	3
5. Dislike their stand on fiscal policy, high interest rates, taxes	3
Total mentioning at least one thing they dislike about the Democratic Party	**37**
Like about the Republican Party	
1. Better chance of peace; Republicans are the party of peace	8
2. Traditional vote (I've always been a Republican)	6
3. Conservative, like conservative wing of the party	6
4. Spend less money, more economy-minded	5
5. Eisenhower	4
Total mentioning at least one thing they like about the Republican Party	**47**
Dislike about the Republican Party	
1. Too good to big business, industry, upper classes	15
2. Republicans bad for common people, poor people, working-class	7
3. Against Republican foreign policy; too much indecision; vacillation; unclear policy	3
4. Dislike stand on tight money, high interest rates	3
5. I just don't like them; lousy party	3
Total mentioning at least one thing they dislike about the Republican Party	**44**
(N)	(1,181)

B. 2000

Like about the Democratic Party	
1. Democrats good for the common people, little people, working people	15
2. Democrats good for poor people, needy people, handicapped	7
3. Democrats good for white collar workers, middle class	5
4. For government activity; supports social programs, spending	4
5. Favor aid to education	4
Total mentioning at least one thing they like about the Democratic Party	**56**

(continued on the next page)

Table 10.1. *Continued*

B. 2000

	Percentage mentioning
Dislike about the Democratic Party	
1. Democrats too much in favor of big government; think government involved in too many things	8
2. Can't trust them; they break their promises	4
3. Too liberal	4
4. Would spend too much	4
5. For higher taxes	3
Total mentioning at least one thing they dislike about the Democratic Party	**43**
Like about the Republican Party	
1. Against government activity; favor reduction in social programs and spending	8
2. They are conservative	6
3. Favor lower taxes	6
4. Efficient, good administration; wouldn't increase national debt	4
5. Generally like their ideas, policies	4
Total mentioning at least one thing they like about the Republican Party	**45**
Dislike about the Republican Party	
1. Too good to big business, corporate rich, upper classes	18
2. Not good for common people, working people	5
3. Against tax reform, won't eliminate loopholes, write-offs	4
4. Oppose legalization of abortion	3
5. Too conservative	3
Total mentioning at least one thing they dislike about the Republican Party	**51**
(N)	(1,799)

Source: American National Election Studies, 1960 and 2000.
Note: Only the top five responses to each question are listed.

conservatism a viable way to get Republicans elected and then govern the nation? A small literature has grown up around these questions, generated partly by various former Bush advisors, partly by academic analysts.[18] Taken as a whole, however, these writings only deepen the mystery. If compassionate conservatism really was a clear and coherent approach to policy and governance, it is striking how little agreement there was, among observers from both inside and outside the administration, as to just what it was. Many of the leading variants, moreover, scarcely seem very new or have other obvious problems.

In the rest of this chapter, I attempt to unravel the nature of compassionate conservatism by examining its intellectual origins: by taking a close

Table 10.2. Public Perceptions about Whether a Presidential Candidate "Really Cares about People Like You"

Year	Candidate	Extremely well	Quite well	Not too well	Not well at all	Average rating
1984	Walter Mondale	14	42	25	7	2.72
	Ronald Reagan	13	32	31	20	2.40
1988	Michael Dukakis	13	44	24	7	2.72
	George H. W. Bush	10	35	29	16	2.43
1992	Bill Clinton	15	46	23	8	2.74
	George H. W. Bush	8	27	36	26	2.17
1996	Bill Clinton	15	42	27	15	2.57
	Robert Dole	7	33	40	15	2.34
2000	Al Gore	15	40	26	13	2.61
	George W. Bush	9	35	31	19	2.35
2004	John Kerry	14	40	28	13	2.58
	George W. Bush	17	29	27	27	2.36
2008	Barack Obama	24	39	23	12	2.76
	John McCain	10	32	37	19	2.33

Source: American National Election Studies.
Note: Question wording was, "I am going to read a list of words and phrases people may use to describe political figures. For each please tell me whether the word or phrase describes the candidate I name. . . . In your opinion, does the phrase 'really cares about people like you' describe [name of candidate] extremely well, quite well, not too well, or not well at all?" "Average rating" figures were computed by assigning a value of 4 for "extremely well" responses, 3 for "quite well," 2 for "not too well," and 1 for "not well at all," and then calculating a mean value for each candidate. "Don't know" responses are not shown in this table nor included in the average rating calculations.

look at the various people and ideas whom Bush read or listened to, who helped shape Bush's approach to domestic policy. In the end, of course, I am most interested in figuring out what Bush himself meant by the phrase, but approaching the question historically can at least give us a sense of the various options that Bush may have considered. As it turns out, this historical tour will also examine all of the major theories advanced by other scholars as to the true meaning of compassionate conservatism.

The Christian Conscience of Doug Wead

The first major strand of compassionate conservatism leads back to a man named Doug Wead. Wead is the sort of person who has worn so many hats and had so many occupations as to defy easy classification. At one time or another, he has been an ordained minister, historian, motivational speaker, presidential assistant, educator, political consultant, author, businessman, political candidate, and organizer of and participant in numerous charitable endeavors.[19] It was in the last of these roles that, in the early 1980s, he first became acquainted with then-vice president George H. W. Bush. When Bush found out about Wead's evangelical religious background, the vice president, who was already planning his 1988 presidential campaign, sought Wead's advice and assistance in trying to build a better relationship with the large evangelical wing of the Republican Party. In 1987, George W. Bush became his father's semiofficial liaison to the evangelical community, a position that effectively made him Wead's immediate superior. Over the next two years, the two men worked closely together, a relationship that was deepened by the younger Bush's recent "born again" experience. For several years, according to Jacob Weisberg, Wead acted as a kind of "surrogate family member" to the vice-president's son: "life counselor, political adviser, spiritual companion."[20] Though Wead played a much smaller part in George W. Bush's 2000 presidential campaign (reportedly having been elbowed aside by Karl Rove),[21] there is little doubt that Wead had a significant influence on the future forty-third president at a crucial point in the latter's political and personal development.

Wead was also the first person to use the phrase "compassionate conservatism" in a more-than-casual sense, as both a consciously intended slogan and a distinctive perspective on politics. Wead first tried out the phrase as the title of a speech he gave in 1976.[22] Its initial appearance in print came in 1985, as a chapter title in a political manifesto that Wead ghostwrote for James Watt, the controversial secretary of the interior during the early years of the Reagan presidency, who had, by that time, been forced out of office and returned to private life.[23] In 1986, Wead wrote an admiring profile of George H. W. Bush for a popular evangelical magazine, in which (apparently at Wead's own instigation) one of Bush's political operatives called the vice president a "compassionate conservative." In 1992, Wead himself ran for Congress from the Sixth District in Arizona, making compassionate conservatism the centerpiece of his campaign.[24] (He won the Republican primary but lost in the general election.)

What did Doug Wead mean by this slogan, to which he obviously accorded a great deal of significance? A close analysis of Wead's writings, particularly his book with Watt and a booklet that Wead wrote to promote his own congressional candidacy, suggests two major points. First, Wead saw compassionate conservatism as a description of his own motives for being a conservative—and an admonition for others on the Right as to what *ought* to motivate them. People should not be conservative, he insisted, "just to protect the status-quo"; conservatives should not invoke the mantra of less government "because they've got a good thing going and they don't want any interference." He specifically criticized the white southern Democrats who came over to the Republican Party in the 1960s because they "saw the conservative movement as a device to maintain segregation." "This," he said, "was tragic for the conservative movement."[25]

By contrast, Wead maintained, compassionate conservatives are "people who are newly committed to meeting the needs of disadvantaged Americans and believe that the modern conservative movement offers their best hope." Reacting to "the evident failure of the great liberal social programs of the 1960s and 1970s," compassionate conservatives believe that it is they, rather than liberals, whose policies would be most beneficial to the true interests of blacks, the poor, the elderly, and the disadvantaged.[26]

Wead's compassionate conservatism also had a strategic component. "Even if we are offended by the liberal charges that we don't care about people," Wead conceded, "that is the public perception, nonetheless."[27] The reason for this perception was that conservatives (or at least the compassionate ones) had done a poor job communicating their message. In particular, Wead argued, conservatives had a tendency to get lost in the details of policy analysis, while liberals understood that the way to win people's allegiance was through their emotions.

> It's not good enough to sit back with a calculator like some accountant and say to blacks, or Hispanics, or to other minorities, "here, take a look, the Democrats have cheated you. Look what liberalism has done to you." . . . People don't relate to Republican accountants, with their dark blue suits and red ties, they want to know how you feel about them, they want to know if you really care. . . . Even while their policies have been wrong, liberal Democrats have been better at identifying with the heart and emotions of the people, of understanding them. And as a good psychologist will tell you, more than anything else, we as people want to be understood. Conservatives are always in danger of winning the argument and losing the hearts of the people.[28]

Though neither Bush nor Rove mentions Doug Wead in their memoirs (perhaps because Wead had by that time committed what the Bushes regarded as an act of rank disloyalty),[29] it is likely that Bush took several things away from his association with Wead. It was Wead who first showed Bush the potential significance of the evangelical vote—and the strategies he should and should not use to court this vote.[30] Second, Wead almost certainly stimulated Bush, who was actively planning his own political career at the time, to think about how to shape his own political identity and about how to reconcile his new Christian faith with some of the harsher aspects of conservative doctrine.

That said, the shortcomings of Wead's vision must have been obvious to Bush—and if not to Bush, certainly to Karl Rove. Perhaps the first question to raise about Wead-style compassionate conservatism is whether it really was anything new or different. Undoubtedly there are people whose conservatism is just a means of protecting their advantages and privileges; there are also libertarians who acknowledge no moral duty to help the poor and who consequently think that government has no right to take away their property, no matter what happens to the poor. But the vast majority of conservatives—particularly those conservatives who have run for office or served in government—have always insisted that their motives were unselfish: that they genuinely believed that welfare hurt the poor and that most government regulations were counterproductive, that the best way to help the poor was to allow them to take full advantage of the opportunities provided by a free-market economic system. Barry Goldwater might have profitably heeded Wead's advice, but every Republican presidential nominee since then could plausibly have said that he was *already* trying to do what Wead recommended.

Anyone who believes that compassionate conservatism is just a new way to dress up old ideas would find ample confirmation in the campaign platform Wead published when he was running for Congress. On virtually every topic, Wead's positions were indistinguishable from standard conservative doctrine.[31] He wanted to reduce domestic spending and cut taxes, including taxes on capital gains, luxury items, and dividend income; he favored congressional term limits, stiffer sentences for convicted criminals, the death penalty, school vouchers, and tort reform; he opposed gun control, "environmental extremists," and legalized abortion.

Wead's strategic advice seems, if anything, even less helpful. As for his premise that conservatives win the policy arguments but lose the emotional battle, one can only say that this is a remarkably common complaint made by losing candidates and parties at both ends of the political spectrum: that the facts and logic are all on their side, but the public is somehow tricked into voting for their opponents.[32] But even if one concedes the point, it is hard to believe that conservatives could overcome this handicap just by, as Wead recommends, "saying that we care."[33] A more comprehensive retooling of the conservative message would seem to be required—but Wead never provides one.

It is hard not to notice, in this respect, that of all the political figures Wead has singled out as "compassionate conservatives," none, with the possible exception of George W. Bush, was particularly successful in courting public support. James Watt was forced out of office (albeit before he collaborated with Wead), partly because of his perceived unwillingness to protect the environment, partly because of an ill-advised joke he made about affirmative action. While George H. W. Bush did get elected president in 1988, that outcome had more to do with the achievements of Ronald Reagan and the Bush campaign's attacks on Michael Dukakis than with the vice president's vague promise that he wanted a "kinder and gentler nation." Four years later, Bush was decisively voted out of office, largely because he was unable to convince the American electorate that he understood or cared about their economic problems. And Wead's own congressional candidacy was unsuccessful. There is no reason to think that any of these men lost support *because* they were described as compassionate conservatives, but neither is there any evidence that they were helped by this label.

Faith-Based Initiatives I: Marvin Olasky

Of all the policy proposals put forward by the 2000 Bush campaign, the one that seemed most distinctive, and that was seen as most emblematic of compassionate conservatism, was its endorsement of so-called faith-based initiatives. Numerous commentators have, in fact, called faith-based initiatives the "centerpiece" of compassionate conservatism.[34] In general terms, the argument was that a great deal of the work performed in America to help the poor and disadvantaged was carried out not by government programs, but by faith-based groups—churches, ministries, religiously-motivated nonprofits—most of whom received no assistance from government and, indeed, sometimes had to fight against the active opposition of various government agencies. Supporters of faith-based initiatives wanted to take better advantage of such groups, by making government more of a help and less of a hindrance. Yet if the major advocates of faith-based initiatives might have concurred on this general diagnosis, they disagreed about the details—about just what uses should be made of the faith-based sector and what role government should play. And to understand the role of faith-based endeavors in compassionate conservatism, it is precisely the disagreements that merit close examination.

The story begins with Marvin Olasky. Like Doug Wead, Olasky has worked in a remarkable variety of occupations: reporter, editor, author, professor, speechwriter, charitable entrepreneur, and college provost.[35] In 1992, Olasky wrote a book called *The Tragedy of American Compassion* that, as he himself would later note, was turned down by a "major publisher" and was finally issued by "a small house with a pea-sized marketing budget."[36] But in a wonderful case study in the modern politics of ideas, the book somehow came to the attention of former secretary of education Bill Bennett, who passed it on to House Speaker Newt Gingrich, who in turn bought a copy for every Republican representative in the 104th Congress.

Another early reader of Olasky's book was Karl Rove. As numerous books have mentioned (including Rove's own autobiography), when George W. Bush first decided to run for governor of Texas in 1993, Rove conducted a kind of policy "tutorial" in which he pushed his candidate to read a number of major books dealing with the problems and issues he was likely to face as governor. The two books that are almost invariably mentioned in this connection are Myron Magnet's *The Dream and the Nightmare* and Marvin Olasky's *The Tragedy of American Compassion*.[37] During the 2000 campaign, it was Olasky who was generally identified in the media as the principal intellectual source of Bush's faith-based policy—and thus as the "intellectual architect" and "godfather" of compassionate conservatism.[38] A lengthy profile of Olasky in the *New York Times Magazine*, for example, was titled "Where W. Got Compassion." As the author of this profile reported, "When I ask one of Bush's top aides to explain what a compassionate conservative administration might look like, he says simply, 'Talk to Marvin.'"[39] During the 2000 campaign, Bush made Olasky the head of his policy subcommittee on religion.[40]

Before taking a close look at Olasky's work, it is worth saying a few words about the other major item on Bush's reading list. The paperback edition of *The Dream and the Nightmare*, published in 2000, proclaims on the front cover that it was "The Book That Helped Make George W. Bush President." On the back cover, Bush describes it as "the most important book he'd ever read with the exception of the Bible." Moreover, "Bush's presidential campaign strategist Karl Rove cites the book as a road map to the governor's philosophy of 'compassionate conservatism.'"[41] Such plaudits notwithstanding, I am not aware of any major Bush policy initiative that can be tied directly to Magnet's work, nor did he receive the kind of media attention that was given to Olasky during the 2000 campaign. Though Magnet's book is, in many respects, the better of the two, its central message was not easily convertible into the kind of policy proposals that would have fit well in a campaign that wanted to expand the Republican base and was organized around the theme of *compassionate* conservatism.

Magnet's argument, in brief, is that the 1960s had brought about a major transformation of American culture that had severe negative consequences for the poor and the homeless. The poor were told that poverty was due to larger societal forces and that their own efforts to lift themselves up were likely to prove ineffective, that welfare was their right and welfare dependency not a problem worth worrying about, and that there was nothing wrong with having children out of wedlock. The homeless were deinstitutionalized, while laws that were designed to secure public order and prevent vagrancy were declared to be cruel and an unconstitutional restriction of personal liberty. Crime and juvenile delinquency were merely forms of political rebellion against an unjust system.

Having devoted most of his book to diagnosis, only in the last three pages does Magnet say anything about solutions:

> Stop doing what makes the problem worse. *Stop* the current welfare system, *stop* quota-based affirmative action, *stop* treating criminals as justified rebels, *stop* letting bums expropriate public spaces or wrongdoers live in public housing at public expense, *stop* Afrocentric education in the schools.[42]

None of these proposals were major themes in the 2000 Bush campaign, nor did he make any sustained effort to accomplish such goals during his eight years in the White House. Early in Bush's presidential memoirs, there is one sentence in which he speaks of a desire to encourage "a new era of personal responsibility," but it is difficult to think of anything concrete he did to follow through on this aspiration.[43] As Rove probably realized, given Bush's unwillingness to own up to, much less pay the penalty for his youthful drug use, and the significant number of ways in which Bush had traded on his family connections to avoid the draft and advance his business career, he was not the best vehicle for a campaign to promote personal responsibility.

To return to Marvin Olasky: in retrospect, it is easy to see why his book so captivated Newt Gingrich, for Olasky presented just the sort of policy analysis that has always characterized Gingrich's own political career: bold, provocative, visionary—but not very practical or well thought-through. The heroes in *The Tragedy of American Compassion* are the private individuals and groups, largely religious in nature, who provided assistance to the poor and disadvantaged from the time America was first settled by Europeans up through the end of the nineteenth century. This private charity, Olasky argued, had several major advantages over the more bureaucratic, governmentally provided welfare system that eventually replaced it. Private help to the poor emphasized a one-on-one, personal relationship between volunteers and recipients, rather than the more tenuous, impersonal links that typically connect government agencies and their clients. Traditional antipoverty efforts thus embodied the original meaning of compassion: *suffering with* the less fortunate; "personal involvement with the needy"; "sympathy that is active and often painful."[44]

Because of their direct, personal involvement with the poor, private actors were able to practice what Olasky called "categorization": the recognition that different individuals may need different kinds of assistance. In particular, since welfare was not then a legally enforceable "right," private charities could withhold aid from those whose bad behavior would only thereby be encouraged or enabled, such as alcoholics and drug addicts or those able-bodied men and women who were simply unwilling to work. Unlike contemporary welfare programs, private assistance was thus able to promote both employment and stronger affiliation between the disadvantaged and their families and communities. Because of their predominantly religious character, charities also recognized that many poor people had unmet spiritual as well as material needs.[45]

Unfortunately (again, according to Olasky), beginning in the late nineteenth and early twentieth centuries, and continuing at an especially rapid pace during the New Deal and Great Society periods, government welfare programs gradually replaced private charities as the principal source of aid to the poor and disadvantaged. The new system, as one might have expected, was more impersonal, less able to draw distinctions between deserving and undeserving recipients. Unlike private charity, government welfare thus promoted family disintegration and offered disincentives to productive employment. In the process, the very notion of compassion was transformed. No longer did the word connote the kind of active, personal, sometimes painful "suffering with" that once animated religious charities. By the late twentieth century, many Americans, especially on the left, saw compassion as little more than a feeling of distant sympathy, measured by one's willingness to vote for large governmental expenditures and then let social workers do all the heavy lifting.

All of which raises the question: If private charity worked so well, why did the state and federal governments get into the welfare business at all? Olasky suggests two answers to this query. First, many of those involved in the fight against poverty were unwilling "to go on patiently helping people, one by one." The process of turning "wilderness into neighborhoods" was simply too slow. As one professor of sociology and social work declared in 1922, "No person who is interested in social progress can long be content to raise here and there an individual."[46]

Even more important, however, according to Olasky, was a new and (in his judgment) antibiblical view of human nature: "The older anthropology saw man as sinful and likely to want something for nothing, if given the opportunity. The new view saw folks as naturally good and productive, unless they were in a competitive environment that warped finer sensibilities. In the new thinking, change came not through challenge, but through placement in a pleasant environment that would bring out a person's true, benevolent nature."[47]

Thus, government gradually took over the work once performed by religious charities. Government provided the poor with money, food, housing, and medical care on an undifferentiated basis, all in the belief that once their material needs were met, all of the other problems associated with poverty would disappear. In fact—and here Olasky joined up with a legion of other critics—exactly the opposite occurred. The modern American welfare system had actually exacerbated the problems of crime, family disintegration, drug abuse, homelessness, and welfare dependency.

And what did Olasky propose to reverse this trend and remedy the current welfare mess? *The Tragedy of American Compassion* does not discuss this issue at any great length. Perhaps, Olasky suggests at one point, government grants could be given to religious service providers without requiring them to abandon their distinctively religious character. Or, maybe the tax code could be changed so as to encourage more charitable giving.[48] It was not until Olasky's second major book on the topic—*Renewing American Compassion*, published in 1996—that it became clear that Olasky's preferred solution was considerably more radical: the complete elimination of government welfare programs:

> It is time now, however, to talk not about reforming the welfare system—which often means scraping off a bit of mold—but about replacing it with a truly compassionate approach based in private and religious charity. Such a system was effective in the nineteenth century and will be even more effective in the twenty-first, with the decentralization that new technology makes possible, if we make the right changes in personal goals and public policy.[49]

Olasky considers a number of specific ways of accomplishing this objective,[50] but his preferred option would be a system of substantial tax credits—in the appendix, he endorses a 90 percent tax credit—for anyone who contributed to a private antipoverty organization. Thus, if someone gave $3,000 to Catholic Charities, the Salvation Army, or a local home for pregnant teenagers, his federal or state tax payments would be reduced by $2,700.[51] Whatever the precise mechanism, "welfare replacement," Olasky assured us, was "necessary," "morally right," "politically possible," and "practical." Even the safety net had to go.[52]

By 2000, when Olasky published his third major book on compassion, poverty, and welfare (*Compassionate Conservatism: What It Is, What It Does, and How It Can Transform America*), he had softened his tone somewhat, perhaps in the interest of helping George W. Bush's presidential campaign. (Bush wrote the foreword to this book, and his performance as governor of Texas was lauded in its longest chapter.) Though he still hoped to replace government welfare with private antipoverty initiatives funded through a system of charitable tax credits, Olasky now emphasized that compassionate conservatism was diverse and pragmatic, and could be brought about through "gradual, sustainable change."[53]

Though Olasky's role in launching compassionate conservatism has often been noted, surprisingly few analysts and commentators have asked what would seem to be the obvious next question: Is he right? Is his history of the transition from private charity to government welfare accurate? Does he provide a plausible solution?

Olasky's work is at its strongest, I would argue, in its recognition that the problems of the contemporary poor are a lot more complicated and deepset than a simple lack of money, a fact that present-day welfare programs (and the left-wing supporters of those programs) are generally unwilling to acknowledge, much less act upon. Olasky also deserves credit for his efforts to publicize and promote the numerous contemporary faith-based endeavors that try, against great odds and with remarkably few resources, to effect real change in the lives of the poor, the homeless, the imprisoned, and the addicted.

The biggest shortcoming of Olasky's work is his assumption that private, faith-based charities were or could be sufficient, by themselves, to handle the massive problems of the American poor. Though Olasky denies that he is "romanticizing the past,"[54] it is difficult to avoid the conclusion that he is, in fact, doing exactly that. Olasky's analysis of the work of religious charities in the nineteenth century is entirely anecdotal. He shows, beyond dispute, that there were a large number of private individuals and groups who tried to provide help to the poor and the unemployed in the pre–welfare state era. What he does not show—does not come close to showing—is that these private charities were enough to relieve the sufferings of even a substantial portion of the truly needy.[55] As virtually every serious history of the late nineteenth and early twentieth centuries agrees, a shockingly large percentage of the US population lived in conditions of severe deprivation: filthy, overcrowded, unsanitary housing; inadequate food and nutrition; high levels of disease and child mortality; and sporadic employment.[56] If the dozens of reports on urban and rural poverty published during this period are even close to being accurate, the inescapable conclusion is that private charities, their best efforts notwithstanding, were simply overwhelmed by the magnitude of the problems they faced. Indeed, it was the leaders of these faith-based charities who often became the most fervent advocates of government welfare programs—precisely because they understood, from direct, personal contact with the poor, that private efforts alone were nowhere near enough.

Some of Olasky's own evidence, properly interpreted, actually shows the extent of the mismatch between private charity and the population that needed serving. In both of his first two books on the subject, Olasky cites the example of the Baltimore Association for the Improvement of the Condition of the Poor, which in 1891 had 2,000 volunteers and made 8,227 "visits" to 4,025 families containing 13,114 persons.[57] But according to the 1890 Census, Baltimore had a total population of 434,439. If we accept Robert Hunter's 1904 estimate that 20 percent of the population in northern industrial cities was poor (other estimates are a good deal higher),[58] the unavoidable conclusion is that this admirable association provided help to only a fraction of the people who needed it—and provided each family with, on average, just two visits a year.

These visits, moreover, seem to have been long on moral exhortation and considerably shorter on material assistance. According to the source Olasky cites, the total cost of fuel, groceries, and other provisions given to those who were "deemed needy and worthy" was $18,980—or about $1.45 per person. Poor persons in Baltimore surely appreciated all the help they could get, but $1.45 per person would hardly have made a dent in most families' penury.[59]

None of this is to deny Olasky's many, well-aimed criticisms of contemporary welfare programs or the plausibility of his insistence that faith-based groups and organizations can make an essential contribution to alleviating many current problems. But it does explain why his call for "welfare replacement" found so few takers, even in the heady days of the "Republican Revolution" in the mid-1990s.

Faith-Based Initiatives II: John DiIulio

Though John DiIulio has denied being "the main mind involved in crafting the president's faith-based and community initiatives,"[60] he clearly was an important intellectual and symbolic force in the development of faith-based policy. On a substantive level, DiIulio helped advise Bush on religion-related issues during the 2000 campaign (he also advised Al Gore), then served as the first head of the White House Office of Faith-Based and Community Initiatives (OFBCI) from January through August, 2001.[61] Symbolically, DiIulio is the best-known exponent of a very different view of what a faith-based policy might have looked like than the one put forward by Marvin Olasky.

DiIulio also played a major role in giving the faith-based policy discussion a substantially greater measure of intellectual heft and academic credibility. Though Olasky also held an academic position (during the 2000 campaign, he was a professor of journalism at the University of Texas), it was the network of conservative activists, think tanks, and policy intellectuals that had seized upon and helped publicize his critique of the welfare state. Academic historians seem to have been generally dismissive of his work.[62] DiIulio, by contrast, had unassailable scholarly credentials.

A Harvard-trained political scientist who was awarded tenure at both Princeton and the University of Pennsylvania, DiIulio first began studying the social effects of religion as a follow-up to his studies of prison management. Where overpromising is standard practice among politicians and (sadly) among an increasing proportion of academic policy analysts, DiIulio's work on faith-based programs has always been notable for a resolute determination *not* to push the evidence farther than it will go, *not* to jump to premature and unsubstantiated conclusions. As a result, DiIulio's writings elicited a remarkable level of respect across the political spectrum.[63] (His performance as the first head of OFBCI, by contrast, received mixed reviews.)

Though both DiIulio and Olasky were proponents of faith-based initiatives, they differed on a number of issues that were central to the design and implementation of any federal faith-based program. First, *what advantage(s), if any, do faith-based groups bring to the delivery of social services?* In Marvin Olasky's work, as we have seen, much of the value of faith-based groups was attributable to their ability to effect a spiritual transformation in those they helped. For this reason, Olasky argued, faith-based programs are *more* successful than their secular counterparts in dealing with groups like addicts, prisoners, and the homeless:

> Judging by the historical record and contemporary testimony, well-managed, faith-based programs are more effective in fighting poverty, on the average, than their nonreligious counterparts. Research studies show that church attendance tracks closely with lower dropout rates, less drug use, and fewer crimes committed. Faith-based organizations have shown that the best way to teach self-esteem and respect for law is to teach that we are esteemed by a wonderful God who set out for us rules of conduct that benefit society and ourselves.[64]

DiIulio was more circumspect on this point. Whether faith-based programs are superior to those without a religious component is, he argued, an inherently difficult question to study in a rigorous, scientific manner, and until recently, few social scientists had shown much interest in the issue. At present, however, "there is no empirical evidence" that programs centered on spiritual transformation produced better results than those that were not "saturated in a particular religion's purposes and practices."[65]

The main advantage of religious congregations and faith-based organizations, according to DiIulio, was their superior capacity to mobilize volunteers. In recent years, a good deal of social science attention has been focused on the theory of *social capital*, an elastic concept that usually refers to the networks, norms, and general sense of trust that allow the people in a society to work together on projects of mutual benefit. And at least in the United States, a great deal of social capital is actually "spiritual capital." As Robert Putnam, the leading academic student of social capital, has summarized the evidence:

> Houses of worship build and sustain more social capital—and social capital of more varied forms—than any other type of institution in America. Churches, synagogues, mosques and other houses of worship provide a vibrant institutional base for civic good works and a training ground for civic entrepreneurs. Roughly speaking, nearly half of America's stock of social capital is religious or religiously affiliated, whether measured by association memberships, philanthropy, or volunteering.[66]

That is to say, a remarkably high percentage of the people who volunteer to work with drug addicts, gang members, prisoners, and the homeless, or who contribute money to organizations that serve such groups, are motivated by religious beliefs and/or work through and give money to religious groups.

DiIulio and Olasky also diverged on another important question: *What kinds of faith-based programs should government try to support?* Based in part on the analysis just described, DiIulio drew a distinction between *faith-based* programs and what he called *faith-saturated* programs. Faith-based programs, as their name implies, include all community-serving work performed by church congregations and religious nonprofits. Faith-saturated organizations, by contrast, "either have no secular or civic purpose, or do not separate secular activities from their sectarian purposes and practices." They "proselytize or promote spiritual transformation as an integral part of their social services."[67]

A paradigmatic example of a faith-saturated program is Teen Challenge. Its stated mission is to provide "an effective and comprehensive Christian faith-based solution to life-controlling drug and alcohol problems"; and as its website makes clear, religion pervades every aspect of its work. Its program is based on "the faith model" rather than "the medical model" of how to help someone who abuses drugs or alcohol. Participants have "little free time, due to a busy schedule" that includes, along with classes, meals, and work projects, "devotions," "discipleship training," "chapel services," and "Bible reading." Moreover, applicants are "carefully informed as to the faith-based nature of the program and that entering a Teen Challenge program is voluntary; however, all aspects of the program are mandatory upon entrance." Teen Challenge attributes its effectiveness to "something (or someone) we call 'the Jesus Factor.' When a person finds a relationship with God everything changes. . . . Newfound life in Christ and learning biblical principles for daily living replace the old lifestyle and the attitudes and behaviors underlying them."[68]

Any attempt by government to support faith-saturated organizations, DiIulio argued, would be politically and legally problematic. It "raises political temperatures and courts constitutional problems." But that's okay, he immediately added, because "faith-saturated organizations are themselves a tiny minority of all community-serving religious nonprofit organizations in America today." The "vast majority" of faith-based groups do *not* demand that those who enter their buildings, eat their food, or participate in their programs take part in religious services or profess a particular faith. Such groups would therefore be suitable recipients of governmental aid.[69] Thus, little would be lost if government assistance were given only to those programs that were *not* faith saturated.

To Olasky, however, such a limitation was a major and highly troubling restriction. Though Olasky never uses DiIulio's terminology, he clearly regards faith-saturated groups as making a distinct and important contribution to the alleviation of many pressing social problems. It is precisely faith-saturated groups that have the capacity to help the real problem cases: the people who have been in and out of drug rehab programs multiple times; the prisoners with a long string of crimes and incarcerations; young people who seem totally without direction or moral compass. Olasky also believed that denying government assistance to all programs that were explicitly and centrally religious would be a civil rights violation, effectively telling religious people—but not those of a secular bent—that they could participate in the public square only if they first renounced all the commitments and identifications that were most important to them.

Finally, Olasky and DiIulio disagreed about *what the role of government should be in encouraging or promoting faith-based organizations*. It is impossible to read Olasky's books without getting the sense that he has a strong animus against government; he clearly wants to keep the role of government as small and unobtrusive as possible. DiIulio, by contrast, often described himself as a "pro-life, pro-poor Democrat,"[70] whose studies and personal experiences had left him with an appreciation of both the assets and liabilities of government. While DiIulio hoped to shift resources to the small, faith-based groups that were really helping the urban poor, he viewed this as supplementing rather than replacing traditional welfare programs. At no point in his writings does DiIulio ever recommend significant cuts in government social spending, at either the federal or state level. Indeed, though he muted this sentiment during his time in the Bush administration, it seems clear that DiIulio would like to see an increase in at least some kinds of government spending.

Given his understanding of the work currently performed by faith-based groups, DiIulio urged the Bush administration to launch its "compassion agenda" via a three-pronged strategy:

1. *Study the Implementation of Existing Faith-Based Laws.* As I will show in more detail in a few pages, Bush was far from being the first person who sought to use religious groups to deliver governmentally financed social services. To the contrary, many religious entities already received government grants to help fund their antipoverty work, and a series of laws had been adopted in the 1990s to extend the practice to a number of additional federal programs. Before any new legislation was enacted, therefore, DiIulio wanted to study whether and how current laws were being carried out.

2. *Establish a Compassion Capital Fund.* DiIulio also wanted the federal government to establish a small "compassion capital fund" that would provide money to groups and organizations that had already shown that they could "tackle critical but unmet social needs on a citywide or national scale." Working with other federal, local, and private agencies, OFBCI would use the money to "support [the] expansion [of these programs], document their operations, monitor their performance, and measure their impact."[71]

3. *Establish Local OFBCI Offices.* Finally, since most federal social service dollars are actually administered by state and local governments, DiIulio hoped to encourage the creation of OFBCI-like agencies in city governments across the country: "Local OFBCI offices would be dedicated to helping small but qualified community-serving programs, religious or secular, access additional public *and* private support with which to better serve their own needy neighbors."[72]

If this agenda seems somewhat less than overwhelming, the reason is that it was deliberately designed to be that way. And this marks one final important difference between the faith-based visions of John DiIulio and Marvin Olasky. The Olasky program, at least as it was laid out in his second book, was definitely not business as usual. It was bold, ambitious, transformational. Careful, prudent academic that he was, DiIulio's plan was substantially more incremental in nature.

DiIulio's claims about what he expected to accomplish were similarly restrained. The goal of faith-based programs DiIulio-style was not to create "faith-favored" federal programs, which would guarantee that a certain amount of money would be given to religious nonprofit organizations, but to ensure that federal programs would be "faith-neutral." If there was a "level playing field," DiIulio argued, some (though by no means all) faith-based groups would apply for money. Based on the preliminary evidence then available, "the best bet . . . was that implementing charitable choice would, over time, result in more money being allocated to religious nonprofits. But not overnight, not on political command, and not unless enough qualified organizations opted to work with Washington. Moreover, it was an informed guess, not a foregone conclusion," that providing more federal money to community-serving urban ministries "would yield measurable and positive results."[73]

All told, it was hardly the stuff of which revolutions are made.

Faith-Based Initiatives III: What Bush Made of It

For the purposes of this book, of course, the most important question to be asked about faith-based initiatives is not what Marvin Olasky or John DiIulio wanted to do but what George W. Bush had in mind. In the most general terms, not surprisingly, Bush's faith-based plan borrowed ideas and program elements from both Olasky and DiIulio. A more revealing summary, I think, is that Bush tried to appropriate Olasky's aura of big, bold, transformational change while actually proposing a set of policy changes that were quite modest and incremental, much like the ones DiIulio had recommended. To paraphrase a line from an old musical, Bush sought to lead a revolution without offending anybody.

To see how Bush dealt with faith-based policy issues, the best place to start is the "Duty of Hope," a speech he gave on July 22, 1999—his first major policy speech during the 2000 campaign and his most detailed discussion of faith-based initiatives. Much of what Bush said about faith-based issues during his eight years in the White House were reprises of this speech. Looking at what Bush said during the campaign also provides a yardstick for comparing what the forty-third president said he wanted to do with what he actually accomplished.

Characteristically, Bush began the substantive part of his speech with the assertion that the proposals he would be unveiling that day were big and bold: "Today I want to propose a different role for government. A fresh start. A bold new approach."[74] Actually, by the end of the twentieth century, government's use of faith-based organizations to deliver social services was a well-established feature of American public policy. In 1996, Catholic Charities USA had received $1.3 billion from federal, state, and local government sources, 64 percent of its total income. The Salvation Army received $245 million from government (16 percent of its income) and the YMCA $203 million (8 percent).[75] Even more directly relevant to what Bush hoped to accomplish, four major federal statutes had been enacted between 1996 and 2000 that included so-called charitable-choice provisions. As originally developed by then-US senator John Ashcroft, charitable choice provisions specified that federal grant-making agencies could not discriminate on the basis of religion against otherwise qualified organizations that served people in need. At the same time, religious organizations that received federal funds had to serve all eligible participants, regardless of their religious beliefs, and could not use federal money to support any inherently religious activity, such as worship services, proselytizing, or religious instruction.

Such statutory language notwithstanding, most informed observers felt that these provisions had not been fully implemented and that the vast majority of faith-based groups had neither applied for nor received federal funds.[76] So there were valid reasons for a presidential candidate to promise that, if elected, he would work to apply and implement this approach more broadly. But absent the kind of thorough dismantling of the American welfare state advocated by Olasky, it was hard to believe that such a proposal was "different," "fresh," or "bold."

Next, Bush offered a general declaration that both Olasky and DiIulio could readily have endorsed: "In every instance where my administration sees a responsibility to help people, we will look first to faith-based organizations, charities and community groups that have shown their ability to save and change lives."[77] Of course, as DiIulio had also argued, this goal was far easier stated than accomplished. Any program that gave faith-based groups exclusive or preferential access to government grants would almost certainly have been declared unconstitutional. The most that Bush could credibly promise was to provide a "level-playing field," in which resources were made available on an equal basis to faith-based organizations, secular charities, and, yes, even those soon-to-be dreaded community organizations. Whether faith-based groups would apply for the money and, if they did, whether they could demonstrate to grant-givers that they were worthy recipients was a different and more daunting challenge.

How much of the available money would actually wind up in the hands of faith-based groups would surely depend, in substantial part, on whether faith-based services really produced superior outcomes—higher cure rates for substance abusers, lower rates of recidivism for prisoners, more unemployed people placed in stable jobs—than their secular counterparts. And on this point, Bush clearly sided with Olasky: "Private and religious groups . . . have clear advantages over government."

> We have found that government can spend money, but it can't put hope in our hearts or a sense of purpose in our lives. This is done by churches and synagogues and mosques and charities that warm the cold of life.
>
> The goal of faith-based groups is not just to provide services, it is to change lives. And lives are changed. Addicts become examples. Reckless men become loving fathers. Prisoners become spiritual leaders—sometimes more mature and inspiring than many of us can ever hope to be.[78]

Exactly what role would government play in Bush's bold, new world? As one might have expected, Bush had no interest in embracing the complete elimination of government welfare programs that Olasky had recommended. Even flirting with this idea (as Newt Gingrich occasionally had done) would have opened Bush up to precisely the kinds of left-wing attacks that would have fatally undermined his claim to be a *compassionate* conservative. On this point, Bush sounded more like DiIulio: "We will recognize there are some things that government *should* be doing—like Medicaid for poor children. Government cannot be replaced by charities—but it can welcome them as partners, not resent them as rivals." More than that, Bush contended, government had an affirmative responsibility to get more resources into the hands of faith-based groups: "It is not enough for conservatives like me to praise these efforts. It is not enough to call for volunteerism. Without more support and resources—both private and public—we are asking them to make bricks without straw."[79]

Specifically, Bush promised that in his first year in office, "we will dedicate about $8 billion . . . to provide new tax incentives for giving, and to support charities and other private institutions." Lest Bush be accused of being a big-spending liberal by his rivals for the Republican nomination, a position paper released along with the "Duty of Hope" speech made clear that most of this money would be devoted to a series of changes in the tax code—tax *cuts*, of course—designed to encourage increased charitable contributions by individuals and corporations. How much new *spending* would occur—if any—was much less clear. Though Bush talked about the need for a compassion capital fund (another nod to DiIulio) and a program to help the children of prisoners, there was nothing to indicate how much money the federal government would provide for these ventures. When everything was taken into account, it is impossible to make a precise estimate of how much additional money Bush hoped to put in the hands of faith-based groups, but measured against the size of the problems Bush himself had outlined, the amounts didn't seem very large.[80]

The one detail in Bush's speech that seemed to be more than business as usual was a promise to "provide for charity tax credits" much like the ones commended by Marvin Olasky. Such credits would have allowed individuals to "give a part of what they owed" in taxes "directly to private and religious institutions fighting poverty." This proposal, had it been seriously advocated, would have meant a radical change in the American welfare system. As Bush himself said, it would have let individual Americans "choose who conducts this war on poverty." But when one examined the fine print, it became clear that Bush was only promising to urge the *states* to adopt these credits. State governments, that is to say, would have borne all the real costs of this proposal—in particular, a very large potential reduction in tax revenues that would probably not have been accompanied by a proportionate reduction in state spending. Bush only committed himself to providing moral support. Needless to say, no state ever responded positively to Bush's exhortation.[81]

When one took a close look at the Bush faith-based initiative, in short, there was a lot less there than met the eye. What it proposed wasn't particularly new or different, and it certainly wasn't very bold. By any reasonable interpretation, the Bush plan seemed likely to do precisely what the then-Texas governor said conservatives shouldn't do: provide faith-based groups with words of praise and encouragement, but not much in the way of tangible resources. To borrow a phrase that Bush himself often used as a pejorative, the president's faith-based plans were merely "small ball." Even if the faith-based initiative had been faithfully enacted and implemented, it is unlikely that it would have had a measurable impact on such problems as substance abuse, poverty, welfare dependency, or crime.

The Bush Faith-Based Initiative: What Became of It

What happened to the Bush faith-based initiative after the president took office is a tale that has already been told several times and in substantial detail.[82] But the story is worth briefly recounting here for the additional insight it provides into the nature and prospects of this aspect of compassionate conservatism.

In July 2001, the House of Representatives passed a faith-based bill, but the vote was sharply polarized along partisan lines. Though Bush would later claim that the bill had been "enacted in a bipartisan way,"[83] Republicans voted for the bill 217 to 4, but Democrats opposed it 15 to 193. The House bill had always been regarded as a tough sell in the Senate, but the odds against it grew substantially more forbidding in late May, when Vermont senator James Jeffords exited the Republican Party and thereby switched control of that body to the Democrats. Though several major efforts were made to put together a bill that was sufficiently conciliatory to pass the Senate, the partisan divide proved too wide to bridge.[84] When the 107th Congress came to an end in late 2002, faith-based legislation died with it.

Having failed to enact faith-based legislation in 2001–2002, the Bush high command never again made a major effort to do so.[85] Instead, they shifted to a different strategy: try to implement as much of the faith-based agenda as possible via administrative action.[86] By late 2002, the administration had already traveled some distance down this path. Just nine days after taking office, Bush had issued two executive orders that created the White House Office of Faith-Based and Community Initiatives and faith-based "centers" in each of five major cabinet departments, and tasked them with "eliminat[ing] regulatory, contracting, and other programmatic obstacles to the participation of faith-based and other community organizations in the provision of social services."[87] Between December 2002 and March 2006, Bush issued four more executive orders, that created faith-based centers in four additional departments and two sub-cabinet agencies, as well as establishing general faith-based policies that all federal departments and agencies were expected to adhere to.[88]

Taken together, these executive orders accomplished most of what the unpassed faith-based legislation would have done with respect to federal bureaucratic rules and procedures. But executive orders could not be used to authorize new appropriations or institute changes in the tax code; these required congressional approval. The former task was done piecemeal, but by the end of Bush's presidency a number of new programs were established generally along the lines indicated in the "Duty of Hope" speech: a compassion capital fund, a program for mentoring the children of prisoners, a voucher program for those seeking treatment for drug or alcohol abuse, a prisoner reentry initiative.[89] And just as one might have anticipated from what was *not* said in that speech, each of these programs was, at least by federal budgetary standards, quite small. In 2008, the Prisoner Reentry Initiative was budgeted at $31 million, Mentoring Children of Prisoners received $49 million, and the compassion capital fund cost

$53 million.[90] The sufficiency of these expenditures is best appreciated when compared to the size of the problems they confronted. In December 2008, for example, the White House's "Final Report to the Armies of Compassion" boasted that the Mentoring Children of Prisoners program had matched 107,000 children with mentors. But according to the 2000 Bush campaign, there were "more than two million children who have one or both parents in prison." In other words, the Bush mentoring program had reached about 5 percent of its target population.[91] In a similar way, the "Final Report" notes that as of September 2008, 15,962 ex-offenders had enrolled in the Prisoner Reentry Initiative. But the same document says that, "Each year, approximately 700,000 inmates are released from prison and return to America's communities." So under the most generous set of assumptions, the prisoner reentry program was serving about 2 percent of the eligible population.[92]

Bush's record at "encouraging an outpouring of [charitable] giving" is similarly checkered. His most important promise of this type—a proposal to allow a charitable deduction for taxpayers who do not itemize—was never enacted. A second proposal, to allow people to make charitable contributions from their individual retirement accounts without paying income tax, was passed as part of a pension reform bill in 2006.[93] No state ever enacted a charitable tax credit, but I'm not sure anyone ever really expected any state to do so.

In addition to his promises of *new* spending and *new* charitable contributions, Bush had also pledged to help faith-based organizations win a larger share of the money from *existing* federal programs, by eliminating the various barriers that had prevented such organizations from participating. Ironically for a Republican president, Bush's greatest success in the faith-based area may have come in the creation of a "faith-based bureaucracy": a set of apparently durable institutions whose principal purpose was to reach out to and advocate for the interests of faith-based groups. Using executive orders, as we have seen, Bush established a White House Office of Faith-Based and Community Initiatives and faith-based centers in eleven departments and agencies. Moreover, when Barack Obama became president, he renamed the White House agency—it is now called the Office of Faith-Based and Neighborhood Partnerships—but otherwise kept both it and the department and agency centers intact.

A similar sort of faith-based infrastructure was created at the state and local level. As of 2005, according to a good study by sociologist Rebecca Sager, thirty-three states had established faith-based "liaison" positions and twenty had some type of formal faith-based office. Sager also found an explosion in faith-based legislation at the state level. And while some of this activity occurred in the final years of the Clinton presidency, the pace clearly accelerated when Bush came to office in 2001.[94]

Many observers have seen these developments as an important achievement. Bush's faith-based initiative, said Nathan Diament of the Union of Orthodox Jewish Congregations, "went a long way, to use the phrase, to 'level the playing field.' They brought in a significant number of new partners by holding these conferences around the country, educating groups. It was useful in terms of enlarging the pool of partners for government." Robert Tuttle, a professor at the George Washington University School of Law, has also credited the Bush effort for undermining and overcoming the "culture of resistance" that had long existed in the federal government toward providing assistance to faith-based organizations: "Measured by that standard, the initiative has been, I think, a success that really doesn't have a parallel in contemporary administrative law, where you have a complete change in culture."[95]

But did the Bush administration succeed in changing the *output* of the federal bureaucracy—the amount of money actually given to faith-based organizations? This is a subject of some dispute. The best-known study of this issue was conducted by the Roundtable on Religion and Social Welfare Policy and made public in February 2006. Looking at 99 discretionary grant programs operated by nine federal departments and agencies, the Roundtable's researchers found that (in the words of the *Washington Post*) "the amount of direct federal grants to faith-based organizations *declined* from 2002 to 2004"—from $669 million in the former year to $625 million in the latter. Actually, the study found that the number and percentage of grants awarded to faith-based organizations had increased modestly. Where faith-based organizations had received 11.6 percent of all grants in 2002, they received 12.8 percent in 2004. During the same time period, however, total funding for these 99 programs had declined. Faith-based organizations, in short, were competing somewhat more effectively for slices of a shrinking pie.[96]

The White House, not surprisingly, disputed these figures. In its most detailed report on the issue, released in March 2006, the Office of Faith-Based and Community Initiatives claimed that the federal government had "awarded more than $2.1 billion in competitive social service grants to faith-based organizations" in 2005, an increase of 7 percent from the previous year. An analysis of a different set of programs found a 14 percent increase in faith-based grants between 2003 and 2004.[97] Another report, issued near the very end of the Bush presidency, said that in the five federal departments that housed the original faith-based centers, the number of grants awarded to faith-based organizations increased from 1,634 in 2003 to 2,281 in 2007, while their total value increased from $477 million to $818 million.[98] Unfortunately, the White House results seem to be based on a shifting set of programs, which obviously complicates comparisons over time, and questions have also been raised about how rigorous the WHOFBCI was in determining which organizations were and were not faith-based.[99] Both the Roundtable and WHOFBCI studies, it should be added, only examined federal programs that gave money directly to the organizations that provided social services. Most federal social service money, however, is given to state and local governments, which then award some of it to contractors and grant recipients. Unfortunately, few state and local governments keep accurate records as to how many of their service-delivery agencies are faith-based.[100]

In the only other study I am aware of that is relevant to this issue, Mark Chaves and Bob Wineburg found that the faith-based initiative had little or no effect on American church congregations. In a survey of congregations conducted in 1988, 3.0 percent said that they received government funding. When this survey was replicated in 2006–2007, 3.5 percent of congregations reported the receipt of government funding.[101]

Though these three studies can be "spun" in different ways, the pictures they paint are not dramatically dissimilar. On the whole, all three studies show, not a lot has changed. Certainly, words like "revolution," "transformation," or "bold, new approach" do not apply. Faith-based organizations appear to be doing a slightly better job of competing for grant money—but only slightly. The White House's 2006 report showed that secular nonprofits were still receiving nearly six times more money from its sample of federal programs than faith-based entities were.[102] As John DiIulio has noted, even the $2-billion-a-year figure cited by the White House "represents a relative pittance," given the hundreds of billions of dollars the federal government gives out every year to governmental, business, and secular nonprofit groups.[103]

I have recounted this history in order to make two final points about the Bush faith-based initiative. First, the Bush plan received a much rockier reception than the president and his advisors had anticipated. During the 2000 campaign, the greater use of faith-based organizations to deliver social services seemed to be a rare point of consensus in an otherwise polarized politics. The four charitable-choice provisions enacted during the Clinton administration had excited little controversy. On May 24, 1999— note that this was two months *before* Bush's "Duty of Hope" speech—Al Gore had given a speech in which he, too, promised that, "If you elect me President, the voices of faith-based organizations will be integral to the policies set forth in my administration."[104] As E. J. Dionne argued in a column several days after Gore's speech, "Think of this [the increased use of faith-based organizations] as the opposite of a wedge issue. On this question, Gore doesn't mind if he and Bush sing from the same hymnal. 'I don't think this should be a political fight,' he says."[105]

In fact, far from being a new policy "paradigm" that would be acceptable to both the political left and the political right, faith-based policy turned out to be one of the most contentious issues the Bush administration dealt with during its first two years in office. The "consensus" came apart at both ends of the political spectrum and many points in between. On the left, once Gore had been defeated and was no longer the Democratic Party's titular leader, many congressional Democrats felt free to voice their long-standing reservations about charitable choice and aid to religious organizations. Liberal Democrats opposed federal support for faith-based initiatives on several grounds. In part, they saw the Bush program as simply one more attempt to undermine the "wall of separation" between church and state. Many Democrats also regarded faith-based policy as little more than a partisan ploy: an attempt to transfer money from a Democratic constituency (traditional public employees and social workers) to a more Republican group (evangelical ministers and churches); and to attract more support from black voters, a group that was both highly religious and overwhelmingly Democratic.

The most potent argument liberals made against faith-based initiatives was the claim that they would result in widespread discrimination in hiring. Since 1964, churches and religious groups had been granted an exemption from the antidiscrimination provisions of federal civil rights legislation. Churches, that is to say, were allowed to require the people they hired to be members of their own faith and to adhere to certain religiously sanctioned standards of behavior, a provision later upheld in a unanimous Supreme Court decision. It was one thing, however, for churches to discriminate when using their own money. It was quite another, many felt, to engage in such practices with tax money. As federal social welfare funds were redirected to faith-based groups, opponents charged, many such organizations would use their hiring discretion to deny jobs to Jews, gays and lesbians, and racial minorities.[106] Many religious groups, of course, saw the matter differently. If faith-based organizations were to act effectively, they argued, they needed to be able to make sure that the people they hired were committed to the organization's mission—in the same way that, for example, Planned Parenthood, which also receives government money, is allowed to insist that all their employees be pro-choice on abortion.

Meanwhile, many conservative evangelicals, once thought to be the prime constituency for faith-based initiatives, also proved to be less than enthusiastic about the idea. Some worried that the receipt of federal money would be accompanied by pressures to water down the religious nature of their services, or would subject churches to a heavy new regimen of federal regulations and audits. ("With the king's shekels come the king's shackles.") Others, including televangelist Pat Robertson, expressed concern about the possibility that federal money would go not only to various types of Christian churches and ministries but also to groups such as Scientologists or Hare Krishnas. These objections aside, most conservative evangelicals just weren't very excited about the whole faith-based issue. As one administration lobbyist would later comment: "Ultimately, there was a conservative base for [faith-based legislation], but it is not at the top of their agenda. . . . They are no longer mobilizable [on the bill]. Why? They are passionate about specific issues, and this is not on their list. They are favorably disposed but not active."[107] One WHOFBCI staffer offered a harsher judgment: The Christian Coalition "would not pay attention because they wanted to abolish welfare, not invite faith-based organizations to participate" in it.[108]

Some critics have charged that faith-based legislation would have proceeded more smoothly if the White House had shown greater leadership, particularly during the early stages of the legislative process.[109] As one Democrat later observed, "The White House allowed the House Republicans to write a bill to alienate Democrats and not attract them. . . . They [House Republicans] hadn't worked hard for bipartisanship, and the scare campaign from civil libertarians worked. The White House should have collaborated with the Democrats and the House Republicans, but that was not the path they chose."[110] The *Washington Post* similarly noted, "Some White House officials say House conservatives overreached when they were writing the bill, giving too much leeway to churches. Some congressional negotiators retort that the president invited trouble by sketching his plan too vaguely."[111]

Perhaps—but I am skeptical that the White House's early strategic missteps are a necessary or sufficient explanation for the controversy that ensued. The Clinton-era charitable choice provisions had been small sections in much larger bills and had therefore attracted little attention.[112] As Bush made faith-based initiatives one of the central issues in his presidential campaign, however, he effectively guaranteed that such provisions would never again sneak by unnoticed. As one of the leading opponents of the faith-based legislation explained, "They were getting [charitable choice] legislation through until it got attention. The more they pressed this, the more it smelled. The more it is discussed, the better the chances are that this idea will collapse."[113] A more moderate House bill would probably still have attracted lots of criticism from the Democratic left, along with objections from conservative groups. The hiring discrimination issue, in particular, was too important to both sides to be quietly swept under the rug.

Second, it is impossible to read the numerous accounts of the Bush administration's handling of faith-based initiatives and not come away with the strong impression that the whole issue was much less important to the administration than one might have anticipated from all the attention it received during the 2000 campaign. The administration's interest in the issue is best described as episodic: marked by occasional bursts of activity but not by the strong, steady commitment that is generally needed to get something accomplished in contemporary Washington. Virtually everyone who has studied the politics of faith-based initiatives has concluded that the issue *was* important to George W. Bush himself.[114] Never having met or interviewed Bush, I am unable to challenge this assessment. But Bush apparently never communicated his personal sense of urgency to his own staff, nor did he monitor his staff closely enough to make sure that the administration's agenda reflected his priorities rather than theirs. As Black, Koopman, and Ryden have noted in their exemplary history of the faith-based controversy:

> To these [White House] staff members, the faith-based initiative was useful as a tool to reward politically and religiously conservative groups seeking greater access to the public square and to political power, and as part of a strategy to appeal to deeply religious ethnic minorities. But they lacked the president's deep belief in the efficacy of faith-based social services. As one WHOFBCI staff person asserted, "Nobody in the administration except George W. Bush [had] any time at all for the faith-based issue; it is, for them, symbolic politics." . . . One close observer of the White House's relationship with Congress on the issue summarized it this way in early 2003: "Very few people in the White House made it a priority. Some wanted to use [the failure to pass faith-based legislation] as a club to beat up on Democrats."[115]

One way to assess the priorities of the Bush administration is to examine what issues the president discussed in his public communications: the speeches, messages, and statements the president made as he attempted to influence public and congressional opinion.[116] As shown in table 10.3, from the day Bush was inaugurated through September 10, 2001, the issue he talked about most often was his tax cut plan. He made thirty-eight speeches and statements in which tax cuts were the principal topic of discussion (i.e., the communication was primarily or exclusively about that topic) and gave the issue some significant mention (more than a passing reference) on fifty-three other occasions. The second most often-discussed issue was education, which received at least some significant mention in eighty-eight of Bush's speeches and messages. The faith-based initiative placed a rather weak third, serving as the principal topic of discussion in seventeen communications and thirty-seven times as a secondary topic.

All of the numbers cited in the preceding paragraph describe the content of Bush's public communications in the approximately eight months before the calamitous events of September 11, 2001. The attacks on the Pentagon and World Trade Center, not surprisingly, dramatically reshaped the president's agenda. As table 10.3 also shows, for the rest of 2001 almost everything the president said or did was connected (or made to seem like it was connected) to the new war on terrorism. Even the "No Child Left Behind" bill, which achieved final passage during this period, received remarkably little public comment from the president.

Though the threat of terrorism never ceased being a major concern for George W. Bush, by mid-2002 it no longer dominated the president's communications agenda in the all-but-exclusive way it had immediately after September 11. Yet even as Bush started to talk about other issues (homeownership, tighter regulation of corporate behavior, welfare reform, the early implementation of the No Child Left Behind law), one issue that did *not* receive much attention was the faith-based initiative. Between June 1 and November 30, 2002, Bush gave just one speech in which the faith-based initiative was among the major topics of discussion.[117] Even in situations where he might easily have raised the issue, he generally didn't. For example, whenever Bush made a speech outside Washington during the summer of 2002, he usually singled out one local volunteer for special recognition and praise, in an attempt to demonstrate the strength and vibrancy of the American spirit in the wake of 9/11. One might have thought that after praising this one "soldier in the army of compassion," Bush could have readily added something like, "But these volunteers need more resources, and that's the purpose of my faith-based legislation." But Bush rarely drew the connection.[118] This pattern held through the rest of the Bush presidency. Every time a bit of space opened up in the president's agenda, such as in early 2005, that space was filled by something other than the faith-based initiative. During the first six months of 2005, Bush delivered forty-two speeches or messages in which social security reform was the principal topic of discussion; the faith-based initiative was the principal topic of just two presidential communications.

Bush's slighting of the faith-based initiative was particularly galling to those who were most invested in the topic. Indeed, this was one subject on which Bush got Marvin Olasky and John DiIulio to agree: both felt that Bush gave short shrift to the issue on which they had once advised him.

Table 10.3. Number of Presidential Communications on Selected Issues, 2001

Dates and topics	Main topic	Secondary discussion	Total
Jan. 20–Sept. 10, 2001			
Tax cuts	38	53	91
Education	24	64	88
Faith-based initiative	17	37	54
Sept. 11–Dec. 31, 2001			
Terrorism	144	37	181
Tax cuts	2	8	10
Education	2	2	4
Faith-based initiative	2	4	6

Source: Compiled by the author from documents in George W. Bush, *Public Papers of the President 2001*, vols. 1 and 2 (Washington, DC: US Government Printing Office, 2003).

In an October 2009 interview, for example, Olasky insisted that compassionate conservatism "did not fail. It was never tried."[119] An even harsher indictment of the Bush faith-based record was delivered by David Kuo, an evangelical Christian who went to work for Bush convinced that the Texas governor was "the real deal . . . the embodiment of the Christian political statesman I had dreamed of finding and dreamed of being."[120] Yet after serving in the Bush administration for two and a half years, including a stint as deputy director of the WHOFBCI, Kuo emerged from that experience thoroughly disillusioned. In his book *Tempting Faith*, published in 2006, Kuo painted an enormously unflattering picture of an administration that had little real interest in helping the poor and disadvantaged, that regarded the faith-based initiative largely as a political vehicle for attracting increased support from minority voters, and that regularly refused to make even the most modest effort to push the faith-based legislation through Congress. Perhaps the most devastating story Kuo tells concerns the passage of the $1.7 trillion tax cut bill in June 2001. The original Senate version of this bill had included the tax incentives for increased charitable giving that Bush had promised in his 1999 "Duty of Hope" speech. When the final bill was negotiated, however, these provisions were dropped—*at the behest of the White House*.[121] In the end, as we have seen, most of these incentives were never enacted.

At a minimum, I think it is highly misleading to claim that the faith-based initiative was the entirety or even the most important element in compassionate conservatism. If one were to make a list of the major domestic policy initiatives pursued by the Bush administration, the list would look something like this:[122]

1. Tax cuts
2. Education reform (i.e., No Child Left Behind)
3. Faith-based initiative
4. Adding prescription drug coverage to Medicare
5. Partially privatizing Social Security
6. Comprehensive immigration reform
7. Relaxation of various federal regulations, especially environmental regulations, in order to promote economic growth and cheaper energy
8. The appointment of more conservatives to the federal judiciary.

Some observers might wish to add or subtract one or more items to or from this list, but few, I suspect, would contest the basic point: that the faith-based initiative was only one of many items on the administration's domestic agenda, that most of what the Bush people wanted to accomplish had nothing to do with the faith-based initiative. After reading David Kuo's book, one might wonder if the faith-based initiative belongs on the list at all.

Karl Rove

Though Karl Rove has rarely been identified as one of the major architects of compassionate conservatism, he clearly did have some significant role in its creation. Whatever else it was or may have become, compassionate conservatism first entered the vocabulary of most Americans when it was put forward as the "mantra" (Rove's word) of the 2000 Bush presidential campaign. In the fourth chapter of his memoirs, Rove provided a list of the "eight hallmarks of a 'Rovian' campaign," the first of which required the campaign to be "centered on big ideas."[123] Given Rove's legendary attention to detail and demand for control over every aspect of the campaigns he ran, he would hardly have allowed compassionate conservatism to play such a central role in the Bush campaign unless he had some idea of what it meant (or at least what *he* thought it meant) and was clearly convinced of its political value.

Perhaps the first thing to notice about Rove's conception of compassionate conservatism is that at no point does he equate it with faith-based initiatives. Faith-based initiatives were clearly *one* element in compassionate conservatism—but not the whole thing nor even its most important component. As Rove put it, "The 2000 Bush campaign was centered on compassionate conservatism, which itself was based on four big foundations: education reform, the faith-based initiative, a generous middle-class tax cut, and Social Security and Medicare reform."[124]

If there was a single core idea that Rove did see as the key to compassionate conservatism, it was the attempt to apply traditional conservative "principles" to new "issues" and "circumstances." Rove's most explicit discussion of the matter is contained in the following two passages from his memoirs:

> "Compassionate conservatism" was a call for a new approach from the right to issues including poverty, education, health care, and a secure retirement. Ignoring these issues all but guarantees that they will be addressed in a way that runs counter to conservative values. . . . By the time Bush used the label, it [compassionate conservatism] had had a solid track record, even occasionally winning Democrats' support. Welfare reform, for example, is "compassionate conservatism." So are school choice and a focus on educational results through an accountability system. Allowing people to save tax-free for their out-of-pocket medical expenses and leveling the playing field so families get a tax advantage for owning health insurance just as companies do are also facets of "compassionate conservatism." Bush wanted to take timeless conservative principles and apply them to the country's new circumstances.[125]

> What the GOP specifically and the conservative movement in general needed were fresh ways to apply their ideas to emerging issues that would appeal to a broad cross-section of voters. . . . Compassionate conservatism provided a framework for carrying conservative principles into a new era and made them relevant to a vast number of Americans.[126]

At least to conservatives, the idea of applying "timeless conservative principles" to "the country's new circumstances" probably sounded attractive enough. Once one turned from a general statement of principles to actual program development, however, it was far from clear just what this entailed. Were school vouchers, which Milton Friedman had famously advocated in 1962, really a "new approach" or a "fresh way" of dealing with the education issue?[127] Was welfare reform a new idea? Most conservatives, of course, would have had no problem relying on long-standing conservative policy prescriptions—but such an approach inevitably raised the question I have already posed with respect to Doug Wead: was compassionate conservatism really new, or just a newer, more attractive label for what most conservatives had long been advocating?

Even more problematic, I would argue, was how to determine whether any given proposal advanced "timeless conservative principles" enough to justify its adoption. Consider, for example, the Medicare prescription drug program that the Bush administration pushed through Congress in 2003. In *Courage and Consequence*, Rove lauds this legislation because it used "market forces" to bring down costs and "provide[d] seniors with a wide range of choices." True—but the law also represented the most significant expansion of a federal entitlement program since the 1960s. Even worse, as we have seen in chapter 5, it was an egregious act of fiscal irresponsibility, taking a program that already had huge unfunded liabilities and increasing its expenditures by more than $50 billion per year, with no attempt to figure out where the additional money would come from. When all the costs and benefits are taken into account, it is surely not obvious, as Rove asserts, that the Medicare prescription drug bill was "one of the best pieces of legislation Bush signed into law" and that it "unleashed results that should make any conservative happy."[128]

As this example suggests, Rovian-style compassionate conservatism frequently seemed to degenerate into a situation where one or two conservative features were added on to an otherwise unassailably liberal program, as if compassionate conservatism could be reduced to the following formula:

ANY LIBERAL PROGRAM + ONE CONSERVATIVE ELEMENT
= COMPASSIONATE CONSERVATISM

The No Child Left Behind law shows the same sort of questionable logic. When Bush signed this bill into law, he agreed to a dramatic expansion of federal spending on education and of federal control over local schools. In addition, the bill included a long list of other concessions to Edward Kennedy and congressional Democrats. A provision for education vouchers, which Rove mentions as a prime example of compassionate conservatism in action, was dropped early in the legislative process, with little apparent objection from the Bush high command. Bush also accepted a provision concerning teacher certification that managed to greatly reduce local flexibility in hiring new teachers, while at the same time exempting veteran teachers from having to meet the higher standards.[129] In return for all this, Bush got—drumroll, please—a lot of testing and a smidgen of accountability (primarily accountability to the federal government, rather than to parents). Yet, in Rove's view, this minimal application of an (allegedly) conservative principle[130] apparently redeemed the entire package, thus making NCLB "one of the great modern domestic policy successes."[131]

So What Was Compassionate Conservatism?

Thus far, we have looked at four possible meanings for compassionate conservatism:

1. Traditional conservatism, albeit with better motives and improved messaging
2 and 3. Faith-based initiatives, in either a pro- or antigovernmental version
4. Conservative principles applied to new issues and circumstances

Which of these best summarizes what George W. Bush himself meant by this elusive term? After several years of research, my answer is: None of the above. At one time or another, Bush can be found saying things that appear to show support for each of these views. Even Doug Wead's "same policies but with a different message" seems to get its props at one point:

> I like to joke that a compassionate conservative is a conservative with a smile, not a conservative with a frown. Some who would agree with a conservative philosophy have been turned off by a strident tone. I have set a different tone. I advocate limited government because too much government limits innovation, restricts competition, and crowds out the market. . . . I worked to reform welfare because I believe it is far more compassionate to help individuals become independent than to trap them in a cycle of dependency and despair.[132]

(Note that also like Wead, Bush actually seems to think that these sorts of arguments are new with him, rather than a long-standing, much-repeated part of conservative rhetoric.) But one never gets the sense that any one of these lines of thought—or all of them together—really explain Bush's domestic policy choices.

To summarize my conclusion in more explicit terms: Compassionate conservatism was a collection of policies that did depart in important ways from conservative orthodoxy. But there was no underlying logic that explained why these particular departures were acceptable and not others, no clear set of guidelines or principles that might have allowed other Republicans or conservatives to follow in Bush's footsteps. In the end, the only thing that united compassionate conservatism's various policy initiatives was the fact that George W. Bush believed in all of them.[133] The compassionate conservative label was adopted largely for political purposes, though it probably also embodied Bush's ambition to give expression to his Christian faith and to leave a mark on history. Yet even its political utility seems to have declined over time. A prominent rhetorical keynote in Bush's 2000 campaign, it became increasingly less significant during the administration's eight years in power.

Before proceeding further, I should first deal with one perception that is likely to be entertained by some readers of this book, especially those on the left side of the political spectrum. This is the contention that Bush was a plain, thorough, unadulterated conservative, in no respects different from most of the other candidates the Republican Party has nominated over the last several decades. And compassionate conservatism was thus a pure smoke screen, cynically designed to give Bush a more attractive image in the 2000 campaign but never intended as a serious philosophy for governing.

There are two major problems with this conclusion. First, it fails to take note of the quite large number of Bush policies that did cut against long-standing conservative principles. For almost two decades, most conservatives had advocated eliminating or greatly reducing the Department of Education. A proposal to *expand* the department's spending and powers, whatever else it was, was definitely *not* standard conservative operating procedure. Indeed, of the eight major items on Bush's domestic agenda listed earlier in this chapter, at least three—No Child Left Behind, the Medicare prescription drug bill, and comprehensive immigration reform—contradicted the positions most of his party had been endorsing just a few years earlier.[134] (Whether faith-based initiatives are compatible with traditional conservative principles depends on whether one proposed to reduce federal social spending, as Olasky favored, or to increase it, à la DiIulio.)

If we widen the scope of our inquiry to include items of somewhat lesser priority, the list of Bush's apostasies grows substantially longer: the hefty increase in agricultural subsidies; the imposition of steel tariffs; the failure to veto any large spending bills during the first six years of his presidency, even when they contained thousands of earmarks or greatly exceeded the spending limits he had initially laid down; the unwillingness to revise Title IX or to offer more than the most tepid opposition to affirmative action; the huge increase in the food stamp program;[135] the 2005 energy bill, which included large subsidies for virtually every form of energy; the 2007 energy bill, which contained both more subsidies and a basketful of new regulations, including the ban on incandescent light bulbs; and the massive corporate bailouts he approved at the end of his second term.[136]

In some of the cases just listed, defenders of the president might be able to excuse his decisions on the grounds of political expediency. Every Republican president of the last seventy years, including Ronald Reagan, has signed on to policies that he was initially opposed to or at least unenthusiastic about, in order to preserve his own or his party's electoral survival or to avoid something even worse. What is noteworthy about George W. Bush, however, is how often his violations of conservative orthodoxy were freely, even proudly chosen. The dramatic expansion of the federal role in education embodied in No Child Left Behind was not just something that happened to occur during Bush's presidency. It was one of his most salient campaign promises in 2000, one of his top legislative priorities during his first year in office. The expansion of Medicare was another major promise from the 2000 campaign, which Bush then worked hard to push through a sometimes-reluctant Congress. And even where Bush was apparently moved by political considerations, he seems to have had a remarkably low threshold for abandoning conservative principles. It is certainly not obvious, for example, that the future welfare of the Republican Party would have been seriously affected if Bush had vetoed the 2005 transportation bill or insisted upon a less generous farm subsidy bill.

Second, portraying Bush as a simple, unreconstructed conservative fails to explain why so many conservatives felt that Bush had betrayed conservatism and the conservative movement. By the end of Bush's second term, there was a small library of books and articles complaining about Bush's abandonment of conservative policies and his apparently enthusiastic embrace of big government, big spending, and big deficits.[137] It is impossible to read a reasonable sample of conservative blogs, conservative journals, and conservative books without becoming aware of this sentiment.

The first key to understanding Bush's actual approach to domestic issues is to recognize that he was not a very ideological or systematic thinker. By ideology, I mean a general, coherent, relatively abstract set of ideas about the role and purpose of government that is supposed to inform one's positions on a variety of specific issues. Bush undoubtedly had firmly held convictions about lots of particular issues, but one never gets the sense that he made much attempt or saw much need to fit them together into a larger whole. As he himself said at one point, "I do not need to explain why I say things. That's the interesting thing about being the president. Maybe somebody needs to explain to me why they say something, but I don't feel I owe anybody an explanation."[138] In this respect, I disagree with a comment made by the late Fred Greenstein of Princeton University, one of the most respected contemporary students of the presidency. In 2004, Greenstein told a *Washington Post* reporter that George W. Bush, unlike his father, "has the vision thing in spades."[139] If by vision one simply means strong opinions about lots of particular policies, Greenstein is no doubt correct. But if vision means a sense of the big picture, an ability to fit particular policy positions into a larger whole, I think Greenstein is quite wrong.

Bush often described his decision-making style by saying that he made decisions on the basis of his "instincts." As noted by Bob Woodward, "Bush had no problem trusting his instincts. It was almost his second religion. In an interview with me . . . on August 20, 2002, he referred a dozen times to his 'instincts' or his 'instinctive' reactions as the guide for his decisions. At one point he said, 'I'm not a textbook player, I'm a gut player.'"[140] One of Bush's press secretaries has similarly commented, "President Bush has always been an instinctive leader more than an intellectual leader. He is not one to delve deeply into all the possible policy options—including sitting around engaging in extended debate about them—before making a choice. Rather, he chooses based on his gut and his most deeply held convictions."[141] Along the same lines, a portrait of the president's decision-making style published in 2004 concluded, "In trying to figure out his position on an issue, Bush, like a lot of other politicians, doesn't so much analyze as look for a hook—a phrase or a way of framing the issue that feels instinctively right to him. In his case, instinct usually takes him to a position where he is in charge and everyone else has to adjust."[142]

Especially at the level of general rhetoric, most of Bush's instincts were undoubtedly conservative. His speeches and press conferences, his campaign biography, and his memoirs are all filled with ritualistic endorsements of limited government, fiscal restraint, free enterprise, and state and local control. And Bush did adhere closely to conservative orthodoxy on a handful of issues, including gun control, taxes, abortion, and the death penalty—generally issues where important Republican constituency groups would have reacted very negatively to any deviation.

But some of Bush's instincts clearly cut in the opposite direction. In particular, much like his father, Bush often responded strongly to stories of individual suffering and misfortune. Michael Gerson, who worked closely with Bush for many years both as his principal speechwriter and as a major policy advisor, has commented, "My experience in the White House policy structure was consistent: President Bush was the most touched by stories of personal suffering, and the most open to government activism that would relieve that suffering."[143] Bush himself said pretty much the same thing in a speech given on Labor Day, 2003: "We have a responsibility that when somebody hurts, Government has got to move."[144]

A good example of this tendency was Bush's 2002 decision, discussed in more detail in chapter 5, to impose tariffs on imported steel. As already noted, almost all of Bush's policy advisors opposed these tariffs; Karl Rove was almost alone in favoring them. But based on long experience with Bush, Rove knew which buttons to push. Where the economists reportedly argued against the tariffs as an instance of "unwarranted protectionism," Rove "helped steer the discussion by asking pointed policy questions of the advisers, making sure that Bush could hear the answers. What would happen, he wanted to know, if the steel companies didn't get relief?"[145]

Faced with the threat of plant closings and unemployed steel workers, Bush opted for tariffs.

There is no doubt that the capacity to respond to evidences of human suffering is an admirable, even essential quality for a president to possess. Few Americans, even on the far-right end of the political spectrum, would want a president who showed not the slightest trace of empathy for the poor, the sick, the vulnerable, and the disadvantaged. But there is also a real danger to this style of decision-making. In particular, it may lead a president to focus too much on the need to relieve immediate, visible suffering—while ignoring negative consequences of equal or greater magnitude just because they are more dispersed, less visible, or more long-term. Indeed, many conservatives have argued that this is the principal difference between liberal and conservative modes of economic analysis. Whereas liberals look only at the immediate consequences of policies like rent control and minimum wage laws, it is alleged, conservatives insist on taking account of their full, less obvious effects, which are (they believe) quite negative.[146]

Steel tariffs are again a good example of the problem. The groups that push for tariffs—in this case, steelworkers and steel mill owners—are very good at calling attention to the immediate harms of *not* restricting foreign imports: the steel plants hovering on the edge of bankruptcy, the longtime workers who will lose their jobs, the cities and contractors that will be affected. But a president will be less likely to hear from all the groups that will bear the *costs* of the tariffs: the manufacturing companies that use steel, many of whom may also face precarious economic circumstances; the workers in those companies; the consumers who will pay higher prices; the industries that will suffer if other countries impose retaliatory tariffs. Economists who study these issues have overwhelmingly concluded that the costs of trade restrictions far outweigh the benefits. A president who was a "textbook player"—or just a more traditional conservative—would have understood this point. Bush, following his instincts, chose to ignore it.

It is also fair to note how often Bush's "instincts" coincided with his political interests. Perhaps Bush really was moved by stories about poor, long-suffering steelworkers—but did he really not notice that the steel industry was concentrated in a small number of states that were crucial to both the 2002 midterms and his own reelection prospects? While Bush may have been instinctively committed to providing a "safety net for farmers," it is hard to believe that he wasn't also aware of the large number of contested Senate races in farm states. And though there is no reason to question the sincerity of Bush's affection for the Hispanic immigrant woman who served as his family's nanny and "second mother," one wonders if he would have drawn the same policy lessons from this experience had he not lived in a state with a large number of Hispanic voters. Like many other politicians, Bush seems to have been quite good at convincing himself that the policies that advanced his political interests could also be justified on their policy merits.

For a president who was fitfully conservative but made decisions based largely on instinct, compassionate conservatism was an ideal slogan. Most obviously, it met Bush's political needs, allowing him to insist that he was, in fact, a conservative while nevertheless putting some distance between himself and congressional Republicans. And precisely because it didn't have a single, clear meaning, virtually any policy Bush decided upon could fit somewhere under compassionate conservatism's capacious umbrella.

Bush's marginal attachment to compassionate conservatism as a general philosophy, as distinct from the individual policies that comprised it, is also shown by its gradual disappearance from his statements and speeches. Compassionate conservatism, as we have seen, was at the heart of Bush's 2000 campaign. It was prominently showcased in his announcement speech; it was the title of the final, forward-looking chapter of *A Charge to Keep*, his campaign biography. Karl Rove himself described it as the "mantra" of Bush's presidential candidacy.

By the time Bush ran for reelection in 2004, compassionate conservatism was still hanging on, but just barely. The phrase is mentioned only once in Bush's acceptance speech at the 2004 Republican National Convention—where Bush appears to provide yet one more definition for the term: "I am running for president with a clear and positive plan to build a safer world and a more hopeful America. I am running with a compassionate conservative philosophy: that government should help people improve their lives, not try to run their lives."[147]

To get a more precise sense of the role compassionate conservatism played in Bush's postconvention campaign, I have examined a sample of twenty-two campaign speeches the president gave between September 1 and November 1, 2004 (election day was November 2).[148] Compassionate conservatism is mentioned once in eight of the twenty-two speeches; it never appears at all in the other fourteen. "Faith-based" programs are mentioned in just two of the speeches. No fair reading of the 2004 Bush campaign, I believe, could conclude that compassionate conservatism was a major theme in the president's quest for a second term.

Even more noteworthy is the fact that *compassionate conservatism is never mentioned at all in Bush's 477-page presidential memoir*. Most of *Decision Points*, it is true, deals with foreign policy. But if compassionate conservatism truly were a well-developed philosophy that explained Bush's approach to domestic policy, one might have thought that he would have snuck in at least a few references to it when discussing his decisions with respect to education, Medicare, Social Security, faith-based programs, or immigration. But the term never appears.

Compassionate Conservatism: The Legacy

In a memoir of his service in the Bush administration, presidential speech-writer Matt Latimer recounts a meeting he had with the president to go over a speech that Bush was scheduled to deliver to the Conservative Political Action Conference. Given the intended audience, Latimer's draft contained numerous references to the conservative "movement." Bush reacted with a mixture of skepticism and irritation.

> "So take out all this movement stuff," he said. "There is no movement."
> He couldn't possibly mean that [Latimer thought]. No conservative movement? He must not have understood what I was trying to say . . .
> Perhaps seeing my confusion, the president tried to explain what he meant. "Look, I know this probably sounds arrogant to say, but I redefined the Republican Party."[149]

In his memoir of the Bush presidency, Karl Rove similarly declares, "he [Bush] did alter the course of the conservative movement that he came to lead. And the direction he steered it in was productive, principled, and healthy for the country."[150]

Both Bush and Rove are, in my opinion, wildly off the mark. The Bush presidency did, it is true, have many lasting consequences for the Republican Party, almost all of them negative. In particular, the Bush record made it considerably more difficult for Republicans to present themselves to the electorate as the guardians of economic prosperity, fiscal rectitude, and US national security. In more positive terms, however, it is difficult to argue that Bush-style compassionate conservatism left any durable impression on either the Republican Party or the conservative movement.

To start with the most basic point: long after Ronald Reagan left office, many candidates for public office, particularly in Republican primaries, proudly assert that they are "Reagan Republicans."[151] Has *any* recent candidate called himself a "Bush Republican"? Or a "compassionate conservative"? In the words of Republican consultant Ed Rollins, "Nobody who's come of age during the Bush era will stand up and say, 'I'm a Bush Republican.'"[152] Even in the contest for the 2008 Republican presidential nomination, while Bush was still in office, the candidates "sounded as if they were trying to succeed Ronald Reagan instead of George W. Bush, whom they didn't mention if they could help it."[153]

If candidates are unwilling to adopt Bush's preferred label or mention his name, have they at least embraced his policies? Have they followed the path he blazed in such areas as education and immigration? Here, too, there is scant evidence that they have. In late 2001, as we saw in chapter 4, No Child Left Behind passed both houses of Congress with large, bipartisan majorities. By Bush's second term, the law was just as widely reviled. In the hyperpartisan environment of contemporary American politics, it is probably no great surprise that Democrats would repudiate the law and thus undermine Bush's attempts to portray himself as "the education president" and a strong, nonpartisan leader. What is more noteworthy for the present discussion is how many Republicans turned against Bush's "signature domestic achievement." A particularly vivid sign of the discontent came in March 2007, when fifty-seven Republican members of the House and Senate introduced a bill that would have allowed states to opt out of the NCLB's testing mandates, in effect gutting the whole law. The bill's cosponsors included the House minority whip and chief deputy whip and one of the senators from Bush's own home state of Texas; a sizable number had voted for the original legislation.[154] Not only did Congress (which was controlled by the Republicans in 2005–2006) refuse to expand the law's reach, as Bush wanted, they were unwilling even to reauthorize the original legislation.

Another useful indicator of the extent of conservative support for the "compassionate conservative" approach to education is provided by the Republican presidential nomination race of 2012. Of the eight major Republican candidates that year, the only one who had a good word to say about No Child Left Behind was Mitt Romney, and even he waffled on the issue as the race progressed.[155] The other seven all argued, with varying degrees of ferocity, that the law was a failure and needed to be done away with entirely or at least drastically revised. Rick Santorum, who had voted for the law in 2001, now said that his vote had been a "mistake" and that "we need to cut and eliminate No Child Left Behind . . . and move [education funding] back to the local level where it belongs."[156] Even Jon Huntsman, who was generally viewed as the most moderate of the GOP presidential contenders, said that "No Child Left Behind hasn't worked for this country. It ought to be done away with."[157]

On immigration, Republicans were never willing to follow Bush's lead. In his 2005 State of the Union speech, Bush had announced that one of his top priorities for the coming Congress was to reform the country's immigration system. The House of Representatives was first to take up the challenge. In December 2005, the House passed a bill that significantly tightened border security and increased the penalties for illegal immigration—but conspicuously did *not* give Bush the guest-worker provision he wanted. Meanwhile, the Senate was proceeding along very different lines. A coalition led by John McCain and Edward Kennedy developed a bill that contained some provisions for stepped-up enforcement (considerably weaker, however, than those in the House bill) but also included a guest-worker program and a path to citizenship for most of the illegal immigrants who already lived in the United States. On May 15, 2006, the president made a nationally televised speech in which he made clear that he wanted a "comprehensive" immigration bill—that is, a bill like the one the Senate was then considering, rather than one that focused only on border security, as the House bill did. Ten days after Bush's speech, in what was widely described as a "bipartisan" effort, the Senate passed the McCain-Kennedy bill, 62–36. The bill undeniably did have some Republican support, but a solid majority of Senate Republicans—32 of 55, or 58 percent—actually voted *against* the measure. It cleared the Senate only because it received the lopsided support of the chamber's Democrats (thirty-eight voted for it, just four against). Bush now hoped to persuade a conference committee to craft a bill closely modeled after the Senate measure—but House Republicans refused to budge. Indeed, the prospects for any kind of compromise were seen as so remote that a conference committee was never even formed.[158] During his presidency, in short, Bush was never able to persuade a majority of Republicans—in either house—to follow his lead on immigration.

In subsequent years, most Republicans continued to reject the Bush position on immigration. After Mitt Romney's defeat in 2012, there was some sentiment among Republican elites, especially those like Rove who had once been part of the George W. Bush administration, that Romney's loss was due to his failure to do better among Hispanic voters.[159] The remedy, Rove and others asserted, was for Republicans to enact some version of "comprehensive immigration reform" that was visibly sympathetic to the concerns and aspirations of illegal immigrants. Once again, however, the majority of Republican elected officials—and, according to the polls, a majority of Republican identifiers—thought otherwise. In June 2013, the Senate passed a comprehensive immigration bill by a 68–32 margin. But much as in 2006, this "bipartisan" measure was supported by all fifty-four Democrats and independents, but just fourteen of forty-six Republicans, an even smaller proportion than in 2006.

Another telling sign of Bush's failure to transform American conservatism was the rise of the Tea Party movement. As Conor Friedersdorf observed:

The Tea Party wasn't just a reaction to President Obama or the financial industry bailouts. As Jonah Goldberg puts it, "a major motivating passion of the tea-party movement was a long-delayed backlash against George W. Bush and his big-government conservatism." Support for the War on Terrorism and the invasion of Iraq caused many conservatives to stay loyal to Bush. But that didn't mean they liked No Child Left Behind, Medicare Part D, the attempt at a guest worker program, TARP, or the Harriet Miers nomination. Especially after the defeat of John McCain, many on the right insisted they'd never again support Bush-Rove conservatism.[160]

Profiles of prominent Tea Party activists often found that, in addition to their dislike of Barack Obama, they had also "lost patience with the [Republican] party for its role in the expansion of government programs and spending. . . . Conservatives reviled President George W. Bush for expanding Medicare and increasing federal spending."[161]

By late 2011 and early 2012, numerous commentators were noting that "the compassionate conservative agenda has virtually disappeared from the Republican Party"; and "Just three years after George W. Bush left the White House, compassionate conservatives are an endangered species."[162] If Bush had "redefined the Republican Party" and "alter[ed] the course of the conservative movement," most conservatives were managing to keep that fact very well-hidden.

As events would prove, however, there was still a bit of life left in the old corpse. In the wake of the Republican Party's unexpectedly weak showing in the 2012 elections, there were signs of a renewed interest in compassionate conservatism. Though the scale of Mitt Romney's loss was not very different from that of John Kerry's in 2004, many Republicans, unlike their Democratic counterparts of eight year earlier, jumped to the conclusion that there was something fundamentally wrong with their party. As the editor of one conservative magazine observed, "To many on the right, the result [of the 2012 presidential election] feels terrifyingly historic, as though it represents an ideological and partisan Rubicon across which the United States has crossed."[163] And while there were, not surprisingly, a variety of diagnoses and remedies, a number of pundits and strategists claimed that what Republicans really needed was a return to the good old days of George W. Bush. The image that Mitt Romney projected to the voters, the argument went, was too harsh, too insensitive, too out-of-touch with the day-to-day concerns of many voters. Future Republican nominees needed to do what Bush had apparently done so successfully in 2000: display a softer, more caring side; show that he, too, felt the voters' pain; show that he was, in a word, compassionate.

I do not wish to overstate the prevalence of this sentiment. After an extensive search on the internet, I have managed to find perhaps a dozen articles or postings after the 2012 election in which the author explicitly endorsed Bush-style compassionate conservatism or claimed that some other Republican or conservative figure had endorsed it.[164] The closest thing I can find to a representative sample of conservative opinion leaders appeared in the January 2013 issue of *Commentary* magazine, in which fifty-three major conservative writers and thinkers were asked to write a short essay on the question, "What is the future of conservatism in the wake of the 2012 election?" Though none of the participants explicitly advocated a return to "compassionate conservatism," two of the fifty-three did urge the Republican Party to display greater compassion. (One even said that compassion was "perhaps the most important conservative principle of all.")[165]

Those commentators who did show a renewed interest in compassionate conservatism, moreover, tended to offer a rather qualified endorsement. A good example is an article written in mid-November 2012 by Jonah Goldberg, probably the best conservative columnist in America today. Goldberg spent much of his column recounting some of the many criticisms of compassionate conservatism he had made during the Bush presidency:

> For years, I've criticized "compassionate conservatism" as an insult to traditional conservatism and an affront to all things libertarian. Bush liked to say that he was a "different kind of Republican," that he was a "compassionate conservative." I hated—and still hate—that formulation. Imagine if someone said, "I'm a different kind of Catholic (or Jew, or American, etc.): I'm a *compassionate* Catholic." The insinuation was—by my lights, at least—that conservatives who disagreed with him and his "strong-government conservatism" were somehow lacking in compassion.[166]

"I still believe all of that," Goldberg now said, "probably even more than I did when Bush was in office. But, as a political matter, it has become clear that he was on to something important. . . . Given the election results, I have to acknowledge that Bush was more prescient than I appreciated at the time." What was appealing about compassionate conservatism, in other words, was that it led to election victories, at least from 2000 to 2004. But there was no indication that Goldberg had changed his mind about any of the major policies associated with the label, such as No Child Left Behind or Medicare Part D or comprehensive immigration reform. Indeed, Goldberg didn't seem entirely convinced that compassionate conservatism was a clearly defined philosophy at all: "Neither critics nor supporters of compassionate conservatism could come to a consensus over the question of whether it was a mushy-gushy marketing slogan (a Republican version of Bill Clinton's I-feel-your-pain liberalism) or a serious philosophical argument for a kind of Tory altruism, albeit with an evangelical idiom and a Texan accent."[167]

And Then Came Donald Trump

As this book was being finished, in the early months of 2020, a great deal has recently been written about how President Trump may, will, or already has redefined the nature of American conservatism. For reasons to be detailed in a moment, reshaping a longtime, well-established political ideology is an enormously difficult undertaking, and I am skeptical that Trump will be successful in this endeavor. But as the preceding section has indicated, whatever Trump manages to accomplish while in the White House, he will not be the person who killed compassionate conservatism. Compassionate conservatism was pretty much dead well before Trump rode down the escalator at Trump Tower and announced his presidential candidacy. By 2009 at the very latest, it was clear that a large part of the Republican base felt betrayed by the Bush presidency and, thus, by the whole Republican establishment, especially on the issue of immigration. If Donald Trump was the candidate best able to exploit this opening, that is because (a) he received such an appallingly disproportionate share of the press coverage and (b) he had few if any ideological convictions to restrain him.

But if there were any lingering doubts on the matter, Trump's nomination and election should have conclusively removed them: George W. Bush failed in his attempt to reshape the governing philosophy of the Republican Party. When Bush exited the White House, American conservatism as an ideology was pretty much the same creature it had been in 1999. Fifty or a hundred years from now, American history textbooks may devote a few sentences to compassionate conservatism and its role in the Bush presidency—or they may not mention it at all. What they are most unlikely to do is accord it the sustained attention that textbooks now give to such ideological/policy movements as Progressivism, New Deal liberalism, or Reagan-style conservatism.

To be fair to George Bush, the task he set for himself always promised to be a very difficult one. Major, well-established political ideologies like liberalism and conservatism are not easy to change. In pushing for a greater federal role in education and an expansion of Medicare, Bush was challenging two important principles that have been part of mainstream American conservatism for at least the last seventy years: opposition to a more powerful federal government and opposition to the growth of the welfare state. When a policy or principle has been part of an ideology for such an extended period of time, there are probably a lot of forces sustaining it. Many opinion leaders and policy intellectuals almost certainly support it; lots of interest groups will have been organized (at least in part) to promote it; and it will probably also have considerable resonance with ordinary voters. Such people and groups are unlikely to change their minds merely because a president of their party claims that he has a better idea. Had No Child Left Behind or the Medicare Modernization Act been a dazzling policy success, perhaps some conservatives would have changed their tune. In fact, NCLB never produced anything like the revolution in educational outcomes that Bush and its supporters had promised. The Bush Medicare bill may have saved a bit of money as compared to the Democratic alternatives, but it still cost a great deal of money and thus deepened the fiscal predicament of a program that already had huge unfunded liabilities.

The faith-based initiative faced a somewhat different set of obstacles. At least in the form that Bush had outlined during the 2000 campaign, there was no compelling reason for conservatives to oppose it. But as I have tried to show in this chapter, that was because the Bush plan was designed more to ward off objections than to have a major impact on the problems it was supposed to address. A scheme more like the one Marvin Olasky had endorsed—where private charity substantially replaced governmental welfare programs—would not have been seen as compassionate. (Nor would it have received congressional approval, even in a Congress where Republicans controlled both the House and the Senate.) The moral of the story is: When dealing with a long-standing, complicated problem like the American welfare system, new ideas that both work and are politically attractive (or at least politically inoffensive) are very hard to come by.

The one issue where Bush may have had some room to maneuver was immigration, where significant numbers of party members could be found on both sides of the issue. Though it would not have been easy, it may have been possible for the administration to work out a compromise that was acceptable to most Americans, in which existing immigration laws were strictly enforced and perhaps tightened while some form of amnesty was granted to the illegals who were already here. But Bush and Rove showed little interest in compromise. They showed little appreciation of the large number of ordinary Republican voters who were genuinely concerned about the problems of illegal immigration. The result was a very one-sided plan under which immigration opponents were expected to swallow amnesty and a new guest-worker program, and given nothing in return except some vague promises of stepped-up enforcement.

Granted the inherent difficulty of the task, Bush made it even more difficult in two ways. First, as I have tried to show in this chapter, compassionate conservatism was never a cohesive, well-defined set of principles and programs. If Rove and Bush really hoped to create a durable Republican majority or to leave a lasting mark on American conservatism, they needed to offer something more than a grab-bag collection of policies united only by their appeal to George Bush's instincts or a vague injunction that Republicans find "fresh ways" to apply "conservative principles" to "emerging issues." Simply put, it is difficult to have ideological heirs when you don't have much of an ideology. Like the great presidents mentioned in the introduction to this chapter, Bush needed to "take the people to school" and teach them something new and important about the problems the nation faced and the role and limits of government. Plainly, compassionate conservatism fell well short of this standard.

Second, even the most principled conservatives might have given a sympathetic look to compassionate conservatism if it had been an obvious political success—just as many Democrats embraced New Deal liberalism after their party posted such thumping victories in 1932, 1934, and 1936. But the electoral record of compassionate conservatism was never terribly impressive, certainly not enough to convince skeptical conservatives that Bush had discovered a sure route to political success. Running as a compassionate conservative, Bush did win an election in 2000—at least in the electoral college—even though most objective indicators seemed to favor the Democrats. The Republicans also posted small gains in both houses of Congress in 2002 and 2004. But even in 2004, in his best electoral showing, Bush couldn't win even 51 percent of the national popular vote. By comparison, Franklin Roosevelt topped out at 60.7 percent in 1936. In any event, the whole house of cards soon came crashing down, as the Democrats won control of the House and Senate in 2006, then added the presidency and a lot more congressional seats in 2008.

The collapse of the Bush presidency owed more to the war in Iraq and the recession that began in late 2007 than to any of the policies that were distinctive to compassionate conservatism—but neither is there much evidence to show that policies such as NCLB, Medicare Part D, or the faith-based initiative helped cushion the blow. In 2000, as shown in chapter 6, Bush did run unusually well among voters who said that education was their most important issue, normally a very Democratic voting bloc. By 2004, however, it was back to business as usual. Though John Kerry had no record of leadership on education issues, 73 percent of education voters cast their ballots for Kerry, versus just 26 percent for Bush. Those who singled out health care as their leading issue also voted overwhelmingly for Kerry, 77 percent to 23 percent. Such results were hardly a persuasive advertisement for the glories of compassionate conservatism.

11

Conclusion

Whatever else may be said of the Bush presidency, it was plainly not a political success. Karl Rove's ambition to engineer the next realignment—to establish a lengthy era of Republican electoral dominance—was always going to be difficult to pull off. As David Mayhew had pointed out, there was no historical precedent for what Rove was trying to accomplish. In every other case, the president who presided over the realignment—Lincoln, McKinley, and Roosevelt—simply tried to cope with a crisis he had inherited from his predecessor (a civil war and the two worst depressions in American history, respectively). Only well after the fact did it become clear that the shape of the party system had been durably transformed. While Bill Clinton's presidency had its share of problems and disappointments, it cannot plausibly be argued that he bequeathed a genuine crisis to George W. Bush.

But it was not unreasonable or overly ambitious to think that the Bush presidency might have left the Republican Party in better shape than it had been in 2001—with an enhanced reputation for dealing with certain kinds of problems, with a somewhat expanded electoral following. In fact, as noted at the end of chapter 2, by the time Bush left the White House the Republican Party had been reduced to its weakest position in several decades. As Barack Obama prepared for his inauguration, many commentators predicted that the country was entering into a new era of reliable *Democratic* majorities.

Did Bush and Rove improve the Republican Party's image or policies in more subtle ways, that may help the party in the longer term? To the contrary, many of Bush's mistakes have continued to plague his party and his country long after he retired to his ranch in Crawford, Texas. By greatly mishandling the postwar occupation in Iraq, Bush largely neutralized at least for a time the Republicans' long-standing advantage as the party better able to protect American national security. Absent such mistakes, it is difficult to imagine that, just seven years after the attacks on the World Trade Center, Americans would have elected a left-wing senator with little foreign policy experience over a legitimate war hero. By reinvigorating the

"Vietnam syndrome," Bush handicapped the capacity of future presidents to fight an aggressive war against terrorism or to intervene in other situations where the American military might make a positive impact, such as peacekeeping and humanitarian missions.

The political failures of the Bush presidency also had their effect on domestic policy. When Bush took office, both he and Rove hoped to bring about significant changes in the nature of American conservatism. There is no evidence that they were successful. Though most Republicans voted for the No Child Left Behind bill, most later came to regard that decision as a major mistake, as the law dramatically increased the federal role in elementary and secondary education while producing few gains in academic achievement or in the Republican Party's appeal to education-minded voters. The faith-based initiative proved to be much ado about very little. By pushing for a tax cut that was no longer justified by economic circumstances as well as increased spending on a wide variety of programs and policies, Bush squandered a sizable budgetary surplus and brought back the era of large, persistent deficits. And Bush was never able to get most Republicans to buy into his immigration policies. The cumulative effect of these policies was to alienate much of the Republican base from the party leadership and thus lay the groundwork for the candidacy of Donald Trump.

And yet, the legend continues. In 2012, journalist Craig Unger wrote a book called *Boss Rove: Inside Karl Rove's Secret Kingdom of Power*. Rove, Unger claimed, was still hatching schemes to take over the Republican Party and then the country. That he had failed to do so when his chief client was president apparently hadn't discouraged Rove (or Unger). By 2008, when Rove became a commentator on Fox News, Unger declared, "Now that he controlled the purse strings to hundreds of millions of dollars, Rove was a kingmaker, a puppet master, not merely a political analyst." By 2012, "Rove had even consolidated the money under his power. He had co-opted the Tea Party, defanging the uncontrollable elements in it, marginalizing their leaders and seizing their resources." It might all sound believable had Unger not also claimed that Rove had consigned Donald Trump "to the dustbin of history."[1]

Though this book has often focused on the work and legacy of Karl Rove, it is important not to lose sight of the fundamentals. The person primarily responsible for these afflictions was not Rove, but George W. Bush. Rove, as I have argued in chapter 7, should have warned Bush about the ways that the botched occupation in Iraq was undermining both his presidency and his party. But such warnings should never have been necessary. A good president would have been more suspicious about Donald Rumsfeld's desire to invade Iraq with a military force that was simply inadequate to the full scope of the task and recognized that many generals were recommending a far larger force. A good president would have spent more time planning the postwar occupation—and then made sure that the leader of the Coalition Provisional Authority followed through on the plans and decisions that were made. A good president would have monitored the situation in postwar Iraq more closely and drawn on sources of information from outside the chain of command.

Though it was not a subject I originally set out to investigate, in examining the Bush presidency I have been repeatedly struck by the number of foolish and highly dysfunctional things George W. Bush believed about governing. These include:

- that it was possible to be a good president without paying much attention to the news;
- that a decision, once made, should never be second-guessed—and that those who did express second thoughts were guilty of either disloyalty or a failure of nerve;
- that the best way to find out about the state of a program or policy was to consult the people who were responsible for devising and implementing it;
- that it wasn't especially important for a president to explain why he had decided upon a particular policy;
- that in choosing subordinates, personal loyalty was more important than previous experience or other marks of demonstrated competence; and
- that his own, relatively uninformed instincts were a sufficient guide for deciding complex policy questions.

As of this writing, Donald Trump's presidency has persuaded many liberals—and, I suspect, many historians—to adopt a somewhat more positive view of the Bush presidency. But even if Trump makes Bush look good by comparison, that should not obscure the fact that Bush was, by almost any other standard, not a very good president. Even Karl Rove, in his memoir, would only call Bush a "consequential" president—not a good or a great one.[2] In that sense, Rove's greatest mistake was simply that he hitched his wagon to the wrong star.

His choice of client aside, Rove was not an innocent bystander as all this was going on. If Rove deserves considerable credit for the Republican Party's successes in 2000 and 2002, he must also bear some of the blame for the predicament the party found itself in as of late 2008. As one of the president's principal domestic policy advisors, he played a major role in pushing some of the administration's least defensible policy decisions, including its support for lax immigration enforcement, steel tariffs, large agricultural subsidies, and a greatly expanded space program. At a time when the war in Iraq was clearly undermining support for both the Bush presidency and the use of American military power abroad, Rove made no apparent effort to warn Bush about these problems until it was too late. The White House communications operation also failed the president in a number of significant ways.

Underlying many of these individual missteps, I believe, were two larger problems. First, Rove failed to appreciate the differences between the politics of campaigning and the politics of governing. As I have shown in some detail in chapters 4 and 5, many effective campaign strategies are likely to result in bad public policy. Yet there is no evidence that Rove recognized this point. As head of the Office of Strategic Initiatives and as deputy chief of staff for policy, Rove continued to pursue the same kinds of appeals he had relied on during his many years as a political consultant.

Second, Rove did his best to make sure that his was the dominant, even the only major voice advising Bush about politics, especially after the departure of Karen Hughes in 2002. By all reports, Rove did not deal well with rivals. As noted in chapter 4, he was a man with a pronounced sense of territoriality, a person often described as a "control freak." Just as presidents generally get economic advice from lots of different economic advisors, and get national security advice from many different foreign policy and defense experts, they should also get political advice from a variety of sources. No one advisor, even someone of Rove's obvious abilities, is infallible. None, as Richard Neustadt warned, has a perspective and set of interests identical to those of the president.[3]

One lesson that should not be drawn from this study, however, is that Bush made a mistake in bringing Rove along with him to Washington or that the president should have made an effort to govern above or without politics. Like Aristotle's moral virtues, both too much and too little politics will serve a president—and the country—poorly. Also like Aristotle's virtues, practicing politics well is not simply a matter of finding a happy medium between two extremes but of doing it "at the right time, toward the right object, toward the right people, for the right reason, and in the right manner."[4]

The titles of chapters 3–10 provide a good summary of my major conclusions in this regard.

Presidents Need Political Help. Political advisors like Rove clearly can perform a number of useful functions for the president: assessing the level of support for and opposition to his policies; monitoring the state of public opinion; determining the best ways to explain and sell his policies; planning and organizing for the next election.

Good Politics Doesn't Always Mean Good Government, or Never Make a Political Consultant One of Your Top Policy Advisors. Political advisors should be given a place at the table when important policy decisions are made, but to make a political consultant a top policy advisor—to make him or her the deputy chief of staff for policy—is likely to produce seriously deficient policy. In too many ways, the incentives and training of political consultants conflict with the requirements of good public policy.

You Can't Nickel and Dime Your Way to a Realignment. Alexander Hamilton was right: The "little arts of popularity" may be enough to build a fine career in the House or the Senate, but being a good president or establishing a durable party majority requires getting the big issues right: peace, prosperity, domestic security, and the national welfare.

When an Administration Is in Crisis and the President Refuses to Acknowledge It, a Political Advisor May Be the Best Person to Warn the President. Presidents, like most human beings, are reluctant to admit their mistakes. Often, they persist with policies well after it has become clear to everybody else that these policies aren't working. For a variety of reasons, a president's political advisors are usually in a particularly good position to alert him to the nature and costs of his mistakes.

Never Forget That War Is a Political Endeavor. President Bush thought he was being noble and principled when he insisted that "politics has no role" in the war on terror. Actually, he was being shortsighted. Particularly for what he himself said would be not a single battle but a lengthy campaign, the president needed to ensure that there was continued political support for the war. In this respect, he clearly failed.

Communication Is Important, but Don't Expect Miracles. A good communications operation cannot turn a seriously botched military operation into a great popular success, but neither should communications be neglected or dismissed as unimportant. When controversies emerge, many people will naturally look to the president for guidance as to how to interpret an issue or respond to his critics. Too often during the Bush presidency, the president's supporters were given no guidance at all.

It's Hard to Have Ideological Heirs When You Don't Have Much of an Ideology. Rove and Bush's claims notwithstanding, the Bush presidency left surprisingly little long-term imprint on conservative and Republican policy ideas. No Child Left Behind was widely repudiated, most Republicans never bought into comprehensive immigration reform, and the faith-based initiative, at least in the version supported by Bush, was unlikely to have much impact on the problems it purported to address, even if it had been fully and faithfully implemented. Beyond the failure of individual policies, Bush was unable to convince his fellow partisans that his general approach to governing—what he called compassionate conservatism—was the road to future success. Indeed, compassionate conservatism never seems to have been a clearly defined set of principles and policies.

These are, of course, generalizations; and like all generalizations, they may not apply in some circumstances. A good politician—a statesman, a Washington, Lincoln, or Roosevelt—is one who knows how to apply the correct lesson in a particular situation. Still, political science can, I believe, contribute to this enterprise by helping make practicing politicians aware of the general dimensions of the problems and challenges they face and, where necessary, by avoiding the bad counsel contained in many of the copybook maxims of our political culture.

That, in any event, has been the hope and intention of this study.

Appendix

A Review of Karl Rove's *The Triumph of William McKinley: Why the Election of 1896 Still Matters*

When a politician or other celebrity writes what purports to be a work of history, it is hard not to treat the book with a considerable measure of skepticism. Too often, such works are little more than an attempt to cash in on the author's fame or were really written by someone else—or both. So the first thing to say about Karl Rove's *The Triumph of William McKinley: Why the Election of 1896 Still Matters* is that this is a serious historical study and that, while he did have the help of six "intern researchers" (duly credited in the acknowledgments), the writing and the ideas are, by all evidence, his own. As the fifty-plus pages of notes indicate, Rove and his research assistants have scoured contemporary newspapers, research libraries, historical societies, and the huge secondary literature on the Gilded Age to construct a remarkably detailed account of how McKinley won the 1896 Republican nomination and how he and his advisors then conducted the general election campaign.

The narrative of the prenomination campaign is particularly well done. McKinley, Rove states, "ran the first modern presidential primary campaign" (108),[1] and Rove, in turn, has fashioned what is, so far as I know, the most detailed account of a presidential nomination campaign conducted during the so-called pure convention system.[2] Unwilling to trust his fate to the Republican bosses in states like New York and Pennsylvania or to the vagaries of a national convention, McKinley put together an unusually active preconvention campaign, the principal elements of which bear a rough resemblance to the way that nomination campaigns are run in the modern, plebiscitary system: begin early; run a national campaign; create a highly disciplined organization. McKinley also did, at least by the standards of the time, a substantial amount of personal campaigning. And he had a knack for finding very talented people to staff his organization, particularly Mark Hanna and Charles Dawes.

A good example of the McKinley campaign in operation was its efforts to line up delegates in the South, a region that after 1876 provided the Republican Party with no electoral votes and very few members of Congress but still accounted for almost a quarter of the national convention votes.[3] Instead of waiting until the convention or offering southern Republicans various forms of boodle, as GOP presidential aspirants typically did, McKinley made an extended trip to the South in the spring of 1895, meeting with party leaders, including many black Republicans. As one party boss who didn't support McKinley would later lament, "He had the South practically solid before some of us awakened" (114). In the end, McKinley won 88 percent of the southern votes on the Republican convention's first (and only) ballot.

The McKinley organization did just as well in the West and almost as well in the Midwest. Thomas Brackett Reed of Maine, who as speaker of the US House of Representatives might have been expected to have widespread national support, won almost no votes outside his home region of New England. The so-called Combine, a group of states characterized by "well-organized, disciplined party organizations tied together by patronage, power, and money" (94), was limited to the votes secured by favorite son candidates in New York, Pennsylvania, and Iowa. McKinley thus became the first nonincumbent candidate since Ulysses S. Grant in 1868 to win a first ballot nomination at a Republican convention.

The main weakness of this book is that too much of it, especially the account of the general election campaign, reads as if it is, consciously or unconsciously, an after-the-fact justification of Rove's own handling of George W. Bush's political fortunes. As befits a political consultant, Rove places great emphasis on the workings of the campaigns waged by McKinley and William Jennings Bryan, his Democratic opponent. He thus substantially undervalues the impact of real-world conditions and events.

Why did McKinley win the presidency in 1896, and by a larger margin than any of the five previous presidential victors? Based on everything we have learned about presidential elections and American voting behavior over the last seventy years, most political scientists today would assign a central role to the state of the economy.[4] What modern-day economists believe was the second worst depression in American history began in early 1893 and continued, with one brief, incomplete period of recovery, until mid-1897. Though there are no official unemployment statistics from this period, two different sets of estimates indicate that national unemployment exceeded 10 percent for five straight years. More than 800 banks failed and 150 railroad companies were in the hands of receivers.[5]

Whether the policies of then-president Grover Cleveland had anything to do with starting or prolonging the depression is an interesting economic question, but politically beside the point. With the Democrats firmly in control of the national government—in 1893–1894, they held not only the presidency but solid majorities in both houses of Congress—they were naturally blamed for it. And given the close connection that has repeatedly been demonstrated between economic conditions and the vote, it would have been very surprising if that party had not been severely punished at the polls. In the 1894 midterm elections, a year and a half before McKinley became his party's national standard bearer, the Democrats lost 116 seats in the US House, the largest congressional seat loss in American history.[6] From this perspective, McKinley's situation in 1896 was similar to that of Franklin Roosevelt in 1932. Once he won the nomination, McKinley was a prohibitive favorite to win the general election as long as he didn't self-destruct. This may be one reason McKinley chose to spend the entire fall campaign at his home in Canton, Ohio. It greatly minimized the chances that he would make a major mistake.

Yet Rove seems determined to suggest that economic conditions were, at most, a minor factor in 1896. In the final chapter of his book, he lists eight reasons why McKinley won, only one of which—"that he was seen as a candidate of change" (370), number six on the list—relates to the state of the economy. (For the full list, see table A.1.) Instead, Rove asserts on several occasions—though he definitely does not *prove*—that Bryan was able to distance himself from his party's record. In Rove's words, "By explicitly repudiating Cleveland's hard-money policies, Bryan separated Democrats from the depression and the unpopular Democrat in the White House on whose watch it happened, undermining Republican arguments that the country needed to change the party that controlled the presidency in order to restore prosperity" (285; a similar claim is made on 239 and 366). No doubt the Democrats hoped that would be the case. But as Adlai Stevenson in 1952 and John McCain in 2008 both learned, it is enormously difficult for a presidential nominee to separate himself from the previous record of his own party. In 1948, sixteen years after Herbert Hoover left office, Harry Truman was able to beat Thomas Dewey by claiming that electing a Republican would bring back the ravages of the Great Depression. Political elites of the time knew that Bryan was, to use Rove's phrase, a "different kind of Democrat" than Cleveland; modern-day historians are also aware of this. But in an era when party symbols loomed so large, education levels were so low, and mass communications so technologically primitive, many ordinary voters probably didn't appreciate or care about the difference.[7]

In a similar way, Rove credits McKinley with conducting "a campaign based on big issues, namely, sound money and protection" (365) but has nothing to say about whether McKinley's positions on these issues offered a sound basis for public policy. Today, the vast majority of conservative economists would argue that tariff barriers, particularly at the level that McKinley favored, would impose far higher costs than benefits on the nation that imposes them. (His decision to impose steel tariffs notwithstanding, George W. Bush usually claimed to support free trade, arguing that "eliminating barriers to trade created new export markets for American producers and more choices for our consumers.")[8] So is it enough to run on "big issues," regardless of whether they are valid issues? In this book, the clear implication, at least for advocates of free market economics, is that big is sufficient.

Rove is also silent about the important economic changes that took place *after* the 1896 election. Like many other realignment scholars, Rove focuses so much attention on one "critical" or "realigning" election as to leave the impression that the whole realignment process was finished by the day after the 1896 election. Again, modern scholarship suggests that such a scenario is unlikely. The depressions that began in 1893 and 1929 gave the party out of power a great opportunity to improve its competitive standing, but in order to become the new majority party, each needed to prove that it could manage the country's economic woes better than the incumbents. Had the 1893 depression persisted, or had the recovery been slow and uneven, voters might have given the Democrats another chance in 1900 or 1904 or perhaps entrusted the reins of government to a third party. In fact, the economy did start to recover soon after McKinley took office; by 1900, when McKinley ran for reelection, the unemployment rate had fallen to 5 percent and fell even further in subsequent years.[9] This was an important reason that "the election of 1896 still matters"—yet Rove has nothing to say about this either.

Though the state of the US economy in 1896 was almost the exact opposite of that which existed in 2000, Rove believes that there are many important parallels between the campaign that brought William McKinley to the White House and the first presidential foray of George W. Bush:

- George W. Bush, Rove says at a number of points in his memoirs, was "a different kind of Republican."[10] So, it turns out, was William McKinley (95, 228, 367).
- McKinley, as we have seen, based his campaign on big issues (365). This, Rove says, is also the first hallmark of a "Rovian campaign."[11] In Bush's case, those big ideas were "education reform, the faith-based initiative, a generous middle-class tax cut, and Social Security and Medicare reform."[12]

- Being a different kind of Republican meant, in McKinley's case, that he tried to "broaden and modernize" his party's appeal (367). (The evidence that McKinley was successful in this regard is more mixed than Rove acknowledges.)[13] Similarly, one of Bush's main selling points to other Republicans, according to Rove, was the claim that Bush could attract support from groups like "women, Hispanics, young people, and others who were not typical Republicans."[14]
- Another key to McKinley's victory, Rove maintains, was that "he ran as a unifier, adopting the language of national reconciliation" (371). That was also the way that Rove tried (mostly) to present George W. Bush in the 2000 campaign, though he was willing to resort to more divisive tactics when that seemed to work to his candidate's advantage. A reporter for the *Washington Post* provided this description of the Bush campaign in the final days before the general election:

> A Bush rally is reminiscent of an "Up With People" concert, with Bush ticking off his hard differences with Gore on taxation and the size of government, but dwelling on his desire to be "a uniter, not a divider," to "raise the spirits of this nation" and "make sure the American dream touches every willing heart." The theme of his campaign tour for the final week is "Bringing America Together."[15]

What really would have made this book worth reading is if Rove had spent some time exploring the central *difference* between McKinley and Bush. The former left his party far stronger than it had been before his election—indeed, the dominant American party for the next thirty-six years. The latter presided over a substantial decline in Republican fortunes. Perhaps that issue will provide the fodder for Rove's next book.

Notes

Chapter 1: Introduction

1. Among other things, Bush won the largest vote percentage ever received by a Republican gubernatorial candidate in Texas and was the first Texas governor to win two consecutive four-year terms.

2. My discussion of the relationship between Hanna and McKinley draws primarily on William T. Horner, *Ohio's Kingmaker: Mark Hanna, Man and Myth* (Athens: Ohio University Press, 2010); Lewis L. Gould, *The Presidency of William McKinley* (Lawrence: University Press of Kansas, 1980); Francis Russell, *The President Makers: From Mark Hanna to Joseph P. Kennedy* (Boston: Little, Brown, 1976), chap. 1; and Stanley L. Jones, *The Presidential Election of 1896* (Madison: University of Wisconsin Press, 1964), chaps. 8, 9, 12, and 20.

3. For a particularly good discussion of the way that Hanna and McKinley were portrayed in contemporary newspapers, especially those owned by William Randolph Hearst, see Horner, *Ohio's Kingmaker*, chap. 5.

4. Rove himself reaches the same conclusion in Karl Rove, *The Triumph of William McKinley: Why the Election of 1896 Still Matters* (New York: Simon & Schuster, 2015), 373–375.

5. On McKinley's decision—against Hanna's advice—not to undertake a national speaking tour of the sort that Bryan was conducting, see Jones, *Presidential Election of 1896*, 277; and Horner, *Ohio's Kingmaker*, 135–137.

6. Jones, *Presidential Election of 1896*, 160–161.

7. Jones, *Presidential Election of 1896*, 276.

8. On the political partnership between Roosevelt and Howe, see, among others, Russell, *President Makers*, chap. 7; Julie M. Fenster, *FDR's Shadow: Louis Howe, the Force That Shaped Franklin and Eleanor Roosevelt* (New York: Palgrave Macmillan, 2009), chaps. 7–14; and Kenneth S. Davis, *FDR: The New York Years, 1928–1933* (New York, Random House, 1985).

9. Horner, *Ohio's Kingmaker*, 138.

10. There is, at present, no published biography of Hamilton Jordan. Jordan himself wrote three memoirs, but all three are limited in scope. One tells the story of his upbringing; the second recounts Jimmy Carter's final year in office; the third describes Jordan's prolonged battle with cancer. See, respectively, Hamilton Jordan, *A Boy from Georgia: Coming of Age in the Segregated South* (Athens: University of Georgia Press, 2015); Jordan, *Crisis: The Last Year of the Carter Presidency* (New York: Putnam, 1982); and Jordan, *No Such Thing as a Bad Day* (Atlanta: Longstreet Press, 2000). The following account draws primarily on contemporary coverage of Jordan and the Carter presidency, especially Jules Witcover, *Marathon: The Pursuit of the Presidency, 1972–1976* (New York: Viking, 1977), chaps. 8, 10, and 15; Aaron Latham, "Hamilton Jordan: A Slob in the White House," *Esquire*, March 28, 1978, 77–85; Nicholas Lemann, "Jordan, Georgia, and the Establishment," *Washington*

Monthly, April 1978, 37–47; and Peter Goldman, "Jimmy Carter's Cabinet Purge" and Melinda Beck, "Deputy President," both in *Time*, July 30, 1979, 22–28, 34–35.

11. The original, untitled Jordan memo, dated November 4, 1972, can be viewed at http://presidentiallibraries.c-span.org/Content/Carter/CarterStrategy.pdf (accessed June 26, 2012).

12. For a more detailed account of the uncertain situation that confronted presidential candidates in 1976 and how the Carter strategy quickly became the "conventional wisdom" about the most effective way to run for a presidential nomination, see William G. Mayer, "Forecasting Presidential Nominations," in *In Pursuit of the White House: How We Choose Our Presidential Nominees*, ed. William G. Mayer (Chatham, NJ: Chatham House, 1996), especially 60–64.

13. On the evolution of the Carter nomination strategy, see Witcover, *Marathon*, chaps. 8, 10, and 15. Excerpts from Rafshoon's media strategy are quoted extensively in the original Jordan memo of November 4, 1972. Tim Kraft's memo on the Iowa campaign, dated August 28, 1975, may be found at http://presidentiallibraries .c-span.org/Content/Carter/CarterIowa.pdf (accessed June 26, 2012).

14. The quotations are from Harold Meyerson, "The Cult of Karl," *American Prospect*, December 30, 2002, 3; and Richard Wolffe and Holly Bailey, "Bush Pops the Bubble," *Newsweek*, May 1, 2006, 27.

15. Jones, *Presidential Election of 1896*, 167.

16. It is striking, for example, how little mention Hanna receives in Lewis Gould's book on the McKinley presidency—and most such references concern the 1896 and 1900 campaigns or the distribution of federal patronage. See Gould, *Presidency of William McKinley*. Herbert Croly, in an early biography of Hanna, takes a somewhat more favorable view of Hanna's time in the Senate, acknowledging that he wasn't much of a force in the Fifty-Fifth Congress (1897–1899) but arguing that he assumed a more prominent role in the Fifty-Sixth Congress (1899–1901). But the only major example of Hanna's congressional leadership that Croly provides is the claim that Hanna influenced the final shape of a bill authorizing the Navy to purchase armor plate. See Herbert Croly, *Marcus Alonzo Hanna: His Life and Work* (New York: Macmillan, 1912), chap. 19.

17. For contemporary coverage of Jordan's growing power within the Carter administration, see "Hannibal Astride the Potomac," *Time*, March 14, 1977, 14; Thomas M. DeFrank, "Ham Jordan's New Suit," *Newsweek*, August 22, 1977, 32; "Ham Jordan: Carter's Unorthodox 'Right Arm,'" *U.S. News & World Report*, February 27, 1978, 33; "Unsinkable Ham Jordan," *Time*, December 4, 1978, 37; and Goldman, "Jimmy Carter's Cabinet Purge."

18. Lemann, "Jordan, Georgia, and the Establishment," 45.

19. See, for example, Burton I. Kaufman, *The Presidency of James Earl Carter, Jr.* (Lawrence: University Press of Kansas, 1993), 46, 77, 80–81, 103, 111, and 191.

20. V. O. Key Jr., "A Theory of Critical Elections," *Journal of Politics* 17 (February 1955): 3–4.

21. This brief synthesis draws primarily on Everett Carll Ladd, *American Political Parties: Social Change and Political Response* (New York: Norton, 1970); Walter

Dean Burnham, *Critical Elections and the Mainsprings of American Politics* (New York: Norton, 1970); Everett Carll Ladd and Charles D. Hadley, *Transformations of the American Party System: Political Coalitions from the New Deal to the 1970s* (New York: Norton, 1975); Jerome M. Clubb, William H. Flanigan, and Nancy H. Zingale, *Partisan Realignment: Voters, Parties, and Government in America* (Beverly Hills: Sage, 1980); and James L. Sundquist, *Dynamics of the Party System: Alignment and Realignment of Political Parties in the United States*, rev. ed. (Washington, DC: Brookings Institution, 1983).

22. Republicans dominated elections between 1860 and 1872—primarily because the most anti-Republican region of the country, the South, had seceded and thus was not participating in presidential and congressional elections. Once the Civil War was over and Reconstruction had run its course, however, Republicans and Democrats competed on remarkably even terms.

23. No presidential candidate during this period won more than 51 percent of the total popular vote.

24. Kevin P. Phillips, *The Emerging Republican Majority* (New Rochelle, NY: Arlington House, 1969). To what extent Phillips was aware of or influenced by the academic realignment literature is unclear. He does refer to V. O. Key's writings at several points (see 195, 282, 335), but *not* to Key's article on critical elections. He also uses the word "realignment" at several points (e.g., 26 and 33) and subscribes to a periodization of American elections identical to that posited by most realignment scholars (see 37).

25. In terms of producing high-quality, capacious, interesting books about contemporary American voting and elections, these years are still, in my view, unrivaled. See especially Richard M. Scammon and Ben J. Wattenberg, *The Real Majority* (New York: Coward-McCann, 1970); Burnham, *Critical Elections*; James L. Sundquist, *Dynamics of the Party System: Alignment and Realignment of Political Parties in the United States* (Washington, DC: Brookings Institution, 1973); Ladd and Hadley, *Transformations of the American Party System*; and Norman H. Nie, Sidney Verba, and John R. Petrocik, *The Changing American Voter* (Cambridge, MA: Harvard University Press, 1976).

26. See David R. Mayhew, *Electoral Realignments: A Critique of an American Genre* (New Haven: Yale University Press, 2002). The quotations in the text are taken from p. 165.

27. In an article published in 1995, I defended the position that realignment was a valid and useful way of understanding American electoral history. See William G. Mayer, "Changes in Elections and the Party System: 1992 in Historical Perspective," in *The New American Politics: Reflections on Political Change and the Clinton Administration*, ed. Bryan D. Jones (Boulder, CO: Westview, 1995), 19–50. While I still hold to that view, I have recently become convinced that the realignment concept, whatever its historical utility, is not very helpful in understanding the changes in American politics that have occurred since 1990. It is worth adding that even if the realignment paradigm is abandoned, it is still possible for one party or the other to establish a period of sustained electoral dominance. No one would deny, for ex-

ample, that Franklin Roosevelt did precisely this in the 1930s, even if one chooses not to call it a realignment.

28. Gould, *Presidency of William McKinley*, 253. On Rove's independent reading course with Gould, see Karl Rove, *Courage and Consequence: My Life as a Conservative in the Fight* (New York: Simon & Schuster, 2010), 131–132.

29. As noted above, some analysts have argued that a Republican realignment occurred in 1968, but this point is by no means universally accepted. The Republicans did win five of the next six presidential elections, but they didn't make gains in party identification until 1984 and didn't win control of both houses of Congress until 1994. By contrast, virtually everyone who subscribes to the realignment synthesis accepts 1896 as a realigning election.

30. See Karl Rove, "What Makes a Great President," speech delivered at the University of Utah, November 13, 2002, available at http://hnn.us/articles/1529.html (accessed June 15, 2012).

31. Nicholas Lemann, "The Redemption," *New Yorker*, January 31, 2000, 62.

32. Joshua Green, "The Rove Presidency," *Atlantic*, September 2007.

33. Richard N. Current, *The Lincoln Nobody Knows* (New York: Hill and Wang, 1958), 187 (emphasis in original).

34. Abraham Lincoln, "Speech in the Illinois Legislature, January 11, 1837," in *The Collected Works of Abraham Lincoln*, ed. Roy P. Basler (New Brunswick, NJ: Rutgers University Press, 1953), 1:65–66.

35. Allegedly. In fact, as Brendan Doherty has recently shown, even after they had been reelected and were constitutionally prohibited from running for a third term, presidents such as Ronald Reagan, Bill Clinton, and George W. Bush did a great deal of campaigning, especially fundraising, for other party candidates and for the national and state party organizations. See Doherty, *The Rise of the President's Permanent Campaign* (Lawrence: University Press of Kansas, 2012), chaps. 2 and 3.

36. This is the first definition listed in *Merriam-Webster's Collegiate Dictionary*, 11th ed. (Springfield, MA: Merriam-Webster's, 2009), 960.

37. As quoted in Mortimer J. Adler, *The Common Sense of Politics* (New York: Holt, Rinehart and Winston, 1971), 7.

38. The tension between power and liberty is the major theme in the republican ideology, as developed in Bernard Bailyn, *The Ideological Origins of the American Revolution* (Cambridge: Harvard University Press, 1967), especially chap. 3.

39. John Trenchard and Thomas Gordon, *Cato's Letters: Or, Essays on Liberty, Civil and Religious, And other Important Subjects*, ed. Ronald Hamowy (Indianapolis: Liberty Fund, 1995 [1755]), 2:678 and 804.

40. So far as I know, the only public mention of this committee's existence is in Mark Halperin and John F. Harris, *The Way to Win: Taking the White House in 2008* (New York: Random House, 2006), 264–265. I am not inclined to think that it deserved more coverage.

Chapter 2: The Rove Record

1. The following discussion draws on William G. Mayer, "The Presidential Nominations," in *The Election of 2000: Reports and Interpretations*, ed. Gerald M. Pomper (New York: Chatham House, 2001), 12–45.

2. John Pitney, as quoted in James Carney, "The Money Chasm," *Time*, July 12, 1999, 28.

3. See especially William G. Mayer, "Forecasting Presidential Nominations," in *In Pursuit of the White House: How We Choose Our Presidential Nominees*, ed. William G. Mayer (Chatham, NJ: Chatham House, 1996), 44–71; Randall E. Adkins and Andrew J. Dowdle, "Break Out the Mint Juleps? Is New Hampshire the 'Primary' Culprit Limiting Presidential Nomination Forecasts?" *American Politics Quarterly* 28 (April 2000): 251–269; Wayne P. Steger, "Do Primary Voters Draw from a Stacked Deck? Presidential Nominations in an Era of Candidate-Centered Campaigns," *Presidential Studies Quarterly* 30 (December 2000): 727–753; and William G. Mayer, "The Basic Dynamics of the Contemporary Nomination Process: An Expanded View," in *The Making of the Presidential Candidates 2004*, ed. William G. Mayer (Lanham, MD: Rowman & Littlefield, 2004), 83–132.

4. I do not include the 2004–2016 nomination races in this part of table 2.2 because those contests were conducted under different campaign finance rules. From 1980–2000, federal law set the individual contribution limit at $1,000. In 2002, however, the Bipartisan Campaign Reform Act doubled the individual contribution limit to $2,000 and then indexed it to inflation. Yet, even though the 2000 Bush campaign operated under more restrictive rules, it still raised more money in 1999 than did John Kerry in 2003, John McCain in 2007, or Mitt Romney in 2011, and came reasonably close to the inflation-adjusted totals achieved by Hillary Clinton and Barack Obama in 2007.

5. See William G. Mayer, "Turning a Candidate into a Lightweight," *New York Times*, February 4, 2000.

6. Dan Balz, "Awash in Money, Bush Needs Message," *Washington Post*, February 3, 2000. In the interests of full disclosure, I should point out that I was one of the persons Balz quoted in this article.

7. Both polls are cited in *Time*, February 14, 2000, 36.

8. These headlines appeared in, respectively, *Washington Post*, February 6, 2000; *New York Times*, February 10, 2000; *Washington Post*, February 11, 2000; *New York Times*, February 11, 2000; and *New York Times*, February 18, 2000.

9. Dick Harpootlian, as quoted in Peter Marks, "Bush and McCain in Ad War, to the Delight of Democrats," *New York Times*, February 12, 2000.

10. Peter Marks, "Harsh, Incessant Wave Crosses South Carolina," *New York Times,* February 18, 2000.

11. See especially Morris Fiorina, Samuel Abrams, and Jeremy Pope, "The 2000 U.S. Presidential Election: Can Retrospective Voting Be Saved?" *British Journal of Political Science* 33 (April 2003): 163–187; James E. Campbell, "The Referendum That Didn't Happen: The Forecasts of the 2000 Presidential Election," *PS: Political Science and Politics* 34 (March 2001): 33–38; Alan Abramowitz, "The Time for

Change Model and the 2000 Election," *American Politics Research* 29 (May 2001): 279–282; Michael S. Lewis-Beck and Charles Tien, "Modeling the Future: Lessons from the Gore Forecast," *PS: Political Science and Politics* 34 (March 2001): 21–23; Christopher Wlezien, "On Forecasting the Presidential Vote," *PS: Political Science and Politics* 34 (March 2001): 25–31; Thomas M. Holbrook, "Forecasting with Mixed Economic Signals: A Cautionary Tale," *PS: Political Science and Politics* 34 (March 2001): 39–44; and Brad Lockerbie, "Forecast 2000: An Afterthought," *American Politics Research* 29 (May 2001): 307–312.

12. For a particularly rich development of this argument, see James E. Campbell, *The American Campaign: U.S. Presidential Campaigns and the National Vote*, 2nd ed. (College Station: Texas A&M University Press, 2008).

13. For examples of Rove drawing attention to the fact that the 2000 Bush campaign performed considerably better than the academic forecasting models had predicted it would, see Nicholas Lemann, "The Controller," *New Yorker*, May 12, 2003; and Karl Rove, *Courage and Consequence: My Life as a Conservative in the Fight* (New York: Simon & Schuster, 2010), 178–179.

14. See Alison Mitchell, "A Confident Bush Says He Can Win California's Vote," *New York Times*, October 31, 2000; Peter Marks, "Bush Has Advertised More in California than in Swing States," *New York Times*, October 31, 2000; and Alison Mitchell, "Bush Returns Fire over Plan for Social Security Overhaul," *New York Times*, November 1, 2000.

15. Prior to the 2000 election, West Virginia had gone Democratic in five of the previous six presidential elections. It had even been carried by Jimmy Carter in 1980 and Michael Dukakis in 1988.

16. On the many significant problems with the Romney campaign, see William G. Mayer, "How the Romney Campaign Blew It," *Forum* 10 (December 2012).

17. All presidential approval rating numbers cited in this chapter are taken from the Gallup Poll. I rely on Gallup data for a number of reasons. In particular, since Gallup was for many decades the only survey organization that asked the presidential approval question, this makes the Bush presidency figures as nearly comparable as possible with the data from earlier presidencies.

18. Nelson W. Polsby, *Congress and the Presidency* (Englewood Cliffs, NJ: Prentice-Hall, 1964), 25.

19. See Marc J. Hetherington and Michael Nelson, "Anatomy of a Rally Effect: George W. Bush and the War on Terrorism," *PS: Political Science and Politics* 36 (January 2003): 37.

20. A good example of Bush's rhetoric on this topic, from which this quotation is taken, is George W. Bush, "Address before a Joint Session of the Congress on the United States Response to the Terrorist Attacks of September 11," September 20, 2001, *Public Papers of the President of the United States: George W. Bush* (hereafter cited as *Bush Public Papers*) (Washington, DC: US Government Printing Office, various years), 2001, 2:1141.

21. During the 2004 presidential campaign, John Kerry, one of the great Monday

morning quarterbacks in all of American politics, criticized Bush for "outsourcing" the final attack on Tora Bora—i.e., for letting it be fought largely by Afghani soldiers and warlords—and thus allowing Osama bin Laden to escape. But at the time that attack was conducted, Kerry, like virtually everyone else, had nothing but praise for Bush's leadership.

22. Larry J. Sabato, "The George W. Bush Midterm: From Popular-Vote Loser to Political Colossus in Two Not-So-Easy Steps," in *Midterm Madness: The Elections of 2002*, ed. Larry J. Sabato (Lanham, MD: Rowman & Littlefield, 2003), 9–10.

23. As quoted in Luke J. Keele, Brian J. Fogarty, and James A. Stimson, "Presidential Campaigning in the 2002 Congressional Elections," *PS: Political Science and Politics* 37 (October 2004): 827.

24. See, in particular, Paul S. Herrnson and Irwin L. Morris, "Presidential Campaigning in the 2002 Congressional Elections," *Legislative Studies Quarterly* 32 (November 2007): 629–648, though this study deals only with House elections. Patrick J. Sellers and Laura M. Denton show that Bush's visits provided favored Senate candidates with a significant increase in media coverage relative to their Democratic opponents, though they do not attempt to assess the electoral impact of that coverage. See Sellers and Denton, "Presidential Visits and Midterm Senate Elections," *Presidential Studies Quarterly* 36 (September 2006): 410–432.

In contrast, Keele, Fogarty, and Stimson claim that while most of the House and Senate candidates Bush campaigned for were successful, this was because Bush only campaigned for candidates who were likely to win. See "Presidential Campaigning." As Herrnson and Morris argue, however, this argument rests on an implausible assumption about the motivations for presidential campaigning. It also, in my opinion, assumes a remarkable level of presidential foreknowledge, such that Rove and the president knew in advance which House and Senate candidates were going to win, even though all the polling and commentary at the time showed these elections to be highly competitive and their outcomes to be uncertain.

For evidence that presidential campaigning had an effect on the vote in midterm Senate elections between 1966 and 1986, see Jeffrey E. Cohen, Michael A. Krassa, and John A. Hamman, "The Impact of Presidential Campaigning on Midterm U.S. Senate Elections," *American Political Science Review* 85 (March 1991): 165–178.

25. The quotations are taken from George W. Bush, "Remarks in a Victory Celebration," November 3, 2004, *Bush Public Papers*, 2004, 3:2936; and "The President's News Conference," November 4, 2004, *Bush Public Papers*, 2004, 3:2943.

26. As quoted in Joshua Green, "The Rove Presidency," *Atlantic,* September 2007 (emphasis in original).

27. I do not include the presidential elections of 2008, 2012, and 2016 in table 2.4 because they were not available for comparison when Rove delivered his postelection analysis. But adding those three elections to the table would not change the general picture. In both 2008 and 2012, Obama ran significantly better than Bush in 2004, no matter how one crunches the numbers. Trump exceeded Bush's electoral college showing, though not his share of the popular vote, total or two-party.

28. All figures in this paragraph are taken from the Illinois State Board of Elections, at www.elections.il.gov/electioninformation/getvotetotals.aspx (accessed July 19, 2012).

29. See Louis H. Bean, *Ballot Behavior: A Study of Presidential Elections* (Washington, DC: American Council on Public Affairs, 1940), chaps. 3 and 4.

30. See Fred Barnes, "The (Finally) Emerging Republican Majority," *Weekly Standard*, October 23, 2003.

31. Fred Barnes, "Realignment, Now More than Ever," *Weekly Standard*, November 22, 2004, 11.

32. Barnes, "Realignment," 11.

33. Dan Balz and Mike Allen, "Four More Years Attributed to Rove's Strategy," *Washington Post*, November 7, 2004.

34. The quotation is from Rove, *Courage and Consequence*, 466. The statistical basis for this pronouncement is discussed in an endnote on p. 560.

35. The literature on these points is voluminous. Among the most influential pieces are David R. Mayhew, "Congressional Elections: The Case of the Vanishing Marginals," *Polity* 6 (Spring 1974): 295–317; Robert S. Erikson, "Malapportionment, Gerrymandering, and Party Fortunes," *American Political Science Review* 66 (December 1972): 1234–1245; and Andrew Gelman and Gary King, "Estimating Incumbency Advantage without Bias," *American Journal of Political Science* 34 (November 1990): 1142–1164.

36. See James E. Campbell, "The Stagnation of Congressional Elections," in *Life after Reform: When the Bipartisan Campaign Reform Act Meets Politics*, ed. Michael J. Malbin (Lanham, MD: Rowman & Littlefield, 2003), 141–158.

37. As table 2.5 indicates, the Democrats actually gained thirty-one seats in 2006, taking thirty from the Republicans and winning the Vermont at-large seat when the incumbent, independent Bernie Sanders, ran for the Senate.

38. Rove, *Courage and Consequence*, 465.

39. The figures given here are based on my own analysis of the complete 2006 House election results, as reported in *Guide to U.S. Elections*, 6th ed. (Washington, DC: CQ Press, 2010), 2:1378–1382.

40. See David J. Hendry, Robert A. Jackson, and Jeffrey J. Mondak, "Abramoff, Email, and the Mistreated Mistress: Scandal and Character in the 2006 Elections," in *Fault Lines: Why the Republicans Lost Congress*, ed. Jeffrey J. Mondak and Dona-Gene Mitchell (New York: Routledge, 2009), 84–100. The quotation in the text is taken from p. 94.

41. See Susan Welch and John R. Hibbing, "The Effects of Charges of Corruption on Voting Behavior in Congressional Elections, 1982–1990," *Journal of Politics* 59 (February 1997): 226–239. Though the authors refer throughout their article to the effects of "corruption," their definition of this term includes "instances of alleged scandals involving morals or crimes not linked to office" (229). For a similar study of an earlier period, see John G. Peters and Susan Welch, "The Effects of Charges of Corruption on Voting Behavior in Congressional Elections," *American Political Science Review* 74 (September 1980): 697–708.

42. This is my own calculation, based on the raw vote totals reported at www
.fec.gov.

43. See the data in Gary C. Jacobson, *The Politics of Congressional Elections*, 7th
ed. (New York: Pearson Longman, 2009), 205–206.

44. For a similar conclusion based on different models and datasets, see Gary
C. Jacobson, "The President, the War, and Voting Behavior in the 2006 House Elections," in Mondak and Mitchell, *Fault Lines*, 128–147.

45. As quoted in Peter Baker, "Rove Remains Steadfast in the Face of Criticism,"
Washington Post, November 12, 2006.

46. The quotations are taken from, respectively, Harold Meyerson, "A Real
Realignment," *Washington Post*, November 7, 2008; John B. Judis, "America the
Liberal," *New Republic*, November 19, 2008, 20; and Hendrik Hertzberg, "Obama
Wins,"*New Yorker*,November 17, 2008.For other post-2008 discussions of realignment,
see Stuart Rothenberg, "Is 2008 a Realigning Election? Numbers Offer Some
Clues," *Roll Call*, November 7, 2008, at www.rollcall.com/2008/11/07/is-2008-a
-realigning-election-numbers-offer-some-clues/; and Barry Gewen, "Has There
Been a Political Realignment?" January 14, 2009, at http://artsbeat.blogs.nytimes
.com/2009/01/14/has-there-been-a-political-realignment/.

47. All of the data cited in this paragraph, like the data in figure 2.1 and table 2.7,
are taken from the Gallup Poll, thus facilitating comparisons across presidencies. For
the full listing of Bush approval ratings, see https://news.gallup.com/poll/116500
/presidential-approval-george-bush.aspx (accessed February 28, 2020).

48. However, Bush's approval numbers, which bottomed out at 25 percent, never
got quite as low as those registered by Nixon (24 percent) or Truman (22 percent).
In the early 1950s and mid-1970s, about 10 to 15 percent of the public generally replied "don't know" to the presidential approval question. By Bush's final years in
office, "don't know" answers usually varied between 3 and 7 percent.

49. Another vehicle for assessing public attitudes toward an ex-president is to
ask survey respondents if they have a "favorable or unfavorable" opinion of him. I
do not use such questions here because it is unclear to what extent they measure
opinions about a former president's performance in the White House as opposed
to opinions about him as a person and/or his conduct since leaving the presidency.
Also, such questions are asked only about living ex-presidents, which we means we
would not be able to compare Bush to Nixon, Ford, or Reagan.

For what it's worth, however, such questions indicate that about 45 to 55 percent
of the American public now views George W. Bush favorably, up from about 35 to
40 percent in the year after he left office.

50. The next several pages draw heavily on Mayer, "How the Romney Campaign."

51. See, respectively, Douglas A. Hibbs, "Obama's Reelection Prospects under
'Bread and Peace' Voting in the 2012 US Presidential Election," *PS: Political Science
and Politics* 45 (October 2012): 635–639; and James E. Campbell, "A First Party-Term
Incumbent Survives: The Fundamentals of 2012," in *Barack Obama and the New
America: The 2012 Election and the Changing Face of Politics*, ed. Larry J. Sabato (Lan-
ham, MD: Rowman & Littlefield, 2013), 59–73.

52. For a fuller examination of the survey record, see Mayer, "How the Romney Campaign," 4–5.

53. Much of the analysis in this section draws on William G. Mayer, "The Nominations: The Road to a Much-Disliked General Election," in *The Elections of 2016*, ed. Michael Nelson (Thousand Oaks, CA: CQ Press, 2018), 29–62.

54. For a more detailed analysis of the factors that propelled Trump to the 2016 Republican nomination, see Mayer, "The Nominations," 29–62.

55. For evidence that the support of party leaders had made a difference in past nomination races, see Marty Cohen, David Karol, Hans Noel, and John Zaller, *The Party Decides: Presidential Nominations before and after Reform* (Chicago: University of Chicago Press, 2008).

56. On the Republican governors' desire to nominate one of their own as the party's 2000 presidential candidate, see Sam Howe Verhovek, "Republican Governors, Wanting One of Their Own, Decided Early on Bush," *New York Times*, November 23, 1999.

57. As quoted in Lou Cannon and Carl M. Cannon, *Reagan's Disciple: George W. Bush's Troubled Quest for a Presidential Legacy* (New York: PublicAffairs, 2008), 321.

58. On Obama's performance as party leader, see William G. Mayer, "With Enemies Like This, Who Needs Friends? How Barack Obama Revived the Republican Party," in *Debating the Obama Presidency*, ed. Steven E. Schier (Lanham, Md.: Rowman & Littlefield, 2016), 103–122.

Chapter 3: Presidents Need Political Help

1. "George W. Bush's Nomination Acceptance Speech," in *American Presidential Campaigns and Elections*, ed. William G. Shade and Ballard C. Campbell (Armonk, NY: M. E. Sharpe, 2003), 3:1050.

2. The full episode is recounted in Dick Morris, *Behind the Oval Office: Getting Reelected against All Odds* (Los Angeles: Renaissance Books, 1999), chap. 12.

3. As quoted in Kathryn Dunn Tenpas, "Words vs. Deeds: President George W. Bush and Polling," *Brookings Review* 21 (Summer 2003): 32–35.

4. Tenpas, "Words vs. Deeds." The quotation at the end of the paragraph appears on p. 35.

5. Some might argue that George Washington is an exception to this statement, but I disagree. Throughout his two terms as president, Washington demonstrated a remarkably sure grasp of the peculiar situation he was in, the limits and opportunities imposed by public opinion, and the consequent need to be constantly aware of the way he presented himself in public. Washington may not have been a partisan, but he was a very deft politician.

6. For a discussion of the various ways that recent presidents have organized their political advisors, see especially Kathryn Dunn Tenpas, "The American Presidency: Surviving and Thriving amidst the Permanent Campaign," in *The Permanent Campaign and Its Future*, ed. Norman Ornstein and Thomas Mann (Washington, DC: American Enterprise Institute and The Brookings Institution, 2000), 108–133;

and Tenpas, "Institutionalized Politics: The White House Office of Political Affairs," *Presidential Studies Quarterly* 26 (Spring 1996): 511–522.

7. For a good discussion of this point, see Paul C. Light, *The President's Agenda: Domestic Policy Choice from Kennedy to Clinton*, 3rd ed. (Baltimore: Johns Hopkins University Press, 1999), 52–59. Another restriction on agenda size that Light does not mention is the news media. Given limits on the total newshole and the number of stories that can fit on the front page of a major newspaper or serve as the lead story on a television broadcast, extensive coverage devoted to one topic means that other issues get crowded out of the public debate.

8. As quoted in David S. Cloud, "U.S. Sees Emirates as Both Ally and, since 9/11, a Foe," *New York Times*, February 23, 2006.

9. See Clark Kent Ervin, "Strangers at the Door," *New York Times*, February 23, 2006.

10. Elisabeth Bumiller and Carl Hulse, "Panel Saw No Security Issue in Port Contract, Officials Say," *New York Times*, February 23, 2006.

11. David E. Sanger and Eric Lipton, "Bush Would Veto Any Bill Halting Dubai Port Deal," *New York Times*, February 22, 2006.

12. See Sanger and Lipton, "Bush Would Veto"; and David S. Cloud and David E. Sanger, "Dubai Company Delays New Role at Six U.S. Ports," *New York Times*, February 24, 2006.

13. Sanger and Lipton, "Bush Would Veto."

14. Shortly after the controversy broke, *National Review* published an article in which they asked five "national security experts," all of whom could be described as ideologically right of center, to assess the issue. Two were opposed to the deal, one was supportive, one offered mixed feelings, and one merely depicted the deal as a payback for recent efforts by Dubai to assist the American war on terror, without indicating whether that was a good or a bad thing. See "Port Insecurity?" February 21, 2006, nationalreview.com/2006/02/port-insecurity-interview.

15. See Cloud and Sanger, "Dubai Company Delays"; David E. Sanger, "Dubai Expected to Ask for Review of Port Deal," *New York Times*, February 26, 2006; Carl Hulse, "In Break with White House, House Panel Rejects Port Deal," *New York Times*, March 9, 2006; and Sanger, "Under Pressure, Dubai Company Drops Port Deal," *New York Times*, March 10, 2006. As promised, in December 2006, DP World sold its American operations to AIG. See Heather Timmons, "Dubai Ports Company Sells Its U.S. Holdings to A.I.G.," *New York Times*, December 12, 2006.

16. Rich Masters, as quoted in Anne E. Kornblut, "Scramble to Back Port Deal: Making of Political Disaster," *New York Times*, February 25, 2006.

17. See the comment by White House press secretary Scott McClellan in Bumiller and Hulse, "Panel Saw No Security Issue."

18. For criticism of Kimmitt's role in the Bush vice-presidential search, see Peter Goldman and Tom Mathews, *The Quest for the Presidency, 1988* (New York: Simon & Schuster, 1989), 316–317; and the comments by Edward Rollins in *Campaign for President: The Managers Look at '88*, ed. David R. Runkel (Dover, MA: Auburn

House, 1989), 211–212. The most telling indicator of how inadequate the vetting process was from a political standpoint came just one day after Quayle's selection was announced, when a major controversy developed over his service in the National Guard. Remarkably, the Bush campaign had almost no solid information on the issue. Instead, shortly after midnight on the same day that Bush was to deliver his acceptance speech, the Bush campaign high command had to send two people over to Quayle's hotel room to grill the Indiana senator about what exactly he and his family had done to get him into the National Guard. See Goldman and Mathews, *Quest for the Presidency*, 325–327; and Jack W. Germond and Jules Witcover, *Whose Broad Stripes and Bright Stars: The Trivial Pursuit of the Presidency 1988* (New York: Warner Books, 1989), 390–391.

19. Of all the accounts of the DP World episode I have examined, only one claims that Rove made any attempt to warn the president about the hornet's nest he was stirring up. See Robert Draper, *Dead Certain: The Presidency of George W. Bush* (New York: Free Press, 2007), 363. Unfortunately, Draper does not indicate the source of this information or whether it was provided while the controversy was still ongoing or only well after the events in question.

20. Perhaps Bush's advisors did issue such a warning and the president simply ignored it. Neither Bush nor Rove mentions the incident in his memoirs.

21. See Elisabeth Bumiller and Marjorie Connelly, "Ports Argument and Iraq Hurt Bush in a New Survey," *New York Times*, February 28, 2006.

22. See the transcript of Bork's interview with Tucker Carlson, "Bork Calls Miers Nomination a 'Disaster,'" October 14, 2005, at http://msnbc.msn.com/id/9623345.

23. George W. Bush, *Decision Points* (New York: Crown, 2010), 100.

24. Karl Rove, *Courage and Consequence: My Life as a Conservative in the Fight* (New York: Simon & Schuster, 2010), 422.

25. In one well-known incident, John Warner, then running for a United States Senate seat in Virginia, was asked about his position on a proposal to grant full congressional representation to the District of Columbia. Turning to his pollster Arthur Finkelstein, Warner responded, "Art, where do we stand?" See Larry J. Sabato, *The Rise of Political Consultants: New Ways of Winning Elections* (New York: Basic Books, 1981), 82.

26. As Morris put it, "We used polling not to determine what positions he [Clinton] would take but to figure out which of the positions he had already taken were the most popular." See Morris, *Behind the Oval Office*, 9.

27. Samuel Kernell, *Going Public: New Strategies of Presidential Leadership* (Washington, DC: CQ Press, 1986). As another indication of its influence and popularity, this book has now gone through four editions.

28. See George C. Edwards, *On Deaf Ears: The Limits of the Bully Pulpit* (New Haven: Yale University Press, 2003).

29. Marc A. Bodnick, "'Going Public' Reconsidered: Reagan's 1981 Tax and Budget Cuts, and Revisionist Theories of Presidential Power," *Congress & the Presidency* 17 (Spring 1990): 13–28.

30. See Benjamin I. Page and Robert Y. Shapiro, "Presidents as Opinion Leaders:

Some New Evidence," *Policy Studies Journal* 12 (June 1984): 649–661; and Benjamin I. Page, Robert Y. Shapiro, and Glenn R. Dempsey, "What Moves Public Opinion?" *American Political Science Review* 81 (March 1987): 32–34.

31. The only recent president who does not seem to have been totally invested in this strategy was George H. W. Bush, who retracted his famous "no new taxes" promise without a word of explanation or justification and then put the final budget package together almost entirely through private negotiations with congressional leaders. But even Bush went public when it concerned an issue he cared about, such as the Gulf War (he gave five nationally televised speeches between September 1990 and early March 1991).

32. George C. Edwards III, *Governing by Campaigning: The Politics of the Bush Presidency* (New York: Pearson Longman, 2007), 29–30.

33. See Mike Allen, "Semantics Shape Social Security Debate," *Washington Post*, January 23, 2005; and Robin Toner, "It's 'Private' vs. 'Personal' in Debate over Bush Plan," *New York Times*, March 22, 2005.

34. The sorts of things I have in mind are amply described in any good introductory text on polling. See, for example, Herbert Asher, *Polling and the Public: What Every Citizen Should Know*, 6th ed. (Washington, DC: CQ Press, 2004).

35. On the unreliability of constituent mail as a measure of public attitudes, see Lewis Anthony Dexter, "What Do Congressmen Hear: The Mail," *Public Opinion Quarterly* 20 (Spring 1956): 16–27; John W. Kingdon, *Congressmen's Voting Decisions* (New York: Harper & Row, 1973), 56–58; Leroy N. Rieselbach, *Congressional Politics* (New York: McGraw-Hill, 1973), 216; and John S. Stolarek, Robert M. Rood, and Marcia Whicker Taylor, "Measuring Constituency Opinion in the U.S. House: Mail Versus Random Surveys," *Legislative Studies Quarterly* 6 (November 1981): 589–595.

36. See the examples cited in James Bovard, *The Bush Betrayal* (New York: Palgrave Macmillan, 2004), chap. 3.

37. According to the Roper Center, where all the old Gallup surveys are archived, the presidential approval question was asked twenty-seven times between 1945 and 1948, and forty-seven times between 1949 and 1952. For a history of the question's development and its use in subsequent presidencies, see George C. Edwards III and Alec M. Gallup, *Presidential Approval: A Sourcebook* (Baltimore: The Johns Hopkins University Press, 1990), 1–3, 185–186.

38. Both figures are based on the comprehensive collection of approval ratings maintained by the Roper Center. See "Job Performance Ratings for President Bush," Roper Center, University of Connecticut, http://webapps.ropercenter.uconn.edu /CFIDE/roper/presidential/webroot/presidential_rating_detail.cfm?allRate=Tru e&presidentName=Bush (accessed August 4, 2011).

39. The three are realclearpolitics.com, pollster.com, and pollingreport.com.

40. The first published article to make this point was Lee Sigelman, "Presidential Popularity and Presidential Elections," *Public Opinion Quarterly* 43 (Winter 1979): 532–534. For updates and extensions of the analysis, see, among others, Alan I. Abramowitz, "An Improved Model for Predicting Presidential Election Outcomes,"

PS: Political Science and Politics 21 (Fall 1988): 843–847; and Michael S. Lewis-Beck and Tom W. Rice, *Forecasting Elections* (Washington, DC: CQ Press, 1992), chap. 2.

41. Again, this conclusion has been documented in a slew of academic studies. See, among others, Edward R. Tufte, "Determinants of the Outcomes of Midterm Congressional Elections," *American Political Science Review* 69 (September 1975): 812–826; Samuel Kernell, "Presidential Popularity and Negative Voting: An Alternative Explanation of the Midterm Congressional Decline of the President's Party," *American Political Science Review* 71 (March 1977): 44–66; Alan I. Abramowitz, "Economic Conditions, Presidential Popularity, and Voting Behavior in Midterm Congressional Elections," *Journal of Politics* 47 (February 1985): 31–43; and Gary C. Jacobson, *The Politics of Congressional Elections*, 7th ed. (New York: Pearson Longman, 2009), 159–161.

42. That is to say, the correlation between presidential approval in June of the election year and the incumbent's share of the two-party popular vote for president is .84. But the correlation between June approval ratings and the number of House seats lost by the president's party is .67, and the correlation between June approval ratings and the number of Senate seats lost is .34.

43. Both quotations are taken from George C. Edwards III, "Presidential Approval as a Source of Influence in Congress," in *The Oxford Handbook of the American Presidency*, ed. George C. Edwards III and William G. Howell (New York: Oxford University Press, 2009), 339, 341.

44. See, respectively, George C. Edwards III, *At the Margins: Presidential Leadership of Congress* (New Haven: Yale University Press, 1989), chap. 6; Edwards, "Aligning Tests with Theory: Presidential Approval as a Source of Influence in Congress," *Congress & the Presidency* 24 (Autumn 1997): 113–130; Douglas Rivers and Nancy L. Rose, "Passing the President's Program: Public Opinion and Presidential Influence in Congress," *American Journal of Political Science* 29 (May 1985): 183–196; Charles W. Ostrom Jr. and Dennis M. Simon, "Promise and Performance: A Dynamic Model of Presidential Popularity," *American Political Science Review* 79 (June 1985): 334–358; ; Paul Brace and Barbara Hinckley, *Follow the Leader: Opinion Polls and the Modern Presidents* (New York: BasicBooks, 1992), chap. 4; and Brandice Canes-Wrone and Scott de Marchi, "Presidential Approval and Legislative Success," *Journal of Politics* 64 (May 2002): 491–509.

45. See Jon R. Bond and Richard Fleisher, *The President in the Legislative Arena* (Chicago: University of Chicago Press, 1990), chap. 7; Mark A. Peterson, *Legislating Together: The White House and Capitol Hill from Eisenhower to Reagan* (Cambridge: Harvard University Press, 1990), esp. chap. 6; Calvin Mouw and Michael MacKuen, "The Strategic Configuration, Personal Influence, and Presidential Power in Congress," *Western Political Quarterly* 45 (September 1992): 579–608; Kenneth Collier and Terry Sullivan, "New Evidence Undercutting the Linkage of Approval with Presidential Support and Influence," *Journal of Politics* 57 (February 1995): 197–209; Jeffrey E. Cohen, Jon R. Bond, Richard Fleisher, and John A. Hamman, "State-Level Presidential Approval and Senatorial Support," *Legislative Studies Quarterly* 25 (November 2000): 577–590; and Jon R. Bond, Richard Fleisher, and B.

Dan Wood, "The Marginal and Time-Varying Effect of Public Approval on Presidential Success in Congress," *Journal of Politics* 65 (February 2003): 92–110.

46. Jon R. Bond and Richard Fleisher, "Presidential Popularity and Congressional Voting: A Reexamination of Public Opinion as a Source of Influence in Congress," *Western Political Quarterly* 37 (June 1984), 303.

47. See Edwards, "Aligning Tests with Theory," 125.

48. See Nelson W. Polsby, *Consequences of Party Reform* (New York: Oxford University Press, 1983), 105–128.

49. Edwards, *Governing by Campaigning*, 234.

50. On the ways that presidents relate to and attempt to use interest groups, see Nelson W. Polsby, "Interest Groups and the Presidency: Trends in Political Intermediation in America," in *American Politics and Public Policy*, ed. Walter Dean Burnham and Martha Wagner Weinberg (Cambridge: MIT Press, 1978), 41–52; Martha Joynt Kumar and Michael Baruch Grossman, "Political Communications from the White House: The Interest Group Connection," *Presidential Studies Quarterly* 16 (Winter 1986): 92–101; Mark A. Peterson, "The Presidency and Organized Interests: White House Patterns of Interest Group Liaison," *American Political Science Review* 86 (September 1992): 612–625; Mark A. Peterson, "Interest Mobilization and the Presidency," and Joan Lucco, "Representing the Public Interest: Consumer Groups and the Presidency," both in *The Politics of Interests: Interest Groups Transformed*, ed. Mark P. Petracca (Boulder, CO: Westview, 1992), 221–241 and 242–262; Joseph A. Pika, "Reaching Out to Organized Interests: Public Liaison in the Modern White House," in *The Presidency Reconsidered*, ed. Richard A. Waterman (Itasca, IL: F. E. Peacock, 1993), 145–168; and Burdett A. Loomis, "Connecting Interest Groups to the Presidency," in Edwards and Howell, *Oxford Handbook of the American Presidency*, 403–424.

51. John Hart, *The Presidential Branch: From Washington to Clinton*, 2nd ed. (Chatham, NJ: Chatham House, 1995), 127.

52. The most complete discussion of the ubiquitous nature of American elections and the effect it has on American government is Anthony King, *Running Scared: Why America's Politicians Campaign Too Much and Govern Too Little* (New York: Martin Kessler Books, 1997). But the general point has long been noted, especially by British observers of American politics. See, for example, Harold J. Laski, *The American Presidency, An Interpretation* (New York: Harper & Brothers, 1940), 64–65.

53. On the increasing length of contemporary presidential campaigns, see Michael G. Hagen and William G. Mayer, "The Modern Politics of Presidential Selection: How Changing the Rules Really Did Change the Game," in *In Pursuit of the White House 2000: How We Choose Our Presidential Nominees*, ed. William G. Mayer (New York: Chatham House, 2000), 1–55. For a discussion of what actually takes place in the third year, see Emmett H. Buell Jr., "The Invisible Primary," in Mayer, *In Pursuit of the White House*, 1–43.

54. See Kathryn Dunn Tenpas, *Presidents as Candidates: Inside the White House for the Presidential Campaign* (New York: Garland, 1997). Tenpas's analysis is updated in Tenpas, "How Incumbent Presidents Run for Reelection," in *The Making of*

the Presidential Candidates 2004, ed. William G. Mayer (Lanham, MD: Rowman & Littlefield, 2004), 133–159.

55. On the historical changes in the organization and management of an incumbent president's reelection campaign, see Tenpas, *Presidents as Candidates*, chap. 1; and Kathryn Dunn Tenpas and Matthew J. Dickinson, "Governing, Campaigning, and Organizing the Presidency: An Electoral Connection?" *Political Science Quarterly* 112 (Spring 1997): 51–66.

56. Marlin Fitzwater, as quoted in Tenpas, *Presidents as Candidates*, 94.

57. See the data in Lyn Ragsdale, *Vital Statistics on the Presidency*, 3rd ed. (Washington, DC: CQ Press, 2009), table 4-10, 204–205.

58. On the origins of the Office of Political Affairs, see Tenpas, "Institutionalized Politics." For a good defense of having such an office, see Edward J. Rollins, "Yes, Play Politics in the White House," *New York Times*, November 21, 2008.

59. For contemporary coverage of the controversy, see Michael A. Fletcher, "White House Had Drug Officials Appear with GOP Candidates," *Washington Post*, July 18, 2007; Bloomberg News, "Cabinet Officials Sent to Campaign at Taxpayer Expense, Report Says," *New York Times*, October 16, 2008; and Eric Lipton, "Bush White House Broke Elections Law, Report Says," *New York Times*, January 25, 2011. The Office of Special Counsel report is available at http://www.osc.gov/docu ments/hatchact/STF%20Report%20Final.pdf. The quotations are taken from the press release accompanying the report.

60. See "The Trail," *Washington Post*, September 22, 2008.

61. Jeff Zeleny, "Obama Will Move Political Operations to Chicago," *New York Times*, January 21, 2011.

62. See Michael D. Shear, "White House Comeback for Political Affairs Office," *New York Times*, January 25, 2014; Edward-Isaac Dovere, "White House to Launch New Political Office," *Politico*, January 24, 2014; and Michael D. Shear, "Obama Official Won't Testify to Congress," *New York Times*, July 16, 2014.

Chapter 4: Good Politics Doesn't Always Mean Good Government

1. The kind of circumstance I have in mind is when a president tries to artificially pump up the economy so that it looks good on election day, knowing that it will probably turn significantly worse once he has been safely reelected. The economic growth spurt the country enjoyed in 1972 was largely of this type.

2. These quotations are taken from, respectively, James Carney and John F. Dickerson, "The Busiest Man in the White House," *Time*, April 30, 2001, 32; Dan Balz, "In New Hampshire, the Spotlight Is on Rove," *Washington Post*, May 8, 2003; Richard Wolffe and Holly Bailey, "Bush Pops the Bubble," *Newsweek*, May 1, 2006, 27; Harold Meyerson, "The Cult of Karl," *American Prospect*, December 30, 2002, 3; Nicholas Lemann, "The Controller," *New Yorker*, May 12, 2003, 71; and S. C. Gwynne, "Genius," *Texas Monthly*, March 2003, 82.

3. See Carney and Dickerson, "Busiest Man," 34; Matt Bai, "Rove's Way," *New York Times Magazine*, October 20, 2002, 56; Michael Wolff, "The Power of Rove," *Vanity Fair*, July 2005, 67; John DiIulio, as quoted in Ron Suskind, "Why Are These

Men Laughing?" *Esquire*, January 2003, 104; James Carney and John F. Dickerson, "W. and the 'Boy Genius,'" *Time*, November 18, 2002, 45; Senator Bill Frist, as quoted in Richard L. Berke and Frank Bruni, "Architect of Bush Presidency Still Builds Bridges of Power," *New York Times*, February 18, 2001; David Kuo, *Tempting Faith: An Inside Story of Political Seduction* (New York: Free Press, 2006), 159; and Scott McClellan, *What Happened: Inside the Bush White House and Washington's Culture of Deception* (New York: PublicAffairs, 2008), 77.

4. Dana Milbank, "Serious 'Strategery': As Rove Launches Elaborate Political Effort, Some See a Nascent Clintonian 'War Effort,'" *Washington Post*, April 22, 2001.

5. Both quotations are taken from Milbank, "Serious 'Strategery.'"

6. As quoted in Berke and Bruni, "Architect of Bush Presidency."

7. See Richard W. Stevenson, "Top Bush Strategist Adds Another Big Hat," *New York Times*, February 9, 2005. The same point was made in Howard Fineman and Michael Isikoff, "King Karl," *Newsweek*, February 21, 2005, 30.

8. Stevenson, "Top Bush Strategist." Contrary to McClellan's statement, President Bush has said that Rove was not included in "national security meetings." See George W. Bush, *Decision Points* (New York: Crown, 2010), 96.

9. Elisabeth Bumiller, "Rove Is Giving Up Daily Policy Post to Focus on Vote," *New York Times*, April 20, 2006.

10. Richard E. Neustadt, *Presidential Power and the Modern Presidents* (New York: Free Press, 1990), 128–129.

11. See especially Norman C. Thomas, "Presidential Advice and Information: Policy and Program Formulation," *Law and Contemporary Problems* 35 (Summer 1970): 540–572; Alexander L. George, "The Case for Multiple Advocacy in Making Foreign Policy," *American Political Science Review* 66 (September 1972): 751–785; Richard Tanner Johnson, *Managing the White House: An Intimate Study of the Presidency* (New York: Harper & Row, 1974); Roger B. Porter, *Presidential Decision Making: The Economic Policy Board* (New York: Cambridge University Press, 1980); Gregory M. Herek, Irving L. Janis, and Paul Huth, "Decision Making during International Crises: Is Quality of Process Related to Outcome?" *Journal of Conflict Resolution* 31 (June 1987): 203–226; Fred I. Greenstein and John P. Burke, "The Dynamics of Presidential Reality Testing: Evidence from Two Vietnam Decisions," *Political Science Quarterly* 104 (1989–90): 557–580; Karen M. Hult, "Strengthening Presidential Decision-Making Capacity," *Presidential Studies Quarterly* 30 (March 2000): 27–46; and Andrew Rudalevige, "The Structure of Leadership: Presidents, Hierarchies, and Information Flow," *Presidential Studies Quarterly* 35 (June 2005): 333–360.

12. See the discussion in "Texas Politics," at www.texaspolitics.laits.utexas.edu (accessed February 1, 2012).

13. One or both of these descriptions are used in, among others, Christopher Hitchens, "Hardball with Chris Matthews," October 30, 2000, as quoted in *The Quotable Hitchens: From Alcohol to Zionism*, ed. Windsor Mann (Cambridge, MA: DaCapo Press, 2011), 38; "The Presidential Bubble," *New York Times*, September 25, 2003; Doug Bandow, "The Conservative Case against George W. Bush," *American Conservative*, December 1, 2003; Mike Allen and David S. Broder, "Bush's Leadership

Style: Decisive or Simplistic?" *Washington Post*, August 30, 2004; and Evan Thomas and Richard Wolffe, "Bush in the Bubble," *Newsweek*, December 19, 2005, 30. During the Bush presidency, there was a website devoted entirely to examples of Bush's general disinterest in information about the policies and issues he dealt with. See www.uncuriousgeorge.org (accessed May 4, 2012).

14. Peter Baker, *Days of Fire: Bush and Cheney in the White House* (New York: Doubleday, 2013), 479.

15. As quoted in Baker, *Days of Fire*, 647.

16. Baker, *Days of Fire*, 516.

17. Frank Bruni, *Ambling into History: The Unlikely Odyssey of George W. Bush* (New York: HarperCollins, 2002), 124 and 125.

18. As quoted in Nicholas Lemann, "Without a Doubt," *New Yorker*, October 14, 2002.

19. This summary of Bush's information and advising routines draws on "Text of Bush Interview," September 22, 2003, at www.foxnews.com/story/0,2933,980 06,00.html; Mike Allen, "Management Style Shows Weaknesses," *Washington Post*, June 2, 2004; Allen and Broder, "Bush's Leadership Style"; Nicholas Lemann, "Remember the Alamo," *New Yorker*, October 18, 2004; Jim VandeHei and Glenn Kessler, "President to Consider Changes for New Term," *Washington Post*, November 5, 2004; James Carney, "Living Too Much in the Bubble?" *Time*, September 11, 2005; Evan Thomas, "How Bush Blew It," *Newsweek*, September 19, 2005, 26; Thomas and Wolfe, "Bush in the Bubble"; James P. Pfiffner, "The First MBA President: George W. Bush as Public Administrator," *Public Administration Review* 67 (January/February 2007): 6–20; Jim Rutenberg, "Ex-Aide Details a Loss of Faith in the President," *New York Times*, April 1, 2007; and Andrew Rudalevige, "'The Decider': Issue Management and the Bush White House," in *The George W. Bush Legacy*, ed. Colin Campbell, Bert A. Rockman, and Andrew Rudalevige (Washington, DC: CQ Press, 2008): 135–163.

20. Thomas and Wolffe, "Bush in the Bubble."

21. McClellan, *What Happened*, 117.

22. For the full text of the order, see http://georgewbush-whitehouse.archives .gov/news/releases/2011/11/2001113–27.html (accessed February 9, 2012).

23. The quotations and most of the other details in this paragraph are taken from the account provided in Barton Gellman and Jo Becker, "'A Different Understanding with the President,'" *Washington Post*, June 24, 2007.

24. The episode is recounted in Baker, *Days of Fire*, 95–97. As Baker notes, Bush had opposed the Kyoto treaty during the 2000 campaign, but both Powell and Rice thought the letter was "unnecessarily provocative," since it made "only passing mention of working with other countries to find alternatives to the flawed pact, and no one had prepared the allies for what was coming." Baker, 96, 95.

25. As quoted in David Rose, "Neo Culpa," *Vanity Fair*, January 2007, 82.

26. As quoted in Lou Cannon and Carl M. Cannon, *Reagan's Disciple: George W. Bush's Troubled Quest for a Presidential Legacy* (New York: PublicAffairs, 2008), 237.

27. Both quotations are taken from Gwynne, "Genius."

28. Melinda Henneberger, "Driving W.," *New York Times Magazine*, May 14, 2000.

29. See Ron Suskind, "Mrs. Hughes Takes Her Leave," *Esquire*, July 2002.

30. This quotation is taken from a memo that John DiIulio sent to reporter Ron Suskind, available at www.esquire.com/features/diilulio (accessed July 11, 2010).

31. This characterization of Cheney is made by, among others, Shirley Anne Warshaw, *The Co-Presidency of Bush and Cheney* (Stanford, CA: Stanford University Press, 2009); Cannon and Cannon, *Reagan's Disciple*, 244; Baker, *Days of Fire*, 6; Paul Kengor, "Cheney and Vice Presidential Power," in *Considering the Bush Presidency*, ed. Gary L. Gregg II and Mark J. Rozell (New York: Oxford University Press, 2004), 160–176; Jack Lechelt, "Vice President Dick Cheney: Trendsetter or Just Your Typical Veep," in *George W. Bush: Evaluating the President at Midterm*, ed. Bryan Hilliard, Tom Lansford, and Robert P. Watson (Albany: State University of New York, 2004), 207–220; and Michael Isikoff and David Corn, *Hubris: The Inside Story of Spin, Scandal, and the Selling of the Iraq War* (New York: Crown, 2006), 414.

32. Joshua Green, "The Rove Presidency," *Atlantic*, September 2007.

33. Baker, *Days of Fire*, 306.

34. Warshaw also claims that Cheney was responsible for the Bush administration's effort to create a more "business-friendly" regulatory environment, claiming that because he ran Bush's transition in late 2000 and early 2001, Cheney was able to stock the administration with a lot of pro-business, antiregulatory appointees. See Warshaw, *Co-Presidency of Bush and Cheney*, chap. 6. Warshaw gives no consideration, however, to a more likely possibility: that Bush himself was always pro-business and antiregulation; and that far from foisting a business-friendly agenda upon an otherwise unwilling administration, Cheney was simply carrying out what had been Bush's intentions all along.

35. Warshaw, *Co-Presidency*, 244–245.

36. The next three paragraphs draw on James Q. Wilson, *Bureaucracy: What Government Agencies Do and Why They Do It* (New York: Basic Books, 1989), especially 55–65.

37. Wilson, *Bureaucracy*, 57.

38. US Senate, Select Committee to Study Governmental Operations with Respect to Intelligence Activities, Final Report, as quoted in Wilson, *Bureaucracy*, 57.

39. Another approach would be to redesign highways and their immediate surroundings, but this task was entrusted to a different agency, the Federal Highway Administration. See Charles Pruitt, "People Doing What They Do Best: The Professional Engineers and NHTSA," *Public Administration Review* 39 (July/August 1979): 363.

40. Wilson, *Bureaucracy*, 62.

41. Pruitt, "People Doing," 363–371.

42. The only campaign I am aware of that actually provided draft bills for the legislation it hoped to enact was the 1994 Contract with America. But this is, in a sense, the exception that proves the rule: the items in the Contract were developed not by candidates or consultants but by the House Republican leadership, which had the full resources of the legislative branch at its disposal.

43. The incident is recounted in DiIulio's memo to reporter Ron Suskind, referenced in note 30 of this chapter.

44. As quoted in Suskind, "Why Are These Men Laughing?"

45. David Frum, *The Right Man: The Surprise Presidency of George W. Bush* (New York: Random House, 2003), 20.

46. Ron Suskind, *The Price of Loyalty: George W. Bush, the White House, and the Education of Paul O'Neill* (New York: Simon & Schuster, 2004), 97.

47. See, for example, the remarkable level of anger and frustration expressed by many neoconservative foreign policy authorities in Rose, "Neo Culpa."

48. As quoted in Peter Baker, "An Unlikely Partnership Left Behind," *Washington Post*, November 5, 2007.

49. On the development and passage of the NCLB legislation, see especially Andrew Rudalevige, "No Child Left Behind: Forging a Congressional Compromise," in *No Child Left Behind: The Politics and Practice of School Accountability*, ed. Paul E. Peterson and Martin R. West (Washington, DC: Brookings Institution Press, 2003), 23–54; and Patrick McGuinn, "The National Schoolmarm: No Child Left Behind and the New Educational Federalism," *Publius* 35 (Winter 2005): 41–68.

50. See Mike Allen, "Bush Tries to Maintain Grade on Education," *Washington Post*, March 3, 2002; Michael A. Fletcher, "Education Law Reaches Milestone amid Discord," *Washington Post*, January 8, 2003; and Richard W. Stevenson, "Amid Criticism, Bush Promises to Produce Education Gains," *New York Times*, January 9, 2003.

51. As quoted in Baker, "Unlikely Partnership."

52. The Bush administration's efforts to reauthorize NCLB are discussed in Paul Manna, *Collision Course: Federal Education Policy Meets State and Local Realities* (Washington, DC: CQ Press, 2011), 61–66.

53. Jonathan Weisman and Amit R. Paley, "Dozens in GOP Turn against Bush's Prized 'No Child' Act," *Washington Post*, March 15, 2007; and Amit R. Paley, "Ex-Aides Break with Bush on 'No Child,'" *Washington Post*, June 26, 2007.

54. Quoted in Baker, "Unlikely Partnership."

55. Frederick M. Hess, "Why LBJ Is Smiling: NCLB and the Bush Legacy in Education," at www.aei.org/print/why-lbj-is-smiling (accessed April 19, 2012).

56. This feature of the NCLB law is criticized in, among others, William J. Bennett and Rod Paige, "Why We Need a National School Test," *Washington Post*, September 21, 2006; John Cronin, Michael Dahlin, Deborah Adkins, and G. Gage Kingsbury, *The Proficiency Illusion* (Washington, DC: Thomas B. Fordham Institute, October 2007), available at http://mail.ofy.org/uploaded/library/The_Proficiency_Illusion .pdf; Paul E. Peterson and Frederick Hess, "Few States Set World-Class Standards," *Education Next* 8 (Summer 2008): 70–73; John E. Chubb, *Learning from No Child Left Behind: How and Why the Nation's Most Important but Controversial Law Should Be Renewed* (Stanford, CA: Hoover Institution Press, 2009), 17–26; Brian M. Stecher, Georges Vernez, and Paul Steinberg, *Reauthorizing No Child Left Behind: Facts and Recommendations* (Santa Monica, CA: Rand Corporation, 2010), 14–15, 56–57; and Manna, *Collision Course*, 47–49, 152–153, 162–163.

57. See Ben Feller, "Huge Gaps in State, Federal Test Scores Cast Doubt over Student Progress," Associated Press, March 3, 2006.

58. Peterson and Hess, "Few States Set."

59. Cronin, Dahlin, Adkins, and Kingsbury, *Proficiency Illusion*, 6.

60. Bennett and Paige, "Why We Need."

61. For examples of this criticism, see, among others, Chester E. Finn Jr. and Frederick M. Hess, "On Leaving No Child Behind," *Public Interest* 157 (Fall 2004): 35–56; Chubb, *Learning from No Child Left Behind*, 26–37; and Stecher, Vernez, and Steinberg, *Reauthorizing No Child Left Behind*, 57–59.

62. See, among others, George W. Bush, "Remarks on Submitting the Education Reform Plan to Congress," January 23, 2001, *Public Papers of the President of the United States: George W. Bush* (hereafter cited as *Bush Public Papers*) (Washington, DC: US Government Printing Office, various years) 2001, 1:11–14; "The President's Radio Address," January 27, 2001, 1:25–26; "Address before a Joint Session of the Congress on Administration Goals," February 27, 2001, 1:140–141; "Remarks at Concord Middle School in Concord, North Carolina," April 11, 2001, 1:384–390; "Remarks on Presenting the National Teacher of the Year Award," April 23, 2001, 1:444–446; and "Remarks to the Business Roundtable," June 20, 2001, 1:705–709.

63. The two quotations are from Bush, "Remarks at Concord Middle School," 1:386; and "Remarks to the Business Roundtable," 1:706 (emphasis added).

64. For a particularly clear explanation of just what NCLB requires local schools and school districts to do, see Manna, *Collision Course*, 22–30.

65. Richard F. Elmore, "Unwarranted Intrusion," *Education Next* 2 (Spring 2002): 31–35.

66. As quoted in McGuinn, "National Schoolmarm," 43.

67. Finn and Hess, "On Leaving No Child Behind," 42.

68. This specific quotation is from "Remarks to the Business Roundtable," *Bush Public Papers*, 2001, 1:706. But almost identical statements can be found in "Remarks on Submitting the Education Reform Plan," 1:13; "Remarks to the National Conference of State Legislators," March 2, 2001, 1:178; and "Remarks at Concord Middle School," 1:386.

69. Rudalevige, "No Child Left Behind," 36.

70. Finn and Hess, "On Leaving No Child Behind," 47.

71. As quoted in Lois Romano, "Tweaking of 'No Child' Seen," *Washington Post*, August 31, 2006. In an interview conducted in early 2012, George W. Bush still refused to acknowledge any major problems with the law. See "'Let's Not Weaken It,'" *Time*, January 23, 2012, 43.

72. The quotation is taken from the transcript of the press conference, available at www.whitehouse.gov/the-press-office/2011/06/29/press-conference-president (accessed September 24, 2011).

73. Howard Kurtz, in particular, has attributed the "aggressive assault on tax breaks for corporate highfliers" to David Plouffe and Dan Pfeiffer, both of whom are long-time political operatives with no apparent training or experience in policy analysis. See Kurtz, "Why the Debt Deal Faltered," *Daily Beast*, July 8, 2011, at

www.thedailybeast.com/articles/2011/07/08/obama-republicans-duke-it-out-in
-public-while-advancing-debt-deal-in-private.html; and Kurtz, "Inside Obama's
Populist Makeover," *Daily Beast*, October 2, 2011, at www.thedailybeast.com/news
week/2011/10/02/inside-obama-s-populist-makeover.html.

74. See, for example, "To Succeed, Serious Negotiations Require a Serious
Negotiating Partner," *New York Times*, June 29, 2011; Richard Rubin and Andrew
Zajac, "Corporate Jet Tax Gets Six Obama Mentions, $3 Billion Estimate," *Bloomberg
News*, June 30, 2011, at www.bloomberg.com/news/2011–06–29/jet-tax-break-cited
-six-times-by-obama-would-cut-debt-by-about-3-billion.html; and Glenn Kessler,
"Takes factchecker banner w/gk mug," *Washington Post*, July 3, 2011.

75. Charles Krauthammer, "The Elmendorf Rule," *Washington Post*, July 8, 2011.

76. See, in particular, his comments in Karl Rove, *Courage and Consequence: My
Life as a Conservative in the Fight* (New York: Simon & Schuster, 2010), 64–66.

77. Rove's leadership of the effort to develop an agenda for the 2004 campaign
is noted in Mike Allen and Kathy Sawyer, "Return to Moon May Be on Agenda,"
Washington Post, December 5, 2003.

78. As quoted in Allen and Sawyer, "Return to Moon."

79. The policy case for small initiatives has been argued most cogently and explicitly by Charles E. Lindblom. See especially "The Science of 'Muddling Through,'"
Public Administration Review 19 (Spring 1959): 79–88.

80. All quotations are from George W. Bush, "Remarks at the National Aero-
nautics and Space Administration," January 14, 2004, in *Bush Public Papers*, 2004,
1:57–58.

81. As quoted in Allen and Sawyer, "Return to Moon."

82. See, for example, Lawrence M. Krauss, "In Search for Life on Mars, Machines
Can Boldly Go Where Humans Can't," *New York Times*, January 6, 2004; and the essay by Robert L. Park in "Human Spaceflight," *CQ Researcher* 19 (October 16, 2009):
877.

83. Rand Simberg, "In Search of a Conservative Space Policy," *New Atlantis* 29
(Fall 2010): 95–100.

84. W. D. Kay, "Space Policy Redefined: The Reagan Administration and the
Commercialization of Space," *Business and Economic History* 27 (Fall 1998), 237.
Barack Obama, whom many Republicans called a socialist, also proved to be a
"champion for the possibilities of capitalism in space." James Muncy, space policy
analyst, as quoted in Christian Davenport, "How Obama Brought Capitalism to
Outer Space," *Washington Post*, October 11, 2016, https://www.washingtonpost
.com/news/the-switch/wp/2016/10/11/how-obama-brought-capitalism-to-outer
-space/?utm_term=.77b67f7be9ab.

85. See George H. W. Bush, "Remarks on the 20th Anniversary of the *Apollo 11*
Moon Landing," July 20, 1989, in *Public Papers of the President of the United States:
George [H. W.] Bush* (Washington, DC: US Government Printing Office, various
years) 1989, 2:990.

86. See William J. Broad, "Diverse Factors Propel Bush's Space Proposal," *New*

York Times, July 30, 1989; and Associated Press, "NASA Plan May Put Man on Mars by 2011," *New York Times*, November 21, 1989.

87. Greg Klerkx, *Lost in Space: The Fall of NASA and the Dream of a New Space Age* (New York: Pantheon Books, 2004), 292. For a similar verdict, see W. D. Kay, *Defining NASA: The Historical Debate over the Agency's Mission* (Albany: State University of New York Press, 2005), 156–158.

88. Bush, "Remarks at NASA," 1:59 (see note 80 of this chapter).

89. "Bush's Space Vision Thing," *New York Times*, January 15, 2004.

90. Review of U.S. Human Spaceflight Plans Committee, "Executive Summary," *Seeking a Human Spaceflight Program Worthy of a Great Nation*, 9, at www.nasa .gov/pdf/396093main_HSF_Cmte_FinalReport.pdf (accessed December 26, 2011; emphasis in original).

91. Joel Achenbach, "Sun Sets on NASA Moon Mission as 2011 Budget Scales Back Goals," *Washington Post*, February 1, 2010.

92. See Kenneth Chang, "NASA Gets New Orders That Bypass the Moon," *New York Times*, October 1, 2010; and "Back to the Past," *New York Times*, October 2, 2010.

Chapter 5: Good Politics Doesn't Always Mean Good Government, Part II

1. This was, of course, one of the central insights behind James Madison's famous analysis of American politics in *Federalist*, no. 10.

2. See, among others, Anthony Downs, *An Economic Theory of Democracy* (New York: Harper & Brothers, 1957), 55–60; James M. Buchanan and Gordon Tullock, *The Calculus of Consent: Logical Foundations of Constitutional Democracy* (Ann Arbor: University of Michigan Press, 1962), chap. 10; and Gordon Tullock, "A Simple Algebraic Logrolling Model," *American Economic Review* 60 (June 1970): 419–426.

3. David Frum, *The Right Man: The Surprise Presidency of George W. Bush* (New York: Random House, 2003), 36.

4. Nicholas Lemann, "The Controller," *New Yorker*, May 12, 2003, 80; Todd S. Purdum, "Karl Rove's Split Personality," *Vanity Fair*, December 2006, 202, 206; and Nicholas Lemann, "Rovian Ways," *New Yorker*, August 27, 2007, 29–30. See also George F. Will, "An Analysis of Roveology," *Newsweek*, July 17, 2006, 70.

5. See Karl Rove, "What Makes a Great President," speech delivered at the University of Utah, November 13, 2002, available at http://hnn.us/articles/1529.html.

6. These last two examples of McKinley's group appeals were mentioned by Rove in an interview in March 1999 reported in James Moore and Wayne Slater, *The Architect: Karl Rove and the Master Plan for Absolute Power* (New York: Crown, 2006), 104.

7. My discussion of the debate on steel tariffs within the Bush administration draws on Richard W. Stevenson, "Recovery Nears, but Its Vigor Is in Doubt, Greenspan Says," *New York Times*, February 28, 2002; Joseph Kahn and David E. Sanger, "Bush Officials Meet to Seek a Compromise on Steel Tariffs," *New York Times*, March 1, 2002; Joseph Kahn and Richard W. Stevenson, "Treasury's Chief Is Said to Fault

Steel Tariff Move," *New York Times*, March 16, 2002; Robert Novak, "Harsh Reaction to Tariff Stuns Bush," *Chicago Sun-Times*, March 17, 2002; Matt Bai, "Rove's Way," *New York Times Magazine*, October 20, 2002, 56; and Ron Suskind, *The Price of Loyalty: George W. Bush, the White House, and the Education of Paul O'Neill* (New York: Simon & Schuster, 2004), 216–221.

8. Powell's comments on the issue are quoted in Suskind, *Price of Loyalty*, 220.

9. See Joseph Kahn, "Bush Moves against Steel Imports," *New York Times*, June 6, 2001.

10. Douglas M. Brattebo, "Ironing Out Reelection: George W. Bush and the Politics of Steel," in *George W. Bush: Evaluating the President at Midterm*, ed. Bryan Hilliard, Tom Lansford, and Robert P. Watson (Albany: State University of New York Press, 2004), 88.

11. The quotation is from "The President's News Conference with President Hosni Mubarak of Egypt," March 5, 2002, *Public Papers of the President of the United States: George W. Bush* (hereafter cited as *Bush Public Papers*) (Washington, DC: US Government Printing Office, various years) 2002, 1:346.

12. See, among others, Robert W. Crandall, "Win for Big Steel Would Cost Jobs," *Chicago Sun-Times*, February 2, 2002; "Man of Steel," *Wall Street Journal*, March 4, 2002; Brattebo, "Ironing Out Reelection"; and James Bovard, *The Bush Betrayal* (New York: Palgrave Macmillan, 2004), chap. 4.

13. See, for example, Neil King Jr. and Robert Guy Matthews, "America Feels Pain of Tariffs on Steel Imports," *Wall Street Journal*, May 31, 2002; Neil King Jr. and Robert Guy Matthews, "So Far, Steel Tariffs Do Little of What President Envisioned," *Wall Street Journal*, September 13, 2002; and Mike Allen and Jonathan Weisman, "Steel Tariffs Appear to Have Backfired on Bush," *Washington Post*, September 19, 2003.

14. Edmund L. Andrews, "Angry Europeans to Challenge U.S. Steel Tariffs at W.T.O.," *New York Times*, March 6, 2002.

15. Andrews, "Angry Europeans."

16. See Elizabeth Becker, "U.S. Tariffs on Steel Are Illegal, World Trade Organization Says," *New York Times*, November 11, 2003; Alan Cowell, "Europeans Warn U.S. on Wider Effects from Steel Tariffs," *New York Times*, November 12, 2003; Elizabeth Becker and David E. Sanger, "President in a Political Vise over Steel Tariff Decision," *New York Times*, December 2, 2003; and Richard W. Stevenson and Elizabeth Becker, "After 21 Months, Bush Lifts Tariff on Steel Imports," *New York Times*, December 5, 2003.

17. See, in particular, Bruce L. Gardner's discussion of what he calls the "farm problem model" in Gardner, "Changing Economic Perspectives on the Farm Problem," *Journal of Economic Literature* 30 (March 1992): 62–101.

18. For a particularly good analysis of these changes, see Bruce L. Gardner, *American Agriculture in the Twentieth Century: How It Flourished and What It Cost* (Cambridge: Harvard University Press, 2002), especially chaps. 2–5.

19. Gardner, *American Agriculture*, 78.

20. See Bruce L. Gardner, "Plowing Farm Subsidies Under," AEI Online, June 22, 2007, at www.aei.org/issue/economics/plowing-farm-subsidies-under-issue.

21. Gardner, *American Agriculture*, 93.

22. Gardner, "Changing Economic Perspectives," 84.

23. Daniel A. Sumner, "Farm Subsidy Tradition and Modern Agricultural Realities," paper prepared for the American Enterprise Institute project on Agricultural Policy for the 2007 Farm Bill and Beyond, 2007, 11, at http://aic.udavis.edu/research /farmbill07/aeibriefs/20070515_sumnerRationalesfinal.pdf (accessed January 20, 2014).

24. The last phrase is quoted from Cato Institute, *Cato Handbook for Policymakers*, 7th ed., 2009, 196, at www.cato.org/cato-handbook-policymakers/cato-handbook -policymakers-7th-edition-2009 (accessed January 20, 2014).

25. Environmental Working Group website, as quoted in Bovard, *Bush Betrayal*, 96.

26. 2012 EWG data can be found at http://farm.ewg.org/region.php?fips=00000 (accessed January 20, 2014).

27. See Mark Arax and Eric Bailey, "Some Farmers Growing Rich on Government Crop Subsidies," *Los Angeles Times*, June 10, 2002.

28. Bruce L. Gardner, "Why Experts on the Economics of Agriculture Have Changed Their Policy Tune," in *The Economics of Agriculture*, vol. 2, *Papers in Honor of D. Gale Johnson*, ed. John M. Antle and Daniel A. Sumner (Chicago: University of Chicago Press, 1996), 225.

29. Daniel A. Sumner, "'The World's Most Outdated Law': Why the Next Farm Bill Should Be the Last," *Atlantic*, April 25, 2013, at www.theatlantic.com/business /archive/2013/04/the-worlds-most-outdated-law-why-the-next-farm-bill-should -be-the-last/275315/.

30. David Orden, Robert Paarlberg, and Terry Roe, *Policy Reform in American Agriculture: Analysis and Prognosis* (Chicago: University of Chicago Press, 1999), 13. "The huge and expensive programs for price supports, market stabilization, and credit provision" are also criticized by Berkeley economist Brian D. Wright in "Goals and Realities for Farm Policy," in *Agricultural Policy Reform in the United States*, ed. Daniel A. Sumner (Washington, DC: AEI Press, 1995), 9–44.

31. The law's formal name was the Federal Agricultural Improvement and Reform Act of 1996. My discussion of the act draws primarily on Sumner, "Farm Subsidy Tradition"; Orden, Paarlberg, and Roe, *Policy Reform*, especially chap. 4 and the appendix; and "Longstanding Farm Laws Rewritten," *Congressional Quarterly Almanac 1996* (Washington, DC: Congressional Quarterly, 1997), 3-15–3-26.

32. Among those who have singled out the Freedom to Farm Act as one of the signature achievements of the Republican Revolution are Michael D. Tanner, *Leviathan on the Right: How Big-Government Conservatism Brought Down the Republican Revolution* (Washington, DC: Cato Institute, 2007), 156; John Boehner and Cal Dooley, "This Terrible Farm Bill," *Washington Post*, May 2, 2002; and Richard E. Cohen and Corine Hegland, "Farm Bill Winners and Losers," *National Journal*, May 11, 2002, 1390. The claim that the 1996 law had tried to "wean" farmers off subsidies is made in, among others, "Reversing Course on Farm Policy," *New York Times*, May 2, 2002; Fred Barnes, "The Pigs Return to the Trough," *Weekly Standard*, May 27, 2002,

12; and Rebecca Adams, "Fear of Budget Constraints in 2002 Galvanizes Farm Bill Supporters," *CQ Weekly*, December 8, 2001, 2901.

33. George W. Bush, as quoted in "Making Hay," *New Republic*, May 20, 2002, 9.

34. Elizabeth Becker, "Bush Gives Tight-Fisted Support to Bigger Farm Subsidies," *New York Times*, November 29, 2001.

35. As subsequent footnotes indicate, my account of the writing of the 2002 farm bill draws primarily on contemporary coverage in *CQ Weekly*, the *Washington Post*, and the *New York Times*.

36. "Stop the Farm Bill," *Washington Post*, May 2, 2002. The final bill did include a provision capping payments to individual farmers at $360,000, but as the *Post* editorial implies, that provision included so many loopholes and exceptions as to effectively nullify the limit. On this point, see Elizabeth Becker, "Accord Reached on a Bill Raising Farm Subsidies," *New York Times*, April 27, 2002; Gebe Martinez and Ted Monoson, "Farm Bill Deal Set for House, Senate As Lawmakers Feel Constituent Pressure," *CQ Weekly*, April 27, 2002, 1086–1087; and David Hosansky, "Farm Subsidies," *CQ Researcher,* May 17, 2002, 440.

37. As quoted in David Rogers, "Bush Embraces Agriculture Bill As Environmentalist Foes Dig In," *Washington Post*, May 2, 2002.

38. Mike Allen, "Bush Signs Bill Providing Big Farm Subsidy Increases," *Washington Post*, May 14, 2002.

39. See Dick Lugar, "The Farm Bill Charade," *New York Times*, January 21, 2002.

40. As quoted in Gloria Borger, "Feeding at the Trough," *U.S. News & World Report*, May 27, 2002, 35. For other discussions of how election-year politics changed Bush's position on the farm bill, see Martinez and Monoson, "Farm Bill Deal"; Gebe Martinez, "Free-Spending Farm Bill a Triumph of Politics," *CQ Weekly*, May 4, 2002, 1147–1149; Hosansky, "Farm Subsidies"; and David Sanger, "Reversing Course, Bush Signs Bill Raising Farm Subsidies," *New York Times*, May 14, 2002.

41. The quoted phrase is taken from Hosansky, "Farm Subsidies," 437. For other discussions of the Republican opposition to the 2002 bill, see Cohen and Hegland, "Farm Bill," 1390; Associated Press, "Bush Makes Hay with Midwest by Signing Farm Bill," *USA Today*, May 13, 2002; Martinez, "Free-Spending Farm Bill"; and Sanger, "Reversing Course."

42. The other change was to delete a provision that would have relaxed restrictions on trading food and medicine with Cuba. The administration's conduct during the conference committee negotiations is discussed in Becker, "Accord Reached"; "Reversing Course on Farm Policy"; Cohen and Hegland, "Farm Bill," 1390; and Martinez, "Free-Spending Farm Bill," 1148.

43. The quotations are taken from, respectively, Barnes, "The Pigs Return"; Borger, "Feeding at the Trough"; Laura D'Andrea Tyson, "The Farm Bill is a $200 Billion Disaster," *Business Week*, June 3, 2002, 26; "Making Hay"; and "Cringe for Mr. Bush," *Washington Post*, May 14, 2002. For other contemporary expressions of opposition to the 2002 farm bill, see "Reversing Course on Farm Policy"; Robert J. Samuelson, "A Sad Primer in Hypocrisy," *Newsweek*, February 11, 2002, 49; and Paul Magnusson, "Farm Subsidies: A Blight on the Economy," *Business Week*, September 9, 2002, 50.

44. Associated Press, "Bush Makes Hay."

45. George W. Bush, "Remarks on Signing the Farm Security and Rural Investment Act of 2002," May 13, 2002, *Bush Public Papers*, 2002, 1:780–783. Like health savings accounts, Bush's proposal would have allowed farmers to set aside up to $10,000 a year in a tax-free account—except that in this case, the money would have been matched by an equal amount from the federal government.

46. As a *Washington Post* editorial correctly responded to this statement, "How can Mr. Bush say this? The essence of the farm law is that it dictates the price that farmers will receive for crops, overriding the 'market realities' that Mr. Bush invokes. These prices are based on haggling among members of Congress; they are the pure essence of anti-market government fiat. Because Congress's chosen prices are above the level that the market would have set, they are certain to stimulate extra production, whatever Mr. Bush says. And extra production will depress market prices." See "Cringe for Mr. Bush."

47. Tyson, "Farm Bill."

48. Bruce Bartlett, *Impostor: How George W. Bush Bankrupted America and Betrayed the Reagan Legacy* (New York: Doubleday, 2006), 92. The same point is made in Julian M. Alston and Daniel A. Sumner, "Perspectives on Farm Policy Reform," *Journal of Agricultural and Resource Economics* 32 (April 2007): 1–19.

49. See, in particular, Michael J. Gerson, *Heroic Conservatism: Why Republicans Need to Embrace America's Ideals (And Why They Deserve to Fail If They Don't)* (New York: HarperCollins, 2007).

50. Amadou Toumani Touré and Blaise Compaoré, "Your Farm Subsidies Are Strangling Us," *New York Times*, July 11, 2003.

51. Tyson, "Farm Bill."

52. My analysis of the Bush administration's arguments for immigration reform is based on the president's public statements on the issue between 2004 and mid-2006. See especially "Remarks on Immigration Reform," January 7, 2004, *Bush Public Papers*, 2004, 1:14–18; "Remarks on Signing the Department of Homeland Security Appropriations," October 18, 2005, *Bush Public Papers*, 2005, 2:1559–1562; "Remarks on Border Security and Immigration Reform in Tucson, Arizona," November 28, 2005, *Bush Public Papers*, 2005, 2:1765–1770; "Address to the Nation on Immigration Reform," May 15, 2006, *Bush Public Papers*, 2006, 1:928–932; "Remarks Following a Tour of the Border in Yuma, Arizona," May 18, 2006, *Bush Public Papers*, 2006, 1:951–956; and "Remarks to the United States Chamber of Commerce," June 1, 2006, *Bush Public Papers*, 2006, 1: 1056–1063.

53. This particular quotation is taken from Bush, "Remarks on Border Security and Immigration Reform," 2:1769. But a similar claim can be found in virtually every one of Bush's speeches on the subject.

54. For an interesting examination of what happened after an immigration crackdown at six meat processing plants, see Jerry Kammer, "The 2006 Swift Raids: Assessing the Impact of Immigration Enforcement Actions at Six Facilities," March 2009, www.cis.org/2006swiftraids (accessed November 11, 2011).

55. George J. Borjas, "Increasing the Supply of Labor through Immigration:

Measuring the Impact on Native-Born Workers," May 2004, available at www.cis .org/articles/2004/back504.html. See also George J. Borjas, Richard B. Freeman, and Lawrence F. Katz, "On the Labor Market Effects of Immigration and Trade," in *Immigration and the Work Force: Economic Consequences for the United States and Source Areas*, ed. George J. Borjas and Richard B. Freeman (Chicago: University of Chicago Press, 1992), 213–244; and James P. Smith and Barry Edmonston, eds., *The New Americans: Economic, Demographic, and Fiscal Effects of Immigration* (Washington, DC: National Academy Press, 1997), 219–228.

56. See Steven A. Camarota and Karen Jensenius, "Jobs Americans Won't Do? A Detailed Look at Immigrant Employment by Occupation," August 2009, www.cis .org/illegalimmigration-employment.

57. Many Democratic commentators also saw Hispanics playing a pivotal role. See, in particular, John B. Judis and Ruy Teixeira, *The Emerging Democratic Majority* (New York: Scribner, 2002).

58. As quoted in David Paul Kuhn, "Rove Leaves during Historic GOP Downturn," *Politico*, August 13, 2007, at www.politico.com/news/stories/0807/5376.html.

59. All figures are based on the exit poll data, available through the Roper Center for Public Opinion Research.

60. All quotations in this paragraph are taken from Bush's "Address to the Nation on Immigration Reform," 1:930.

61. See Bush's comments in "Remarks at the Laredo Border Patrol Sector Headquarters and an Exchange with Reporters in Laredo, Texas," *Bush Public Papers*, 2006, 1:1086.

62. See Jessica Vaughn, "Shortcuts to Immigration: The 'Temporary' Visa Program Is Broken," January 2003, at www.cis.org/TemporaryVisaProgram-Broken.

63. Nathan Thornburgh, "Can a Guest Worker Program Work?" *Time*, May 24, 2007.

64. See Bush, "Address to the Nation on Immigration Reform," 1:928–929.

65. Rove, *Courage and Consequence: My Life as a Conservative in the Fight* (New York: Simon & Schuster, 2010), 469.

66. All quotations are from "President's Radio Address," May 20, 2006, *Bush Public Papers*, 2006, 1:977.

67. See, for example, "Address to the Nation on Immigration Reform," 1:931; "The President's Radio Address," December 3, 2005, *Bush Public Papers*, 2005, 2:1804; and "The President's Radio Address," March 25, 2006, *Bush Public Papers*, 2006, 1:571.

68. Steven A. Camarota, "Analysis of the Senate Amnesty Plan: S2611 Repeats Many of the Mistakes of the Past," July 18, 2006, https://cis.org/Analysis-Senate -Amnesty-Plan. Others making the same point include Edwin Meese III, "An Amnesty by Any Other Name . . . " *New York Times*, May 24, 2006; and Mark Krikorian, "None Dare Call It Amnesty," February 21, 2007, http://www.cis.org/node/431.

69. This particular quotation is from "President's Radio Address," May 20, 2006, *Bush Public Papers*, 2006, 1:976, but the same statistic is cited in "President's Radio Address," March 25, 2006, 1:571; "Remarks on Immigration Reform and a Question-

and-Answer Session in Irvine, California," April 24, 2006, *Bush Public Papers*, 2006, 1:784; "Remarks at a Republican National Committee Gala," May 17, 2006, *Bush Public Papers*, 2006, 1:948; "Remarks on Immigration Reform and a Swearing-In Ceremony for W. Ralph Basham as Commissioner of Customs and Border Protection in Artesia, New Mexico," June 6, 2006, *Bush Public Papers*, 2006, 1:1079; and "Remarks on Immigration Reform in Omaha, Nebraska," June 7, 2006, *Bush Public Papers*, 2006, 1:1093.

70. The quotation is from Rove, *Courage and Consequence*, 467. For similar claims by Bush, see, among others, "Remarks on Signing," 2:1560–1561; "Remarks at a Naturalization Ceremony," March 27, 2006, *Bush Public Papers*, 2006, 1:574–575; and "Address to the Nation on Immigration Reform."

71. See www.cbp.gov/xp/cgov/border_security/border_patrol/ (accessed November 13, 2011). By way of comparison, a 1998 publication by the Immigration and Naturalization Service defined the Border Patrol's mission this way: "The major objectives of the Border Patrol are to prevent illegal entry into the United States, interdict drug smugglers and other criminals, and compel those persons seeking admission to present themselves legally at ports of entry for inspection." See US Immigration and Naturalization Service, *Statistical Yearbook of the Immigration and Naturalization Service, 2000* (Washington, DC: US Government Printing Office, 2000), available at www.dhs.gov/xlibrary/assets/statistics/yearbook/1998/ENF98text.pdf.

72. For further details, see "Biography of James Ziglar," *Immigration Daily*, at www.ilw.com/immigrationdaily/News/2001,0803-Ziglar.shtm (accessed March 16, 2012); Eric Schmitt, "Immigration Nominee Could Face Firestorm at Hearing Today," *New York Times*, July 18, 2001; and Eric Schmitt, "Bush Choice Pledges Kinder, Gentler I.N.S.," *New York Times*, July 19, 2001.

73. Schmitt, "Immigration Nominee Could Face Firestorm."

74. Somini Sengupta, "I.N.S. Urges Immigrants to Report the Missing," *New York Times*, October 6, 2001.

75. David Johnston, "6 Months Late, I.N.S. Notifies Flight School of Hijackers' Visas," *New York Times*, March 13, 2002.

76. Details on Myers's biography are taken from Dan Eggen and Spencer S. Hsu, "Immigration Nominee's Credentials Questioned," *Washington Post*, September 20, 2005; "Withdraw Myers," *National Review*, September 22, 2005, at http://old.nationalreview.com/editorials/editors200509221416.asp; and The White House, "Julie Myers: Assistant Secretary of Homeland Security for U.S. Immigration and Customs Enforcement," at http://georgewbush-whitehouse.archives.gov/government/j-myers-bio.html (accessed March 8, 2012).

77. Charles Showalter, as quoted in Eggen and Hsu, "Immigration Nominee's Credentials."

78. As quoted in "Withdraw Myers."

79. "Withdraw Myers." Many other conservatives also opposed her nomination. See, for example, Michelle Malkin, "No More Cronyism: Bush DHS Nominee Doesn't Deserve the Job," September 20, 2005, at http://michellemalkin.com/2005/09/20

/no-more-cronyism-bush-dhs-nominee-doesnt-deserve-the-job; and "Julie Myers: Not Qualified," at http://archive.redstate.com/story/2005/9/21/13359/4429 (accessed February 23, 2012).

Myers's appointment was also an enormous political risk. Though it never became a major theme in post-9/11 media coverage, several studies had shown that foreign-born al-Qaeda terrorists who committed crimes in the United States, including the 9/11 hijackers, were able to enter and then remain in America by manipulating US immigration laws and/or by violating them outright with impunity. See especially Steven A. Camarota, *The Open Door: How Militant Islamic Terrorists Entered and Remained in the United States, 1993–2001*, Center for Immigration Studies Paper No. 21, May 2002, at www.cis.org/articles/2002/Paper21/terrorism.html. In the event of another terrorist attack on American soil, Myers's appointment would have been a very inviting target of criticism.

80. The phrase is quoted from Rachel L. Swarns, "Failed Amnesty Legislation of 1986 Haunts the Current Immigration Bills in Congress," *New York Times*, May 23, 2006.

81. On the failure to seriously enforce the border security parts of the IRCA, see Dan Cadman, "Lessons Learned by an Insider in the 30 Years Since IRCA," October 26, 2016, https://cis.org/Cadman/Lessons-Learned-Insider-30-Years-IRCA; Brad Plumer, "Congress Tried to Fix Immigration Back in 1986. Why Did It Fail?" January 30, 2013, https://www.washingtonpost.com/news/wonk/wp/2013/01/30/in-1986-congress-tried-to-solve-immigration-why-didnt-it-work/?utm_term=.709df1045153; and Caroline Mimbs Nyce and Chris Bodenner, "Looking Back at Amnesty Under Reagan," May 23, 2016, https://www.theatlantic.com/notes/2016/05/thirty-years-after-the-immigration-reform-and-control-act/482364/.

82. Both figures are taken from Plumer, "Congress Tried to Fix."

83. Cadman, "Lessons Learned by an Insider."

84. Swarns, "Failed Amnesty Legislation."

85. Mark Krikorian, "'Give Me the Tools': They Have Them So Use Them," July 2007, www.cis.org/node/450.

86. As quoted in Michael Sandler, "Immigration Debate Focuses on Those in U.S.," *CQ Weekly*, November 7, 2005, 2964.

87. I know a number of observers who still maintain that Bill Clinton offered a serious deficit reduction proposal during the 1992 campaign. I strongly disagree. For a detailed analysis of his plan, which concludes that it was composed largely of smoke, mirrors, and wishful thinking, see William G. Mayer, "Why Presidents Break Promises," in *Readings in Presidential Politics*, ed. George C. Edwards III (Belmont, CA: Thomson Wadsworth, 2006), 20–25. The definitive proof of the Clinton plan's essentially frivolous nature is, of course, the fact that once Clinton was in office and decided that a serious deficit reduction effort was necessary, he discarded most of his campaign platform and put forward a plan that had both substantially lower levels of new spending and a broad-based tax increase instead of a middle-class tax cut.

88. My account of the making and breaking of Bush's "no new taxes" promise

draws on Bob Woodward, "Making Choices: Bush's Economic Record," *Washington Post*, October 4–7, 1992; Richard Darman, *Who's in Control? Polar Politics and the Sensible Center* (New York: Simon & Schuster, 1996), chaps. 10–13; Peggy Noonan, *What I Saw at the Revolution* (New York: Random House, 1990), chap. 17; and Jack W. Germond and Jules Witcover, *Mad as Hell: Revolt at the Ballot Box, 1992* (New York: Warner Books, 1993), chap. 2.

89. For the text of Bush's acceptance speech, see *Congressional Quarterly Weekly Report*, August 20, 1988, 2353–2356.

90. Germond and Witcover, *Mad as Hell*, 30.

91. The division between the economic policy team and the political consultants is a major theme in Bob Woodward, *The Agenda: Inside the Clinton White House* (New York: Simon & Schuster, 1994).

92. Suskind, *Price of Loyalty*, 117. Though written by Suskind, this book is largely based on O'Neill's recollections.

93. Peter Baker, *Days of Fire: Bush and Cheney in the White House* (New York: Doubleday, 2013), 233.

94. This is, for example, the assessment of Lou Cannon and Carl M. Cannon, *Reagan's Disciple: George W. Bush's Troubled Quest for a Presidential Legacy* (New York: PublicAffairs, 2008), 15.

95. See, for example, Baker, *Days of Fire*, 292–293.

96. See Robert J. Samuelson, "Who Will Say No?: Retirement Benefit Costs Are Out of Control," *Washington Post*, December 15, 2004.

97. As quoted in "U.S. Heading for Fiscal Trouble?" *60 Minutes*, March 4, 2007, at www.cbsnews.com/stories/2007/03/01/60minutes/main2528226.shtml.

98. Rove, *Courage and Consequence*, 374. For a nonpartisan endorsement of Rove's claim, see Mort Kondracke, "Medicare Drug Plan Ought to be Model for Health Reform," *Roll Call*, June 11, 2009.

99. This estimate should always have had an asterisk next to it. The prescription drug plan did not actually go into effect until 2006, so the costs for 2004 and 2005 were comparatively negligible.

100. See Amy Goldstein and Juliet Eilperin, "Medicare Drug Cost Estimate Increases," *Washington Post*, January 30, 2004.

101. All cost figures in this and the next paragraph are taken from *2019 Annual Report of the Boards of Trustees of the Federal Hospital Insurance and Federal Supplementary Medical Insurance Trust Funds*, table III.D.3, p. 103, available at cms. gov/Research-Statistics-Data-and-Systems/Statistics-Trends-and-Reports/Reports TrustFunds/Downloads/TR2019.pdf (accessed March 7, 2020). All numbers refer only to the costs to the federal treasury. Small amounts of additional money are derived from premiums paid by the recipients and contributions by state governments.

102. See Mark R. Levin, "Ronald Reagan and George W. Bush," March 18, 2011, at www.humanevents.com/article.php?id=42377.

103. Shailagh Murray, "Funding for Alaskan Bridges Eliminated," *Washington Post*, November 17, 2005.

104. Rove, *Courage and Consequence*, 414.

105. For contemporary coverage of the controversy, all of which records not a word of criticism from the Bush administration, see Bill Marsh, "Fresh Pork, Coming to a District Near You," *New York Times*, August 7, 2005; Jeffrey H. Birnbaum, "Congress Pigs Out on Pork-Barrel Projects," *Washington Post*, September 5, 2005; Carl Hulse, "Senate Retains Money for Disputed Alaska Bridges and Other Pet Initiatives," *New York Times*, October 21, 2005; Shailagh Murray, "For a Senate Foe of Pork Barrel Spending, Two Bridges Too Far," *Washington Post*, October 21, 2005; Shailagh Murray, "Some in GOP Regretting Pork-Stuffed Highway Bill," *Washington Post*, November 5, 2005; Murray, "Funding for Alaskan Bridges"; and Carl Hulse, "Two 'Bridges to Nowhere' Tumble Down in Congress," *New York Times*, November 17, 2005.

106. See George W. Bush, "Remarks on Signing the Safe, Accountable, Flexible, Efficient Transportation Equity Act: A Legacy for Users in Montgomery, Illinois," August 10, 2005, *Bush Public Papers*, 2005, 2:1322.

107. For a nice discussion of this problem, see James L. Sundquist, *The Decline and Resurgence of Congress* (Washington, DC: Brookings Institution, 1981), esp. chap. 7. It is also a major theme in David R. Mayhew, *Congress: The Electoral Connection*, 2nd ed. (New Haven: Yale University Press, 2004), esp. at 53–59 and 127–130.

108. Bush finally cast his first veto in July 2006—but that veto was directed at a bill that would have changed federal policy with regard to stem-cell research. In short, Bush never vetoed a bill on fiscal grounds during the entire time that the Republicans held majorities in the House and/or the Senate.

109. See "Big-Government Conservatives," *Washington Post*, August 15, 2005.

110. Birnbaum, "Congress Pigs Out."

111. A classic discussion of this last problem is James Q. Wilson, "Crime and the Criminologists," *Commentary*, July 1974.

Chapter 6: You Can't Nickel and Dime Your Way to a Realignment

1. Alexander Hamilton, James Madison, and John Jay, *The Federalist Papers*, ed. Clinton Rossiter (New York: Signet Classic, 2003 [1788]), 412.

2. Karl Rove, *Courage and Consequence: My Life as a Conservative in the Fight* (New York: Simon & Schuster, 2010), 238–239.

3. A similar question was included in the 2008 and 2012 exit polls, but "education" was not among the issues listed.

4. The polls referred to are, respectively: Lake Snell Perry & Associates survey for *Education Week*, January 22–28, 2003 (n=1050, registered voters only); Hart and Teeter Research Companies survey for the Educational Testing Service, May 25-June 2, 2004 (n=1309); and Winston Group survey for New Models, July 23–24, 2003 (n=1000, registered voters only).

5. I have looked through five major books on the 2004 election, and have found not a single reference in any of them to the Bush space initiative. See James W. Ceaser and Andrew E. Busch, *Red over Blue: The 2004 Elections and American Politics* (Lanham, MD: Rowman & Littlefield, 2005); William Crotty, ed., *A Defining*

Moment: The Presidential Election of 2004 (Armonk, NY: M. E. Sharpe, 2005); Paul R. Abramson, John H. Aldrich, and David W. Rohde, *Change and Continuity in the 2004 Elections* (Washington, DC: CQ Press, 2006); Institute of Politics, *Campaign for President: The Managers Look at 2004* (Lanham, MD: Rowman & Littlefield, 2006); and Michael Nelson, ed., *The Elections of 2004* (Washington, DC: CQ Press, 2005).

6. According to the *Public Papers of the President*, Bush mentioned the space program in just two statements through the remainder of 2004, both of which were fairly short and seem to have been issued as press releases rather than delivered orally by the president himself. See George W. Bush, "Statement on Signing the NASA Flexibility Act of 2004," February 24, 2004, *Public Papers of the President: George W. Bush* (Washington, DC: US Government Printing Office, various years) (hereafter cited as *Bush Public Papers*) 2004, 1:265; and "Statement on the Report of the Commission on Implementation of United States Space Exploration Policy," June 16, 2004, 1:1065. Even on July 21, when Bush posed for pictures with Neal Armstrong, Buzz Aldrin, and Michael Collins on the thirty-fifth anniversary of the first moon landing, he apparently made no attempt to make a pitch for his proposal to return to the moon.

7. See Elisabeth Bumiller and Richard W. Stevenson, "A Trusted Bush Aide to Return, but Not to Washington," *New York Times*, March 28, 2004.

8. See George W. Bush, "Remarks Accepting the Presidential Nomination at the Republican National Convention in New York City," September 2, 2004, *Bush Public Papers*, 2004, 2:1855–1863.

9. This is my own calculation, based on the daily approval numbers reported at www.realclearpolitics.com/epolls/other/obama_vs_bush_election_day_job_approval.html (accessed March 5, 2014).

10. Harris Interactive survey of January 14-15, 2004 (n=1003).

11. As quoted in David E. Sanger, "Bush Puts Tariffs of as Much as 30% on Steel Imports," *New York Times*, March 6, 2002.

12. Richard W. Stevenson, "Steel Tariffs Weaken Bush's Global Hand," *New York Times*, March 6, 2002.

13. As quoted in "Steel Thyself, Karl Rove," *Wall Street Journal*, August 6, 2003.

14. I am implicitly drawing here on the framework for analyzing group interests and public policy first presented in James Q. Wilson, *Political Organizations* (Princeton, NJ: Princeton University Press, 1995 [1974]), chap. 16.

15. Neil King Jr. and Robert Guy Matthews, "So Far, Steel Tariffs Do Little of What President Envisioned," *Wall Street Journal*, September 13, 2002.

16. Neil King Jr. and Robert Guy Matthews, "America Feels Pain of Tariffs on Steel Imports," *Wall Street Journal*, May 31, 2002.

17. Mike Allen and Jonathan Weisman, "Steel Tariffs Appear to Have Backfired on Bush," *Washington Post*, September 19, 2002.

18. For references to some of these estimates, see "Man of Steel?" *Wall Street Journal*, March 4, 2002; and Joseph Kahn and Richard W. Stevenson, "Treasury's Chief Is Said to Fault Steel Tariff Move," *New York Times*, March 16, 2002.

19. Allen and Weisman, "Steel Tariffs Appear."

20. See, for example, David Hosansky, "Farm Subsidies," *CQ Researcher*, May 17, 2002; and Mike Allen, "Bush Signs Bill Providing Big Farm Subsidy Increases," *Washington Post*, May 14, 2002.

21. The quotation is taken from "Longstanding Farm Laws Rewritten," *Congressional Quarterly Almanac 1996* (Washington, DC: Congressional Quarterly, 1997), 3–15.

22. See Gebe Martinez, "Farm Bill Now Tops Senate Agenda but GOP Is Likely to Filibuster," *CQ Weekly*, December 1, 2001, 2840.

23. Richard E. Cohen and Corine Hegland, "Farm Bill Winners and Losers," *National Journal*, May 11, 2002, 1390.

24. Republican National Committee, *Growth and Opportunity Project*, 4, 8, at http://goproject.gop.com/ (accessed February 28, 2014).

25. See, in particular, Steve Sailer, "Bush Didn't Win 44% of Hispanic Vote—The Smoking Exit Poll," November 10, 2014, www.vdare.com/articles/bush-didnt-win -44-of-hispanic-vote-the-smoking-exit-poll; Ruy Teixeira, "44 Percent of Hispanics Voted for Bush?" November 24, 2004, www.alternet.org/story/20606/44_percent _of_hispanics_voted_for_bush; and Roberto Suro, Richard Fry, and Jeffrey Passel, "Hispanics and the 2004 Election: Population, Electorate and Voters," Pew Hispanic Center Report, June 27, 2005, www.pewhispanic.org/2005/06/27/hispanics-and -the-2004-election.

26. See Henry Flores, "The 2004 WCVI National Latino Election Day Exit Poll," at http://wcvi.org/latino_voter_research/polls/national/2004/flores.html (accessed February 14, 2014).

27. See, for example, Steven Malanga, "Hispanic Voting Myths," *City Journal*, Autumn 2007, at www.city-journal.org/html/17_4_sndgso2.html.

28. See Suro, Fry, and Passel, "Hispanics and the 2004 Election," 11–13.

29. See Sailer, "Bush Didn't Win 44%"; and Teixeira, "44 Percent of Hispanics." For other analyses of how well George W. Bush "really" fared with Hispanic voters in 2004, see Richard S. Dunham, "Did Hispanics Really Surge to Bush?" *Business Week*, November 22, 2004; Darryl L. Fears, "Pollsters Debate Hispanics' Presidential Voting," *Washington Post*, November 26, 2004; Richard Nadler, "Bush's 'Real' Hispanic Numbers," *National Review*, December 8, 2004, at http://old.national review.com/comment/nadler200412080811.asp; John F. Harris, "Bush's Hispanic Vote Dissected," *Washington Post*, December 26, 2004; and David L. Leal, Matt A. Barreto, Jongho Lee, and Rodolfo O. de la Garza, "The Latino Vote in the 2004 Election," *PS: Political Science and Politics* 38 (January 2005): 41–49.

30. For a good critique of the Velasquez Institute poll, see Warren J. Mitofsky, "Comment on 'The Latino Vote in 2004,'" *PS: Political Science and Politics* 38 (April 2005): 187–188.

31. As one piece of evidence on this point, in both 2000 and 2004, Bush fared substantially better among Hispanic respondents who were interviewed in English than among those who were interviewed in Spanish. See, for example, the data reported in Kate Kenski and Russell Tisinger, "Hispanic Voters in the 2000 and 2004 Presidential General Elections," *Presidential Studies Quarterly* 36 (June 2006), table 2, 197.

32. Actually, given the argument made earlier about the distinctive political attitudes held by Hispanics who live in heavily Hispanic areas, it is likely that the Velazquez Institute poll *over*estimates the percentage of 2004 Hispanic voters who based their vote on immigration policy.

33. For those interested in replicating my results, I am referring here to responses no. 1016 and 1017 in the ANES coding scheme. There is also a code—no. 1247—which indicates that the candidate or party in question was good for Hispanics generally, but without mentioning any specific issue. Exactly one Hispanic respondent in the 2004 ANES gave this as a reason for liking Bush.

34. In a similar way, Marisa A. Abrajano, R. Michael Alvarez, and Jonathan Nagler have concluded that Bush ran well among Hispanics in 2004 due to the greater-than-usual salience of moral values and national security issues. Unfortunately for my purposes, their conclusion is derived from an analysis of the 2004 NEP data, which, as noted in the text, did not include immigration policy on its "most important issue" checklist. But if the Velasquez Institute poll's finding that only 3 percent of Hispanics thought immigration to be the most important issue is anywhere close to being accurate, Abrajano, Alvarez, and Nagler's results would have been substantially unaffected if immigration had been listed in the NEP poll. See "The Hispanic Vote in the 2004 Presidential Election: Insecurity and Moral Concerns," *Journal of Politics* 70 (April 2008): 368–382.

35. See George Hawley, "Pro-Immigration Congressional Republicans Do Not Perform Better among Latino Voters," Center for Immigration Studies Backgrounder, February 2013, https://cis.org/sites/cis.org/files/hawley-latino-voters.pdf.

36. Both quotations are from James G. Gimpel, "Immigration Policy Opinion and the 2016 Presidential Vote: Issue Relevance in the Trump-Clinton Election," Center for Immigration Studies Backgrounder, December 2017, https://cis.org/sites/default/files/2017–12/gimpel-2016-vote.pdf.

37. Gallup survey of October 14–16, 2004 (n = 1,013).

38. Pew Research Center survey of October 16–19, 2008, likely voters only (n = 3,016).

39. CBS News/*New York Times* survey of January 12–17, 2012 (n = 1,154).

40. CNBC survey of March 19–22, 2012, conducted by Hart and McInturff Research Companies (n = 836). According to the Roper Center's iPOLL database, prior to this poll, there were thirteen national survey questions from 2009 to 2012 in which respondents were asked whether Bush or Obama was more to blame for the federal deficit. (Some of these questions, like the CBS News/*New York Times* poll quoted in the text, also allowed respondents to blame other entities, such as Congress or "Wall Street banks and financial companies.") In all thirteen instances, more people blamed Bush than Obama.

41. The same point has been made in Molly Ball, "There's Nothing Better than a Scared, Rich Candidate," *Atlantic*, October 2016, 54–63.

Chapter 7: When an Administration Is in Crisis and the President Refuses to Acknowledge It

1. This definition is taken from *Merriam-Webster's Collegiate Dictionary*, 11th ed. (Springfield, MA: Merriam-Webster, 2009), 296.

2. In brief, "groupthink" is a condition where members of a small "in-group" strive so hard to preserve their own internal cohesion that it overrides "their motivation to realistically appraise alternative courses of action." For an argument that groupthink has been the cause of many presidential policy mistakes, see Irving L. Janis, *Groupthink: Psychological Studies of Policy Decisions and Fiascoes* (Boston: Houghton Mifflin, 1982). The definition quoted above appears on p. 9.

3. Confirmation bias is the tendency to search for, interpret, favor, and recall information in a way that supports a person's prior beliefs, opinions, and preferences. For a good discussion of the general phenomenon as well as the claim that it has sometimes led to bad public policy decisions, see Raymond S. Nickerson, "Confirmation Bias: A Ubiquitous Phenomenon in Many Guises," *Review of General Psychology* 2 (June 1998): 175–220. Though she never uses the term confirmation bias, many of the examples Barbara W. Tuchman discusses would clearly seem to fit the description. See Tuchman, *The March of Folly: From Troy to Vietnam* (New York: Random House, 2014).

4. Some might argue that Clinton's real problem was that he put forward a complicated, big-government health-care plan based on an untested theory about how to control health-care costs. But, of course, it was his wife's task force that developed this plan, while most of the president's more experienced advisors—including Lloyd Bentsen, Leon Panetta, Donna Shalala, and Alice Rivlin—were largely excluded from the deliberations. See, for example, the discussion in Haynes Johnson and David S. Broder, *The System: The American Way of Politics at the Breaking Point* (Boston: Little, Brown, 1996).

5. The New Hampshire primary was on March 12, 1968; Johnson's nationally televised address, in which he announced that he was "taking the first step to de-escalate the conflict," came on March 31. The connection between these two events is discussed in Don Oberdorfer, *Tet!* (Garden City, NY: Doubleday & Company, 1971), 275–277, 293–294, 299–302.

6. A number of recent presidents have done their best to disguise their political roots. Ronald Reagan in particular often sought to portray himself as just a concerned citizen who had made a brief detour into politics—"a 'citizen-politician' who had answered a call to public duty" and "would return to his basic calling after serving." But the facts of Reagan's biography tell a different story. Though Reagan had a long career in movies before he first sought public office, he was, particularly by the standards of the 1940s and 1950s, a very political member of the acting profession. As Reagan's most perceptive biographer has noted, "Despite his own disclaimers, Reagan has been a political person all his life." See Lou Cannon, *Reagan* (New York: G. P. Putnam's Sons, 1982), 71–72. There is, in any event, no doubt that politics was Reagan's principal occupation in the fourteen years before he was elected president.

7. For a detailed account of this episode and of Rove's role in it, see Peter Baker, *Days of Fire: Bush and Cheney in the White House* (New York: Doubleday, 2013), 409.

8. Those who think I am exaggerating here should consult Howard Zinn's *A People's History of the United States* (New York: HarperCollins, 1999). Just as I have suggested in the text, Zinn takes a highly critical view of literally *every* war in which the United States has been involved. The War of 1812, he asserts, "was not (as usually depicted in American textbooks) just a war against England for survival, but a war for the expansion of the new nation, into Florida, into Canada, into Indian territory" (p. 127). The Civil War was "not a clash of peoples . . . but of elites. The northern elite wanted economic expansion—free land, free labor, a free market, a high protective tariff for manufacturers, a bank of the United States" (189). American participation in World War II was largely an exercise in hypocrisy, since our record for aggressive military interventions in foreign countries and mistreatment of minorities was not much different than Nazi Germany's (408–409). Moreover, the United States had "clearly provoked the war with Japan," including the attack on Pearl Harbor, by imposing an embargo on scrap iron and oil in the summer of 1941, "a clear and potent threat to Japan's very existence" (411). The two original participants in the Korean War, North and South Korea, were morally indistinguishable; the only noteworthy effect of US involvement "was to reduce Korea, North and South, to a shambles, in three years of bombing and shelling" (427–428). Similar or even harsher judgments are rendered about the US role in the Spanish-American War (302–312), World War I (359–374), and the Vietnam War (469–501). Lest one think that Zinn assumes this stance because he is a pacifist, he offers a quite positive assessment of the Chinese civil war that brought Mao Tse-tung and the Communists to power in 1949. The Communist movement had "enormous mass support." When the war was over, China had "the closest thing, in the long history of that ancient country, to a people's government, independent of outside control" (427).

9. The best contemporary statement of the reasons for invading Iraq, which one hopes will be required reading for all historians who choose to write about that conflict, is Kenneth M. Pollack, *The Threatening Storm: The Case for Invading Iraq* (New York: Random House, 2002).

10. This curious incident is described in Pollack, *Threatening Storm*, 68–70.

11. See, among many others, Thomas E. Ricks, *Fiasco: The American Military Adventure in Iraq* (New York: Penguin Books, 2007); Michael R. Gordon and Bernard E. Trainor, *Cobra II: The Inside Story of the Invasion and Occupation of Iraq* (New York: Pantheon Books, 2006), especially chap. 6; Bob Woodward, *State of Denial* (New York: Simon & Schuster, 2006); Larry Diamond, *Squandered Victory: The American Occupation and the Bungled Effort to Bring Democracy to Iraq* (New York: Times Books, 2005); Lou Cannon and Carl M. Cannon, *Reagan's Disciple: George W. Bush's Troubled Quest for a Presidential Legacy* (New York: PublicAffairs, 2008), chap. 7; Terry H. Anderson, *Bush's Wars* (New York: Oxford University Press, 2011), chaps. 2–4; David Rieff, "Blueprint for a Mess," *New York Times Magazine*, November 2, 2003, 28; and James Fallows, "Blind into Baghdad," *Atlantic*, January 2004. Even Stephen F. Knott, whose book is intended to defend Bush against the

criticisms of other historians, is unwilling to endorse the conduct of the postwar occupation in Iraq, instead conceding that the occupation was based on "an overly optimistic" notion of how easy it would be to build a "functioning democracy" in Iraq and criticizing Bush for his excessive loyalty to Donald Rumsfeld. See Knott, *Rush to Judgment: George W. Bush, the War on Terror, and His Critics* (Lawrence: University Press of Kansas, 2012), 144, 142.

12. Both quotations are taken from Ricks, *Fiasco*, 111 and 109–110. The second person quoted is Lt. Gen. Joseph Kellogg. The lack of planning for the postwar occupation is also a frequent theme in Baker, *Days of Fire*, 207–208, 221, 224–225, and 246.

13. Michael R. Gordon, "The Strategy to Secure Iraq Did Not Foresee a 2nd War," *New York Times*, October 19, 2004.

14. See, for example, the Rand Corporation study quoted in Ricks, *Fiasco*, 78–79.

15. This incident is recounted in Woodward, *State of Denial*, 126–129; Gordon and Trainor, *Cobra II*, 158–159; and Ricks, *Fiasco*, 102–104. Garner was also ordered to remove a second State Department employee, Meghan O'Sullivan, but Rumsfeld later relented.

16. Baker, *Days of Fire*, 285.

17. The quotation is from Diamond, *Squandered Victory*, 299. See also Cannon and Cannon, *Reagan's Disciple*, 199–200.

18. As quoted in Rieff, "Blueprint."

19. Anderson, *Bush's Wars*, 152.

20. See especially Diamond, *Squandered Victory*, 39–45.

21. This is a major theme in Diamond, chap. 10.

22. Anderson, *Bush's Wars*, 153.

23. See United Nations Security Council, Resolution 1483 (2003), at www.un .org/Docs/journal/asp/ws.asp?m=s/res/1483(2003).

24. The polls, which were conducted by the Iraqi Centre for Research and Strategic Studies, are discussed in Diamond, *Squandered Victory*, 51.

25. Eric Schmitt and David E. Sanger, "Looting Disrupts Detailed U.S. Plan to Restore Iraq," *New York Times*, May 19, 2003.

26. Diamond, *Squandered Victory*, 305.

27. Probably the most preposterous example of this sort of thinking occurred just before the war began, when one outside expert argued for the need to pay Iraqi civil servants after the war so they would continue to do their jobs—a proposal that Rumsfeld strongly resisted. When someone else suggested that there would be riots if the civil servants didn't get paid, Rumsfeld reportedly replied that "this could be used as leverage to get the Europeans to pick up the burden." See Diamond, *Squandered Victory*, 31.

28. Most of the details noted here, including the quotation from Colonel T. X. Hammes, are taken from Ricks, *Fiasco*, 216. See also Woodward, *State of Denial*, 245–248.

29. Baker, *Days of Fire*, 332–333.

30. Baker, 494.

31. For the full text of the interview, see www.foxnews.com/story/0,2933
,98006,00.html (accessed January 18, 2012) (emphasis added).

32. As quoted in Cannon and Cannon, *Reagan's Disciple*, 249.

33. As quoted in Woodward, *State of Denial*, 326.

34. Baker, *Days of Fire*, 452.

35. As quoted in Peter Baker, "A President Besieged and Isolated, Yet at Ease,"
Washington Post, July 2, 2007.

36. Karl Rove, *Courage and Consequence: My Life as a Conservative in the Fight*
(New York: Simon & Schuster, 2010), 477.

37. Rove, *Courage and Consequence*, 476.

38. More precisely, Mueller found that support for the war declined with the
logarithm of the cumulative number of American casualties. As the total number
of casualties increased by a factor of ten, support for the war decreased by about 15
percentage points. In other words, "the public is sensitive to relatively small losses
at the start of the war but only to rather large ones toward its end." See John E.
Mueller, *War, Presidents, and Public Opinion* (New York: John Wiley & Sons, 1973),
59–62.

39. As noted in the text, Mueller's study was based almost entirely on an analysis
of polling data from the Korean and Vietnam wars. He did take a brief look at similar data from World War II and noted that they seemed to follow a different pattern;
however, he made no real attempt to explore or account for the differences. See
War, Presidents, and Public Opinion, 63–65. In a later book, Mueller argued that the
Korea-Vietnam pattern also applied to public attitudes about the 1991 Gulf War, but
that the drop-off in support was much smaller because the United States suffered
substantially fewer casualties. See John Mueller, *Policy and Opinion in the Gulf War*
(Chicago: University of Chicago Press, 1994), 76–78.

40. The literature on this subject is voluminous. Among the most important contributions that would have been available before the beginning of the Iraq war are
Bruce W. Jentleson, "The Pretty Prudent Public: Post Post-Vietnam American Opinion on the Use of Military Force," *International Studies Quarterly* 36 (March 1992):
49–74; Andrew Kohut and Robert C. Toth, "Arms and the Public," *Foreign Affairs* 73
(November/December 1994): 47–61; Steven Kull, "Misreading the Public Mood,"
Bulletin of the Atomic Scientists 51 (March/April 1995): 55–59; Steven Kull, "What
the Public Knows That Washington Doesn't," *Foreign Policy* 101 (Winter 1995–1996):
102–115; Eric V. Larson, *Casualties and Consensus: The Historical Role of Casualties
in Domestic Support for U.S. Military Operations* (Santa Monica, CA: RAND, 1996);
Bruce W. Jentleson and Rebecca L. Britton, "Still Pretty Prudent: Post-Cold War
American Public Opinion on the Use of Military Force," *Journal of Conflict Resolu-
tion* 42 (August 1998): 395–417; Peter D. Feaver and Christopher Gelpi, "A Look at
. . . Casualty Aversion: How Many Deaths are Acceptable? A Surprising Answer,"
Washington Post, November 7, 1999; James Burk, "Public Support for Peacekeep-
ing in Lebanon and Somalia: Assessing the Casualties Hypothesis," *Political Science
Quarterly* 114 (Spring 1999): 53–78; Philip Everts, "When the Going Gets Rough:
Does the Public Support the Use of Military Force?" *World Affairs* 162 (Winter

2000): 91–107; and Louis Klarevas, "The 'Essential Domino' of Military Operations: American Public Opinion and the Use of Force," *International Studies Perspectives* 3 (November 2002): 417–437. For a good review of this literature, see Christopher Gelpi, Peter D. Feaver, and Jason Reifler, "Success Matters: Casualty Sensitivity and the War in Iraq," *International Security* 30 (Winter 2005–2006): 7–46.

41. In addition to the works listed in note 11 above, also see three books by Bob Woodward: *Bush at War* (New York: Simon & Schuster, 2002); *Plan of Attack* (New York: Simon & Schuster, 2004); and *The War Within: A Secret White House History, 2006–2008* (New York: Simon & Schuster, 2008).

42. See, in particular, Anderson, *Bush's Wars*, 104; and Woodward, *Plan of Attack*, 200, 333.

43. The memo is mentioned in Gordon and Trainor, *Cobra II*, 152. On Rove's reconsideration, see Woodward, *Plan of Attack*, 430.

44. See Woodward, *State of Denial*, 362; and Baker, *Days of Fire*, 453.

45. The best account of these early efforts to reexamine American strategy in Iraq is Woodward, *War Within*, chaps. 1–20.

46. Woodward, *War Within*, 102.

47. John M. Broder, "Bush Works to Solidify Base with a Defense of Rumsfeld," *New York Times*, November 2, 2006. Bush and his top aides would later claim that the 2006 elections had no effect on the decision to accept Rumsfeld's resignation. See George W. Bush, "The President's News Conference," November 8, 2006, *Public Papers of the President of the United States: George W. Bush* (hereafter cited as *Bush Public Papers)* (Washington, DC: US Government Printing Office, various years) 2006, 2:2055; Jim Rutenberg, "Removal of Rumsfeld Dates Back to Summer," *New York Times,* November 10, 2006; and Woodward, *War Within,* 196–197, 205. Maybe, but there are some grounds for skepticism. An important part of Bush's self-image, as we have seen, was that he did the "right thing" regardless of politics. Claiming that he had decided to replace Rumsfeld before the 2006 elections allowed him to preserve this opinion. One wonders if Bush would have stuck with the decision to replace Rumsfeld—which had not yet been made public—had the Republicans suffered only minor losses in the 2006 elections.

48. Bush, "President's News Conference," November 8, 2006, *Bush Public Papers*, 2006, 2:2058.

49. George W. Bush, "Address to the Nation on Military Operations in Iraq," January 10, 2007, *Bush Public Papers*, 2007, 1:16–20.

50. The changes in on-the-ground military strategy received less attention at the time but were clearly critical to the results documented in table 7.2. For further details, see, in particular, Woodward, *War Within*, chaps. 32–41; Michael R. Gordon and Bernard E. Trainor, *The Endgame: The Inside Story of the Struggle for Iraq, from George W. Bush to Barack Obama* (New York: Pantheon Books, 2012), chaps. 14–21; and Thomas E. Ricks, *The Gamble: General David Petraeus and the American Military Adventure in Iraq, 2006–2008* (New York: Penguin Press, 2009), chaps. 1–4.

51. US Government Accountability Office, "Securing, Stabilizing, and Rebuilding Iraq," GAO-07-1195, September 2007, at www.gao.gov/new.items/d071195.pdf.

52. See, for example, Karen DeYoung and Thomas E. Ricks, "Report Finds Little Progress on Iraq Goals; GAO Draft at Odds with White House," *Washington Post*, August 30, 2007; and Associated Press, "Congressional Body Finds Iraq Fails to Meet Most Goals Laid Out by Lawmakers," *New York Times*, August 30, 2007.

53. See Michael E. O'Hanlon and Jason E. Campbell, "Iraq Index: Tracking Variables of Reconstruction & Security in Post-Saddam Iraq," July 31, 2008, p. 13; and December 18, 2008, p. 14, both available at www.brookings.edu/about/centers /saban/iraq-index.

Chapter 8: Never Forget That War Is a Political Endeavor

1. As quoted in Richard L. Berke, "Bush Adviser Suggests War as Campaign Theme," *New York Times*, January 19, 2002.

2. See especially Eliot A. Cohen, *Supreme Command: Soldiers, Statesmen, and Leadership in Wartime* (New York: Free Press, 2002); Andrew J. Polsky, *Elusive Victories: The American President at War* (New York: Oxford University Press, 2012); James M. McPherson, *Tried by War: Abraham Lincoln as Commander in Chief* (New York: Penguin, 2008); and Joseph E. Persico, *Roosevelt's Centurions: FDR and the Commanders He Led to Victory in World War II* (New York: Random House, 2013). Though the essays in it are not as analytical, see also Joseph G. Dawson III, ed., *Commanders in Chief: Presidential Leadership in Modern Wars* (Lawrence: University Press of Kansas, 1993).

3. Polsky, *Elusive Victories*, 323.

4. The italicized phrase is quoted from Polsky, 25. Persico makes the same point when he examines Roosevelt's performance as a "home front leader charged with motivating, marshalling, and inspiring a people at war." *Roosevelt's Centurions*, xvi.

5. Carl von Clausewitz, *On War*, trans. Michael Howard and Peter Paret (Princeton, NJ: Princeton University Press, 1976), 87.

6. Though Bush had repeatedly deplored "nation building" during his 2000 presidential campaign, his plan to "transform Iraq into a liberal society that would be a beacon to the oppressed masses of the Middle East" required exactly that. But his defense secretary, Donald Rumsfeld, was never committed to this goal and instead believed that the US military should withdraw from Iraq as soon as possible and allow the Iraqis to work out their own destiny—even though such an approach would almost certainly not have produced a functioning democracy, at least in the short run. Yet Bush never seemed to notice the divergence, much less act to correct it. For a good discussion of the problem, see Polsky, *Elusive Victories*, chap. 5. (The phrase quoted above appears on 288.)

7. John G. Nicolay and John Hay, *Abraham Lincoln: A History* (New York: Century, 1890), 4:359–360.

8. George W. Bush, "Address Before a Joint Session of the Congress on the United States Response to the Terrorist Attacks of September 11," September 20, 2001, in *Public Papers of the President of the United States: George W. Bush* (hereafter cited as *Bush Public Papers*) (Washington, DC: US Government Printing Office, various years), 2001, 2:1141–1142 (emphasis added).

9. For a good, if somewhat dated, discussion of the controversy, see Richard N. Current, *The Lincoln Nobody Knows* (New York: Hill and Wang, 1958), chap. 6.

10. See Abraham Lincoln, "First Inaugural Address—Final Text," March 4, 1861, in *The Collected Works of Abraham Lincoln*, ed. Roy P. Basler [hereafter cited as *Collected Works*] (New Brunswick, NJ: Rutgers University Press, 1953), 4:263.

11. See William G. Mayer, "Was the Civil War a Just War? Lincoln's Case against Secession," unpublished manuscript.

12. McPherson, *Tried by War*, 7.

13. McPherson, 22.

14. Cohen, *Supreme Command*, 37. Cohen also argues that the military performance of the politician-generals was better than many historians have recognized; see 35–37.

15. Lincoln's skill as an "astute and dexterous operator of the political machine" is a major theme in David Herbert Donald, *Lincoln Reconsidered: Essays on the Civil War Era* (New York: Random House, 2001), chap. 12.

16. See "Letter to His Mother," December 1, 1861, in *The Correspondence of John Lothrop Motley*, ed. George William Curtis [hereafter cited as *Motley Correspondence*] (New York: Harper & Brothers, 1889), 46.

17. "Reply to Emancipation Memorial Presented by Chicago Christians of All Denominations," September 13, 1862, in Basler, *Collected Works*, 5:422. For a very similar argument, see John Lothrop Motley, "Letter to His Second Daughter," January 13, 1862, in *Motley Correspondence*, 2:54–55. It should be noted that the need to prevent foreign intervention on behalf of the Confederacy was also used as an argument *against* emancipation. Some British leaders, it was claimed, believed that emancipation would lead to a violent insurrection by the freed slaves and would therefore do their best to prevent it. For a thorough discussion of the issue, see Louis P. Masur, *Lincoln's Hundred Days: The Emancipation Proclamation and the War for the Union* (Cambridge, MA: Harvard University Press, 2012), 139–150; and Allen C. Guelzo, *Lincoln's Emancipation Proclamation: The End of Slavery in America* (New York: Simon & Schuster, 2004), 224–225.

18. All quotations from the Emancipation Proclamation are based on the text reported in Basler, *Collected Works*, 6:28–31. Slavery was also still legal in Delaware in 1863, but most of the state's slaves had been freed by that time and there was little support for secession.

19. William Seward, as quoted in McPherson, *Tried by War*, 109.

20. As quoted in George C. Gorham, *Life and Public Services of Edwin M. Stanton* (Boston: Houghton, Mifflin: 1899), 2:220–221.

21. Guelzo, *Lincoln's Emancipation Proclamation,* 225 (emphasis in original).

22. Henry Adams Letter to Charles Francis Adams, January 23, 1863, in *A Cycle of Adams Letters: 1861–1865*, ed. Worthington Chauncey Ford (Boston: Houghton Mifflin, 1920), 1:243.

23. For a good discussion of these four letters and of Lincoln's public letters more generally, see Guelzo, *Lincoln's Emancipation Proclamation*, 203–212.

24. See especially Harold Holzer, *Lincoln and the Power of the Press: The War for*

Public Opinion (New York: Simon & Schuster, 2014); and Harry J. Maihafer, *War of Words: Abraham Lincoln and the Civil War Press* (Washington, DC: Brassey's, 2001).

25. The fullest account of this episode is in Holzer, *Lincoln and the Power of the Press*, 186–194. At the time, it was not especially unusual for politicians to own or edit newspapers. According to Maihafer, Hannibal Hamlin, Lincoln's vice president, and four members of Lincoln's original cabinet "had been editors at one time or another." *War of Words*, 35. What is noteworthy about Lincoln's ownership of the *Illinois Staats-Anzeiger* was that he kept it secret.

26. Roosevelt's performance before September 1939 is, in my judgment, far less commendable. His actions and statements during the Munich crisis of September and October 1938 are particularly deplorable. He sent a telegram to both Hitler and Chamberlain urging them to find a "peaceful, fair, and constructive settlement," but he offered no specific suggestions and also made clear that the United States would "assume no obligations in the conduct of the present negotiations." FDR supported Chamberlain's decision to go to Munich for one last set of discussions with Hitler, and after the agreement had been finalized and the Sudetenland had been handed over to the Nazis, Roosevelt sent a private message to Chamberlain saying, "I fully share your hope and belief that there exists today the greatest opportunity in years for the establishment of a new order based on justice and on law." See Robert A. Divine, *The Reluctant Belligerent: American Entry into World War II* (New York: John Wiley & Sons, 1965), 54–55.

27. Almost all of these steps are discussed in any good analysis of American foreign policy in the years preceding World War II. My own list draws especially on Divine, *Reluctant Belligerent*; Persico, *Roosevelt's Centurions*, chaps. 1–4; Kenneth S. Davis, *FDR: Into the Storm 1937–1940* (New York: Random House, 1993), chaps. 13–15; and Davis, *FDR: The War President 1940–1943* (New York: Random House, 2000), chaps. 2–6.

28. All quotations from Roosevelt's September 11, 1941, speech are based on the text given in *FDR's Fireside Chats*, ed. Russell D. Buhite and David W. Levy (Norman: University of Oklahoma Press, 1992), 188–196.

29. Davis, *FDR: The War President*, 172 (emphasis in original). Davis, I think one can say, is generally sympathetic with this criticism.

30. As quoted in Davis, *FDR: The War President*, 253.

31. Results are taken from Gallup surveys no. 243, July 31–August 4, 1941; and no. 242, July 24–29, 1941. Sample size for both surveys was approximately 1500.

32. Persico, *Roosevelt's Centurions*, 160.

33. These numbers are based on the list of fireside chats given in Buhite and Levy, *FDR's Fireside Chats*.

34. For a nice sampling of statements by Bush, Cheney, et al. that progress was being made in Iraq, see Michael Isikoff and David Corn, *Hubris: The Inside Story of Spin, Scandal, and the Selling of the Iraq War* (New York: Crown, 2006), 313, 315, 321, 336, 339, 383, 395, and 413.

35. The Success Offensive, the Tet Offensive, and the impact that both had on American public opinion are analyzed in William G. Mayer, *The Changing American*

Mind: How and Why American Public Opinion Changed between 1960 and 1988 (Ann Arbor: University of Michigan Press, 1992), 234–246.

36. The attempt to increase presidential power, especially with respect to foreign policy and the war on terrorism, is a major theme in many books on the Bush presidency. See, in particular, Charlie Savage, *Takeover: The Return of the Imperial Presidency and the Subversion of American Democracy* (New York: Little, Brown, 2007); and James P. Pfiffner, *Power Play: The Bush Presidency and the Constitution* (Washington, DC: Brookings Institution Press, 2008).

37. The final clauses in this sentence are an almost exact quotation of the advice that Cheney gave to incoming White House chief of staff James Baker in mid-November 1980. See Savage, *Takeover*, 43.

38. This is a major theme in Andrew Rudalevige, *The New Imperial Presidency: Reviving Presidential Power after Watergate* (Ann Arbor: University of Michigan Press, 2005).

39. See Jackson's concurring opinion in *Youngstown Sheet & Tube Co. v. Sawyer*, 342 U.S. 579 (1952), at 635.

40. Both officials are quoted anonymously in Mike Allen and Juliet Eilperin, "Bush Aides Say Iraq War Needs No Hill Vote," *Washington Post,* August 22, 2002.

41. All quotations are from George W. Bush, "Remarks Following a Meeting with Congressional Leaders and an Exchange with Reporters," September 4, 2002, *Bush Public Papers,* 2002, 2:1523–1524.

42. Karlyn Bowman, "Public Opinion on the War in Iraq," March 19, 2009, 3, at www.aei.org/publication/public-opinion-on-the-war-in-iraq/.

43. See Gallup surveys of September 24–26, 2004 (n=1006) and October 14–16, 2004 (n=1013).

44. The Annenberg data are reported in Bowman, "Public Opinion on the War," 163.

45. George W. Bush, "Detention, Treatment, and Trial of Certain Non-Citizens in the War against Terrorism," Military Order of November 13, 2001, at https://georgewbush-whitehouse.archives.gov/news/releases/2001/11/20011113-27.html.

46. See Department of Defense, "Military Commission Order No. 1," March 21, 2002, at news.findlaw.com/hdocs/docs/dod/dod032102milcomord1.pdf.

47. See *Hamdan v. Rumsfeld*, 548 U.S. 557 (2006). The quotation from the Geneva Conventions is at 630.

48. All quotations are taken from the Military Commissions Act of 2006, https://www.loc.gov/rr/frd/Military_Law/pdf/PL-109-366.pdf (accessed April 17, 2017).

49. Scott Shane and Adam Liptak, "Shifting Power to a President," *New York Times*, September 30, 2006.

50. The partisan breakdown of the votes is reported in *CQ Weekly,* October 2, 2006, 2645; and October 9, 2006, 2712.

51. The history and import of the Foreign Intelligence Surveillance Act of 1978 are discussed in Pfiffner, *Power Play*, 172–174; and Rudalevige, *New Imperial Presidency*, 109–113.

52. See Peter Baker and Charles Babington, "Bush Addresses Uproar over Spying," *Washington Post*, December 20, 2005.

53. James Risen and Eric Lichtblau, "Bush Lets U.S. Spy on Callers without Courts," *New York Times*, December 16, 2005.

54. See, for example, Elisabeth Bumiller, "Bush Sees No Need for Law to Approve Eavesdropping," *New York Times*, January 27, 2006. A detailed examination of the administration's arguments can be found in Pfiffner, *Power Play*, 174–182.

55. Sheryl Gay Stolberg and David E. Sanger, "Facing Pressure, White House Seeks Approval for Spying," *New York Times*, February 20, 2006.

56. Adam Liptak and Eric Lichtblau, "U.S. Judge Finds Wiretap Actions Violate the Law," *New York Times*, August 18, 2006.

57. Eric Lichtblau and David Johnston, "Court to Oversee U.S. Wiretapping in Terror Cases," *New York Times*, January 18, 2007.

58. James Risen, "Legislation Seeks to Ease Rules on Domestic Spying," *New York Times*, April 14, 2007.

59. The FISA court ruling is discussed in Eric Lichtblau and Mark Mazzetti, "Broader Spying Authority Advances in Congress," *New York Times*, August 4, 2007.

60. James Risen, "Bush Signs Law to Widen Reach for Wiretapping," *New York Times*, August 6, 2007.

61. Pfiffner, *Power Play*, 191.

62. Tim Starks, "Democrats Seek Last Word on FISA Bill," *CQ Weekly*, August 13, 2007, 2470.

63. All quoted material is from *2008 CQ Almanac*, 110th Congress, 2nd session (Washington, DC: Congressional Quarterly, 2009), 6–12.

64. *2008 CQ Almanac*, H-146 and S-37.

65. See Savage, *Takeover*, 220–223.

66. As quoted in Joby Warrick and Dan Eggen, "Hill Briefed on Waterboarding in 2002," *Washington Post*, December 9, 2007.

67. George W. Bush, *Decision Points* (New York: Crown Publishers, 2010), 180.

68. The two definitions are taken from Marvin Kalb, "It's Called the Vietnam Syndrome, and It's Back," January 22, 2013, at www.brookings.edu/blogs/up-front/posts/2013/01/22-obama-foreign-policy-kalb; and William Safire, *Safire's New Political Dictionary* (New York: Random House, 1993), 844. Most sources who use the term clearly have a quite similar idea in mind. See, for example, George C. Herring, "The Vietnam Syndrome," in *The Columbia History of the Vietnam War*, ed. David L. Anderson (New York: Columbia University Press, 2011), 409–429; Max Boot, "The Incurable Vietnam Syndrome," *Weekly Standard*, October 19, 2009, at www.weeklystandard.com/Content/Public/Articles/000/000/017/059wcvib.asp#; and Patrick Hagopian, *The Vietnam War in American Memory: Veterans, Memorials, and the Politics of Healing* (Amherst: University of Massachusetts Press, 2009), chap. 1.

This is not, however, the only way the term has been defined. Originally, the phrase was used to refer to a cluster of attitudes and behaviors—including boredom, alienation, and resentment—that were said to characterize soldiers who had just returned from serving in Vietnam. See Ralph Blumenthal, "'Syndrome' Found in Returned G.I.'s," *New York Times*, June 7, 1971; and "What 'Post-Vietnam Syndrome'?" *Science News*, September 29, 1979, 213. More recently, Eliot Cohen has used the Vietnam syndrome to describe the belief that presidents should not second guess or interfere with the strategic and tactical decisions of their top military commanders and advisors. See Cohen, *Supreme Command*, 199–203; and Rich Lowry, "Bush's Vietnam Syndrome," *National Review*, December 27, 2006, at www.nationalreview .com/article/219591/bushs-vietnam-syndrome-rich-lowry.

69. For the exact wording and full results for both questions, see Mayer, *Changing American Mind*, 435.

70. As quoted in Herring, "Vietnam Syndrome," 414.

71. The surveys referred to are: Gallup polls of March 11–14, 1983 (n = 1,558); July 29–August 2, 1983 (n = 1,565); and September 9–12, 1983 (n = 1,574); Harris surveys of April 29–May 1, 1983 (n = 1,250); and August 18–22, 1983 (n = 1,257); and ABC News/*Washington Post* poll of May 11–15, 1983 (n = 1,501).

72. See George H. W. Bush, "Remarks to the American Legislative Exchange Council," March 1, 1991; and George H. W. Bush, "Radio Address to United States Armed Forces Stationed in the Persian Gulf Region," March 1, 1991; both *in Public Papers of the President of the United States: George [H. W.] Bush* (Washington, DC: US Government Printing Office, 1992), 1991, 1:197 and 207.

73. As quoted in Herring, "Vietnam Syndrome," 417.

74. Richard Holbrooke, *To End a War* (New York: Random House, 1998), 217.

75. Boot, "Incurable Vietnam Syndrome."

76. See Opinion Dynamics survey of April 21–22, 1999 (n=942).

77. Herring, "Vietnam Syndrome," 421.

78. My discussion of the Rwandan genocide draws especially on Samantha Power, "Bystanders to Genocide," *Atlantic*, September 2001, 84–108; and Alan J. Kuperman, *The Limits of Humanitarian Intervention: Genocide in Rwanda* (Washington, DC: Brookings Institution Press, 2001).

79. Power, "Bystanders to Genocide," 84.

The number of Rwandan lives that might have been saved by an American intervention is a matter of some dispute. Alan Kuperman has argued that, given the speed with which the genocide transpired, the lack of early information about it, and the inherent delays involved in sending American forces to a Central African country without a modern airport system, most victims would have already been killed by the time US help arrived. But Kuperman does believe that US intervention might have saved between 75,000 and 125,000 lives. See *Limits of Humanitarian Intervention*, chap. 7. He also concludes that the "genocide might have been averted . . . if [the UN assistance mission] had been reinforced several months before the outbreak of violence" (97). Such a reinforcement had in fact been proposed—and the Clinton administration (and others) opposed it. In a 2013 interview, former President Clinton gave his opinion that, "If we'd gone in sooner, I believe we could have saved at least a third of the lives that we lost"—about 270,000 persons. See

"Bill Clinton: We Could Have Saved 300,000 Lives in Rwanda," March 13, 2013, at www.cnbc.com/id/100546207.

80. Bill Clinton, *My Life* (New York: Alfred A. Knopf, 2004), 593.

81. Julie Pace, "Analysis: Obama Crosses Own Red Line with Syrian Deployment," October 31, 2015, at bigstory.ap.org/article/03de1bc8bca74ebc855ccd3c2465b088/analysis-syria-deployment-obama-crosses-own-red-line (accessed November 1, 2015).

Chapter 9: Communication Is Important, but Don't Expect Miracles

1. I am not the only person to notice this pattern. See, among others, Kevin Liptak, "Six Times Obama Blamed the Message, Not the Policy," December 21, 2015, www.cnn.com/2015/12/21/politics/obama-communications-strategy/; and Jenna Lifhits, "8 Times Obama Blamed His Problems on Messaging," January 5, 2016, at freebeacon.com/politics/8-times-obama-blamed-his-problems-on-messaging.

2. As quoted in "Obama, the Salesman: 'Sometimes I Forgot Part of My Job Is Explaining to the American People,'" July 22, 2011, at blogs.abcnews.com/politicalpunch/2011/07/obama-the-salesman-sometimes-i-forgot-part-of-my-job-is-explaining-to-the-american-people.html.

3. From an interview on "CBS This Morning," as quoted in Lindsey Boerma, "Obama Reflects on His Biggest Mistake as President," July 12, 2012, at www.cbsnews.com/obama-reflects-on-his-biggest-mistake-as-president.

4. From an interview with NBC News, as quoted in Sarah Kliff, "VIDEO: Watch Obama (Kinda, Sorta) Apologize to Americans Losing Their Health Plans," November 7, 2013, https://www.washingtonpost.com/2013/11/07/video-watch-obama-kinda-sorta-apologize-to-americans-losing-their-health-plans.

5. From an interview on CBS News, November 9, 2014, as reported in Liptak, "Six Times Obama Blamed."

6. Karen DeYoung, "Obama's Big Push on ISIS Strategy," *Washington Post*, January 1, 2016.

7. Martha Joynt Kumar, *Managing the President's Message: The White House Communications Operation* (Baltimore: Johns Hopkins University Press, 2007), 71–72.

8. Kumar, *Managing the President's Message*, 75.

9. Kumar, 72.

10. See Kumar, 136–137.

11. The two quotations are from, respectively, Mark McKinnon, as quoted in Ron Suskind, "Mrs. Hughes Takes Her Leave," *Esquire*, July 2002; and an unnamed "longtime observer" quoted in David Frum, *The Right Man: The Surprise Presidency of George W. Bush* (New York: Random House, 2003), 39–40. For other, similar comments about the Bush-Hughes relationship, see John Dickerson, "Losing His Mittens," *Time*, May 6, 2002, 30; and Elisabeth Bumiller, "An Influential Bush Adviser, Karen Hughes, Will Resign," *New York Times*, April 24, 2002.

12. Scott McClellan, *What Happened: Inside the Bush White House and Washington's Culture of Deception* (New York: PublicAffairs, 2008), 80.

13. The balance between Rove and Hughes is noted in Frum, *Right Man*, 39–40; McClellan, *What Happened*, 83; and Suskind, "Mrs. Hughes."

14. At the outset of the Bush presidency, Hughes had two titles: director of communications and counselor to the president. On October 2, 2001, she ceded the former title to Dan Bartlett while retaining the latter title. Bartlett did not officially become a counselor to the president until January 2005, at which point Nicolle Wallace became director of communications.

15. See, for example, Elisabeth Bumiller, "Minus One, Bush Inner Circle Is Now Open for Sharp Angling," *New York Times*, July 15, 2002; Bumiller, "Influential Bush Advisor"; and Dickerson, "Losing His Mittens."

16. The books referred to are by Karl Rove, Dick Cheney, Condoleezza Rice, George Tenet, Scott McClellan, Joseph Wilson, Peter Baker, and Michael Isikoff and David Corn. (Full citations can be found elsewhere in the notes to this chapter.) Rice's book does include one enigmatic sentence in which she says that during Bush's trip to Africa immediately after the sixteen words controversy broke, "reporters were peppering Ari [Fleischer, Bush's press secretary] and Karen with questions about Niger and uranium." See Condoleezza Rice, *No Higher Honor: A Memoir of My Years in Washington* (New York: Crown, 2011), 224. While Rice does not indicate which Karen she is referring to, it cannot have been Hughes as Hughes herself has informed me that she did not accompany Bush on his July 2003 trip to Africa. Karen Hughes, personal communication to the author, June 14, 2017.

17. McClellan, *What Happened*, 80 (emphasis added).

18. For further details on both incidents, see Peter Baker, *Days of Fire: Bush and Cheney in the White House* (New York: Doubleday, 2013), 211–212 and 578–579.

19. See, for example, James Moore and Wayne Slater, *Bush's Brain: How Karl Rove Made George W. Bush Presidential* (Hoboken, NJ: John Wiley & Sons, 2003); Lou Dubose, Jan Reid, and Carl M. Cannon, *Boy Genius: Karl Rove, the Brains behind the Remarkable Political Triumph of George W. Bush* (New York: PublicAffairs, 2003); and Craig Unger, *Boss Rove: Inside Karl Rove's Secret Kingdom of Power* (New York: Scribner, 2012).

20. Over the course of a month and a half, the *New York Times* asserted that Ken Lay and other Enron executives had given Bush "more than $550,000," "$623,000," "more than $700,000," and "nearly $2 million." So far as I can determine, no corrections were ever issued or explanations offered for the conflicting numbers. See, respectively, Elisabeth Bumiller, "Enron Contacted Two Cabinet Officials before Collapsing," *New York Times*, January 11, 2002; Don Van Natta Jr., "Aides Deny Any Duty to Tell Bush of Enron Calls," *New York Times*, January 14, 2002; Don Van Natta Jr., "Enron Spread Contributions on Both Sides of the Aisle," *New York Times*, January 21, 2002; and Joseph Kahn and Jeff Gerth, "Collapse May Reshape the Battlefield of Deregulation," *New York Times*, December 4, 2001.

21. On these points, see Van Natta, "Enron Spread Contributions"; John Schwartz and Richard A. Oppel Jr., "Foundation Gives Way on Chief's Big Dream," *New York Times*, November 29, 2001; Jeff Gerth, "Enron and Cheney Aides Met 4 Times," *New*

York Times, January 9, 2002; and Don Van Natta Jr. and Leslie Wayne, "Several Administration Officials Held Enron Shares," *New York Times*, January 18, 2002.

22. See Bumiller, "Enron Contacted Two Cabinet Officials"; and David E. Sanger and David Barboza, "In Shift, Bush Assails Enron over Handling of Collapse," *New York Times*, January 23, 2002.

23. Don Van Natta Jr., "White House Could Be Sued on List Access," *New York Times*, January 26, 2002.

24. The poll results referred to in this paragraph were taken from, respectively, Gallup Poll of February 8–10, 2002 (n = 1,001); CBS News poll of February 24–26, 2002 (n = 861); *Washington Post* poll of February 19–21, 2002 (n = 756); and Princeton Survey Research Associates poll of September 26–27, 2002 (n = 1,011).

25. Though the Sarbanes-Oxley bill passed both houses of Congress by overwhelming margins in July 2002, by the end of the decade many conservatives—and some liberals—were complaining that the bill dramatically increased auditing costs for publicly traded companies and thus denied many small and midsize companies access to public capital markets. See, for example, David Addington, "Congress Should Repeal or Fix Section 404 of the Sarbanes-Oxley Act to Help Create Jobs," Heritage Foundation, September 30, 2011, http://www.heritage.org/node/12725; and Adam Ingeles and Frank Gonzalez, "Dodd-Frank Isn't the Only Financial Law Trump Should Change," *The Hill*, February 3, 2017, http://thehill.com/pundits-blog/finance/317798-dodd-frank-isnt-the-only-financial-law-trump-should-change. For a contrary view, see Greg Farrell, "Sarbanes-Oxley Law Has Been a Pretty Clean Sweep," *USA Today*, July 30, 2007; and Michael W. Peregrine, "Tread Lightly When Tweaking Sarbanes-Oxley," Harvard Law School Forum on Corporate Governance and Financial Regulation, April 12, 2017, https://corpgov.law.harvard.edu/2017/04/12/tread-lightly-when-tweaking-sarbanes-oxley/. Those who believe that Sarbanes-Oxley has been an "overcorrection" to Enron et al. may rewrite the last sentence in the text paragraph to read: "Had Bush been able to shift the blame for Enron to the Democrats, he might have been in a stronger position to negotiate a less burdensome version of the Sarbanes-Oxley bill."

26. My account of the Enron scandal draws especially on Malcolm S. Salter, *Innovation Corrupted: The Origins and Legacy of Enron's Collapse* (Cambridge: Harvard University Press, 2008), 1–153; Peter C. Fusaro and Ross M. Miller, *What Went Wrong at Enron* (Hoboken, NJ: John Wiley & Sons, 2002); and Thayer Watkins, "The Rise and Fall of Enron," http://www.sjsu.edu/faculty/watkins/enron.htm (accessed June 26, 2017).

27. All of these ventures are examined in Salter, *Innovation Corrupted,* 28–45. The estimate for total losses is given on p. 46.

28. Salter, 135.

29. As cited in Salter, 149.

30. My analysis of the Tyco scandal draws especially on Catherine S. Neal, *Taking Down the Lion: The Triumphant Rise and Tragic Fall of Tyco's Dennis Kozlowski* (New York: Palgrave Macmillan, 2014); Jerry W. Markham, *A Financial History of Modern U.S. Corporate Scandals: From Enron to Reform* (Armonk, NY: M. E. Sharpe,

2006), 235–245; Anthony Bianco, William Symonds, and Nanette Byrnes, "The Rise and Fall of Dennis Kozlowski," *BusinessWeek*, December 23, 2002, 64–77; and James B. Stewart, "Spend! Spend! Spend!" *New Yorker*, February 17 and 24, 2003, 132–147.

31. Markham, *Financial History*, 235–236.

32. Neal, *Taking Down the Lion*, 65, 77.

33. These early accusations are nicely summarized in William C. Symonds, "Tyco: Aggressive or Out of Line?" *BusinessWeek*, November 1, 1999, 160–165.

34. See Stewart, "Spend! Spend! Spend!" 147.

35. Thomas Curren, as quoted in Associated Press, "Ex-Tyco Executives Get Up to 25 Years in Prison," September 20, 2005, www.nbcnews.com/id/9399803/ns/busi ness-corporate_scandals/t/ex-tyco-executives-get-years-prison/#.WYFOJITyuJA.

36. The book referred to is Neal, *Taking Down the Lion*.

37. These incidents are described in considerable detail in Stewart, "Spend! Spend! Spend!"; Neal, *Taking Down the Lion*, 67–71 and 109–119; and Alex Berenson and Carol Vogel, "Ex-Tyco Chief Is Indicted in Tax Case," *New York Times*, June 5, 2002.

38. *The People of the State of New York against L. Dennis Kozlowski and Mark H. Swartz* [hereafter cited as *New York against Kozlowski and Swartz*], Indictment No. 5259/02, at news.findlaw.com/wsj/docs/tyco/nykozlowski91202ind.pdf (accessed August 2, 2017).

39. *New York against Kozlowski and Swartz*, 10–22.

40. For details, see Neal, *Taking Down the Lion*, 167.

41. My discussion of the WorldCom scandal draws primarily on Lynne W. Jeter, *Disconnected: Deceit and Betrayal at WorldCom* (Hoboken, NJ: John Wiley & Sons, 2003); Markham, *Financial History*, 330–354; and contemporary coverage in the *New York Times*.

42. Simon Romero and Alex Berenson, "WorldCom Says It Hid Expenses, Inflating Cash Flow, $3.8 Billion," *New York Times*, June 26, 2002; Barnaby J. Feder and Seth Schiesel, "WorldCom Finds $3.3 Billion More in Irregularities," *New York Times*, August 9, 2002; and Kurt Eichenwald and Seth Schiesel, "S.E.C. Files New Charges on WorldCom," *New York Times*, November 6, 2002.

43. For some examples from the first six months of 2002, see *Public Papers of the President of the United States: George W. Bush* [hereafter cited as *Bush Public Papers*] (Washington, DC: US Government Printing Office, various years), 2002, 1: 42, 124, 356–359, 368–369, 405, 1072, and 1082–1083.

44. Both quotations are taken from "The President's News Conference," July 8, 2002, *Bush Public Papers*, 2002, 2: 1185–1187.

45. George W. Bush, "Remarks on Corporate Responsibility in New York City," July 9, 2002, *Bush Public Papers*, 2002, 2: 1194.

46. See Richard L. Berke, "Greed, Pain, Excesses. Oh, What a Lovely Issue," *New York Times*, January 27, 2002.

47. Richard Clarke, "Testimony before the 9/11 Commission," March 24, 2004, http://www.americanrhetoric.com/speeches/richardclarke911commissiontesti mony.htm.

48. "Excerpts from Attorney General's Testimony on September 11 and Counterterrorism," *New York Times*, April 14, 2014.

49. As quoted in Eric Lichtblau, "White House Criticizes Justice Department over Papers," *New York Times*, April 30, 2004.

50. George J. Tenet, "Written Statement for the Record of the Director of Central Intelligence before the Joint Inquiry Committee," October 17, 2002, as quoted in Rich Lowry, *Legacy: Paying the Price for the Clinton Years* (Washington, DC: Regnery, 2003), 306.

51. The Deutch Rules are also sometimes referred to as the "Torricelli Principle," after New Jersey congressman Robert Torricelli, who first leaked information about the Guatemala case and then led the fight for remedial action. For a good account of the rules, from which the quotation in the text is taken, see Christopher Vallandigham, "Deutch Rules," in *The Central Intelligence Agency: An Encyclopedia of Covert Ops, Intelligence Gathering, and Spies*, ed. Jan Goldman (Santa Barbara, CA: ABC-CLIO, 2015), 1:107–111.

52. As quoted in Bill Gertz, *Breakdown: How America's Intelligence Failures Led to September 11* (Washington, DC: Regnery, 2002), 68.

53. National Commission on Terrorism, *Countering the Changing Threat of International Terrorism*, June 2000, at https://www.hsdl.org/?abstract&did=992. For other criticisms of the Deutch Rules and the development of a risk-averse, "politically correct" mentality at the CIA, see, among others, Melissa Boyle Mahle, *Denial and Deception: An Insider's View of the CIA from Iran-Contra to 9/11* (New York: Nation Books, 2004), chap. 16; John Miller, Michael Stone, and Chris Mitchell, *The Cell: Inside the 9/11 Plot, and Why the FBI and CIA Failed to Stop It* (New York: Hyperion, 2002), 133–134 and 329–330; and Gertz, *Breakdown*, 66–70.

54. For a particularly detailed report on the Khobar Towers investigation, see Elsa Walsh, "Louis Freeh's Last Case," *New Yorker*, May 14, 2001.

55. Mike Rolince, as quoted in Lowry, *Legacy*, 311.

56. As quoted in Miller, Stone, and Mitchell, *Cell*, 188. Miller is the ABC reporter who interviewed bin Laden.

57. See his comments in Al Gore, *The Assault on Reason* (New York: Penguin, 2007), 140–142 and 178–180.

58. For a full discussion, see Miller, Stone, and Mitchell, *Cell*, chap. 13. The three quotations in this paragraph are taken, respectively, from pp. 195, 205, and 194.
The US embassy in Dar es Salaam, Tanzania, was also bombed that day, but the authors seem to regard that attack as less obviously preventable.

59. As quoted in Richard L. Berke, "Bush Adviser Suggests War as Campaign Theme," *New York Times*, January 19, 2002.

60. George W. Bush, "Address before a Joint Session of the Congress on the State of the Union," January 28, 2003, *Bush Public Papers*, 2003, 1:88.

61. Joseph C. Wilson IV, "What I Didn't Find in Africa," *New York Times*, July 6, 2003.

62. As quoted in Richard Leiby and Walter Pincus, "Retired Envoy: Nuclear Report Ignored," *Washington Post*, July 6, 2003.

63. See Wilson, "What I Didn't Find"; and Joseph Wilson, *The Politics of Truth: Inside the Lies that Led to War and Betrayed My Wife's CIA Identity* (New York: Carroll and Graf, 2004), 21 and 25. Wilson probably used such terminology because, according to his op-ed, he was sent to Niger to investigate a "memorandum of agreement that documented the sale of uranium yellowcake . . . by Niger to Iraq in the late 1990s." His official mission, in other words, was to look into a claim that a transaction of some kind had actually taken place. Still, one might have thought that before accusing the president of deliberate, outright deception, he would have paid closer attention to the exact words the president used.

64. The back-and-forth on this issue between the CIA and British intelligence is described in Walter Pincus, "CIA Asked Britain to Drop Iraq Claim," *Washington Post*, July 11, 2003; and Glenn Frankel, "Allies Didn't Share All Intelligence on Iraq," *Washington Post*, July 17, 2003.

65. See, for example, Dan Balz and Walter Pincus, "Why Commander in Chief Is Losing the War of the 16 Words," *Washington Post*, July 24, 2003; Baker, *Days of Fire*, 279; and Russ Hoyle, *Going to War: How Misinformation, Disinformation, and Arrogance Led America into Iraq* (New York: St. Martin's Press, 2008), 357. Rove's assessment of the White House response is also quite critical; see Karl Rove, *Courage and Consequence: My Life as a Conservative in the Fight* (New York: Simon & Schuster, 2010), 320, 321.

66. See, respectively, Rice, *No Higher Honor*, 222–223; George Tenet, *At the Center of the Storm: My Years at the CIA* (New York: HarperCollins, 2007), 456; and Dick Cheney, *In My Time: A Personal and Political Memoir* (New York: Threshold Editions, 2011), 404.

67. Rove, *Courage and Consequence*, 331.

68. Walter Pincus, "White House Backs Off Claim on Iraqi Buy," *Washington Post*, July 8, 2003. A separate statement sent to the *New York Times* was perhaps slightly more nuanced: "The information [about Iraqi attempts to buy uranium in Africa] is not detailed or specific enough for us to be certain that attempts were in fact made." In other words, "we couldn't prove it, and it might be wrong." See David E. Sanger, "Bush Claim on Iraq Had Flawed Origin, White House Says," *New York Times*, July 8, 2003.

69. See Rice, *No Higher Honor*, 223.

70. As quoted in Walter Pincus and Dana Milbank, "Bush, Rice Blame CIA for Iraq Error," *Washington Post*, July 12, 2003.

71. George W. Bush, "Remarks Following Discussions with President Yoweri Kaguta Museveni of Uganda and an Exchange with Reporters in Entebbe, Uganda," July 11, 2003, in *Bush Public Papers*, 2003, 2:860.

72. The most detailed evidence about how the vice president's office responded to the sixteen words controversy comes from testimony at Scooter Libby's trial. See David E. Sanger and David Barstow, "Iraq Findings Leaked by Aide Were Disputed," *New York Times*, April 9, 2006,; Carol D. Leonnig and Amy Goldstein, "Ex-Aide Says Cheney Led Rebuttal Effort," *Washington Post*, January 26, 2007; Neil A. Lewis, "Ex-

Cheney Aide Contradicts Libby's Version of Events," *New York Times*, January 26, 2007.

73. The CIA director's expectations in this regard are set forth in Tenet, *At the Center*, 458–459.

74. "Statement by George J. Tenet Director of Central Intelligence," July 11, 2003, https://www.cia.gov/news-information/press-releases-statements/press-release-archive-2003/pr07112003.html.

75. White House objections to Tenet's statement are discussed in Michael Isikoff and David Corn, *Hubris: The Inside Story of Spin, Scandal, and the Selling of the Iraq War* (New York: Crown, 2006), 275; and Tenet, *At the Center*, 461–466.

76. Wilson's assertion that he had "every confidence" that his report was communicated to the appropriate officials is taken from his "What I Didn't Find in Africa." His claim that the alleged effort to secure uranium was a "fundamental justification" for the war is from Leiby and Pincus, "Retired Envoy." All other quotations are from "Statement by George J. Tenet."

77. See David E. Sanger and James Risen, "C.I.A. Chief Takes Blame in Assertion on Iraqi Uranium," *New York Times*, July 12, 2003; and Walter Pincus and Dana Milbank, "Bush, Rice Blame CIA for Iraq Error," *Washington Post*, July 12, 2003. The *Times* article mentions that Wilson's mission was undertaken "apparently without the knowledge of Mr. Cheney or Mr. Tenet," but does not note that Wilson's column had asserted otherwise.

78. "Statement by George J. Tenet."

79. Precisely for that reason, I have not attempted here to pronounce judgment on the issue. As discussed later in the text, an "Additional Views" section in a report by the Senate Committee on Intelligence concluded that Wilson's wife had, in fact, suggested the plan to send him to Niger. But Isikoff and Corn argue that Valerie Wilson's role was misinterpreted and that she was, in fact, no more than a "conduit" between the CIA and her husband. See *Hubris*, 93–94 and 235–236.

80. See "Intelligence Identities Protection Act of 1982," Public Law 97–200, at https://www.gpo.gov/fdsys/pkg/STATUTE-96/pdf/STATUTE-96-Pg122.pdf (accessed May 15, 2017).

81. The fullest description of Valerie Plame Wilson's position at the CIA is in "Unclassified Summary of Valerie Wilson's CIA Employment and Cover History," which can be viewed in "Valerie Plame, Covert after All," May 30, 2007, http://www.salon.com/2007/05/30/plame_46/. The description of her job as "an analyst, not a spy" is from Robert Novak, who attributed it to a "confidential source at the C.I.A." See Eric Lichtblau and Richard W. Stevenson, "White House Denies a Top Aide Identified an Officer of the C.I.A.," *New York Times*, September 30, 2003.

82. Barton Gellman and Dafna Linzer, "A 'Concerted Effort' to Discredit Bush Critic," *Washington Post*, April 9, 2006.

83. Fleischer's efforts to spread the word are detailed in Amy Goldstein and Carol D. Leonnig, "Former Press Secretary Says Libby Told Him of Plame," *Wash-*

ington Post, January 30, 2007; and Neil A. Lewis, "Ex-Bush Aide, in Testimony, Contradicts Libby's Account," *New York Times*, January 30, 2007.

84. Isikoff and Corn, *Hubris*, 272.

85. Numerous sources have described Cheney as being at the center of the effort to discredit Wilson and his wife. See, among others, Gellman and Linzer, "A 'Concerted Effort'"; McClellan, *What Happened*, 171; and Leonnig and Goldstein, "Ex-Aide Says Cheney." The "discredit, punish, or seek revenge" quotation is from Patrick Fitzgerald, in the Gellman and Linzer article.

86. Robert D. Novak, "Mission to Niger," *Washington Post*, July 14, 2003.

87. For Novak's testimony about the sources for his column, see CNN, "Columnist Testifies Rove Confirmed Plame Was CIA," February 14, 2007, www.cnn.com /2007/POLITICS/02/12/cia.leak/index.html?eref=yahoo. For Rove's version, see Rove, *Courage and Consequence*, 328–329.

88. The fullest account of Rove's conversation with *Time* reporter Matthew Cooper is in Isikoff and Corn, *Hubris*, 272–275. In a file Cooper later sent to his magazine, he says that Rove initially would say only that "Wilson was not sent by the director of the CIA or by Dick Cheney and when it comes out who sent him, it will be embarrassing." Only when Cooper "pressed" Rove for more details did Rove say that Wilson had been sent by his wife.

89. Matthews's version of this conversation is recounted in Isikoff and Corn, *Hubris*, 297. Rove's version is in *Courage and Consequence*, 345–346.

90. See David E. Sanger, "National Security Aide Says He's to Blame for Speech Error," *New York Times*, July 23, 2003.

91. See Mike Allen and Dana Priest, "Bush Administration Is Focus of Inquiry," *Washington Post*, September 28, 2003.

92. The claim that Valerie Wilson's life was put in danger by the disclosure was often made by critics of the Bush administration. The example quoted in the text is from Sen. Charles Schumer (D-NY), in Allen and Priest, "Bush Administration Is Focus." So far as one can determine from the available press coverage, no attempt was ever actually made on her life.

93. US Senate, Select Committee on Intelligence, *U.S. Intelligence Community's Prewar Intelligence Assessments on Iraq*, 108th Cong., 2d sess., 2004, p. 14.

94. Select Committee on Intelligence, *U.S. Intelligence Community's*, 46, 443, 445. The first two quotations in this paragraph are from the full committee report; the others are from the "Additional Views" of Senators Pat Roberts, Christopher Bond, and Orrin Hatch.

95. "Review of Intelligence on Weapons of Mass Destruction," Report of a Committee of Privy Counsellors, July 14, 2004, p. 123. The full text of the report can be found at news.bbc.co.uk/nol/shared/bsp/hi/pdfs/14_07_04_butler.pdf.

96. See, for example, William Safire, "Sixteen Truthful Words," *New York Times*, July 19, 2004; "The Yellowcake Con," *Wall Street Journal*, July 15, 2004; and Hugh Hewitt "Four Facts and Five Conclusions," *Weekly Standard*, July 14, 2004, www .weeklystandard.com/four-facts-and-five-conclusions/article/5542.

97. Howard Kurtz, "Boston's Bloggers, Filling in the Margins," *Washington Post*, July 26, 2004.

98. Both quotations are from Richard W. Stevenson and David Johnston, "New Reports Reopen Debate Over Whether Iraq Sought Uranium in Niger," *New York Times*, July 18, 2004.

99. Kumar, *Managing the President's Message*, 104.

100. Both quotations are from David Kay. The first is taken from "Transcript: David Kay at Senate Hearing," January 28, 2004, www.cnn.com/2004/us/01/28 /kay.transcript. The second is from Walter Pincus and Dana Milbank, "Arms Hunt in Iraq to Get New Focus," *Washington Post*, January 24, 2004.

101. For some data on this point, see Lou Cannon and Carl M. Cannon, *Reagan's Disciple: George W. Bush's Troubled Quest for a Presidential Legacy* (New York: Public-Affairs, 2008), 194–195.

102. This particular quotation comes from Bush's acceptance speech at the Republican National Convention, August 3, 2000, as archived at www.presidency .ucsb.edu/ws/index.php?pid=25944. But the line was apparently a regular part of Bush's stump speech. See Frank Bruni, "Bush Calls on Gore to Denounce Clinton Affair," *New York Times*, August 12, 2000.

103. McClellan, *What Happened*, 161–162.

104. As reported in Cannon and Cannon, *Reagan's Disciple*, 71–72.

105. David Kay, Testimony before the Senate Armed Services Committee, January 28, 2004, at www.cnn.com/2004/US/01/28/kay.transcript.

106. As quoted in James Risen, "Ex-Inspector Says C.I.A. Missed Disarray in Iraqi Arms Program," *New York Times*, January 26, 2004.

107. Rove, *Courage and Consequence*, 333–335.

108. William J. Clinton, "Remarks at the Pentagon in Arlington, Virginia," February 17, 1998, in *Public Papers of the President of the United States: William J. Clinton* [hereafter cited as *Clinton Public Papers*] (Washington, DC: US Government Printing Office, various years), 1998, 1:232.

109. William J. Clinton, "Address to the Nation Announcing Military Strikes on Iraq," December 16, 1998, in *Clinton Public Papers*, 1998, 2:2183.

110. Clinton, "Address to the Nation," 2:2184.

111. William J. Clinton, "Letter to Congressional Leaders on Continuation of the National Emergency with Respect to Iraq," July 28, 2000, in *Clinton Public Papers*, 2000–2001, 2:1503 (emphasis added).

112. Peter Feaver, "The Fog of WMD," *Washington Post*, January 28, 2004 (emphasis added).

113. Harry S. Truman, *Memoirs*, vol. 2, *Years of Trial and Hope* (Garden City, NY: Doubleday & Company, 1956), 306.

114. For the text of UN Security Council Resolution 687, adopted April 3, 1991, see www.un.org/Depts/unmovic/documents/687.pdf. The investigatory rights later granted to UNSCOM are listed in "United Nations Special Commission," at www.un.org/Depts/unscom/General/basicfacts.html (accessed January 27, 2016).

115. R. Jeffrey Smith and Glenn Frankel, "Saddam's Nuclear-Weapons Dream: A Lingering Nightmare," *Washington Post*, October 13, 1991.

116. William J. Broad, "U.N. Says Iraq Was Moving Toward More Potent Bombs," *New York Times*, October 15, 1991.

117. For various estimates of the size of the Iraqi nuclear program, see Smith and Frankel, "Saddam's Nuclear-Weapons"; and Michael R. Gordon and Bernard E. Trainor, *The Generals' War: The Inside Story of the Conflict in the Gulf* (Boston: Little, Brown, 1995), 457.

118. Gordon and Trainor, *Generals' War*, 458.

119. All quotations are taken from Paul Lewis, "U.N. Aides Discover Atom Arms Center Concealed by Iraq," *New York Times*, October 8, 1991.

120. Zeev Schiff, as quoted in Smith and Frankel, "Saddam's Nuclear-Weapons."

121. George Tenet, *At the Center*, 330.

122. See "Text of David Kay's Unclassified Statement," October 2, 2003, at www.cnn.com/2003/ALLPOLITICS/10/02/kay.report/.

123. As quoted in Richard M. Stevenson, "Iraq Illicit Arms Gone before War, Inspector States," *New York Times*, January 24, 2004.

124. As quoted in Douglas Jehl and Eric Schmitt, "Rumsfeld and Tenet Defending Assessments of Iraqi Weapons," *New York Times*, February 5, 2004.

125. See *Bush Public Papers*, 2004, 1:129–138, 143–149.

126. George W. Bush, "Remarks Prior to Discussions with President Aleksander Kwasniewski of Poland and an Exchange with Reporters," January 27, 2004, *Bush Public Papers*, 2004, 1:138–141.

127. See, in particular, "Remarks Following a Meeting with Economists and an Exchange with Reporters," January 30, 2004, *Bush Public Papers*, 2004, 1:164–165; and "Remarks Following a Cabinet Meeting and an Exchange with Reporters," February 2, 2004, *Bush Public Papers*, 2004, 1:170–171.

128. See George W. Bush, "Remarks at a Bush-Cheney Reception in Old Greenwich, Connecticut," January 29, 2004, *Bush Public Papers*, 2004, 1:159–164.

129. Katharine Q. Seelye and David M. Halfinger, "Democratic Contenders Attack Bush on Iraq, Terrorism, Trade and Economy," *New York Times*, January 30, 2004.

130. Mike Allen, "Bush Stands Firmly Behind His Decision to Invade Iraq," *Washington Post*, February 6, 2004.

131. All quotations are from George W. Bush, "Remarks at the Port of Charleston, South Carolina," February 5, 2004, in *Bush Public Papers*, 2004, 1:188.

132. See Jehl and Schmitt, "Rumsfeld and Tenet Defending"; and Douglas Jehl, "Tenet Concedes Gaps in C.I.A. Data on Iraq Weapons," *New York Times*, February 6, 2004.

133. For the full text of this interview, see "Interview with Tim Russert on NBC's 'Meet the Press,'" February 7, 2004, at http://www.presidency.ucsb.edu/ws/?pid=75523.

134. George W. Bush, "Remarks to Military Personnel at Fort Polk, Louisiana," February 17, 2004, *Bush Public Papers*, 2004, 1:231.

135. See, for example, *Bush Public Papers*, 2004, 1:249, 252, 260, 271, 280, and 307.

136. Rove, *Courage and Consequence*, 342–343.

137. See, in particular, John R. Zaller, *The Nature and Origins of Mass Opinion* (New York: Cambridge University Press, 1992).

138. See especially George C. Edwards III, *On Deaf Ears: The Limits of the Bully Pulpit* (New Haven: Yale University Press, 2003).

139. See Benjamin I. Page and Robert Y. Shapiro, *The Rational Public: Fifty Years of Trends in Americans' Policy Preferences* (Chicago: University of Chicago Press, 1992), especially chap. 2.

140. On how the characteristics of elite commentary can determine the impact of rally point events, see Richard A. Brody and Catherine R. Shapiro, "A Reconsideration of the Rally Phenomenon in Public Opinion," in *Political Behavior Annual*, ed. Samuel Long (Boulder, CO: Westview Press, 1989), 2:77–102.

141. Frum, *Right Man*, 20.

Chapter 10: It's Hard to Have Ideological Heirs When You Don't Have Much of an Ideology

1. Marc Landy and Sidney Milkis, *Presidential Greatness* (Lawrence: University Press of Kansas, 2000). The quoted phrase appears on 6.

2. The line comes from Roosevelt's address to Oglethorpe University, May 22, 1932, in *The Public Papers and Addresses of Franklin D. Roosevelt*, vol. 1 (New York: Random House, 1938), 646.

3. For a good argument along these lines, see Hugh Heclo, "One Executive Branch or Many?" in *Both Ends of the Avenue: The Presidency, the Executive Branch, and Congress in the 1980s*, ed. Anthony King (Washington, DC: American Enterprise Institute, 1983), 26–58.

4. Robert Ajemian, "Where Is the Real George Bush?" *Time*, January 26, 1987, 20.

5. See, for example, Dilys M. Hill, "Domestic Policy," in *The Bush Presidency: Triumphs and Adversities*, ed. Dilys M. Hill and Phil Williams (New York: St. Martin's Press, 1994), 134–161; Kerry Mullins and Aaron Wildavsky, "The Procedural Presidency of George Bush," *Political Science Quarterly* 107 (Spring 1992): 31–62; and Michael Duffy and Dan Goodgame, *Marching in Place: The Status Quo Presidency of George Bush* (New York: Simon & Schuster, 1992).

6. John Sununu, as quoted in Duffy and Goodgame, *Marching in Place*, 82.

7. In addition to the forecasting articles listed in the next footnote, see Seymour Martin Lipset, "The Significance of the 1992 Election," *PS: Political Science and Politics* 26 (March 1993): 7–16; John C. Whitehead, "Considerations on the Eve of the 1992 Presidential Election," *Presidential Studies Quarterly* 23 (Winter 1993): 37–40; and Marc J. Hetherington, "The Media's Role in Forming Voters' National Economic Evaluations in 1992," *American Journal of Political Science* 40 (May 1996): 372–395.

8. See, for example, Ray C. Fair, "The Effect of Economic Events on Votes for President: 1992 Update," *Political Behavior* 18 (June 1996): 119–139; Richard F. Gleisner, "Economic Determinants of Presidential Elections: The Fair Model," *Po-*

litical Behavior 14 (December 1992): 383–394; Alberto Alesina, John Londregan, and Howard Rosenthal, "The 1992, 1994 and 1996 Elections: A Comment and a Forecast," *Public Choice* 88 (July 1996): 115–125; and Tim Fackler and Tes-min Lin, "Political Corruption and Presidential Elections, 1929–1992," *Journal of Politics* 57 (November 1995): 971–993.

9. Excerpts from Bush's June 12, 1999, speech in Cedar Rapids, Iowa, as reported in the *New York Times*, June 20, 1999.

10. Results are taken from, respectively, Louis Harris & Associates poll of February 11–15, 1999 (n = 1,007); *Los Angeles Times* survey of February 12, 1999 (n = 664); and ABC News poll of February 6–7, 1999 (n = 803).

11. See Richard L. Berke, "Attention-Seeking Republicans Attack One of Their Own," *New York Times*, January 25, 1999.

12. See Mark D. Brewer, *Party Images in the American Electorate* (New York: Routledge, 2009), especially table 2.4, p. 18.

13. See, for example, Donald R. Kinder, "Presidential Character Revisited," in *Political Cognition*, ed. Richard R. Lau and David O. Sears (Hillsdale, NJ: Lawrence Erlbaum, 1986), 233–255; and Carolyn L. Funk, "Bringing the Candidate into Models of Candidate Evaluation," *Journal of Politics* 61 (August 1999): 700–720.

14. In 1984 and 1988, the ANES also included a set of questions asking respondents how "compassionate" each of the presidential candidates was. In both years, the Democratic candidate was seen as more compassionate.

15. See Opinion Dynamics survey of May 18–19, 2004 (n = 900).

16. Notice in this respect that not only are Democrats seen as consistently more caring than Republicans but that the various candidates within each party are pretty much rated the same. Thus, Bill Clinton, who reputedly had such a great capacity to "feel your pain," was seen as no more empathetic than the allegedly more wooden Michael Dukakis.

17. This phrase is used in Karl Rove, *Courage and Consequence: My Life as a Conservative in the Fight* (New York: Simon & Schuster, 2010), 128 and 158.

18. The major Bush advisors who contributed to compassionate conservatism are discussed in the text. For academic analyses of compassionate conservatism, see especially Steven M. Teles, "The Eternal Return of Compassionate Conservatism," *National Affairs* 1 (Fall 2009); John J. DiIulio Jr., "The Political Theory of Compassionate Conservatism," *Weekly Standard*, August 23, 1999; W. W. Riggs, "Compassionate Conservatism Meets Communitarianism," in *George W. Bush: Evaluating the President at Midterm*, ed. Bryan Hilliard, Tom Lansford, and Robert P. Watson (Albany: State University of New York Press, 2004), 29–38; Gertrude Himmelfarb, "Compassionate Conservatism: Properly Understood," *Weekly Standard*, January 14, 2013; Clifford Orwin, "Compassionate Conservatism: A Primer," *Defining Ideas*, March 1, 2011, at www.hoover.org/publications/defining-ideas/article/68921; and Kevin Kruse, "Compassionate Conservatism: Religion in the Age of George W. Bush," in *The Presidency of George W. Bush: A First Historical Assessment*, ed. Julian E. Zelizer (Princeton: Princeton University Press, 2010), 227–251.

19. This account of Wead's career and relationship with the Bush family draws on

Jacob Weisberg, *The Bush Tragedy* (New York: Random House, 2008), chap. 3; Doug Barton, "Wead Helps Keep the Faith in Politics," *Insight on the News*, May 14, 2001; "Biography of Doug Wead," www.dougwead.com/biography.htm (accessed November 19, 2010); "Interview with Doug Wead," conducted on November 18, 2003 and archived at www.pbs.org/wghb/pages/frontline/shows/jesus/interviews/wead .html; and "Doug Wead—CCA's President," www.canyonville.net/the-doug-wead -school (accessed January 5, 2011).

20. Weisberg, *Bush Tragedy*, 88.

21. See Lois Romano and Mike Allen, "Secret Tapes Not Meant to Harm, Writer Says," *Washington Post*, February 21, 2005; Weisberg, *Bush Tragedy*, 95–96.

22. See Burton, "Wead Helps Keep the Faith"; and Doug Wead, personal communication to the author, November 24, 2010.

23. Some sources claim that compassionate conservatism's first appearance in print occurred in 1981, when Vernon Jordan, then-president of the Urban League, was quoted in a news report as saying, "I do not challenge the conservatism of this Administration [i.e., the Reagan administration]. I do challenge its failure to exhibit a compassionate conservatism that adapts itself to the realities of a society ridden by class and race distinction." See Sheila Rule, "At Urban League, Mondale Derides Reagan Values," *New York Times*, July 23, 1981.

There is no evidence, however, that Jordan invested this phrase with any special significance, much less that he was advocating some kind of variant version of traditional conservatism. Indeed, his initial disclaimer notwithstanding, the full statement from Jordan (only part of which I have quoted here) suggests that Jordan was in fact challenging Reagan's conservatism—and wanted to replace it with something much like traditional liberalism.

24. See, respectively, James G. Watt with Doug Wead, *The Courage of a Conservative* (New York: Simon and Schuster, 1985), esp. chap. 4; Doug Wead, "George Bush: Where Does He Stand?" *Christian Herald* 109 (June 1986): 14–17 (the description of Bush as a compassionate conservative is on p. 16); and Doug Wead with Billy Childers, *It's Time for a Change* (Mesa, AZ: Doug Wead for Congress Committee, 1992).

25. Wead, *It's Time for a Change*, 1–2.

26. Watt with Wead, *Courage,* 49.

27. Watt with Wead, 50.

28. Wead, *It's Time for a Change*, 2.

29. From 1998 to 2000, Wead secretly taped a series of telephone conversations he held with George W. Bush—and then, in 2005, played some of them for the *New York Times*. See David D. Kirkpatrick, "In Secretly Taped Conversations, Glimpses of the Future President," *New York Times*, February 20, 2005; and David D. Kirkpatrick, "From Psst to Oops: Secret Taper of Bush Says History Can Wait," *New York Times*, February 24, 2005.

30. Given Wead's own religious commitment, his advice in this regard is strikingly nuanced. In particular, he urged both Bushes to court evangelicals early, subtly, and outside of the public spotlight, and appreciated that overt public pandering

to evangelicals could hurt a candidate with the rest of the electorate. See, in particular, his comments in "Interview with Doug Wead."

31. An interesting exception was Wead's support for agricultural subsidies, which most economists, liberal and conservative, see as one of the least defensible forms of government spending. See Wead, *It's Time for a Change*, 36.

32. For an example from the left side of the political spectrum, see Barney Frank, *Speaking Frankly: What's Wrong with the Democrats and How to Fix It* (New York: Times Books, 1992).

33. Wead, *It's Time for a Change*, 2.

34. See, for example, Amy E. Black, Douglas L. Koopman, and David K. Ryden, *Of Little Faith: The Politics of George W. Bush's Faith-Based Initiatives* (Washington, DC: Georgetown University Press, 2004), 2.

35. Details on Olasky's biography are taken from David Grann, "Where W. Got Compassion," *New York Times Magazine*, September 12, 1999, 62; and Michael King, "The Last Puritan," *Texas Observer*, May 14, 1999.

36. Marvin Olasky, *Compassionate Conservatism: What It Is, What It Does, and How It Can Transform America* (New York: Free Press, 2000), 4.

37. Among the many sources that highlight the role of these two books in Bush's preparation for his 1994 gubernatorial campaign are Rove, *Courage and Consequence*, 83; James Moore and Wayne Slater, *Bush's Brain: How Karl Rove Made George W. Bush Presidential* (Hoboken, NJ: John Wiley & Sons, 2003), 169; Steven E. Schier, *Panorama of a Presidency: How George W. Bush Acquired and Spent His Political Capital* (Armonk, NY: M. E. Sharpe, 2009), 101; Ronald Kessler, *A Matter of Character: Inside the White House of George W. Bush* (New York: Sentinel, 2004), 58; and Robert Draper, *Dead Certain: The Presidency of George W. Bush* (New York: Free Press, 2007), 44.

38. Olasky is described as the "intellectual architect" of compassionate conservatism in Gary Gerstle, "Minorities, Multiculturalism, and the Presidency of George W. Bush," in *The Presidency of George W. Bush: A First Historical Assessment,* ed. Julian E. Zelizer (Princeton: Princeton University Press, 2010), 354n18. For claims that Olasky was the "godfather" of compassionate conservatism, see Grann, "Where W. Got Compassion"; and Riggs, "Compassionate Conservatism," 31.

39. Grann, "Where W. Got Compassion."

40. Grann.

41. Myron Magnet, *The Dream and the Nightmare: The Sixties' Legacy to the Underclass* (San Francisco: Encounter Books, 2000 [1993]), front and back covers.

42. Magnet, *Dream and the Nightmare*, 236–237 (emphasis in original).

43. George W. Bush, *Decision Points* (New York: Crown, 2010), 36.

44. This is a point that Olasky emphasizes in every one of his books on the subject. See Marvin Olasky, *The Tragedy of American Compassion* (Washington, DC: Regnery Gateway, 1992), 196–198; Olasky, *Renewing American Compassion* (New York: Free Press, 1996), 34–36; and *Compassionate Conservatism*, 2.

45. My summary of Olasky's argument draws especially on Olasky, *Tragedy of American Compassion*, chaps. 1 and 6.

46. The passages quoted here come from Olasky, *Renewing American Compassion*, 64; and Olasky, *Tragedy of American Compassion*, 137.

47. Olasky, *Renewing American Compassion*, 64.

48. Olasky, *Tragedy*, 224, 226.

49. Olasky, *Renewing American Compassion*, 26. See also Olasky, "The New Welfare Debate: How to Practice Effective Compassion," *Imprimis*, September 1995.

50. There are, Olasky writes, "at least four ways to use government to promote the delivery of resources to programs that can provide effective compassion" (*Renewing American Compassion*, 182). But two of the four are essentially the same: federal tax credits and state tax credits. Olasky's endorsement of the other two mechanisms—vouchers and "giving religious groups equal access to funding under the Ashcroft [charitable choice] provision"—is considerably more restrained. Giving social service vouchers to welfare recipients and drug addicts, Olasky recognizes, would be considerably more complicated than using vouchers to enhance parental choice in elementary and secondary education (pp. 185–186). As the subsequent discussion will make clear, Olasky is even more skeptical of the value of the kind of charitable choice provisions originally developed by John Ashcroft.

51. It is important to emphasize here that Olasky is proposing a tax *credit* for private antipoverty contributions, and not just a tax *deduction*. To clarify the difference, imagine a person with a total income of $100,000 who makes a $10,000 contribution to an antipoverty group. Assume further—just to make the math simple—that there is a flat, 20 percent income tax, with no exemptions or other deductions. If taxpayers merely received a tax *deduction* for their antipoverty contributions, then this person would subtract $10,000 from his total income and pay a 20 percent tax on the remaining $90,000. He would thus pay the government $18,000 in taxes. But if a 90 percent tax *credit* were in operation, this same taxpayer would subtract 90 percent of his $10,000 contribution directly from the $20,000 in taxes he would otherwise have paid. He would thus pay the government only $11,000 in taxes. In short, under a tax deduction for charitable contributions, a person who contributed $10,000 would have his taxes reduced by just $2,000. Under a 90 percent tax credit, this person would get a tax reduction of $9,000. Obviously, the tax credit would act as a much more substantial incentive for charitable contributions—and bring about a much larger reduction in federal revenues.

52. See Olasky, *Renewing American Compassion*, 26–27 and 99–101.

53. See Olasky, *Compassionate Conservatism*, 18–20.

54. Olasky, *Renewing American Compassion*, 80.

55. Olasky is also wrong in his frequent assertion that previous histories of American poverty have largely ignored the work of private charities in attempting to relieve the sufferings of the poor. To the contrary, *every* history of poverty I have consulted devotes considerable attention to the efforts of private charities—and invariably concludes that they were simply inadequate to deal with the problem. See, in particular, Robert H. Bremner, *From the Depths: The Discovery of Poverty in the United States* (New York: New York University Press, 1956), chap. 3; Michael B.

Katz, *In the Shadow of the Poorhouse: A Social History of Welfare in America*, rev. ed. (New York: BasicBooks, 1996), chap. 3; and James T. Patterson, *America's Struggle against Poverty in the Twentieth Century* (Cambridge, MA: Harvard University Press, 2000), chap. 2.

56. See, for example, Jacob A. Riis, *How the Other Half Lives: Studies among the Tenements of New York* (New York: Penguin Books, 1997 [1890]); Patterson, *America's Struggle*, chap. 1; Bremner, *From the Depths*; and Katz, *In the Shadow*, chaps. 1–4.

57. Olasky, *Tragedy of American Compassion*, 80; and *Renewing American Compassion*, 43.

58. Hunter's work is discussed in Patterson, *America's Struggle*, 6–12.

59. All information in this paragraph is taken from Charity Organization Society, *Directory of Charitable and Beneficent Organizations of Baltimore and of Maryland* (Baltimore: Friedenwald, 1892), 23–25. As noted in the text, this is the same source from which Olasky derived all his information about the Association for the Improvement of the Condition of the Poor. See *Tragedy of American Compassion*, 251n1. (Olasky actually cites the second edition of the *Directory*, but all the numbers he lists are the same as in the edition I have consulted.)

The actual amount of assistance contributed to those families receiving aid was probably greater than $1.45 per person, since families deemed unworthy were apparently given nothing. But even if aid were given to only a third of the persons visited, the lucky recipients would still have received just $4.35 per person. Of course, the more selective the aid, the more families that would have been given nothing but moral exhortation.

60. See John J. DiIulio Jr., *Godly Republic: A Centrist Blueprint for America's Faith-Based Future* (Berkeley: University of California Press, 2007), 96.

61. My account of DiIulio's career and involvement with the faith-based issue draws primarily on Tim Stafford, "The Criminologist Who Discovered Churches," *Christianity Today*, June 14, 1999, 34–39; Elizabeth Becker, "An Ex-Theorist on Young 'Superpredators,' Bush Aide Has Regrets," *New York Times*, February 9, 2001; John J. DiIulio Jr., "Why Judging George W. Bush Is Never as Easy as It Seems," in *Judging Bush*, ed. Robert Maranto, Tom Lansford, and Jeremy Johnson (Stanford: Stanford University Press, 2009), 294–310; and DiIulio, *Godly Republic*.

62. See, for example, Robert Westbrook, "Dubya-ism," *Christian Century*, September 13–20, 2000, 912–916. Westbrook is a professor of history at the University of Rochester. The most revealing indication of how the history profession reacted to Olasky's work is that, so far as I can tell, none of his books on compassion has ever been reviewed in an academic history journal. *The Tragedy of American Compassion* was, however, reviewed—positively—in both *Public Choice* and *American Scholar*.

63. An exception is Bob Wineburg, *Faith-Based Inefficiency: The Follies of Bush's Initiatives* (Westport, CT: Praeger, 2007).

64. Olasky, *Compassionate Conservatism*, 19–20.

65. DiIulio, *Godly Republic*, 161. Wineburg has accused DiIulio of having prematurely claimed in 1999 that "scientific studies testify to the efficacy of faith-

based efforts"—a conclusion, according to Wineburg, that DiIulio later had to retract. See Wineburg, *Faith-Based Inefficiency*, 53–55. Wineburg was referring to an op-ed by DiIulio, "Two Million Prisoners Are Enough," *Wall Street Journal*, March 12, 1999. But Wineburg's criticism seems to me both an overreaction to one sentence and a failure to distinguish between what DiIulio would later call "organic religion" and "programmatic religion." See DiIulio, "The Three Faith Factors," *Public Interest* 149 (Fall 2002): 50–64.

I have read every major article DiIulio wrote on this topic during the late 1990s and early 2000s and have found them consistent with the conclusion reached in his 2007 book, though at times he seems a bit more optimistic that the evidence will *eventually* show faith-based programs to be superior to their secular counterparts. See especially the following works by DiIulio: "Three Faith Factors"; "Know Us by Our Works," *Wall Street Journal*, February 14, 2001; "Godly People in the Public Square," *Public Interest* 141 (Fall 2000), 113–114; and "Not by Faith Alone: Religion, Crime, and Substance Abuse," in *Sacred Places, Civic Purposes: Should Government Help Faith-Based Charity?*, ed. E. J. Dionne Jr., and Ming Hsu Chen (Washington: Brookings Institution Press, 2001), 86–88.

66. Robert Putnam, *Better Together: Report of the Saguaro Seminar*, as quoted in DiIulio, *Godly Republic*, 155.

67. The first quotation is from DiIulio, *Godly Republic*, 159–160; the second is from DiIulio, "Getting Faith-Based Programs Right," *Public Interest*, no. 155, Summer 2004, 79.

68. All quotations are taken from the Teen Challenge Website: http://teenchallengeusa.com (accessed July 1, 2013).

69. DiIulio, *Godly Republic*, 161.

70. See, for example, DiIulio, "Why Judging," 295.

71. DiIulio, *Godly Republic*, 126–127.

72. DiIulio, *Godly Republic*, 128 (emphasis in original).

73. *Godly Republic*, 140.

74. All quotations from the "Duty of Hope" speech and the position paper that accompanied it are taken from 2000 Bush for President, *Renewing America's Purpose: Policy Addresses of George W. Bush, July 1999–July 2000* (Washington, DC: Republican National Committee, 2000), 109–131.

75. Figures are taken from Black, Koopman, and Ryden, *Of Little Faith*, 21.

76. This is the consensus conclusion of most scholars who have studied charitable choice. See, in particular, Black, Koopman, and Ryden, *Of Little Faith*, 58–65; DiIulio, *Godly Republic*, 110–112, 123–125; DiIulio, "Getting Faith-Based Programs," 77–78; and Rebecca Sager, *Faith, Politics, and Power: The Politics of Faith-Based Initiatives* (New York: Oxford University Press, 2010), 31–32. There are dissenters, however. See, for example, Mark Chaves, "Going on Faith: Six Myths about Faith-Based Initiatives," *Christian Century*, September 12–19, 2001, 20.

77. Bush for President, *Renewing America's Purpose*, 112.

78. Bush for President, *Renewing America's Purpose*, 112, 113.

79. Bush for President, *Renewing America's Purpose*, 114.

80. See Bush for President, *Renewing America's Purpose*, 115–116, 121–123. It is important to note that the $8 billion figure mentioned in Bush's speech represents the amount of money lost to the federal treasury, *not* the amount actually received by faith-based organizations.

81. The position paper that accompanied the "Duty of Hope" speech said that states would be permitted "to offset the costs of this credit by using money from the Temporary Assistance to Needy Families (TANF) program." See Bush for President, *Renewing America's Purpose*, 122. But this offer would have been attractive only if states had large amounts of unspent welfare money lying around. It didn't funnel any new money to the states—which meant that even with this provision, the costs of the tax credits would still have been borne entirely by state governments.

82. See, in particular, Black, Koopman, and Ryden, *Of Little Faith*; Jo Renee Formicola, Mary C. Segers, and Paul Weber, *Faith-Based Initiatives and the Bush Administration: The Good, the Bad, and the Ugly* (Lanham, MD: Rowman & Littlefield, 2003); DiIulio, *Godly Republic*; and David Kuo, *Tempting Faith: An Inside Story of Political Seduction* (New York: Free Press, 2006).

83. See, for example, George W. Bush, "Statement on House of Representatives Action on the Faith-Based and Community Initiative," *Public Papers of the President of the United States: George W. Bush* (hereafter cited as *Bush Public Papers*) (Washington, DC: US Government Printing Office, various years), 2001, 2:872; and "The President's Radio Address," 2:991.

84. For a full account of the faith-based initiative's travails in the Senate, see Black, Koopman, and Ryden, *Of Little Faith*, chap. 4.

85. Though a number of good books have been written about how the faith-based initiative fared during Bush's first two years in office, there is surprisingly little written about what happened in the following six years. Probably the best overall assessment of faith-based policy during the Bush presidency is David J. Wright, "Taking Stock: The Bush Faith-Based Initiative and What Lies Ahead," June 11, 2009, Roundtable on Religion and Social Welfare Policy, Nelson A. Rockefeller Institute of Government, State University of New York, at www.rockinst.org/pdf /faith-based_social_services/2009–06–11-taking_stock_faith-based_office.pdf. See also Douglas L. Koopman, "The Status of Faith-Based Initiatives in the Later Bush Administration," in *Church-State Issues in America Today*, ed. Ann W. Duncan and Steven L. Jones (Westport, CT: Praeger, 2008), 167–193; and Amy E. Black and Douglas L. Koopman, "The Politics of Faith-Based Initiatives," in *Religion and the Bush Presidency*, ed. Mark J. Rozell and Gleaves Whitney (New York: Palgrave Macmillan, 2007), 155–175.

86. For a more detailed discussion of how this was accomplished, see Anne Farris, Richard P. Nathan, and David J. Wright, "The Expanding Administrative Presidency: George W. Bush and the Faith-Based Initiative," August 2004, Roundtable on Religion and Social Welfare Policy, Rockefeller Institute of Government, State University of New York, 1–16, at www.rockinst.org/pdf/federalism/2004-08-the_expanding _administrative_presidency_george_w_bush_and_the_faith-based_initiative.pdf.

87. See executive orders nos. 13198 and 13199, both issued on January 29, 2001. The quotation in the text is from no. 13198.

88. The executive orders referred to are nos. 13279 and 13280 (both issued on December 12, 2002), 13342 (June 1, 2004), and 13397 (March 7, 2006).

89. For an analysis of the new appropriations created in connection with the Bush faith-based initiative, see Wright, "Taking Stock," 58–69; and the White House, "Innovations in Compassion: The Faith-Based and Community Initiative: A Final Report to the Armies of Compassion," December 2008, archived at www .readysandiego.org/resources/innovations_in_compassion.pdf.

90. Figures are taken from White House, "Innovations in Compassion," 44nii.

91. Actually, the percentage is almost certainly smaller. The 107,000 figure includes all children of prisoners who were matched with a mentor at any time between 2003 and 2008. But the two million figure is the number of children who had one or both parents in prison *at a single point in time*. When one takes into account the turnover in the target population that occurred over a six-year period—from new births, children becoming adults, and parents newly incarcerated or released from prison—the total number of children needing mentors over this period is probably closer to four million.

92. All figures are taken from White House, "Innovations in Compassion," 8.

93. See Wright, "Taking Stock," 21–22.

94. See Sager, *Faith, Politics, and Power*, especially chaps. 3 and 4.

95. Diament and Tuttle are both quoted in Wright, "Taking Stock," 81.

96. All results are taken from Lisa M. Montiel and David J. Wright, "Getting a Piece of the Pie: Federal Grants to Faith-Based Social Service Organizations," February 2006, Roundtable on Religion and Social Welfare Policy, Nelson A. Rockefeller Institute of Government, State University of New York, at www.rockinst.org/pdf /faith-based_social_services/2006-getting_a_piece_of_the_pie_federal_grants _to_faith-based_social_service_organizations.pdf. The quotation in the text is from Alan Cooperman, "Grants to Religious Groups Fall, Study Says," *Washington Post*, February 15, 2006.

97. See White House Office of Faith-Based and Community Initiatives, "Grants to Faith-Based Organizations Fiscal Year 2005," March 9, 2006, at http://georgewbush -whitehouse.archives.gov/government/fbci/final_report_2005.pdf. The quotation in the text is from a speech by George W. Bush in which he announced the WHOFBCI results. See "Remarks at the White House National Conference on Faith-Based and Community Initiatives," March 9, 2006, *Bush Public Papers*, 2006, 1:425.

98. White House, "Innovations in Compassion," 32.

99. Both criticisms are made in Wright, "Taking Stock," 73.

100. This point is made in DiIulio, *Godly Republic*, 139.

101. See Mark Chaves and Bob Wineburg, "Did the Faith-Based Initiative Change Congregations?" *Nonprofit and Voluntary Sector Quarterly* 39 (April 2010): 343–355. This study too has an important limitation. Chaves and Wineburg surveyed church *congregations*, but according to the Montiel and Wright study, only about 10 percent of faith-based grant awards went to congregations. Most

went to "independent, religiously affiliated organizations." See Montiel and Wright, "Getting a Piece," 9.

102. See WHOFBCI, "Grants to Faith-Based Organizations."

103. DiIulio, *Godly Republic*, 139.

104. As quoted in Black, Koopman, and Ryden, *Of Little Faith*, 76.

105. E. J. Dionne Jr., "Al Gore Speaks for Himself," *Washington Post*, May 28, 1999. Some commentators did recognize, however, that beneath the surface agreement, Bush and Gore had very different intentions with respect to the role of faith-based organizations. See, for example, Joe Loconte, "Bush vs. Gore on Faith-Based Charity," *American Enterprise*, June 2000, 26–28.

106. The issue is substantially more complicated than the brief discussion in the text indicates. For further details, see Formicola, Segers, and Weber, *Faith-Based Initiatives*, 74–77; Black, Koopman, and Ryden, *Of Little Faith*, 249–253; and John Orr, "Religion-Based Discrimination in Charitable Choice: A Guide for the Perplexed," Center for Religion and Civic Culture, 2002, at http://crcc.usc.edu/resources/pub lications/religion-based-discrimination-in-charitable-choice-a-guide-for-the -perplexed.html. The Supreme Court case referred to in the text is *Corporation of the Presiding Bishop v. Amos*, 483 US 327 (1987).

107. Ralph Benko, as quoted in Black, Koopman, and Ryden, *Of Little Faith*, 102–103.

108. As quoted in Black, Koopman, and Ryden, *Of Little Faith*, 209.

109. This criticism is made in both Black, Koopman, and Ryden, *Of Little Faith*; and DiIulio, *Godly Republic*.

110. Will Marshall, president of the Progressive Policy Institute, as quoted in Black, Koopman, and Ryden, *Of Little Faith*, 208.

111. Mike Allen, "Bush Aims to Get Faith Initiative Back on Track," *Washington Post*, June 25, 2001.

112. On this point, see Black, Koopman, and Ryden, *Of Little Faith*, 51–62.

113. Rep. Robert C. Scott (D-Va), as quoted in Wright, "Taking Stock."

114. As Black, Koopman, and Ryden note, "Friend and foe alike did not doubt the president's sincere belief in the effectiveness of faith-based programs." See *Of Little Faith*, 111. Even David Kuo, one of the sharpest critics of the administration's handling of the faith-based issue, has concluded, "No one who knows him [Bush] even a tiny bit doubts the sincerity and compassion of his heart." See Kuo, "Please, Keep Faith," February 2005, at www.beliefnet.com/News/Politics/2005/02/Please -Keep-Faith.aspx.

115. Black, Koopman, and Ryden, *Of Little Faith*, 111.

116. As indicated in the text, the statistics cited in the next three paragraphs come from an analysis of Bush's public communications, as reported in *Bush Public Papers*. I count all communications that were initiated by the president—i.e., all except his responses to questions posed by reporters.

117. The speech referred to is George W. Bush, "Remarks on the Faith-Based Welfare Initiative in Milwaukee," July 2, 2002, *Bush Public Papers*, 2002, 2:1162–1168. One day earlier, when Bush spoke at a forum on inner-city compassion, just two of

the sixty-five paragraphs in his transcribed speech dealt explicitly with the faith-based initiative. See "Remarks at a Rally on Inner-City Compassion in Cleveland, Ohio," July 1, 2002, 2:1153–1160.

118. See, for example, George W. Bush, "Remarks to the Community in Little Rock, Arkansas," June 3, 2002, *Bush Public Papers*, 2002, 1:923–927; "Remarks at the Marks Street Senior Recreation Complex in Orlando," June 21, 2002, 1:1038–1041; "Remarks at High Point University in High Point, North Carolina," July 25, 2002, 2:1287–1293; "Remarks at Madison Central High School in Madison, Mississippi," August 7, 2002, 2:1357–1364; and "Remarks to the Community in Louisville, Kentucky," September 5, 2002, 2:1530–1536.

119. Olasky's comments came in an interview with Mike Huckabee aired on October 10, 2009, as quoted in "Provost Olasky on Huckabee Show," at www.tkc .edu/media/archives2.asp?id=159. As for DiIulio, by mid-2002 he had already become disillusioned by Bush's failure to follow through on the promises of his "compassion agenda." See, for example, his comments in the "confidential memo" he wrote to reporter Ron Suskind on October 24, 2002, available at www.esquire .com/features/diilulio. For a good summary of DiIulio's later views on the Bush presidency, see DiIulio, "Why Judging."

120. Kuo, *Tempting Faith*, 115.

121. The story is told in Kuo, *Tempting Faith*, 160–162.

122. The order in which these policies are listed is *not* significant: i.e., items at the top of the list are not presumed to be more important than those near the bottom.

123. The quoted phrases are taken from Rove, *Courage and Consequence*, 122 and 65.

124. Rove, *Courage and Consequence*, 66.

125. Rove, *Courage and Consequence*, 158–159.

126. Rove, *Courage and Consequence*, 248.

127. Milton Friedman, *Capitalism and Freedom* (Chicago: University of Chicago Press, 1962), chap. 6.

128. Rove, *Courage and Consequence*, 372–373.

129. NCLB required new teachers to be state-certified, to pass competency tests in the subject(s) they taught, and, in middle schools and high schools, to have majored in or done graduate study in their area(s) of specialization. But a provision known as HOUSSE (High Objective Uniform State Standard of Evaluation) allowed states to develop much weaker, alternative procedures for "veteran" teachers. HOUSSE was strongly supported by teachers' unions and included in the final bill largely at the behest of Sen. Kennedy. As Stanford professor Terry Moe lamented, "The HOUSSE provisions create a loophole big enough to drive three million veteran teachers through." For further details, see Frederick M. Hess, "Why LBJ Is Smiling: NCLB and the Bush Legacy in Education," American Enterprise Institute, December 11, 2008, at www.aei.org/print/why-lbj-is-smiling; Paul Manna, *Collision Course: Federal Education Policy Meets State and Local Realities* (Washington: CQ Press, 2011), 30 and 100–101; and Ben Feller, "Ed. Dept. Eases Teacher Quality Rule," Associated Press, September 7, 2006. The Moe quotation is taken from Hess.

130. I describe accountability as an "allegedly" conservative principle only to make the point that while most conservatives probably do think accountability is a good thing, no great conservative thinker I am aware of has ever claimed that accountability was a core conservative principle. The word is not listed at all, for example, in the index to Russell Kirk, *The Conservative Mind: From Burke to Eliot*, 7th rev. ed. (Washington, DC: Regnery, 1985); or George H. Nash, *The Conservative Intellectual Movement in America since 1945* (New York: Basic Books, 1976).

131. Rove, *Courage and Consequence*, 237–239.

132. George W. Bush, *A Charge to Keep* (New York: William Morrow, 1999).

133. Jimmy Carter's policy preferences were described in very similar terms in James Fallows, "The Passionless Presidency," *Atlantic*, May 1979, 42.

134. Those who insist that Bush was no more than a standard, garden-variety conservative might reply that both No Child Left Behind and the Medicare prescription drug bill received overwhelming Republican support when they were passed by the Senate and House of Representatives. But as numerous accounts of those bills make clear, many Republicans had reservations about the legislation—reservations that they stifled only in order to assist a Republican president. Frederick M. Hess, for example, has written the following about NCLB: "Bush's leadership largely quieted 'big government' concerns among conservatives who had helped sink Clinton's less ambitious 1999 proposal. Eager to support the new president, conservatives who had backed the 1994 pledge to abolish the Education Department swallowed their doubts—allowing Bush to win landmark legislation that would have floundered in a Republican Congress if Gore had won the election." See Hess, "Why LBJ Is Smiling."

135. Though many Republicans criticized Barack Obama for the enormous increase in the number of food stamp recipients that occurred during his presidency, the increase actually began under George W. Bush. In 2000, the last year of the Clinton presidency, 17,194,000 people were enrolled in the food stamp program. By 2008, that number had jumped to 28,223,000, a 64 percent increase. Between 1994 and 2000, by contrast, the number of food stamp recipients had declined by 37 percent. See the data at www.fns.usda.gov/pd/snapsummary.htm (accessed January 1, 2014).

136. This list is an attempt to summarize the major, contemporary conservative criticisms of the Bush domestic record. See, among others, Jonah Goldberg, "George W. Bush, Preservative: Has Government Become the *Answer?*" January 21, 2004, at http://old.nationalreview.com/goldberg/goldberg200401211053.asp; Ilya Somin, "George W., Richard Nixon, and Big Government Conservatism," May 4, 2006, at www.volokh.com/posts/1146756572.shtml; George F. Will, "Bush's Budget Battle," *Washington Post*, February 18, 2005; and Rich Lowry, "Big Government Falls Flat: It's Not So Strong," February 21, 2006, at http://old.nationalreview.com/lowry/lowry200602210811.asp.

137. As noted in the text, the literature on this point is huge. See, among many others, Bruce R. Bartlett, *Impostor: How George W. Bush Bankrupted America and Betrayed the Reagan Legacy* (New York: Doubleday, 2006); Richard A. Viguerie,

Conservatives Betrayed: How George W. Bush and Other Big Government Republicans Hijacked the Conservative Cause (Los Angeles: Bonus Books, 2006); James Bovard, *The Bush Betrayal* (New York: Palgrave Macmillan, 2004); Herman Cain, "Compassionate Conservatism Lost," November 8, 2006, at http://townhall.com /columnists/hermancain/2006/11/08/compassionate_conservatism_lost/page /full; and Mark R. Levin, "Ronald Reagan and George W. Bush," *Human Events*, March 18, 2011, at www.humanevents.com/2011/03/18/ronald-reagan-and -george-w-bush. For some additional examples, see Lou Cannon and Carl M. Cannon, *Reagan's Disciple: George W. Bush's Troubled Quest for a Presidential Legacy* (New York: PublicAffairs, 2008), xii and 321–322.

138. As quoted in Mike Allen and David S. Broder, "Bush's Leadership Style: Decisive or Simplistic?" *Washington Post*, August 30, 2004.

139. See Mike Allen, "Management Style Shows Weaknesses," *Washington Post*, June 2, 2004.

140. Bob Woodward, *State of Denial* (New York: Simon & Schuster, 2006), 11.

141. Scott McClellan, *What Happened: Inside the Bush White House and Washington's Culture of Deception* (New York: PublicAffairs, 2008), 127.

142. Nicholas Lemann, "Remember the Alamo," *New Yorker*, October 18, 2004.

143. Michael J. Gerson, *Heroic Conservatism: Why Republicans Need to Embrace America's Ideals (and Why They Deserve to Fail If They Don't)* (New York: Harper One, 2007), 156.

144. George W. Bush, "Remarks on Labor Day in Richfield, Ohio," September 1, 2003, in *Bush Public Papers*, 2003, 2:1078.

145. Matt Bai, "Rove's Way," *New York Times Magazine*, October 20, 2002, 56.

146. Probably the best single statement of this argument is Henry Hazlitt, *Economics in One Lesson* (New York: Three Rivers Press, 1946). As Hazlitt summarizes his "lesson," *"The art of economics consists in looking not merely at the immediate but at the longer effects of any act or policy: it consists in tracing the consequences of that policy not merely for one group but for all groups"* (p. 17, emphasis in original).

147. George W. Bush, "Acceptance Speech to the Republican National Convention," September 2, 2004, at www.washingtonpost.com/wp-dyn/articles/A574 662004Sep2.html.

148. I drew the sample from *Bush Public Papers*, 2004, vols. 2 and 3. After excluding all obviously noncampaign related documents (messages to Congress, letters to other public officials, joint statements with foreign dignitaries, statements issued to observe religious holidays or the deaths of famous Americans) and the three presidential debates (where the topics were determined more by the questioners than by the candidates), I was left with 128 speeches, the vast majority of which were identified as "remarks" delivered at a particular city. To ensure a proper distribution of statements from different points in the fall campaign, I then selected every sixth speech for closer analysis. I read each statement for any mention of "compassionate conservatism" or "faith-based" initiatives, programs, or organizations.

149. Matt Latimer, *Speech-Less: Tales of a White House Survivor* (New York: Three Rivers Press, 2009), 250.

150. Rove, *Courage and Consequence*, 247.

151. See, for example, Adam Nagourney, "Issue by Issue, First Lady Details Differences with Giuliani," *New York Times*, October 17, 1999; David Kocieniewski, "Whitman and Forbes, Separated Now by Political Ideology," *New York Times*, November 9, 1999; Richard L. Berke, "Bush Supporters in State of Shock over Twin Losses," *New York Times*, February 24, 2000; Dana Milbank, "What Makes a Real Reagan Republican," *Washington Post*, May 27, 2012; and Cannon and Cannon, *Reagan's Disciple*, 322–323.

152. As quoted in Craig Unger, *Boss Rove: Inside Karl Rove's Secret Kingdom of Power* (New York: Scribner, 2012), 202.

153. Cannon and Cannon, 257–258.

154. See Jonathan Weisman and Amit R. Paley, "Dozens in GOP Turn Against Bush's Prized 'No Child' Act," *Washington Post*, March 15, 2007; and Amit R. Paley, "Ex-Aides Break with Bush on 'No Child,'" *Washington Post*, June 26, 2007.

155. The eight presidential candidates whose views on NCLB I examined were Mitt Romney, Rick Santorum, Newt Gingrich, Rick Perry, Jon Huntsman, Herman Cain, Ron Paul, and Michelle Bachman. In a book published in 2010, Romney said that, "Former president George W. Bush was right to champion the No Child Left Behind legislation . . . Only the federal government had the clout to force testing through the barricade mounted by the national teachers' unions." See Mitt Romney, *No Apology: The Case for American Greatness* (New York: St. Martin's Press, 2010), 219. By October 2011, however, Romney was saying that "we need to get the federal government out of education." As quoted in Trip Gabriel, "G.O.P. Anti-Federalism Aims at Education," *New York Times*, October 9, 2011.

156. For various quotations from Santorum on No Child Left Behind, see http://2012.republican-candidates.org/Santorum/Education-issue.php (accessed July 9, 2013); and http://2012election.procon.org/view.answers.election.php?question ID=1724 (accessed July 9, 2013).

157. The quotation is from a GOP debate in Ames, Iowa, August 11, 2011, as quoted in www.ontheissues.org/2012/Jon_Huntsman_Education.htm.

158. For the legislative history of the various immigration bills, see Alex Wayne, "Getting Tough on Illegal Immigration," *CQ Weekly*, December 26, 2005, 3396–3397; Jonathan Weisman, "House Votes to Toughen Laws on Immigration," *Washington Post*, December 17, 2005; Jim VandeHei and Jonathan Weisman, "On Immigration, Bush Seeks 'Middle Ground,'" *Washington Post*, May 16, 2006; Elizabeth B. Crowley and Michael Sandler, "Senate Plunges Back into Debate," *CQ Weekly*, May 22, 2006, 1400–1402; Michael Sandler, "Tough Immigration Conference Looms," *CQ Weekly*, May 29, 2006, 1473; and Michael Sandler, "GOP Move Delays Conference on Bill," *CQ Weekly*, June 26, 2006, 1785.

159. See, for example, Linda Chavez, "Hispanic Panic," *Commentary*, December 2012, 20–23; and Michael Gerson and Peter Wehner, "How to Save the Republican Party: A Five-Point Plan," *Commentary*, March 2013, 13–20.

160. Conor Friedersdorf, "Why a Newt Gingrich Candidacy Would Doom the Tea Party," December 6, 2011, at www.theatlantic.com/politics/archive/2011/12

/why-a-newt-gingrich-candidacy-would-doom-the-tea-party/249534/. Other commentators who made the same point include Julian E. Zelizer, "It's Tea Party vs. Bush *and* Obama," November 1, 2010, at www.cnn.com/2010/OPINION/11/01/zel izer.tea.party.bush/index/html; David Friedman, "George Bush and the Tea Party Movement," at davidfriedman.blogspot.com/2010/09/george-bush-and-tea-party -movement.html (accessed July 14, 2013); Timothy Dalrymple, "The Tea Started Brewing under Bush," October 25, 2010, www.patheos.com/Resources/Additional -Resources/Tea-Started-Brewing-Under-Bush.html; and Michael Hirsh, "George W. Bush: He Gave Rise to the Tea Party," *National Journal*, October 3, 2013.

161. The quotations come from a profile of Keli Carender, who reportedly led the first Tea Party rally, in Kate Zernike, *Boiling Mad: Inside Tea Party America* (New York: Times Books, 2010), 15–16.

162. The quotations are taken from Jim Wallis, "The Disappearance of the Compassionate Conservatives," December 8, 2011, at www.huffingtonpost.com /jim-wallis/the-disappearance-of-the_b_1137208.html; and Amy Sullivan, "Is Compassionate Conservatism Dead?" January 29, 2012, at http://usatoday30.usatoday .com/news/opinion/forum/story/2012–01–29/compassionate-conservatism -bush-santorum-republican/52873150/1.

163. John Podhoretz, "The Task," *Commentary*, January 2013, 1. Another good example can be found in the December 3, 2012, issue of *National Review*, the cover of which reads, "Conservatives suffered a terrible defeat on November 6, and there is no point pretending otherwise."

164. In addition to the Jonah Goldberg column discussed below, see Ben Smith, "Compassionate Conservatism Is Back," March 18, 2013, www.buzzfeed.com/ben smith/compassionate-conservatism-is-back; Dana Milbank, "'Compassionate Conservatism' Revival Lacks Passion," April 27, 2013, www.columbian.com/news/2013 /apr/27/compassionate-conservatism-revival-lacks-passion; Elias Isquith, "GOP Plan: Bring Dubya Back," *Salon*, June 15, 2013, www.salon.com/2013/06/15/gop _plan_bring_dubya_back/; Tom Benning, "Top Bush Adviser Karen Hughes Implores GOP to Re-Embrace Compassionate Conservatism," *Dallas Morning News*, January 31, 2013, http://trailblazerblog.dallasnews.com/2013/01/top-bush-adviser -karen-hughes-implores-gop-to-re-embrace-compassionate-conservatism.html/; Joseph Perkins, "Defending Compassionate Conservatism," *Orange County Register*, December 7, 2012, www.ocregister.com/articles/compassionate-380014-conser vative-party.html; Tom Benning, "Exclusive: As His Presidential Library Debuts, George W. Bush Prepares to Return to Public Stage on His Own Terms," *Dallas Morning News*, April 13, 2013, www.dallasnews.com/news/politics/headlines/20130413 -exclusive-as-his-presidential-library-debuts-george-w.-bush-prepares-to-return -to-public-stage-on-his-own-terms.ece; Matt K. Lewis, "To Modernize, the GOP Must Embrace Compassionate Conservatism," *The Week*, November 19, 2012, http:// theweek.com/bullpen/column/236572/to-modernize-the-gop-must-embrace -compassionate-conservatism; William Schambra, "Genuine Compassionate Conservatism Could Do Wonders for Poor Americans," May 1, 2013, http://philan thropy.com/article/To-Help-the-Poor/138943/; George Seay, "Retaking the Faith-

Based Initiative," *American Conservative*, January 31, 2013, www.theamerican conservative.com/articles/retaking-the-faith-based-initiative-5934; Ashley Portero, "Cantor Makes Pitch for Compassionate Conservatism to 'Make Life Work' for Americans," *International Business Times*, February 5, 2013, www.ibtimes .com/cantor-makes-pitch-compassionate-conservatism-make-life-work-ameri cans-full-text-1063682; and Rick Klein, "For George W. Bush Legacy, 'Compassionate Conservatism' Is Back," ABC News, April 25, 2013, http://abcnews.go.com/blogs /politics/2013/04/for-george-w-bush-legacy-compassionate-conservatism-is-back/.

165. See John Podhoretz, "What Is the Future of Conservatism in the Wake of the 2012 Election?–A Symposium," *Commentary*, January 2013, 14–53. The two symposium participants who urged conservatives to be more "compassionate" without actually using the phrase "compassionate conservatism" were Michael Gerson (p. 24) and James K. Glassman (p. 25). Both had held positions in the George W. Bush administration, and Glassman was then director of the George W. Bush Institute. Two other contributors—John B. Taylor (p. 49) and Tevi Troy (p. 50)—explicitly used the phrase "compassionate conservatism," but not in a way that could reasonably be read as an endorsement of the idea.

166. Jonah Goldberg, "Compassionate Conservatism Redux," *National Review*, November 16, 2012, at www.nationalreview.com/articles/333504/compassionate -conservatism-redux-jonah-goldberg.

167. Goldberg, "Compassionate Conservatism Redux."

Chapter 11: Conclusion

1. Craig Unger, *Boss Rove: Inside Karl Rove's Secret Kingdom of Power* (New York: Scribner, 2012), 218 and 252.

2. Karl Rove, *Courage and Consequence: My Life as a Conservative in the Fight* (New York: Simon & Schuster, 2010), 518.

3. Richard E. Neustadt, *Presidential Power and the Modern Presidents* (New York: Free Press, 1990), 129.

4. Aristotle, *Nichomachean Ethics*, trans. Martin Ostwald (Indianapolis: Liberal Arts Press, 1962), bk. 2, chap. 6.

Appendix: A Review of Karl Rove's *The Triumph of William McKinley: Why the Election of 1896 Still Matters*

1. All page references are to Karl Rove, *The Triumph of William McKinley: Why the Election of 1896 Still Matters* (New York: Simon & Schuster, 2015).

2. Historical studies of the presidential nomination process conventionally divide the years since 1832 into three major periods or systems: the pure convention system (1832–1908); the mixed system (1912–1968); and the plebiscitary system (1972 to the present). See, for example, Byron E. Shafer and Elizabeth M. Sawyer, *Eternal Bandwagon: The Politics of Presidential Nomination* (forthcoming).

3. For purposes of this appendix, the South is defined as the eleven former Confederate states. Though in 1896 it was in the process of becoming even more lopsid-

edly Democratic in its voting, the South did not provide a single electoral vote to a Republican presidential candidate between 1880 and 1916.

4. As indicated, there is a very large literature on the relationship between the state of the economy and presidential and congressional voting. For two good overviews of the field, see Edward R. Tufte, *Political Control of the Economy* (Princeton: Princeton University Press, 1978); and Douglas A. Hibbs Jr., *The American Political Economy: Macroeconomics and Electoral Politics* (Cambridge: Harvard University Press, 1987). For evidence about the effect of economic conditions on the vote in the 1890s, see David W. Brady, *Critical Elections and Congressional Policy Making* (Stanford: Stanford University Press, 1988), 168–170, 194; and Samuel T. McSeveney, *The Politics of Depression: Political Behavior in the Northeast* (New York: Oxford University Press, 1972), esp. chap. 7.

5. The two sets of unemployment estimates, one by Stanley Lebergott and the other by Christina Romer, are reported in Romer, "Spurious Volatility in Historical Unemployment Data," *Journal of Political Economy* 94 (February 1986), 31. On the severity of the depression, see Charles Hoffmann, "The Depression of the Nineties," *Journal of Economic History* 16 (June 1956): 137–164.

6. Estimates of the Democratic seat loss in 1894 vary a bit depending on the base against which the 1894 election results are compared. The number given here is taken from Harold W. Stanley and Richard G. Niemi, eds., *Vital Statistics on American Politics 2015–2016* (Washington, DC: CQ Press, 2015), table 1-17.

7. The difference in information levels and ideological sophistication between political elites and the mass public is also a major theme in contemporary voting studies. Philip E. Converse, in particular, has often warned about the dangers involved in inferring the motivations for mass behavior on the basis of elite ideology. See especially Converse, "The Nature of Belief Systems in Mass Publics," in *Ideology and Discontent*, ed. David E. Apter (London: Free Press, 1964), 206–261.

8. The quotation is from George W. Bush, *Decision Points* (New York: Crown, 2010), 38.

9. A number of economic historians have argued that the recovery had little to do with McKinley's pro-gold standard, high-tariff policies, but he was in the White House when the recovery occurred and was consequently given credit for it.

10. See Karl Rove, *Courage and Consequence: My Life as a Conservative in the Fight* (New York: Simon & Schuster, 2010), 122, 128, and 158.

11. Rove, *Courage and Consequence*, 65.

12. Rove, 66.

13. As the national popular vote totals make clear, McKinley ran well ahead of the five previous Republican presidential candidates. But detailed voting studies generally conclude that McKinley increased the GOP vote share across the board, rather than showing a particular appeal to specific groups such as Catholics. See, for example, V. O. Key Jr., "A Theory of Critical Elections," *Journal of Politics* 17 (February 1955): 3–18; and Jerome M. Chubb, William H. Flanigan, and Nancy H. Zingale, *Partisan Realignment: Voters, Parties, and Government in American History* (Boulder, CO: Westview Press, 1990), chap. 3.

14. Rove, *Courage and Consequence*, 128.

15. Mike Allen, "Style Counts, Strategists Say," *Washington Post*, November 1, 2000. It was during the final week, it should be noted, that Bush lost what had once been a fairly substantial lead in the polls.

Index

Numbers in italics refer to pages with figures or tables.

Doolittle, Jimmy, 181
Dowd, Matthew, 53
Draper, Robert, 326n19
Dream and the Nightmare, The (Magnet),
262–263
Dubai, 56
Dubai Ports World, 56–61, 326n19
Duberstein, Ken, 162
Dukakis, Michael, 256
"Duty of Hope" (Bush speech), 272–275,
284

economy
presidential election of 1896 and, 101,
310–311, 312
presidential election of 1992 and,
250–251
presidential election of 2012 and, 45–46
presidential elections and the
economic well-being of the
electorate, 45
public perception of the Democratic
Party and economic fairness, 253
education policy
importance in modern presidential
elections, 131, *133*
traditional party images regarding,
134
See also No Child Left Behind Act
Education Trust, 90
Edwards, George C., 63, 69
Edwards, James, 118
Eisenhower, Dwight D., *41*, 153
election forecasting, 23–24, 31–32
electronic surveillance program, 190,
194–196, 197
Elmore, Richard, 91
El Salvador, 198, 200, *201*
Emancipation Proclamation, 173, 176–177,
356n17
Emerging Republican Majority, The
(Phillips), 9
empathy, 253, 255–256, 372n16
enhanced interrogation techniques, 190,
196–197
Enron Corporation, 209–210, 211–212, 214,
215, 216
Environmental Protection Agency, 82
Environmental Working Group, 106
equilibrium analysis, 102
European Union, 104
evangelical Christians, 257–261,
373–374n30

Every Student Succeeds Act (2015), 89
executive orders, Bush's faith-based
initiatives and, 276

faith-based bureaucracy, 277–278
faith-based initiatives
Bush's handling of as president, 275–285
Bush's proposals for during the 2000
presidential campaign, 272–275
critics of, 279, 280–281, 376–377n65
John DiIulio and, 267–272
failure of compassionate conservatism
and, 300, 304
Marvin Olasky and, 261–262, 263–267,
300
Rove's notion of compassionate
conservatism and, 285–286
faith-based laws, 271
faith-based organizations, government
and, 273, 278–279
faith-based programs, 269
faith-saturated programs, 269–270
Farm Security and Rural Investment Act
(2002), 108–111, 149–150
farm subsidies, 104–111, 139–141, 149–150,
293
FBI. *See* Federal Bureau of Investigation
Feaver, Peter, 235
Federal Bureau of Investigation (FBI),
194, 217, 219
federal deficit, 119–127, 146–149
Federal Emergency Management Agency,
155
Federalist no. 68, 130
Feith, Douglas, 129
"Final Report to the Armies of
Compassion," 277
Finkelstein, Arthur, 326n25
Finn, Chester E., Jr., 91
fireside chats, 182
fiscal policy, 119–127
Fitzgerald, Patrick, 227
Fleischer, Ari, 65, 223, 227
Fleisher, Richard, 69
Foley, Mark, 50
food stamp program, 382n135
Forbes, Steve, 19, 21
Ford, Gerald, *43, 44*, 45, 71, 122–123, 190
Foreign Intelligence Surveillance Court,
194–195
foreign policy
Bush legacy and the 2012 presidential
election, 46

failures of the Bush administration in, 87–88

See also Iraq war

Foreign Surveillance Act (1978), 194

Fort Sumter, 174

Fox News, 304

Fox News/Opinion Dynamics polls, *59, 185,* 199

France, 178, 180

Freedom to Farm Act (1996), 107–108

Friedersdort, Conor, 296

Friedman, Milton, 286

Frist, Bill, 57

front-porch campaigns, 3, 17

Frum, David, 87, 99, 246

Fuller, Craig, 120

Gallup/ORC polls, *244*

Gallup Poll
    on Bush and the Enron Corporation scandal, 210
    on the Bush legacy and the federal deficit, 149
    on Bush's post-presidential image, 42–44
    changing public attitudes about Bush's honesty, *244*
    on the federal deficit issue and the 2004 election, 147, 148
    presidential approval ratings and, 66–67, 320n17
    on public opinion regarding the Iraq war, 183–184, *185,* 186, 187, *188*
    on public opinion regarding the No Child Left Behind Act, 132, *136*
    on the Vietnam syndrome, 198
    during World War II, 180–181, 182, *183*

Gardner, Bruce, 106

Garner, Jay, 157

Gates, Robert, 167, 199

General Social Survey, 135–136

Geneva Conventions, 193

Georgia, 140, 150

Gephardt, Richard, 136–137

Gerard, Leo, 137

Gergen, David, 247

Gerson, Michael, 291, 386n165

Gettysburg Address, 173

Gibbs, Robert, 65

GI Bill of Rights, 182

Gillespie, Ed, 77

Gimpel, James, 145

Gingrich, Newt, 262, 263

Glassman, James K., 386n165

Going Public (Kernell), 63

Goldberg, Jonah, 297, 298–299

Goldwater, Barry, 249, 260

Gonzales, Alberto, 195

Gordon, Michael, 236

Gore, Al
    campaign fund raising for the 2000 presidential election, 19, *20*
    John DiIulio and, 267
    election forecasting with the 2000 presidential election and, 23–24
    faith-based initiatives and, 279–280
    presidential approval ratings and, 67
    public perceptions of, *256*
    September 11 terrorist attacks and, 219
    weapons of mass destruction issue and, 233

Gorelick, Jamie, 217

Gould, Lewis, 10, 316n16

government
    campaign consultants and the requisites of good government, 75
    faith-based initiatives and, 263–267, 270–271
    faith-based organizations and, 273, 278–279
    relationship of politics to, 74–75

Government Accountability Office, 57, 168

Graham, Bob, 233

Great Britain
    Lincoln's pursuit of the Civil War and, 174, 176–177
    Franklin Roosevelt's pursuit of aid for during World War II, 178–179, 180
    sixteen words controversy and, 220–222, 230

Greenberg, Stan, 122

Greenspan, Alan, 103

Greenstein, Fred, 290–291

Grenada, 172

Gresham's Law, 74

group politics
    differing perspectives of political consultants v. policy advisors regarding, 98–102
    farm subsidies and, 104–111, 139–141, 293
    immigration policy and, 111–119, 141–146
    Rove's focus on, 99–101, 102
    steel tariffs and, 102–104, 138–139, 291–292

NIE. *See* National Intelligence Estimate

Niger, sixteen words controversy and, 221, 223, 227, 229

9/11 Commission, 56, 216–217

Nixon, Richard
impact of Watergate on success rate with Congress, 69
post-presidential image of, 42, *43, 44*
presidential approval ratings, 41, 67, 69
Watergate crisis and, 69, 153, 154

No Child Left Behind Act (2001)
compassionate conservatism and, 287, 289, 290, 300, 301–302
High Objective Uniform State Standard of Evaluation provision, 381n129
policy-making driven by political considerations and, 88–92, 94
political consequences for Bush, 131–134, *136*
presidential communications about following 9/11, 283
Republican reservations about and eventual rejection of, 295–296, 304, 382n134

Noonan, Peggy, 120, 122

North Africa invasion, 181

Novak, Robert, 227, 228

NSA. *See* National Security Agency

nuclear weapons, Iraq and, 235–237

Nye, Joseph, 161

Obama, Barack
economic well-being of the electorate and, 45
federal deficit and, 123, 147, 149
food stamp program and, 382n135
midterm elections of 2010 and, 68–69
Office of Faith-Based and Neighborhood Partnerships and, 277
Office of Political Affairs and, 73
Office of Public Engagement and, 71
Patient Protection and Affordable Care Act, 49–50
political use of tax policy, 93–94
poor communication as an excuse for flawed policies, 203–204
post-presidential image of, 42, *43, 44*
presidential approval ratings and, 41, 67, 68–69
presidential election of 2008, 38, 39

presidential election of 2012, 45–46
public perceptions of, 256
space policy and, 96–97, 336n84
Viet-Iraq syndrome and, 202

O'Brien, Ed, 136

Office of Faith-Based and Community Initiatives
Bush's creation of, 276, 277
John DiIulio as head of, 86–87, 267, 268, 271
on government funding to faith-based organizations, 278, 279
David Kuo as director, 284
proposal for local offices, 271

Office of Faith-Based and Neighborhood Partnerships, 277

Office of Political Affairs, 73–73, 77

Office of Political Strategy and Outreach, 73

Office of Public Liaison/Office of Public Engagement, 71, 77

Office of Public Opinion Research, 182–183

Office of Strategic Initiatives (OSI), 77, 82, 306

Office of Strategic Services, 84

Oklahoma, 90

Olasky, Marvin
Bush's slighting of faith-based initiatives and, 284
charity tax credits and, 265, 275, 375n51
differences with John DiIulio's notion of faith-based initiatives, 268, 269, 270, 271–272
influence on Bush's notion of faith-based initiatives, 272, 273, 274, 275
lack of response from the history profession to the work of, 376n62
notions of faith-based initiatives, 261–262, 263–267, 300

O'Neill, Paul, 87, 103, 123

On War (Clausewitz), 171

Opinion Dynamics poll, 255–256

Orden, David, 107

OSI. *See* Office of Strategic Initiatives

Ostrom, Charles W., Jr., 69

Oxfam, 160

Paarlberg, Robert, 107

Page, Benjamin I., 63

Paige, Rod, 90

Panama, 172

Panetta, Leon, 122
partisan realignment
    concept and historical overview of, 8–9
    Democratic Party and the 2008
        presidential election, 39–40
    importance of big issues in, 307
    William Mayer on, 317–318n27
    See also Republican realignment
party systems, 9
Patient Protection and Affordable Care
    Act, 49–50
Pearl Harbor, 181
Peninsular and Oriental Steam
    Navigation, 56
People's History of the United States, A
    (Zinn), 351n8
Perle, Richard, 82
Persico, Joseph, 181
Peterson, Mark A., 69
Peterson, Paul E., 90
Petraeus, David, 167
Pew Hispanic Center, 143
Pew Research Center, 59, 147, 232
Pfeiffer, Dan, 335–336n73
Phillips, Kevin, 9, 317n24
Plouffe, David, 335–336n73
policy
    appropriate place of political
        consultants in policy making, 128
    consequences of placing politics over
        policy, 127–129
    poor communication as an excuse for
        flawed policies, 203–204
    presidents and the importance of
        policy over popularity, 130–131,
        150–151
    presidents and the selling of, 62–65
    relationship of politics to, 74–75
    See also domestic policy; foreign
        policy
policy advisors
    assessment of the individual value
        and appropriate roles of, 306–307
    differences with political consultants
        (see political consultants v. policy
        advisors)
    dynamics of the Rove-Cheney
        relationship in the Bush
        administration and, 83–84
    presidential decision-making in the
        Bush administration and, 80–83
    Rove compared to other historical
        figures, 6–7

Rove's role as and influence in the
    Bush administration, 74, 75–77,
    82–83
political consultants
    appropriate place in policy making,
        128
    assessing support and opposition,
        61–62
    assessment of the individual value
        and appropriate roles of, 306–307
    Bush and the Dubai Ports World
        episode, 56–61
    defining the boundaries of the
        possible, 55–61
    monitoring the nation's political
        pulse, 65–70
    outreach to interest groups, 70–71
    planning for the next election, 71–73
    presidents and the need for, 55
    presidents in crisis and, 154–155
    selling the president and the
        president's program, 62–65
    See also campaign strategists; political
        consultants v. policy advisors
political consultants v. policy advisors
    appropriate place of political
        consultants in policy making, 128
    assessment of the individual value
        and appropriate roles of, 306–307
    consequences of placing politics over
        policy, 127–129
    differences in measuring the value of
        domestic policy, 92–97
    differences in understanding and
        handling the details of domestic
        policy, 85–92
    differing notions of political time and
        its consequences for fiscal policy,
        119–127
    differing perspectives on group
        politics, 98–119 (see also group
        politics)
    overview of the importance of
        differences between, 84–85
    Rove's failure to distinguish between,
        306
political feedback, 66
political generals, 174–175
political power, politics and, 13–14
politics
    consequences of placing politics over
        policy, 127–128, 129
    definitions of, 13

Bush's creation of military
commissions and, 81–82
Kyoto climate change treaty and,
332n24
sixteen words controversy and, 222,
223–224, 225, 362n16
weapons of mass destruction issue
and, 237
Rivers, Douglas, 69
Rivlin, Alice, 122
Robertson, Pat, 281
Rockefeller, Jay, 233
Roe, Terry, 107
Rollins, Ed, 294
Romney, Mitt
Hispanic vote in 2012 and, 141, 145,
146, 296
loss in the 2012 presidential election,
297, 298
view of the No Child Left Behind Act,
295
Roosevelt, Franklin Delano
Louis Howe and, 4, 6–7
Munich crisis of 1938 and, 357n26
presidential election of 1936 and, 301
presidential ideology and, 249
use of subordinates as president, 83
war as a political enterprise and,
178–184
Roper Center, 46–47
Rose, Nancy L., 69
Rotherham, Andy, 91
Roundtable on Religion and Social
Welfare Policy, 278, 279
Rove, Karl
ambition of and drive to control,
82–83, 207
Bridge to Nowhere project and, 126
Bush administration fiscal policy and,
122, 125, 126
Bush's gubernatorial election of 1998
and, 16–17
Bush's presidential communications
and, 205, 206–207, 246
Bush's response to Hurricane Katrina
and, 155
compared to other figures as a
campaign strategist, 2–5
compared to other figures as a policy
advisor, 6–7
compassionate conservatism and, 252,
257, 285–287, 293, 294, 301
dynamics of the Rove-Cheney

relationship in the Bush
administration, 83–84
failure of the Bush presidency and,
303–306
failure to provide Bush with political
advice during the Iraq occupation
crisis, 163–166, 168, 169
failure to separate political consulting
from policy advising, 306
Fox News and, 304
group politics and Bush
administration immigration policy,
112–113, 114, 115, 118
group politics and Bush
administration steel tariffs,
103–104, 138, 291–292
importance placed on group politics
by, 99–101, 102
interest in and study of William
McKinley, 10–11, 100–101
job titles held by in the Bush
administration, 77
William Mayer and, 14–15
Medicare prescription drug program
and, 125, 287
midterm elections of 2002 and, 26,
27–28
midterm elections of 2006 and, 34–35,
38
Harriet Myers Supreme Court
nomination and, 62
No Child Left Behind Act and, 130
Office of Public Liaison and, 71, 77
Marvin Olasky and, 262
presidential election of 2000 and,
16–25
presidential election of 2004 and,
28–29, 31, 94
presidential election of 2008 and, 38,
39
presidential election of 2012 and, 296
presidential polling and, 53, 54
prominence and reputation of, 1–2
on Republicans and the terrorism
issues, 220
role and influence as senior policy
advisor to Bush, 74, 75–77, 82–83
selling the president's program and,
64
sixteen words controversy and, 223,
227, 228, 368n88
The Triumph of William McKinley,
309–313

Rove, Karl, *continued*
    Doug Wead and, 258, 259, 260
    weapons of mass destruction issue
        and, 233, 242
    "What Makes a Great President"
        speech, 10
    See also Republican realignment
Rudalevige, Andrew, 92
Rumsfeld, Donald
    crisis of the Iraq war and, 153
    failure of the US postwar occupation
        of Iraq and, 157, 158, 160, 163, 166,
        189, 304–305, 352n27
    military commission policy and, 193
    policy credentials as an advocate for
        the Iraq war, 129
    resignation of, 166, 167, 354n47
    view of the postwar occupation of Iraq
        as unnecessary, 355n6
    weapons of mass destruction issue
        and, 238, 241
Russert, Tim, 241
Russia, 104
Rwandan genocide, 201–202, 360–361n79
Ryden, David K., 282

Sabato, Larry, 27
Sager, Rebecca, 277–278
Sailer, Steve, 143
Salter, Malcolm, 212
Salvation Army, 273
Samuelson, Robert, 124
Santorum, Rick, 295
Sarbanes-Oxley Act, 210, 363n25
Saudi Arabia, Khobar Towers bombing,
    218–219
scandals
    Bush administration responses to
        corporate scandals, 208–216
    midterm elections of 2006 and, 35–36
school vouchers, 286, 287
Schumer, Chuck, 184
Schwarzkopf, Norman, 236
Second New Deal, 249
Securities and Exchange Commission, 214
Selective Service Act (1941), 179, 180–181
Senate Committee on Agriculture,
    Nutrition, and Forestry, 108
Senate Select Committee on Intelligence,
    229
September 11 terrorist attacks
    Bush administration failures to assign

blame for the attacks to Clinton,
    216–220
Bush presidential approval ratings
    and, 26–27, 40
impact on Bush's presidential
    communications, 283
Vietnam syndrome and, 199–200
Seward, William, 176
Shapiro, Robert Y., 63
Shehhi, Marwan al-, 116
Sherman, John, 3
"shoot on sight" policy, 179
Simberg, Rand, 95
Simon, Dennis M., 69
sixteen words controversy, 207, 220–231,
    362n16, 366n63
slavery, Lincoln's pursuit of the Civil War
    and, 174, 175–177
social capital, 269
social programs. *See* faith-based
    initiatives
Social Security, 64, 70, 95, 249
Somalia, 199, 219
Souter, David, 62
South Carolina, Fort Sumter and, 174
South Carolina primary, 22–23, 47
South Dakota, 140
Soviet Union, US military assistance to
    during World War II, 179, 180, 181
Space Exploration Initiative, 96
space policy, 95–97, 134–137, 336n84,
    347n6
special purpose entities (SPEs), 211, 212
Stalin, Joseph, 13
Stanton, Edwin, 176
State of the Union address (2003),
    220–222. *See also* sixteen words
    controversy
steel tariffs, 102–104, 138–139, 291–292
Steeper, Fred, 53
Stevenson, Adlai, 67, 311
Stimson, Henry, 180, 181
Stone, Michael, 219
Strategery Group, 206
Success Offensive, 190
Sullivan, Terry, 69
Sumner, Daniel, 106–107
Supreme Command (Cohen), 79
"surge" strategy, 64, 167–168, 186–188
Suskind, Ron, 87
Swartz, Mark, 213, 214
Syria, 202

ks, gathered before the skinners were through with their work; they
lly stayed at a wary distance, but the handsome ravens, glossy-hued
n white napes. long-billed, long-winged, and short-tailed, came round
re familiarly.

th so much game available he found that he rarely had to stalk.
ng was from a long range, but by maneuvering, and never walking
t toward the quarry, he was usually able to collect whatever specimen
turalist desired. Sometimes he shot well, sometimes he did not. Fail-
vere confessed in his diary. One entry noted, "Missed steinbuck [an
pe], pig, impala and Grant: awful."
lls were noted in terms of the game, distances, his position when
ing, and where the bullet struck. On one very successful day the diary
read: "Hartebeest, 250 yards, facing me; shot through face, broke neck.
a, very large, quartering, 160 yards, between neck and shoulder. Buck
t, 220 yards, walking, behind shoulder. Steinbuck, 180 yards, standing,
d shoulder."
enerally, each head of game that he collected cost him "a goodly
ber of bullets." But the expenditure of a few cartridges was "of no con-
ence whatever compared to the escape of a single head of game which
ld have been bagged." Because shooting at a long range required run-
, his proportion of misses was sizeable, and there were "altogether too
y even at short ranges."
As in his ventures in the West, he would have preferred to go out by him-
but he was not in the Dakotas or the Rockies. He was in Kitanga, and
meant being accompanied by natives who knew the land and the ways
he East African hunt that began before the tropic sun rose to flame over
brink of the world as strange creatures rustled through the brush or fled
ly in the long grass before the light grew bright and revealing.
Here, in the still heat of noon when he sat beneath a tree, with his water
teen, lunch, and a volume from the Pigskin Library at hand, he could
r through his pocket telescope to watch the herds of game that hardly
Americans had ever heard about, and very few had seen for themselves,
ng down or standing drowsily in the distance. Then, as the afternoon
ned and a red sunset paled to amber and opal, he returned to Sir Alfred's
me with whatever the vast, mysterious African landscape had provided in
phies.

Bret Harte poems, *Tales of the Argonauts* and *Luck of Roaring
   Camp*
Mark Twain's *Huckleberry Finn* and *Tom Sawyer*
Crothers' *Gentle Reader* and *Pardoner's Wallet*
Bunyan's "Pilgrim's Progress"
Macaulay's History, Essays, and Poems
The Federalist
Gregorovius's *Rome*
Cooper's *Pilot*
Thackeray, *Vanity Fair* and *Pendennis*
Dickens, *Mutual Friend* and *Pickwick Papers*
Alfred Thayer Mahan, *The Influence of Seapower Upon History
   1660–1783*, a book that was of great influence in Roosevelt's
   vision of an American two-ocean navy built on the role of
   the battleship.

These books were for use, not ornament, Roosevelt pointed out, and one
or more of them would be "either in my saddle pocket or in the cartridge-
bag." Reading would be done "while resting under a tree at noon, perhaps
beside the carcass of a beast I had killed, or else while waiting for camp to be
pitched." As a result, "the books were stained with blood, sweat, gun oil,
dust, and ashes." He chose pigskin bindings because ordinary coverings
"either vanished or became loathsome, whereas pigskin merely grew to look
as a well-used saddle looks."

With the camp well established, Roosevelt and Kermit rode out on the afternoon of the third day on their first African hunt, guided by their host, Sir
Alfred Pease and a friend, Clifford Hill. Along with gun bearers and porters
to carry in the game they ventured across desolate flats or short grass until
the ground began to rise at places into low hills (called koppies) with rock-
strewn tops. Soon they began to see game, but the flatness of the country
and the absence of cover made stalking difficult.
    Among sparsely scattered, stunted, scantily leaved mimosas were herds
of hartebeests, wildebeests, and small parties of two kinds of gazelles
(Thompson and Grant, named for the discoverers of the species). Peering
across the bare plain through a rain squall, Roosevelt saw a fine Grant and
began stalking it. When he fired his Springfield, he underestimated the
range. His bullets fell short and the gazelle raced away. Aiming for a smaller

gazelle buck and shooting "for the table," he felled it at 225 yards. But what the specimen collector really desired were a wildebeest bull and cow. The powerful, ungainly variety of the brindled gnu or blue Wildebeest of South Africa, with shaggy manes, heavy forequarters and generally bovine look were "interesting creatures of queer, eccentric habits" that at a distance reminded him of the bison of the Great Plains.

In an account of the quest for the benefit of Americans who eagerly awaited the reports he'd agreed to provide *Scribner's Magazine* he wrote:

> I first tried to get up to a solitary old bull, and after a good deal of maneuvering, and by taking advantage of a second rain squall, I got a standing shot at him at four hundred yards, and hit him, but too far back. Although keeping a good distance away, he tacked and veered so, as he ran, that by much running myself I got various other shots at him, at very long range, but missed them all, and he finally galloped over a distant ridge, his long tail twitching, seemingly not much the worse. We followed on horseback, for I hate to let any wounded thing escape to suffer. But meanwhile he had run into view of Kermit, and Kermit, who is of an age and build which better fit him for successful breakneck galloping over unknown country dotted with holes and bits of rotten ground, took up the chase with enthusiasm. Yet it was sunset, after a run of six or eight miles, when he finally ran into and killed the tough old bull, which had turned to bay, snorting and tossing its horns.

A wildebeest cow that Roosevelt shot at and missed was killed by Sir Alfred Pease just before sundown. Both it and the bull were fat and in fine condition, providing meat for dinner and their skins for the National Museum.

By the law of the veldt, Roosevelt noted, because his shot had been the first to hit the bull, he was entitled to claim the kill. Yet in reality, he wrote, "the credit was communistic, so to speak, and my share was properly less than that of the others" on the hunt.

The next day the hunting party rode about sixteen miles to Pease's farm (to Roosevelt it was a ranch, "as we should call it in the West") in the hills of Kitanga. Always careful to set the scene, Roosevelt dutifully recorded, "The house was one story high, clean and comfortable, with a veranda running round three sides; and on the veranda were lion skins and the skull of a rhi-

noceros. From the house we looked over hills green valley below, with its flat-topped acacias, evening we could see, scores of miles away, the sn imanjaro turn crimson in the setting sun. The tv when night fell, stars new to northern eyes flashe

The veranda also provided Roosevelt a sight while seated in a rocking chair at Sagamore Hill. hartebeests came "right up to the wire fence, two-s itself." On long afternoons "in plain view, on th "black-and-white-striped zebra, and ruddy hartebe

Unless there was a lion or rhinoceros hunt invol sevelt went out accompanied only by a few native He felt that riding through teeming herds of gam steps of time for sixty or seventy years, and being white men first came to Africa. He enjoyed "a pecul: in "the wild, lonely country," with only his "silent b alert to everything, he provided this vividly poetic outing, from the climate to the kill:

> When the sky was overcast it was cool and ple country; as soon as the sun appeared the vertical trop quiver above the scorched land. As we passed down a through aromatic shrubs and the hot, pleasant fragr When we came to a nearly dry watercourse, there rushes, beautiful lilies and lush green plants with st great deep-green fig trees, or flat-topped mimosas. In n there were sure to be native beehives; these were sectic hung from the branches; they formed striking and cha of the landscape. Whenever there was moisture there v liant of hue and many of them sweet to smell; and bi kinds abounded. When we left the hills and the wooded might ride hour after hour across the barren desolation c herds of zebra and hartebeest stared at us through the the zebra, with shrill, barking neighs, would file off acros the high-withered hartebeests, snorting and bucking, wo confused mass, as unreasoning panic succeeded foolish shot anything, vultures of several kinds, and the tall, hic

10

★ ★ ★

The Lions of the Kapiti

A
FTER NIGHT FELL, Theodore Roosevelt heard hyenas. Although he had yet to see one, he'd listened to hair-raising tales about their savagery. The wild creatures were always lurking on the threshold of Nairobi, and often crossed it. Just a few months before his arrival, one had crept into a hut on the outskirts of the town and seized and killed a man. When one of Sir Alfred's native hunters was attacked as he slept beside a campfire, part of his face was torn off. In 1908 and throughout the early part of 1909, as sleeping-sickness ravaged the region, hyenas had grown constantly bolder. They haunted camps where the stricken lay, burst into huts, and carried off their helpless prey.

It was with great pleasure and parental pride, therefore, that Roosevelt looked on as Kermit killed one. Coming across the hyena in a dry creek bed, known as a donga, he galloped after it. The chase was a long one. Twice the hyena got onto such rocky ground that he almost outran his determined pursuer. At last, after covering nearly ten miles, Kermit ran into it in the open, shooting from the saddle as it shambled along at a canter, growling with rage and terror.

Regarding hyenas with contempt, Roosevelt described them as hideous spotted beasts that were a dreadful curse to the weak and helpless, but "too cowardly ever to be a source of danger to a hunter." When he inquired of veteran hunters as to which African animals they knew to be the most dangerous to men, he found a wide difference of opinion. The territorial governor placed the buffalo first, then the elephant, lion, and rhinoceros. Another professional hunter and writer on the topic of African game put the rhino first. But for the hunter whom Roosevelt most admired, Frederick Selous, it was the lion. Allowing that opinions on the relative prowess and ferocity of the various animals were based on personal experience, Roosevelt wrote that what must be kept in mind was that "surrounding conditions, the geographical locality, and the wide individual variation of temper within the ranks of each species must all be taken into account."

Consequently, he concluded that "the weight of opinion among those best fitted to judge is that the lion is the most formidable opponent of the hunter, under ordinary conditions."

As evidence, he noted that during the last three or four years, in German and British East Africa and Uganda, more than fifty men had been killed or mauled by lions, buffaloes, rhinos, and elephants, but that "the lions have much the largest list of victims to their credit."

Everywhere he went he'd found signs that the lion was lord and that his reign was cruel. Lions took livestock of settlers, ravaged the herds and flocks of natives, and preyed at will on swarming zebras and kongoni. Observing the remains of a zebra that had been killed not more than eighteen hours earlier, he found the stripped bones all in place and the skin still on the lower legs and head. The zebra was lying on its belly, the legs spread out, the neck vertebra crushed. From this Roosevelt deduced that the lion had "sprung clean on it, bearing it down by his weight while he bit through the back of the neck, and the zebra's legs had spread out as the body yielded under the lion."

Brimming with excited anticipation of a lion hunt, he told a companion, "If only I can get *my* lion I shall be happy—even if he is a small one—but I hope he will have a mane."

Initial hunting sojourns proved disappointing. The ravines they beat either had no lions, or efforts to make them leave a particularly difficult hill or swamp failed. But if anybody knew just the right place to seek them, Roosevelt believed, it was Sir Alfred Pease. Confident that he would get his lion, he and Kermit set out again with Sir Alfred in charge of an all-day hunt. In the party were Lady Pease, their daughter, a fellow-guest named Medlicott, another amateur hunter named Percival, and several Masai beaters, gun bearers, porters, and dogs.

After pausing for lunch under a great fig tree at the foot of a high, rocky hill, the party followed a long dry donga with low, steep banks and here and there patches of brush that might hold hyena, cheetah, wild dog, or lion. Soon, in the sandy bed, Sir Alfred discerned lion spoor, then the footprints of a big male and those of a lioness. As the hunters walked cautiously along each side of the donga, with their horses following close behind, the dogs began to show signs of scenting the lions.

As beaters thrashed away at each patch of brush, shouted, and threw stones, Roosevelt and the others stood watching any probable exit with rifles at the ready. After a couple of false alarms the dogs drew toward one patch, their hair bristling, and showing such eager excitement that Roosevelt knew "something big was inside."

"Simba!" shouted a beater, pointing to the patch of bushes just across a small ravine.

Shifting position, Roosevelt peered eagerly at the spot for several moments before he caught a glimpse of tawny hide.

As the lion moved, someone yelled, "Shoot!"

Roosevelt fired. So did Kermit.

Out of the brush came not the hoped-for big lion, but two large cubs. Each was so badly wounded, Roosevelt recorded, that they had to be "finished off." But even if they'd not been shot, he added, the mastiff-sized cubs "were too big to take alive."

With remarkable understatement, Roosevelt wrote, "This was a great disappointment."

Because it was well on in the afternoon, and the country most apt to harbor lions had proved unrewarding, it seemed to Roosevelt that he would not have another chance that day. But Sir Alfred was not so easily discouraged. Although he said nothing, he intended to have another try. As he rode toward another donga, Roosevelt and the others followed at a canter. When they reached the shallow donga, Pease found the spoor of two large lions. With "every sense acock," Roosevelt recalled, the hunters dismounted and approached the first patch of tall bushes. But shouts and thrown stones produced no result.

Again disappointed, Roosevelt got back on his horse, a stout and quiet sorrel named Tranquility. About a quarter-mile farther along the donga, out of a patch of tall, thick brush, he heard loud gruntings and crashings. Off Tranquility in an instant, he waited, uncertain whether he would see the lions charging out ten yards distant or running away.

"Fortunately, they adopted the latter course," he wrote in an account of the encounter. As only the accomplished author of three books on big-game hunting could, he captured the thrill of the moment:

> Right in front of me, thirty yards off, there appeared, from behind the bushes which had first screened him from my eyes, the tawny, galloping form of a big maneless lion. Crack! the Winchester spoke; and as the soft-nosed bullet ploughed forward through his flank the lion swerved so that I missed him with the second shot; but my third bullet went through the spine and forward into his chest. Down he came, sixty yards off, his hind quarters dragging, his head up, his ears back, his jaws open and lips drawn up in a prodigious snarl, as he endeavored to turn his face to us. His back was broken; but of this we could not at the moment be sure, and if it had been merely grazed, he might have recovered, and then, even though dying, his charge might have done mischief. So Kermit, Sir Alfred, and I fired almost together, into his chest. His head sank, and he died.

Unhit, the second lion to emerge from the brush galloped across the plain. When a few shots missed, Roosevelt and the others leapt onto their horses to try to ride him down over a plain that sloped gently upward for three-quarters of a mile to a low crest. Topping the hill, both Kermit and Pease fired again and missed. With Miss Pease riding close behind Tranquility, and Medlicott keeping up, Roosevelt saw the lion loping along close behind a few kongoni. In hot pursuit of the speeding lion in a downhill race, he gained rapidly until the lion suddenly halted in long grass in a slight shallow.

Dismounted, Roosevelt found him difficult to discern. Concerned that the lion might charge, and certainly outrun him, he decided to stay put and rely on his marksmanship, rather than try to vault back onto Tranquility. He would write of this decision, "Now, an elderly man with a varied past which includes rheumatism does not vault lightly into the saddle; as his sons, for instance can; and I had already made up my mind that in the event of the lion's charging it would be wise for me to trust to straight powder rather than to try to scramble into the saddle and get under way in time."

Kneeling, Roosevelt was still unable to see the lion. But it suddenly stood, looking first at one group of horses and then at the other. His tail was flashing to and fro, his head held low, while his harsh and savage growling

Future naturalist, hunter, and explorer Theodore Roosevelt, nicknamed "Teedie," at age five.

Striking an adventuresome pose before scaling the Matterhorn in 1881.

Following the deaths, on the same day, of his wife and mother in 1884, Roosevelt dropped out of politics. He headed west to start a cattle ranch and to hunt for the big game that roamed the mountains and prairies.

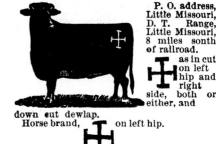

CHIMNEY BUTTE RANCH.
THEODORE ROOSEVELT, Proprietor.
FERRIS & MERRIFIELD, Managers.

P. O. address, Little Missouri, D. T. Range, Little Missouri, 8 miles south of railroad.

as in cut on left hip and right side, both or either, and down cut dewlap.
Horse brand, on left hip.

The first public advertisement for Roosevelt's "Chimney Butte Ranch," 1884.

Roosevelt and his cow pony, named "The Big D."

President Roosevelt and
hunter-friends with
Roosevelt's prized
coyote in 1905.

At dinner during a Colorado bear hunt.

The caption for this J. N. Darling cartoon in the *Des Moines Register and Leader* was: "I wish I could get someone at the White House who could cook like this."

When President Roosevelt announced that he was going on a bear hunt in Texas, J. S. Cobb of the Rochester, New York, *Herald*, called this cartoon "The arrival."

T.R. (left) posing with famed naturalist John Burroughs (with beard) at Yellowstone, 1903.

SENATO CAMERA

Cartoon by Gaido in the Turin, Italy, newspaper *Pasquino,* titled "Roosevelt's first hunting," was captioned: "Before going to hunt in Africa, Teddy wants to practice with his Redskins (Senate and House)."

This cartoon by F. C. Gould in London's *Westminster Gazette* saw ex-President Roosevelt leading "a quiet life."

This unflattering Italian newspaper cartoon predicted: "Roosevelt out of the White House will be able to devote himself to his favorite sport which he adores."

Opera star and talented cartoonist Enrico Caruso drew this caricature of Roosevelt for *La Follia di New York*, wishing Roosevelt "Bon voyage! and good luck in Africa."

"Teddy at home in Africa," by Burton Link in the *Pittsburgh Press*.

C. H. Cunningham of the *Washington Herald* drew a cartoon map of Africa with frightened animals running for their lives as Roosevelt casts an ominous shadow over the continent.

MEETING OF SOVEREIGNS IN THE CENTER OF AFRICA
His Majesty the King of the Desert: "In the name of that Nobel whose prize covers you with glory, O Teddy, I implore you to spare other thousands of my subjects." (From *Pasquino*, Turin, Italy.)

"The King is dead; long live the King!" by Robert Minor Jr., *St. Louis Post-Dispatch*.

The Stars and Stripes flew over Roosevelt's tent and always led the way as his safari crossed East Africa. The picture was snapped by Kermit Roosevelt.

Roosevelt, dressed for the hunt, photographed by traveling companion and hunter Edmund Heller.

"Bwana Makuba" poses for
Kermit's camera with one of his
big lions.

Father and son with their first
African buffalo.

Roosevelt and a dead
"tusker."

Rowland R. Murdoch of the *Pittsburgh Press* made a play on words by naming this drawing "How the artist understands 'T. R. in Cartoon.'"

"Steady, Kermit. We must have one of these." (From *Punch*, London.)

"The mighty hunter returns" in *Il Fishietto* (Turin, Italy)
showed Roosevelt posing with a slain lion while Kermit
gets a photo.

"DEE-LIGHT-ED!" by W. P. Canfield, *Pittsburgh Sun*.

"BACK IN THE OLD PLACE!" by Nelson Harding, *Brooklyn Eagle*.

In a cartoon called "Civilization at last," in the *San Francisco Call*, J. C. Terry depicted Roosevelt cursing an uncooperative bow tie and a racist view of African natives celebrating Roosevelt's departure.

The question marks in this cartoon by J. C. Terry refer to Roosevelt's Sphinx-like silence about whether he would run for president in 1912. He did, as the candidate of the Progressive (Bull Moose) Party, but lost, coming in second after Woodrow Wilson and ahead of President William Howard Taft.

Roosevelt (left) crossing from Chile into Argentina on November 20, 1913. The men with him are members of the Argentine reception committee.

Roosevelt (left) with Colonel Rondon at a camping place on the River of Doubt, photographed by the expedition's chief naturalist, George Cherrie.

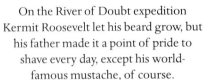

On the River of Doubt expedition Kermit Roosevelt let his beard grow, but his father made it a point of pride to shave every day, except his world-famous mustache, of course.

Roosevelt and Brazilian Army Colonel Rondon on January 9, 1914, with a bush bear killed by Roosevelt. He called it a "very pretty and graceful creature."

Having nearly died, and after twice asking Kermit to leave him behind in the Brazilian jungle, Roosevelt returned in triumph to the United States, but had lost a lot of weight. The effects of malaria and continuing problems with an injured knee that later became infected are believed to have contributed to his death on January 6, 1919.

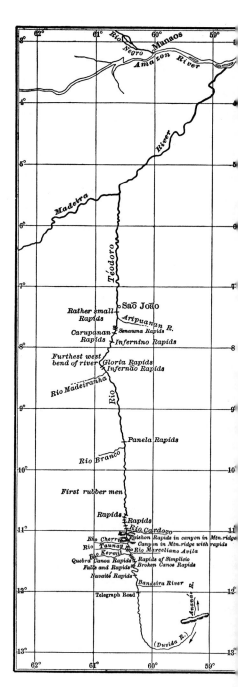

Map of the River of Doubt, re-named Rio Roosevelt and later Rio Teodoro. It was drawn by Roosevelt on the basis of notes in his journal and on those of Kermit and the expedition's naturalist, George Cherrie.

rolled thunderously over the plain. When he turned toward Roosevelt and Roosevelt's sais (horse-watcher), ironically named Simba, his tail was lashing quicker and quicker, a sign that he was preparing to charge. Resting an elbow upon Simba's bent shoulder, Roosevelt took steady aim and fired. The bullet struck between neck and shoulder. The lion fell over on his side, one foreleg in the air, but recovered enough to stand facing the man who'd shot him and growl hoarsely. Expecting a charge, Roosevelt fired again, breaking the lion's back just behind the shoulders. Standing over the body, he gave the lion a coup de grace.

"These were two good-sized maneless lions," Roosevelt wrote of the kills, "and very proud of them I was."

With two porters carrying each lion, and two others bearing the skins of the two cubs, the party started back to camp at dusk on a trail that was soon illuminated by a brilliant tropic moon. It was a scene that stirred both Roosevelt's sense of place and his unflagging romanticism. He noted that the "stalwart savages who carried the bloody lion skins swung along at a faster walk as the sun went down and the moon rose, chanting in unison, one uttering a single word or sentence and the others joining in a deep-toned, musical chorus."

Nor did Roosevelt-the-historian and self-appointed instructor of his readers pass up an opportunity to teach. "The men on a safari, and indeed African natives generally," he wrote, "are always excited over the death of a lion, and the hunting tribes then chant their rough hunting songs, or victory songs, until the monotonous, rhythmical repetitions make them grow almost frenzied."

Ever the naturalist, he continued, "The ride home in the moonlight, the vast barren landscape shining like silver on either hand, was one to be remembered; and above all, the sight of our trophies and of their wild bearers."

Three days later, Roosevelt, Sir Alfred Pease, Medlicott, Edmund Heller, Clifford and Harold Hill, and a small army of porters, beaters, and bearers established a fresh camp at a water hole in a little stream called Potha by a hill of the same name. Teamed in riding out with Kermit and Medlicott, Roosevelt dismounted at a likely place for lions and soon heard the distant shouts of beaters coming toward him. But the only game he saw were mountain reedbuck does that he chose not to shoot. But Kermit, with keen eyes following a male cheetah, "bowled it over in good style as it ran, then, moments later, killed a reedbuck and a steinbuck."

At that moment, a 150 yards away on the opposite side of the hill, Harold Hill shouted, "Lion!"

Unable to see it at first, Roosevelt thought he'd sighted the lion and fired, but the bullet was aimed too high. When the startled quarry moved, the next shot hit behind his shoulders. Assessing the trophy, Roosevelt was disappointed to find that it was a half-grown male, which Roosevelt deemed "not much of a trophy."

After lunch under a tree overlooking a long, wide valley, Roosevelt and Harold Hill stationed themselves on one side of the valley, while Kermit and Sir Alfred took positions on the opposite side, and waited for the beaters to do their work, starting at the lower end of the valley and slowly and noisily beating toward them in tall grass. Presently, Hill directed Roosevelt's attention to two lions, but it took Roosevelt a few seconds to realize that a dim yellow smear in the yellow-brown grass was a lion. Having difficulty getting a bead on it, he overshot. When the lion jumped up and faced in the direction of the rifle's crack, it growled, lowered its head with its tail straight up, and charged at a trot. Before it could reach galloping speed, Roosevelt took aim with his Winchester and fired a soft-nosed bullet between neck and shoulder. The lion went down with a roar, but Roosevelt was taking no chances. He shot twice more. But before he was able to approach the dead lion, Hill shouted another alert. This time it was a lioness.

Walking toward Hill, Roosevelt discerned the lion clearly. Facing him, the lion snarled as Roosevelt aimed at her chest. What followed was, in Roosevelt's astonished description, "a series of extraordinary antics, tumbling about on her head, just as if she were throwing somersaults, first to one side and then to the other." He fired again, but managed to shoot between the somersaults and miss. As the shot seemed to bring her to herself, she charged toward the line of beaters, then suddenly sank down in the high grass. Approaching warily, Roosevelt and the others found her alive, half crouched, half sitting, head down. Recognizing that the lioness still had strength "to do mischief," he sent a fatal bullet through her shoulders.

Weighed in camp, the full-grown lioness was 283 pounds. The male that Roosevelt had difficulty in seeing at first, although only half-grown, tipped the scale at nearly 400 pounds. In the light of the full moon and the glow of the campfire, Roosevelt again observed the victory dance of the natives as the firelight "gleamed and flickered across the grim dead beasts and the shining eyes and black features of the excited savages."

Next morning, the hunters started for another water hole about eight miles away at a rocky hill called Bondoni. The move afforded Roosevelt-the-intrepid-diarist an opportunity to record the formidable task of uprooting a safari camp. He wrote, "When we were to march, the camp was broken as early in the day as possible. Each man had his allotted task, and the tents, bedding, provisions, and all else were expeditiously made into suitable packages. Each porter is supposed to carry from fifty-five to sixty pounds, which may all be in one bundle or in two or three."

From the start of the journey into the heart of Africa, Roosevelt had placed above his tent an American flag. But he found that his pride in the Stars and Stripes was equaled by porters who carried it at the head or near the head of the line of march. After it in single file came a long line of bearers, some blowing horns or whistles and others beating small tomtoms. At intervals during the trek some suddenly began to chant. Headmen carried no bundles, tent boys little if anything, and the horse-tending saises concerned themselves only with tending them.

Roosevelt found the outfits of the natives so fascinating that in an article for *Scribner's Magazine* (and the subsequent book, *African Game Trails*) he described the clothing at some length. Expressing amazement that a porter "thought nothing whatever of walking for hours at mid-day under the equatorial sun with his head bare," or trudging solemnly and proudly along either with an umbrella open or furled as if it were "a wand of dignity," Roosevelt expounded on the head gear of other natives that "varied according to the fancy of the individual." He wrote with amusement:

Normally it was a red fez, a kind of cap only used in hot climates, and exquisitely designed to be useless therein because it gives absolutely no protection from the sun. But one [man] would wear a skin cap; another would suddenly put one or more feathers in his fez; and another, discarding the fez, would revert to some purely savage headdress which he would wear with equal gravity whether it were, in our eyes, really decorative or merely comic. One such headdress, for instance, consisted of the skin of the top of a zebra's head, with the two ears. Another was made of the skins of squirrels, with the tails both sticking up and hanging down. Another consisted of a bunch of feathers woven into the hair, which itself was pulled out into strings that were stiffened with clay. Another was really too intricate for description because it included the man's natural hair, some strips of skin, and an empty tin can.

Many years before Americans could subscribe to *National Geographic* magazine to read about the mysterious African continent, its animals, its people, and their ways, Roosevelt gave them a keen sense of being with him on his historic safari. From its start as an idea, throughout his planning, on the day of his departure, and as he proceeded, the thrilling odyssey of their beloved "Teddy" was eagerly followed in press reports. As the fifty-year-old ex-president and his energetic second son plunged into an adventure that was excitedly shared, if vicariously, by countless countrymen, Henry Cabot Lodge wrote to Roosevelt that Americans "follow it all with the absorbed interest of a boy who reads 'Robinson Crusoe' for the first time."

Theodore Roosevelt Jr., who had passed up the chance to go to Africa because he had fallen in love, was greatly amused to learn that the father he knew as "Big Bear" had gotten a new name from the Africans, "Bwana Makuba," meaning "Great Master." Ted also learned that Big Bear was having "a bully time," and that Kermit was "as hardy as a bullmoose" and the admiration of everyone on the safari. The favorite of the gun bearers, twenty-year-old Kermit was, Big Bear reported, "cool and daring." His African given-name was "Bwana Medogo," or "the young master." Later, Kermit was called "Bwana Morodadi," meaning "the Dandy." But on occasion his father found him "a little too reckless and keeps my heart in my throat," but he was able to "outrun, when after a wounded beast, or outlast, in a day's or week's tramp, any man, black or white, in the outfit."

And what an outfit the Roosevelt safari was! With the American flag aloft at the head of the march, it could easily have been mistaken by the native population for yet another colonial army set on the total conquest and subjugation of their continent. It was an image that certainly fit into Theodore Roosevelt's view of the world and its peoples.

As he had embraced the policy of "Manifest Destiny" in which white Americans believed they were entitled to fill up the lands from the Atlantic to the Pacific, from Canada to Mexico, even if that meant the eradication of the Indians and their culture if it came to that (as it very nearly did), Roosevelt looked upon East Africa as ripe for civilization. With no apologies, he declared, "It is a white man's country." His vision encompassed imposition of the better life for the original inhabitants as could be found in Africa wherever the English flag flew.

But it was not the Union Jack that preceded "Bwana Makuba" Roosevelt as the biggest safari ever mounted in East Africa wended its way from the hospitality of Sir Alfred Pease's comfortable ranch toward the foot of Kilimakiu Mountain. The route took him across bare plains thickly covered with short grass. All around the long safari he observed herds of hartebeests, zebras, gazelles, and wildebeests. Occasionally they crossed the trails of natives, "worn deep in the hard soil by the countless thousands of bare or sandaled feet that had trodden them." Africa, he lectured his readers, "is a country of trails." Across the high veldt, in every direction, ran the "tangled trails of multitudes of game that have lived thereon from time immemorial."

Through all the epochs of Africa, neither natives nor animals had witnessed such a panoply of grandeur as that of Theodore Roosevelt's safari. When it made camp at Kilimaiku, it was in a grove of shady trees. From it at sunset, Roosevelt looked across the vast plain and marveled as the far-off mountains grew umber and purple as the light waned. Established near an ostrich farm belonging to Captain Arthur Slatter, Roosevelt's new host, the camp was also close to a tribe of the Wakamba. When its chief paid a call, he presented Roosevelt with a traditional welcoming gift, "a fat hairy sheep, of the ordinary kind" in that part of Africa where, Roosevelt noted, "the sheep very wisely do not grow wool."

The headman, wearing khaki clothing, proudly showed the honored guest an official document which confirmed him in his position by the direction of the government, and required him "to perform various acts, chiefly in the way of preventing his tribespeople from committing robbery or murder, and of helping to stamp out cattle disease."

The natives were to Roosevelt's eyes "wild savages with filed teeth, many of them stark naked, though some of them carried a blanket," whose heads were "curiously shaved so that the hair tufts stood out in odd patterns." They carried small bows and arrows with poisoned heads.

What the headman and his entourage thought of Roosevelt in his hunting garb, toothy grin, mustache, eyeglasses, and bubbling personality was not recorded.

The following morning, accompanied by Captain Slatter and the requisite retinue of bearers and porters, Roosevelt rode out to hunt.

11

★ ★ ★

I Am Not a Rhinoceros
Mind-Reader

O N DROUGHT-STRICKEN GROUND that was largely open, but thinly covered in part by bush, meager forest, and scattered mimosa trees, Roosevelt and the others were guided by Captain Slatter among herds of zebras and hartebeests. But it was a small herd of the type of antelope called the eland that triggered Roosevelt's interest. There were about a dozen cows with reddish-looking coats. The pelts of two huge bulls were salty blue with great dewlaps hanging down and legs that seemed too small for their massive bodies.

As Roosevelt crept toward them he was struck by their likeness to great, clean, handsome American cattle of the Great Plains and thought the eland ought to be domesticated. Grazing or resting, they switched their long tails at swarms of pestering flies. Firing at them, he misjudged the distance. The shot sent the eland running, with a few of the cows bolting in such a hurry that as they skipped over those that were in their way, Roosevelt was surprised by the agility of such large animals. A few hundred yards distant, they settled into the slashing trot that was their usual gait, then disappeared over the brow of a hill.

That morning, Roosevelt noted, was "a blank," with no game killed, but early in the afternoon, they found the elusive herd around a tree in an open space that prevented Roosevelt and his companions from getting close.

Undaunted by the distance, Roosevelt felt "warranted" in shooting. Although he wanted a bull, he had to settle for a "fine cow" that stood about a quarter of a mile away.

A moment later, a Wakamba man rushed forward to excitedly report that on a hillside three-quarters of a mile away he'd seen a rhinoceros. Racing to the spot with Captain Slatter and a couple of gun bearers, Roosevelt soon saw his first rhino in the wild. The hulking animal was standing in open country a short distance away, with the wind blowing from him to the hunters.

To Roosevelt the big beast stood like "an uncouth statue, his hide black in the sunlight, looking like a monster surviving over from the world's past, from the days when the beasts of the prime ran riot in their strength, before man grew so cunning of brain and hand as to master them." So little did the rhino dream of the hunters' presence, Roosevelt noted, "that when we were a hundred yards off he actually lay down."

Walking lightly, and with every sense keyed up, the human stalkers at last reached a patch of brush. Releasing the safety lock on a double-barreled Holland rifle, the first time he'd used the gun, Roosevelt stepped to one side of the brush to get a clear aim. Suddenly, the rhino jumped to his feet with "the agility of a pony." Roosevelt fired the right-hand barrel and sent the shot into the rhino's lungs. Wheeling round with blood spurting from its nostrils, the rhinoceros galloped forward. Firing the left-hand barrel, Roosevelt hit it between neck and shoulder, a shot that tore into the rhino's heart.

Looking back on the "wicked charge," Roosevelt said, "I am not a rhinoceros mind-reader, and its actions were such as to warrant my regarding it as a suspicious character." The rhinos, he decided, "are truculent, lumbering beasts, much the most stupid of all the dangerous game I know." If it had been a lion the first bullet would have knocked all the charge out of it, but the vitality of the rhino was so great that one shot from the hard-hitting Holland rifle could not stop it outright.

When a group of Wakamba skinners returned to camp, the rhino's meat was divided among them and the white hunters, with the Makamba feasting on their portions in their camp. As Roosevelt went to bed, he could still hear the drumming and chanting.

The next afternoon found him looking down the barrel of his rifle at giraffes, but they were "such enormous beasts" that he thought they were closer than they were. When his shot missed, they broke into their "leisurely looking gallop" and disappeared among the mimosas.

"Of all the beasts in an African landscape," Roosevelt wrote, "none is more striking than the giraffe." Because of its height and keen vision, no animal was harder to approach unseen. Observing them through army field glasses, he saw "a striking-looking animal and handsome in its way." But its length of leg and neck and sloping back made it appear awkward even at rest. Yet when alarmed and stirred to action, it could take off, not in its long swinging pace or walk, but in a peculiar gallop or canter.

"The tail is cocked and twisted," Roosevelt noted, "and the huge hind legs are thrown forward well to the outside of the forelegs. The movements seem deliberate and the giraffe does not appear to be going at a fast pace, but if it has any start a horse must gallop to overtake it. When it starts on this gait, the neck may be dropped forward at a sharp angle with the straight line of the deep chest, and the big head is thrust in advance."

Disappointed that he'd missed his chance, he was out the next day with Captain Slatter. While eating lunch under a huge fig tree on a hill about three miles from camp, he scanned the country with field glasses and spotted a herd of eland and three giraffes about a mile and a half away. He wanted to kill a bull eland, but he wanted a giraffe even more. His goal was to collect a bull and cow for the museum in whose name he'd ventured into Africa. With the Winchester loaded with full metal-jacketed bullets, he approached the stately trio, moving in a straight line with Captain Slatter and natives. As they neared their quarry, the giraffes "showed symptoms of uneasiness." As a smaller one bolted, the others shifted positions slightly. Dropping to a knee, Roosevelt took a bead on the large bull's shoulder with the rifle's 300-yard sight and got off one shot. It struck where he'd aimed, but all three giraffes ran in their rocking-horse canter. Chasing them, Roosevelt chambered a soft-nosed bullet and fired at one of the smaller giraffes. It was a long shot, between 400 and 500 yards, but the bullet brought it down. As the others fled, he jumped on Tranquility and rode full speed after them.

The pursuit proved harder than expected. Although the bull was wounded and lagging in its desperate flight, it put on a spurt. Believing he was close enough to get off a telling shot, Roosevelt leapt from Tranquility and opened fire. The bull dropped, but as Roosevelt remounted the horse, the giraffe struggled to his feet and bounded off and disappeared with the second in a thicket of trees at the bottom of a valley. Tearing after them, Roosevelt spurred Tranquility and scrambled through a dry donga, then up the other side, determined to get close enough to the bull to finish him off.

But the usually reliable sorrel horse, as Roosevelt colorfully described what happened, "did not quite like the look of the thing ahead of him." The horse did not refuse to come up to the giraffe, but he evidently felt that, with such an object close by, it behooved him to be careful as to what might be lurking in the brush and trees. When Tranquility shied away at every bush or clump of trees, Roosevelt jumped off with rifle in hand and fired one at the bull giraffe. This time it went down for good.

At the very same time, Roosevelt learned, another giraffe hunt was going on, involving Kermit and their intrepid companions on this part of the safari, Sir Alfred Pease and Medlicott. They'd come across a dozen giraffes on the open plains. As the hunt began, Kermit had found himself alone, galloping after a giraffe and firing again and again with his Winchester. When his horse gave out, he jumped off, and as Roosevelt proudly noted, "being an excellent long distance runner," chased the giraffe on foot for more than a mile. The race ended with wounded giraffe slowing down, stopping, and falling dead.

The bullets retrieved from Kermit's and Roosevelt's giraffes were saved, in keeping with Roosevelt's decision, made before he'd left for Africa, to preserve as many as possible of the bullets that brought down quarry in order to assess what could be done by the different types of rifles used on the expedition.

It was on this portion of the year-long odyssey that the natives honored the white hunters with Swahili names, and became so impressed with Kermit's prowess that thereafter he was, to them, Bwana Medogo, the young master.

While Kermit and the party moved on to the next destination, Roosevelt took time off from hunting to visit the American Mission Station at Machakos. Accompanied by Sir Alfred, he found the little town "both interesting and attractive." He also admired the manner in which the ancient native village on the old route taken by Arab caravans engaged in the slave trade was being run by the British. It was here that Roosevelt found evidence justifying the tenets of a philosophical view of the world known as Social Darwinism. In applying the evolutionary theories that Charles Darwin had advanced in *Origin of Species* and *The Descent of Man,* the Social Darwinists of the years of Theodore Roosevelt's youth had argued that various peoples were at different stages in the evolutionary process. Because some were far more advanced than others, it went without saying that white Europeans, and their American cousins, stood at the top of the evolutionary ladder.

They therefore had the moral duty to protect their interests and lead infe-riors toward higher civilization, as English colonialists and Christian mission-aries were doing in Machakos.

Writing about his visit, Roosevelt was a Social Darwinist in full bloom, but not without handing out some advice to His Majesty Edward VII's gov-ernment. He wrote:

> The English rule in Africa has been of incalculable benefits to the Africans themselves, and indeed this is true of most European nations. Mistakes have been made, of course, but they have proceeded at least as often from an unwise effort to accomplish too much in the way of benefi-cence, as from a desire to exploit the natives. Each of the civilized nations that has taken possession of any part of Africa has had its own peculiar defects. Some of them have done too much supervising and ordering the lives of the natives, and in interfering with their practices and customs, even when of an immoral and repulsive character, and to do no more than what is obviously necessary, such as insistence upon keeping the peace and preventing the spread of cattle disease. Excellent reasons can be advanced in favor of this policy, and it must always be remembered that a fussy and ill-considered benevolence is more sure to awaken resent-ment than cruelty itself; while the natives are apt to resent deeply even things that are obviously for their ultimate welfare. Yet I cannot help thinking that with caution and wisdom it would be possible to proceed somewhat farther than has yet been the case in the direction of pushing some of the least of the East African tribes; and this though I recognize fully that many of these tribes are of a low and brutalized type. Having said this much in the way of criticism, I wish to add my tribute of unstinted admiration for the disinterested work being done, alike in the interest of the white man and the black, by the government officials whom I met in east Africa. They are men in whom their country [Eng-land] had every reason to feel a just pride.

Constantly describing Africans as "wild" and "savages" in his writings about the safari, Roosevelt was, of course, a man in step with his times and, therefore, a man who by standards of enlightened people of a century later would be called a racist, just as today's environmentalists and wildlife preser-vationists deem Roosevelt's hunting an outrageous slaughter of animals for the pleasure of showing his trophies and bragging about his manliness. Yet, is it fair to fault Theodore Roosevelt for holding the prevailing beliefs, and prejudices, of his times from the vantage point of one whose present existence lay in a future that Roosevelt couldn't envision? It seems especially egregious to look back on his safari as a year-long bloody campaign against innocent animals when at that time he was engaged in what he and his sponsors believed was an educational enterprise. Had television been available, he certainly would have ventured into Africa, and on his later expedition in the uncharted jungles of Brazil, with video equipment and come back to produce documentaries for Public Television, had it been around then. He should be credited for taking with him not only guns, but photographic equipment. Nearly ten years before his African adventure, he'd declared from Sagamore Hill, "More and more, as it becomes necessary to preserve the game, let us hope that the camera will largely supplant the rifle."

As Theodore Roosevelt found much to praise, and to criticize, in the colonialism that was represented by the English rule in East Africa on his visit to the village of Machakos, he met in American missionaries a group of white men whose "work among the savages" offered many difficulties that often met with "dishearteningly little reward." Again a man of his time, and as a Christian, he saw nothing wrong with efforts to convert the people of Africa to the Cross. While he endorsed proselytizing, he cautioned against "zealous missionaries, fervent in their faith," who did not always find it easy to remember "that savages can only be raised by slow steps" and that "empty adherence to forms and ceremonies" amounted to nothing, and that the "gradual elevation of mind and character is a prerequisite to the achievement of any kind of Christianity which is worth calling such." Nevertheless, he wrote, "after all this has been said, it remains true that the good done by missionary effort in Africa has been incalculable."

After returning from Machakos, and spending the night at Sir Alfred Pease's home, he set out with Kermit across the Athi Plains in a grand procession of horses, porters, bearers, and equipment, with the U.S. flag unfurled at the head of the impressive retinue, for a place owned by Mr. and Mrs. W.N. McMillan in the beautiful Mua Hills, known as Juja Farm.

12

★ ★ ★

Land of the Masai

L YING ON THE EDGE of the Athi Plains near the junction of the
Nairobi and Reworo Rivers, the home of Roosevelt's welcoming countrymen, the McMillans, Juja Farm was typical of those of the white settlers. The one-story house with a broad, vine-shaded veranda was surrounded by numerous out-buildings, cornfields, flocks and herds of animals,
and a vegetable garden tended by "unsmiling Kikuyu savages." One that
especially fascinated Roosevelt evidently had been so attracted by the shiny
surface of a tobacco can that he wore it on one ear as a complement to a curiously carved wooden drum on the other. Another native, whose arms and
legs were "massive with copper and iron bracelets," was naked except for a
blanket that he wore except when he used a lawn mower. For this task he
wrapped the blanket around his neck and the handle of the lawn mower, in
Roosevelt's words, "with the evident feeling that he had done all that the
most exacting conventionalism could require."

House boys and gun-bearers, and most of the boys caring for the horses,
were Somalis. Men and women field workers were Kikuyus. Herders were
Masai. The former Little Missouri cattle rancher found them to be "wild hea-
then of the most martial type." Observing that they looked carefully after
the cattle, and were delighted to join the chase of dangerous game, but thoroughly despised regular work, Roosevelt wrote, "Sometimes when we had
gathered a mass of Kikuyus or of our own porters to do some job, two or

three Masai would stroll up to look on with curiosity, sword in belt and great spear in hand." In their erect carriage they had a fearless bearing in which the hero of the San Juan Heights discerned "a soldierly race."

In temporary residence at Juja Farm when Roosevelt arrived in mid-May was his friend Frederick Selous. His purpose was to join McMillan on a safari in company with one of the most notable professional hunters of East Africa, H. Judd. Eager to learn from him, Roosevelt and Kermit went hunting with him almost every day. Rising before dawn, they took an east-ward course toward the mountain mass called Donyo Sabuk in search of waterbuck and impala, in Roosevelt's view the most beautiful of all the ante-lope. About the size of the American white-tailed deer that was so familiar to Roosevelt, they had annulated horns that formed a single spiral. Their coat was as shiny as satin with contrasting shades of red and white.

What surprised Roosevelt about the impala and other African antelope was that they succumbed to wounds quicker than similar American game. In citing the shooting of an impala buck as evidence of this unexpected behavior, he described creeping up an anthill to get a shot at the animal from about 250 yards. The buck dropped, and while putting in another cartridge he said to Judd that he didn't like to see an animal drop like that, so instanta-neously, as there was always the possibility that it might only be creased, and that if an animal so hurt got up, it always went off exactly as if unhurt. Roo-sevelt wrote:

When we raised our eyes again to look for the impala, it had vanished. I was sure that we would never see it again, and Judd felt much the same way, but we walked in the direction toward which its head had been pointed, and Judd ascended an ant hill to scan the surrounding country with his glasses. He did so, and after a minute remarked that he could not see the wounded impala; when a sudden movement caused us to look down, and there it was, lying at our very feet, on the side of the ant hill, unable to rise. I had been using a sharp-pointed bullet in the Springfield, and this makes a big hole. The bullet had gone too far back, in front of the hips. I should not have wondered at all if the animal had failed to get up after falling, but I did not understand why, as it recovered enough from the shock to be able to get up, it had continued to travel, instead of falling after going one hundred yards.

Another impala buck that Roosevelt shot also showed an "unexpected softness" as it succumbed to a wound which Roosevelt believed would not have felled either a white-tailed or black-tailed deer at home.

Having claimed two impala, Roosevelt returned to the place where he and Judd had left their horses. They discovered the boys who tended the horses exclaiming that they had seen a large snake nearby. When Roosevelt looked for it, he found a python coiled up in long grass under a small tree. Perhaps recalling his encounters with Dakota rattlesnakes, he chambered his gun with a solid bullet and fired into the middle of its body. To his surprise, the snake lashed at him with open jaws, and then, recoiling, glided forward.

"I did not think it was charging," Roosevelt wrote. "I thought it was merely trying to escape. But Judd, who was utterly unmoved by lion, leopard, or rhino, evidently held this snake in respect, and yelled at me to get out of the way. Accordingly, I jumped back a few feet, and the snake came over ground where I had stood; its evil genius then made it halt for a moment and raise its head to a height of perhaps three feet, and I killed it by a shot through the neck."

When Roosevelt picked it up, first by the tail and then by the head, the porters were aghast that he would touch it. "It was," Roosevelt noted calmly, "only twelve feet long."

A close call for Kermit was with a leopard. Hunting in a ravine with McMillan and a few natives, Kermit observed the leopard slinking through bushes, then lost sight of it. Supposing that the leopard had sought cover in a large thicket, the beaters went to work in hopes of driving it out. But without a warning snarl, the leopard lunged into the open and charged at Kermit. With an icy calm as the leopard came within six yards, Kermit shot it in the chest. Seemingly unfazed, it continued its forward rush. Unmoving, Kermit fired a crippling shot into its hips.

Excited by the sight of the charge and the way in which it was stopped, the beaters rushed jubilantly forward, only to discover that the leopard wasn't finished. Though crippled, it lunged at one of the beaters. Although shot again by McMillan, the thrice-wounded leopard managed to run down the beater and sink fangs and claws into the man's leg. Wrenching free, the beater heard the bang of McMillan's rifle, but rather than dropping, the leopard retreated into the thicket. As the wounded beater was taken away and dogs were sent to sniff out what all in the party expected to be a carcass, the leopard darted from the brush and again raced toward Kermit. With a single shot, Kermit killed it. A female, it weighed just under sixty pounds, but although it was small, Theodore Roosevelt was so impressed by the tale of the struggle that he admiringly wrote that Kermit's first bullet "would have knocked the fight out of any animal less plucky and savage than the leopard." There was, he said, "not even in Africa, a beast of more unflinching courage than this spotted cat."

With a far larger trophy in mind, Roosevelt rode off one day with Judd, the famed hunter's Masai gun-bearer, and two of Roosevelt's bearers in search of the animal that ancient Greeks found living in streams and had named "hippopotaus," the Greek for "riverhorse." The species abounded in the rivers of Juja farm, along with the scaled, gaping-mouthed, river-god of the old kingdoms of Egypt, the fearsome crocodile.

Noiselessly approaching a great pool in which they expected to find hippopotami, the party advanced with utmost caution to a steep bank of the pool and a sight that was, Roosevelt thought, "typically African." The scene he described was both primeval and could have been a descriptive passage for scenarists of yet long-in-the-future African adventure *Tarzan* movies:

> On the still water floated a crocodile, nothing but his eyes and nostrils visible. The bank was covered with a dense growth of trees, festooned with vines; among the branches sat herons; a little cormorant dived into the water; and a very small brilliantly colored kingfisher, with a red beak and large turquoise crest, perched unheedingly within a few feet of us. Here and there a dense growth of tall and singularly graceful papyrus rose out of the water, the feathery heads, which crowned the long smooth green stems, waving gently to and fro.
>
> We scanned the waters carefully, and could see no sign of hippos, and, still proceeding with utmost caution, we moved a hundred yards farther down to another lookout. Here the Masai detected a hippo head a long way off on the other side of the pool; and we again drew back and started cautiously forward to reach the point opposite which he had seen the head.

Just as they reached the point where they'd intended to turn toward the pool, they heard a succession of snorts and the sound of trampling of heavy feet and of a big body being shoved through dense tropical brush.

"Shoot, shoot," shouted Judd.

Suddenly, it was not a hippo that appeared, but a rhinoceros, twitching its tail and twisting its head from side to side. As it crashed toward Roosevelt and the others, Roosevelt thought it did not have very good horns, and would rather not have killed it. But faced with no alternative, "for it showed very symptom of being bent on mischief," and with the hulking animal less than forty yards away, he fired with his Winchester. Two full-jacketed bullets struck between the neck and shoulder, bringing the lumbering rhino to a halt. A third and fourth bullet hit its flank. The rhino then disappeared with a crash of branches into a dense thicket of thorn-bushes, reeds, and small, low-branching trees.

Examining the grass at the far end of the thicket, Roosevelt and Judd found so much blood that it was clear the rhino had been badly hit. With his heavy double-barreled Holland at the ready, Roosevelt moved gingerly through the grass, peering into the thicket and "expectant of developments." He wasn't disappointed. Hearing furious snorting and crashing directly opposite him in the thicket, he brought up his rifle. But the rhinoceros broke out of the cover, some thirty yards away. Firing both barrels, Roosevelt hit it behind the shoulder. Wheeling round, the rhino struggled back into the thicket. A crashing of brush signaled that it had fallen. When Roosevelt crept under the branches and saw the rhino on the ground, he thought it was dead. Taking no chances, he loaded the gun and fired a heavy bullet into it. An old female that was smaller than the rhino bull he'd already claimed, it had a front horn that measured fourteen inches (the bull's horn was nineteen inches) and weighed almost a ton.

"Now I did not want to kill this rhinoceros," Roosevelt wrote, "and I am not certain that it really intended to charge us. It may very well be that if we had stood firm it would, after much threatening and snorting, have turned and made off; veteran hunters like Selous could, I doubt not, have afforded to wait and see what happened. But I let it get within forty yards, and it still showed every symptom of meaning mischief, and at a shorter range I could not have been sure of stopping it in time."

To kill the rhino he'd needed eight bullets, five from the Winchester and three from the Holland. In keeping with his policy of comparing the effects of various bullets, he concluded that with the full-jacketed Winchester bullets he had inflicted wounds from which the rhino would have died in a short time. But it was the Holland that provided an immediate kill. From this study he recognized that the Winchester and Springfield did admirably against giraffes, elands, and lions, but for heavy game, rhinos and hippos, his rifle of choice ought to be the Holland. Ultimately, he noted, the determining factor would always be the quality of the man behind the gun.

That afternoon Roosevelt and Judd were out again, looking for hippos in the Rowero River. With light failing, and no hippos encountered, Judd announced that he was going home, but as he took a last look around, he dropped to his knees and beckoned to Roosevelt. Creeping forward on all fours, Roosevelt peered toward an object in the stream. About fifty yards off, he saw a hippo looking toward him, ears up and nostrils, eyes, and forehead above the surface. He aimed at the center of the head. The hippo sank without a splash. Informed by Judd that when a hippo was killed, it sank and that the body would not surface for several hours, Roosevelt went back to the McMillan house with the intention of returning to the spot in the morning.

Accompanied by Judd and a group of porters, and joined by R.J. Cuninghame, in a very leaky boat, they soon found the dead hippopotamus. A cow, it weighed almost 3000 pounds. A full-jacketed Winchester bullet had gone into the brain, where the jacket remained lodged as the remainder of the bullet plowed into the neck to break the atlas vertebra.

Having claimed a hippo and rhinoceros, Roosevelt departed Juja Farm and moved to the neighboring estate of Hugh H. Heately, a Roosevelt admirer who'd invited him to hunt African buffalo. Comprising 20,000 acres between the Rewero and Kamiti Rivers, and stretching seventeen miles, Heatley's property was a thriving farm with large herds of cattle, a dairy, hundreds of cultivated acres, and an impressive game preserve. With the party's tents pitched by the Kamiti, Roosevelt could not ride out in any direction without seeing swarms of hartebeest and zebra.

But he was after buffalo. Esteemed by many professional hunters as the most dangerous game, the species was nothing like the bison of the American West. With a coat of black hair, it had massive horns. Seeking them on the morning after making camp, Roosevelt, Kermit, their host (Heately), Cuninghame, and a neighbor of Heatley (identified by Roosevelt only as a Boer farmer), proceeded to a swamp that promised buffalo. The Roosevelts carried double-barrel Hollands, with Winchesters as backups. Grazing close to the edge of the swamp were four bulls, staring sullenly at the intruders. Instead of fleeing into cover of papyrus reeds, the herd moved to open country. Grateful for their luck, Roosevelt and Kermit opened fire. The result was three "fine trophies," one old bull and two young.

Three days later, Roosevelt sought a buffalo cow. What the party encountered was a herd lying in a curving, dry watercourse flanked by high banks and dotted with patches of high grass and papyrus. As the hunters crept toward the buffalo, one of the huge animals saw the crouching figures and reacted in a way that caused the herds to rise from their beds. They were at a long range for heavy rifles, but Roosevelt and the others had no choice but to fire. Two bulls were hit, but as they stumbled Roosevelt was startled to see not half a dozen buffalo rising from the grass, but scores of them bolting to their feet. He aimed at a cow and wounded it, but now his attention was distracted from his expected prize by the sight of the wounded bulls turning in a quarter-circle and drawing into a phalanx facing him and his companions with outstretched heads, a sure sign of defiance.

With teasing understatement, Roosevelt would write of that moment, "It was not a nice country on which to be charged by the herd, and for a moment things trembled in the balance."

In describing the thrill of going into battle in Cuba, Roosevelt would say in the autobiography that he would publish in 1913 that all men who feel any power of joy in battle know what it is like when the wolf rises in the heart. He called it three-o'clock-in-the-morning courage, and it was to him the most desirable kind. He'd shown it by leading the Rough Riders up Kettle Hill in the San Juan Heights. Now, discerning "a perceptible motion of uneasiness" in men, white and black, who stood in the path of menacing African buffalo, he called out, "Stand steady! Don't run!"

Knowing that any kind of movement would invite a charge, Cuninghame shouted, "And don't shoot."

After a few tense, expectant seconds, it was the buffalo herd that moved; first those that had not been wounded, then the two injured bulls. With the peril passed, Roosevelt turned his attention to finishing off the cow. Later that day, after collecting several different animals that he wanted, he returned to the place of the stand-off with the herd. Having "a vaguely uncomfortable feeling that as it grew dusk the buffalo might possibly make their appearance again," he found a number of them. "It seemed very strange that after the experience in the morning any of the herd should be willing to come out in the open so soon," he wrote. "But there they were. They were grazing to the number of about a dozen." Looking at them through field glasses, he could see them looking at him. For a moment he wondered if they might charge. "But it was only curiosity on their part," he recorded, "and after having grazed their fill, they sauntered back to the swamp and disappeared."

Camp was broken the next morning, providing Roosevelt another opportunity to watch the porters at work. Through the eyes of the man of his times that he was, they were "strapping grown-up children" who "felt as much pleasure and excitement over breaking camp after a few days' rest as over reaching camp after a fifteen-mile march." On this occasion, after they had made up their loads, "they danced in a ring for half an hour, two tin cans being beaten into tomtoms." As they strode off in a long line with a white man's burdens, each greeted Roosevelt with a smile as they said, "Yambo, Bwana!"

So far the Roosevelt safari had collected hundreds of specimens that had to be recorded and shipped from Nairobi. It was, Roosevelt noted, a task of "herculean proportions." He found the city of Nairobi so "very attractive" and "most interesting" that he believed the city and all of East Africa were ideal for settlement as a white man's country, and that the region was an ideal "playground alike for sportsmen, and for travelers who wish to live in health and comfort, and yet see what is beautiful and unusual."

With the classifying and packing of specimens completed, and on the move again on June 5, 1909, the Roosevelt expedition began a trek across sixty miles of waterless country called "the thirst."

13

★ ★ ★

Crossing the Thirst

HAD THEODORE ROOSEVELT been able to travel in the manner he preferred when on a hunt in the Dakotas—alone—the sixty-mile trek across the arid wasteland would have been made in one night. Instead, he set off in the company of stalwart son Kermit; intrepid R.J. Cuninghame; and the leathery veteran of hunts in the Australian outback and East Africa, Leslie Tarlton. With them were a "fine young colonial Englishman" named Ulyate; seasoned hunters Alden Loring and Edmund Heller; three other white wagon drivers, two of them English and the third a Boer; a boy from the Cape of Africa; a Kaffir wagon-driver; 196 porters; numerous askaris, tent boys, gun bearers, and saises; and various natives described in the usual Roosevelt way as "primitive savages in dress and habit, but coming from the cattle-owning tribes." Huge wagons, with white tops or "sails," were drawn by teams of oxen.

Because of the heat and blazing sun, they moved mostly at night. Horses were loaded lightly. Each man took only what he could carry. Roosevelt and Kermit each had an army overcoat, rifle, and cartridges. As they pushed steadily across the plain, the dust rose in clouds under a spectral moon and the stars of the Southern Cross.

This was not the first time Theodore Roosevelt had gazed in wonder at the constellation. Eleven years earlier, aboard the troopship *Yucatan*, bound for Cuba, with the wolf rising in his warrior's heart, he'd written to his sister Corinne, "All day we have steamed close to the Cuban coast, high barren looking mountains rising abruptly from shore, and at a distance looking much like those on Montana. We are well within the tropics, and at night the Southern Cross shows low above the horizon." The evening before, he'd gazed from the ship "through a sapphire sea, wind-rippled under an almost cloudless sky." There were some forty-eight craft in all, in three columns, the black hulls of the transports setting off the gray hulls of men-of-war. He watched "the red sun sink and the lights blaze up on the ships, for miles ahead and astern," while the band played piece after piece, from the "Star Spangled Banner" at which everyone rose and stood uncovered. It was a great historical expedition, Roosevelt wrote, "and I thrill to feel that I am part of it."

People might perceive in Theodore Roosevelt a blood-thirsty slaughterer of animals, but he knew how to set a scene.

Now, at intervals he heard the barking call of hyenas and shrieks of jackals. Overhead, plains plover circled. When the sun came up, the porters received rations of water and food, then lay down to sleep. Horses were fed and got half a pail of water.

Three-quarters of the way into the journey, black clouds gathered and thickened in the west, promising rain. Making good time, riding in advance of the lumbering wagons, Roosevelt and Kermit reached a fording place on the Suavi River and made camp. Seven and a half hours later, the porters arrived in excellent spirits, the Stars and Stripes waving, to an accompaniment of chanting and horn-blowing. The wagon train appeared in midmorning. After a day's rest, the safari pushed on with the expectation of two days of easier travel to the Guaso Nyero, a rapid little river edged by yew trees and wooded cliffs.

"It was cool, rainy weather, with overcast skies and misty mornings, so that it seemed strangely unlike the tropics," Roosevelt noted. "The country was alive with herds of Masai cattle, sheep, and donkeys. The Masai, herdsmen by profession and warriors by preference, were stalwart savages, and showed the mixture of types common to this part of Africa, which is the edge of an ethnic whirlpool."

The safari was in "high feather." After nightfall the camp fires blazed in the cool air as the white hunters stood or sat around the blazes to do what Roosevelt liked most about being among such men—listening to and joining in the swapping of hunting tales. Cuninghame and Tarlton spun accounts of hunting elephants in the Congo. Loring and Heller spoke of Rocky Mountain hunts, the deserts of the Mexican border which were familiar to Kermit, and Alaska, where Roosevelt might have gone had he not become enthralled with Africa.

All these naturalists exhibited interest not only in big game, but many small mammals. Their catches ranged from big-eared mice and those with spiny fur, rats striped like chipmunks, and large cane rats to meercats, akin to the mongoose. Large game was not plentiful, but on one outing Kermit killed the party's first topi. The bull was, Roosevelt recorded, "a beautiful animal the size of a hartebeest, with satin-sheened coat."

Desiring a topi himself, Roosevelt soon encountered a herd of the shy, agile creatures in an open area that afforded him no cover. Aware of him as he maneuvered their way, the topi let him get within 600 yards. They stood motionless, as if tempting him to shoot. Uncertain of the range, Roosevelt fired more times than he cared to remember before getting a "handsome cow." Feeling delighted, he returned to camp and sat at the mouth of his tent to enjoy himself, not only with thoughts of his prize, but in taking a book from the Pigskin Library. The selection had been added to during the journey, including a copy of *Alice's Adventures in Wonderland* and *Louves de Macnecoul*, by Alexander Dumas, presented to Roosevelt at Port Said by the brother of an old and valued friend who had been the French ambassador to the United States, and vice-president of President Theodore Roosevelt's group of friends and tennis players, known then as Roosevelt's "Tennis Cabinet."

If members of the Roosevelt safari had inquired of Kermit about his father's game of tennis, they might have been told that the children of a father who advocated "the strenuous life" were expected to take part in all kinds of sports, both individual and team. For Sagamore Hill tennis, there was a makeshift dirt court. Kermit's older brother Ted remembered it as a place where moles traversed regularly, giving the court an uneven surface. In addition, it was so well shaded that moss grew over it. The branches of the trees were so low that there was a special rule that when a ball hit a branch and might have gone in it was a 'let.' The children batted the ball in whatever fashion seemed best. "While Father played with us whenever he had the time, and was always welcome," Ted wrote in a family memoir. "His method of playing was original, to say the least. He gripped the racquet halfway up the handle with his index finger pointed back. When he served he did not throw the ball into the air, but held it in his left hand and hit it from between his fingers. In spite of this, and in spite of his great weight, he played a surprisingly good game. We used him as a sort of milestone of progress. When we were able to beat him in singles it was equivalent to having passed the entrance examinations to college."

In winter the children's strenuous life included hikes through the snow, sledding, and snowball fights. When their father came home one day with "snowshoes" which had been given to him by a Norwegian diplomat, they were introduced to a new sport that would be known in the future as skiing. When old enough to hold a rifle, the Roosevelt boys were introduced to the adventures of hunting and exploration, so that when Ted and Kermit were adults, following their valiant service in the army during World War I, they teamed for big-game hunts and exploring in the Himalaya mountains of Central Asia. But because falling in love had stood in the way of Roosevelt's namesake joining his father in Africa in 1909, it was the second son about whom Roosevelt joyfully wrote after his account of getting a prize topi, "The next day was Kermit's red-letter day."

Riding with Leslie Tarlton, Kermit killed two cheetahs and "a fine maned lion" that was better than any that the safari had so far collected. Roosevelt recorded that on the same day "I merely got some ordinary game," then proudly described Kermit having seen the lion feeding, then galloping a mile in pursuit of the big male. When it suddenly turned to charge, Kermit got off a crippling shot, then a fatal one. Although nearly a foot longer than any lion Roosevelt had claimed, Kermit's prize was so thin as to be called gaunt and weighed only 412 pounds. Still, in a photograph taken by Kermit, the lushly maned lion appeared formidable, even though dead.

After five days camped by the Guaso Nyero the hunt had resulted in the collection of heads and pelts of fourteen animals of ten different species. With the meticulousness of little Teedie Roosevelt's entries into his note-books, Theodore Roosevelt's journal recorded not only the safari's trophies, but details of how they were gotten. In the register were: "one lioness, one hyena, one wart-hog boar, two zebra, two eland, one wildebeest, two topi, two impala, one Roberts' gazelle, one Thompson's gazelle."

Making it clear that he had killed "nothing that was not absolutely needed, both for scientific purposes and for food," and that skin of every animal was preserved for the museum, he recorded how each prize had been obtained. He wrote:

> Except the lioness and one impala (both of which I shot running), all were shot at rather long ranges; seven were shot standing, two walking, five running. The average distance at which they were shot was a little

over two hundred and twenty yards. I used sixty-five cartridges, an amount which will seem excessive chiefly to those who are not accustomed actually to count the cartridges they expend, to measure the distances at which they fire, and to estimate for themselves the range, on animals in the field when they are standing or running a good way off. Only one wounded animal got away; and eight of the animals I shot had to be finished with one bullet—two in the case of the lioness—as they lay in the ground. Many of the cartridges expended really represented range-finding.

Perhaps because Roosevelt told his stories of hunting in Africa in the articles he sent back for publication at the time in *Scribner's Magazine*, and their later compilation in the book *African Game Trails* in 1910, he devoted less than two pages of his 1913 autobiography to his year in Africa. But the stories he chose to relate in it were about the charges by the elephant that "came through the thick brush to my left like a steam plow through a light snow-drift," and the rhinoceros that "charged with the utmost determination." In comparing these harrowing close calls with his confrontation more than twenty years earlier with a charging grizzly bear, he still considered the grizzly's attack his "only narrow escape."

As to the debate among hunters regarding which African animal was the most dangerous, he came down on the side of those who cited the lion, even though, he pointed out, "I personally had no difficulties with lions."

For readers who might shiver in revulsion at the thought of killing wild animals, except in self-defense, of course, Roosevelt revealed empathy for the creatures he killed, and found in their violent deaths, whether at the hands of man or as a part of nature, a lesson for humans, snug in their homes in modern cities. "Watching the game," he wrote, "one was struck by the intensity and the evanescence of their emotions. Civilized man now usually passes his life under conditions which eliminate the intensity of terror felt by his ancestors when death by violence was their normal end, and threatened them every hour of the day and night. It is only in nightmares that the average dweller in civilized countries now undergoes the hideous horror which was the regular and frequent portion of the ages-vanished forefathers, and which is still the everyday incident in the lives of most wild creatures. But the dread is short-lived, and its horror vanishes with instantaneous rapidity."

14

★ ★ ★

With Rifle and Camera

THE ROOSEVELTS' NEXT CAMP was in the middle of a vast plain by limestone springs at one end of a line of dark acacia trees. The day after setting up the camp he rode out, hoping to get either a rhino or a cow giraffe. The day was cloudy and cool and the game shy. Although the safari needed meat, Roosevelt was unable to get within fair range of wildebeest, hartebeest, topi, or large gazelle. He succeeded in claiming only two tommy gazelles, one with a good shot as the animal ran, but he got it, he confessed, after his first shot had missed in a "rather scandalous fashion" while the quarry was standing.

In maneuvering toward a herd of giraffes he found himself being "played around" with by a wildebeest bull. Within two hundred yards of Roosevelt's little Springfield rifle, it pranced, flourishing its tail, tossing its head, and uttering its grunting bellow as if it knew Roosevelt would not shoot at him. The wildebeest was right. Roosevelt was more interested in the giraffes. There were seven, a medium-size bull, four cows, and two calves. Roosevelt's intent was to collect two cows and a young one for the museum. After he shot the three he wanted, he marveled that the remaining four did not run.

Because they stayed, exhibiting what Roosevelt called "tameness bordering on stupidity," Kermit was able to shoot them with a camera. After the exercise of much patience, he managed to get within fifty yards of the bull and take several pictures. Never without a camera, carried by one of the porters, Kermit proved to be a talented photographer whose photos were not limited to showing the animals that were killed. His pictures recorded all kinds of wildlife and birds in their habitats, as well as vistas of the African landscapes and action shots of the safari on the move across plains, fording streams, and encamped. Many of the pictures, of course, captured Roosevelt striking a victorious pose with particularly prized specimens at his feet.

One day when Roosevelt was preparing to shoot at a bull rhino with a stubby horn, and Kermit readied his camera to capture the rhino with a camera, Kermit exclaimed, "Look at him, standing there in the middle of the African plain, deep in prehistoric thought." The photo he got was of the rhino's left profile, the short grass of the plain beneath him and against a cloudless sky. Another photo taken at the same time caught the bull, a cow, and a calf, widely separated in a scene that appeared to Roosevelt to not have changed since the pliocene age, while "the rest of the world, for good or evil," had gone forward.

Kermit's lens also caught giraffes and wildebeest herds for photos that in Roosevelt's book were captioned "at home." Other pictures immortalized a wounded lioness in deep grass as she prepared to charge, and a head-on, angry rhino that was captioned "coming on."

Had audiotape recorders been available, Roosevelt certainly would have preferred to use such a machine to capture the sounds made by the animals, rather than to attempt to describe them in prose. He noted that zebras were the noisiest game. After them came the wildebeest's "queer grunt." The topi uttered only a kind of sneeze, as did the hartebeest. But no sound was as thrilling as the roar of a lion.

A perpetual source of wonder was the difference in the behavior of individuals within the same species, and in behavior of the same individual at different times, such as wariness when going for water, when they rested, and when they showed their ferocity. He also observed how their appearance seemed to change, depending on the light. "At one moment the sun would turn the zebras of a mixed herd white," he noted, "and the hartebeest straw-colored, so that the former could been seen much farther than the latter; and again the conditions would be reversed when under the light the zebras would show up gray, and the hartebeest as red as foxes."

Having collected almost all the specimens of the common type desired by the sponsoring museum, Roosevelt and his safari marched north from the Sotik plain toward Lake Naivasha.

★ ★ ★

"Two or three times we crossed singularly beautiful ravines, the trail winding through narrow cliffs that were almost tunnels, and along the brinks of sheer cliffs, while the green mat of trees and vines was spangled with many colored flowers," Roosevelt wrote of the trek. "Then we came to barren ridges and bare, dusty plains; and at nightfall pitched camp near the shores of Lake Naivasha." He found it "a lovely sheet of water surrounded by hills and mountains, its shores broken by rocky promontories, and indented by papyrus-fringed bays."

To reward the porters for their hard work and good conduct he gave them twenty-five sheep. The men improvised long chants in his honor, then "feasted royally."

For a day of hippo hunting, Roosevelt, Kermit, Cuninghame, and the usual number of natives set out in a steam launch. The boat was provided by a pair of English brothers named Attenborough. To start a farm in Africa one had given up mining in the California Sierras after twenty years and the other had retired from His Majesty's Navy in the rank of commander. Roosevelt saw in them "just the men for work in a new country—for a new country is a poor place for the weak and incompetent, whether of body or mind." As the steam launch plied the waters of a lagoon, Roosevelt was surprised and delighted to see a big hippo walking entirely out of the water on the edge of the papyrus at the far end of a little bay that was filled with waterlilies. Until that moment all the hippos he'd encountered had been submerged with only their eyes and nostrils in view. When the launch was maneuvered to within a few rods of the hippo, Roosevelt switched to the launch's rowboat. As he steadied himself in the bow with the small Springfield rifle in hand, Cuninghame steered. Kermit readied his camera.

To Roosevelt the hippopotamus was a "self confident, truculent beast" that went under water once or twice, only to pop out of the papyrus and wade along the water, its massive body in full view. Cuninghame rowed closer into shallower water, but still more than a hundred yards from the hippo. As it turned as if to break into the papyrus, Roosevelt fired into its shoulder. A truculent beast indeed, it plunged into the water, and with its huge jaws agape, surged straight at the boat, floundering and splashing through the water lilies, bent on mischief. Instead of trying to reach deeper water, and despite being shot again, the hippo continued on. Aimed at its open mouth, Roosevelt fired one more. The jaws closed, Roosevelt noted, "with the clash of a sprung bear trap." The next bullets slammed at the base of an ear, dropping the hippo in its tracks.

While this drama unfolded, Kermit was so busy snapping pictures that he saw the hippo only through his viewfinder. Putting down the camera, he joined in the hard work of dragging the hippo from among the water lilies and tethering it to the back of the launch. Back at camp, the natives welcomed Roosevelt and his prize with a half-hour chant, praising Bwana Makuba for his feat. But Roosevelt did not think much of hippo-hunting. He regarded it as not a very attractive sport, primarily because he usually had to wait an hour or more before finding out if he'd been successful because, as noted earlier, a hippo killed in water sank immediately, only to bob to surface a day later. He also didn't like not knowing if he'd shot a bull or cow because all he could see of the hippo when he shot was a portion of the head sticking above the water. As the time he had to get off a shot was brief, any hesitation ensured that the hippo escaped. This meant that two or three hippo might be killed before the right specimen was secured. This was, the conservationist felt, a waste of wildlife.

But there were times when going after a hippo could afford, as he wrote, "interesting and exciting incidents." The one he had in mind involved him, Cuninghame, and the two Attenborough brothers. They'd started out early in the launch, towing the big, clumsy rowboat manned by a trio of strong porters who knew how to row. Steaming down the lake about fifteen miles, they entered a wide bay that was indented by smaller bays, lagoons, and inlets, all fringed by the ever-present papyrus. Leaving the launch for the rowboat, they immediately heard a hippo, hidden in the green vastness on their right. There were eight hippos, floating with heads above the water. Roosevelt shot one, hoping that it was a bull and disappointed that it was a cow.

Later, in the rowboat with two rowers who did not speak English, he made out about a dozen hippo, two or three of them very big. When he shot the largest, it disappeared in the water. As the rowers brought the boat to the spot, Roosevelt directed one of the rowers to probe the water with a pole. The porter did as told and poked the submerged body, then with a look of alarm on his face, found enough English vocabulary to shout that the hippo was alive.

"Sure enough," Roosevelt recorded for his eventual readership, "bump went the hippo against the bottom of the boat, the jar causing all to sit suddenly down."

Another bump shook the boat, followed by the shallow, muddy water boiling as hippos on all sides, above and below the surface, scattered. As the two horrified rowers struggled to take the boat "out of the dangerous neigh-borhood," Roosevelt shot at the head of a hippo that appeared to his left. As the hippo made off in frantic haste, Roosevelt had no idea whether he'd hit it. What happened next was described as only Roosevelt could:

> I had small opportunity to ponder the subject, for twenty feet away the water bubbled and a huge head shot out facing me, the jaws wide open. There was no time to guess at its intentions, and I fired on the instant. Down went the head, and I felt the boat quiver as the hippo passed underneath. Just here the lily pads were thick; so I marked its course, fired as it rose, and down it went. But on the other quarter of the boat a beast, evidently of great size—it proved to be a bull—now appeared, well above the water; and I put a bullet into its brain.
>
> I did not wish to shoot again unless I had to, and stood motionless, with the little Springfield at the ready. A head burst up twenty yards off, with a lily pad plastered over one eye, giving the hippo an absurd resem-blance to a discomfited prize-fighter, and then disappeared with great agi-tation. Two half-grown beasts stupid from fright appeared, and stayed up for a minute or two at a time, not knowing what to do. Other heads popped up, getting farther and farther away. By degrees everything van-ished, the water grew calm, and we rowed over to the papyrus, moored ourselves by catching a hold of a couple of stems, and awaited events. Within an hour four dead hippos appeared: a very big bull and three big cows. Of course, I would not have shot the latter if it could have been avoided; but under the circumstances I do not see how it was possible to help it. The meat was not wasted; on the contrary it was a godsend, not only to our own porters, but to the natives round about, many of whom were short on commons on account of the drought.
>
> Bringing over the launch we worked until after dark to get the bull out of the difficult position in which he lay. It was nearly seven o'clock before we had him fixed for towing on one quarter, the rowboat towing the other, by which time two hippos were snorting and blowing within a few yards of us, their curiosity as much excited as to what was going on. The night was overcast; there were drenching rain squalls, and a rather heavy sea was running, and I did not get back to camp until after three. Next day the launch fetched the rest of the hippo meat.

From Lake Naivasha, the safari proceeded to the railroad town of the

same name. There they read news of the outside world from the only newspaper they ever saw, the New York *Oswego Gazette,* that was mailed on a regular basis to Alden Loring. It was now late July 1909 and three months since
Roosevelt had debarked the German steamer *Admiral* at Mombasa.

On July 24, in order to ship fresh specimens and trophies to the United
States, Roosevelt was again in Nairobi and reunited with Frederick Selous,
the McMillans, and Judd. It was race week in the colorful city. White army
officers, government officials, and farmers and wives went to the races on
ponies, and a few on camels, or drove there in rickshaws, a cart called a
gharry, in bullock-towed two-wheel carriages known as tongas, and occasionally in automobiles. The races were carried out in the most sporting
spirit. Kermit demonstrated the horsemanship his father had seen that all his
children develop, and deported himself admirably in what Roosevelt termed
the "capital fun."

On the fourth of August Roosevelt was back at Lake Naivasha after stopping on the way to lay a cornerstone of a new mission building. While
waiting for the safari to get ready for its next leg, and as Kermit went off on a
camping trip, Roosevelt spent a couple of days trying for singsing waterbuck.
He missed a bull and wounded another that he did not get, but he succeeded
in shooting a fine waterbuck cow at a hundred yards, and a buck tommy,
both for food.

A four-day march from Naivasha brought the safari to Neri, in the high
plateaus and mountain chains of the Aberdare range. Their last camp at that
spot was at an altitude of about ten thousand feet. The air was so cold that
water froze in wash basins. Fog and rain shrouded the landscape. There was
not much game. The land was Kikuyu country. The natives welcomed the
Bwana Makuba with one of their dances at a ceremony arranged by the district commissioner. Two thousand warriors, naked or half so, with faces and
legs painted red and yellow, chanted in unison, danced rhythmically in rings
while drums throbbed and horns blared. Women shrilled approval and also
danced, while Masai tribesmen circled and swung in a pantherlike dance of
their own. The dancing continued in their camps, late into the night, long
after Bwana Makuba had gone to bed.

Two days later, the clouds lifted. The safari rose from camp in bright sunlight, ahead of them in the distance the high rocky peaks of Mount Kenya.

15

★ ★ ★

Most Interesting of
All the Animals

WITH KERMIT AND LESLIE TARLTON heading north on a safari of their own, Roosevelt, Cuninghame, and Heller traveled for two days through well-peopled farm country in which Kikuyu women worked the fields with hoes, because, Roosevelt observed, "among the Kikuyus, as among other savages, the woman is the drudge and beast of burden." The trail led by clear, rushing streams that formed the headwaters of the Tana River. On the afternoon of the second day the party struck upward among the steep foothills of Mount Kenya and pitched camp by the green wall of tangled forest.

Elephants on his mind, Roosevelt had observed along the route the devastation they had wreaked in farm fields in nighttime rampages, known as "shambas," in which the elephants had pillaged the crops. In his travels Roosevelt found that no other animal, including the lion, was so constant a theme for talk around campfires of African hunters and in the native villages as the elephant. "It is, not only to hunters, but to naturalists, and to all people who possess any curiosity about wild creatures and the wild life of nature," he wrote, "the most interesting of all animals."

After two days of rain that followed the setting up of the camp in an open glade on the mountainside, Cuninghame and a native guide called an 'Ndorobo, set off to look for signs that elephants were nearby. Rain was still falling when Roosevelt, Heller, and Cuninghame tramped in single file through forest that was too thick for horses. Clad in a khaki-colored shirt and khaki trousers that buttoned down the legs, wearing hobnailed shoes and a thick slouch hat, with a book from the Pigskin Library in his kit, Roosevelt climbed in and out of the deep ravines and waded through swift streams for three hours on a route along the edge of the woods. When the sun came out, they plunged into a forest that was a riot of twisted vines and interlacing trees and bushes.

On finding elephant spoor, Cuninghame and the 'Ndorobo minutely examined the dung, then tested the wind by lighting matches to see which way the smoke blew. The frustration of the trek was noted in Roosevelt's account. He wrote, "Each time after an hour's stealthy stepping and crawling along the twisted trail a slight shift of wind in the almost still air gave our scent to the game, and away it went before we could catch a glimpse of it; and we resumed our walk."

As evening fell, they pitched camp beside a little brook at the bottom of a ravine. They dined "ravenously" on bread, mutton, and tea. Two hours after leaving camp in the morning, all the frustration and impatience of yesterday vanished with today's discovery of the fresh signs of between ten and fifteen elephants. Around noon they were heard thrashing around in the woods. They were moving slowly. Roosevelt listened to the crack of tree branches and the elephants' "curious internal rumblings." Carefully, with every sense alert, Roosevelt and his two knowing companions kept pace with the yet unseen quarry. With double-barreled rifle in hand, Roosevelt stepped in the huge footprints left by the elephants, confident that where such a great weight had pressed there were not sticks left to crack under his feet to alert the quarry.

He wrote, "It made our veins thrill thus for half an hour to creep stealthily along, but a few rods from the herd, never able to see it, because of the extreme denseness of the cover, but always hearing first one and then another of its members, and always trying to guess what each one might do, and keeping ceaselessly ready for whatever might befall."

Where the trail took a twist to one side, suddenly there was before Roosevelt, about thirty yards in front, part of the massive gray head of an elephant resting its tusks on the branches of a young tree. A bull with good ivory, it turned in Roosevelt's direction. Roosevelt raised his gun and aimed for an eye, but a little to the side, hoping to send the bullet into the brain. He struck where he'd aimed, but he merely stunned the elephant. As it stumbled forward, half falling, a second bullet "sped true," as the rifleman described the shot, and as Roosevelt lowered the gun from his shoulder, he "saw the great lord of the forest come crashing to the ground."

With both barrels of the rifle emptied, Roosevelt watched as the thick bushes parted to his left, revealing the vast bulk of a charging bull elephant that was so close to Roosevelt that it could have knocked him down with a swipe of his thick trunk. Leaping aside, Roosevelt dodged behind a tree, frantically ejected the two shells from the rifle's barrels, and reloaded. But it was Cuninghame, firing twice, who stopped the charge. The wounded elephant wheeled and ran for thick cover. Unable to follow him, Roosevelt heard him trumpet shrilly. Then all sounds ceased.

Having wisely run for safety when the elephant first crashed from the trees, the 'Ndorobo reappeared to go forward in search of the elephant's trail. He soon returned to report evidence that the elephant had fled fast, but that great amounts of blood marked the route. Rather than go after the wounded giant, Roosevelt decided to tackle the formidable job of collecting the skin of the dead bull for mounting in the museum. Of killing his first elephant, Roosevelt chose an odd noun for a man who professed great respect for "the great lord of the forest." He wrote "I felt proud indeed as I stood by the immense bulk of the slain *monster* [emphasis added] and put my hand on the ivory. The tusks weighed a hundred and thirty pounds. There was the usual scene of joyful excitement among the gun bearers—who had behaved excellently—and among the wild bush people who had done the tracking for us."

When some of the 'Ndorobo looked for the bull that Cuninghame had shot to see if it had fallen, they found that it had traveled steadily, even though its wounds were probably fatal, but the searchers found no carcass. Leaving Cuninghame and Heller to skin the bull and to do the time-consuming curing of the hide, and then transport it to Neri, Roosevelt took one porter and a guide and returned to the base camp. Reaching it in early afternoon, he sent natives back to the scene of the elephant skinning to deliver a week's supply of provisions, tents, and fresh clothing for Cuninghame, Heller, and their workers. He then enjoyed the luxuries of a shave and a warm bath. The next day was devoted to writing, accepting the accolades of a visiting Kikuyu chief, and preparing for the next adventure, a fortnight-long safari that he would lead himself.

* * *

The immediate destination was Neri. There he added to his entourage a pair of young Scotsmen who spoke the local language. He also assembled fifty Kikuyus to supplement his Swahili porters, and a "head tent boy," an Arab named Ali. The only significant event on the first afternoon was finding "safari" ants, so-called because they moved on foraging expeditions in immense numbers. Roosevelt observed with amused fascination as one of the porters of the human safari laid two twigs on the ground as a peace-offering to the ants, stating that since the ants were on safari, too, it was wise to propitiate them, although it's highly unlikely that the man actually said "propitiate."

After camping for an evening in a forest glade, the Roosevelt safari came out onto plains on which there were no human inhabitants, hardly any game, and no lions. Camp was pitched by a cold stream that was one of the headwaters of the Guaso Nyero. To the east rose the crags and snowfields of Mount Kenya. Roosevelt had been told to expect to hunt in a dry season, but found rains that often turned torrential. During one especially heavy storm, Ali rushed into Roosevelt's tent exclaiming about "a big snake up high." Deciding this was definitely worth investigating, Bwana Makuba exited the tent, looked up, and saw a huge, funnel-shaped, whirling, dark cloud careering across the sky. Fortunately, it passed to one side of the camp harm-lessly.

On another occasion there was such a violent thunderstorm that the natives cowered in fear. "In this desolate and lonely land the majesty of the storms impressed on the beholder a sense of awe and solemn exaltation," Roosevelt-the-naturalist recorded in an almost biblical prose. "Tossing their crests, and riven by lightning, they gathered in their wrath from every quarter of the heavens, and darkness was before and under them; then, in the lull of a moment, they might break apart, while the sun turned the rain to silver and the rainbows were set in the sky; but always they gathered again, menacing and mighty—for the promise of the [rain]bow was never kept, and ever the clouds returned after the rain."

Once as he rode alone facing Mount Kenya "the clouds tore asunder, to right and left, and the mountain towered between, while across its base was flung a radiant arch. But almost at once the many-colored glory was dimmed; for in splendor and tenor the storm that rode in front shrouded all things from sight in thunder-shattered sheets of rain."

On these days alone in the wilderness, happy and content as he had been on his solitary hunts in his beloved, but now lost, American West, he enjoyed being "entirely by myself," except for his native followers. But as he ventured out with them, the gunbearers, sais, and the skinners walked silently, on the lookout for game, until he called a halt and returned to camp. On the front peak of his little triangular tent, called a "thorn boma," flew the American flag.

Late in the afternoon of September 3, 1909, Cuninghame and Heller caught up with the safari to be greeted "joyfully." Next morning, they started toward Mera, a small settlement in the Kenya foothills. Awaiting them were Kermit and Tarleton, eager to relate their own hunts. With Kermit and Tarleton striking out again on their own hunts, Roosevelt and the others spent two weeks hunting elephants and rhinos. Riding through tall grass, which often rattled in the wind, Roosevelt thought about rattlesnakes in the West. Although he knew that no African snakes had rattles, his "subconscious senses" always put him at attention if he heard anything resembling the threatening noise of a rattler.

While at Mera he received a cable informing him that Admiral Peary had reached the North Pole. Perhaps wishing he could have joined that expedition, he recalled that a year before, as President of the United States, he'd said good-bye to Peary at Oyster Bay as Peary started on his Arctic quest on a ship named *Roosevelt*.

On a hunt from Mera, Roosevelt claimed two ostriches and on the same day took a giraffe. A different species than the giraffe he'd hunted south of Kenya, it was a "reticulated" species, so-called because its coloring consisted of a network of reticulation of white lines. It was a type of giraffe that naturalists were eager to obtain and study.

When this phase of Roosevelt's safari ended at Neri on October 20, 1909, after a march through mist and rain across the cold Aberdare tablelands, Roosevelt again admired the blue waters of Lake Naivasha. After a brief pause at Neri, he headed for Nairobi and a reunion with Kermit. Exhilarated by a month-long hunt with Leslie Tarleton, son told father about killing the "great koodoo." With spiral horns and striped coat, the animal was, in Theodore Roosevelt's opinion, "the stateliest and handsomest antelope in the world."

Kermit had turned twenty on October 10. Sixteen days later he was again with father for the next adventure in the company of Tarlton and Edmund Heller. The following day was his father's fifty-first birthday, but because they spent it marching hard toward the Uasin Gishu plateau and the 'Nzoi

River Roosevelt was disappointed that he had no chance to celebrate the occasion by taking a hunt. He'd marked his fiftieth as president by riding his jumping horse, Roswell, over all the hurdles in Rock Creek Park in Washington. Now he was pushing on among rolling hills and along valleys and ravines on a route that crossed and re-crossed the Equator.

As on the Aberdares and the slopes of Mount Kenya, the nights were sometimes so cold that he was glad to have brought a mackinaw and a lumberman's jacket that had been a gift from a dear friend, Jack Greenway, who'd ridden with Roosevelt's Rough Riders. When Roosevelt opened his diary to note the events of the first day of November 1909, his African safari was in a landscape that reminded him of northern California. Some of the hills were bald. Others were wooded at the top. There were wet meadows, hillsides covered with rank, thick-growing grass that alternated with stretches of forest of stately cedars, yews, and tall laurel-leaved olive trees.

It was a land rich in game, including a large party of the despised hyena in a lair laid in the wet seclusion of some reed beds. As natives beat the brush, the hyenas bolted into the clear, allowing both Roosevelts to claim one. The next day, Roosevelt decided, "it was Kermit's turn for a giraffe." After a spirited chase, during which Roosevelt's horse, Tranquility, put both his front feet into a hole and dumped Roosevelt to the ground, Kermit and Tarlton were in a race with a wounded bull giraffe. When it suddenly came to a standstill, looking as if it had had enough and decided to charge, Kermit leaped from his horse and felled it. The kill of the "fine specimen" meant that the safari had to stop so that the giraffe hide could be preserved. The pause allowed Roosevelt to switch from big-game hunter to quiet observer of the region's lush flora, and to write about it at length and in meticulous detail. He noted that some of the acacias "had put forth their small, globular, yellow blossoms, just as the acacias of the Athi Plains were doing in the previous May," and blue lupins were flowering, "for it is cool, pleasant country."

But hunting was not completely forgotten. To "fill out the series of specimens of the big hartebeest and the oribi" needed by the National Museum, Roosevelt and son took advantage of the leisure time to hunt them. The meat of the oribis were reserved for the white men's table, set up in Roosevelt's tent in a way that Colonel Roosevelt of the now-legendary Rough Riders saw as the "officers' mess." His faithful tent boy, "Good Ali," saw to it that the table was adorned by bowls of sweet-scented jessamine.

Kermit's two gun-bearers were Juma Tohari, a "coal-black Swahili Moslem," and "a Christian negro" named Kassitura from Uganda. Roosevelt was pleased that both men were as eager to serve Kermit as those who looked after Bwana Makuba. From time to time Roosevelt gave them chocolate in colorful wrappers, then delighted in watching them puzzling over their pictures of ladies, gentlemen, little girls, and wild beasts.

From the giraffe camp the safari traveled two days to the 'Nzoi River. Until now they'd been on waters that either vanished in the desert or flowed into the Indian Ocean. The 'Nzoi, a rapid, muddy river that passed south of Mount Eglon and emptied into the Victoria Nyanza lake, was part of the watershed of the Nile River. The territory was rife with game, from lions that Roosevelt heard roaring at night, to troops of elephants who marked their passage by tearing off the tops of small thorn trees. Seeing the evidence, Roosevelt marveled over how the elephants could swallow such prickly "dainties" armored with needle-like spikes. Hartebeests were many in number, along with topi, oribi, and herds of zebras.

Nor were the area's birds overlooked, especially honey birds. Before starting for Africa, Roosevelt had been encouraged by naturalist John Burroughs to look into the bird's habits. One whose existence Burroughs had doubted, the species got its name from its facility in finding honey. Camped by the 'Nzoi, Roosevelt found the noisy birds almost a nuisance because they continually accompanied him as he hunted. They flew from tree to tree, never ceasing their harsh chatter.

One day as the honey birds vexed him, and a line of a hundred porters fanned out across a large swamp, Roosevelt shot a couple of bushbuck. After the drive was over Kermit shot a female leopard as she stood on the side of an anthill. Then he had a close call when a wounded singsing buck charged him. But the day turned out to be one on which Roosevelt found himself benefitting from honey birds. They led Kermit and some porters to a bee hive. After the porters smoked out the inhabitants, the hive provided enough honey to be a welcome accompaniment to Roosevelt's lunch.

A few miles beyond the swamp they encountered a small herd of elephants in the open. Roosevelt counted eight cows and two calves, moving slowly and feeding on the thorny tops of mimosa trees. Desiring to photograph them, Kermit wanted to move closer. Having obtained all the elephants he needed for the museum, Roosevelt was content to observe them as their great ears flapped and trunks lifted and curled.

On the way back to camp he saw a white man on the trail ahead and was surprised that he was Carl Akeley, out from New York City on a mission on behalf of the American Museum of Natural History. His goal was elephants, he explained, as Roosevelt remembered that it had been a year ago that Akeley's vivid descriptions of the glories of Africa had persuaded Roosevelt to abandon plans to hunt in Alaska. Now, when Akeley asked Roosevelt to join him in a hunt for elephants, Roosevelt happily agreed. The hunt began the next morning. In addition to Akeley and Roosevelt were Kermit and Tarlton, traveling light. They found elephants around noon, standing in a clump, each occasionally shifting its position or lazily flapping an ear in a grassy area dotted by mimosas. Akeley wanted two cows and a calf. The hunters advanced to within twenty-five yards of them. Standing on an anthill, Roosevelt prepared to shoot.

Tarlton shouted, "Look out! They are coming for us."

Regarding an elephant charge at such close range "a serious thing," Roosevelt stood his ground and shot a menacing cow in the forehead. The elephant lurched heavily forward to her knees. A volley from everyone finished it, while sending the other elephants scurrying as fast as possible for safety. As they turned to run, Roosevelt felled a second cow. Meanwhile, Kermit used a Winchester to kill a bull calf. With a camp set up a hundred yards from the carcasses, Tarlton and Akeley, "working like a demon," had them skinned by nightfall. Before long a pack of hyenas gathered in the dark to quarrel among themselves as they gorged on the remains.

Pleased to have assisted Akeley, Roosevelt left him by the 'Nzoi to go to Lake Sergoi on a two-day march. Not a true lake, but a reed-filled pond, it was the limit at which Englishmen and Boers had settled. But there was a store kept by a South African of Scottish lineage who met Roosevelt with "a kind courtesy." Anticipating Roosevelt's arrival, the English commissioner of the district had arranged for a group of warriors of the Nandi tribe to show Roosevelt how they hunted lions with spears.

The next day, November 20, 1909, Roosevelt and several other white settlers set out on horseback to catch up with Nandi hunters already in the field. The action began around noon when a maned lion rose a quarter of a mile ahead of the line of Nandi and galloped off through high grass. Roosevelt and the others tore after him on horseback. He was, observed Roosevelt, "a magnificent beast, with a black and tawny mane; in his prime, teeth and claws perfect, with mighty thews, and a savage heart."

He was lying near a hartebeest on which he had been feasting. Until this very moment, Roosevelt mused, "his life had been one of unbroken career of rapine and violence; and now the maned master of the wilderness, the terror that stalked by night, the grim lord of slaughter, was to meet his doom at the hands of the only foes who dared molest him."

But not without a tremendous fight. As the Nandi encircled him, the lion rose to his feet. The lush mane bristled. His tail lashed. The great head hung low, fangs revealed. Facing first one way and then another, he grunted and roared. With an eye as true as the lens of Kermit's camera, and invoking the experience of years of hunting dangerous game and then writing about them in articles and books, Roosevelt recorded the drama this way:

It was a wild sight; the ring of spearmen, intent, silent, bent on blood, and in the center the great man-killing beast, his thunderous wrath growing ever more dangerous.

At last the ring was complete, and the spearmen rose and closed in. The lion looked quickly from side to side, saw where the line was thinnest, and charged at his topmost speed. The crowded moment began.

In writing about a moment twelve years and five months earlier when he had raced on horseback and then afoot in the lead of Rough Riders and other soldiers of the U.S. Army to the top of Kettle Hill in the San Juan Heights of Cuba, Roosevelt had called it "my crowded hour." For the remainder of his life he would try to recapture the thrill of it, to feel once more the wolf rising in his heart. In pursuit of that need he'd come to Africa. In the first line of the foreword to the book he would title *African Game Trails,* he exclaims, "I speak of Africa and golden joys; the joy of wandering through lonely lands; the joy of hunting the mighty and terrible lords of the wilderness, the cunning, the wary, and the grim."

He'd come to Africa with an arsenal of guns and fitted out the grandest safari ever seen to that time, and possibly of all time, to discover "these greatest of the world's great hunting grounds." But he closed the foreword to the book by confessing, "There are no words that can tell the hidden spirit of the wilderness, that can reveal its mystery, its melancholy, its charm."

The hunter who wandered through the lands of Africa, he said, would see sights which ever afterward remain fixed in his mind. On November 20, 1909, he witnessed just such a scene as Nandi warriors, with only their shield and spears held steady, ringed a lion and then braced themselves for its maddened attack. Merely an observer at this point, Roosevelt saw, then wrote:

Bounding ahead of his fellows, the leader reached toward throwing distance; the long spear flickered and plunged; as the lion felt the wound he half turned, and then flung himself on the man in front. The warrior threw his spear; it drove deep into the lion, for entering at one shoulder it came out of the opposite flank, near the thigh, a yard of steel through the great body. Rearing, the lion struck the man, bearing down the shield, his back arched; and for a moment he slaked his fury with fang and talon. But on the instant I saw another spear driven clear through his body from side to side; and as the lion turned again the bright spear blades darting toward him were flashes of white flame. The end had come. He seized another man, who stabbed him and wrenched loose. As [the lion] fell he gripped a spearhead in his jaws with such tremendous force that he bent it double. Then the warriors were round and over him, stabbing and shouting, wild with furious exaltation.

From the moment when he charged until his death I doubt whether ten seconds had elapsed, perhaps less; but what a ten seconds!

The wounded Nandi were treated. Roosevelt promised to reward their bravery with a heifer. Noting that the men prized their cattle more than their wives, Roosevelt was greeted with broad smiles. Then the warriors raised their shields above their heads and chanted a victory song while they danced around the dead lion. It was a celebration of triumph, Roosevelt wrote, that ended "a scene of as fierce interest and excitement as I ever hope to see."

The Nandi marched back to the camp by themselves, carrying the two wounded men on their shields. When Roosevelt tried to get them to remain for a few days to serve as beaters, they declined, unless they would be allowed to kill whatever lions they encountered. Roosevelt was not interested in being a "mere spectator at any more hunts, no matter how exciting—though to do so once was well worthwhile."

The only lion Roosevelt found appeared for an instant at a swamp. He got off one shot that ought to have hit him, but didn't. Efforts to drive the lion in the open by setting fire to the grass failed. The lion was not seen again.

On the last day of November, with genuine regret, Roosevelt said goodbye to his East African safari because on the next phase of the odyssey he could take only a few of his personal attendants. The porters, beaters, and saises had been with him more than seven months. Not one had been killed, either by accident or in an attack by an animal.

Ahead of Roosevelt lay Uganda and the Nile Valley.

16

★ ★ ★

Tales by Poe on the Upper Nile

THE FIRST TEN DAYS of December were spent in beautiful farm country at Njoro on the edge of the Mau escarpment. Roosevelt's host was Lord Delamere. A renowned big-game hunter, he'd bagged fifty-two lions before turning his attention to wheat-growing and was a leader in the work of "taming the wilderness" and "conquering for civilization the world's worst spaces." To Roosevelt he was "a most useful settler, from the standpoint of the all-round interests" of East Africa. To Roosevelt's delight, Lady Delamere had a large library.

Four days passed hunting bongo in the dense forest to avail. But on this fruitless outing Roosevelt observed the resting stance of a dozen 'Ndorobo men as they stood on one leg "like storks." He was also fascinated by squat, woolly, funny animals called tree hyraxes that the natives called "Teddy bears." But it was the bongo, along with the giant hog, that Roosevelt saw as the region's "big game." Again, his efforts at hunting ended in disappointment. This was not the case with Kermit. On a hunt with Lord Delamere he succeeded in collecting one bongo, a fine cow. Following this success, Kermit hunted at the coast near Mombasa, the city where the Roosevelt expedition had begun.

Kermit's objective was sable. He traveled on his own with two gun bearers and a few Swahili porters. After marching from Mombasa and crossing a harbor in a dhow, they arrived in a village in time to observe, and for Kermit to photograph, a ritual dance at the funeral of a chief's dead son.

Kermit reported that the dance "had more life and go to it" than any he'd seen in the ballrooms of New York and Harvard student soirees at Cambridge. The dirge music, he told his father, "had such swing and vivacity" that it was almost as lively as a comic opera.

Arriving in Nairobi, Roosevelt had a reunion with Cuninghame and Tarlton. With three other naturalists they were engaged in sending specimens to America and in preparations for the next trek, into Uganda, by way of Lake Victoria Nyanza. The safari departed on December 18. Sailing on "a smart little steamer" for twenty-four hours, they landed at Entebbe, the seat of the British governor of Uganda. The next morning they crossed the Equator for the last time. They headed north to the native town of Kampalla. The ruler of Uganda, Roosevelt learned, was a boy king. He also found that Ugandans had proved so accessible to Christianity that Kampalla was the headquarters of missions of the Church of England and the Vatican. "For their good fortune." he wrote of the native population, "England has established a protectorate over them."

Well aware of the distinguished stature of their visitor, the missionaries of both faiths received Roosevelt by waving American and British flags. Native children who attended the mission schools sang "The Star Spangled Banner." Also greeting Roosevelt at the Church of England Mission was "Mother Paul." Having met her in New York before leaving for Africa, he'd promised to call on her in Kampalla to "look into the work she, and the sisters associated with her, were doing." Mother Paul had a surprise for Roosevelt. She had received, she said, a "goodwill letter" from two of "the Finest" (the nickname, and the boast, of the New York Police Department). The writers had been members on the force when Roosevelt was the president of a four-commissioner governing Police Board (1895–1897).

When the British commissioner, a man named Knowles, arranged a hunt for sitununga, a bigger relative of the bushbuck, Roosevelt and Kermit eagerly accepted the invitation, and the help of a hundred natives. Only Kermit managed to shoot one of the elusive animals. The next day, the safari left Kampalla for Lake Albert Nyanza. The journey encompassed a holiday that was Theodore Roosevelt's favorite: Christmas. But with a pang of nostalgia he wrote, "There is not much use in trying to celebrate Christmas unless there are small folks to hang their stockings on Christmas Eve, to rush gleefully in at dawn the next morning to open the stockings, and after breakfast to wait in hopping expectancy until their elders throw open the doors of the room in which the big presents are arranged, those for each child on a separate table."

Even though his second son and now grown-up "bunnie" Kermit was with him this may have been the only time in Africa that Theodore Roosevelt felt seriously homesick. Offsetting the longing for Sagamore Hill was his recognition that Kermit had proven himself to be a boon companion and an excellent hunter.

Pressing northward about forty miles from the coast, Roosevelt and Kermit usually got in two or three hours of hunting each day. They were in elephant country on the morning of the twelfth of December when they struck camp with information that a herd was nearby. Not much later, they heard four or five of them feeding in the thick jungle. The sounds indicated that they were about half a mile away. Presently, one of the natives crouched and beckoned to Roosevelt. Peering through dense foliage, Roosevelt "caught the loom of the tusker." Evidently catching the scene of humans, the elephant "assumed the offensive." With huge ears cocked at right angles to his head and trunk hanging down, he charged "full tilt." Coming on steadily, silently, and at a great pace, his feet swishing through the long grass, he looked to Roosevelt like a "formidable monster." At forty yards Roosevelt aimed at the huge head and let loose with one barrel of the Holland rifle. As the elephant stopped, a bullet from Kermit's Springfield slammed into its head. When the elephant wheeled, Roosevelt emptied the second barrel between neck and shoulder. Three more shots by Kermit struck, but the elephant spun around and crashed away. Because there was not much daylight remaining, the trail was difficult to follow. When the elephant's lumbering in the jungle thicket gave him away, Kermit crept forward and Roosevelt slipped within a dozen feet of the elephant as he stood on the other side of a group of small, twisted, vine-matted trees. Father and son fired together. The mighty bull threw up his trunk, crashed over backward, and lay dead on his side among the bushes. "A fine sight he was," Roosevelt wrote, "a sight to gladden any hunter's heart, as he lay in the twilight, a giant in death."

The scene was memorialized by a camera that captured Roosevelt in a pith helmet and khakis, left hand in a pocket, the right arm bent by his side as Roosevelt leaned on the carcass.

After leaving the elephant camp the safari journeyed in country that was mostly covered with open forest, chiefly acacia trees. At one place the woods reminded Roosevelt of regions of Texas and Oklahoma. It was a pleasant ride along the road in early mornings, with the safari coming behind, but noontime became very hot under the glare of a brazen equatorial sun. When it moved lower, they sallied forth to hunt in jungle so thick that without the guidance of natives there was little success. Ten days out of Kampalla they crossed the little Kafu River and entered a native kingdom, under British protectorate but separate from Uganda, named Unyoro. In its main settlement, Hoima, Roosevelt was greeted by British officials, a few missionaries, and the Christian king, to whom Roosevelt served five o'clock tea.

After a pause to hunt, the safari continued into a new year. At noon on January 5, 1910, it reached Butiaba on the shores of Lake Albert Nyanza. To get from the lake named for Prince Albert's wife, Queen Victoria, they'd marched 160 miles. The landscape around Butiaba and Lake Albert Nyanza shimmered in the white, glaring heat, but when the sun went down, the land to the west, Roosevelt wrote, "was kindled in ruddy splendor."

Boats took them to the Lado country and the saffron-hued river Zaire and northward to the Victorian Nile, "alive with monstrous crocodiles, and its banks barren of human life because of the fly whose bite brings the torment which ends in death."

As Roosevelt began this final phase of his expedition he took from the Pigskin Library *Tales of Mystery and Imagination* by Edgar Allan Poe.

As the safari sailed northward, the waters of Lake Albert Nyanza stretched "beyond the ken of vision," Roosevelt observed, "to where they were fed by streams from the Mountains of the Moon." On his left hand rose the frowning ridges on the other side of which forests of the Congo lay like a shroud over the land. Entering the White Nile, they steamed past many hippos that roared from reed beds, then snorted and plunged beside the boat. Arriving at Koba, they were met by six professional elephant hunters who made a living poaching ivory in the Congo. Still in British territory 48 hours after leaving Butiaba on Lake Albert Nyanza, the safari left its small flotilla of boats and set up a permanent camp in good game country with no native villages in the region. Roosevelt and Kermit usually went out together with gun-bearers to shoot a buck for food. Roosevelt wore his customary khaki outfit while Kermit strode along in front in short trousers and leggings, but knees bared.

The purpose of making this camp was a search for the so-called "white," or "square-nosed," rhinoceros. Almost exterminated by hunting in South Africa, and unknown north of the Zambezi River, it was even scarce in the narrow ribbon of territory on the left bank of the Upper Nile. Conceding that "it would certainly be well if all killing of it were prohibited until careful inquiry has been made as to its numbers and exact distribution," Roosevelt believed that he had an obligation to science to collect an example of the rare species.

He got his chance. Along with Kermit and native trackers after hours of seeking signs of the rhino under burning sun in grass that was higher than their heads, one of the natives pointed toward a thorn tree about sixty yards away. Mounting a low anthill, Roosevelt saw the rhino, "rather dimly through the long grass." Lying asleep on its side, the female rhino looked like a giant pig. Evidently sensing peril, it lurched to a sitting position with its big ears turned forward. With a shot from the Holland, Roosevelt "knocked it clean off its feet." Squealing loudly, the rhino staggered ten yards, then collapsed. But with Roosevelt's shot, four other rhinos appeared out of the grass. As they fled in panic, Kermit wounded a bull and followed it a long way, but couldn't overtake it. (The body was found ten days later.) Meanwhile, Roosevelt killed a calf that was apparently that of the cow that he'd killed with the one shot.

No longer the hunter, but a naturalist, he observed and recorded the unique aspects of the white rhinoceros. It stood higher than the common rhino and was shorter in length. The most interesting difference to Roosevelt was a huge "ungainly, square-mouthed head" lacking the "curved, prehensile development which makes the upper lip of a common rhino look like the hook of a turtle's beak."

At night in the riverside camp Roosevelt listened to the grunts and brays of venturesome hippos splashing and wallowing among the reeds. During one unforgettable night, in addition to the hippo chorus came the roaring of lions and elephants, driving home to Roosevelt that he was, indeed, "in the heart of the African wilderness."

He was also no longer in healthy East Africa. Although he and Kermit continued to be in robust health, others in the party suffered with dysentery, fever, and sun prostration. While in Uganda, one of the gun bearers had died, and on a march from Koba to Nimule four porters had succumbed to dysentery.

On February 17, 1910, the safari left the tiny village of Nimule on a ten-day march across a barren and arid land to Gondokoro, during which the Roosevelts hunted game for meat and the collections of their sponsoring museum. Awaiting them at Gondokoro was a boat that had been sent by the British head man in that region of the Sudan, Major-General Sir Reginald Wingate. The boat was provided to Roosevelt for a Nile River voyage to the storied city of Khartoum.

But before going down the Nile Roosevelt intended to collect the handsomest, largest, and least known of African antelopes, the giant eland. Because all the other white men in the party were down with dysentery and fever, the hale and hearty Roosevelt father and son went out with sixty Ugandan porters, a dozen pack mules, and several little riding mules. Also part of the entourage were seven native soldiers of the Belgian Congo, led by a corporal. The weather was very hot, and the landscape a waste of barren desolation. There was ample game to supply meat for the campfires, but the quarry crowding Roosevelt's imagination was the giant eland. For two days he left camp before sunrise with gun bearers and a guide, only to spend a day of tracking with glimpses of eland but no opportunity to shoot.

At eight in the morning on the third day the tracker found the spoor of a lone bull. By half-past noon Roosevelt knew he was "close on the beast." Then he glimpsed the eland. The tense excitement that ensued is vivid in his account of the hunt:

> Taking advantage of every patch of cover I crawled toward it on all-fours, my rifle too hot [from the sun] to touch the barrel, while the blustering heat of the baked ground hurt my hands. At a little over a hundred yards I knelt and aimed at the noble beast; I could now plainly see his huge bulk and great, massive horns, as he stood under a tree. The pointed bullet from the little Springfield hit a trifle too far back and up, but made such a rip that he never got ten yards from where I was standing; and great was my pride as I stood over him, and examined his horns, twisted almost like a koodoo's, and admired his size, his finely modeled head and legs, and the beauty of his coat.

On the first two days Kermit had killed two eland, a cow on the first day and a bull on the second. With pride in his son, Roosevelt wrote, "Kermit could see game, and follow tracks, almost as well as his gun-bearers, and in a long chase could outrun them. On each day [of the hunts] he struck the track of the eland, and after a while left his gun-bearers and porters, and ran along the trail accompanied only by a native guide."

Returning to the camp on that third day, Roosevelt found R.J. Cuninghame in better health, while Alden Loring and others remained seriously sick. But by the last day of February they were able to join Roosevelt and Kermit as they started down the Nile.

17

★ ★ ★

Reunion at Khartoum

GLIDING NORTHWARD on the Nile, with stops now and then for hunts, Roosevelt spent time seated on the foredeck of the steamer gazing at the long, glistening river and recalling a boy called Teedie heading up the Nile from Cairo 37 years before. Looking back over the past year, he felt proud and satisfied with his accomplishment. In the company of Smithsonian scientists, 15 native soldiers, 260 porters, and a handful of white hunters, he and Kermit had claimed 512 animals, including 17 lions, 11 elephants, 20 rhinos, 8 hippos, 9 giraffes, 47 gazelles, 20 zebras, and thousands of specimens of birds and other small creatures for the enlightenment of perhaps millions of Americans who could never see them in the wild.

He also felt heartened by improvement in the health of his companions. He credited their rebounding from fever and dysentery to a case of champagne that he had opened at Gondoroko. Evidently remembering the disastrous effects of a bottle of whiskey on his guide during a hunt in the West, he had decided that on the African trip the only liquor he would carry for emergencies would be brandy and champagne. But in the eleven months of hardgoing in difficult terrain he'd sipped only six ounces of brandy, believing that hot tea would do him more good. In that time Kermit had been ill once, and only for three days, and Roosevelt for five days. He attributed his own fever not to Africa, but to a recurrence of a fever he'd contracted in Cuba. The attacks he had in Africa were "very slight" and nowhere near as severe as a fever he'd experienced while bear hunting early one spring in the Rockies.

Much worse than any fever was a longing for home that became more pronounced as the end of the African year approached. In mid-February 1910 he'd written to Andrew Carnegie, "I am homesick for my own land and my own people! Of course it is Mrs. Roosevelt I most want to see; but I want to see my two youngest boys [Archie and Quentin]; I want to see my house, my own books and trees, the sunset over the sound from the window in the north room, the people with whom I have worked, who think my thoughts and speak my speech."

In November 1909 he'd written to Edith, "Oh, sweetest of all sweet girls, last night I dreamed that I was with you, and that our separation was but a dream, and when I waked up it was almost too hard to bear."

As the Nile steamer neared Khartoum, he eagerly looked forward to seeing Edith in the flesh. She would be there to welcome him, along with her mother and daughter Ethel. Archie and Quentin would not be present because they'd had to go back to the United States to school. Nor would Ted be there. While his father and brother had been adventuring in Africa, the love for Eleanor Alexander that had kept him from joining the expedition had been formalized by their engagement, with the wedding in abeyance until the groom's father returned home.

When Edith gave Roosevelt this news, he thought about his own marriage and wrote to Eleanor, "There is nothing in the world that equals the happiness that comes to lovers who remain lovers all through their wedded lives, and who are not only devoted to each other, but wise and forbearing and gentle, as well."

To Ted he wrote of the wife who had let him go off to Africa for a year, "Greatly tho I have Mother I was at times thoughtless and selfish, and if Mother had been a mere unhealthy Patient Griselda, I might have grown set in selfish and inconsiderate ways. Mother, always tender, gentle and considerate, and always loving, yet when necessary pointed out where I was thoughtless and therefore inconsiderate and selfish, instead of submitting to it. Had she not done this it would in the end have made her life much harder, and mine very much less happy."

But going back to the bliss of life at Sagamore Hill was not to be an immediate thing. The voyage to the United States with Edith, Kermit, and Ethel would include a lengthy passage through the cities of Europe that would announce to Americans and the world that Teddy Roosevelt had emerged from the wilderness just as he'd entered it—brash, daring, and ready to speak his mind.

It became "a grand tour" that one writer said was "rich months, with emperors and kings, presidents and cheering thousands." When in Rome, he turned down an audience with Pope Pius X after the Pope demanded that he not agree to see a group of American Methodists, one of whom had offended His Holiness by calling him "the whore of Babylon." Roosevelt then snubbed the Methodists with equal pleasure.

Warmly received in Paris, he spoke at the Sorbonne on the "Duties of Citizenship." In the speech he voiced a philosophy which had characterized his life:

> It is not the critic who counts, not the man who points out how the strong man stumbled or whether the doer of deeds could have done better. The credit belongs to the man who is actually in the arena; whose face is marred by dust and sweat and blood; who errs and comes up short again . . . who knows the great enthusiasms, the great devotions, and spends himself in a worthy cause; who at least knows in the end the triumph of high achievement; and who, at worst, if he fails, at least fails while doing greatly, so that his place shall never be with those cold and timid souls who know neither victory nor defeat.

Visiting the country of his Dutch ancestors, he marveled at the tulips of Holland's annual flower show. Moving northward to Stockholm, Sweden, he donned a suit of white-tie-and-tails to accept the Nobel Peace Prize, a ceremony belatedly held in recognition of his mediation of a treaty of peace that had ended the Russo-Japanese War of 1905. His acceptance speech called for the limitation of naval armaments by the European Powers, and formation of a "League of Peace," that would be backed by force if necessary. "The ruler or statesman who should bring about such a combination," he predicted, "would have earned his place in history for all time and his title to the gratitude of mankind."

Going on from Sweden to Germany, the former president paid a call on a ruler who was busily building battleships. Kaiser Wilhelm was so impressed by his illustrious guest, and with himself, that he gave TR a photograph that was taken as they met. The inscription read, "When we shake hands we shake the whole world."

The penultimate stop en route home was England, where Alice joined him, Edith, Ethel, and Kermit. He arrived in time to be designated by President Taft to represent the United States at the funeral of King Edward VII. A week and a half later he was given a rare honor for an American of giving an address at London's historic Guildhall. In the speech the man who'd helped end Spanish sovereignty in Cuba, and who had recently been a visitor to British East Africa and British-dominated Egypt, lectured the government of the new king, George V. He told the astonished, assembled dignitaries in their regal robes, "Now, either you have the right to be in Egypt or you have not; either it is or it is not your duty to establish and keep order." If they were not prepared to rise to their responsibilities they should get out, but he hoped that in the interest of civilization, and with "fealty to your own great traditions," that they would not.

After delivering the Romanes lecture at Oxford University, he took some ribbing from the Archbishop of York. "In the way of grading which we have at Oxford," he said, "we agreed to mark the lecture 'Beta Minus,' but the lecturer 'Alpha Minus.' While we felt that the lecture [on the subject "Biological Analogies to History"] "was not a very great contribution to science, we were sure that the lecturer was a very great man."

On June 18, 1910, "the great man," as Ted called his father, returned to New York City and a tumultuous welcome. As the steamer *Kaiserin Auguste Viktoria* sailed into the harbor, she was saluted by the battleship *South Carolina* and a flotilla of destroyers and yachts decked with banners and blowing whistles." When the ship docked at the Battery it was to a roaring reception by the people on the wharf. Following the welcoming speeches and a parade of horse-drawn carriages, marchers, and five hundred Rough Riders who had come to New York from all over the country, the Roosevelts gathered for lunch at 433 Fifth Avenue in a house built by Ted's fiancee's great-grandfather. After the meal, they took a ferry and train to Oyster Bay. Two days later, at the Fifth Avenue Presbyterian Church, Ted and Eleanor were married.

Speaking to the welcoming crowd on the day he set foot on American soil for the first time in a year, Theodore Roosevelt had declared that it was peculiarly the duty of a man who had been president of the United States to be nothing more than a private citizen. But before he had sailed for home he had a visit in Europe from an ally in his years as a politician. Gifford Pinchot had rushed across the Atlantic in a veritable panic to report that Roosevelt's heir in the White House, President William Howard Taft, had not only abandoned Roosevelt's progressive policies, but was acquiescing in everything Congress was doing to uproot everything Roosevelt had done as president.

Roosevelt listened, then renounced the implication of Pinchot's visit that he rescue the Progressive Party by getting back into the political fray. But his dockside pledge that he intended to be only a private citizen fell on deaf ears. He found himself besieged by old friends and allies to ride to the rescue of the Progressives. For reasons known only to him, but widely speculated upon by allies, old enemies, and Roosevelt biographers, he changed his mind about going quietly into private life. In pondering Roosevelt's reversal, Wall Street tycoon J.P. Morgan, who knew a thing or two about human nature, expressed a not untypical Morgan view that a man always has two reasons for what he does, "a good one and the real one."

The explanation for Roosevelt's abrupt turnaround in the minds of his foes was that he, like Julius Caesar and every ruler since, was ambitious. On the contrary, wrote Roosevelt's old and steadfast friend and veteran of the West, novelist Owen Wister, Roosevelt's change of plans demonstrated "the strongest element of his character," both a sacrifice to obvious duty and the performance of a plain obligation to his ideals. In a memoir, *My Friendship with Roosevelt,* published 30 years after Roosevelt's death, Wister wrote that the "real reason" for his change of mind "was the same reason that a duck takes to water." He explained the Roosevelt character this way:

> Among all his bents, historical, zoological, whatever, he was the preacher militant perpetual, and to be in a fight for his beliefs was his true element. In the appeals made to him [before his decision to get back into politics] the water had not come quiet so close to the duck. [Then he had been dragged] to the edge of a definite pond, and into the pond he plumped. . . . And then, the pond flowed steadily into a brook, and the brook speedily into a river, and down the river he went toward a sea that neither he nor friend nor enemy dreamed of.

On September 21, 1910, Roosevelt wrote to Henry Cabot Lodge, "The fight is very disagreeable. Twenty years ago I would not have minded in the least . . . but it is not the kind of fight into which an ex-President should be required to go. I could not possibly help myself."

One thing led to another—the pond into a brook, the brook into a river, and the river into a sea—and by 1912, Theodore Roosevelt was the nominee of a revitalized Progressive Party for president of the United States.

As a third-party candidate he would run against Taft and the Democratic standard-bearer, Woodrow Wilson. Acknowledging that "the great bulk of my wealthy and educated friends regard me as a dangerous crank," the old warrior asserted that he wanted to find a remedy for evils which, if left unremedied, would in the end do away not only with wealth and education, but with pretty much all of civilization. "It is a fight that must be made, and it is worth making, and the event lies on the knees of the gods."

For the now grown-up and mostly independent bunnies of Sagamore Hill the tumult of Big Bear running for office was a familiar phenomenon. But for Ted's wife, and mother of little Grace Roosevelt as they set foot in the house in the summer of 1912, the scene encountered was a shock. Eleanor wrote in her autobiography:

> It was the first time I had been there when the entire family was at home. Before twenty-four hours passed I realized that nothing in my bringing up as an only child had in any way prepared me for the frenzied activity into which I was plunged. Something was going on every minute of the day. The house was full of people. Conferences went on all day. The telephone never stopped ringing. In the evenings my father-in-law received the newspapermen. At first I thought everyone would be tired when the day was over and would go to bed early, but I soon found out that nothing of the kind could be expected. The Roosevelt family enjoyed life too much to waste time sleeping. Every night they stayed downstairs until nearly midnight; then, talking at the top of their voices, they trooped up the wide uncarpeted stairs and went to their rooms. For a brief moment all was still, but just as I was going off to sleep for the second time they remembered things they had forgotten to tell one another and ran shouting through the halls. I tried going to bed with cotton in my ears, but it never did any good.

The Roosevelt family had weathered other campaigns, and no matter how this contest came out, they were certain everything would be fine. However, their confidence was shaken on October 12 with horrifying news that as Roosevelt left the Hotel Gilpatric in Milwaukee for a speech at a campaign rally, a man wielding a pistol had lurched out of a crowd of well-wishers and fired a shot into Roosevelt's chest. The terrifying report was quickly followed by word that he not been killed, or even seriously wounded, but had actually delivered his speech. He began by saying to the audience, "I shall ask you to be as quiet as possible. I don't know whether you fully understand that I have just been shot; but it takes more than that to kill a Bull Moose." The speech went on for an hour and a half with Roosevelt repeatedly brushing aside appeals that he stop and get himself to a hospital. His survival was attributed to his good physical condition and to the fact that the text of his speech had been tucked into an inside pocket and had blunted the impact of the bullet.

Expressions of admiration for this latest demonstration of courage by the hero of San Juan Hill by the American people did not translate into sufficient votes to enter the Roosevelt name in the annals of American history as the first president to serve a third term. "We have fought the good fight, we have kept the faith," he said to an old friend a few days after losing to Wilson, "and we have nothing to regret."

Seven months later from Sagamore Hill, Roosevelt announced that he was in receipt of an invitation from the governments of Brazil, Argentina, and Chile to visit those countries for the purpose of delivering a series of lectures. Anticipating a chance for yet another adventure, he said, "I have to go. It's my last chance to be a boy."

PART FOUR

To Be a Boy Again

18

★ ★ ★

Merely Deferred

I F ANYONE could get Theodore Roosevelt to take a break from his presidential activities for a few minutes in the waning months of 1908 it was John Augustine Zahm. Roosevelt and the vigorous, rosy-cheeked, blue-eyed, fifty-five-year-old Roman Catholic priest with a mane of white hair had been, as Roosevelt put it, "cronies for some time, because we were both of us fond of Dante and of science." The president was such an admirer of Zahm's book, *Evolution and Dogma,* that he'd regularly commended it to other theologians. He also liked that Zahm had gotten his early education in Ohio in "old-time American fashion in a little log school."

Discovering that he had a religious calling, Zahm chose to enter the priesthood. He was ordained in the Congregation of the Holy Cross in 1875. Two decades later, as Teddy Roosevelt garnered fame in leading the Rough Riders to glory, Father Zahm found himself elected head of the order's American province's hospitals, orphanages, and schools, including a small seminary named Notre Dame in the little Indiana town of South Bend.

Determined to make it equal to any "community of saints and scholars" in the United States, he spent money so freely to modernize the schools facilities that his superiors feared he would bankrupt the order. At their urging, and on the advice of doctors who said he was having a nervous breakdown, he left Notre Dame in 1906. Instead of resting and recuperating in the Caribbean, he threw himself into almost a frenzy of explorations in

Venezuela and Colombia. The expedition encompassed the daunting heights of the Andes Mountains and the mysteries and dangers of the Amazon River.

Toward the end of 1907 when he was planning another such expedition, he returned to the United States with the intention of finding as a companion for the odyssey a man who had "made nature study a predominant part of his life-work." Recognizing that the only man who qualified was Theodore Roosevelt, he arrived at the White House to propose that Roosevelt enlist in the venture, once he was "free from presidential cares." In addition to scientific aspects of the journey that Zahm knew would appeal to Roosevelt, he was prepared to stress that such a trip by the ex-president would have political and diplomatic benefits for the United States in its often touchy relations with Latin America. To help sell this idea he brought along John Barrett, whom Roosevelt knew as the director-general of the Pan-American Union.

It was not so much the prospects of improving U.S. south-of-the-border relations that appealed to Roosevelt as he listened to Zahm and Barrett, but Zahm's colorful, exciting accounts of South America's wildlife. At some point Roosevelt exclaimed that he had always wanted a chance to hunt the South American jaguar. Unfortunately, he informed his guests, he was at that very time engaged in planning a post-presidency year-long African safari.

Disappointed, Father Zahm left the White House with every indication from Roosevelt that the South American adventure wasn't being abandoned, but "merely deferred."

Back from Africa in 1910, and hailed for the accomplishment by his always-admiring countrymen, Roosevelt found that his published accounts of the safari had made him better off financially than at any time since he'd lost a large part of his wealth in the Dakota ranching enterprises. Royalties from his two-volume *African Game Trails,* compiled from the magazine articles for *Scribner's,* were expected to garner him $40,000. Compensation as a contributing editor for *The Outlook* magazine came to $12,000 a year. Other funds flowed in for lectures and other writings. Among the latter was a monumental monograph (40,000 words) on "Revealing and Concealing Coloration in Birds and Animals." While drafting it, he confided to Ted that he expected the work to "attract frenzied dissent and tepid assent among obscure zoological friends here and abroad."

Following his second-place finish in the 1912 presidential race, Roosevelt received a note from Father Zahm. It wished him "every blessing for 1913," then went on to exclaim that Roosevelt "made history as you probably never did during the year just closing." Zahm expected him to "make more during the years to come."

The adventuresome priest certainly had his finger firmly on the American pulse. A poll by *Independent* magazine in the spring of 1913 discerned that five years after Roosevelt left the White House he was, in the opinion of the public, "America's most useful citizen." If requests that Roosevelt make speeches were a measure of popularity, Theodore Roosevelt had nothing to worry about. In February 1913 alone he had to turn down 171 such invitations simply because his engagement calendar was already filled. Edith worried that he was "working like a steam engine" and looked "tired and jaded—having far too much to do."

One of the matters on his mind was an invitation that had come near the end of the 1912 campaign. It arrived on the letterhead of the Historical and Geographical Society of Rio de Janeiro. The Brazilian group proposed a series of Roosevelt lectures in the spring and summer of 1913. Accompanying the solicitation was an offer from the president of Brazil of a hunting trip in his country. These enticements were followed in January by a letter from the Museo Social of Argentina stating that if Roosevelt should go to South America, he would find a warm welcome from a population that had "heard so much about you, your public career and the high ideals you stand for." And if he came, said Dr. Emilio Frers, president of the Museo Social, he would, of course, be paid a honorarium. For three speeches Frers proposed a fee of $6,000, to be paid in U.S. gold dollars.

Although disinclined to give "merely an ordinary speech or to go on an ordinary trip," Roosevelt saw in the invitation an opportunity to visit his intrepid companion in Africa. At that time a supervisor for the Anglo-Brazilian Iron Company in Sao Paulo, Kermit had gone to Brazil after graduating from Harvard. With the idea of a South American adventure percolating in his thoughts, Roosevelt received a letter from Kermit in April 1913 about a hunting trip Kermit had made. Roosevelt replied, "The forest must be lovely. Sometime I must get down to see you, and we'll take a fortnight's outing, and you shall hunt and I'll act as what in the North Woods we used to call 'wangan [wagon] man' and keep camp."

There now occurred an amazing coincidence. With the fires of a new adventure rising like a wolf in a warrior's heart, Roosevelt remembered his friend Father Zahm and wondered if the time had come to rekindle the "merely deferred" idea of a Roosevelt-Zahm expedition in South America. Always a man to be sure he had his ducks in a row, and appreciating the value of having the assistance of the professional naturalists of a distinguished museum for what he saw as a scientific undertaking, he contacted Frank Chapman of the American Museum of Natural History in New York City.

When they met for lunch in early June, Chapman informed Roosevelt that a few days earlier he had gotten the same request for the museum's advice on choosing a naturalist. The query had come from Father Zahm. The priest had also told Chapman that he was planning to go to Sagamore Hill to tell Roosevelt of his intention of at last launching the South American expedition, in the hope that Roosevelt was now prepared to join it. Chapman told Zahm that he could save himself the trip to Oyster Bay. "Colonel Roosevelt is going to take luncheon with me here tomorrow," he explained, "and I shall be glad to have you join us."

As Roosevelt entered the museum's dining room just before one o'clock in the afternoon of June 6, 1913, he was astonished to find Zahm with Chapman. Striding toward Zahm, he said, "You are the very man I wished to see. I was just about to write you to inform you that I think I shall, at last, be able to take that long-talked-of-trip to South America."

With the expedition approved by museum president Henry Fairfield, Chapman prepared a list of professional naturalists who were ready to enlist in the expedition, subject to Roosevelt's approval. He gladly accepted the recommendations of George K. Cherrie and Leo E. Miller. "No two better men could have been found," Roosevelt wrote. "Both were veterans of the tropical American forests."

Miller was young, but he was enthusiastic and had good literary as well as scientific training. Working in the Guiana forests at the time, he would join Roosevelt and the others in Barbados. Cherrie was older. After twenty-two adventurous years of collecting in the American tropics that included the birth of his second of six children in a South American jungle camp, three months in a South American prison, and a brief career as a gun-runner during a revolution, he had achieved immortality as a naturalist by naming a new species of ant-thrush for the chief who'd been the beneficiary of the illicit trade in weaponry.

To arrange the expedition's equipment Chapman proposed Anthony Fiala. A former Arctic explorer, he was well known to Roosevelt as a member of the New York squadron in the Spanish-American War. Another army veteran, Jacob Sigg, had experience as a hospital nurse and a cook. A major part of his duties would be to serve as personal attendant to Father Zahm. Roosevelt's secretary, Frank Harper, was also enlisted in the party.

In composition, Roosevelt noted, the expedition was typically American. He meant that its members symbolized the wide variety of people from all over the world who had formed the ingredients for a unique stew in what was called the American melting pot. Roosevelt noted that he and Kermit were "of the old Revolutionary stock, and in our veins ran about every strain of blood that there was on this side of the water in colonial times." Cherrie's father was Irish, his mother a Scot. Father Zahm was part Alsacian, part Irish. Leo Miller's father had emigrated from Germany and his mother from France. Fiala's parents were Bohemian. Harper was born in England, and Sigg in Switzerland. Just as varied as these men's ethnicity were their religions. Zahm and Miller were Roman Catholic; Cherrie a Presbyterian; Sigg, Lutheran; Fiala a Baptist; and the Roosevelts belonged to the Dutch Reformed Church.

Except for 16-bore shotguns belonging to each of the naturalists, the weaponry for the sojourn was furnished by the Roosevelts. Kermit brought two Winchesters, a pair of shotguns (his 12-gauge and a 16-gauge), and two pistols (Colt and Smith & Wesson). Roosevelt brought his beloved and trusty Springfield rifle. Equipment consisted of canvas canoes, tents, ropes and pulleys, light cots and hammocks, and "plenty of cheesecloth" for screening the tents and making protective nets for hats to fend off mosquitoes. The choice of clothing was "to each his own." Roosevelt packed the kind of khaki gear he'd worn in Africa: U.S. Army flannel shirts, a couple of silk ones for dressing to be received by South American officialdom, a pair of hob-nailed boots with leggings. A pair of laced leather boots that came nearly to his knees were the recommendation of the naturalists for protection against snake bites. Although the intention was to live off the land, provisioner Anthony Fiala packed U.S. Army emergency rations and 90 cans of victuals for the subsistence of five men for five days.

The official purpose of the venture, beginning after Roosevelt's lecture tour, was to be the collection of specimens of fauna and flora in the region between the Paraguay River and the Amazon. The starting point was to be at Asuncion in Paraguay. To prepare for the trip, as he had done prior to going to Africa, Roosevelt immersed himself in the geography and topography of "the most extensive stretches of tropical forest to be found anywhere." His intention was to go up the Paraguay as far as it could be navigated, trek overland to one of the sources of the mighty Amazon, build canoes "on the spot," and descend the world's longest and most perilous river.

With customary Rooseveltian zest, he wrote to Father Zahm, "I don't in the least mind risk to my life, but I want to be sure that I am not doing something for which I will find my physical strength unequal." A letter to Kermit brimmed with excited anticipation. "I cannot tell you how I am looking forward to seeing you," he wrote, adding that he hoped that Edith would go with him, "but it is possible she may not." The letter continued, "It won't be anything like our African trip. There will be no hunting and no adventure so that I will not have the pang I otherwise would about not taking you along— which of course would never do."

Perhaps as a test of his stamina, he set out in the summer with Archie, age nineteen, and fifteen-year-old Quentin for a hunting excursion in the Arizona desert, hoping to shoot mountain lions. And no trip into the Southwest could be taken without taking time for a nostalgic reunion with men who had been with him as Rough Riders in Cuba. The journey included sightseeing at the Grand Canyon, the nearby Painted Desert, and exploration of a Hopi Indian village, where he was given the honor of admission to a sacred room to witness a tribal snake dance. While on the cougar-hunts he carried no gun and left the shooting to the boys. On the way back east from his last hunting trip in the West he stopped in Chicago to meet with leaders of the Progressive Party, but his mind was already far ahead of him, fixed on the challenges that awaited him in the jungles of South America. The date for his departure was to be October 4, 1913. En route to his last chance to be a boy he would mark his fifty-fifth birthday. He carried more than 200 pounds on a five-feet-eight-inch frame. Because of a blow while boxing in the White House, he had lost sight in the left eye. The vigorous life he encouraged in everyone had resulted in his own body being scarred, battered, and plagued with rheumatism that provoked him to complain that he felt like "a worn-out and crippled old man." Also a plague were lingering effects of having been hit by a trolley car in Pittsfield, Massachusetts, in 1902 in which doctors had to cut down to the shin bone, permanently damaging it. The injury remained so troubling that in 1908, the year before the start of the African safari, he told Kermit that if anything happened "there is always a chance of trouble which would be serious."

In South America, Kermit would recall the words with a chilling sense of having been given a grim prophecy.

19

★ ★ ★

A Difficult Trip Ahead

WHEN ROOSEVELT told people who speculated about what he would do as an ex-president that he had no intention of sitting in a rocking chair on the piazza at Sagamore Hill and letting the rest of the world get along as best it could without him, no one in the United States was less surprised, and none happier, than newspaper reporters, whom Roosevelt delighted in calling "idiots of the press"; their editors; and photographers (Roosevelt's term was "Kodak creatures").

Acutely conscious of having been regarded as "a great story" from the autumn of 1880 when he had plunged into the decidedly ungentlemanly arena of politics to his astonishing African safari and then his presidential bid in 1912, he'd hoped to avoid pestering from the press about his next great adventure by keeping it a secret until the very last minute, and possibly until he had already sailed away. But four days before the embarkation date of Saturday, October 4, 1913, the *New York Times* announced in bold headlines:

ROOSEVELT SAILS SATURDAY
Heads Exploring Expedition of Amazon

Consequently, what had been planned as a Progressive Party political dinner in the roof-top "Garden of Dance" of the New York Theater in Manhattan, with a speech by the party's once-and-possibly-future (1916) presidential candidate, became a raucous send-off to the ever-surprising and apparently tireless exponent of the strenuous life. A *Times* reporter gushed, "The Colonel has had many a great ovation, but never so boisterous and hearty as this one." Although he denied rumors that his hat would be in the ring three years hence, he promised that when he came back from South America, he would devote himself "with whatever strength I have to working with you for this [Progressive] cause."

The hat on Roosevelt's freshly barbered head on October 4 was not his political one. It was a buff-toned, stylish complement to a gray business suit with a carnation in the lapel. As he stepped from an automobile onto Pier 8 in Brooklyn, a dock worker appreciated that it was not a politician, but a man with a boyish heart who rushed toward the gangplank of the Lamport and Holt steamer *Vandyck*. "Good boy, Teddy," the docker yelled, "shoot 'em in the eye." A reporter covering the departure for the *New York Tribune* thought that the hero of San Juan Heights and recent intrepid African big-game hunter was not "the same strenuous Roosevelt of 1909."

As if determined to prove that he was up to the challenge physically, Roosevelt proved to be an exuberant and energetic voyager as the *Vandyck* headed south. On one memorable night he amused the other passengers by dancing the hornpipe. In a tug of war between married men and bachelors he anchored the husbands' end of the rope with his 220 pounds. Hoping to bring down his weight, he took daily brisk walks around the promenade deck. When he played shuffleboard and other deck games with people half his age, Edith was pleased to observe him thoroughly enjoying himself. She wrote to his sister Anna, "I haven't heard him laugh for years."

When he wasn't playing, he dictated articles for the *Outlook,* read several books at once, and conducted daily conferences on the expedition. In a letter to Ted's wife Eleanor he wrote, "It is not exploration work exactly, but it is pioneer work, and the collection of birds and mammals ought to be of some value."

Six days out of New York the ship arrived at Bridgetown, Barbados, where Leo Miller came on board. At age twenty-six, he brought his reputation as an expert naturalist with the American Museum. It was said that his exploits in the remotest part of southern Venezuela so impressed Sir Arthur Conan Doyle, best-known as the creator of Sherlock Holmes, that Conan Doyle patterned a mysterious, dinosaur-populated land in his non-Sherlockian novel *The Lost World* on Miller's account of a "country, and of the people and the animal life inhabiting its virgin fields" about which very little was known.

After a shipboard conference on October 11, Miller reported to his museum boss, Frank Chapman, "Our trip promises to be a great thing, and we are eager to start work."

Roosevelt sent a message to the Foreign Minister of Brazil, Lauro Muller, concerning the expedition's needs when the party landed in Rio de Janeiro. "My hope is to make this trip not only an interesting and valuable one from a scientific viewpoint," he said, "but of real benefit to Brazil, in calling attention to the ease and rapidity with which the vast territory can be traversed, and also to the phenomenal opportunities for development which she offers."

With a demonstration of a lifetime of caution, if not outright pessimism about what the future held, he advised Frank Chapman, "We have a difficult trip ahead of us. We will have all kinds of troubles, with waterfalls, showers, shallows, fevers, and the like, and we may not be able to get beyond the Amazon Valley." He added, "When we will get home I have no idea."

Before he could throw himself into the challenge, however, he had commitments in the form of the daunting schedule of speaking and public appearances that had provided the impetus for the sojourn to South America. He would have the much-anticipated happy reunion with his second son in Bahia, the oldest city in what was then Brazil, but later part of the future Salvador.

When Roosevelt laid eyes on Kermit, now twenty-four, he thought Kermit didn't look as healthy as he would have liked. This appearance was the result of a fall. A few months earlier, he'd plummeted forty feet from a suspended ninety-foot steel beam that was part of a bridge-building project. Landing on rocks, he had suffered two broken ribs, several broken teeth, and a dislocated knee. Although he had not expected to accompany Roosevelt on the venture into the wilderness, his mother had asked him to go along to "take care of Father." Therefore, instead of a fortnight of hunting, as Roosevelt had planned, Kermit found himself delaying marriage to Belle Willard (daughter of the U.S. ambassador to Spain and owner of Washington's Willard Hotel), and taking a leave of absence from the Anglo-Brazilian Iron Company.

Two days after leaving Bahia, the Roosevelt expedition reached Rio de Janeiro to find a welcome by the Brazilians that Father Zahm described as having "all the wild enthusiasm of a national holiday." Among the greeters was Lauro Muller. The government official informed Roosevelt that he had arranged that on the headwaters of the Paraguay River, at the town of Cac-

eres, Roosevelt would be met by a Brazilian army officer, Colonel Candido
Mariano de Salva Rondon. Recalling this turn of events, Roosevelt wrote,
"My exact plan of operations was necessarily a little indefinite." Now he
found that Muller's offer of help made it possible for the trip to be "of much
more consequence" than he'd originally planned. Roosevelt wrote:

> He told me that he would cooperate with me in every way if I cared to
> undertake the leadership of a serious expedition into the unexplored por-
> tion of western Matto Grasso, and to attempt the descent of a river which
> flowed nobody knew whither, but which the best-informed men believed
> to be a very big river, utterly unknown to geographers. I eagerly and
> gladly accepted, for I felt that with such help the trip could be made of
> much scientific value, and that a substantial addition could be made to
> the geographical knowledge of some of the least-known parts of South
> America. Accordingly, it was arranged that Colonel Rondon and some
> assistants and scientists should meet me at or below Corumba, and that
> we should attempt the descent of the river, of which they had already
> come across the headwaters.

This abrupt change of plans did not sit well with the expedition's official
sponsor. When Henry Fairfield Osborn of the American Museum of Natural History learned of the alteration in the itinerary, he had a horrible vision
of the beloved icon of American heroism lying dead in a South American
jungle. He shot off a threat to Roosevelt that the museum would not
"assume part of the responsibility for what might happen in case he [Roo-
sevelt] did not return alive."

The return message, sent to Frank Chapman, was a sample of Roosevelt
bravado: "Tell Osborn I have already lived and enjoyed as much of life as any
nine other men I know; I have had my full share, and if it's necessary for me
to leave my bones in South America, I am quite ready to do so."

With the museum's backing intact, Roosevelt would first have to travel
through Brazil, Uruguay, Argentina, and Chile for six weeks of speaking
engagements. Consequently, Cherrie, Miller, Fiala, and Sigg left him at Rio
de Janeiro to wait for him at Corumba. Father Zahm saw it as "a continuous
ovation as well as a triumphal march." Roosevelt would write, "In all the
South American countries there is more pomp and ceremony in connection
wth public functions than with us, and at these functions the liveried ser-

vants, often with knee-breeches and powdered hair, are like those seen in familiar European functions; there is not the democratic simplicity which better suits our own habits and ways of thought. But the South American often surpasses us, not merely in pomp and ceremony but in what is of real importance, courtesy; in civility and courtesy we can well afford to take lessons from them."

During the two months before starting from Asuncion, in Paraguay, for the journey into the interior, he complained that he was kept so busy that he had little time to think of natural history. "But in a strange land a man who cares for wild birds and wild beasts," he noted, "[he] sees and hears something that is new to him and interests him."

As the time neared when he and Kermit would again brave the wilds, Edith Roosevelt prepared to leave husband and son and return to Sagamore Hill. "We're both feeling quiet and sad," Kermit wrote to his fiancee about Edith's leaving. She sailed on the steamer *Orcoma* from Valparaiso on November 26. Ten days later, Roosevelt, Kermit, Father Zahm, and Frank Harper took a train to Asuncion, Paraguay.

On the afternoon of December 9, 1913, they left behind "the attractive and picturesque city of Asuncion to ascend the Paraguay" on a gunboat-yacht of Paraguay's president. It was a "most comfortable river steamer" on which the food was good and the quarters clean. From its deck during three days of steaming northward toward the Tropic of Capricorn Roosevelt saw "fairly well-settled country, where bananas and oranges were cultivated and other crops of hot countries raised."

With him on the boat was an old Western friend, Tex Rickard, but now the owner of a sprawling cattle ranch near Concepcion. When the boat docked there at daybreak on the third day, Rickard accompanied Roosevelt ashore for a walking tour of a town that had been founded by Spanish conquistadores three-quarters of a century before the English and Dutch landed in North America. With sightseeing and official receptions completed, it was back to the gunboat. At noon on the twelfth it crossed the Brazilian border and the eagerly anticipated rendezvous with Colonel Rondon. On December 15 in Corumba they were greeted by George Cherrie, Leo Miller, Anthony Fiala, and Jacob Sigg. The naturalists informed Roosevelt that they had already collected eight hundred specimens of animals and birds.

* * *

Roosevelt's planning for the expedition included a deal with *Scribner's Magazine* for a series of articles. Like those he'd provided about his African adventure the essays would then be compiled into a book (*Through the Brazilian Wilderness*). By the time he arrived at Corumba he'd sent off the first, titled "The Start." With the second, "Up the Paraguay," went a letter to his editor, Robert Bridges. Roosevelt wrote, "This is all so different from my African trip!" He also expressed some doubt whether what he'd written in the essay "is satisfactory or not." The task that faced Bridges as he read the dispatches was not the quality of Roosevelt's prose, but the challenge of correctly interpreting Roosevelt's handwriting. Transposed to typeface, the series would begin running in the magazine in April 1914.

When "Up the Paraguay" appeared it gave readers an introduction through Roosevelt's eyes to "the piranha or cannibal fish, the fish that eats men when it can get the chance." There is no way of knowing how many people shivered with horror in snug American homes as they read:

> They are the most ferocious fish in the world. Even the most formidable fish, the sharks or the barracudas, usually attack things smaller than themselves. But the piranhas habitually attack things much larger than themselves. They will snap a finger off a hand incautiously trailed in the water; they mutilate swimmers. In every river town in Paraguay there are men who have thus been mutilated; they will rend and devour alive any wounded man or beast; for blood in the water excites them to madness. . . . Most predatory fish are long and slim, like the alligator and pickerel. But the piranha is a short, deep-bodied fish, with a blunt face and a heavily undershot or projecting lower jaw which gapes widely. The razor-edged teeth are wedge-shaped like a shark's, and the jaw muscles possess great power. The rabid, furious snaps drive the teeth through flesh and bone. The head with its short muzzle, staring malignant eyes, and gaping, cruelly armed jaws, is the embodiment of evil ferocity; and the actions of the fish exactly matches its looks.

Along with the second essay went 80 photographs taken by Kermit. The captions were written by Roosevelt. The one for a picture of a piranha said, "Maneating fish: see his teeth!"

These hungry, swarming inhabitants of the waters in the vicinity of Corumba continued to fascinate Roosevelt as he and the other explorers prepared for the next leg of the expedition. If someone dropped something of value in the water and waded in to retrieve it, he did so "very slowly and quietly, avoiding every possibility of disturbance, and not venturing to put his hands into the water." Nobody could bathe because scrubbing hands with soap "immediately attracted the attention of the savage little creatures, who darted to the place, evidently hoping to find some animal in difficulties."

Menacing piranhas aside, Roosevelt, Colonel Rondon, and other members of the party left Corumba by boat on December 17 to venture down the Paraguay River to one of its many tributaries, this one called the Taquary. The "noxious creatures" that attracted Roosevelt's eyes were cayman crocodiles, known locally as "jacares." They sometimes darted into the stream, looking like "miniatures of the monsters of the prime," and oblivious to the bullets fired at them by Roosevelt and the others. When a cayman was hit by a long .22-caliber bullet, it slid into the water and "at once forgot everything except its greedy appetite." Roosevelt observed it seizing "fish after fish, holding its head above water as soon as its jaws had closed on a fish" until a second bullet killed it.

Almost as interesting to Roosevelt as the cayman was the "giant antbear," known in the region as the "tamandua bendeira." They were easy game. Out in the open marsh the animal "could neither avoid observation, nor fight effectively, nor make good its escape by fight." It was "curious" to Roosevelt to "see one lumbering off at a rocking cantering, the big bushy tail held aloft," and on one occasion battling hunting-hounds by suddenly throwing itself on its back, evidently hoping to grasp the dog with its paws, or rearing to strike its assailant.

But none of these unique animals tempted Roosevelt's hunter's nature as much as the jaguar. Setting out to get one at three in the morning, Roosevelt was accompanied by Kermit, Colonel Rondon, two native jaguar hunters, dogs, and a boy carrying the saddle bags containing lunch. "As our shabby little horses shuffled away from the ranch-house," Roosevelt wrote of the start of his quest, "the stars were brilliant and the Southern Cross hung well up in the heavens, tilted to the right. The landscape was spectral in the light of the waning moon."

Hour after hour the hunters "shogged along" as night gave way to an overcast day, but with the sun breaking through here and there to light fields of papyrus that were a reminder of Africa. At last, on the edge of a patch of jungle, they found fresh jaguar tracks. With the hounds loosed, the party followed through ponds and long, winding bayous and islandlike stretches of tree-covered land. As the pace quickened, the dogs led the hunters through a marsh toward a taruman tree. Among its forked limbs, Roosevelt saw "a beautiful picture." The spotted coat of the big, lithe, formidable cat fairly shone as the jaguar snarled at the dogs below.

Fearing that if the jaguar descended, the hounds would be unequal to the challenge, and the jaguar would get away, Roosevelt raised the little Springfield rifle that had never failed him in Africa, sighted the jaguar from 70 yards, and fired. The jaguar fell from the tree "like a sack of sand through the branches, and although it staggered to its feet it went but a score of yards before it sank down." To Roosevelt the jaguar was "the king of South American game, ranking on an equality with the noblest beasts of the chase of North America, and behind only the huge and fierce creatures which stand at the head of the big game of Africa and Asia."

Roosevelt's jaguar was an adult female, "heavier and more powerful than a full-grown male cougar, or African panther or leopard." As Roosevelt knelt behind its carcass, holding its head erect in his right hand and grasping the Springfield in the left, Kermit snapped a picture that would be captioned "Colonel Roosevelt and the first jaguar."

The next day it was Kermit's turn. Around ten in the morning they were at a long, deep, winding bayou when they found tracks. After a long pursuit, they found a huge male jaguar high in the branches of a fig tree. They later learned that it was "a well-known" jaguar that had been raiding cattle herds and had killed a few cows and a young steer. A bullet from Kermit's 405 Winchester ended its cattle-killing career. With all the keenest of observations made by Teedie Roosevelt when he examined the body of the seal laid out on ice in front of a Broadway fish store, Theodore Roosevelt noted Kermit's prize for the record:

> He was heavier than the very big male horse-killing cougar I shot in Colorado, whose skull Hart Merriam reported as the biggest he'd ever seen; he was very nearly double the weight of any of the male African leopards we shot; he was nearly or quite the weight of the smallest of the adult African lionesses we shot while in Africa. He had the big bones, the stout frame, and the heavy muscular build of a small lion; he was not lithe and slender and long like a cougar or leopard; the tail, as with all jaguars, was short, while the girth of the body was great; his coat was beautiful

with a satiny gloss, and the dark-brown spots on the gold of his back, head, and sides were hardly as conspicuous as the black of the equally well-marked spots against a white belly.

During this respite before launching the primary goal of the expedition, the exploration of the unknown river whose headwaters had been discovered by Colonel Rondon, Roosevelt exhibited his skills as a naturalist in observations of the birds, insects, and other wildlife around Corumba, from the noisy howler monkeys, the armadillo, and huge anthills to the blunt-nosed, short-eared, water-living, piglike rodents called the capybara. He also spent a delightful, and rather nostalgic, afternoon watching the South American version of the Wild West cowboy, "the gaucho." Riding into a big square corral near the ranch house where Roosevelt was a guest, they demonstrated the "agility, nerve, and prowess" of North American cattle herders as they drove a small herd of calves, yearlings, and two-year-olds in for branding. They differed from Dakotas cowboys only in skin color—the gauchos were mainly of Indian or Negro descent—and in a lack of boots. "Their bare feet must have been literally as tough as thorn," Roosevelt noted, "for when one of them roped a big bull he would brace himself [on bare feet], bending back until he was almost sitting down and digging his heels into the ground, and the galloping beast would be stopped short and whirled completely round when the rope tautened."

Roosevelt's stay at the ranch ended just before Christmas. He was back in Corumba on December 24. The plan for the expedition required that it reach the headwaters of the unknown river that was their destination by late February, before the rainy season.

Homesick for the love of his life, Kermit dashed off a reassuring letter to Belle Willard. "You must be sure to realize that there's not the slightest danger for me in this trip," he wrote, "for the tropics agree with me."

His father agreed with this assessment of Kermit's condition. In a Christmas Eve letter to "Darling Edith," he wrote:

Kermit is now in first rate shape, and as tough as hickory, and I never felt in better health—in spite of being covered with prickly heat—so if you do not hear from me to the contrary you can safely assume that this condition of things is permanent. Of course we have not yet really begun the expedition proper as yet, and there will be many disagreeable experiences; but we are being hardened under exceptionally unpleasant conditions, and so far have had no hardships whatever. Kermit, Harper, Miller and I, with some of the Brazilians, who are capital fellows and great chums of Kermit, are returning from a delightful week at a huge ranch in the marshes of the Taquary River. . . . We each killed a jaguar, [Kermit's] being an exceptionally large one and mine a good average one; and we were in the saddle eight or ten hours a day . . . Kermit is his own mother's son! He is to me a delightful companion; he always has books with him; and he is a tireless worker. He is not only an exceptionally good and hard hunter, but as soon as he comes in he starts at his photographs or else at the skins, working as hard as the two naturalists.

When Roosevelt, Kermit, and the entire party boarded the river boat *Nyoac* on Christmas day, the shallow little steamer was crammed with men, dogs, rifles, partially cured skins of the specimens that had been collected, scores of boxes of provisions, ammunition, tools, tents, cots, bedding, clothes, saddles, hammocks, and all the items deemed necessary by outfitter Anthony Fiala for a trip through the "great wilderness" for which the Brazilian term was "matto grasso."

The sky was brilliantly clear. The early morning was cool and pleasant. Roosevelt and his companions sat on the forward deck, admiring the trees on the brink of sheer riverbanks, the lush grass of the marshes, and seemingly countless water birds. The boat would be piloted by two men, one black and one white.

Colonel Rondon ignored the colorful scene, preferring to read Thomas à Kempis. Kermit, Cherrie, and Miller squatted on a deck above the boat's paddle wheel while putting the final touches on the curing of the two jaguar skins. Fiala checked and double-checked the piles of equipment and supplies. Only "good little Father Zahm," because of his age and physical frailty, was not working hard. And, Roosevelt had assured Edith in his letter, everything possible was being done for the comfort, in little ways that meant much "to a man of my age on a rough trip."

That evening on the afterdeck as the boat pushed against the current of the Paraguay, the explorers dined in the open amid decorative green boughs and rushes. On both sides of the river was a fertile land, pleasant to live in, and there to provide a living to any settler who was willing to work. In Roosevelt's view there was no doubt that the country would soon be opened up by railroads, just as the American West had been, with the result that ambitious people would flood in to exploit the land by farming and mining. Roosevelt believed, as he had felt in East Africa, that South America "has a great future."

It was possible that in his own future lay hardship, Roosevelt realized, but for now "the day was our own, and the day was pleasant."

The former president of the United States proposed toasts to the health of the present one, Woodrow Wilson, and to the ever-helpful and accommodating president of Brazil.

20

★ ★ ★

"I'm bully!"

O N DECEMBER 28, 1913, Theodore Roosevelt was a guest at the ranch of Joao de Costa Marques and his son, who was secretary of agriculture of the Matto Grasso. Another guest was the president of the region. As a welcome for Roosevelt a great rodeo was arranged, followed by a hunt. The event afforded Roosevelt a chance to realize his long-held dream of killing a peccary (a boar) in native fashion with a jaguar spear. Two days later, chased by dogs, the animal was at bay in a half-hollow stump when Roosevelt set aside a rifle, "borrowed" a spear, and "killed the fierce little boar therewith."

Continuing through jungle so thick that "machetes were constantly at work" to clear a path, Roosevelt, Kermit, Colonel Rondon, and Marques's son waded across hip-deep marshes while vexed by swarms of mosquitoes and stinging fire ants. But pestering of insects couldn't compare to the pain Roosevelt suffered when he discovered that a prized pocket watch which had kept reliable time in battles of the Spanish-American War and during the year-long trek in Africa "came to an indignant halt."

When the party failed to return to the *Nyoac* at the expected hour, the steamer's worried captain ordered the boat's whistle to be sounded again and again. As Roosevelt finally climbed aboard, Anthony Fiala gazed at the dripping-wet, mud-spattered, welt-reddened, portly figure and gasped, "Are you all right, Colonel?"

Beneath a droopy gray mustache, the world's most famous set of teeth was revealed by a satisfied grin as Roosevelt exclaimed, "I'm *bully!*"

Looking across the dinner table at Roosevelt's disheveled figure, Leo Miller thought, "Good heavens, there sits an ex-president of the United States, and I have never seen a more dilapidated individual."

Having marked the turning of the calendar from 1913 to 1914, the expedition proceeded up the Paraguay River toward the town of Sao Luis de Caceres and the beginning of the search for the route of a river that was so mysterious that Rondon has named it Rio du Duvida (River of Doubt). Writing to his mother on January 3, Kermit reported that, except for a hurt knee, gotten when he'd jumped off the boat, "Father's in fine shape." He added, "A little less to eat and drink won't hurt anyone, and will improve Father's figure. How long this trip will take seems to be getting more doubtful every day; tho I think Rondon is putting an outside estimate on everything so as to have Father prepared for the longest & worst."

The strategy agreed upon by Roosevelt and Rondon on reaching Caceres was to divide the expedition: Leo Miller and Father Zahm leading a party to chart Rio Gy-Parana; Roosevelt, Kermit, Rondon, Cherrie, and Fiala would enter the River of Doubt. The rendezvous point at the conclusion of these explorations was to be the city of Manaos.

Because Caceres was the last point at which collected specimens could be sent to New York, Cherrie and Miller packed up more than a thousand birds and mammals. Roosevelt was so impressed by their work that he wrote to Henry Fairfield Osborn suggesting that it would be "a matter of justice that the men who undergo the hardship and discomfort of work in the field should be permitted themselves to describe the animals they have collected" in their own book.

"The quaint old-fashioned little town" of Caceras, on the outermost fringe of the Matto Grasso, Roosevelt noted, was "the last town we should see before reaching the villages of the Amazon." Just as fascinated by the town's inhabitants as he'd been by the natives of Africa, he saw pretty faces of women, "some dark, some light," looking out lattice-shuttered windows in white or blue one-story, red tile–roofed houses that had "come down from colonial days and tracing back through Christian and Moorish Portugal to a remote Arab ancestry." But he also discerned "the spirit of the new Brazil." Symbolized by "a fine new government school and its principal, an earnest man doing excellent work," the school represented to Roosevelt "the new educational movement which will do so much for Brazil."

From Caceres the expedition would enter the region of explorations by Colonel Rondon that had resulted in the discovery of the existence of the River of Doubt. His original purpose, eighteen years earlier, had been to open telegraph lines through the vast wilderness known as the "matto grasso." In 1907 he'd been sent by the Brazilian government to explore the uncharted region and to map it for the first time. In carrying out this mission Rondon proved to be exactly the kind of man that appealed to Roosevelt's own concept of hardy, adventurous manhood.

They were laudable traits that Roosevelt had found in Kermit. As the Roosevelt scholar Edward J. Renehan Jr., author of a book about Roosevelt's four sons titled *The Lion's Pride,* wrote for the Theodore Roosevelt Association's Internet Web site, "It seemed it was always Kermit—the lucky one, his brothers called him—who got to go along with TR on his most splendid adventures." Like all the Roosevelt boys, Kermit "shared his father's love of the outdoors and physical activity." No one in the family had been surprised by Kermit's enthusiastic embrace of the African expedition, or that he'd enlisted for the Brazilian adventure.

But on the verge of beginning the thrust into the unknowns of the River of Doubt, Kermit became ill. Although he thought he was simply coming down with a bad cold, the illness was a recurrence of malaria, contracted soon after he'd arrived in Brazil to work for the iron company. Felled in Caceres by a raging fever that reached 102 degrees, he laid in a hammock for four days while Roosevelt felt "utterly miserable with worry." Kermit's fever broke on January 12. Four days later, Roosevelt wrote to his youngest son, Quentin, "So far there have been no hardships, although of course there has been some fatigue and some discomfort." Telling Quentin it was the last letter he would receive for a while, and that "I think it will take six weeks to two months in getting to you," he expressed the hope that "not long after that I will be able to send a telegram to Mother announcing that I have gotten out of the wilderness and am about to sail for home."

While Kermit rebounded from his malaria, Roosevelt was dismayed when his secretary, Frank Harper, suddenly exhibited all its symptoms. Worried, and aware that Harper hadn't been cut out for the arduous demands of wilderness living, Roosevelt proposed that Harper leave the expedition. He departed on January 18 for Caceres with five crates of specimen skins and Leo Miller's living trophy of the expedition, a giant turtle named Lizzie.

Roosevelt's account of this portion of the expedition made no mention of the reason for Harper's departure. He said only that at Tapirapuan, named for the River of Tapirs, "we broke up our baggage—as well as our party." He explained, "All the skins, skulls and specimens, and all the baggage not absolutely necessary, were sent back down the Paraguay and to New York, in charge of Harper."

As previously agreed, the expedition was split in two. The larger group left Tapirapuan on January 19. Roosevelt's party, including Kermit, Rondon, Father Zahm, Cherrie, and Anthony Fiala, departed two days later for an expected month-long march to the headwaters of the River of Doubt. In addition to Kermit's photographic record of the expedition, there would be pictures captured by a movie camera that equipment manager Anthony Fiala had thought to add to his list of necessities and creature comforts. Roosevelt's contingent surpassed the size of the African safari, but instead of using native bearers, it had 98 mules and 70 oxen to carry Fiala's outfittings and cans of food on a journey of nearly 300 miles.

While there was no problem with the mules, about half the oxen had to be "broken in." Observing this process, Roosevelt found a comparison between the pack-men and cowboys in the West. As the oxen "bucked like wild broncos" and scattered their loads over the corral, the pack-men "were not only masters of their art, but possessed tempers that could not be ruffled."

This was not true of Kermit. Infuriated by the delay in starting, he wrote in exasperation to his far-away and sorely missed bride-to-be, "I have been ready to kill the whole lot, and all the members of the expedition." But once they were on the move he was feeling better, emotionally and physically, so that when his indomitable father broke into recitations of the favorite poetry of the parent, the son happily joined him.

From Tapirapuan their direction was northward to and across a highland (Plan Alto) from which flowed the affluents of the Amazon to the north and the Plate River to the south. The level country was a great natural pasture that reminded Roosevelt of Texas and Oklahoma. He saw a future in the region for stock-raising and expected the river to ultimately become a source of electric power. The proponent of the manifest destiny of the people of the United States to fill up a continent said of the Plan Alto, "It is fine country for settlement."

On January 24, 1914, after a sixteen-mile trek over the plains, camp was set up on the banks of the Rio Perdiz. Having marched fourteen hours without a meal, Roosevelt recorded, the party "feasted royally on beans and rice and pork and beef, seated around oilskins spread upon the ground." A campfire that evening passed in a traditional Roosevelt fashion when surrounded by other outdoorsmen of swapping stories of their adventures. Always a great listener who would recount others' stories in his hunting books, he did so with many of the tales he absorbed around the campfires in Brazil. But during those evenings nobody surpassed his own spellbinding yarns of roughing it in the West and hunting big game in Africa. His enchanted audience of Brazilians had a word for him: *pandego*. Kermit translated it from Portugese to mean "life of the party."

When a camp was broken in the morning, Roosevelt found the activity a "picturesque sight." He also enjoyed the breakfasts of rice, beans and crackers, with canned corned beef, and salmon or any game that had been shot, all washed down by coffee and tea. While mules and oxen were being packed, he usually sat down somewhere to write for *Scribner's*. Kermit saw it as "paying for his fun."

With the expedition on the move again, Kermit left the line of march astride "a big, iron-mouthed, bull-headed white mule" to hunt pampas deer. When he rejoined the party late in the afternoon, he had two bucks behind his saddle. Roosevelt pronounced the venison "delicious."

Riding day after day across the seemingly endless flats of grass and low, open, scrubby forest, Roosevelt took in the scenery with a naturalist's interest. He noted the flowers ("the most beautiful being the morning-glories"), "bastard rubber trees," and dwarf palmetto, but saw very little bird or animal life. "Yet the desolate landscape had a certain charm of its own," he wrote, "although not a charm that would be felt by any man who does not take pleasure in mere space, and freedom and wildness, and in plains standing empty in the sun, the wind, and the rain."

The Plan Alto bore some resemblance to the country west of the White Nile, home of the giant eland. But these Brazilian plains offered no big game, "no chance of seeing the towering form of the giraffe, the black bulk of the elephant or buffalo, the herds of straw-colored harte-beests, or the ghostly shimmer of the sun glinting on the coats of roan and eland as they vanished silently in the gray sea of withered scrub."

There was one feature that the Plan Alto shared with the African landscape. It had an "abundance of anthills, some as high as a man." Known to the Brazilians as "carregadores," or porter ants, these "inveterate burden-carriers" toted bits of leaves and blades of grass to their underground homes. They also took an interest in gnawing off snippets of clothing, requiring Roosevelt and the others to guard their vulnerable belongings. Of great interest, also, were black ants that were an inch and a quarter long and "very vicious" with a poisonous bite; grasshoppers as large as sparrows; and praying mantises. Especially fascinating was "an extraordinary colony of spiders." Discovered at a camping sight one early afternoon, the colony was among some dwarf trees at the edge of a pool of water. Although it appeared to have been abandoned, its occupants suddenly emerged by the hundreds at dusk from daytime hiding places in tree leaves to repair old webs or spin new ones.

Roosevelt diligently recorded for his eventual readers, "Each spun his own circular web, and sat in the middle; and each web was connected on several sides with other webs, while those nearest the tree were hung to them by spun ropes, so to speak. The result was a kind of sheet of web consisting of scores of wheels, in each of which the owner and proprietor sat."

Roosevelt did not note how long he watched the spiders. But when darkness fell and rain began, he was in place to record that the spiders were "still out, fixing their webs, and pouncing on the occasional insects that blundered into the webs."

More than a century later, a reader of Roosevelt's account can only wonder that a former president of the United States, champion of "the square deal" for every American, advocate of a foreign policy of speaking softly while carrying a big stick, and believer that the white man had a duty to carry his civilization and the gospel of Jesus Christ to the remotest corners of the globe, could spend an afternoon transfixed by spiders.

It's reasonable to assume that Theodore Roosevelt did not expect his writings about the expedition to Brazil, the safari across East Africa, and his adventures in the West to be read by several succeeding generations. He was speaking, as Roosevelt biographer H. W. Brands wrote in an introduction to a reprint of Roosevelt's *Through the Brazilian Wilderness*, to the people who never would have seen most of what he described.

After a late start on December 29, the expedition marched for six hours to reach one of the most spectacular natural wonders of the world, a waterfall named Salto Bello. Near a small native village, the wide cataract was a sheer drop of forty or fifty yards. Vine-covered cliffs flanked it as the river, "after throwing itself over the rock wall," rushed off in long curves at the bottom of a thickly wooded ravine, the white water churning among the black boulders."

The men of the settlement operated a ferry across the Rio Sacre. Parecis Indians, they were "an unusually cheerful, good-humored, pleasant-natured people" with bad teeth, but who otherwise "appeared strong and vigorous." They demonstrated their vitality by playing a kind of soccer in which only their heads were allowed to touch the ball. "It is hard to decide," Roosevelt wrote of the unique sport, "whether to wonder most at the dexterity and strength with which it is hit or butted with the head, as it comes down through the air, or at the reckless speed and skill with which the players throw themselves headlong on the ground to return the ball if it comes low down. Why they do not grind off their noses I cannot imagine."

Having breakfast on benches set under trees by the waterfall, with its roar "lulled to a thunderous murmur," Roosevelt believed there could have been no more picturesque place to have his morning repast. He would soon find himself awed by an even greater spectacle in the form of the Falls of Utiarity. The site had been discovered on his earlier explorations by Colonel Rondon and named for a local breed of falcon.

"Lovely though we had found Salto Bello," Roosevelt wrote of the new vista, "these falls were far superior in beauty and majesty. They are twice as high and twice as broad; and the lay of the land is such that the various landscapes in which the waterfall is a feature are more striking." Excepting Niagara, he doubted that there was a waterfall in North America outranking it "if both volume and beauty are considered." As Roosevelt and Kermit admired "one sunset of angry splendor," they contrasted "this going down of the sun, through broken rain clouds and over leagues of wet tropical forest, with the desert sunsets we had seen in Arizona and Sonora. and along the Guaso Nyiro north and west of Mount Kenya."

After days and nights of relentless rain, the weather improved enough on February 2 for Roosevelt to go hunting. But the only game he found was a "rather hairy armadillo." Back at the camp, he held it by its "flexible tail" and presented it to Leo Miller to add to their collection.

Two events at the falls plunged Roosevelt into unusual sadness. The first was receipt of a telegram notifying him that his niece, Margaret Roosevelt, who had been a traveling companion for Edith to and from South America, had died of typhoid fever shortly after returning to New York. The second unsettling occurrence involved Father Zahm. The elderly, ailing priest who had been the impetus for Roosevelt's venture into the Brazilian wilderness announced that if he were to continue on the expedition, he would need a special chair that would be carried by four Parecis men. When Rondon heard of the idea, he rejected it. He told Zahm that the idea went against the democratic principles of the Parecis. Roosevelt sided with Rondon. He ordered Zahm back to Tapirapuan. Zahm replied that leaving was "the greatest disappointment of my life." As in the earlier departure of Harper, Roosevelt's published account of Zahm's leaving did not give the reason. He wrote, "From here Father Zahm returned to Tapirapuan, accompanied by Sigg." But in a memorandum that was signed by all the remaining men of the expedition, Roosevelt noted for the record, "Every member of the expedition has told me that in his opinion it is essential to the success and well being of the expedition that Father Zahm should at once leave it and return to settled country."

On February 4 the diminished party arrived at the Burity River. As the new encampment was being established, Roosevelt wrestled with another personnel problem. This one concerned Anthony Fiala. The veteran of explorations in the Arctic had proven to be, in the opinion of Leo Miller, "incompetent to do a single thing" on an expedition in the Brazilian tropics. Much of the equipment he'd brought from New York had turned out to be useless. But in deciding that Fiala should also leave the expedition, Roosevelt could not bring himself to send Fiala home. Instead, Fiala was assigned to a secondary expedition down the Papagaio River and into the Juruena and Tapajos. Roosevelt explained it as "performing a necessary part of the work of the expedition." It was a feeble attempt at all-around face-saving, and everyone recognized it. That night George Cherrie confided to his journal, "I think his going had a saddening effect on all of us."

In addition to Roosevelt, the remaining North Americans were Kermit, Cherrie, and Miller. Roosevelt later justified the trimming of the party by writing, "We have weeded out everyone unfit for exploration." Also left behind on orders from Colonel Rondon were "all luxuries" and half the party's baggage. Kermit wrote to Belle Willard, "We've been going through a regular course of shedding men and provisions." Roosevelt's account of the process needed only two sentences: "Here we had to cut down our baggage and rearrange the loads for the mule-train." And "Each of us got rid of everything above the sheer necessities."

After traveling 230 arduous miles in nineteen days, the greatly trimmed and lightened venture in exploration arrived at the banks of the upper Rio Juruena. One of the five known tributaries of the Amazon, it flowed only 150 miles from Roosevelt's goal—the unknown and enticing waterway with a name that was ominous in both languages of the expedition: "Rio du Duvida" in Portugese and "River of Doubt" in English. But the Brazilian government had given its pledge that should Roosevelt and his companions succeed in finding where the river went, it would be given a new name in honor of its illustrious explorer: "Rio Teodoro."

21

★ ★ ★

All Well and Cheerful

TRAVELING THROUGH a tropical wilderness in the rainy season on a journey of discovery and scientific observation, when the amount of baggage must be strictly limited, Theodore Roosevelt mused as his pared-down expedition rested by yet another Brazilian river, "entails not only a good deal of work, but also the exercise of considerable ingenuity if the writing and photographing, and especially the preservation, if the specimens are to be done in satisfactory shape."

Just how difficult the going could be was reinforced for Roosevelt in a message waiting for him at a station of the Brazilian telegraph service for whom Colonel Rondon had worked in extending lines into the Matto Grasso. In doing so, Roosevelt believed, Rondon had founded "the Brazilian school of exploration" in an enterprise that previously had been left to foreigners. The telegram read by Roosevelt was from Anthony Fiala. It contained the disturbing news that in going down the Papagaio there'd been a "misadventure." In rough rapids a few miles below a waterfall, two of the party's canoes had been upset at the cost of half the party's provisions, all of Fiala's baggage, and, most distressing of all, Fiala had nearly drowned.

The incident provided Roosevelt an opportunity to educate the eventual readers of his articles for *Scribner's Magazine* of the hazards of descending a "swift, unknown river rushing through uninhabited wilderness." Failure to remember this fact, he counseled, "is one of the obstacles in the way of securing a proper appreciation of the needs and the results of South American exploration."

Assessing how well his expedition had done in under three months, Roosevelt noted that more than 300 mammals had been collected, and about five times that number of birds. But now they stood on the verge of the most exciting part of the odyssey.

To be starting the last leg of the trip was for Kermit "a great relief." Since leaving Rio de Janeiro five months ago, he wrote to Belle, he had been continually afraid that the hard-working pack train might give out completely, or at least cause a very long delay. But now, he wrote, "we're here and ready to start down the river, and each day brings me nearer to you, my own dearest dearest Belle."

Writing to Edith, Roosevelt announced:

> Here we are ready to start down the Duvida, all well and cheerful. No one has an idea, or at least every body has half a dozen,—which comes to the same thing—,as to where the Duvida goes. . . . It is almost impossible even to guess at the amount of time it will take to go down it. If things go in the best way possible I think we may be in Manaos in a month and a half; two months is really the most probable, tho three or four is possible.

The assertion "all well and cheerful" was not true concerning Kermit. Roosevelt had been worried enough about Kermit's health that since the stop at Tapirapuan he'd suggested to Kermit that he go "straight on out" of the expedition. The idea certainly proved to be a temptation. Longing to be with Belle, Kermit confessed to her in a letter, "I have hated this trip." But the love and loyalty of a son, and his promise to Edith to take care of Father, had persuaded him that quitting "would be far worse than never to have come at all."

Making him more miserable were a recurrence of malarial fever and saddle sores that developed into boils. They were so painful that he couldn't get a good night's sleep and had to stand in the stirrups when he rode. He complained to Belle, "We keep crawling along, gradually cutting down the distance to the Duvida, but oh so slowly." He confessed, "I'm afraid I'm not very much of an explorer at present." While everyone else was hoping that the River of Doubt would turn out to be long and important, all he asked was that it "be short and easy to travel."

An obvious result of the nineteen-day trek from Tapirapuan to Rio

Juruena on Roosevelt that Kermit welcomed was a diminished waistline. The weight loss was a legacy not only of the physical demands of such an arduous trip, but the consequence of a limitation to two meals a day, breakfast and dinner. When the expedition arrived at Juruena station and Colonel Rondon declared that the mid-day repast could be restored during the brief respite, the announcement was greeted with delight by the expedition, with one notable exception. As Roosevelt insisted on continuing the twice-a-day policy, the only person who dared to confront him on the matter was Kermit. If Father chose to limit himself to two meals, said the son, "there was no reason why he should force fasting upon the rest of us."

Already at the Juruena station was a segment of the expedition that had continued on from Tapirapuan while Roosevelt's contingent took a longer route to carry out explorations and specimen collections. Led by two officers of the Brazilian army (Captain Amilcar and Lieutenant Lyra), the train of ox-drawn wagons carried material that would be needed going down the River of Doubt. Roosevelt was relieved that Amilcar reported the loss of only three oxen and their loads. After a short rest, Amilcar and his men and animals were off again, heading for the point at which the expedition planned to enter the unknown river.

In addition to meeting Amilcar at Juruena, Roosevelt found himself introduced to a few of the local natives. Members of the Nhambiquara tribe who'd met Rondon during his earlier explorations of the region, they had a reputation for ferocity. But Roosevelt found them "very friendly and sociable." He attributed their present peaceable demeanor to the civilizing effect of Colonel Rondon's "unwearied thoughtfulness and good temper, joined with his indomitable resolution." Roosevelt also noted that Rondon had never killed one of the Nhambiquaras.

"Nowhere in Africa," Roosevelt observed, had he and Kermit "come across wilder or more absolutely primitive savages, although these Indians were pleasanter and better-featured than any of the African tribes at the same stage of culture." Both sexes were "well-made and rather good-looking, with fairly good teeth, although some of them seemed to have skin diseases. They were a laughing, easy-tempered crew, and the women were as well-fed as the men, and were obviously well-treated, from the savage standpoint."

Accustomed to beholding naked natives, Roosevelt was fascinated and amused to see that the only raiment on most of the men was a string worn around the waist, while the women "did not wear a stitch of any kind anywhere on their bodies." The men had holes in their lips into which decorative reeds were thrust.

Roosevelt wrote, "It seems like a contradiction in terms, but it is nevertheless a fact that the behavior of these completely naked women and men was entirely modest. There never was an indecent look or a consciously indecent gesture."

Roosevelt soon discovered that some of the picturesque visitors were thieves. On the morning after a night of native dancing and singing for the entertainment of the white explorers, Colonel Rondon found that a native had made off with one of Rondon's dogs. "Probably the temptation had proved irresistible to one of their number," Roosevelt noted forgivingly, "and the others had been afraid to interfere, and also afraid to stay in or return to our neighborhood. We had not time to go after them; but Rondon remarked that as soon as he came again to the neighborhood he would take some soldiers, hunt up the Indians, and reclaim the dog."

While the natives were in the camp, Kermit made good use of his camera to photograph them in their "Adam and Eve" attire, but when the negatives were bundled up to be sent in the next packet of Roosevelt's writings for *Scribner's,* Kermit made sure that the pictures went with a note stating that he wanted the negatives returned.

Roosevelt's article, "Across the Nhambiquara," dealt with the natives in the preachy tone he'd adopted when writing about African natives. "In spite of their good nature and laughter," he declared, "their fearlessness and familiarity showed how necessary it was not to let them get the upper hand."

On the afternoon of February 15, 1914, the expedition reached Campos Novo. It was in a large basin, several miles wide, and crossed by several brooks; the grassy land surrounding the small outpost provided food for the expedition's pack animals, and for a variety of farm animals, including goats, pigs, turkeys, and milch cows, allowing Roosevelt to have a drink of refreshing "delicious" milk, his favorite beverage after coffee. (That he always enjoyed a cup of coffee had been made known to the American people by the makers of Maxwell House coffee. After he'd finished a cup of that brand at a famous hotel, a waiter asked if he wanted another. Roosevelt asked the name of the coffee company. Told that it was Maxwell House, he said not only that he would like another cup, but that the coffee was "good to the last drop." This off-hand accolade immediately became the motto of Maxwell House coffee, and remains so.)

Cooking accommodations at Campos Novos consisted of two kitchens. One was in the open air. The other was under a shelter of ox hide. Roosevelt found the view over surrounding hills "lovely." He was pleased that as he ate he wasn't bothered by insects. Always interested in the birds of a region, he thought "the most conspicuous" species was a huge oriole that was the size of a small crow, with a naked face, a black-and-red bill, and variegated plumage of green, yellow and chestnut. There were also "a tiny soft-tailed woodpecker, no larger than a kinglet; a queer humming-bird with a slightly flexible bill; and many species of ant-thrush, tanager, manakin, and tody." Very interesting to him was the "false bell-bird, a gray bird with loud, metallic notes" that explained its name.

After a hunting-outing from the camp one day with a small Luger belt-rifle, Kermit came back with "a handsome curassow, nearly as big as a turkey" from which the cook made a thick Brazilian soup with rice. Of this "delicious canja" Roosevelt declared "there is nothing better of its kind." The uncooked remains of the curassow went into the specimen collection. Looking back on that afternoon's work, Roosevelt noted that it had produced "nine species new to the collection, six new genera, and a most excellent soup."

On the march again, the expedition arrived at Vilhena, another telegraph station, near a small river that Colonel Rondon had named "Twelfth of October," because he'd reached it on the date known as the day Christopher Columbus discovered the "New World." What is amazing about Roosevelt's recording of these facts is that one of the most well-read and history-minded Americans, and arguably the most intellectual president to that time, with the possible exception of Thomas Jefferson, confessed that until Rondon explained the naming of the river Theodore Roosevelt "had never known" what day it was that Columbus had landed in America.

From Vilhena the trek turned northward across a grassy plateau, a region of forests, and after three days, a beautiful open country on either side of a little brook that was known as one of the headwaters of the River of Doubt. With a camp established, Kermit ventured out alone and came to a small settlement inhabited by twenty or thirty men, women, and children of the warrior-like Nhambiquaras. Kermit rode into their camp with a manner that his father described as that of all "honest folk in the wilderness," meaning that Kermit "advanced ostentatiously in the open, calling out to give warning of his coming." In the land of the Nhambiquras, Roosevelt advised, it was considered not only against etiquette, but might prove "very unhealthy," to come through the woods toward them "without loudly announcing one's presence."

The naked Nhambiquaras greeted Kermit as a friend while plying him with pineapple wine. When time came for Kermit to return to his own camp, half a dozen men and boys went with him. Welcomed hospitably, they were invited to join Kermit, Roosevelt, and the others for a meal. Because Nhambiquara males adorned themselves with long reeds that pierced their lips, Roosevelt suggested that they might eat more comfortably if they removed them. The suggestion was answered with laughter. Roosevelt concluded that a Nhambiquara man taking out the reed "would have been bad manners—like using a knife as an aid in eating ice cream."

After supper, the guests danced beside the campfire, impressing Roosevelt with the rhythm and "weird, haunting melody of their chanting." While most of the Americans and Brazilians enthusiastically joined in the dancing, Roosevelt and Rondon watched appreciatively and applauded enthusiastically.

Again on the move, through alternate spells of drenching rain and blazing sunlight, the expedition came to a telegraph station at Bonofacio. It was a collection of thatched one-room cabins connected by a stockade. After breakfast a group of Nhambiquaras strolled in; the men put on an exhibition of archery that Roosevelt judged "not very good." From Bonofacio the expedition traveled about seven miles, crossing rolling prairies dotted with trees and clumps of shrub, to a brook that flowed into the River of Doubt, only a few miles away. On a page of his journal dated February 23, 1914, an exultant George Cherrie wrote, "At last we have arrived at the end, or rather the virtual end, of our long overland journey. Thirty-three days in the saddle since leaving Tapirapuan. We now have only two short marches of 7 or 8 miles each to the banks of the Duvida, where we begin the canoe journey down its unknown length."

22

★ ★ ★

The Oxford Book of French Verse

O N FEBRUARY 24, 1914, Roosevelt's expedition kept its rendezvous with Captain Amilcar by a brook that flowed into the River of Doubt. Six miles from the stream, the party divided. Amilcar and Leo Miller would march three days to Gy-Parana River and descend it. Roosevelt, Kermit, Cherrie, and Rondon would head for the Duvida with a doctor and sixteen paddlers for the party's seven canoes. If they found within a few days that the Duvida fed into the Gy-Parana, the Madeira, or into the Tatpajos, they would know that it was not a river worth exploration and turn their attention to another mysterious waterway. The Ananas, its outlet was also unknown. The group would carry provisions for fifty days, but not full rations. On the way they would live primarily on fish, game, nuts, and palm tops. Their kit consisted of tents, bedding, medicines, instruments for determining their geographical position, and an assortment of books.

Should the party run into trouble, such as losing men or canoes in the rapids, or if any of the men got sick, Roosevelt noted coldly, "the loads would lighten themselves." Everyone was armed. The guns were intended for shooting game for food and self-defense. Demonstrating his capacity for always anticipating disaster, Roosevelt allowed that if the expedition were to lose its boats in falls or rapids, or have to make "too many and too long portages, or were brought to a halt by impassable swamps, then we would have to reckon with starvation as a possibility." Anything might happen. They were about to go into the unknown.

No one could say what the future held. "That was why," he wrote, "the river was rightly christened the Duvida."

Shortly after mid-day on February 27, they started down the river. The point from which they departed was about 12 degrees 1 minute south and 60 degrees 15 minutes longitude west of Greenwich. Their course was northward toward the equator. Of the seven canoes, one was small, one was "cranky," and two were old, waterlogged, leaky, and lashed together. The other three were good. Kermit went in the smallest of these. Rondon, Lieutenant Lyra, and three men to paddle took the next largest. Roosevelt, Cherrie, and a doctor, Alexander Lambert, took the largest with three men as paddlers. The rest of the boats carried the baggage.

A "strapping set" of expert river-men and men of the forest, the paddlers were as "lithe as panthers and brawny as bears" and "swam like water-dogs." "Equally at home with pole and paddle, with axe and machete," they reminded Roosevelt of pirates in pictures by Howard Pyle or Maxfield Parrish. He later learned that one of them really was a pirate and that another was "worse than a pirate," although why this was so Roosevelt did not explain.

Surveying of the river was done by Rondon and Lyra, with Kermit assisting by using a sighting rod. Lyra had a device to establish distance. Rondon recorded the data. Because of the twists and turns of the river, Kermit had to land nearly a hundred times in only nine and one-third kilometers in just half a day. Riding ahead of them, Roosevelt assumed the role of naturalist and found it "interesting work, for no civilized man, no white man, had ever gone down or up this river or seen the country through which we were passing." With all the diligence that had been shown by Teedie Roosevelt in keeping his notebooks on the subjects of a dead seal and the birds of the Nile River when he was ten, the grown-up veteran of warfare in fetid Cuban jungles and leading a great safari over game-rich African plains and down rivers teeming with hippos and crocodiles recorded the flora of the banks of the River of Doubt:

> The lofty and matted forest rose like a green wall on either hand. The
> trees were stately and beautiful. The looped and twisted vines hung from
> them like great ropes. Masses of epiphytes grew both on the dead trees
> and the living; some had huge leaves like elephants' ears. Now and then

fragrant scents were blown to us from flowers on the banks. There were not many birds, and for the most part the forest was silent; rarely we heard strange calls from the depths of the woods, or saw a cormorant or ibis.

When Roosevelt's party halted after a couple of hours to wait for the surveyors to catch up, their canoes were moored to trees. Axemen hacked out a clearing for a campsite. Tents were pitched, the luggage brought ashore, and fires kindled. Kermit and the others arrived just before nightfall. The stars of Roosevelt's first night on the river of his quest were brilliant and a new moon hung in the west. "It was a pleasant night, the air almost cool," Roosevelt wrote, "and we slept soundly."

In the morning as the surveyors pushed off, Cherrie went collecting birds in the woods. The most interesting to Roosevelt of those brought back were a brilliant turquoise-blue cotinga with a magenta-purple throat, and a big woodpecker, black above and cinnamon below with an entirely red head and neck. Leaving camp at noon, Roosevelt saw more birds and heard howler monkeys from the depth of the forest. Noting again the nature of the surrounding trees, he saw places where palms stood close together, "towering and slender, their stems a stately colonnade, their fronds an arched fretwork against the sky." The say was overcast, with rain showers, but when the sun broke through rifts in the clouds, its light "turned the forest to gold." In midafternoon the explorers in their canoes came to the mouth of a large, swift stream that Roosevelt thought was undoubtedly the known Bandeira whose headwaters they had crossed ten days before. According to Nhambiquaras, Roosevelt recalled, the Bandeira flowed into the Duvida. The expedition camped beside it that evening, and in the morning they dove into its depths to bathe. In two days going down the Duvida, they'd covered sixteen and a half kilometers.

March 1, 1914, dawned rainy. Moving somewhat west of north, they made more than twenty kilometers and camped close beside the river so that their "swimming-bath was handy." When one of the barefoot paddlers stepped on a poisonous coral snake, Roosevelt stomped on it with a booted foot. The snake bit it harmlessly. The incident provided Roosevelt an opportunity to note the dead snake's coloring, and that in the dark and tangled woods "anything motionless, especially if partially hidden, easily eludes the eye."

Always interested as much in the sounds of a forest as he was in its birds and animals, Roosevelt did not hear "such a chorus of birds and mammals"

as he had occasionally heard on the overland trek across the Brazilian high-
lands, when more than once he'd been awakened by the howling, screaming,
yelping, and chattering of monkeys, toucans, macaws, parrots, and para-
keets. But in this river-edging forest in the daytime there was mostly silence.
And at night the strange cries and calls came from frogs and insects that died
away at midnight, leaving the land silent again.

In this encampment the expedition experienced its first crisis. During the
night an army of carregadores ants took a liking for the doctor's undershirt
and devoured it. The also ate holes in his mosquito netting, and even partook
of the strap of Lyra's gun case. But morning dawned with little rain,
allowing Roosevelt and the others to drift and paddle delightfully down the
river. Until mid-afternoon the current was not very fast, but then its flow
quickened. "Faster it went, and faster," Roosevelt noted, "until it ran like a
mill-race."

Hearing the roar of rapids ahead, the rowers made for the shore on their
right. After going twenty kilometers that day, Roosevelt and his companions
assessed the situation and agreed that the rapids were "a serious obstacle."
About a mile of the river had many curls and a number of falls, some six feet
high. They would be impossible to run in the canoes. This meant that they
would have to be carried around the mile-long rapids. Doing so took all day
on March 3 and 4 and the morning of the fifth.

Dragging the heavy dugout canoes, Roosevelt said with unusual understatement, "was labor." To get around the obstacle a road had to be chopped
through the jungle and a bed of hundreds of cut tree trunks laid to function
as rollers, placed about two yards apart. The boats were lifted from the river
with block and tackle. The men then harnessed themselves two by two on a
drag rope while another used a hewn log as a lever to coax the boat along.
"Bumping and sliding," it was "twitched through the woods."

In describing the portage for his *Scribner's* readers, snug in their comfortable American homes, the proponent of the strenuous life could not resist a
lecture. He wrote:

> Looking at the way the work was done, at the good-will, the
> endurance, and the bull-like strength of the camaradas [the Brazilian
> boatmen], and the intelligence and the unwearied efforts of their com-
> manders [Kermit and Lyra], one could but wonder at the ignorance of
> those who do not realize the energy and the power that are so often pos-

sessed by, and that may be so readily developed in, the men of the tropics. Another subject of perpetual wonder is the attitude of certain men who stay at home, and still more the attitude of certain men who travel under easy circumstances, and who belittle the achievements of the real explorers of, the real adventurers in, the great wilderness. The imposters and romancers among explorers or would-be explorers and wilderness wanderers have been unusually prominent in connection with South America (although the conspicuous ones are not South Americans, by the way); and these are fit subjects for condemnation and derision. But the work of the genuine explorer and wilderness wanderer is fraught with fatigue, hardship, and danger. Many of the men of little knowledge talk glibly of portaging as if it were simple and easy. A portage over rough and unknown ground is always a work of difficulty; and of some risk to the canoe; and in the untrodden, or even in the unfrequented, wilderness risk to the canoe is a serious matter.

In the times when Roosevelt set up his portable table and laid out sheets of foolscap and carbon paper to keep his writing commitment to *Scribner's,* Colonel Rondon enjoyed observing him. "I used to love to watch him think," he recalled. "A person could watch Roosevelt think! It was a very amusing sight, for he always gesticulated. He would be alone, not saying a word, yet his hands would be moving, and he would be waving his arms and nodding his head with the greatest determination, as though arguing with some-body."

In the portage of the rapids (called the Navaite Rapids) the canoe in which Roosevelt had been traveling was split in a way that raised grave doubts that it could be repaired. One of the already water-logged boats sank, requiring "more work in raising it."

After a lively debate among the explorers as to where each thought the River of Doubt would lead them, the expedition started downstream again on March 5. Their hands and faces were swollen from insect bites and stings. The current was swift, the water deep, as it meandered "hither and thither," but always in the general direction of east of north. The surveying canoes went first, while Roosevelt "shepherded" two pairs of lashed cargo canoes. At the end of half a day, they'd gone twelve kilometers.

Eight days on the river had left them where they'd started, in the sense that they still had no idea where they were going, and therefore no concept of how long the trip would take them. Roosevelt mused, "We did not know whether we had one hundred or eight kilometers to go."

Having completed the portage, they returned the boats to the river and made good time, covering nineteen kilometers, with a brief break to pillage a "bee tree" for honey. The tree was hacked open to reveal a nest built by the stingless bees in a hollow. Roosevelt noted that the honey was sweet yet with a tart flavor, and that the comb from which it was drawn differed from the combs he'd known elsewhere. Its honey cells were very large, while the brood cells were small and in a single row instead of a double row. Just as fascinating to him was a huge tree toad, the size of bullfrog, sitting upright— "not squatted flat"—on a rotten tree limb. When he stirred it up, it jumped to a small twig, catching hold with disks of its fingertips, and balancing itself with unexpected ease for so big a creature.

Back in his canoe at three o'clock, Roosevelt felt the current quicken. When the canoe passed over "decided ripples," he heard the roar of rapids ahead. With the river now racing, he directed the rowers into a bank. A quarter of a mile of reconnoitering revealed that there were big rapids that would certainly doom any canoe that ventured into them. With everyone in the expedition camped where Roosevelt had landed, Kermit, Rondon, and Lyra boated ahead as far as wisdom dictated, then returned to camp with their dismaying findings. The rapids continued a long way, with falls and steep pitches of roiling water.

At this point, Roosevelt calculated, the expedition had gone almost exactly 100 kilometers, but because of the snaking river, they were only about fifty kilometers north of their starting point.

After returning from a hunt which resulted in a jacu for dinner, Kermit reported that on this five- or six-kilometer venture downstream he'd found another steep rapids that would have to be gone around. This required three days of portaging (March 7, 8, and 9). To pass the time as the young men struggled to heave the heavy boats and all the cargo out of the river and up its banks Roosevelt read Kermit's copy of *The Oxford Book of French Verse*. Consequently, readers of his account of this interlude for *Scribner's* were treated to this:

> Eustache Deschamp, Joachim de Bellay, Ronsard, the delightful but appalling Villon, Victor Hugo's "Guitare," Madame Desbordes-Valmore's lines on the little girl and her pillow, as dear little verses about

a child as ever were written—these and many others comforted me much, as I read them in head-net and gauntlets [defenses against insects], sitting on a log by an unknown river in the Amazonian forest.

Happily and eagerly afloat once more on March 10, Roosevelt spotted a small cayman, known as a jacare-tinga. Progress was slow. Each set of rapids meant unloading the canoes and the camaradas carrying them past the turgid obstacle on their shoulders. At one point three canoes were paddled ahead by two naked rowers per boat. A pair of double, lashed-together canoes were let down the stream by ropes. When one of them was swamped, strenuous efforts were needed to rescue it. Working with the camaradas, Kermit came out of the water with his torso, arms, and legs blistered by insect bites.

The following morning brought "a serious misfortune." During the night, one of the old, leaky dugouts, one of the biggest cargo-carriers, had broken from its mooring and had dragged another boat downstream with it. A canoe was launched to retrieve them, but it struck boulders and was quickly smashed in a raging rapid. Fragments floated away. Roosevelt decided to give the site a name: Broken Canoe Rapids.

He wrote, "It was not pleasant to have to stop for some days; thanks to the rapids, we had made slow progress, and with our necessarily limited supply of food, and no knowledge whatever of what was ahead of us, it was important to make good time. But there was no alternative. We had to build either one big canoe or two small ones."

In heavy rain the men explored in different directions for good canoe trees. They found three suitable ones near the camp and the axemen immediately attacked them, supervised by Colonel Rondon. At the same time Kermit and Lyra went in opposite directions in search of game for food. Lyra bagged a jacu. Kermit shot two monkeys.

With the canoe-builders still hard at work on March 12, Roosevelt spent the day hunting in the silent forest. All went well until he burst through a tangle of foliage and disturbed a nest of wasps. Their "resentment was active," causing him to lurch into a tree containing a small party of carnivorous foraging ants. Grasping a branch as he stumbled, he shook down a shower of fire ants. The bite of one of the giant insects stung "like a hornet" and continued to hurt three hours later. Returning to camp, he found the canoe-builders still at work, rolling and shifting a huge, heavy tree trunk to position it for the axemen. After nightfall some of the men held candles as others chopped away to hollow out the wood, while the flicker of the lights showed the tropical forest rising in the surrounding darkness.

At mid-day on the fourteenth, in a torrential downpour, the finished dugout was dragged to the river and launched. The resumed expedition passed large whirlpools in the swollen, swift river. The heavily loaded canoes rode low so that when they raced through rapids they took on a great deal of water. In one set of big ripples Roosevelt's canoe was nearly swamped. Forging through the dangerous rapids was deemed necessary because no one knew where they were going or whether they had sufficient provisions to survive. Unless they made up time, it was likely that they would run short of food. At day's end they had gone nearly sixteen kilometers. Everyone's clothing was soaked by the river water, rain, and sweat. And when they put them on the next morning they were still wet.

The morning of March 15 began well. As usual, Kermit took the lead in a canoe that was the smallest and least seaworthy. With him were his dog, Tigueiro, and two black Brazilians, Joao, the helmsman, and Simplicio, the bowsman. While Kermit went ashore on an island to see what might be the best course to proceed, the Brazilians were to take the boat to the opposite bank. Before they'd gone a dozen yards, they found themselves caught in a whirlpool and pushed into rapids. Swept over them, but with the boat still upright and afloat, the two men fought to get it to land. They'd almost done so when another whirlpool dragged the boat to midstream where the dugout filled and turned over. Joao managed to swim ashore, but Simplicio was swept away, never to be seen again. Stranded on the island, with the 405 Winchester rifle that he'd carried through Africa and on hunts on the West, Kermit succeeded in reaching the overturned dugout, only to be swept off the rolling boat and whirled away. Losing his grip on the rifle, he barely kept his head above water. Weighted by his jacket, he tore it off. Gasping for breath, he fought the current and made it to shore. Safe on land, and seeing that his dog was also dripping wet, he realized that Triguiero had plunged into the river in an effort to save him.

The spot where Simplicio was lost was marked with a wooden post with an inscription in Portugese: "In these rapids died poor Simplicio." Because the man was unmarried, the money that he would have been paid at the end of the expedition was sent by Roosevelt to his mother. In recounting the tragedy in an article for *Scribner's* Roosevelt wrote, "On an expedition such as ours death is one of the accidents that may at any time occur, and narrow escapes from death are too common to be felt as they would be felt elsewhere. One mourns sincerely, but the mourning cannot interfere with the labor. We immediately proceeded with the work of the portage."

The next day brought two more calamities. The first involved a dog named Lobo that belonged to Rondon. While the colonel was supervising the portage of one of the new canoes, the dog wandered into the forest. When Rondom heard it yelping with pain, he rushed in the direction of the sound and found Lobo dead, shot with two arrows by Indians who'd fled. But this tragedy was eclipsed by a disaster with one of the new dugout canoes. Large and heavy, it had been made of wood that would not float. When its weight snapped a mooring rope, it sank in the rapids, taking with it the rope and a set of pulleys.

This "very bad thing," as Roosevelt called the loss, meant that it would be physically impossible to hoist the big canoes up even small hills. Worried about running out of supplies, he decided it was not wise to spend four days building a replacement canoe, especially since the murder of Lobo indicated the presence of possibly hostile Indians in the neighborhood. He also realized that the four remaining canoes could not carry all the loads and all the men, even if the loads were cut by leaving material behind.

The site of this disaster was named Broken Rope Rapids.

But the reality of the situation was truly grim. In eighteen days they had used more than a third of their food. They'd gone 125 kilometers, with the probability that they faced five or seven times that distance to go. Two weeks had been spent descending no more than seventy yards of rapids. Four canoes had been lost. And one man was dead. In a country of wild Indians who shot well with their bows and arrows, Roosevelt reasoned, it "behooved us to go warily, but also to make all speed possible, if we were to avoid serious trouble."

23

★ ★ ★

A River of Real Importance

T HE IMMEDIATE RESULT of the loss of the rope and block and tackle was a convening of a late-night discussion of what George Cherrie called "ways and means" of continuing. It ended with agreement that only vitally needed baggage and supplies would be floated on four canoes lashed together to form a balsa (raft), each with three paddlers. Roosevelt and Doctor Cajazeira would travel on the raft. The others (thirteen) would walk along the shore.

The expedition's position, wrote Cherrie that night in his journal, "is really a very serious one." Provisions were decreasing daily. It was not possible to go back. "The journey ahead is undoubtedly *a very long one*," he continued. "The difficulties to overcome can only be judged by what we have passed through!"

Almost sixteen years earlier on a steamy July day in 1898, Colonel Theodore Roosevelt had led his Rough Riders and other Americans in a race to the summit of Kettle Hill in the San Juan Heights of Spanish Cuba. With the wolf rising in his heart, he'd known his "crowded hour." On March 17, 1914, about three hours after sunrise on the River of Doubt, he found himself on an overloaded raft as a trio of straining paddlers struggled to maneuver it around a raging and roaring stretch of water. Unwieldy and clumsy, the lashed-together canoes were hard to handle. As they came to a sharp bend they were caught by the swift current. With no alternative but to run a string of crashing, boulder-strewn rapids, Roosevelt and the doctor helped the laboring camaradas by paddling hard. The raft went "scraping and bumping" through one rapid after another in a frenzied attempt to guide the careening canoes toward the nearest riverbank.

Watching with horror in a single file from the shore were Kermit, Colonel Rondon, Cherrie, and Lyra, with nine camaradas, Unable to help, they saw their leader's raft swept along and slammed into a boulder. How it survived the crash no one could explain, but it did, and after a few minutes Roosevelt was on land, safe but soaked. Roosevelt would write of his brush with death that he'd been "within an ace of coming to grief," that they had "got through by the skin of our teeth," and "It was a narrow escape from grave disaster."

With all the loads taken out, and the empty canoes run through less dangerous channels between a cluster of islands, the party made camp by a small river with a low waterfall and many fish that were "delicious eating." Because the stream was a discovery, Rondon gave it a name that thrilled Roosevelt and surprised his son: Rio Kermit. Convinced that this newly named waterway was evidence that the Duvida had no connection with any other river, Rondon said, "There was no longer any question that the Duvida was a big river, a river of importance."

Before camp was broken the next day (March 18), Rondon had a bugler summon everyone around him to hear him declare that henceforth the River of Doubt would be known as "Rio Roosevelt." That said, he called for three cheers for President Roosevelt, three cheers for the United States of America, and three cheers for Kermit. Roosevelt responded by waving his hat and leading a chorus of "hip, hip, hurrah" for Rondon, Brazil, the Brazilian Telegraph Commission, Doctor Cajazeira, Lieutenant Lyra, and the camaradas. When Lyra pointed out that the cheers had omitted Cherrie, the naturalist promptly received his due.

Although Roosevelt wrote that naming the river after him "was a complete surprise," he had known all along that if the Duvida turned out to be, indeed, an unknown river, it would be named the Roosevelt. Yet in his story of the re-naming, he said he believed "River of Doubt" was "an unusually good name; and it is always well to keep the name of this character." But, he wrote, because his "kind friends insisted otherwise," it would have been "churlish" of him to "object longer."

That a river or stream would be named for Kermit had also been decided long before the expedition began was evidenced by Rondon producing a plaque bearing the name "Rio Kermit" to be nailed to a marker post.

When the expedition resumed, the explorers found signs that they were not the only people in the region. Indian villages were seen along the river, but no inhabitants. Assuming that they'd retreated to the forest, Rondon left peace offerings of an axe, knife, and glass beads. The gesture was fine with Roosevelt, but worried about the presence of Indians that might be hostile, and concerned about the state of supplies, he insisted that the expedition proceed as quickly as possible. His anxiety over Indians was soon reinforced by the finding of footprints and a few more abandoned settlements. He also heard voices of unseen people coming from the jungle.

While these concerns were genuine, it's arguable that Roosevelt was increasingly eager to go home. Having seen his beloved Kermit come close to being killed, he lived in dread that he might have to tell the mother of his children that her second son had died on an expedition that Kermit had never wanted to join, and had postponed his marriage to do so in order to keep his promise to his mother to watch over Father. Now, with lurking Indians on his mind, he confided to his journal, "I cannot accept the prospect of having my son's life threatened constantly by the presence of Indians, more than the life of any other member of the expedition, whenever his canoe goes out in front."

With the existence of the Rio de Duvida as an important river confirmed, he now saw no reason why the expedition should not move rapidly along, noting only the most significant of its features and leaving further exploration to others.

Kermit was also impatient. Frustrated by the pace on March 22, he wrote in his diary, "Off with a good many delays." At his father's insistence he was no longer the spearhead of the flotilla of canoes as it moved ahead. But if he shared his father's worries about hostiles in the forest, he did not show those concerns. When he had time on his hands, he ventured away on a hunt, with his faithful dog Trigueiro his only company. Whatever game he shot was certainly welcome, and needed. With half the expedition's provisions gone, either consumed or lost, Cherrie reckoned that they had rations for no more than twenty-five days.

The frustration Roosevelt felt about the slow progress was expressed in a diary note on March 24. They had come "only a trifle over 160 kilometers," and "thanks to the character and number of rapids," they had "three or four times the distance yet to go before coming to a part of the river where we might hope to meet assistance." The ordeal was also taking a toll on the camaradas. Kermit recorded, "Hard work; men disanimated."

On March 25 Cherrie noted, "There is a feeling of great depression in our camp tonight." But the following day, he cast aside his gloom and exulted in a startling archaeological find. On huge granite and quartzite rocks he discovered a series of carved concentric rings and three sets of what seemed to be the letter M, or perhaps inverted Ws. They were so unquestionably of ancient origin that Roosevelt mused about a moment "in a very remote past some Indian tribes of comparatively advanced culture had penetrated to this lovely river, just as we had now come to it."An even more rewarding discovery that day on the forest floor was a harvest of Brazil nuts that provided a welcome supplement to a dinner of cooked palm tops and two piranha that had been caught by one of the boatmen. Dessert was two tablespoons of honey for each man. "So we all had a feast," Roosevelt recorded, "and everybody had enough to eat and was happy."

After naming the stop "Camp of Indian Inscriptions," the expedition set out on March 27, 1914, and came to another rapids at a cost of two more destroyed boats. When paddlers became trapped in the debris, Roosevelt, Kermit, Cherrie, and others plunged into the treacherous current to rescue them. Up to his armpits and barely able to maintain his footing, Roosevelt slipped and stumbled against a boulder, re-injuring the knee that had been badly hurt in the 1902 carriage accident. While Dr. Cajazeira swabbed the gashed right knee with antiseptic and bandaged it, Roosevelt blamed the injury on clumsiness. Limping to his boat to resume the day's journey, he described the wound as "somewhat bothersome." Just ten minutes later, the expedition was forced to stop by another daunting rapids.

Plagued by torrential rains and swarming insects, and confronted with "all the unpleasant possibilities ahead," a decision was made to "cut to the bone" and throw away everything but the barest necessities. Two tents were kept, one for Roosevelt and a larger one for everyone else. In addition to the wet clothes on his back Roosevelt had a pair of pajamas, a spare pair of underwear, wash kit, a pocket medicine case, some adhesive plaster, needles and thread, his purse containing a letter of credit to be used at the end of the journey, and an extra set of eyeglasses. He also carried a cartridge bag, head net, and gauntlets.

Lightened to the limit, the expedition spent the final days of March getting to the foot of rapids in a gorge with walls too steep to be traversed, forcing the party to climb a rock-strewn, forest-clad mountain. Roosevelt's reward for making the ascent on his aching injured leg was "a beautiful view of the country ahead." Through an opening in the trees at the edge of a cliff he gazed at ranges of low mountains about the height of the lower ridges of the Alleghenies. "It was well worth seeing; but, beautiful although the country ahead of us was," he noted. "its character was such as to promise further hardships, difficulty, and exhausting labor, and especially further delay; and delay was a serious matter to men whose food supply was beginning to run short, whose equipment was reduced to the minimum, who for a month, with the utmost toil, had made very slow progress, and who had no idea of either the distance or the difficulties of the route in front of them."

As formidable as the challenge was, one of the main purposes of the expedition was not abandoned. Between navigating dangerous rapids and dealing with unexpected problems, the work of collecting specimens continued. Roosevelt noted with satisfaction that George Cherrie's "unwearied efforts" as the expedition's professional naturalist were rewarded from time to time by a species new to the collection. Roosevelt also found Cherrie to be a good man to talk to at the end of an arduous day. They chatted about their views of life, of a man's duty to his wife and children, responsibilities to humankind in general, duty to one's country in peace and war, and, of course, natural science.

Camped at the foot of the gorge on the last day of March, Roosevelt went to his tent in a thunderstorm and found his cot and bedding soaked. He had to sleep rolled up in a blanket. Except for the injured knee, he slept "comfortably enough" and awoke ready for whatever came next. Two mornings later, thinking he'd put his clothing out of reach of insects, he discovered that both termites and carregadores had chewed holes in a boot, the leg of one of his underpants, and a handkerchief. He noted, "I now had nothing to replace anything that was destroyed."

On the move on April 2, the expedition had spent "exactly a month going through an uninterrupted succession of rapids." In that time they had come only about 100 kilometers, and had descended nearly 150 kilometers from their point of departure. Four original canoes had been lost, along with the dugout built in the forest. A man was dead. And so was Rondon's little dog. "Most of the camaradas were downhearted, naturally enough," Roosevelt wrote, "and occasionally asked one of us if we really believed that we should ever get out alive; and we had to cheer them up as best we could."

Adopting the tone of a teacher as he wrote about the adventure so far, and assuming that someone would eventually read about it, he explained:

> Such an exploring expedition as that in which we were engaged of necessity involves hard and dangerous labor, and perils of many kinds. To follow downstream an unknown river, broken by innumerable cataracts and rapids, rushing through mountains of which the existence has never been even guessed, bears no resemblance whatever to following even a fairly dangerous river which has been thoroughly explored and has become in some sort a highway, so that experienced pilots can be secured as guides, while the portages have been pioneered and trails chopped out, and every dangerous feature of the rapids is known beforehand. In this case no one could foretell that the river would cleave its way through steep mountain chains, cutting narrow clefts in which the cliff walls rose sheer on either hand. When a rushing river thus "canyons," as we used to say out West, and the mountains are very steep, it becomes almost impossible to bring the canoes down the river itself and utterly impossible to portage them along the cliff sides, while even to bring the loads over the mountain is a task of extraordinary labor and difficulty. Moreover, no one can tell how many times the task will have to be repeated; or when it will end; or whether the food will hold out; every hour of work in the rapids is fraught with the possibility of the gravest disaster, and yet it is imperatively necessary to attempt it; and all this is done in an uninhabited wilderness, or else a wilderness tenanted only by unfriendly savages, where failure to get through means death by disease and starvation.

Such wilderness exploration, said the hero of the San Juan Heights, was as "dangerous as warfare" and the "conquest of nature demands the utmost vigor, hardihood, and daring, and takes from the conquerors a heavy toll of life and health."

Roosevelt found no more telling evidence of this reality than his wounded right leg. If it had been injured on an adventure in the pine woods of Maine or somewhere on the prairies of the West, rather than in the relentless humidity of the Brazilian jungle, healing would have been expected to be constant and complete. But each day as Dr. Cajazeira examined it and changed the dressing he found little improvement. George Cherrie observed Roosevelt and concluded that he was a very sick man.

Recovery had been complicated two days after Roosevelt's collision with the boulder. On March 28 an attack of malaria resulted in his temperature rising to 105 degrees. For Kermit it was a "particularly black night." His account of those hours revealed why:

> The fever was high and father was out of his head. Doctor Cajazeira, who was one of the three Brazilians with us, divided with me the watch during the night. The scene is vivid before me. The black rushing river with the great trees towering high above the bank; the sodden earth under foot; for a few moments the stars would be shining, and then the sky would cloud over and rain would fall in torrents, shutting out the sky and trees and river.
>
> Father first began with poetry; over and over again he repeated "In Xanadu did Kubla Khan a stately pleasure dome decree," then he started talking at random, but gradually he centred down to the question of supplies, which was, of course, occupying every one's mind. Part of the time he knew that I was there, and he would then ask me if I thought Cherrie had had enough to eat to keep going. Then he would forget my presence and keep saying to himself: "I can't work now, so I don't need much food, but he and Cherrie have worked all day with the canoes, they must have part of mine."

At one point a few hours later, with Kermit and Cherrie standing by his cot, Roosevelt said, "Boys, I realize that some of us are not going to finish this journey."

He looked intently at Cherrie.

"I want you and Kermit to go on," he continued. "You can get out. I will stop here."

Cherrie had no doubt that Roosevelt was contemplating suicide. From that moment on both he and Kermit kept an eye on him to prevent him, in Cherrie's words, "from carrying out what he felt was necessary," that he must "relieve the party of what he considered a burden."

Years earlier in contemplating the heroic deeds of Rough Riders and other soldiers in the jungles of Cuba on a mission to kick out Spain, Colonel Theodore Roosevelt had witnessed a kind of bravery that he defined in his autobiography, published just before he'd launched his quest to be a boy again. He called it "three o'clock in the morning courage." It was, he said, "the most desirable kind." In an essay for *The Outlook* magazine in 1895 he'd written about the man "who is not frightened by the sweat and the blood, and the blows of friends and foes; who haunts not the fringy edges of the fight, but the pell-mell of men."

Certainly, no man had measured up to that Rooseveltian standard better than Kermit.

Like all the four sons of Theodore Roosevelt, he shared a love of the out-doors and physical activity. But the fair-haired boy (the only son with blond hair), he was also the most sensitive of the children for whom the best companionship was found in his imagination. His mother looked into Kermit's "big, dark eyes, full of poetry" and described him as "a good deal of a hermit" who "never need to retire to a cloister for a life of abstraction." Yet Kermit became a fierce defender of his controversial father as a young boy (he'd beaten up a boy who'd criticized Roosevelt), the valued companion in Africa and now the Amazon jungles of Brazil. To his older and younger siblings he was "the lucky one" who got to go along on Father's most exciting adventures.

Again and again, when it was touch and go whether the expedition could get around a rapids, Kermit's valor had often made the difference. He'd spent days stripped to the waist in water. His clothes were never dry. Bruises on his bare feet and scores of insect bites had become festering sores. What little he had for food he'd readily shared with camaradas, who emulated the gun bearers of Africa by adoring him. Frequently, it had been Kermit's Winchester rifle that provided meat for meals. And, Roosevelt could never forget, his second son had delayed his marriage to come along on a trip in the unknown to "look after Father."

That Kermit Roosevelt would now leave his father to die was, of course, as impossible as getting Theodore Roosevelt's permission to be carried. Rejecting the suggestion, he was on his feet as the battered and dispirited expedition dragged the five surviving canoes past yet another waterfall to find a new obstacle in the form of another portage that would require at least two more days of risking lives and canoes. At one point Kermit worried that the strain on Roosevelt was so great that his heart might give out.

"Men very disheartened," Kermit noted in his journal. "Hard work. Wet all day; half ration." The only smoker among the explorers then recorded the sad fact that he'd smoked his last pipeful of "Injus Bill" tobacco. But he had the consolation of a bottle of Scotch whiskey, the last of three. Watching

Kermit and Cherrie sipping the precious remainder, Roosevelt smiled and said, "I am sorry I can't enjoy that, but I wouldn't if I could. It would take too much away from your pleasure."

By April 1 Kermit and Lieutenant Lyra succeeded in hauling the expedition's five canoes around the last of the impeding falls. They had worked for four days to do so. Ahead of them lay other challenges, among them a chasm filled with rapids and falls. Forced to camp on April 2, they'd gone less than two miles. As the encampment was being organized, Kermit went hunting. He returned with a small turtle and a strange-looking fruit that was new to the naturalists. The turtle was boiled into a soup for breakfast.

But it wasn't the turtle soup and the sweet fruit that made the day remarkable for the discouraged, bedraggled, weary, and hungry men of the expedition. "Under such conditions," Roosevelt wrote, "whatever is evil in men's natures comes to the front."

The "strange and terrible tragedy" on this day was a homicide.

24

★ ★ ★

Murder in the Jungle

O NE OF THE CAMARADAS was "a man of pure European blood." Named Julio, he was "a very powerful fellow and had been importunately eager to join the expedition." Because he came with the reputation of being a good worker, Roosevelt had gladly enlisted him. But before long, Roosevelt recognized that Julio, "like so many men of higher standing," had no idea what such a venture really meant. Under the strain of toil, hardship, and danger his true nature emerged in which Roosevelt discerned "depths of selfishness, cowardice, and ferocity." He shirked all work and shammed sickness. Nothing could make him do his share, yet he was constantly begging for favors, so that after out of the goodness of his heart Kermit shared his rapidly dwindling supply of tobacco with him, Julio expected to receive more. Julio "threw all his tasks on his comrades," Roosevelt wrote, and, moreover, "he stole their food as well as ours." To Roosevelt this was "next to murder as a crime and should by rights be punished as such."

A dramatic contrast to Julio was a large black man named Paixao. A corporal and acting sergeant in the engineer corps of the Brazilian army, he had worked so hard that when his only pair of pants had become torn to tatters, Roosevelt gave him his spare trousers. One of the most admirable traits that the former commander of the Rough Riders found in Paixao was that he was a figure with military bearing. Also a stern disciplinarian, he was a man of action who stood ready to deal with miscreants by doling out appropriate punishment. Consequently, one evening when he caught Julio stealing food, he punched Julio in the mouth.

"Julio came crying to us, his face working with fear and malignant hatred," Roosevelt noted, "but after investigation he was told that he had gotten off uncommonly lightly." He spoke as a former deputy sheriff in the Dakota Badlands, veteran of two years as head of the New York Police Department, and an ex-president who frequently had to sit in judgment of men who had been convicted of federal crimes and appealed to him for executive clemency. One of them was a former member of the Rough Riders who had committed armed robbery. Roosevelt pardoned him and later appointed him to a high official position in which he rendered such good service that Roosevelt lauded him in his autobiography as a man whom, "as a soldier, as civil officer, as citizen, and as a friend, I valued and respected."

In the autobiography, published as the Brazilian expedition was being planned, Roosevelt wrote on the general subject of crime and punishment:

> Now I suppose some good people will gather from this that I favor men who committed crimes. I certainly do not favor them. I have not a particle of sympathy with the sentimentality—as I deem it, the mawkishness—which overflows with foolish pity for the criminal who cares not at all for the victim of the criminal. I am glad to see wrong-doers punished, The punishment is an absolute necessity from the standpoint of society; and I put the reformation of the criminal second to the welfare of society. But I do desire to see the man or woman who has paid the penalty and who wishes to reform given a helping hand—surely every one of us who knows his own heart must know that he too may stumble, and should be anxious to help his brother or sister who has stumbled. When the criminal has been punished, if he then shows a sincere desire to lead a decent and upright life, he should be given the chance, he should be helped and not hindered; and if he makes good, he should receive that respect from others which so often aids in creating self-respect—the most valuable of all possessions.

Hoping that Julio had learned a lesson from Paixao's punch in the mouth and that Julio would reform his ways, Roosevelt prepared himself for the next portage. But another member of the expedition, named Pedrinho, caught Julio pilfering some of the men's dried meat. Pedrinho reported this to Paixao. Because everyone was busy loading canoes, Paixao let the incident pass. But a while later, he upbraided Julio for lagging behind and slacking in his work. Paixao had just put down a load of cargo. As he departed to get another, he left his rifle on the ground.

Nearby, Roosevelt, Rondon, and Lyra were seated, waiting for the work to be completed. Engaged in conversation, no one paid any attention to Julio as he marched into camp, muttering to himself as usual, put down his load, picked up Paixao's carbine, and strode back to the trail.

A short time later, a shot rang out.

Rushing into camp from the trail, several of the men exclaimed in unison that Paixao was dead and that Julio had shot him and fled into the woods.

Roosevelt ordered a messenger to find Kermit and Cherrie and tell them to stay where they were and guard the canoes and provisions. Roosevelt, limping on his bad leg and with his revolver belted to a hip, and Dr. Cajazeira—"an absolutely cool and plucky man"—hurried as fast as possible to the scene of the crime. They found Paixao on the ground "in a huddle, in a pool of his own blood, where he had fallen, shot through the heart."

Roosevelt feared that Julio had run amuck and intended to take more lives, and that his next victim would probably be Pedrinho. With this dreadful scenario in mind, and worried that Julio might have returned to the camp to lay an ambush for Pedrinho, Roosevelt and the doctor returned to the camp and found no one there. Presently, the camaradas strode into the camp to report "the welcome news" that they'd found the carbine.

Relieved that abandonment of the rifle meant there would be no more killings, Roosevelt demonstrated a talent for deductive reasoning in a criminal investigation that readers of fiction had been relishing in American editions of short-stories and novels by Sir Arthur Conan Doyle concerning "the world's first private consulting detective," Mr. Sherlock Holmes of 221-B Baker Street, London, and his cohort in crime-solving, Dr. John H. Watson. A comparison of Theodore Roosevelt as sleuth in a Brazilian jungle to Sherlock Holmes is even more delicious because his investigative companion was also a physician.

Examining the clues, Roosevelt deduced:

> The murderer had stood to one side of the path and killed his victim, when a dozen paces off, with deliberate and malignant purpose. Then evidently his murderous hatred had at once given way to his innate cowardice; and, perhaps hearing some one coming along the path, he fled in

terror into the wilderness. A tree had knocked the carbine from his hand. His footsteps showed that after some rods he had started to return, doubtless for the carbine, but had fled again, probably because the body had then been discovered. It was questionable whether or not he would live to reach the Indian villages, which were probably his goal. He was not a man to feel remorse—never a common feeling; but surely that murderer was in a living hell, as, with fever and famine leering at him from the shadows, he made his way through the empty desolation of the wilderness.

As Roosevelt investigated and deduced, the expedition's cook quoted the melancholy proverbial philosophy of a native proverb: "No man knows the heart of any one." Then he said with deep conviction a ghostly belief that sent a shiver down Roosevelt's back of the kind that Edgar Allen Poe hoped to cause in readers of *Tales of Mystery and Imagination,* even if they read the stories in a Brazilian jungle. "Paixao is following Julio now, and will follow him until he dies," the cook declared grimly, pointing to the dead body. "Paixao fell forward on his hands and knees, and when a murdered man falls like that his ghost will follow the slayer as long as the slayer lives."

Roosevelt chose not to hunt for Julio. If he were captured, he would have to be guarded day and night on an expedition where there were always loaded firearms about. As a prisoner he might grab a weapon and kill someone else. He couldn't be shackled in a canoe that might overturn, dooming him to drowning. Nor could he climb cliffs with bound hands and feet. And standing watch over him would be an additional and severe burden on men already stretched to the limit. But neither could Julio be put to death legally, although he was a soldier who in cold blood had murdered another soldier. No one knew how many weeks of journeying remained. The food was running low. Sickness was appearing among the men. The first duty was to save them. Whether the murderer lived or died in the wilderness was of "no moment," compared to doing everything possible to secure the safety of the rest of the party.

Paixao was buried where he fell. This was in accord with Roosevelt's lifelong belief that "where a tree falls there let it lay." The shallow grave was dug by the same men who had used their axes and skills to turn trees into dugout canoes. Reverently and carefully, the body "which but half an hour before had been so full of vigorous life" was in the ground beneath a mound with a rude wooden cross over him. A volley was fired in tribute to a brave and loyal soldier who had died performing the greatest and finest accomplishment in Theodore Roosevelt's lexicon: duty.

"Then we left him forever," he wrote, "under the great trees beside a lonely river."

Not knowing if Julio were alive, and if so, where he might be lurking to heave rocks down on the expedition, or to steal a canoe in the dead of night, the expedition remained on high alert for two days. On the morning of the third day, as the flotilla of four canoes floated down the river, Julio appeared on a bank from a thicket of trees. Waving arms and shouting, he begged to surrender and be taken aboard. Roosevelt gazed at him and saw "an arrant craven at heart, a strange mixture of ferocity and cowardice." The canoes passed by. At the first halt, Rondon explained that he hadn't picked up Julio because Rondon wished to consult with Roosevelt "as the chief of the expedition." Roosevelt gave his reasons against rescuing Julio, but because Rondon was the superior officer of both murderer and victim, he would not object to whatever Rondon chose to do out of his duty as an officer and according to the laws of Brazil.

At the next camp Rondon sent two expert woodsmen to look for Julio.

In perhaps the coldest line in Roosevelt's account of the trip down the River of Doubt, and possibly with righteous satisfaction, Roosevelt wrote, "They failed to find him."

Under way again, the expedition at first found no good place to camp, but eventually came to a place at the foot of a steep cliff that provided a narrow, boulder-covered slope where it was possible to sling hammocks and a "slanting spot" for Roosevelt's cot. Battered and sagging, the bed looked to Roosevelt like a broken-backed centipede. The next day, Kermit and Cherrie found a new location that was not much better. Despite Kermit suffering an attack of fever, and Cherrie and Lyra plagued by dysentery, the camp was arranged. Roosevelt's "bothersome" leg was tended by the doctor. The wound was inflamed. That night Roosevelt's temperature shot up. But because Roosevelt's teeth were chattering so much, the doctor had to measure it by placing the thermometer in an armpit. It registered 100.4 degrees. Cajazeira covered him with a blanket and insisted that he down half a gram of quinine salts in a cup of water.

When the expedition left a camp that the doctor termed a "disagreeable bivouac," the camaradas had to carry Roosevelt to his canoe and place him on a bed of crates. Readers of *Scribner's Magazine* would eventually be told,

"It is not ideal for a sick man to spend the hottest hours of the day stretched on the boxes in the bottom of a small open dugout, under the well-neigh intolerable heat of the torrid sun of the mid-tropics, varied by blinding, drenching downpours of rain."

He longed for "a big Maine birch-bark," such as that in which he once went down the Mattamakeag at high water. It would have slipped down the rapids "as a girl trips through a country dance."

On Palm Sunday (April 5, 1914) Roosevelt's fever was down and Kermit was feeling well enough to go with Rondon and Lyra to reconnoiter the river ahead. They came back to make the heartening announcement that "after these rapids we're out of the hills." Cherrie's diary notation that evening saw brighter prospects. "The mountains, that have so long hemmed us in," he wrote, "seem to be falling away from the river. The river seems to be broadening."

Five days later, Kermit had a recurrence of fever. It reached 104 degrees, requiring the doctor to inject him with quinine every six hours. Although Kermit declared himself "feeling better" in the morning, he had head and back aches and was too weak to work. He crawled into a canoe and covered himself with a tarpaulin. Ordinarily his dog would have settled next to him, but that morning Trigueiro evidently had other things on his mind. As the boats floated away, no one noticed the dog was not with them. When they did, there was no going back to look for him.

On Saturday, April 11, Kermit's continuing distress over the fate of the pet that plunged into a raging river in an attempt to help its master avoid drowning galvanized Roosevelt into action. As head of the expedition, he insisted that Rondon send out a party of camaradas to look for Trigueiro. This meant delaying the start of the next part of the journey, with very little likelihood that the dog would be found, or that he was alive. The expedition waited all day, but just as the sun was setting the searchers returned, preceded by Trigueiro, who greeted Kermit in dog fashion by licking his beaming face.

The reunion took place at the expedition's twenty-eighth camp. For the first time there were no roaring rapids. But even more exciting to the men of the expedition than the return of Kermit's dog was a report by one of the men who'd gone off fishing that he'd found that a vine had been cut by an axe or knife at a place reachable only by canoe. And a post at the spot had been carved with the initials A.J. Because the local Indians did not have boats, this discovery meant that the vine must have been cut by someone who had come up the river, and that the voyager was most likely looking for rubber trees to tap.

Venturing ahead with great excitement on April 12 (Easter), the expedition came to a newly built house in a planted clearing. No one was at home, except for a couple of watchdogs. Contents of the house suggested that it was occupied by a man, woman, and child, and that they had only just left. An hour farther downstream stood a house belonging to an elderly black man. He welcomed these surprising men who had come *down* the river with "the innate courtesy of the Brazlian peasantry" that Roosevelt had hoped Americans would emulate.

In mid-afternoon the voyagers stopped at a "picturesque" house of palm thatch, but its occupants appeared to have hastily evacuated in fear of an Indian raid. When they came back and discovered that white men were their guests, they were hospitable and communicative. They invited them to spend the night.

During forty-eight days, covering 300 kilometers of "absolutely unknown ground," Roosevelt and the others had seen no other human being. Six weeks had been spent slogging their way through a seemingly interminable series of rapids on a river about the size of the Rhine or Elbe, of which no geographer had any idea of its existence.

With deserved pride, Roosevelt wrote, they were putting on the map a river that appeared on no map published in Europe, or the United States, or that any map of Brazil recognized.

"I esteemed it a great piece of good fortune to be able to take part in such a feat," he said while acknowledging that it was an achievement that represented "the capping of a pyramid" which during the previous seven years had been guilt by Colonel Rondon and the Brazilian Telegraphic Commission.

The expedition had passed the period of peril and possible disaster.

There might still be risks ahead to individuals, and some difficulties and annoyances for everyone, but there was no longer the least likelihood of calamity for the expedition as a whole.

Its triumphant leader wrote, "The wearing work, under very unhealthy conditions, was beginning to tell on everyone. Half the camaradas had been down with fever and were much weakened; only a few of them retrained their original physical and moral strength. Cherrie and Kermit had recovered; but both Kermit and Lyra still had bad sores on their legs, from the bruises received in the water work. I was in worse shape."

The aftereffects of the fever still hung on. The leg which had been hurt while working in the rapids with the sunken canoe had developed an abscess that "the good doctor" had cut open to insert a drainage tube. He credited Cajazeira for "unwearied care and kindness" and praised Kermit, Cherrie, Rondon, and Lyra for taking care of him without mentioning (perhaps because he didn't remember, or chose not to recall) the night when the doctor's patient pleaded to be left behind in order not to jeopardize the welfare of the others. He chose instead to assert that it was such a man's "duty to go forward, if necessary on all fours, until he drops."

He minimized his perilous situation, and his heroism, by telling his readers, "Fortunately, I was put to no such test. When my serious trouble came we had only canoe-riding ahead of us."

Now the north was "calling strongly to the three men of the north— Rocky Dell Farm to Cherrie, Sagamore Hill to me; and to Kermit the call was stronger still," because of a wedding.

"In our home country spring had now come," he wrote movingly and with Rooseveltian romanticism, "the wonderful northern spring of long glorious days, of brooding twilights, of cool delightful nights. Robin and bluebird, meadow-lark and song sparrow, were singing in the mornings at home; the maple-buds were red; windflowers and bloodroot were blooming while the last patches of snow still lingered; the rapture of the hermit-thrush in Vermont, the serene golden melody of the wood-thrush on Long Island, would be heard before we were there to listen. Each man to his home, and to his true love! Each was longing for the homely things that were so dear to him, for the home people who were dearer still, and for the one who was dearest of all." His beloved Edith.

And the children he'd once again left behind, as so often during their growing up, save one, "the lucky one" named Kermit, in order to grab a last chance to be a boy again.

25

★ ★ ★

A Wedding in Spain

A MONTH BEFORE the men of the expedition discovered that the worst of their journey was behind them, the *New York Times* had published (on March 23) an alarming headline:

ROOSEVELT PARTY LOSES EVERYTHING
IN RAPIDS OF A BRAZILIAN RIVER;
MEMBERS OF PARTY PROBABLY SAFE;
MAY BE ON AN UNKNOWN RIVER

Five days later, Anthony Fiala was in the town of Santarem and able to send a cable to the newspaper: "The Roosevelt party is in good health, exploring the Duvida River." He added, "It is expected to reach Manaos early in April."

But on the very day when Fiala's confidence-instilling message was sent (March 28), Theodore Roosevelt was so despondent because of his crippling leg injury and malarial fever that he proposed to Kermit and Cherrie that for their sake and the expedition's they should "go out" and leave him to die in the jungle.

That he had come through that crisis and survived others during an arduous month of navigating a continually dangerous river had demanded of everyone a twenty-four-hour-a-day demonstration of "three o'clock in the morning courage," and the unflinching devotion of a son and an indomitable doctor. During the thirty days between Fiala's telegram to New York and the expedition's return to a semblance of civilization, there had been other crises. Rondon thought Roosevelt "never was himself again." Although the leg-wound had begun to heal, he suffered from an infection of cellulite tissue that was so painful he was often unable to sit. Cherrie noted that because he was unable to eat properly he'd lost one-fourth of his weight and become so thin that his clothes "hang like bags on him."

But now the end of the ordeal was near. With the help of a "first-class waterman, cool, fearless, and brawny as a bull," as a guide, the expedition passed that last of the dangerous rapids on April 26. The paddles were plied with hearty goodwill, with Cherrie and Kermit, as usual, working like the camaradas, as the canoes "went dancing down the broad, rapid river." At one o'clock in the afternoon the boats reached the mouth of the Castanho River and an army camp with flags of the United States and Brazil flying over it. Rifles fired a salute in welcome.

As the boats landed, the men of the expedition looked back on the two months they'd spent in canoes. From February 27 to April 26 they had traveled more than 750 kilometers on a river that could no longer be called "unknown." Now it was "Rio Roosevelt." (The name proved to be so cumbersome for the Portugese tongue that it was soon changed to "Rio Teodoro.")

Upon arriving at the "attractive camp," commanded by one of Rondon's lieutenants by the name of Pyrineus, Roosevelt learned that Anthony Fiala had gone home, but that Leo Miller was at Manaos, and that the camp was only four hours above the river hamlet of Sao Joao, a port of call for rubber steamers, from which he could travel to Manaos in two days. Roosevelt also rejoiced to learn that Captain Amilcar, the head of the party that went down the Gy-Parana River, was all right. After spending his last night under tent canvas Roosevelt boarded a steamer at Sao Joao for Manaos and a reunion with Leo Miller.

When the river steamer *Cidade de Mandaos* moored at half-past two in the morning of April 30, 1914, Roosevelt had to be taken ashore on a stretcher. Shortly after the boat docked, Kermit was handed a bundle of letters from his fiancee. Belle had sent them from London and Madrid, where, she informed him, she expected to marry him in June. Though very ill, Roosevelt cabled Edith, "Successful trip," without revealing how sick he was. He then marshaled enough strength to dictate a telegram to Lauro Muller. To the Brazilian official who more than any other had made the expedition possible he reported:

> We have had a hard and somewhat dangerous but very successful trip. No less than six weeks were spent slowly and with peril and exhausting labor forcing our way down through what seemed a literally endless succession of rapids and cataracts. For forty-eight days we saw no human being. In passing these rapids we lost five of the seven canoes with which we started and had to build others. One of four best men lost his life in the rapids. Under the strain one of the men went completely bad, shirked all his work, stole his comrades' food and when punished by the sergeant he with cold-blooded determination murdered the sergeant and fled into the wilderness, Col. Rondon's dog, running ahead of him while hunting, was shot by two Indians; by his death he in all probability saved the life of his master. We have put on the map a river of about 1500 kilometers in length running from just south of the 13th degree to north of the 5th degree and the biggest affluent of the Madeira. Until now its upper course has been utterly unknown to everyone, and its lower course altho unknown for years to the rubber-men utterly unknown to all cartographers. . . .
>
> My dear Sir, I thank you from my heart for the chance to take part in this great work of exploration.

When the last zoological specimen was noted for the record, the expedition's collection consisted of more than 2500 birds, nearly 500 mammals, and an assortment of reptiles and fish. Many of them were new to science.

Before Roosevelt could depart Manaos for the port city of Belen and then back to the United States he had to face the ordeal of an operation to treat his abscessed leg. With that done, and feeling better than he had in weeks, he was carried to the freighter *Dunstan* and placed in the captain's quarters at the skipper's insistence. On the fourth day he was able to get around with a cane. On May 5 he left the ship walking. Two days later, the Roosevelt expedition came to an end with a formal ceremony and a personal farewell to the camaradas. Kermit translated as his father told them, "You are all heroes." Each was given two gold sovereigns as mementoes.

Dr. Cajazeira lectured his patient about the importance of continuing to take his quinine.

When Roosevelt invited Colonel Rondon to visit Sagamore Hill some day, Rondon gave a reply that indicated he was not unfamiliar with the politics of Theodore Roosevelt's country. "I shall be there," he said, "when you are once again elected president of the United States."

When Colonel Roosevelt of the Rough Riders returned from his crowded hour in Cuba, he'd bounded down the gangplank of the ocean steamer *Miami* at Montauk, Long Island, on August 15, 1898, exclaiming, "I feel as big and as strong as a bull moose." He'd made the same boast on his return from Africa. On May 19, 1914, family, friends, and other welcomers, as well as newspaper reporters, saw a far different figure. Clothing sagged on an almost gaunt frame. His sunburned face showed fatigue. He favored his right leg, but when Ted offered an arm to lean on, it was brushed away as Roosevelt snapped, "I can take care of myself."

Asked if he planned to run for president in 1916, he said that the only plans he had were to go to Washington to address the National Geographic Society and answer any question on geography "from any reputable man," and to travel to Spain for the wedding of his second son.

In his talk to the nation's leading geographers, many of whom had expressed concerns about the truth of his claim to have explored an unknown river, he used the analogy of having put the cap on a pyramid that had been built by Colonel Rondon and the Brazilian Telegraph Commission. Charting the Duvida in chalk on a blackboard, he gave a detailed description of the expedition and its work that together dispelled the geographer's doubts. When reports of their embrace of Roosevelt's claims reached London, they were quickly followed by an invitation to present his findings to the Royal Geographical Society.

But first there was a wedding to attend in Spain.

Because Edith didn't feel up to an ocean crossing so soon after the death of her sister, and still emotionally drained by the ordeal of months of not knowing if she would ever see her husband and son again, Roosevelt was accompanied by Alice (now the wife of Congressman Nicholas Longworth). The nuptials of Kermit Roosevelt and Bella Willard were a civil ceremony on June 11. That night Roosevelt happily wrote to Edith, "I never saw two people more in love with each other."

On the evening of June 16, 1914, the man who had once told the English to do their duty to Egypt or leave that country spoke to English scientists about the River of Doubt. His audience were members of the same venerated society of geographers that in 1872 had at first rejected the claim by American journalist Henry Morton Stanley that he had found the "missing" explorer and missionary Dr. David Livingstone alive in an African village. When he entered the hall, he was given the kind of reception he would have received had he walked into a convention of the Progressive Party, prepared to announce his candidacy for president in 1916. Part of his warm welcome may also have been acknowledgment that he was the former president of the United States and Nobel laureate. Certainly the sustained ovation recognized the courage shown by a man of his age in venturing into unexplored Brazilian jungles. In introducing the guest of honor the president of the Royal Society recognized that "he must have overcome great difficulties."

Settled expectantly in the crowded, small hall, the geographers were taken into those jungles and onto the Duvida—400 miles by dugout canoe in relentless tropical heat, soaked by drenching rains and raging rapids, stung and bitten by voracious insects, bruised and battered in body and sometimes in spirit, with occasionally faltering courage, with no turning back and no idea where it all would end, whether dead or alive.

"It was," said one of the previous doubters to reporters after the Society adjourned, "a very good lecture."

Nagged by a recurrence of the jungle fever, Roosevelt sailed from England on June 18 on the German liner *Imperator*. Although tired and vexed by a hoarse throat, he genially accepted rounds of applause from his fellow passengers whenever he entered a dining room for a meal. One of the passengers was the world's most famous magician and escape artist, Harry Houdini.

What the passengers didn't know, and certainly Roosevelt didn't, was that Houdini had memorized a picture of a hand-drawn map by Roosevelt of the Duvida that had been obtained by a London newspaperman, and shown to Houdini. What he had in mind, in the certainty that at some point in the crossing the passengers would demand a performance of his famous mind-reading act, was inveigling Roosevelt to participate in the act by picturing in his own head the course of what was now the most famous river in the world. Unaware that a trick was being played on him and the audience, Roosevelt agreed to visualize the river's route. In a "trance," Houdini proceeded to draw the memorized map on a slate. Gazing at it in wide-eyed wonder,

Roosevelt exclaimed, "That was the most amazing thing I've ever seen."

In November 1914 the articles Roosevelt had written for *Scribner's* became a book, *Through the Brazilian Wilderness*. It was dedicated "with esteem, regard, and affection by their friend" to Lauro Muller, Colonel Rondon, Amilcar, Lyra, Dr. Cajazeira, and "our companions in scientific work and in the exploration of the wilderness."

"Throughout the body of the work," he said in the preface, "will be found reference after reference to my colleagues and companions of the expedition, whose services to science I have endeavored to set forth, and for whom I shall always feel cordial friendship and regard."

Roosevelt's book was followed in the spring of 1916 by Father Zahm's memoir of the expedition, titled *Through South America's Southland*. The valiant priest who had encouraged Roosevelt to make the trip informed him that he was thinking about another venture. This idea, an exploration of the Rio Negro into Venezuela, he said, "becomes more and more dominant from day to day."

Zahm was not alone in contemplating another adventure. In December 1914 Roosevelt inquired if Henry Fairfield Osborn and the American Museum of Natural History would be interested in sponsoring a six-month odyssey to the South Pacific. Offering to finance it by again writing a series of articles for *Scribner's*, Roosevelt wrote, "I believe I could make a trip that would be worth while, and that it would do credit to the Museum." His envisioned a journey to Polynesia in 1918. But world events scuttled the project. With European powers engaged in a war that Roosevelt expected to soon involve the United States, he turned his attention to what he might do to contribute to the defeat of Germany and her allies. With the wolf rising in his heart, he asked President Woodrow Wilson to allow him to raise a regiment, as he had done in 1898. Having promised American voters in 1912 that he would keep the country out of the war, Wilson greeted the idea of Teddy Roosevelt leading an army with horror.

Disappointed by the rejection, but not surprised by it, Roosevelt wrote to Kermit, "I had hoped that we might round out Africa and South America by a 'greater adventure' together."

A consolation that spring was the awarding to Theodore Roosevelt by the American Geographical Society of a new David Livingstone Gold Medal for exploration. In accepting it, he said it really belonged to Colonel Rondon. He was gratified that the same gold medal was given to Rondon, through the Brazilian ambassador to the United States, in August 1918.

By then, the United States was in "the Great War" to "save the world for democracy," and Roosevelt's sons, Kermit, Ted, Archibald, and Quentin, were in it. Kermit had gone to war even before American entry by serving with British forces in Mesopotamia, then switching to the U.S. Army to fight in France beside his brothers. Meanwhile, Ted had distinguished himself as the only Reserve officer to command a Regular unit in combat. Archie was so severely wounded that he was declared 100 percent disabled and sent home. The youngest, Quentin, had joined the fight as an Army Air Services pilot and been killed in action at the age of twenty.

Roosevelt wrote to an old Rough Rider comrade, "It is bitter that the young should die." But there were "things worse than death," continued the broken-hearted but proud father, "for nothing under Heaven would I have had my sons act otherwise than as they acted. They have done pretty well haven't they? Quentin killed, dying as a war hawk should . . . over the enemy's lines; Archie crippled, and given the French cross for gallantry; Ted gassed once . . . and cited for 'conspicuous gallantry'; Kermit with the British military cross; and now under Pershing."

As Americans welcomed Armistice Day, Roosevelt found himself in the hospital. He was there to be treated for anemia, vertigo (caused by an old ear infection), the leg troubles left over from his last chance to be a boy, and general signs of physical exhaustion. In the previous six weeks he had been on a whirlwind speaking tour. In Alliance, Nebraska, he had demanded a total American victory so that no nation would ever dare to "look cross-eyed at us."

Republicans attending a party rally held in Carnegie Hall on October 28 hoped that he would announce his candidacy for president in 1920. They were heartened by his attack on the conduct of the war by President Wilson. To his delight and relief Republicans swept to victory in congressional elections in what he considered a repudiation of Wilson's war policies, and therefore vindication of his own relentless criticism of it. To one of the doctors attending him in the hospital he said of Wilson, "I would like to be left alone in this room with our great and good president for about fifteen minutes, and then I would be cheerfully hung."

Informed that he would have to remain hospitalized for some time, he kept busy with correspondence, drafting magazine and newspaper articles, and greeting well-wishers who came to call. Informed by doctors that they could do no more for his condition, he was discharged. Offered a wheelchair, he shrugged off an assisting hand and snapped, "Don't do that. I am not sick, and it will give the wrong impression."

In a letter to Ted he said it would be "a couple of months before I am in any kind of shape." But it didn't matter, he added, because "this happens to be the very time when I do not care to speak or to take an active part in politics."

On the day of New Year's Eve came an envelope from France containing France's official commemoration in the form of a citation for Quentin's sacrifice for French freedom.

January 1, 1919, was passed sitting on a sofa in the old nursery of the Sagamore Hill house and looking out a south-facing window. On the third a rheumatic specialist came to look him over. The next day, Edith wrote Kermit that his father was "having a horrid painful time."

Roosevelt stated on the fifth that he felt a little better. That day he was visited by the British poet Alfred Noyes. He then dictated a letter to Kermit and spent eleven hours honing proofs of a *Metropolitan Magazine* article and an editorial for the *Kansas City Star* newspaper on the subject of the League of Nations.

That evening as Edith sat nearby, playing solitaire, he said to her, "I wonder if you will ever know how much I love Sagamore Hill."

When he complained to her of "a terribly odd feeling," as if his heart and breathing were about to shut down, she woke the nurse and later summoned a doctor. The physician gave him a shot of morphine. His valet, James Amos, put him to bed around midnight. As the servant settled into a chair to sleep, a lamp was on. Roosevelt said, "James, please turn out that light."

He died in his sleep of a coronary artery embolism.

Archie cabled Kermit and Ted at their camp near Coblenz: "The old lion is dead."

EPILOGUE

NEWS OF BWANA MAKUBA'S death reached Ted in the early evening while Kermit was not in camp. Ted found him later that night in his tent, sipping wine. "We sat up the rest of the night and talked," Kermit wrote to their mother. "Father somehow was very near, and as if he would never be far. I don't feel sorry for him; he wouldn't want it, that would be the last thing. There never was anyone like him, and there won't be. . . . [I]t is foolish to think of oneself, but you will know how the bottom has dropped out for me; at first it was complete, but comes the realization that father could never really die, and that even though I can't bother him about every little decision, when a really vital one comes he will be there as unfailing as ever."

Kermit organized and ran the Roosevelt Steamship Company. He was the father of Kermit Jr., Joseph Willard, Belle Wyatt, and Dirck. Among his circle of literary friends were his father's old pal Rudyard Kipling, the poet Edwin Arlington Robinson (Kermit had gotten Roosevelt to give him a government job), William Butler Yeats, Gertrude Stein, Alexander Woollcott, famed as founding member of the Algonquin Round Table wits of the 1920s, and other stars in the literature of the hard-drinking Jazz Age. Using his literary skills, he published his own memoir of Africa with Bwana Makuba and other adventurers in *The Happy Hunting Grounds.*

Taking a respite from his shipping firm, Kermit accompanied brother Ted in a hunting-exploring expedition to the Himalayan Mountains and later to China in a quest for a Giant Panda for display in Chicago's Field Museum. The brothers published their adventures in books titled *East of the Sun and West of the Moon,* and *Trailing the Giant Panda.* The outfitter for the first expedition was Anthony Fiala.

Increasingly, Kermit showed the same dark moods of his Uncle Elliott, who had become an alcoholic and died in an epileptic seizure. Some scholars of the Roosevelt family of Sagamore Hill theorize that Roosevelt had chosen Kermit as his confidante in an attempt to protect him from the demons that had plagued Elliott.

The hope proved unavailing. The dark side of Kermit recognized by his mother, and so feared by Father, emerged in bouts of heavy drinking and infidelity to Belle that threatened their marriage. With his business hit hard by the effects of the Great Depression, and unable to write because of drinking, he periodically left Belle for a woman named Carla Peters, just as his uncle had been alcoholic and had taken a mistress.

When the Second World War broke out in September 1939, Kermit sought the assistance of his friend, Winston Churchill, to obtain a commission in the British Army. Churchill knew of Kermit's valor under the Union Jack in fighting on the Near East front in the last war. But the man appealing to Churchill in 1940 was a shadow of the dashing hero who had captured Turks by waving an officer's baton at them. Churchill recognized Kermit's condition as the toll taken by alcohol on him physically and spiritually, and that by volunteering Kermit was expressing a no-longer-young man's need to prove that he could still be the heroic figure of the Great War, the "lucky one" who'd dared the wilds of Africa and Brazil with his father, and as the younger brother who'd conquered the Himalaya Mountains with Ted.

If Churchill saw Kermit as a man verging on the brink of doom, and hoped to aid him in getting a commission, he soon had reason to believe that his faith was justified. Kermit proved he still possessed the quality of valor by taking part in a plan of Churchill's to thwart an invasion of Norway by the Soviet Union. But before the mission could be mounted, Norway surrendered to Germany. When a second British attempt to get a hold in Norway in which Kermit took part failed and required evacuation of British commandos, Kermit helped to extricate the men and equipment. He carried some of the wounded on his back. He'd done this while staying sober.

Sent on a mission to North Africa in 1940, Kermit found German patrols, but none of the exciting action he desired. Bored, he resumed drinking and became ill. Sent back to England, he was diagnosed with a flare-up of malaria he'd contracted while on the Brazil expedition. He was also found to have an enlarged liver. Because of these illnesses he was discharged from the army in early 1941. Back in New York in June and reunited with Belle, he vanished almost immediately.

An appeal by Belle to President Franklin D. Roosevelt put the FBI on his trail. Agents found him in July, beaten up after a fight with a taxi driver. After two commitments to the care of a sanitarium, he went to California with Carla Peters in early 1942. When the FBI traced him again, agents reported finding him "stumbling drunk" and reciting Edwin Arlington Robinson's poem, "Richard Cory," about a young man who seemed to have everything but went home one night and put a bullet through his head.

Appeals by Belle and brother Archie to FDR and General George C. Marshall resulted in Kermit being sent to an army air corps base at Fort Richardson, Alaska. He had no specific duty, but he persuaded pilots to take him along on bombing missions against Japanese forces on small islands in the Aleutians. He also helped organize Eskimos and Aleuts into a militia, in case the Japanese attempted to overrun the islands. Sober and feeling good about himself, he wrote to Ted that the war was his "fountain of youth." But he was soon dropping in at Nellie's diner in Anchorage and drinking a few glasses of wine.

Years of hard liquor had left him severely weak, with his stomach distended and arms and legs shockingly thin. Almost any task left him exhausted.

On the night of June 3, 1943, he said to a friend, "I wish I could sleep."

Not long after saying goodnight to the friend, he emulated "Richard Cory" by closing the door of his quarters, placing his Colt Army .45 pistol under his chin, and putting a bullet in his head. In keeping with his father's maxim that where a tree falls, "there let it lay," he was buried at Fort Richardson in Grave 72, Plot A, marked by a plain white army headstone.

The enterprising outfitter of the Brazilian adventure, Anthony Fiala, outlived Theodore Roosevelt by thirty-one years. Well into his eighties, he died in 1950. Among his lifetime of treasures was one of the last letters written by Roosevelt. Dated three days before Roosevelt's death, it praised Fiala's work with a small arms maker during the war.

Jacob Sigg, the Swiss valet for Father Zahm, died at age 65 in Patino, Paraguay, where he'd settled into a quiet life of farming with his wife.

After nearly 40 expeditions in his beloved South America, and with more than 120,000 birds collected in his career as a naturalist, George Cherrie had been the American consul in La Guaira, Venezuela, when news came to him on January 6, 1919, that Roosevelt was dead. The intrepid scientist who refused to abandon Roosevelt in the Brazilian jungle lived until 1948. He died at age 83 in the same year that Edith Roosevelt passed away at Sagamore Hill.

Four years later, death claimed Leo Miller. He'd left his position with the American Museum of Natural History to go into business and lecture from time to time on "The Truth about the River of Doubt." When asked about Theodore Roosevelt, he usually answered, "For a long time it seemed that it could not be possible that a man like that could ever die."

Colonel Rondon became one of the most honored men in Brazilian history. Proclaimed "Civilizer of the Wilderness," made a marshal of Brazil, and with a city named for him, called Rondonia and located in the western part of Matto Grasso, he died at the age of 90 in 1958.

Roosevelt's secretary, Frank Harper, lived the longest after the expedition. He died in a nursing home in Santa Monica, California, in 1971.

As to the former River of Doubt, two attempts by expeditions sent out by the Brazilian government to follow Rio Teodoro met with failure. The first expedition never returned and was presumed to have been killed by Indians. The second was abandoned mid-way out of fear of meeting the same fate. Not until 1927 would there be a successful venture. Led by a British explorer, Commander George M. Dyott, at the request of the Roosevelt Memorial Association (later the Theodore Roosevelt Association), its purpose was to produce a film record of the route for a series of documentaries on Roosevelt's life. Finally, in 1992, the New Century Conservation Trust and the Theodore Roosevelt Association launched an expedition headed by Charles T. Haskell and Elizabeth C. McNight, with Roosevelt's great-grandson, Tweed Roosevelt, in the vanguard. A high-tech enterprise, it had sturdy inflatable rafts that were impervious to the pounding of rapids and crashes into boulders. Global positioning satellites eliminated any doubt as to where the expedition was at all times.

Tweed Roosevelt said of following his illustrious ancestor's route, "They were explorers, while we were merely adventurers, and there is a world of difference." In a foreword to historian Joseph R. Ornig's book, *My Last Chance to Be a Boy: Theodore Roosevelt's South American Expedition of 1913–1914*, published in 1994, Tweed noted that Roosevelt had been five years older than himself, and sixty-five pounds heavier, and "in much worse shape," but had survived with grace and humor.

He certainly had. On the day of his return to New York, May 19, 1914, he stood still for a photographer to snap a picture of him. Wearing a baggy coat and vest, necktie, and white shirt with a collar that was too loose, under a big soft hat with upturned brim, a cord dangling from his pince-nez glasses, and with droopy gray walrus mustache and tired-looking expression, he gazed intently at the cameraman and declared, "I am worth more than several dead men yet."

AUTHOR'S NOTES

TRYING TO GET TO KNOW Theodore Roosevelt, and in seeking to understand him, an author does not today, and never has, set off into unexplored territory. The trail was blazed and marked by the man himself. Very little of what Theodore Roosevelt did in his life went unrecorded in his own hand and spoken words. Historian Stephen E. Ambrose hit the Theodore Roosevelt nail squarely on the head by asserting that he "stands alone, unchallenged by any other twentieth-century president, as a writer and scholar." Certainly, he has no equal as a prodigious, prolific writer of letters, magazine articles, essays, monographs, biographies, histories, speeches, and books. Forty-two titles range in subjects from glorious sea battles in the War of 1812, jungle skirmishes in Cuba, the lives of a British reformer-turned-tyrant (Cromwell) and two American politicians (Thomas Hart Benton and Gouverneur Morris), his own hunting adventures, and the monumental *The Winning of the West,* to the thrills of a year-long African safari and his nearly fatal last chance to be a boy by chasing a river named Doubt.

Library and archive files bulge with his papers, photographs, and other memorabilia. They are found in the Theodore Roosevelt Collection of the Houghton Library at Harvard, the Library of Congress, American Museum of Natural History in New York, Scribner's Archives at Princeton, the University of Virginia Library in Charlottesville, Virginia, and at Sagamore Hill and the Theodore Roosevelt Birthplace national historic site where Teedie Roosevelt started his Roosevelt Museum of Natural Science. Many of his thousands of letters, official and to friends, family, and his beloved children, have been culled and published. Friends of his, colleagues, foes, critics, admirers, and companions on his hunts and other adventures wrote about him.

Countless accounts of the adventures of Theodore Roosevelt are found in newspapers and magazines from his time, and since then, along with innumerable Roosevelt biographies. He is one of literature's most fascinating and enduring subjects. His life has been attractive not just to writers about history, but to those who make it. Every subsequent president of the United States turned to him, either for inspiration and guidance, or to borrow a ringing phrase. In the eight decades since his death he has remained an icon of American culture and remains highly ranked as a leader and popular heroic figure.

No one cannot admire a president who could say about the Panama Canal, "While the Congress debated, the canal was built." And there's not a man of middle age, or older, who cannot understand Roosevelt's need to grab a last chance to be a boy again. Who but Theodore Roosevelt could have a cuddly stuffed toy bear named after him, and not be offended?

Yet few people who think they know all about Theodore Roosevelt realize that after he left the White House he went off to Africa for a year of exploration, big-game hunting in the name of science, and self-discovery. Or that he very nearly died in pursuit of the course of an unknown Brazilian river because he thought it would be fun. But surprisingly, except for brief summaries in biographies, a scholarly book by Joseph R. Ornig on the Brazilian expedition, and a greatly abridged *The Hunting and Exploring Adventures of Theodore Roosevelt Told in His Own Words*, edited by Donald Day, with an introduction by Elting E. Morison, there has been until now no single-volume, comprehensive telling of Roosevelt's life as explorer, hunter, and adventurer in the wilds of his own country, Africa, and South America.

My principle sources were Roosevelt's own accounts found in *Hunting Trips of a Ranchman, The Wilderness Hunter, Outdoor Pastimes of an American Hunter, African Game Trails, Through the Brazilian Wilderness, A Book-Lover's Holiday in the Open,* and his autobiography. Articles by him were published in the magazine *The Outlook* and the *Geographical Journal* of London. Other material appeared in many contemporary magazine and newspaper articles, essays, and interviews. There are also official reports and speeches made by Roosevelt's traveling companions.

The African safari was written about by Kermit Roosevelt in *The Happy Hunting Grounds*. Books touching on the exploration of the River of Doubt were published by Frank M. Chapman (with a Roosevelt introduction), Paul Russell Cartwright, Joseph L. Gardner, Edward J. Goodman, and Leo Miller.

I'm also grateful for the insights provided by Roosevelt biographers Lawrence F. Abbott, H.W. Brands, Hermann Hagedorn, William Henry

Harbaugh, William Draper Lewis, Nathan Miller, Edmund Morris, Sylvia Jukes Morris (a biography of Edith Roosevelt), Henry Pringle, Edward J. Renehan Jr. (*The Lion's Pride: Theodore Roosevelt and His Family in Peace and War*), Corrine Roosevelt Robinson (TR's sister), Roscoe William Thayer, R.L. and C.C. Wilson, and Owen Wister (*Roosevelt, The Story of a Friendship*).

Thanks, too, to Jake Elwell and Olga Wieser of Wieser & Wieser Literary Agency for their steady encouragement and always-wise counsel.

Photographs and cartoons in this book are from my collection, assembled throughout a lifetime of admiring Theodore Roosevelt, and in the course of gathering material for my other books on him: *Commissioner Roosevelt: The Story of Theodore Roosevelt and the New York City Police, 1895–1897; Colonel Roosevelt: Theodore Roosevelt Goes to War, 1897–1898; The Bully Pulpit: A Teddy Roosevelt Book of Quotations*; and my first mystery novel, teaming a young Theodore Roosevelt and incipient detective named Sherlock Holmes, *The Adventure of the Stalwart Companions*.

Being enamored with Roosevelt has also resulted in the only biography of his namesake, *Theodore Roosevelt Jr.: The Life of a War Hero*, a large portion of which deals with Ted's Asian explorations with the "lucky one" of the Roosevelt "bunnies," the indomitable, heroic, and ultimately tragic Kermit.

On February 18, 1918, lying in a bed in New York's Roosevelt Hospital (built by one of his cousins), suffering with the "old Brazilian trouble," Roosevelt had written to his "Dearest Kermit" with the U.S. Army in France and provided a fitting way to end this book. "Well, old side partner," he said, "your letters are perfectly delightful and surely you must know how my heart thrills with pride whenever I think of you."

SELECTED BIBLIOGRAPHY

Abbott, Lawrence F. *Impressions of Theodore Roosevelt*. Garden City, N.Y.: Doubleday, Page & Company, 1920.

Brands, H. W. *TR: The Last Romantic*. New York: Basic Books, 1997.

Chapman, Frank M. *Autobiography of a Bird Lover*. New York: Appleton Century Co., 1935.

Cutright, Paul Russell. *Theodore Roosevelt the Naturalist*. New York: Harper & Brothers, 1956.

Day, Donald, editor. *The Hunting and Exploring Adventures of Theodore Roosevelt Told in His Own Words*. New York: The Dial Press, 1955.

Gardner, Joseph L. *Departing Glory: Theodore Roosevelt as Ex-President*. New York: Charles Scribner's Sons, 1973.

Goodman, Edward J. *The Explorers of South America*. New York: The MacMillan Co., 1972.

Hagedorn, Hermann. *The Roosevelt Family of Sagamore Hill*. New York: The MacMillan Co., 1954.

Harbaugh, William Henry. *Power and Responsibility: The Life and Times of Theodore Roosevelt*. New York: Farrar, Straus and Cudahy, 1961.

Harlow, Alvin F. *Theodore Roosevelt: Strenuous American*. New York: Julian Messner, Inc., 1943.

Jeffers, H. Paul. *The Bully Pulpit: A Teddy Roosevelt Book of Quotations*. Dallas, Texas: Taylor Publishing Company, 1998.

———. *Colonel Roosevelt: Theodore Roosevelt Goes to War, 1897–1898*. New York: John Wiley & Sons, Inc., 1996.

———. *Commissioner Roosevelt: The Story of Theodore Roosevelt and the New York City Police, 1895–1897*. New York: John Wiley & Sons, Inc., 1994.

———. *Theodore Roosevelt Jr.: The Life of a War Hero*. Novato, CA: Presidio Press, Inc., 2001.

Miller, Nathan. *Theodore Roosevelt: A Life*. New York: William Morrow, 1992.

Miller, Leo E. *In the Wilds of South America*. New York: Charles Scribner's Sons, 1918.

Morris, Edmund. *The Rise of Theodore Roosevelt*. New York: Coward, McCann & Geohegan, 1979.

Morris, Sylvia Jukes. *Edith Kermit Roosevelt: Portrait of a First Lady*. New York: Coward, McCann & Geohegan, 1980.

Pringle, Henry F. *Theodore Roosevelt: A Biography*. New York: Harcourt, Brace & Co., 1931.

Roosevelt, Kermit. *The Happy Hunting Grounds*. New York: Charles Scriber's Sons, 1920.

Roosevelt, Theodore. *African Game Trails: An Account of the African Wanderings of an American Hunter-Naturalist*. New York: Charles Scribner's Sons, 1910; Cooper Square Press, 2001.

———. *A Book-Lover's Holiday in the Open*. New York: Charles Scribner's Sons, 1919.

———. *Hunting Trips of a Ranchman*. New York: The Modern Library (reprint) 1998.

———. *Letters*. Edited by Elting R. Morison and John Blum. 8 vols. Cambridge: Harvard University Press, 1951–54.

———. *Outdoor Pastimes of an American Hunter*. New York: Charles Sribner's Sons, 1902.

———. *Ranch Life and the Hunting Trail*. New York: Charles Scribner's Sons, 1925.

———. *Theodore Roosevelt: An Autobiography*. Charles Scribner's Sons, 1913.

———. *Through the Brazilian Wilderness*. New York: Charles Scribner's Sons, 1914; Cooper Square Press, 2001.

———. *The Wilderness Hunter*. New York: The Modern Library (reprint), 1998.

Wister, Owen. *Roosevelt, The Story of a Friendship*. New York: MacMillan, 1930.

INDEX

ABOUT THE AUTHOR

A broadcast journalist for more than three decades, H. PAUL JEFFERS has published over fifty works of fiction and nonfiction, including biographies; histories of the FBI, Scotland Yard, and the Great Depression; "true crime" studies; mysteries; historical westerns; and young adult non-fiction. His other Roosevelt books are *Theodore Roosevelt Jr.: The Life of a War Hero; Commissioner Roosevelt; Colonel Roosevelt;* and *The Bully Pulpit: A Teddy Roosevelt Book of Quotations.*

Other biographies include *An Honest President: The Life and Presidencies of Grover Cleveland; Diamond Jim Brady: Prince of the Gilded Age; The Napoleon of New York: Fiorello La Guardia;* and *Sal Mineo: His Life, Murder and Mystery.*

Before becoming a full-time author, he was a TV news producer and reporter in Boston, producer/writer/editor for the ABC and NBC radio networks, and the only person to hold the position of news director at both of New York City's all-news radio stations. He has taught writing and journalism at New York University, City College of New York, Syracuse University, and California State University at Long Beach.

He lives in New York City.